PICTORIAL HISTORY
OF THE JEWISH PEOPLE

For Ethel Frimet
MY BELOVED DAUGHTER

*Behold the rock from which you are hewn
and the source which gave you birth.*

Books by Nathan Ausubel

SUPERMAN: LIFE OF FREDERICK THE GREAT
VOICES OF HISTORY (Annual Series)
A TREASURY OF JEWISH FOLKLORE
A TREASURY OF JEWISH HUMOR
PICTORIAL HISTORY OF THE JEWISH PEOPLE

.

PICTORIAL HISTORY *of the* *Jewish People*

FROM BIBLE TIMES TO OUR OWN
DAY THROUGHOUT THE WORLD

by Nathan Ausubel

CROWN PUBLISHERS, INC.   NEW YORK

SPECIAL PICTURE CREDITS

The map of Palestine on page 5 is from *Israel: A History of the Jewish People*, by Rufus Learsi, copyright 1949 by the author, and used by permission of author and publisher, The World Publishing Company. The map, "Western Russia and the Jewish Pale," on page 231, is reprinted by permission of Random House, Inc., copyright 1939 by Catherine Drinker Bowen.

Acme News Pictures: photograph on page 322 of Jewish and Arab *Knesset* deputies.

Ewing Galloway: photographs on page 16 of Rachel's Tomb, and on page 64 of Pool of Siloam.

Matson Photo Service: photograph on page 229 of Samaritan Highpriest.

Press Association: photographs on page 316 of Arab mob burning Jewish shop and on page 317 of young Haganah members.

Pix, Inc.: photographs on page 139 of Ari Synagogue; on page 222 of Cochin Jews; on page 226 of Ghriba Synagogue and worshipers (Island of Djerba); on page 227 of Sahara oasis; and on page 264 of Warsaw Ghetto destroyed.

Foto Riwkin (Stockholm): photographs on page 2 of Israeli soldier; on page 3 of Jewish children; on page 56 of Temple Area, Jerusalem; on page 39 of Jewish Cemetery, Jerusalem; and on page 316 of Tel-Aviv celebration.

Harry Rubenstein: photographs on page 286 of Triangle Waist Co. fire, strikers' demonstration, and David Dubinsky.

Sovfoto: photographs on page 2 of Emil Hilels; on page 247 of Mme. Molotova and Kaganovich; on page 248 of sheepbreeder; on page 249 of Birobidjan Museum; on page 252 of Lina Stern, Abram Jaffe, David Oistrakh and Botvinnik; on page 253 of Eisenstein and Ehrenburg; on page 258 of Gen. Shmushkevich; on page 259 of Gen. Dovator and Fisanovich; on page 265 of pyre of Vilna Jews and Sutzkever.

Eastfoto: photographs on page 269 of Minc, Rakosi and Pauker.

Three Lions Agency: photograph on page 83 of Kfar Birim Synagogue.

Underwood & Underwood: photographs on page 8 of Canaanite altars; on page 15 of Machpelah Cave; on page 30 of Wilderness of Sin; on page 43 of Megiddo Excavations; on page 53 of King Solomon's Quarries; on page 55 of Rock of Moriah; on page 80 of "Street of Columns"; on page 217 of Tomb of Ezekiel scribes; on page 218 of Jewish houses, Bagdad; on page 305 of Djemal Pasha before Mosque of Omar; on page 308 of immigrants in Haifa; on page 313 of Arab riot, Jaffa; and on page 327 of Damascus Gate.

Wide World: photographs on page 156 of Dreyfus reinstated; on page 202 of Mussolini; and on page 255 of a Jew ordered by Nazi to scrub street.

Library of Congress Catalog Card Number: 52-10777

ISBN: 0-517-097575

Printed in the United States of America

Thirty-second Printing, June, 1979

Contents

WHO ARE THE JEWS?

Who really are the Jews?

Many definitions have been offered. Some of the most frequently heard are: that they are a nation, that they are a people, that they are a religious group, that they are a race, that they are a language-culture group, that they are an historic phenomenon which cannot properly be labeled or described.

Jews themselves are wide apart in their thinking about it. Every definition that is offered seems to exclude or contradict the others. This in itself is ample proof of the confusion that exists in many people's minds concerning who and what Jews are.

Let us examine several of the most widely held beliefs about who the Jews are.

Even before modern Israel was established as a state, it was a quite commonly held belief that Jews were a nation. Probably the first instance in modern times in which this conception appeared, partly with the connotation of a distinctive group, was in the official documents of the Dutch East India Company during the seventeenth century, where Jews were referred to regularly as "members of the Jewish nation."

Nevertheless, today there are a sizable number of Jews who do not consider themselves at all as "members of the Jewish nation." In the United States, for instance, perhaps most Jews claim their nationality to be American, although they readily admit, and are even proud of, their Jewish ancestry, culture and religion. The same thing holds true in

THESE ARE JEWS

The Talmudist.

Myra Hess, English pianist.

Rabbi Alexander D. Goode, one of four chaplains who went down with the troopship *Dorchester*, February 3, 1943.

ARE THE JEWS A NATION?

One of the most popular views is that the Jews are a nation. That is why, when asked what their nationality is, many Jews promptly answer, "Jewish."

With the establishment of modern Israel many Jews have been strengthened in their conviction that the Jews are a nation with Israel as the *national* Jewish homeland. In fact, the Government of Israel currently gives this view official approval; it holds that every Jew who settles in Israel automatically becomes a citizen of Israel unless he states in writing that he does not wish to relinquish the citizenship he already holds in another country.

other countries of the world: they consider themselves to be nationals of those countries as well as Jews.

ARE THE JEWS A RELIGIOUS GROUP?

There are a number of people today who say that the only link that unites the scattered communities of Jews throughout the world is their religion. It is the *Torah,* and the observance of religious rites and customs, they insist, that have preserved the Jewish people and its identity through all the trials and tribulations of several thousand years. They are equally certain that it will be the Jewish religion alone, insofar as it continues to command the loyalty of Jews, that will preserve this Jewish identity in the future.

However, there is a strongly dissenting view held by other Jews. They challenge the claim that Jews are solely a religious group. They maintain that there are as many Jews who are non-observant as there are religious-minded, and therefore this definition clearly does not provide for those without religious affiliation, conviction or practice.

ARE THE JEWS A RACE?

Perhaps the most widely held view of all is that the Jews form a distinct race by themselves. One constantly meets Jews who refer to themselves as belonging to "the Jewish race." Many Christians, on the other hand, think of Jews as being members of "the Semitic race."

To speak precisely, in the language of the anthropologists, there is no such thing as "a Jewish race." The idea of "a Semitic race" is also a fiction. Furthermore, they contend, there is no "Aryan race" either. The words "Semitic" and "Aryan" were originally used by philologists to describe certain language groups, and not races at all.

The anthropologists agree that the Jews sprang from the Mediterranean sub-division of the Caucasoid race. It is assumed that they, as Hebrews, appeared some thousands of years ago, a small part of the migratory movement of the

however, reveal different physical characteristics. This, say the anthropologists, is unquestionably due to the fact that, besides influences of climate and diet, the Jews since earliest times have been fused with other racial blends wherever they have lived through the centuries. This fusion occurred in many ways: through voluntary or involuntary acceptance of the Jewish faith; through intermarriage even though there were and are restrictions against it, through involuntary interbreeding which took place everywhere in times of public disorder. Thus, many Polish Jews today are indistinguishable in type from many Christian Poles, many Ukrainian Jews look like Don Cossacks, many French Jews look like so many other Frenchmen, and quite a few German Jews have all the characteristics claimed by the Nazis as being "Nordic."

ARE THE JEWS A LANGUAGE-CULTURE GROUP?

Perhaps, then, the identity of the Jews lies in their ethnic group life and their culture. However, Jews have been widely dispersed throughout the globe for many centuries. They do not constitute a single ethnic language group (Semitic, for instance) but a large and extraordinary aggregation of ethnic language units. By the very nature of their historic experience

THESE ARE JEWS

An Israeli soldier.

Dr. James Simon, German philanthropist.

Emil Hilels, Russian pianist.

semi-nomadic Hyksos, and under the name of Israelites, settled along the coastal plains of Canaan. When the Kingdom of Judah was established, its people were known as Jews. After the destruction of the Jewish state by the Romans in 70 c.e., the Jews were dispersed to all the far corners of the earth. They migrated in large numbers to such various places as Rome, Egypt, Babylonia, Syria and the Aegean Islands, where Jewish communities had already been in existence for a long time. They also founded new ones in Spain, the Rhineland, Italy, France, England and Poland.

While many Jews today are considered, in a biologic sense, as belonging to the Mediterranean sub-division of the Caucasoid race common to that particular area, other Jews,

in different parts of the world at different times and under the impact of diverse civilizations, these units are seen as being only loosely related to one another. Even the blends of physical types vary in different parts of the world.

The variety of languages, of "mother-tongues" as it were, which the Jews of the world speak is quite staggering, and it has been this way for thousands of years. To whatever extent in their religious and intellectual life, at home and in the synagogue, Jews may have used Hebrew, "the sacred tongue," the language they used in their daily lives was that of the people among whom they lived. Only in ancient Israel, as is also true today in modern Israel, was Hebrew the national language of the Jews. Later on, after the Return of the Exiles from Babylon, it was displaced as the language of the people in Judea by Aramaic, or "*Targum* speech." Hebrew was used then, as it has been ever since until its revival as a living tongue in the nineteenth century, as the language of prayer and of sacred literature, but Jews used the language of the country in which they lived for speech and writing. We thus have entire bodies of Jewish literature written originally in many languages: in Hellenistic Greek (Philo), Arabic (Maimonides), Persian, Yiddish and Ladino, German, French, Spanish, Portuguese and many others. Consequently, one can hardly refer to the Jews as being a single ethnic or language group. And to call them an aggregation of loosely related ethnic language groups is quite meaningless.

The Falashas, the Jews of Abyssinia, for example, pray in Ethiopic *Gheez* but they speak in *Amharic*, the native tongue of the district in which they live. They are swarthy in complexion and have black curly hair, although their features are generally delicate. In their appearance, dress, culture and mode of life they are hardly to be distinguished from other groups in that region of Africa.

The same is true of all other Jews elsewhere, whether in Iran or Switzerland, in K'ai-feng-fu or Italy, in the United States or Sweden. Diversities are sometimes as great, or even greater, among separate Jewish ethnic groups as similarities.

What is it then that they have in common?

First of all, say these scholars, they draw from a common group awareness—a consciousness of *being Jews*. This state

ARE THE JEWS A PEOPLE?

There are those who hold that the wide distribution of the Jews throughout the world has made of them a variegated though unified people—in fact, a global people. It is argued that whether a Jew lives in Israel or in India, in the United States or in Sweden, whether his native tongue is Persian or English, Dutch or Chinese, he still remains a Jew. Nonetheless, he continues to be a national of the country in which he has been born or naturalized. His attachment to his Jewish identity and his fraternal concern for the welfare of Jews everywhere do not in the least diminish his devotion to the nation of which he is a citizen. It is pointed out that those most loyal to their Jewish group-identity frequently make the most exemplary citizens—for instance, Haym Salomon and Justice Louis D. Brandeis in the United States, Sir Moses Montefiore in England, Moses Mendelssohn in Germany and Adolphe Crémieux in France. The two loyalties are not considered either divisive or incompatible, but on the contrary complementary, one enriching the other.

The ancestry of the 11,558,830 Jews estimated in 1952 to be scattered throughout the world goes back by tradition to the Patriarch Abraham, the first Jew. He and his descendants were known as Hebrews until the time of Jacob, when he was given the name of Israel. All his descendants were called Israelites. When the kingdom of *Yehuda*, or Judah, was established in the southern part of Palestine, its people were given

THESE ARE JEWS

Danny Kaye, American actor.

Israeli children.

of thinking and feeling about one's self and one's group is shared by many such widely different individuals as Albert Einstein, the physicist, and the *Tat*-speaking "Mountain-Jew" from the Caucasus, as fashionable Lady Reading in her London mansion and the trinket-bedecked Jewess of the Libyan cave-dwellers, as Mischa Elman, the violinist, and the turbaned Jewish horn-blower in an Afghan marketplace. In greater or lesser measure, each of them is linked up in some way with the historic Jewish past. Whether Jews are familiar with this past or not, they, or their ancestors, have had a common Jewish cultural heritage and a religion from which to draw and together to establish a common group identity.

the name of Yehudim, Judeans or Jews. Yet always, and wherever they may have been dispersed, they regarded themselves as a people, it is maintained. Their descendants, products of whatever biologic mixtures, language-cultures and civilizations in various parts of the world, are considered Jews whether they are religious or not, Zionists or non-Zionists.

In conclusion: who really are the Jews? Some say that this question cannot be fully answered because Jews are an historic phenomenon which cannot properly be labeled or described. Possibly, as we pursue the course of Jewish life and destiny through the ages in *Pictorial History of the Jewish People*, the Jewish identity may appear a little less involved and baffling.

THE LAND OF ISRAEL

ITS TOPOGRAPHY

In the earliest times the country was known as the *Land of Canaan*. When the Israelites settled it after the Egyptian Bondage they renamed it the *Land of Israel*. Then, in the period of its political decline as a Jewish state, when the Romans subjugated it nineteen hundred years ago, they called it Palestine (Philistia, i.e., the land of the Philistines, although the Philistines occupied only the southern portion of the coastal region). Since then, and until the establishment of the modern state of Israel in 1948, the land has been universally known as Palestine.

Despite its small territorial area, Palestine has often played a significant role in the world drama of mankind. There are a variety of reasons to explain this historical paradox, the geographic location of Palestine being probably the most important of them.

By all standards, Palestine is actually a tiny country, consisting of little more than 10,000 square miles, or about the area of the state of Vermont. Nonetheless, its position as a land-corridor, linking up three continents—Africa, Asia and Europe—gives it even today a unique strategic-military importance. In their quest for world power, the great nations of antiquity—Egypt, Assyria, Babylonia, Greece and Rome—were obliged to deploy their armies through the narrow coastal

words of Job, "man is born for trouble even as the sparks fly upward." But, in a constructive sense, the ancient Jews also developed a hatred of war and inhumanity, and inversely, a passion for universal peace and social justice.

The coastal region of Palestine served perhaps as vital a function as a commercial route as it did as a military highway. Along it the caravans of many peoples, laden with a great variety of goods, proceeded to other lands.

A LAND OF MILK AND HONEY

In ancient times Palestine was much more fruitful than it is today. The Bible constantly refers to it as the Promised Land of man's desiring and dreams:

"A land of wheat and barley, and fig trees and pomegranates, a land of olive oil and honey."

By and large, Palestine is a narrow upland strip consisting of a stony plateau some 150 miles long, of low limestone hills that are barren and forbidding, but happily broken in many places by broad deep valleys, such as Esdraelon, Jezreel and Sharon. These are fertile and wooded and green, and grateful to the eye in the blinding glare of the semi-tropic sun.

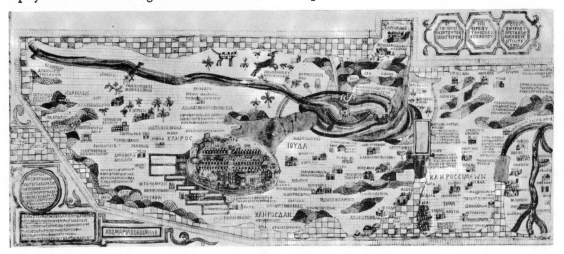

The Medeba (Mosaic) Map, the oldest map of Palestine in existence. Found in the Transjordan Church of Medeba, built in the 5th or 6th century c.e.

plain of Palestine in order to invade other lands. Consequently, there was hardly a time when the tread of foreign hosts, marching on their way to war and conquest, was not heard in the land. Each time they passed they left behind them a swath of devastation and mourning, for conquerors are no respecters of the weak. In a way, this direct, though harsh, contact with other people proved beneficial to the ancient Jews. For one thing, it drew them out of their narrow tribal provincialism. It brought them into contact with other and sometimes more advanced cultures, gave them a world view and consequently influenced their manner of life.

However, it was unavoidable that they also should have derived from their peculiar geographic situation and historic experience a tragic sense of life, an awareness that human affairs were unpredictable and hazardous, and that, in the

The stony plateau slopes gently to the Mediterranean in the west. In the east, the far end of the Jordan valley sets Palestine's boundary where the ancient lands of Gilead and Bashan began. Its northernmost borders touch on Lebanon and Syria;

Vignette from a 13th-century German *Haggadah* ms.

its southernmost part is the Negev, "the barren land," the Beersheba region where the Patriarchs Abraham, Isaac and Jacob made their home. It is a wilderness even today, stretching from the hills of Judea in the north to the port of Elath on the Gulf of Akaba, an arm of the Red Sea, in the south.

Although it is only a little country, Palestine has a wide variety of climates. Generally speaking, it is a hot country. On the high plateau the summer is almost uniformly cool and dry. In the plain stretching along the Mediterranean coast the weather is usually warm and humid, yet the nights are pleasantly cool. However, in the Jordan valley near the Dead Sea the climate changes dramatically; it suddenly becomes semitropical and even torrid. It has often been remarked that the climate of Palestine resembles that of Florida and southern California and has similar vegetation.

When it rains in Palestine it rains long and steadily, from October until April. This constitutes the "winter" season. The other six months make up the "dry" or "summer" season. The rainfall is usually heavy on the plateau and along the seacoast but it is very slight in the Negev. That is why, until recently, the entire Negev area had the aspect of an unyielding rocky wilderness.

At all times water in Palestine had to be carefully conserved, stored in cisterns and reservoirs to be used by both men and beasts. As a result of neglect and abuse through

The Negev wilderness.

many centuries, much of the land, fertile and verdant as it was at one time, eroded and turned into a wilderness. Forests began to disappear, except in Galilee; and to the east of the Jordan River, trees became a rarity. While these parts did not turn literally into desert land they, nevertheless, did become rocky and sandy. Because there was no irrigation and little rainfall, as in the Negev, the topsoil vanished. For many centuries, until the Zionist settlers appeared, the jackals and the hyenas vied fiercely with the Arab nomads for sheer physical survival.

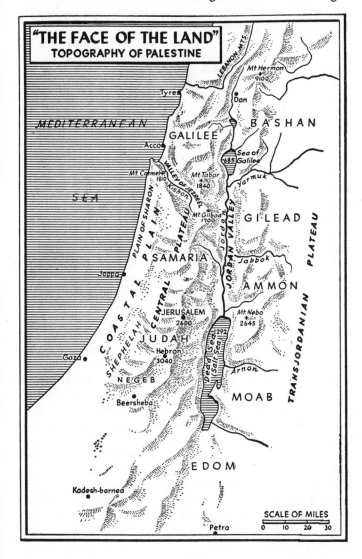

Graphic Associates

Galilee.

The River Jordan.

The Dead Sea.

Palestine is poor in natural waterways. The most important rivers are the Jordan, Kishon, Arnon and Yarmuk; the principal lakes are the Dead Sea, the Sea of Galilee or Lake Kinnereth (in Hebrew, "Lake of the Harp") and Lake Huleh.

The Jordan River knifes through the stony hills and sandy *wadis,* and follows a serpentine course through a long stretch of the country. Only a narrow stream, it is fed by the melting snows from the slopes of Mount Hermon in the Lebanon. It then meanders through Lake Huleh and the swampy Huleh plain. There it begins to sink and the temperature begins to rise sharply. Near the Sea of Galilee where the riverbed falls about 700 feet below sea-level the climate changes suddenly to semitropical and finally to tropical after it falls into the Dead Sea, which is nearly 1,300 feet below sea-level, the lowest in the world.

PLANTS AND ANIMALS

Palestine's diverse physical characteristics inevitably must result in a wide range of plant life. Actually, more than 2,000 varieties of plants have been counted by botanists. These run from temperate to tropical in classification.

Since Galilee and the eastern regions have natural forests even today, they must have been luxuriant in ancient times. The trees mentioned in the Bible, *Mishna* and *Talmud* are probably the same as those found today—oleander, terebinth, monk's pepper, acacia, willow, poplar, pine, balsam, apple of Sodom, sycamore, cypress, cedar, ash, oak and palm. This

Left. Grapes of modern Israel. *Right.* Coin (dinar) Bar Kochba revolt, 132-135 C.E.

unusual variety of trees in such a small area is accounted for by different temperatures and amounts of precipitation.

The same conditions are equally true of the fruit trees that are found in various parts of the country: apple, orange, lemon, St.-John's-bread, pomegranate, almond, olive, date-palm, fig, mulberry and various kinds of nuts. Grape-growing, in Bible times as well as today, was an important horticultural pursuit, especially in the fertile valleys.

Grains and vegetables were also grown in considerable quantity, and though several varieties of wheat were grown, the poor could not afford to eat it. They ate barley, as the modern poor of Europe eat potatoes. Wheat was raised mostly for the consumption of the well-to-do and for purposes of foreign trade.

Other crops mentioned in the *Mishna* and *Talmud* are corn, maize, millet and lentils (Esau's celebrated "mess of pottage" for which he sold his birthright was lentils), cucumbers, horsebeans, chickpeas, watercress, all kinds of melons, garlic and onions. The "spices of the East," on which Europeans of later centuries set such a high premium, grew profusely, especially nutmeg, cumin, pepper, ginger, hyssop, saffron, thyme, mint and dill.

All kinds of flowering bushes grew in ancient Israel. Thyme and cactus, sage and laurel relieved the harsh landscape of the stony highlands. Even in districts with little rainfall, as in Beersheba, vegetation, such as wormwood and the Rose of Jericho, held on tenaciously. The most common flowers were the Rose of Sharon that grew in the Valley of Sharon in Judea and the lily of the valley (both flowers immortalized in the *Song of Songs*), the iris, hyacinth, crocus, anemone, as well as a great profusion of wild flowers that grew in the meadows and along lake and river banks.

Whether it was a semi-nomadic pastoral economy or in later centuries a simple agricultural one, the inhabitants of ancient Palestine always engaged in animal husbandry. They kept flocks of sheep and goats and herds of cattle, raised chickens, fattened geese and ducks, caught fish and tended beehives. They domesticated many animals and imported other species from foreign lands.

Sheep and goats constituted, in number and in value, the most important of all these animals. A practical sage of the *Talmud* saw fit to recommend them as a short-cut to prosperity. "Whoever wishes to become rich," he wrote, "let him devote himself to the raising of small animals." The reason for this enthusiasm, no doubt, was that the sheep and goats served many useful purposes. They supplied wool for clothing, meat for the table, and the milk of the goats was for drinking and for the making of cheese. The tender meat of the goat kid was a highly prized delicacy. Goat hides were also used as containers to hold wine and water.

Besides sheep and goats there were the ox, which drew the plow and the laden cart, and the bull, which was merely used for breeding purposes. Amusingly, the *Mishna* and the *Talmud* repeatedly are obliged to discuss all kinds of problems of civil and criminal law that resulted from the high frequency of bull or ox-goring. Herds of cattle grazed in the valleys. The "fatted calf" was more than a figure of speech. It served as the *pièce de résistance* of every important festivity. King Solomon's royal table, the chronicler notes, groaned under its weight, although the plain people had to be satisfied with a hen or a rooster on festivals or on days of celebration.

Just as it is today, the little ass was the mainstay of trans-

6

Beast of burden.

portation. It was a patient hard-working beast of burden, although difficult to handle because of its temperament.

After the ass, the camel, "the ship of the desert," was the most widely used animal for carrying heavy loads over long distances. The horse, oddly enough, was used principally for military purposes, for the chariot and for cavalry. The finest horses came from other countries. Because of his notorious love of luxury and military power, King Solomon kept a large stable of Egyptian horses at Meggido.

There were many wild animals and beasts of prey in the Land of Israel, according to the Bible chroniclers. Some of those mentioned can no longer be found in Palestine, for instance, the leopard, the crocodile and the ostrich. The lion is mentioned about 130 times in the Holy Scriptures. In the Mesopotamian area of the ancient Semitic world the lion towered as a symbol of strength and majesty.

The attributes of the lion and of other wild animals became Hebraic figures of speech. In extolling the virtues necessary to the would-be pious man the *Talmud* gives this piece of zoological advice: "Be courageous as a leopard, be swift as an eagle, nimble as a stag, and strong as a lion, in order that you may fulfill the will of Your Father in Heaven."

Then, of course, there were the foxes, "the little foxes," the hyenas and the jackals who prowled in packs, the bats, gazelles, stags, hinds, ibexes, eagles, ravens, owls, snakes, lizards and scorpions. There have always been our present crop pests—the locusts and the grasshoppers; also spiders, wasps, hornets, bees and a great variety of creeping things. But these unpleasant insects were counter-balanced by the concrete and agreeable presence of animals whose flesh was considered a gourmet's delicacy—partridges, pheasants, quail and perhaps peacocks.

ISRAEL'S NEIGHBORS

To place the matter in its right focus: the ancient Israelites were only a part of a larger population-pattern that formed the mosaic of peoples in ancient Palestine. There were numer-

ous tribal units and federations among whom the land was divided. The natural terrain, a maze of stony ridges, of gray wilderness and of deep valleys, lent itself to an easy isolation of one group from the others. Besides the Israelites, there were the Canaanites, Ammonites, Moabites, Amorites, Edomites, Hittites, Jebusites, Horites, Phoenicians and Philistines. Every little corner had its prince, every town its kingdom. The Philistines themselves were divided into five "states." It is easy to see how these small peoples were prey for invaders.

Ethnic Semitic types. *Left.* Sumerian, C. 2600 B.C.E. (*Metropolitan Museum*) *Center.* C. 1200 B.C.E. *Right.* C. 28th-26th century B.C.E.

With the exception of the Philistines, all these groups drew from the common source of religion, language and culture we call Semitic. Actually, by their fundamental ties, nearly all these various groups were related to the same ethnic culture family. But, by living apart, they insulated themselves to some degree against one another's influence, and so gradually developed their own group characteristics and traditions.

All these tribal groups spoke Semitic tongues of greater or lesser similarity, so that it was not too difficult for one group to understand the others. Despite the division among them, and notwithstanding the stern prohibitions in the Mosaic Law, intermarriage with the other groups and idol worship went on all the time among the ancient Israelites.

Similarity of Israelites and Canaanites. *Left.* Two Israelite warriors (First Temple Period). *Right.* Canaanite warrior.

It goes without saying that no people ever lives in a vacuum, completely sealed off from the rest of mankind. Deep were the influences of the dominant civilizations of antiquity —Egypt and Babylonia-Assyria. These profoundly left their stamp on Jewish life and thought, as we shall see.

Undoubtedly, during the earliest period and before they evolved their own individuality as a people, the Israelites, in their way of life, beliefs, occupations, language and customs, were hardly distinguishable from the Canaanite groups. When the Israelites first crossed the Jordan under Joshua to fight for the land they found numerous Canaanite communities occupying the lowlands from the Jordan to the Mediterranean Sea and from the foot of Mt. Hermon in the north to the southern end of the Dead Sea. The Ammonites lived in the hills surrounding them—a warlike people. The Phoenicians, a trading and maritime people, occupied the northern stretch of the coastal region. Living so close together, the cultural fusion of these groups, including the Israelites, was inevitable and unavoidable. The periodic invasions of Palestine by the Egyptians, even before the Bondage in Egypt, turned many of these groups into vassals of the Pharaohs.

There is also ample archaeological proof that Egyptian beliefs and ways were grafted onto the cultures of all the tribal groups in Canaan. The influence of the Hittite and Babylonian-Assyrian religions and civilizations was perhaps even greater than the Egyptian, owing in part at least to ethnic and language kinship, which did not exist with Egypt.

Astarte.
(First Temple Period.)

All the peoples of Palestine, like peoples everywhere in antiquity, were idol-worshippers. They had a vast and incongruous pantheon of major and minor deities. Frequently these bore similar Semitic names and had similar divine attributes. Among the Canaanites, a male deity was sometimes called a *baal* and a female one a *baalat*. They were designated by various other names, too, by *el* (god) or *adon* (lord). The worship of the female goddess of fertility, Ishtar, or Astarte (Hebrew, Ashtoreth), was borrowed from the Babylonians, and was widespread in Canaan. This held true among the Israelites at fairly late periods, even as late as the Exile.

These divinities, major and minor, were worshipped with invocations, propitiations, incantations and bloody sacrifices "in high places," on rocks, on pillars, on stone altars and before trees.

The gods were masters of everything through their agents, the priests. They could demand all that the people possessed: the first-fruits of all produce and the firstlings of all animals. There was no such thing as a unified religion with a consistent set of beliefs. Each city had its own supreme *baal* or *ashtoreth*.

Canaanite altars.

Nature worship and animism led the Canaanites to attempt to placate the spirits and demons of nature, that were believed to dwell in every rock, tree and river, with all manner of gifts and sacrifices: of incense and even of children. The Philistines and Phoenicians who inhabited the seacoast of Palestine, and therefore were maritime and fishing peoples, worshipped fish, a mainstay of their daily diet. The goddess Atargatis of the Aramaeans in southern Syria was a fish-deity; she was represented with a human face and the scaly tail of a fish. A sacred fish, symbolizing her, was kept in a pond adjoining her temple and was eaten ritually by priests in a solemn religious ceremony. In Ascalon, a coastal city where the Philistines lived, a similar deity, also in the form of a woman with a fishtail, was worshipped. Dagon (*dag* means "fish" in Hebrew and in other Semitic tongues), the chief god of Philistia, was also represented with a fishtail, and here, too, sacred fish were eaten in a ritual performed by the priests.

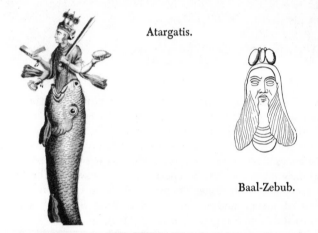

Atargatis.

Baal-Zebub.

The Philistines, apparently afraid of it, worshipped a fly-god at Ekrom. They called him *Baal-Zebub* (or Baal-Zebul, Lord Prince). In the New Testament this Philistine fly-god was transformed into Beelzebub, prince of the demons. Bulls and cows, of course, were worshipped widely in the same way as fish, primarily because they were sources of sustenance. The Aramaeans worshipped the storm god *Hadad* enthroned on a bull. The worship of the golden calf by the Israelites in the desert was no mere accident.

Babylonia and Assyria, in their religion as in their art, were very similar. The priests, a dominant force in those empires, constituted a hereditary clergy, the high priest being the king himself. They, too, like the priests of Egypt, worshipped with chanting of hymns and with the recitation of magic formulas.

Oddly enough, these sometimes sound ethical overtones which the Israelites, in their later more developed period, merely increased and deepened. One of the beliefs, for instance, which the Jews later adopted, was that a man who causes unjust grief or injury to others is punished by the gods with illness of body and soul.

The star and moon worship of the Babylonians had a profound effect on Jewish beliefs. The Babylonians were convinced that the celestial bodies held the secrets of man's future. They also believed that there was a mysterious connection between the destinies of people and the motion of the stars. They conceived of the souls of the dead as winging their solitary way to the starry regions to live there in perfect bliss forever. The virtuous and the heroic, in their passing, were invariably transformed by the gods into indestructible, luminous stars.

From the worship of the stars sprang astrology, the Babylonian "science" of seeking the chart of man's unknown future in the celestial orbs. It is interesting to note that in the Bible astrologists were called Chaldeans, and this usage has come down to recent times.

While the Egyptian genius, more than 4,000 years ago, excelled in sculpture and painting, architecture and science, its religion, as has so often happened in the case of other great civilizations, suffered from stagnation and primitive magic. There were, in fact, many religions in ancient Egypt, each with a great profusion of gods. Each locality had its own favorite deities, and with them a bewildering confusion of beliefs—concerning the universe, life and death, and the nature of the soul.

Egypt was a priest state; it was also a slave state. Its economy was built on the back-breaking toil of untold millions. The ruling classes, as in ancient Athens, were cultured and far in advance of their times. But the great majority of the people were backward and oppressed, kept purposely ignorant and superstitious.

Perhaps more than any other people the Egyptians were nature worshippers in the most aboriginal sense. All their deities, demons and spirits represented the forces of nature, the sun, moon and stars, rivers, animals and trees.

Egyptian priest presenting an official and his son to the god.

Metropolitan Museum

Even more pervasive among the people was the worship of the god of death. The Egyptians considered their houses as only temporary habitations and themselves as travelers passing through a world in which they were strangers. Their tombs, however, they looked upon as being their everlasting homes. That is why the rich often lavished more care on their places of burial than on their homes.

This brief summary of the beliefs of the Israelites' neighbors is essential to an understanding of the religious growth of the Israelites. More important still, it sets the background for the epoch-making and historically unprecedented discovery by the ancient Jews of an ethical God. This One God was a Supreme Being who expected the life of Man to be hallowed by the daily practice of the arts of peace and righteousness, of social justice and of human brotherhood. This universal child of God is best characterized by the poetic Talmudic tradition: "When God made the first man, He fashioned him out of the dust that He had gathered from all the countries of the world."

Egyptians at prayer.

From left to right. Ugaritic divine couple, Syria, c. 2000-1800 B.C.E. Syrian winged male sphinx, c. 1200 B.C.E. Egyptian goddess, Sekhmet. Hittite god Teshub, c. 1400 B.C.E.

THE CREATION AND THE FIRST MEN

The Creation of Man.   *Michelangelo (Sistine Chapel)*

The traditional Jewish belief is that God existed in timelessness before He created the world. He created it out of chaos by His divine will and He shaped it into harmony. In fact, He talked it into being. God said, "Let there be light: and there was light." Similarly, "By the word of the Lord were the heavens made; and all the hosts of them by the breath of his mouth." In this manner, the Book of Genesis records, He brought into existence both Night and Day, Earth and Sea and Heaven, all manner of vegetation and produce, the animals on land, in the sea and in the air.

God Creates Man

But the most important act of creation and the crowning point of his labors the Lord left for the very end of the Sixth Day. Then He said: "Let us make man in our image."

So He proceeded to form the first man out of dust, and in His own divine likeness, and He breathed the breath of life into his nostrils, and man became "a living soul."

The Lord called the first man Adam because He had formed him from *adamah*, which in Hebrew means "earth." And this lowly origin of man was called to his attention each time that he grew too haughty. The Lord put Adam over all other creatures in the world and told him to multiply his seed and to enjoy the fruits of the world. To increase his bliss He made for him the Garden of Eden, which He bade him tend and cultivate and enjoy. Only one fruit was forbidden: "the fruit of the tree of knowledge of good and evil."

God fashioned for Adam a woman from a rib in his side and He called her Eve, because she was to be the mother of all mankind. And Eve was Adam's companion and she shared with him the innocent bliss of the universe.

The Fall of Man

One day Eve was tempted by a serpent, who urged her to eat the forbidden fruit from the tree of knowledge, "then your eyes shall be opened, and ye shall be as gods, knowing good and evil."

She listened to the serpent's seductive words and she tasted, and induced Adam to taste, the fruit: "And the eyes of them both were opened. . . ."

Then the Lord's anger fell upon them and they ran to hide themselves from His wrath among the trees. Why had they done it? asked the Lord. "The serpent beguiled me, and so I did eat," Eve excused herself.

Miniature from a Hebrew ms. anthology of the Bible. 1288 c.e.
British Museum

Thereupon, the Lord decided to punish them, and He passed sentence upon them: For all the days of their lives they would have to earn their bread by the sweat of their brows and eat it in sorrow. And because they had fallen from divine grace He drove them with a flaming sword out of the Garden of Eden and into the unpredictable hazards of the mortal world.

Thereafter, Adam and Eve experienced every manner of joy and grief that is the lot of all humankind. They toiled and moiled in order to live and bring up their two sons. Cain, the elder, was a tiller of the soil and Abel was a shepherd. But between the two brothers there was a great rivalry, and on the part of Cain a bitter enmity for his younger brother.

One day, Abel the shepherd brought a sacrifice to the Lord of the fat firstlings of his flock. Cain the tiller, too, offered a sacrifice of his fruits. But the Lord accepted Abel's offering only—Cain's he rejected. At this Cain felt humiliated, and he was filled with a desperate resentment of Abel. Whose fault

Adam and Eve Driven Out of Paradise. *Dürer*

was it if not his own? the Lord chided him. As long as he continued in the path of sin he would not be favored.

From that time on Cain plotted vengeance on his brother.

Cain Kills Abel

Then one day when the two were alone in the field, "Cain rose up against Abel, his brother, and slew him." The Lord then descended upon Cain and asked him sternly: "Where is Abel, your brother?" "I know not," answered Cain. "Am I my brother's keeper?"

His reply angered the Lord. "What have you done?" He rebuked him. "The voice of your brother's blood cries out to me from the ground."

The crime of the fratricide could not go unpunished, lest evil triumph in the world. And so the Lord pronounced a curse on Cain, the ageless curse upon the murderer. Henceforth, Cain was to be "a fugitive and a wanderer on earth."

A time came when the Lord regretted that He had ever created wretched men, for as they increased in number and their possessions multiplied, they grew in wickedness.

The earth had become corrupt and was filled with violence. According to Jewish tradition, the people of that generation were haughty, licentious and without shame. They mocked at the Lord and at everything righteous. Therefore, the Lord resolved: "I will destroy them with the earth."

Noah, the Ark and the Flood

Only one, Noah, "was a just man." He walked in the ways of the Lord. Therefore the Lord loved him, and only him would he spare from destruction. He bade Noah build a three-story ark of gopher wood. He instructed him to seal it both outside and inside with pitch, in order to make it waterproof. He told him to ready it for a long sea voyage.

Noah built the ark, and all the wicked came to watch him at his labors and to jeer at him. At the Lord's bidding Noah entered the ark with his wife and his three sons, Ham, Shem and Japheth, and also their three wives. In addition, Noah took into the ark with him a male and female of every living species of animal.

Then, at the bidding of the Lord, the waters began to rise. After seven days they were at flood-tide. Furthermore, "the windows of heaven were opened" and it rained forty days and forty nights. The ark was then lifted up and swept away by the flood, which covered everything.

The Flood. *Michelangelo (Sistine Chapel)*

Mount Ararat.

For 150 days the flood raged. After that the waters abated and the ark rested on the mountain of Ararat. Noah sent out a dove to see if the flood had receded. It came back, for the flood was still strong. A week later, he sent the dove out again and when she returned—"lo, in her mouth was an olive-leaf plucked off." The following week Noah sent the dove out once again. It did not return and thereby Noah knew that the waters had at last abated. And so he and his kin left the ark, rejoicing. With them went all the animals, as the Lord had commanded, in order that, in a world cleansed of its evil, "they may breed abundantly."

At first the descendants of Noah were blessed and they multiplied. They lived in peace and harmony with one another, for they all "spoke one language" and worshipped the Lord. But with the passage of time all this changed. Corruption and evil once again were rife on the earth.

The Tower of Babel

In the land of Shinar near the Euphrates River, where Noah's descendants lived, the people were filled with pride and arrogance. They said to one another: "Let us build us a city and a tower, with its top in heaven."

Jewish tradition calls the men who built the Tower of Babel, *Dor Haflagah*, "the generation of secession." They were men determined to secede from God's rule of the world. The *Midrash* puts the following argument into the mouths of these rebels: "He—God—has no right to choose the upper world for Himself, and to leave the lower world to us. Therefore, we will build a tower, with an idol on the top holding a sword, to appear as if it intended to war with God."

When the Lord heard the great commotion in the land of Shinar, He came down to investigate. Indignant at the arrogance of the rebels, he was resolved to confound them. He confused them so in their speech that one could no longer understand the other. Chaos reigned and the ambitious project had to be abandoned.

AS HISTORIANS VIEW IT

All people have their creation-myths, say the historians. Therefore, the creation-story narrated in the Bible merely follows the pattern in which peoples and groups of men, feeling overwhelmed by the mystery of life and the orderly vastness of the universe, try to explain their origin.

It is perhaps not accidental, point out the historians, that there is a striking similarity between the creation-story in the Bible and some of the cosmological myths of other peoples of antiquity.

There is, for instance, an early Egyptian myth which describes Re, the sun-god in the Egyptian pantheon, as having created the world and mankind by means of his divine powers and his will. Another Egyptian myth ascribes the creation of the world to the god Thoth, who was credited with supreme magic powers. Oddly enough, Thoth, somewhat

Babylonian cylinder-seal.

like the Lord in the Bible, intoned all creation into existence chanting magic formulae until the universe was completed.

Another striking parallel is found in the Finnish epic poem, *The Kalevala*. There, "the wise and truthful" bard, Wainemoinen, struck his harp and sang the world into being.

Philo, the great neo-Platonic philosopher and rabbi who flourished in Alexandria almost two thousand years ago, first propounded a view that has now been quite generally accepted by advanced Bible scholars. He wrote: "It is folly to suppose that the universe was made in six days, or in time at all." The Bible story of creation, he averred, was merely an allegory, and was not to be taken literally. Its aim was to point out by means of symbolism that God's way in everything was perfect and harmonious, and that He was always creating order out of chaos, in the universe and in man's affairs.

The story of the flood, too, has analogies in ancient mythology. A Babylonian cuneiform tablet, with the text of a Sin-Flood incident similar to that recorded in the Bible, was unearthed in 1872. This version is considered even more ancient than that of the Bible. It, too, comments sadly on the corrupt spirit that took hold of the first created men. They were disobedient and ungrateful to the gods for all that they had done for them. The gods, therefore, resolved to be done with them, to drown them and wipe them from the earth.

However, there was some disagreement in the divine council: the deity of the underground waters, Ea, asked pertinently: what would happen to the world if all mankind were destroyed? She, therefore, secretly revealed the plan of the gods in a dream to Utnapishtim, who, like Noah, built an ark and took along with him animals and birds of every species. Then the god Marduk let loose the flood.

After six days of being tossed about on the flood-waters, "the huge boat" finally rested on Mount Nisir. Utnapishtim then sent out a dove to find out if it would be safe for him to emerge. Finding no resting-place, the dove returned. Then Utnapishtim sent out a swallow, but it, too, returned. Finally a raven was let loose, and he did not return. Then Utnapishtim knew for certain that the time had come for him to leave the ark in safety. So he, his family, and all the animals stepped onto dry land, and offered a sacrifice of thanksgiving.

That the Tower of Babel story, when stripped of its legendary elements, was at least based on architectural reality, has become evident in recent decades of archaeological discovery. Ruined Towers of Babel, or *ziggurats*, have been located in various parts of Babylonia. They all seem to have had a similar design, and were built on "stages." One tower, found at Borsippa, and first mentioned by Rabbi Benjamin of Tudela, the tireless traveler of the twelfth century, has been attributed inconclusively to Nebuchadnezzar. It was built in seven stages, presumably to symbolize the Seven Heavens.

THE FIRST HEBREWS

Abraham

The Bible describes the Patriarch Abraham as being the first Hebrew. When he was a young man, his father Terah took his household, including Abraham, Abraham's wife Sarah, and his nephew Lot, on a journey to the land of Canaan. But they never reached their destination. Instead they stopped halfway at Haran and settled there.

Unfortunately, in the Biblical narrative there is no reference made to Abraham's early life. The Jewish folk-fancy of later days, however, attempted to fill this gap by means of moral-istic and wise tales that have become traditional. Ancient

Priest and worshipper before the sun god, Shamash. (Seal from the reign of Ur-Engour, c. 2300 B.C.E.)   *British Museum*

sources, like the *Talmud* and *Midrash*, embellish every remembered tale of Abraham's boyhood with all the warmth and lyricism of which a grateful people was capable toward its founder.

These folk-reconstructions tell how, even as a lad, Abraham showed the traits of "a wise man." At fourteen he had not only discovered the emptiness of idol-worship but had demonstrated successfully to the farmers of Chaldea better methods for cultivating the soil.

Now it so happened, relates a tradition in the *Talmud*, that the Chaldeans were moon-worshippers who believed in astrological prediction, and young Abraham was carried away by this religious enthusiasm. He, too, became a star-gazer.

Abraham Discovers the One God

One night, when the crescent of the new moon appeared red in the sky, Abraham went out to inquire of the stars whether the crops planted that season would yield a good harvest. As he tried to divine the answer from the stars, he was filled with consternation: he knew suddenly that he had been deluded. It was then that the Lord revealed Himself to Abraham for the first time.

Abraham, the ancient tradition continues, was contrite before the Lord. He implored forgiveness for having, in his ignorance, followed false gods. Henceforth, he swore, he would abandon the lifeless idols of Chaldea and worship only the Lord. And so, at fourteen, he went forth into the world as a missionary to the idolators to teach the way of the Lord.

There are many incidents related in the *Talmud* and *Midrash* which attempt to illustrate the nature of the conflicts into which young Abraham was flung as a result of his doubts about the divinity of his father's idols. For instance, one legend, in which Abraham's father, Terah, is a maker and seller of idols, tells how an old man once went into Terah's shop to buy an idol. Since Terah was out, the boy Abraham waited on him. The old man chose his idol carefully.

"How old are you?" asked the boy.

"Seventy years," replied the man.

"Fool! How can you worship a god who is so much younger than you?" young Abraham jeered at him. "You were born seventy years ago, but this idol was made only yesterday!"

At this, the old man threw down his idol in disgust and walked away.

The Bible story, however, tells us that after the death of his father in Haran, Abraham felt free at last to lead his own life, to explore a new conception which his conscience had opened to him.

The Lord once more appeared to Abraham and commanded him: "Get thee out of thy country, and from thy kindred, and from thy father's house, unto the land that I will show thee. And I will make of thee a great nation, and I will bless thee, and make thy name great."

Abraham, Sarah and his nephew, Lot, depart from Haran for Canaan. (Mosaic from Church of San Marco, Venice.)

Abraham did as the Lord bade him. But when he reached Canaan, the country the Lord spoke of, he found a great famine. Accordingly, he thought it prudent to migrate with his household to Egypt, where he prospered in cattle, in gold and in silver. But his prosperity gave him no pleasure. He longed for the land of Canaan which the Lord had promised him would be an inheritance to his descendants forever.

In the years that followed, Abraham and his nephew Lot lived side by side. Their flocks increased and they grew in power, but their irritation with each other grew with their prosperity. Matters reached a head when their herdsmen started to quarrel. It was then Abraham decided to part company with his kinsman, and Lot chose to settle among the inhabitants of Sodom.

Sodom and Gomorrah

Now, Sodom and its companion city Gomorrah were evil cities in the eyes of the Lord. An ancient tradition recorded in the *Talmud* says that each man hated his neighbor, and all acts of human kindness were despised. Local custom made them punishable by death if discovered. Justice was not only blind and cruel but also corrupt.

When the Lord made known to Abraham His unalterable intention to destroy those wicked cities, Abraham was horrified. Vainly he implored: "Wilt thou indeed sweep away the righteous with the wicked?" He further asked: "Shall not the Judge of all the earth do justly?"

Lot's Flight from Sodom. *Doré*

But the Lord remained adamant. Had He found but ten righteous men in all of Sodom, He assured Abraham, He would gladly have spared the entire city.

Accordingly, two angels descended upon Sodom and Gomorrah, unloosed a rain of fire and brimstone upon them, and utterly destroyed them. But taking into consideration the great merit of Abraham, the Lord agreed to spare the lives of Lot, his wife and their two daughters, who were permitted to flee the city.

As Lot and his household reached the outskirts of the burning city, his "wife looked back from behind him, and she became a pillar of salt."

Isaac

Because Sarah had not borne any children, Abraham complained to the Lord. Had He not promised him that his seed would be as numerous as the stars and as countless as the sands of the sea?

"Behold, to me Thou hast given no seed," he lamented.

Seeing how deeply Abraham yearned for a son, Sarah persuaded him to wed her handmaiden, Hagar, who bore him a son, Ishmael. And when Sarah saw that her handmaiden had borne a son while she remained barren, she felt so humiliated and jealous that she treated Hagar harshly.

Hagar in the Desert. *Corot* *Metropolitan Museum*

When Sarah finally conceived and gave birth to a son, Isaac, she said to Abraham with resolution: "the son of this bondswoman shall not be heir with my son. . . ."

And Abraham, who was weak before Sarah's onslaught, drove Hagar into the wilderness of Beersheba, where she strayed, abandoned and alone, with her boy Ishmael. The Lord, however, saved them through an angel.

The Sacrifice of Isaac

Probably the one incident in the Hebrew Scriptures which has most deeply stirred the emotions and the imagination of all generations of Jews was Abraham's attempted sacrifice of his beloved son Isaac. This was because of the moral and human problems the incident posed so dramatically. For one thing, it was the supreme test of faith. For another, it stood for the most poignant renunciation of self any human being could be called upon to make for his faith.

One day the Lord revealed Himself to Abraham, the Bible story goes. "Take now thy son," He commanded, "thine only son, whom thou lovest, Isaac, and get thee unto the land of Moriah; and offer him there for a burnt-offering upon one of the mountains which I will tell thee of."

Abraham obeyed the Lord implicitly, even though his heart was breaking.

The Book of Genesis tells in detail how Abraham built a sacrificial altar on Mount Moriah, piled wood on it, and then

bound Isaac and laid him on the wood. The terrible moment came at last. As Abraham reached out his hand for the sacrificial knife, it is told in the *Talmud*, the angels in heaven started to weep. And as they wept, their tears flowed down to earth and fell on Isaac's eyes. So moved was the Lord by His angels' grief that He instantly sent the Archangel Michael winging down to earth. Swiftly Michael gripped Abraham's outstretched hand and restrained the knife poised to slay. "For now I know," murmured the angel to Abraham, "that thou art a God-fearing man."

In commemoration of Abraham's exemplary faith, it became a tradition on *Rosh Hashanah,* the Jewish New Year, to read aloud in the synagogue that chapter of the Book of Genesis which tells of the sacrifice of Isaac. And when the *shofar,* the ram's horn, is solemnly blown at the end, then Abraham's descendants are comforted in the knowledge that because of his steadfast faith they will be protected for that year against all tribulation.

Just as the Lord was humane and gentle, so was Abraham, says the *Midrash:* "Until Abraham's time the Lord was known only as the God of heaven. When He appeared to Abraham He became the God of the earth as well as of heaven, for he brought Him near to man."

In time Abraham was recognized as the prototype of the ideal righteous man. "Whosoever has a kind eye, a simple

Child sacrifice was practiced among the Canaanites, Babylonians and other neighboring peoples to the East, as evidenced by this detail from a Babylonian cylinder dating back approximately to the time of Abraham.

Machpelah. An interior view of the mosque built by Arabs over the traditional site of the Cave of Machpelah. Moslems, too, consider the Hebrew Patriarchs and Matriarchs as their illustrious ancestors.

heart and a humble spirit . . . is a disciple of Abraham," say the sages in the *Ethics of the Fathers.*

The time came when Sarah sickened and died and Abraham buried her in the cave called Machpelah which he had bought from some Hittites in Hebron. Later he and Isaac and Jacob and their wives were buried there.

Perhaps it was Sarah's death which made Abraham realize it was time to find a wife for Isaac. He therefore instructed his steward, Eliezer, to go to Nahor in Mesopotamia, where Abraham's kinsmen lived, and to bring back a proper wife for his son.

Rebekah

When Eliezer reached the outskirts of Nahor "he made his camels to kneel down . . . by a well of water at the time of the evening . . . that women go out to draw water."

Isaac's meeting with Rebekah.

As he did so, a girl arrived carrying a pitcher upon her shoulder. She went down to the well and filled it. As she turned to leave, Eliezer went toward her and said: "Let me, I pray thee, drink a little water of thy pitcher." And she said: "Drink, my lord." After he was through drinking she drew more water from the well and slaked his camels' thirst. Eliezer marveled greatly at her kindness and as a token he put a gold earring into her ear and golden bracelets on her hands, for he knew that at last he had found the proper wife for his master's son.

The girl's name was Rebekah. She was the daughter of Bethuel, the Aramaean, and a kinswoman of Abraham's. So Eliezer was full of rejoicing and took her back with him to the land of Canaan.

Now, "Isaac went out to meditate in the field at the eventide: and he lifted up his eyes and saw, and behold, the camels were coming." When, in turn, Rebekah noticed Isaac, she dismounted from her camel. Then Isaac led her into his departed mother's tent and Rebekah "became his wife, and he loved her."

Isaac's life was rather uneventful. The Lord was with him in everything he did. He increased his inheritance from his father and never had to journey outside Canaan.

Jacob and Esau

For many years Rebekah was barren, but at last she gave birth to twins. The firstborn was named Esau and the brother, Jacob. The brothers were opposites. Esau was a fierce warrior and a hunter. He was devoted to his father, whose favorite he was, and he supplied him with the finest game, which Isaac liked exceedingly. Jacob, on the other hand, was gentle and quiet. He pursued the arts of peace. He was a shepherd, and his mother's favorite.

One day Esau came home from the hunt, faint with hunger, and found Jacob preparing some pottage of lentils. Almost overcome by the smell of the food, Esau asked Jacob for a mess of the pottage, and Jacob answered, "Sell me first your birthright." At that moment, the birthright mattered little to Esau, who thought he would die of hunger. He agreed to sell it to Jacob, and when Esau swore to abide by the sale, Jacob fed him.

As Isaac grew old and infirm, he became quite blind. When he felt the shadow of death stealing upon him, he called Esau to him. He asked him to hunt for some venison, and to prepare a dish of it "such as I love, and bring it to me, that I may eat; that my soul may bless thee before I die."

Rebekah, who had overheard the conversation, confided it promptly to Jacob. She urged him to impersonate Esau before

A birthright for a mess of pottage.

his father in order that he might receive the blessing instead. Jacob demurred. He argued: "Esau, my brother, is a hairy man, and I am a smooth man. My father peradventure will feel me, and I shall seem to him as a mocker; and I shall bring a curse upon me and not a blessing."

"Upon me be thy curse," Rebekah reassured him.

Ill at ease with the deception she asked him to work, Jacob followed his mother's instructions. He brought her two tender kids with which she prepared a tasty dish for Isaac, the kind she knew he was fond of. To add a realistic touch to the impersonation, Rebekah made Jacob put on Esau's clothes. As a further safeguard, she tied the hairy skin of the two kids on Jacob's hands and around his neck. Then he went in to see Isaac.

"My father," he said.

"Who art thou, my son?" asked Isaac.

"I am Esau, thy firstborn; I have done according as thou badest me. Arise, I pray thee, sit and eat of my venison, that thy soul may bless me."

"How is it that thou hast found it so quickly, my son?" asked Isaac in wonder.

"Because the Lord thy God sent me good speed," answered Jacob.

"Come near, I pray thee, that I may feel thee, my son, whether thou be my very son Esau or not."

Jacob went near and Isaac felt him. "The voice is the voice of Jacob, but the hands are the hands of Esau," he said suspiciously. Again he touched Jacob's hands, but when he found that they were hairy, he was reassured.

"Come near now and kiss me, my son," Isaac said to him.

Then Isaac folded him into his arms and blessed him. When Esau discovered Jacob's deception he hated Jacob with a terrible hatred.

"Let the days of mourning for my father be at hand; then will I slay my brother Jacob," he thought in his heart.

When Rebekah learned of Esau's murderous intention, she hurried Jacob off on a visit to her brother Laban in Haran.

Jacob's Dream: The Ladder

Jacob journeyed with as great speed as possible from Beersheba to Haran. As night began to fall, he laid his head on a stone and went to sleep. And as he slept, he had a dream in

From "The Second *Haggadah*," c. 1300. *Germanic National Museum, Nuremberg*

which appeared the reassuring theme in the lives of all the three patriarchs—that of the Lord's Promise. And Jacob dreamed he saw a ladder. The bottom rung rested on the earth, the topmost reached into heaven. And on it was a procession of angels, ascending and descending constantly.

Suddenly Jacob became aware that "the Lord stood before him."

He heard Him say: "I am the Lord, the God of Abraham thy father, and the God of Isaac. The land whereon thou liest, to thee will I give it, and to thy seed. And thy seed shall be as the dust of the earth and thou shalt spread abroad to the west, and to the east, and to the north and to the south.

And in thee and in thy seed shall all the families of the earth be blessed. And, behold, I am with thee and will keep thee whithersoever thou goest and will bring thee back unto this land; for I will not leave thee until I have done that which I have spoken to thee of."

When Jacob awoke in the morning he must have felt profoundly stirred by his dream. He interpreted it to be a personal revelation from the Lord. In recognition of this awesome event he "took the stone that he had put under his head and set it up for a pillar and poured oil upon the top of it." He called the place *Beth-el*, the "House of God."

This was the beginning of a new phase in Jacob's life, accidental and owing to his flight from Esau's vengeance.

Jacob and Rachel

As Jacob reached Haran, he saw a girl approach. She was leading a flock of sheep to the well. Jacob saw that she was beautiful, and her charm attracted him. Eager to bring himself to her attention, he rolled away the stone that covered the mouth of the well and he watered her flock. Later, when he discovered that she was his cousin Rachel, the daughter of his uncle Laban, "Jacob kissed Rachel, and lifted up his voice, and wept."

After the fresco in the Loggia di Raffaello, the Vatican, planned and supervised by Raphael.

When finally he met his uncle Laban, Jacob proposed: "I will serve thee seven years for Rachel, thy younger daughter." If he said explicitly "younger," it was because Laban also had an older daughter, Leah, who was not at all beautiful.

And so, for seven long years Jacob served Laban faithfully and well, "and they seemed to him but a few days, for the love he had for her [Rachel]." When he went to claim Rachel for his wife, Laban consented promptly to give his daughter in marriage. But on the morning after the wedding night, Jacob made a startling discovery: Laban had deceived him, had married him off not to Rachel but to his elder daughter, Leah, with the "weak eyes."

This piece of duplicity only fanned the flame of Jacob's love for Rachel. Although outraged by Laban's treachery, he nonetheless agreed to work another seven years for Rachel. All in all, he served Laban twenty years—fourteen for his two wives and six for the flock of goats and sheep he earned from his father-in-law in lieu of wages. Then Jacob departed for the land of Canaan.

Now he was rich, and in the course of time he grew richer. Numerous were his flocks, his oxen and asses, his menservants and his maidservants. He even acquired two more wives besides Rachel and Leah. These were the latter's handmaidens, Bilhah and Zilpah, who also bore him sons.

Traditional Rachel's tomb on the road to Bethlehem.

At the time of Jacob's return to Canaan with his household he was the father of eleven sons: Reuben, Simeon, Levi, Judah, Issachar, Zebulun, Gad, Asher, Dan, Naphthali, Joseph, and a daughter, Dinah.

During the journey from Haran southward to Canaan, Rachel gave birth to Benjamin. Her other child was Joseph. But, as Benjamin came into the world, she departed from it. Deep was Jacob's grief at Rachel's passing. Of all his wives, it was she whom he had really loved. He mourned her, and then he laid her in a grave on the road to Bethlehem. Over the grave he set a pillar of stone as a memorial.

Jacob's old but unforgotten feud with Esau was suddenly revived when he heard that Esau was hastening toward him with an armed band. Jacob trembled for his life and the lives of his family, for he well remembered Esau's great enmity. To mollify Esau, Jacob sent messengers with costly gifts to him.

The night before their expected meeting, Jacob was full of foreboding. He went off by himself to meditate and plan for the ordeal.

Jacob Becomes "Israel"

The Bible chronicler relates how, as Jacob meditated, he met an angel. He wrestled with him in mortal combat until the break of day. When the angel saw that he could not prevail, he implored Jacob: "Let me go, for the day breaketh."

But Jacob was filled with despair when he remembered what terrible end awaited him in the morning. So he cried out to the angel: "I will not let go of thee, except that thou bless me."

Since the angel had no choice, he blessed Jacob: "Thy name shall be called no more Jacob, but Israel; for thou hast striven with God and with man and hast prevailed."

From "The Second *Haggadah*," c. 1300. *Germanic National Museum, Nuremberg*

From that moment on, Jacob was no longer afraid of Esau and of his vengeance. Now his name was Israel and not Jacob, and Esau could do him no harm.

When the two brothers met at last, it was without any lingering bitterness. They embraced and wept on each other's necks and were reconciled.

Joseph and His Brothers

Once again the drama of rivalry and strife between brothers is repeated because of the favoritism shown a particular son by a doting parent.

"Now Israel [i.e., Jacob] loved Joseph more than all his children, because he was the son of his old age: and he made him a coat of many colors. And when his brethren saw that their father loved him more than all his brethren, they hated him, and could not speak peaceably unto him."

It is interesting to note at this point that the sages of the *Talmud*, in spite of the awe and reverence in which they held the Patriarch Jacob, greatly disapproved of the favoritism he showed Joseph. They deemed it unjust toward the other sons, for a father should love all his children equally, they said.

As Joseph grew older, the envy of his brothers toward him intensified. He himself unintentionally helped to increase it because of a remarkable gift for interpreting dreams and for the prophetic quality of his own dreams.

Unaware of the hostility he would arouse, Joseph once described to his brothers a dream in which it was hinted that he would reign over them.

In this dream Joseph saw them binding sheaves of wheat in the field. Suddenly his own sheaf stood up, but the sheaves of all his brothers prostrated themselves in homage to him. When Joseph repeated this dream to Jacob, his father, too, thought it was strange. "Shall I and thy mother and thy brethren indeed come to bow down ourselves to thee to the earth?" asked Jacob ironically.

One day, while his brothers were grazing their father's flocks near Shechem, Jacob sent Joseph to them to inquire if all went well with them. When they saw Joseph approaching they started to jeer: "Behold, this dreamer cometh." They hurriedly put their heads together and plotted to slay him and to throw his body into a pit where no one would find it. But the eldest, Reuben, was horrified. After much pleading, he induced the others not to kill Joseph but to hide him instead in a pit.

Soon after, the brothers sold Joseph to some passing Ishmaelite merchants in a camel caravan on its way from Gilead to Egypt with spices, balm and ladanum.

Now the brothers were in a quandary: how were they to break the news to their father? So they held counsel together and decided on a deception: they took Joseph's "coat of many colors," which had made them so envious before, slaughtered a he-goat and dipped the coat in its blood. Then, pretending deep grief, they brought the coat to Jacob, who immediately concluded that a wild beast had devoured Joseph.

Then Jacob lamented and wept for his son.

In the meantime the Ishmaelites had reached Egypt and had sold Joseph as a slave to Potiphar, the captain of Pharaoh's guard. Joseph's unusual abilities soon attracted his master's attention, and Potiphar appointed him the steward of his household. As a result of his excellent management Potiphar's riches multiplied. He had full confidence in Joseph's honesty and entrusted everything to him.

Joseph and Potiphar's Wife

Potiphar's wife, to whom legend gave the name Zuleika, had fallen in love with Joseph, for he was very handsome. But Joseph spurned her love. Goaded by her unrequited passion, Zuleika made a display of her feelings for him at every opportunity. She pursued him, but Joseph eluded her.

When Zuleika finally concluded that her efforts were in vain, she plotted vengeance. She charged Joseph before Potiphar with misconduct. Potiphar believed her and cast Joseph into the palace prison.

This Jewish-Persian miniature represents Zuleika and a companion watching Joseph curiously through a lattice grill. *In lower right,* Joseph is shown in prison. (With text from a Persian poem by Jami, 17th century, written in Hebrew characters.)

Joseph's charm and intelligence favorably impressed the keeper of the prison. He treated him with kindness and left the management of all the other prisoners to him.

By chance, there were two important personages among the prisoners, Pharaoh's chief chamberlain and chief baker, who somehow had suffered their royal master's displeasure.

One day, they both had dreams which Joseph promptly interpreted for them. He predicted that within three days the royal chamberlain would obtain his freedom and the royal baker would be hanged.

It happened exactly as Joseph predicted. The baker was hanged. When the chamberlain was leaving the prison, restored to his favored position by Pharaoh, Joseph begged him: "Think of me when it shall be well with thee, and show kindness unto me, I pray thee, and make mention of me unto Pharaoh, and bring me out of this house." But the royal chamberlain so rejoiced over his good fortune, he forgot all about Joseph.

Pharaoh's Dream

Two years later Pharaoh had a very disturbing dream. He saw himself standing at the river's edge. Seven fat cows came out of the water to graze in the meadow. Thy were soon followed by seven lean cows. Thereupon, an astonishing thing happened: the seven lean cows devoured the seven fat cows. And, at this point, Pharaoh woke up.

Deeply troubled, he summoned all the magicians of Egypt. When they were assembled he told them this and yet another dream about seven withered ears of corn devouring seven perfect ones. Then the chief chamberlain suddenly recalled the wonderful interpreter of dreams, "the Hebrew Joseph," and he told Pharaoh about him.

So the king of Egypt sent for Joseph "and they brought him hastily out of the dungeon: and he shaved himself, and changed his raiment, and came in unto Pharaoh."

Joseph readily interpreted Pharaoh's dreams. He said that the two dreams were really one, that the seven lean cows and the seven withered ears of corn meant only one thing—that seven years of famine would come to Egypt. But these would be preceded by seven years of plenty. And when the seven years of famine finally came they would devour all the substance of the seven years of plenty. Joseph, therefore, advised Pharaoh to prepare himself against the famine during the years of plenty by appointing a competent administrator who would see that all surplus grain was stored away in order "that the land perish not through the famine."

Pharaoh was completely charmed by Joseph and appointed him vizier, governor of his kingdom "and he made him ruler over all the land of Egypt."

Joseph was then only thirty years old.

He set to work immediately and filled the granaries during the seven years of plenty. When the seven years of famine arrived, there was bread for all Egypt. But in all the other lands there was great hunger. Then "all countries came into Egypt to Joseph to buy corn, because the famine was so sore in all lands."

In the Land of Goshen

In Canaan, too, the famine raged. Jacob said to his sons: "I have heard that there is corn in Egypt: get you down there, and buy. . . ."

And Jacob's ten sons started out on their journey to Egypt. But Jacob would not permit them to take along little Benjamin, his youngest son, for he trembled greatly for his safety.

When the brothers reached Egypt they went to see Joseph, "for he it was that sold corn to all the people of the land." Now they did not recognize Joseph in the great vizier of Egypt, but he recognized them readily. Nonetheless, he "made himself strange unto them and spoke roughly unto them," and charged them with being spies.

"Nay, my lord, but to buy food are thy servants come . . . thy servants are twelve brethren, the sons of one man in the land of Canaan."

If that were so, asked Joseph, where was the twelfth brother? And, of course, Joseph missed his own beloved Benjamin, born of the same mother, Rachel. The only way they could prove that they were honest men and not spies, recommended Joseph, was to go back to Canaan and bring back with them their missing brother. To make sure that they would return he kept Simeon, one of the brothers, as a hostage.

At first Jacob refused to let Benjamin go, but when the famine got worse and all the grain the brothers had brought back with them from Egypt had been eaten up, he reluctantly allowed his sons to take Benjamin with them into Egypt.

As soon as Joseph saw Benjamin in the midst of his brothers, he invited them to dine with him. Then, pointing to Benjamin, Joseph asked: "Is this your youngest brother, of whom ye spoke unto me?"

And when they said that he was, Joseph was overcome with emotion, "and he sought where to weep; and he entered into his chamber, and wept there."

Still Joseph did not wish to reveal his identity. He ordered the steward of his house to fill his brothers' sacks with food, and in the mouth of each sack to place each man's money. "And put my cup, the silver cup, in the sack's mouth of the youngest, and his corn money."

At the break of dawn the brothers started out on their return journey to Canaan. But they had not gone very far when Joseph sent his steward in pursuit of them. He searched

Joseph's Stratagem.   *Francesco Ubertini Bacchiacca*

their sacks and looked for the silver cup. Of course, he found it in Benjamin's sack.

So all the brothers were hauled back again before Joseph, "and they fell before him on the ground."

Then Joseph revealed himself. He wept aloud and said: "I am Joseph your brother, whom you sold into Egypt." He forgave them and comforted them.

Joseph bade them return immediately to Canaan and to

tell his father in his name: "God hath made me lord of all Egypt; come down unto me, tarry not."

Joseph's brothers hastened to break the joyous news to their father. "Joseph is yet alive," they told him, "and he is governor over all the land of Egypt."

At first Jacob would not believe it, but finally he was convinced. He gathered his entire household, and it numbered seventy souls. Then he set out for Egypt to be reunited with his son, Joseph.

And so Jacob and his sons dwelt in the land of Goshen which is in Egypt. But when he began to feel the shadow of

Joseph Reveals Himself. *Doré*

death resting upon him, he did not want to be buried among strangers in Egypt. Therefore, he instructed Joseph that as soon as he had died he was to carry his remains back to Canaan and lay them in the Cave of Machpelah. "Bury me with my Fathers," he implored.

Jacob took farewell of all his kith and kin, gave them his last counsel, and "everyone according to his blessing he blessed them."

In the fullness of time, Joseph, too, died. They embalmed his body and put it in a sarcophagus, and it rested in Egypt. But when the Israelites departed from Egypt centuries later, they bore Joseph's remains with them to the land of his fathers.

Generation after generation of the children of Israel appeared in the land of Goshen. They were fruitful and they multiplied, "and waxed exceedingly mighty." So notes the Biblical chronicler.

Jacob Is Carried Home. (By an unknown Jewish folk artist, early 19th century.)

AS HISTORIANS VIEW IT

There are historians who have expressed serious doubt that the Hebrew Patriarchs—Abraham, Isaac and Jacob—ever really lived. They consider them ordinary folk-myths, like Romulus whom "a wolf suckled" and whom the Romans deified as their founder. These historians also point out that, outside of the Scriptures, no mention of them is to be found in any ancient records. For them this fact is conclusive evidence that the Patriarchs never existed.

An entirely different school of scholarship answers this skeptical view in this fashion: true enough, Biblical tradition lies embedded in myth and legend, but for all that, it has frequently turned out to be as authentic and reliable, in an historic sense, as the best tested documents. Granted even that the Patriarchs never lived, the fact that for thousands of years Jews of every generation have revered them as the Fathers of their stock and religion lends them a reality as profound as if they had actually lived—the reality of a great cultural and religious influence.

These historians emphasize another point: that the chronicler of the Book of Genesis treats the Patriarchs not as if they were myths but as well-remembered people who had the vices and virtues of ordinary human beings. And even if elements of myth and legend do enter the narrative, they in no way obscure the essential reality of the Patriarchs, particularly since their story has been kept alive by the oral tradition of the Jews, a tradition preserved by an unfading folk-memory made perhaps more persistent by a will to remember consecrated by religion.

The conduct of the Patriarchs and the analysis of their motives, say these historians, are time and again presented in the most unflattering way in the Bible. This portrayal makes them out as neither heroes nor paragons of virtue, but as well-meaning though erring, groping men. They are drawn with restraint, sometimes with brutal objectivity, but always with a rugged truthfulness. They are basically good men with a hunger for righteousness and a compelling need to find the Lord, but they lack insight into themselves. They are moved to act, like most men, by mysterious passions which they themselves neither understand always nor are capable of controlling. Their characters are full of contradictions and their worship of the Lord is marked by confusion and inconsistency. They are at once humane and cruel, righteous and corrupt, morally weak and strong, primitive and progressive, thirsty for truth and sly at working for their material interests.

In short, they are portrayed in the Bible as human beings. Their traits of character and their attitudes of mind must not, however, be judged by those of our own age, for history, despite the general belief, does not repeat itself. Abraham, Isaac and Jacob, in order to be understood, must be evaluated in the context of the society in which they lived, and by that society's standards.

The Habiru

In the opinion of some scholars who believe that the story of Abraham is essentially true, it would be unrealistic to attempt to fix a specific date for his life. However, because he was a semi-nomadic chieftain at about the same time as the vast migratory movement of the Habiru (for an account of this migration, see page 25) they assume that he must have lived sometime between 2000 and 1700 B.C.E.

Frequent references to these Habiru are found in very ancient records. They date from the middle of the Third to almost the close of the Second Millennium B.C.E.—a time-range of more than a thousand years. Some of the references bear a striking similarity to the experiences, the way of life and the manner of thinking and feeling of the Old Testament accounts of Abraham, Isaac and Jacob.

A leading architect of Israelite destiny was Jacob's favorite son Joseph. Persistent attempts have been made in recent years to prove that he was an historical character. It is argued with some heat by the skeptics that it is indeed surprising that in the well-documented history of ancient Egypt there should not have been found a single reference to such an august personage as Joseph, the vizier to a Pharaoh. Besides, they ask, how could an Israelite, an alien son of a despised nomad tribe, become sufficiently acceptable to such a highly cultured people as the Egyptians as to be elevated over them as their "governor"?

In partial answer to the last question it has been pointed out that there are two el-Amarna tablets of the period 1400-1370 B.C.E. which refer to a royal governor of Egypt who bore a Semitic name. It is not at all improbable that during the domination of Egypt by the Hyksos, the Semitic kinsmen of the Israelites, an Israelite such as Joseph may have held a high position.

Woolley's Discoveries

To add fuel to the scholars' controversy about Joseph, the eminent English archeologist, Sir Leonard Woolley, has discovered new and surprising evidence. He excavated in Alalakh, Syria, a statue of its king, Idrimi. It also bore an inscription, recorded during the Second Millennium B.C.E., in which King Idrimi gave a brief sketch of his own strange life and career. He speaks of a rebellion in the home of his parents which led to a quarrel with his envious brothers. Afterwards, he fled for his life into the desert where he lived with nomad tribesmen. Among them he earned a great name as an interpreter of dreams. He became a diviner of mysteries by looking into the intestines of a lamb. The flight of birds made clear to him the most obscure meanings of events yet to happen. After many years, Idrimi returned to his native city at the head of a victorious host. Although he recognized his brothers they did not recognize him. Because he was a great-hearted person he was magnanimous to them. He forgave them their past treachery, the cause of the hardships he had had to endure for so many years. In fact, in the end, he even rewarded them handsomely.

The remarkable similarity between the autobiography of Idrimi and the Bible story of Joseph is so striking that it has not been easy to dismiss as mere coincidence. It has, however, proved nothing conclusive about the historicity of the Israelite in Egypt who was "second only to Pharaoh."

Other Gods

Some historians of religion, pointing to certain references in the Bible, reach the conclusion that neither Abraham nor, for that matter, his immediate descendants really believed in One Supreme Being. Instead of having discovered monotheism, as is so often claimed for them, the faith of the first Jews, they say, was one of monolatry, which means the worship of a chief or favorite deity. The chief deity of the Patriarchs, of course, was the Lord. But this worship of the Lord did not prevent many from paying homage to other and less esteemed gods. The older *Baal*-worship went right on in the midst of their acclaim of the One God. For mystical reasons, Jews are not allowed to speak God's real name aloud. When, therefore, they speak it, they say "Adonay." The word "Jehovah" came into use among Christians only after 1518 when Peter Galatin, Pope Leo X's confessor, introduced it.

In more than one way, and like their Canaanite kinsmen, many Israelites remained primitive animists or nature-worshippers. They erected *asheras* (sacred trees and tree-trunks on "high places") to protect them against the evil spirits and demons they believed infested all creation. They rigidly observed a variety of tribal prohibitions (*taboos*) in the regulation of their daily lives out of fear of reprisal and punishment by the *baalim* or gods. They practiced primitive magic with exorcisms, incantations, talismans and disguises. Changing Jacob's name to Israel is one instance and with the change his entire personality was altered.

Household idols, the *teraphim,* were often worshipped side by side with the Lord. Rachel stole her father's precious *teraphim* (to discourage him from idolatry, Jewish tradition holds), which led him to go in angry pursuit of Jacob. How persistent and widespread idol-worship and magic must have been among the Israelites is revealed in the Bible when it describes the religious climate in the Kingdom of Judah during the reign of Josiah (639-608 B.C.E.) more than a thousand years after the Patriarchs are assumed to have lived.

"Moreover, the workers with familiar spirits, and the wizards, and the images, and the idols, and all the abominations that were spied in the land of Judah and in Jerusalem, did Josiah put away, that he might perform the words of the law which were written in the book that Hilkiah the priest found in the House of the Lord."

Other primitive customs and practices of the Canaanites were made part of the religious ways of many early Israelites. They brought sacrifices of animal blood, oil, fruits, vegetables and grain on the top of *mazzebot* (s.-*mazzebah*) which were stone pillars set up in fields and on high places.

Ethical Monotheism

There was, of course, nothing unusual in the manner in which the early religion of Israel was "blended." It was a process common to all religions since the beginning of time. Each faith borrowed generously from the others. Thus, in antiquity, the attributes of one god imperceptibly fused with those of other gods. Elements drawn from one belief were easily mixed with another. For these reasons, some of the beliefs and practices of the Israelites which go back to their tribal, idol-worshipping days survived in their religion in a disguised and shadowy form.

It was not until its "purification" of idolatrous elements by the preaching of the Prophets and by the devoted work of Ezra and the scribes who compiled and edited the Bible during the fifth century B.C.E. that the worship of One God, for which Moses had striven, was at last achieved. Only then could one, with justice, describe the religion of Israel as *ethical monotheism*—the supreme contribution of the Jewish people to the progress of mankind.

SLAVES IN EGYPT

Egyptian wall-painting of Semitic slaves at construction work.
Metropolitan Museum

A new and plaintive note is sounded by the Bible narrator with the words: "Now there arose a new king over Egypt, who knew not Joseph." Dark clouds, ominous for the children of Israel, begin to gather over the fateful Egyptian sky. The descendants of Joseph and his brothers, living so tranquilly in the fat pasture lands of Goshen, are abruptly deprived of the free status they had enjoyed. The reigning Pharaoh feels insecure. He has had forebodings of trouble to come because the Israelites have been multiplying too rapidly. He fears they may some day feel strong enough to rebel against his rule. And because of this fear Pharaoh resolves to reduce them to abject bondage and impotence.

In the years which followed, the Israelites felt on their backs the stinging lash of their Egyptian taskmasters who "made their lives bitter with hard bondage, in mortar and in brick, and in all manner of service in the field." But uppermost in Pharaoh's mind was the need to curb the Jews' natural increase. He therefore decreed that all Israelite male children were to be put to death at birth. It is at this juncture that the epic of Moses the Liberator begins.

Moses in the Bulrushes

A male child had been born to Jochebed and Amram, Israelite slaves of the tribe of Levi. Trembling for the infant's life, his mother had secreted him for three months. No longer able to conceal him, she placed him in "an ark of bulrushes" and laid it hopefully among the reeds at the

river bank. When Pharaoh's daughter went down to bathe, she found the infant and was so enchanted with him that she decided to adopt him. She named him "Moses." That was, she said, "because I drew him out of the water."

Although raised and educated in the royal household as an Egyptian, Moses somehow discovered his kinship with the Israelite slaves. Far from running away from his identity Moses was irresistibly drawn to explore it further. But he became fully aware of it only after he had experienced a shattering emotional crisis.

This took place one day after he had gone out to watch the Israelite slaves "and looked on their burdens." Suddenly Moses saw an Egyptian taskmaster beating a slave. At this a searing indignation flamed up within him. Now he knew that the helpless slave being beaten was one of his own brothers. Now he knew with certainty that he himself was no Egyptian but an Israelite.

In a passion Moses turned on the Egyptian and slew him. Then, afraid of the consequences, he concealed the body in the sand. But the murder was soon discovered and Moses fled for his life into the desolate hills of Midian. There he married Zipporah, the daughter of Jethro, a Midianite priest. He led the life of a simple shepherd, grazing his father-in-law's flock. Yet he could not forget his people suffering in bondage. It gave him no peace, for it had left an indelible impression on his spirit.

From a 16th century *Haggadah.*

The Lord Reveals Himself to Moses

One day Moses had driven his father-in-law's goats and sheep up the slope of Mount Horeb. There, in the great silence and loneliness that dwells in both man and nature, the Lord revealed Himself directly to Moses in a burning thorn bush. The Lord spoke: "I am the God of your father, the God of Abraham, the God of Isaac, and the God of Jacob." And God went on to tell Moses how He had heard the cries of affliction of the Israelite slaves in Egypt, and that He was resolved to deliver them out of the hand of the oppressor. More than that. He solemnly vowed that He would lead them, a free people at last, into the heritage He had promised their forefathers—into "a land flowing with milk and honey."

Wood engraving by Hans Holbein the Younger

Humbly Moses accepted his election to be the instrument of the Lord's will in the liberation of his people.

Now Moses was "slow of speech," so the Lord delegated his brother Aaron to "be to you a mouth." And Moses gathered the children of Israel and spoke to them about the Lord's intentions. They believed in Moses and had faith in the Lord.

Moses and Pharaoh

Then, with Aaron at his side, he went to Pharaoh. He demanded of him: "Thus saith the Lord, the God of Israel: Let My people go. . . ."

Pharaoh merely laughed. Who was this man Moses and who was his God of Israel to command him thus! So his heart grew harder against the slaves, and he ordered still harsher treatment of them.

Moses grew disheartened. He had made a dismal failure of his mission. Pharaoh had laughed . . . instead of liberating the slaves he had only increased their burdens because Moses had interceded for them. Now his fellow Israelites no longer believed in his leadership. He, Moses, had led them to doubt entirely the existence of the Lord!

Once more the Lord revealed Himself to Moses as he grieved. He commanded him to rise up and go again to the king of Egypt to demand that he free the slaves. This time the Lord armed Moses with a symbol of His divine majesty.

He gave him "the Rod of the Lord" with which to perform wonders before Pharaoh in order to overawe him.

Moses performed many wonders before Pharaoh. But Pharaoh called upon the priests of Egypt to perform the same wonders, which they did by means of their magic art, and Pharaoh was reassured that the Lord of Moses possessed no greater powers than the gods of Egypt. So he hardened his heart still more against the Israelite slaves and increased their burdens. Even after Moses brought down on the land a series

A grotesque from a Hebrew parchment *Haggadah* ms. of the 13th century, illustrating one of the ten plagues.

of nine frightful plagues and pests, Pharaoh was unconvinced. Then the Lord's patience came to an end. He decided to have Moses bring before Pharaoh decisive proof of His power. First He commanded that each Israelite bring a sacrifice of a lamb, a yearling without blemish. With its blood each man should stain the signposts and lintels of his house. With that accomplished, the Lord told Moses, He would pass through the land and smite all the first-born of the Egyptians, both men and beasts. However, where he could see the doorway stained with the blood of the sacrifice—"I will pass over you" and because the Lord "passed over" the homes of the Israelites and spared their first-born the festival of Passover was established. It was to be celebrated by Jews for all time in joyous commemoration of the Lord's loving mercy in freeing them from their bondage "with a mighty hand."

At the hour of midnight the Lord slew all the first-born of Egypt, even Pharaoh's own son. "We are all dead men," cried the Egyptians. The king himself was filled with terror. Hastily, in the middle of the night, he summoned Moses and Aaron. "Rise up," he implored them, "get you forth from among my people, both you and the children of Israel."

Pharaoh Implores Moses to Leave Egypt with Israelites.   *Doré*

Limestone relief: Semitic (possibly Israelite) captives led to Egypt by Pharaoh Horemheb, founder of the 19th dynasty, who invaded Palestine. 14th century, B.C.E.

Rijksmuseum van Oudheden te Leiden

The Exodus

Because the Egyptians were frightened they were eager to be rid of the Israelites. To hasten their departure they pressed upon them much gold and silver, jewels and fine clothes, which explains why, when they departed from Egypt, they were rich in possessions. They drove before them herds of cattle and flocks of sheep and goats. Then, too, many of the liberated slaves, out of hatred for their oppressors, despoiled them of their wealth and carried it off triumphantly.

The Book of Exodus notes that at the time of their departure the Israelites had dwelled in the land of Egypt four hundred and thirty years. When the patriarch Jacob first came down into Egypt with his household it numbered but seventy souls. Now, when their descendants were leaving into freedom they counted 600,000 men, but not including boys and women. In addition, there went forth with them "a mixed multitude" of non-Israelites, probably slaves themselves, who had cast in their lot with them in the uprising.

The Israelites went forth rejoicing. But soon their laughter became stilled. The gravity of their situation at last began to dawn on them. They now had to face the grim problems of survival. For instance, there was the need of avoiding clashes with the powerful forces of the Philistines. Moses therefore prudently decided that the Israelites were not to proceed to Canaan by the direct short route northwards. Instead he planned to take a circuitous course from one wilderness into another and from oasis to oasis. This roundabout wandering was to last forty years before they were ready to cross into the Promised Land.

But while the Israelites were making slow progress out of Egypt, Pharaoh had ample time to sober up from his panic. He gathered a mighty host, including numerous chariots and horsemen, and went in pursuit of the Israelites.

He overtook them as they lay encamped on the western shore of the Red Sea. When they saw the Egyptian army draw near they were gripped by panic.

The Crossing of the Red Sea

At the bidding of the Lord, "Moses stretched out his hand over the sea; and the Lord caused the sea to go back by a strong east wind all the night and made the sea dry land."

The Children of Israel crossed safely over to the eastern shore. When the Egyptians tried to follow them in the morning the waters receded and engulfed them all.

The drowning of the Egyptian host.

Then, seeing that the mighty hosts of the enemy had drowned, Moses raised his voice in a song of thanksgiving:

I will sing unto the Lord, for He is highly exalted;
The horse and his rider has He thrown into the sea.

And the Israelites sang jubilantly with him.

And Miriam the Prophetess, the sister of Moses, took a timbrel in her hand, and all the women went out after her. The Israelites danced and rejoiced and Miriam sang aloud the Song of Moses.

Miriam's song of triumph.

24

AS HISTORIANS VIEW IT

Who exactly were the Hebrews? Where did they originate? And how did they come to settle in the land of Goshen, which lies in the eastern delta of the Nile Valley?

In recent years there has been piling up an impressive body of evidence, historical as well as archaeological, regarding this people. Remarkably enough, it tends to support the central theme of the Biblical narrative.

True, by no stretch of the imagination can this evidence be considered entirely conclusive. No documentary proof has thus far been presented of the Israelite settlement in Egypt. History has shed no light whatsoever on the life and personality of Moses, not even a hint that he ever really existed. In fact, in no writing extant today is there even a mention of the Exodus. But the fact that such evidence has not thus far been unearthed is no indication that many of the incidents in the Bible narrative did not actually take place. Perhaps in time the proof will appear. Nonetheless the available evidence today does point to a core of historic truth in the Bible account of the Bondage and the Exodus.

The most vivid of all these materials presented by the historians are the wall-paintings and the sculptured reliefs in limestone that were wrought by the hands of unknown Egyptian artists contemporary with those dim and distant events. These portrayals are surprisingly realistic and give one a sense of the authentic about the Jewish Bondage.

It was, relatively speaking, only yesterday that the earth, hiding the secrets of many vanished civilizations, began to yield up to the archaeologists material corroboration of some basic facts of Biblical and related history. For example, it was as recent as 1901 that the stone stele of Hammurabi was dug up. It revealed for the first time the Babylonian lawgiver's celebrated code in cuneiform writing. Furthermore, crowning the column stood a sculptured full-length figure of Hammurabi receiving the laws directly from the Sun-god, Shamash.

Hardly a year passes which does not bring to light new proof to buttress in some essential way events, personalities, places and conditions mentioned in the Bible. And so with time, the Scriptural picture gets fuller, more detailed and also more authentic than many a skeptic thought it to be. In fact, the view of some historians of culture is that aside from all the myth and magic with which the folk memory of a people tends to glorify its remote origins, at the core there remains a fidelity to real events and actual people.

To return to the original question: who were the first Hebrews? The answer must remain in the twilight zone of speculation. Just the same, the prevailing opinion of most serious scholars today links up the early-known movements of the Hebrews with the mass migration of the Habiru.

Who were the Habiru? The word itself, it is believed, refers neither to a race, a people, a nation nor even to an ethnic culture group. It was apparently a Semitic word applied loosely to all nomads. Specifically, it referred to nomads who came from beyond the Jordan or the Euphrates in Central Asia. They were vast migratory groups of uprooted tribes and peoples driven to wandering by King Hunger, or by a lust for plunder, or by the blows of superior enemies.

The migrations of the Habiru, driving their herds and flocks before them, did not take place at one time or in a specific area. They flowed in irregular waves of advance and recession during a long period of time and over a sizable part of the Middle East. It can well be imagined that the wanderings of the Patriarchs Abraham, Isaac and Jacob must have been a part of this vast Habiru migration.

Let us take, for instance, the highly civilized Egyptians. They lived in an advanced society with an agricultural and commercial economy. They boasted great cities, were proficient in engineering, astronomy and in the arts. Naturally, they had nothing but scorn for the rude nomads.

Although the Habiru were of diverse ethnic origins, they were in some degree linked together by the use of languages having a common Semitic character, by similar beliefs, myths and nature worship. Whether driven on by the need for new grazing lands for their herds and flocks or whether they were moved by a desire for conquest and plunder, they gradually swarmed over an area of what is now Anatolia, Syria and Palestine. Many of these groups settled there and led a semi-nomadic existence. Others, however, continued their migratory movement southward through Palestine. Perhaps they came to Egypt when the Hyksos wrested the power from the feeble hands of the then-reigning Pharaoh in about 1720 B.C.E. For about 170 years the Hyksos, who were largely Semitic, ruled over the Egyptian Empire and infused new vigor into its civilization.

It is widely believed that the settlement of the Israelites in the land of Goshen, as it is related in the Bible, may have taken place at some time during the conquest or rule of Egypt by the Hyksos.

After the Egyptians had finally overthrown the foreign invaders in 1580 B.C.E. they drove them back through Palestine and into Syria.

In recent times thoughtful students of Bible history have come more and more to the belief that not all the Israelites during the Egyptian Bondage were descendants of Jacob and his sons. Probably later arrivals, Israelites from neighboring parts of Palestine and Syria, constantly joined the patriarchal clan of Jacob in Goshen. This is a possible surmise from Egyptian records, from wall-paintings and sculptural reliefs. While Jacob and his household had migrated to the fertile Delta region in order to improve their desperate condition, probably the vast majority of other arrivals did not come out of their own free will, but perhaps as deportees, since it was the fixed state policy of the Egyptian Pharaohs to break up the Hyksos and allied Habiru strength in the north by forcibly transplanting them in Egypt. These deportations, it appears, went on for six centuries. The first one resulted from the invasion of Palestine by King Thutmose III in 1550 B.C.E., and the last from King Shishak's invasion during the last quarter of the tenth century B.C.E., when Rehoboam ruled as King of Judah.

The Pharaoh of the Exodus

When it was exactly that the Bondage in Egypt began, how long it lasted and the date of the liberation—all this still remains inconclusive. One thing is generally agreed upon—the overthrow of the Hyksos rule in Egypt led to the enslavement of the Israelites in Goshen. It is widely held that it was Seti I who instituted the Bondage. His successor, Rameses II (1292-1225 B.C.E.), presumably was the Pharaoh of the Exodus. He, with his entire army, according to the Bible story, was drowned when he pursued the Israelites across the Red Sea, which gives rise to the speculation that the Exodus occurred in 1225 B.C.E.

Though many years have passed since archaeologists unearthed in Goshen the sites of *Per Rameses*, "The House of Rameses," and its twin store-city of *Pithum* or *Pi-Tum*, "The

National Museum, Cairo

Rameses II.   *Museo Egizio, Turin*

House of the God Tum," there are still many skeptics who doubt that this corroborates the Bible account of the bitter toil of the Israelite slaves who built the cities of Pithum and Rameses for Pharaoh. We know that Rameses II suffered from a building mania, and that these two store-cities were a part of his staggering construction program. It can therefore be said with reasonable certainty that it was he who was the Pharaoh of the Exodus and not Thutmose III or Merenptah, the son of Rameses II, as some scholars claim.

Pharaoh Merenptah, who is not mentioned in the Bible, may have quite another distinction in the history of the Israelites.

The stele shown here, discovered by Professor Flinders Petrie in Merenptah's mortuary temple at Thebes, bears an inscription listing Merenptah's military triumphs and concludes:

Canaan is plundered . . .
Carried away is Askelon.
Gezer is taken.
Yenoam is no more.
Israel is desolated, its seed is not.
Palestine is become as a widow for Egypt.

This inscription, the only known extra-Biblical contemporary reference to Israel, establishes the presence of Israelites in Palestine in Merenptah's time (he died 1215 B.C.E.). Quite obviously, the inscription does not refer to the Israelites of the Exodus. It does suggest the possibility that some Israelites were living in Canaan during the Bondage.

Egyptian soldiers in combat with unidentified enemies. Sandstone relief from the Temple of Rameses II at Thebes. Perhaps the same Egyptians who presumably pursued the Israelites across the Red Sea.

Canaanite (Israelite?) lords bringing gifts as tribute to Pharaoh. (From a wall-painting on a Theban grave. c. 1400 B.C.E.)

PESACH (PASSOVER)

The most beloved of all the Jewish festivals is *Pesach* or Passover. It celebrates, and symbolizes, freedom, the value most cherished among Jews for more than three thousand years: their longing for freedom. That is why it is referred to as "The Festival of Liberation."

Jewish families on *Pesach* night have always gathered together to relive in recollection their most unforgettable historic experience: their bondage in Egypt and their liberation.

Passover did not always hold this significance for Jews. It had quite a different character in the days when the Temple in Jerusalem stood. Then it was considered as the first of the year's three great harvest festivals. It celebrated the gathering in of the spring barley from which most of the bread of the people was made. It culminated with a gigantic pilgrimage to the sanctuary in Jerusalem and was marked by dramatic rites of spring.

In preparation for the Festival each householder was obliged to slaughter a lamb or a goat, a yearling "without blemish," which he brought as a sacrifice to the Lord. The blood of the animal he smeared over the sideposts and the lintel of the door in grateful imitation of his ancestors in Egypt when the Lord passed over the houses of the Israelites but killed all the first-born of the Egyptians.

The Book of Exodus gave precise directions how the paschal lamb was to be eaten: "And they shall eat the flesh in that night, roast with fire; its head with its legs and with the inwards thereof. And ye shall let nothing of it remain until the morning; but that which remaineth of it until the morning ye shall burn with fire."

On the second day of the Festival in ancient times a sheaf of the harvested barley was brought as "an offering made by fire, a burnt offering." This was presented on the Temple altar amidst impressive priestly rites and the singing of the Levites. From this one can see that, notwithstanding the Festival's formal commemoration of the Exodus from Egypt, it retained basically its original harvest character.

Pesach, the Festival of Liberation as we know it today, achieved its social and spiritual significance only after the Temple lay in ruins and the Jewish people was scattered far and wide. The bringing of a sacrifice in a central sanctuary was no longer possible. Therefore, the celebration became a festival of reunion for all the members of the family.

Succeeding generations keenly felt their rootlessness and the bitter persecution they were subjected to everywhere. The Bondage in Egypt then became more than a national religious memory. Every Jew who felt his torment and humiliation in the *Galuth*, the Exile, considered himself in more than a symbolic sense "a slave in Egypt." The liberation that had come to his ancestors he looked upon as a divine sign and promise of the eventual "redemption" of the Jewish people from suffering and its restoration in the land of Israel.

Medieval *seder*.   *British Museum*   *Seder* of Hadhrami Jews.   A modern *seder* in the U.S.A.
Courtesy of B. Manischewitz Co.

The Seder

As a substitute for the Passover sacrifices and rites in the Temple, the latter-day sages of the *Talmud* who flourished during the first centuries after the Destruction established the institution of the *Seder*. This was the religious service for the home. Since that time the *Seder* has served as "the heart" of the Festival celebration for Jews in every part of the world.

The rabbis provided the ritual for the *Seder*, which means "order," with a special prayer-book called the *Haggadah* ("recital" or "story") consisting first of an anthology made up of varied materials of a narrative in epic style, then prayers, benedictions and psalms of praise and thanksgiving. As a sop to the children, it concluded with several merry nursery rhymes and jingles. Yet the burden and the refrain of the whole service are found in the recital of the tribulations the Israelite slaves had suffered in Egypt and how, because of His love and mercy, the Lord had led them out of their bondage "with a mighty hand."

"Liberation" now became the principal theme of the Festival of Passover. It was an ideal lovingly to be preserved and handed down in perpetuity like an inheritance from father to son and from generation to generation. This was a unique consecration of an entire people to an ideal value. The rabbis of the *Talmud* laid down the injunction to all Jewish fathers for all time that on the first two nights of the Festival: "You shall recite the story to your son, saying: 'I am telling it to you because of what the Lord did for me when I came out of Egypt.'"

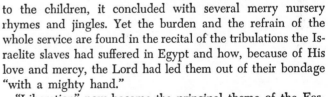

Decorative figures from medieval *Haggadahs*.

27

Baking *matzohs* (old style), Utrecht, 1657.

Baking *matzohs* (modern style).
Courtesy of B. Manischewitz Co.

Passover begins on the eve of the fourteenth day of *Nissan* (March-April) and lasts eight days, the eighth day having been added during the Middle Ages. But Jews of modern Reform congregations observe only seven days. The first two days and the last two are traditionally considered as full holy days; the intervening ones are only half holy days. The advent of the Festival is marked by elaborate preparations. This held particularly true in other days when Jewish life in the ghettos was intensely religious and the community was both more integrated and single-minded. Special dishes, cooking utensils and silver are used for the entire period. There are special wine bottles, *matzoh* covers, a special *kiddush* goblet, or benediction cup, for the head of the household. The festive table, too, is arranged in a way reserved for the *Seder* service and feast.

The night before Passover Eve, in those homes where tradition is closely followed, the ceremony of *bedikat chametz* takes place. The head of the household makes a diligent search in all possible places for *chametz*, leavened bread. This is because throughout the eight days of Passover only *matzoh*, unleavened bread, may be eaten. Not a single crumb of bread is allowed to remain in the home. The custom since ancient

times is for the searcher to carry a candle with him, and to sweep any bread crumbs he finds into a wooden spoon with a whisk made of several chicken or goose feathers. At the outset, as a symbol of his search, he places a crumb on a window sill. When he is through he returns and brushes it ceremoniously into the spoon, as he pronounces the benediction: "Blessed be Thou . . . Who hast commanded us to remove the leaven." The following morning, the leaven he has put aside is burned, and the ritual law requires that unleavened bread may not be eaten after mid-morning on that day.

In keeping with the humane and libertarian spirit of the Festival it is obligatory for those with means to supply the poor with *matzohs*, wine and other holy day necessities, so that they, too, may be able to celebrate the *Seder* properly.

Passover wine jug.

Passover *kiddush* goblet.

Distributing *matzohs* to the poor, c. 1200. (From Spanish illuminated *Haggadah*.)

British Museum

This Passover benevolence is provided for by a special fund collected from the worshippers in the synagogue.

For the rites of the *Seder* service a number of symbolic foods are required: a shank bone of a roasted lamb, recalling the paschal lamb that was sacrificed in ancient times; a roasted egg—an explanation is that the egg symbolizes Israel: the longer you cook it the harder and more indestructible it

Passover platter, German, 18th century.

Matzoh cover, Galicia, 18th century.

becomes; a piece of *moror*, or horseradish, to recall the bitter life of Israel during the Egyptian bondage. Also required are a sprig of *karpas*, or parsley, and a patty called *charoseth*, which is a mixture of ground apples, raisins, almonds, cinnamon and wine, symbolizing the brick and mortar the Israelites were forced to make in Egypt. All of these foods are put in a special Passover plate and placed upon the *matzoh* cover under which lie three *matzohs*.

The *Seder* rites also require the use of wine—for "The Four Cups" which are drunk in the course of the service. It is specially prepared for the use of Passover according to ritually prescribed methods.

Around the narrator—usually the head of the household, dressed in the *kittel*, the white robe worn on the Day of Atonement in the synagogue—the rest of the family is gathered at the festive table. Originating in Graeco-Roman times, and in imitation of the way they banqueted then, the custom is for the head of the household to recline on cushions placed at his left side. This is meant as a sign of ease and of his free status. Wine cups or glasses are filled for everyone. There is a special cup for Elijah in the center of the table. It is reserved for him as a memorial to the Jewish expectation of the coming of the Messiah of which the Prophet is to be the forerunner.

After the benediction, the drinking of the first cup of wine and the eating of parsley, the master of the household breaks the center *matzoh*. It is customary for him to hide a part of it, the *aphikomon* (Greek for dessert). Festival folk tradition, which is always gay, requires that the children make a diligent search for it. It is a form of treasure hunt designed

to sustain their interest in the long prayer-service. At the conclusion of the *Seder*, whoever has possession of the *aphikomon* receives a reward.

The service continues in a serious vein as the reader of the service lifts the *matzoh* from the table and to an ancient musical mode intones from the *Haggadah*: "Lo, this is as the bread of affliction which our forefathers ate in the land of Egypt! Let all who are hungry enter and eat of it, and all who are needy let them come and celebrate the Passover!"

At this point it is the custom for the youngest child to ask his father "The Four Questions" about the why and wherefore of the celebration of Passover. The *Haggadah*, in a quaint folkloristic style, describes four kinds of sons who might be asking these questions: the wise son, the wicked son, the fool and the child still unable to phrase the questions properly. To the last one especially the father must patiently and lovingly "explain the matter fully, as it is said, And thou shalt relate to thy son fully on that day." In this manner, not only the memory of the liberation but also an understanding of its significance would be forever preserved among all generations of Jews.

And so, in this gentle spirit, the father goes on to narrate to his children in melancholy but exalted cadence the story of the Bondage in Egypt and of the Liberation which followed. Psalms of joy and of praise are intoned. The family service finally ends on a note of gaiety. Grown-ups and children together blend their voices in the singing of medieval Hebrew nursery rhymes. This is because *Pesach* is basically the festival for children, designed to help them to know and to cherish their people's traditions of equality and freedom.

The wise.

The wicked.

The fool.

The child.

WANDERING IN THE WILDERNESS

The Wilderness. Looking east over the route taken by the Israelites to the Promised Land.

The Ordeals of Israel

Tortuous and slow was the wandering of the Israelites through the wilderness. Life was hard, and what lay before them was unknown and dark with danger. They found it difficult to fit into the new conditions of life. Formerly they had been slaves, had known a fixed existence in the towns and cities of Egypt. Now necessity had turned them into a horde of nomads. Without rest they were forced to drive their herds and flocks before them, urgently seeking new grazing lands and water-wells.

Men without roots, homeless and landless, they went in search of the Fertile Valley, the object of all mankind's dream-yearnings. It was a hunger for permanence and security.

The wandering Israelites formed an unruly "congregation" of family-clans, tribes and allies. They had to meet with crisis after crisis. It wasn't long after the crossing of the Red Sea that the Israelites became mutinous and rebelled against Moses' leadership. There was a shortage of food and water and they heaped bitter reproaches on him. "You have brought us forth into this wilderness to kill this whole assembly with hunger!" they accused him. They dwelled nostalgically upon the supposed security they had found in Egypt. They even glorified the conditions of their bondage "when we sat by the fleshpots, when we did eat bread to the full."

The Scriptural narrator is overawed by the Lord's unflagging love and Moses' capacity to endure the doubters, the mutineers and the grumblers. He records the great number of miracles God performed on their behalf to fulfill His oft-repeated promise to set them up as His people in the land of Canaan.

This is what happened when the Israelites were encamped at a place called Rephidim on the edge of the wilderness of Sin. They were almost ready to stone Moses because they

30

could not find water to drink. Now, even more than ever, did they doubt the existence of the Lord. "Is He among us, or not?" they asked gibingly of Moses.

Once, according to the chronicler, the Lord was forced to come to their aid and work a miracle. He bade Moses strike a rock on Mount Horeb with the Rod of the Lord. As soon as Moses had struck the rock in the sight of all the people, water began to gush forth and the people slaked their thirst. Later, when they murmured against Moses because they had nothing to eat, the Lord caused another miracle to happen: manna, a strange but palatable food, began to rain from the sky.

For a little while at least after that, they believed in the

The Israelites Gather Manna.
From a woodcut by Hans Holbein the Younger

Lord. But, no sooner did the tingling memory of the last miracle wear off than they were consumed with doubt all over again.

Wherever they went the Israelites found themselves not wanted, were considered trespassers. Almost every step of the way they were forced to fight hostile tribes in a life-and-death struggle for the few and far-between water-wells. At first they could not cope with the onslaughts of these enemies who enjoyed better group-unity and were skilled in desert warfare.

The Bible chronicler points out that when the Israelites

Battle with Amalek.   *Millais*

were hard pressed, the Lord sustained them by means of miracles. For instance, when the Amalekites swooped down on their encampment at Rephidim, the Israelites, under Joshua's military leadership, put up a desperate but futile defense. Therefore, at the Lord's bidding, Moses ascended a hill that overlooked the field of battle. When he raised aloft the Rod of the Lord, Israel prevailed. When he grew weary and lowered his arms, the Amalekites won the upper hand. For that reason Aaron and Hur stationed themselves on either side of Moses, and hour after hour they supported his arms upraised to heaven until the Amalekites were slain to the last man.

The Lord's Covenant with Israel

The most significant event for the Israelites, and for their descendants down through the ages, was their consecration as "a kingdom of priests, and a holy nation," that took place at the foot of Mount Sinai.

According to the Scriptural account this happened in the third month after the departure from Egypt amidst supernatural drama and was accompanied by all the manifest signs of the Lord's presence in their midst. He descended in a great burst of flame. The mountains smoked and quaked with a mighty inner rumbling. Lightning rent the sky, and the earth was convulsed by thunder. And above all the wondrous sights and sounds the blast of the heavenly *shofar* was heard. The Lord was on the Mount!

The multitude of Israelites was overcome by these signs and tokens of the Lord's power. They were in a mood now to accept instruction from Moses in the Ten Commandments. And Moses taught them:

> I am the Lord thy God: thou shalt have no other gods before Me.
> Thou shalt not make unto thee a graven image, nor any manner of likeness.
> Thou shalt not take the name of the Lord thy God in vain.
> Remember the Sabbath day to keep it holy.
> Honor thy father and thy mother.
> Thou shalt not murder.
> Thou shalt not commit adultery.
> Thou shalt not steal.
> Thou shalt not bear false witness.
> Thou shalt not covet.

This was the covenant entered into between the Israelites and the Lord. To solemnize the occasion they erected an altar at the foot of the Mount. Upon it they brought sacrifices: burnt-offerings and peace-offerings. And if they would keep His commandments faithfully as their way of life, the Lord promised them: "you shall be my own treasure from among all peoples."

Because the Ten Commandments were merely rudimentary, Moses went up again to the summit of Mount Sinai in order to receive further instruction from the Lord in the *Torah*. This time, his disciple, Joshua, son of Nun, went up with him.

For six days a cloud obscured the Mount. But on the seventh day the Lord called to Moses from the midst of the cloud and He bade him come into it. Then for forty days and forty nights Moses stayed within the cloud and was not seen by the Israelites. During this time he neither ate nor drank, only receiving instruction from the Lord.

Moses receiving tablets from God.
Julius Schnorr von Karolsfeld

Historians point out certain superficial resemblances between the laws of Moses and those of the Babylonian King Hammurabi. There is also some similarity in the manner in which the two acquired their codes. Above the stele of Hammurabi's Code in cuneiform writing the Babylonian king is shown in sculptured relief receiving the code from the hand of the sun-god, Shamash.
The Louvre

When the Israelites saw that Moses was away so long, they became restive. Rebel leaders seized control of the camp. They went to Aaron and clamored: "Up, make us a god who shall go before us; for as for this Moses, the man that brought us up out of the land of Egypt, we know not what is become of him."

Afraid, Aaron submitted to the mutineers and asked them to bring him their gold earrings. With a graving tool he made for them a sculptured calf of gold. Before it he raised an altar on which the Israelites offered sacrifices. They chanted: "This is thy God, O Israel, which brought thee up out of the land of Egypt."

And while the Israelites were worshipping the Golden Calf, the Lord continued to instruct Moses in His laws and precepts. When He had finished, He gave him "the tables of stone written with the finger of God" (i.e., The Ten Commandments) to present to the people as an everlasting memorial. Through the ages the Jews have never ceased marveling over the intimacy which existed between the Lord and

Moshe Rabbenu, "our teacher Moses." The narrator in the Bible explains this relationship by the fact that the Lord loved Moses and because of it He spoke with him "face to face, as a man speaks to his friend."

The Worship of the Golden Calf

Holding the stone "tablets of the testimony" in his arms, Moses descended the Mount, followed by his disciple Joshua.

As they approached the camp of the Israelites they heard a great tumult. When they drew still nearer they recoiled in horror. The Israelites were dancing wildly. Round and round they leaped and whirled. In their midst stood a golden calf which they were adoring. When Moses saw this he was engulfed by grief. His "anger waxed hot and he cast the tablets out of his hands and broke them beneath the Mount."

Then he came to Aaron, his brother the high priest, to whose care he had entrusted the people while he was away on Mount Sinai. Moses reproached him bitterly. Why had he allowed the children of Israel to sink back into idolatry? What would others say now concerning their steadfastness toward the Lord? Aaron's sin was unpardonable, said he, since he had let Israel "loose for a derision among their enemies."

Moses saw plainly that this was not merely a rejection of the Lord by the people but also a rebellion against his own leadership. At all costs and by the most drastic means, he decided, the insurrection had to be put down, or all his fondest dreams for the people would be shattered. He soon saw that not all the tribes had joined the rebellion. There were still strong elements on whose loyalty he could count. Moses therefore stationed himself within the gate of the camp. "Who is on the Lord's side," he cried out, "let him come unto me."

In answer to his call, the men of his own tribe of Levi rallied round him. A fierce struggle with the mutineers followed, for three thousand men lay dead when the day drew to an end. The uprising was crushed for the time being.

When morning came, Moses assembled all of Israel. Now his initial anger and despair had dissipated themselves. The bloody events of the previous day filled him with sorrow.

Moses destroys the tablets.

Egyptian sculpture depicting calf-worship.

Compassion for Israel's backwardness pointed out to him his only course of action: "You have sinned a great sin," said he to the people. Yet this did not mean that all was lost, that they would forevermore remain irredeemable. He himself was prepared to share the blame with them, in fact, to take it all upon himself if need be. "I will go up unto the Lord," he comforted them, "peradventure I shall make atonement for your sin."

Once again Moses climbed up to the summit of Sinai to speak to the Lord, to intercede for his backsliding people.

It is this image of Moses as their defender that the plain Jewish folk have cherished most through the ages. He understood, therefore he forgave. He loved them, therefore he was ready to sacrifice himself for them. He was of flesh and blood himself, therefore he could understand their human frailties.

The Lord yielded to the pleading of Moses. He could not act otherwise because He is "merciful and gracious, long-suffering, and abundant in goodness and truth; keeping mercy unto the thousandth generation, forgiving iniquity and transgression and sin."

For a second time Moses hewed "two tables" out of stone like the first that he had broken. At the Lord's command he inscribed "the ten words" upon them. With his mission accomplished he began to descend the Mount. Eagerly now, the people accepted the *Torah* from him. Unbeknown to himself, his extraordinary experience had altered his appearance.

Moses presents the *Torah* to the Israelites at Mount Sinai. (Miniature, Sarajevo *Haggadah*, Spanish, 13th Century.)

"Moses knew not that the skin of his face sent forth beams and the Israelites were afraid to draw near him."

The Ark of the Lord

Quite obviously, the experience with the Golden Calf had shaken Moses to his innermost being. He had to recognize at last that the Israelites' past history and bondage as slaves among a people that worshipped rivers, animals and trees, could not properly be ignored. It was too much of him to expect that they could make the transfer in one leap from primitive animism to the abstract idea of One Supreme Being who was universal, harmonious and just. Apparently, the people needed a tangible and symbolic evidence of the reality of the Lord. Like all their contemporaries, they could believe only what they could find out through their senses. Because they could see the Egyptian and other gods, could touch them and feel them, could set before them food to eat and wine to drink, therefore, they considered them real. But as for this Israelite God, they had only Moses' own fervent assurance that He was, and always will be. This explains, in part, why they were so easily provoked into doubting the Lord's existence every time they met with some physical difficulty.

And so, at the Lord's bidding, Moses set about creating a sanctuary for public worship which would be visible to the eye, real to the touch and therefore convincing. This task he assigned to the master craftsman, Bezalel, who was filled "with the spirit of God, in wisdom, and in understanding, and in knowledge, and in all manner of workmanship."

The prime purpose of the sanctuary was to provide a fitting and awesome repository for the stone Tables of the Testimony, or the Ten Commandments, the object of highest veneration for ancient Israel. Centuries later, a Talmudic sage tried to epitomize their supreme importance in geometric metaphor:

Palestine is the center of the world.
Jerusalem is the center of Palestine.
The Temple is the center of Jerusalem.
The Holy of Holies is the center of the Temple.
The Ark is the center of the Holy of Holies.
In the center of the Ark rests the stone called "The Foundation Stone of the World."

So precise and detailed is the Biblical description of the way the Israelite artists, craftsmen, smiths, weavers and dyers made the Ark, the tentlike Tabernacle which housed it, the sacrificial altar, the holy vessels and the High Priests' sacerdotal garments and ornaments that it has been possible for modern artists to make reconstructions of them.

The Ark was made of acacia wood. Its inside and outside surfaces were overlaid with gold. Two figures of cherubim with outspread protecting wings, and sculptured in gold, surmounted the rectangular Ark. It was here that the stone tables were stored and where the Lord had told Moses ". . . I will meet with thee, and I will speak with thee from above the Ark-cover."

The Ark was a portable chest. It was designed expressly to fit into the wandering movements of the Israelites. Therefore, two staves of acacia wood overlaid with gold were fitted into four golden rings on the sides. By that means the Ark was carried from place to place.

The Ark was not meant merely to hold the Ten Command-

The Tabernacle.

ments. By its protective magic powers it was also to serve as the supreme talisman for Israel against its enemies. For example, during the days of Samuel, when the Israelites were hard pressed in battle against the Philistines, the Elders of Israel decided as a last desperate measure: "Let us fetch the Ark of the covenant of the Lord of Shiloh unto us, that He may come among us, save us out of the hand of our enemies . . . And when the ark of the covenant of the Lord came into the camp, all Israel shouted with a great shout, so that the earth rang."

The historic importance of the Ark ceased after Temple times. One view is that when Pharaoh Shishak carried off Rehoboam, King of Judah, into Egypt, he also took along the Ark as a trophy of war. From that time on it disappeared from Jewish life.

Death of Moses

The long wanderings of the Israelites at last came to an end. They had reached their goal. Opposite them, beyond the wooded left bank of the Jordan River winding its serpentine

The High Priest in the Sanctuary of the Tabernacle.

course among the hills of Moab, beckoned the Promised Land.

Moses was old now and the time had come for him to depart from the world. He, therefore, assembled all the people and instructed them in the ways of the righteous and the pious. He directed how they should govern themselves when at last they had conquered Canaan.

When he was through with his teaching of the people, notes the chronicler, the Lord resolved that it was time for Moses to die. He bade him ascend to the summit of Pisgah on Mount Nebo in the land of Moab, not far from Jericho, across the River Jordan. From this commanding height Moses looked out upon the Promised Land which the Lord had sworn He would give as an inheritance to the seed of Abraham.

Then the Lord told Moses that he was about to die "and be gathered unto thy people."

Jewish tradition cannot contain its grief when it considers Moses' destiny. Was it just of God to have Moses die at the very hour that he was standing on the threshold of the Promised Land? Was it not the height of cruelty to show him the Promised Land and then not allow him to enter it after all his years of fidelity to the Lord and of struggle and self-denial for Israel?

A poetic elaboration of the Biblical recital of the death of Moses is found in the *Midrash*. It describes the final anguish of Moses. Desperately he struggled to stave off the extinction of his physical being. He tried to temporize with God, to refute His Divine reasoning with logical arguments, to appeal to His Divine mercy with the pathos of his frustration.

"Must I die now, after all the trouble I have had with the people?" he asked of God. "I have seen their suffering, why should I not also see their joy?·You have written in the *Torah*: 'In the same day thou shalt give him his hire.' Why do you not give me the reward of my toil?"

The answer did not come. It was merely implied in the Lord's silence: the reward of man's toil must be found only in the doing.

Jewish tradition becomes sorrowfully poetic when it describes Moses' last moment. God bent over him like a father over his child. He kissed his lips, and took his soul away.

At that very moment a voice sounded from above and was heard by all the Israelites. "Woe, woe!" it lamented. "Moses, the great teacher of Israel, is dead!"

The children of Israel grieved for Moses, their teacher, for thirty days in the plains of Moab. Where was he buried? "No man knoweth of his sepulchre unto this day." Yet all men remember him.

SUCCOTH (SUCCOS)

Like *Pesach* and *Shavuoth*, *Succoth*, The Feast of Tabernacles, began as an agricultural festival. It celebrated the final gathering of the harvest in the land of Israel. That is why it is frequently referred to in ancient writings as "The Feast of Ingathering" and sometimes in rapturous terms as "The Season of Our Joy." However, with the passage of the centuries the festival acquired a new and profounder significance. Actually, this was the imposition of a spiritual meaning upon the original naturalistic one.

The Bible gives the reason for this new meaning plainly. It states that on the fifteenth day of the seventh month, Tishri, "when ye have gathered in the fruit of the land . . . ye shall dwell in booths seven days; all that are Israelites born shall dwell in booths: That your generations may know that I made the children of Israel live in booths when I brought them out of the land of Egypt."

Once again we are faced here with the reminder to the Jews that they had at one time been slaves in Egypt. It was deemed necessary by Israel's religious teachers that the memory of its bondage in Egypt be stamped forever on the people's thoughts. It was to be recalled to them unforgettably by means of customs and ceremonies in the synagogue and at home. The *succah*, remarked Philo of Alexandria, was intended to be lived in by rich and poor alike because it served as an instrument of democratic leveling and taught "equality, the first principle and beginning of justice."

In the days of the Temple, *Succoth* marked one of the three annual festival-pilgrimages to Jerusalem. Of the three, it was celebrated with the greatest festivity and elaborateness and the people participated more fully and directly in the great religious drama enacted in the Temple courts and sanctuary. Therefore, because it eclipsed all the other festivals the people simply referred to it as "The Festival." But after the destruction of the Temple and of the Jewish state, *Succoth* lost much of its importance. Dispersed to all the far corners of the earth, Jews were not allowed by their oppressors to continue as tillers of the soil. Therefore, this feast day which was so intensely agricultural in its earlier character, began to lose much of its meaning. The harvest

A *succah* interior, Amsterdam, 18th century.   *Bernard Picart*

rites, as performed in the Temple, could no longer have much real significance, except as a sentimental memory, to a people so divorced from nature and the soil.

Precise instructions were laid down for building the festival booth or *succah*. Whether in Bagdad or Kharkov, in Berlin or Kansas City, the structural lines and materials used remained very similar. It was to be no less than four feet long and four feet wide and not more than twenty-five feet in height. Its roof had to be covered with green branches, just as in a wandering shepherd's shelter. The green cover was to offer protection against the sun, yet allow the stars to shine through at night. The interior decorations were principally festoons of fruits and flowers.

There are certain distinctive rites performed at home and in the synagogue on *Succoth* that date back to the time of the Second Temple. Then the Jews used to march in procession around the sanctuary altar carrying four kinds of greens symbolic of nature. These were the *lulab*, a palm branch; the *ethrog*, a sweet-smelling variety of citrus; *hadas*, myrtle twigs; and *arabah*, willow branches. And, as they made the circuit around the altar, they waved their palm branches and raised their voices in supplication:

> I beseech Thee, O Lord, grant salvation!
> I beseech Thee, O Lord, grant prosperity!

Seven times they thus made the circuit, or *hakafoth*, around the altar. And for countless generations, this ceremony

Lulab and *ethrog* (became symbols of Judaism, as evidenced by this coin from the Bar-Kochba revolt, 132-135 C.E.)

Citron vender outside the Great Synagogue, Tel Aviv.

Circuit around the altar in Amsterdam synagogue, 1724.
Bernard Picart

has been observed by Jews everywhere and unchanged in any essential manner.

Succoth lasts seven days, the final day being called *Hoshana Rabba*, "The Great Salvation." Following an ancient tradition, on that day the final decree concerning the fate of the worshippers for the year to come is sealed in Heaven. In the synagogue that morning, after the seven circuits have been made, the worshippers pick up a bundle of willow branches, called *hoshanahs* ("Save, O Lord!") and beat them vigorously upon the floor or praying desks three times, crying out: "A voice proclaims glad tidings." This ancient formula signifies that the final decree for the year will be merciful and just. In East European countries until the Hitler era it was the custom to eat *kreplach*, triangles of chopped meat and onions boiled in dough, and honey from the comb, so that they might leave a sweet taste in the mouth as a cheering omen of a good and tranquil year ahead.

SHAVUOTH

The consecration of Israel as "a holy people" at the foot of Mount Sinai when Moses presented it with the stone-tables of the Covenant is commemorated in the Festival of *Shavuoth*, the two-day "Feast of Weeks," often referred to in sacred Hebrew writings as *zeman matan toratenu*, "the season when our *Torah* was given us."

Like other Jewish festivals with a deeply religious and national content, *Shavuoth*, too, had an agricultural origin farther back than the days of Moses. Its other ancient name was *Hag Habikkurim*, "Festival of the First Fruits."

The Jews of later Hellenic times who spoke Greek called it Pentecost, The Fiftieth Day, because it took place fifty days after the offering of the barley-sheaf in the Temple on the first day of the Festival of Passover. This means that *Shavuoth* was celebrated on the sixth day of the third month, *Sivan* (May-June).

The Rabbinic sages, wishing to inspirit this harvest festival with a higher religious meaning, concluded that the departure of the Israelites from bondage in Egypt was only the prelude to their liberation. They could not be considered really free, the rabbis went on to express themselves in a striking paradox, until they voluntarily had taken upon themselves the redeeming "yoke" of the *Torah*. And *Shavuoth* commemorates the day on which they accepted the "chains of liberation."

While the Temple still stood in Jerusalem, *Shavuoth* was celebrated as the second of the yearly pilgrimage-festivals

to the Holy City. It culminated at the Temple altar with the offering of the first fruits of the summer season. In later times, when the synagogue took the place of the Temple for congregational worship, the agricultural rites of ancient times were perpetuated symbolically by decorating homes as well as houses of worship with greenery and flowers. Otherwise, *Shavuoth* had lost its original primitive character. Thenceforth, it was observed only as the day on which Israel had received the *Torah*.

In the synagogue during this festival of consecration, the Book of Ruth is read aloud to the assembled worshippers. The story it tells is considered highly appropriate for the occasion, because it has a harvest setting and because the climax in the pastoral romance is reached when Ruth, a non-Israelite gleaner in the fields, is converted to a belief in the One God.

Beginning with the Middle Ages, this theme of consecration was carried over into the field of child-education. It was customary for Jewish parents in Europe to start their small boys in *cheder*, the religious school, on *Shavuoth*. This, too, was designed to have a symbolic meaning for the children. It was as if they, too, were standing before the Lord on Mount Sinai. By commencing the study of the *Torah* on that day they were thus consecrating themselves to its preservation forever. From this custom there developed still another of very recent date, but it is observed in Reform and Conservative congregations: that of the group-confirmation of boys and girls during the Festival.

In East European countries it was the time-honored custom on *Shavuoth* for pious Jews to leave the drab ghetto-towns where they lived and to make their way into the nearby woods and fields. The *cheder*-boys, led by their religious teachers, would march there, too, in procession, singing gaily all the way. And so, in a setting of blossoming fields and shimmering woodland, recalling to them the agricultural manner of their ancestors' life in Bible times, both old and young would chant *Akdamut*, a song of praise in Aramaic, which extols the Lord's greatness, His loving-kindness and bounty.

Ruth gleaning in the field. (From a Hebrew manuscript, France, c. 1750.)

THE CONQUEST OF CANAAN

JOSHUA

Joshua ben Nun, Moses' disciple, who eventually took up the burden of Moses' leadership, is described as "a man in whom is the spirit . . . the spirit of wisdom." To him also, as to Moses, were ascribed prophetic and supernatural powers. These gifts were granted him by the Lord, according to Scripture, in order that he might fulfill his divinely appointed mission to help conquer Canaan for Israel. This mission he began immediately when the period of mourning for Moses had come to an end.

Joshua had been one of the "spies" Moses had sent out earlier to investigate the fertility of the Promised Land. These scouts had penetrated as far as the valley of Eshcol and had returned to camp with huge clusters of grapes the

The grapes of Eshcol.

sight of which had delighted the hearts of the Israelites and made them impatient to take over the land without delay. While Moses was still alive, the Israelite tribes had made two attempts to battle their way into Canaan from the south, but they were beaten back. This time Joshua was determined

The Jordan near Jericho.

to make a supreme effort to gain a foothold in the land by crossing the Jordan at a fordable point some miles from where the Jabbok River flows into it.

Joshua's main military objective at the moment was to seize the city of Jericho which lay across the river beyond its western bank. After two spies had brought back the information he required about the city's defenses, he made the army and the people ready for fording the river.

Before the advancing army came the priests bearing the Holy Ark to give it divine protection. They stationed themselves in midstream and allowed the army to pass before them and to draw heart from the Ark's presence. When they had all crossed the river, followed by the entire people, they rested at the town of Gilgal. Since it was the season of Passover, they celebrated it in the plain of Jericho, their feast consisting of *matzohs* and parched corn.

The Battle of Jericho

The attack on Jericho began early in the morning. The priests took up their previously assigned station with the Ark of the Lord. Seven priests marched before it with *shofars*, or ram's horns, in their hands. At a given signal from Joshua they started blowing upon their horns, and continued without a pause while the armed men of Israel who both preceded and followed the Ark were making a complete circuit of the walls of Jericho. This tactic they repeated each day for six days. On the seventh and final day they marched around the city walls not once but seven times with the priests as

The walls of ancient Jericho.

usual blowing upon the horns. And at the seventh circuit Joshua commanded the entire people to shout with all their might.

"So the people shouted and the priests blew the horns. And it came to pass, when the people heard the sound of the horn, that the people shouted with a great shout, and the wall fell down flat."

THE LAND IS DIVIDED

The Israelites captured Jericho and went on taking fortress-city after fortress-city, so that the people of Gibeon that lay in the Israelites' way grew afraid and made peace with them. When Adoni-zedek, the king of Jerusalem, heard of the Gibeonites' faint-hearted capitulation he was infuriated and decided to wreak vengeance upon them. For this purpose he made an alliance with other Amorite rulers like himself, with the kings of Hebron, Jarmuth, Lachish and Eglon. With their combined armies he then marched on Gibeon. When Joshua heard of the threat to his new allies, he quickly marshaled Israel's army and hastened to Gibeon's assistance.

It was at Makkedah that the battle was joined. On this critical occasion Joshua revealed his supernatural powers. We read in the Bible of the exhortation Joshua made as night began to fall and the tide of battle flowed on inconclusively:

Sun, stand thou still upon Gibeon;
And thou, Moon, in the valley of Aijalon.
And the sun stood still, and the moon stayed,
Until the nation had avenged themselves of their enemies.

The battle was fought with savage brutishness, so characteristic of ancient times. It was either kill or be killed. The Israelites put the enemy to the sword without flinching. Had the enemy been victorious, the Israelites, too, would have been murdered, man by man.

The fortified city-kingdoms of Libnah, Lachish, Eglon, Hebron and Debir fell one by one. The Israelites fought their way victoriously right down to Kadesh-barnea in the south and to Gaza in the west. The tribe of Judah seized Hebron for itself. From there it radiated northward towards the plain of Esdraelon. The Israelites routed a number of petty kinglets at Lake Merom and burned Hazor, slaying all its inhabitants.

Joshua made the fortress-town of Gilgal the military and political seat of his leadership. From it he carried on the war of conquest and ruled the tribes. Later on, he found it more desirable to move his center of government and the Holy Ark to the fortified city of Shiloh. There he built a sanctuary which housed the Ark and its Tabernacle. Shiloh served as the holy city of the Israelites for some two hundred years until the Temple in Jerusalem was built by Solomon.

Joshua distributed the land among the people in gradual stages, bit by bit, as fast as it was conquered. He had each tribe draw lots for the various districts they were to occupy. The tribe of Reuben, for instance, was given land beyond the Jordan; the tribe of Gad received half the territory of Gilead, about half of Ammon and the land along the banks of the winding Jordan up to Lake Kinnereth in Galilee. The half tribe of Manasseh was allotted the other half of Gilead and all of Bashan. Settled thus outside the borders of Canaan, these tribes remained somewhat unconcerned about the trials and misfortunes that beset the main body of Israel as it desperately fought its way into the interior.

The most valuable part of the country, the entire coastal region, was denied the Israelites. The northern part was firmly held by the Phoenicians; and the southern by the Philistines. Furthermore, the Israelites did not have a firm hold on their conquered land. Reuben, Gad and Manasseh were constantly plagued by the attacks of Moab and Ammon. In the southern territory Judah was harried by the Edomites and the Amalekites, but especially by the unceasingly relentless Philistines.

Most significant is the fact that everywhere the Israelite victors went they embraced the culture of the local peoples among whom they found themselves. Formerly, they had been wandering shepherds, but as soon as they settled down in fixed localities they readily adopted the agricultural way of life of their Canaanite neighbors. This cultural absorption was quite thorough-going. Canaanitish in design were their houses, furniture and clothing. Similarly their manner of cultivating the soil, the Hebrew language they spoke, the musical instruments they played, the weapons with which they fought. They even adopted some of the Canaanite deities and rites. To be sure, they still believed in the Lord, but they considered Him as only the mightiest of their gods. Outside of their monolatrous worship of the Lord there was little else in their religion to distinguish them from other tribes on both sides of the Jordan.

The mountain ridges that isolated many parts of the country proved a great setback to the development of a unified group life for the Israelites, whether politically, culturally, religiously or even militarily. Contact with one another being difficult, each tribe had to fend for itself. Only on rare occasions, whenever an overwhelming and common danger seemed to threaten them all, did they close ranks.

The readiness with which the Israelites intermarried with the Canaanites disturbed Joshua greatly. When he was well on in years and felt that his time to die was near, he assembled all of Israel for the last time in a solemn convocation. He warned them that, if they continued to intermarry at the rate they were doing, Israel would soon be lost. Their Canaanite and other neighbors, he assured them, would become "a snare and a trap unto you, and a scourge into your sides, and pricks in your eyes, until ye perish from off this good land. . . ."

Therefore he implored them to swear a solemn oath: "The Lord our God will we serve, and unto His voice will we hearken."

They swore as he asked, but they soon forgot their oath.

THE RULE OF THE JUDGES

When Joshua was laid to rest, a new era began for the Israelites. Joshua had succeeded only in a partial conquest of the land. It was the greater task of his successors, the *Shofetim*, or Judges, to complete his work and to consolidate Israel's power as a nation.

The institution of these Judges was of tribal origin. It dated back to the time of Moses. When the government of Israel became too difficult for him to run single-handed, he had appointed "able men" from among the people. Their chief duty was to "judge the people at all seasons." Actually, they were just sub-leaders to whom he had delegated some of his burdens in ruling the people.

Moses himself performed the duties of chief Judge. Making important decisions and issuing judgment on infractions of religious, civil and criminal laws seemed to be the most important functions of a ruler in a primitive tribal society. But these judgments were often charged with an extra-legal content, a deep religious and prophetic conviction. Whether it was Moses, Joshua or the Judges, seeking judgment also meant "inquiring of God." Thus we see in the early judicial practices of Israel the beginning of an ethical relationship between God's will and man's social dealings, a relationship which, in the course of several centuries, was destined to blossom into a conception of human relations which mankind had never known before.

The Prophetess Deborah

No one can fix a definite date for the rule of the five Judges of Israel. A reasonable assumption is that it took place sometime between the twelfth and the eleventh century B.C.E.

An early Judge, oddly enough, was a woman: Deborah the Prophetess. This would indicate that in the democratic social organization of early Israel, women occupied, if not an equal position with men, at least a higher one than among other peoples.

The Book of Judges recounts how for twenty years the tribes of Israel groaned under the yoke of the Canaanite king, Jabin. His general, Sisera, had subdued them in a

Deborah and Barak.

series of clashes. And so King Jabin had extorted enormous tribute from them year after year. However, Israel's desperate need created a natural leader to win back its independence: Deborah the Prophetess. To use a modern comparison, she was very much like Joan of Arc. The plight of her fellow-Israelites moved Deborah so deeply that she was ripe for divine revelation. The Lord appeared to her one day and pointed out her sacred duty—to lead a revolt against the king of Canaan. She persuaded a tribal chieftain, Barak, to join her with ten thousand men drawn from the tribes of Naphtali and Zebulun. Several of the other tribes held back and would not support her. Undaunted because the Canaanites greatly outnumbered the Israelites, Deborah marshaled her force on Mount Tabor which rises at the rim of the Plain of Esdraelon. Her plan was to try and lure the Canaanite general Sisera to the river Kishon and there ambush him.

Now the reason why so many of the tribes would not support Deborah's revolt was that they stood in mortal fear of Canaanite military prowess, especially of their "chariots of iron." In other weapons as well the Israelites felt their inferiority to the enemy. As a fixed agricultural people of long duration and possessing a higher material culture than the Israelites, the Canaanites had better means as well as knowledge to develop the arts of war and for producing superior weapons.

Sisera assembled a great host and nine hundred chariots against Deborah and Barak. Lifted up by Deborah into a heroic mood, the Israelites poured down the slopes of Mount Tabor upon the enemy and routed them.

Sisera fled on foot with Barak in pursuit of him. As he passed the tent of Jael, the wife of Heber the Kenite who was not an Israelite at all, he asked her to hide him in her tent. The Song of Deborah, probably the most ancient portion of the Bible because it was composed in saga-form by a contemporary, tells the whole tale most vividly:

Water he asked, milk she gave him;
In a lordly bowl she brought him curd.
Her hand she put to the tent-pin,
And her right hand to the work-men's hammer;

And with the hammer she smote Sisera, she smote
   him through his head,
Yea, she pierced and struck through his temples.

Gideon

The defeat of the Canaanites did not put an end to the tribulations of the Israelites. There remained other enemies to harass them, most of all the Amalekites, Moabites and the Midianites, three powerful tribal kingdoms lying along the eastern bank of the Jordan.

For seven years the Midianites had been a source of great trouble to the Israelite tribes. They constantly were preying upon them, especially during the harvest season, when they descended upon their fields and stripped them clean of all their grain and produce.

At this time Gideon was Judge of Israel. The Book of Judges tells how the Lord revealed Himself to him and elected him to serve as His instrument for the crushing of the Midianites.

Out of thirty-two thousand men from the most reliable tribes Gideon carefully selected three hundred who he considered possessed the most spirit, strength and skill. These he divided into three bands, each under a separate commander. Every man was provided with a horn, a jar and a torch.

Gideon then cautioned them to watch him closely, and to do whatever he did.

When darkness fell he led them towards the foe. They stole along silently until suddenly they saw Gideon raise the horn to his lips and blow a mighty blast on it. All three hundred men then blew on their horns. Gideon smashed his jar, they proceeded to smash theirs. When he raised his torch and brandished it, they did likewise. They then descended upon the enemy shouting as one man: "The Sword of the Lord and of Gideon!"

The unexpected loud noises and the moving torches confused the Midianites. They could make out neither friend nor foe, and they fled in panic. Gideon then drove them down into the Jordan valley, and by a swift maneuver he blocked their path of escape and routed them.

The people jubilated over the victory and tried to reward Gideon. They asked him to become their king, but Gideon replied: "I will not rule over you, neither shall my son rule over you; the Lord shall rule over you."

In these simple words Gideon uttered the dislike for kings that had become traditional in the democratic society which Moses had established. This aversion stemmed from the belief that a leader exercised power only by the will of the people, and that he was its servant and not its master. More-

Gideon defeats the Midianites.

over, his power to lead and govern was not unlimited. It was expected that he, like the humblest Israelite, conduct himself according to the laws of Moses.

The Philistines

Of all the enemies of Israel during the two hundred years it took to conquer and settle Canaan, the Philistines were the most bitter and also the most formidable. Unlike the other peoples who inhabited the country, they were not related to the Israelites by language or culture. They had come as invaders in the twelfth century from the island of Crete where already a civilization of a high order had long been in existence. In a relatively short time they had succeeded in conquering the southern portion of the coastal plain. They then established themselves as a federation of five city-states that, in its political organization, was far in advance of any existing before that time in Palestine.

The Philistines were a warrior people. They were highly advanced in battle tactics and in the weapons they used. Against them the Israelites proved no match. It was natural that in the course of time the latter should have resigned themselves to the humiliating role of vassal.

Samson

The Book of Judges tells a number of tales about a real hero of extraordinary strength who arose to put new heart into the supine tribes of Israel. While he never succeeded in breaking the power of the Philistines, his successful harassment of them raised the spirit of resistance among his own people. He proved that the Philistines were not as invincible as they had thought.

This "strong man" hero was Samson. He judged Israel for twenty years neither wisely nor well.

For a holy man as he purported to be, a Nazirite who had taken ascetic vows to the Lord, he showed himself extraordinarily weak in character. Upon the slightest provocation he abandoned himself to the most primitive passions. He engaged without scruple in the mass-slaughter of human beings. Furthermore, as the leader of his people he should have set an example of loyalty to the Lord and to Israel. Instead he revealed a persistent fondness for Philistine women.

Samson's feats of strength are illustrated by a number of legends. One day, while walking past the vineyards of Timnah, "behold, a young lion roared against him . . . and he

40

rent him as one would have rent a kid." On another occasion, when he allowed the Philistines to bind him with new ropes, he snapped them "as flax that was burned with fire." And then, to revenge himself for this piece of impudence, he picked up a jawbone of an ass and laid about him among the Philistines. "With the jawbone of an ass have I smitten a thousand men!" he rejoiced.

Samson's carnal temptation, which led to his inglorious and premature downfall, was the Philistine woman, Delilah. In her his mortal enemies thought they had found at last the means of trapping him and settling accounts with him. The Philistine rulers said to this temptress: "Entice him, and see wherein his great strength lieth, and by what means we may prevail against him, that we may bind him to afflict him."

Samson slays the Philistines.

The Babylonian hero and "strong man," Gilgamesh, with a lion cub. He defeated the Elamites and was chosen king. Like Samson he, too, fought lions and slayed countless enemies.

"Tell me, I pray thee," she asked Samson, "wherein thy great strength lieth, and wherewith thou mightest be bound to afflict thee."

Samson was evasive. The first time he told her that if he were tied with seven fresh bowstrings he would not be able to break loose. With the Philistines nearby Delilah tied him with bowstrings. When she called out to him: "The Philistines are upon thee, Samson!" he rose up and snapped the bowstrings "as a string of tow." The second time he told her the newly twisted ropes would prove beyond his strength, and the third time that "if thou weavest the seven locks of my head with the web" of the loom, he would not be able to break loose. Nonetheless, both times he extricated himself without difficulty, of course to the chagrin of Delilah and the Philistines.

But Delilah was determined to worm the secret out of him. Daily she nagged, wheedled and coaxed until finally he confessed that his strength lay in his long unshorn hair. "If I

be shaven then my strength will go from me, and I shall become weak, and be like any other man."

Delilah took him at his word. While he slept with his head resting in her lap she "had the seven locks of his head shaven off . . . and his strength went from him."

The Philistines then emerged from their place of hiding, laid hold of Samson and bound him securely. He struggled desperately but could not break his bonds as he had before. The Philistines gouged out his eyes. They bore him to Gaza in triumph. There they bound him with fetters of brass and threw him into prison. The Judge of Israel was now reduced to the labor of a mule. He was harnessed to a treadmill and round and round he staggered, grinding corn for the Philistines.

The capture of this feared and hated enemy caused great rejoicing among the Philistines. Thousands of them, including their foremost men, gathered in the great temple of Dagon to offer a sacrifice of thanksgiving. In the midst of their jubilation they cried out: "Call for Samson, that he may make us sport!" So they fetched the blind Samson from his prison, stood him between the pillars and mocked at him and humiliated him.

Then Samson raised his voice in a mighty outcry. In agony

41

he called to the Lord: "O Lord God, remember me, I pray Thee, and strengthen me, I pray Thee, only this once, O God, that I may be this once avenged of the Philistines!"

Taking firm hold of the two middle pillars upon which the temple rested, Samson cried out: "Let me die with the Philistines!" Straining with all his ebbing might, he pushed, and the pillars broke. The temple tottered and crashed. It became a tomb for Samson and all the Philistines that were there.

Samuel

Upon the death of Samson, the harassment by the Philistines increased. Israel's lot became even more intolerable than before. The High Priest and Judge at Shiloh during that period was Eli. In a pitched battle with the Philistines the Israelites were badly beaten and their generals, Eli's sons Hophni and Phinehas, were slain. In the popular mind, the crowning point of the disaster was the capture of the Holy Ark. When news of it and of the death of his sons was brought to Eli he fell dead.

It was most fortunate for the tribes of Israel that at this time there arose a great and selfless leader to guide them. He was Samuel, the son of Hannah of the tribe of Ephraim. After she had been childless for many years, Samuel was born to assuage her grief. To keep a vow she had made that if the Lord blessed her with a son she would consecrate him to His service, she had brought the child Samuel to Eli, the High Priest.

Because his sons were dissolute men and Samuel was full of righteousness and wisdom, Eli had trained him to be his successor. Even as a boy he wore the linen *ephod*, or apron, of a priest, and he ministered at the sacrificial altar. As he grew older he was filled with the prophetic spirit. His election by the Lord was recognized and acclaimed by all of Israel. The divine revelations he received in later years when he became Eli's successor, he imparted to the people for their instruction and rule.

However, the attacks by the Philistines throughout Samuel's long leadership of Israel did not abate. Although the Philistines returned the Holy Ark after a series of disasters had

convinced them that their retention of it was the cause, matters still did not go well with Israel after that.

Like all religious leaders of ancient Israel, Samuel attributed the misfortunes that befell the people to their disobedience of the Lord and to their worship of other gods. Twenty years after the Ark had been returned by the Philistines, Samuel admonished Israel: "If ye do return unto the Lord with all your heart, then put away the foreign gods and the Ashtaroth from among you, and direct your hearts unto the Lord, and serve Him only; and He will deliver you out of the hand of the Philistines."

Apparently, Samuel had initiated and successfully carried through a program of religious purification, for the chronicler does record how the Israelites put away for the time being their Canaanitish idol-worship of the *Baalim* and the *Ashtaroth* "and served the Lord only."

The turning point in the dismal position of the tribes occurred at the decisive battle of Mizpah. Samuel, to carry out his program of religious purgation, had assembled all Israel at Mizpah for a day of general fasting and repentance. Sacrifices were brought and public atonement was recited. "We have sinned against the Lord," murmured all Israel contritely.

When the Philistines heard that all Israelites had gathered for penitence in Mizpah they considered it a marvelous opportunity for a surprise attack to destroy them. Quickly they assembled their forces. "And when the children of Israel heard it, they were afraid. . . ."

But Samuel would not permit them to give way to panic. Serenely he offered a sacrifice upon the altar of the Lord and called on Him to come to Israel's aid. When the attack finally came, the Lord "thundered with a great thunder . . . upon the Philistines . . . and they were smitten down before Israel."

Samuel was the last of the Judges. He was the first of the Prophets of Israel. He not only tried to cleanse its religion of idolatry, but he wisely used the religion as a unifying agent to draw the still loosely linked tribes closer together and thus to weld them into a people.

Samuel and Eli.   *John Singleton Copley*
Wadsworth Atheneum, Hartford

42

DAILY LIFE IN ANCIENT ISRAEL

Portrayal of inhabitants of ancient Canaan, possibly Israelites, or at least of tribes akin to them in language, culture and mode of life. *Above.* Advance to battle, or a military parade. *Below.* Farmers with ducks. (From the Megiddo ivories, 12th or 11th century B.C.E.) *Oriental Institute, University of Chicago*

When the Egyptians, Assyrians, Persians, Greeks and Romans held overlordship in turn over Palestine, they imposed their cultures on the Jewish people. By contrast, when the Israelites subdued the Canaanite inhabitants, they absorbed the Canaanite culture. This was due chiefly to the fact that the Israelite conquerors had come into the settled, predominantly agricultural land as a nomadic people. The Canaanite culture they found there was, of course, more developed than their own.

The Israelites did not become farmers overnight. Their transformation from herdsmen was a slow process. In fact, the light rainfall and the large area of wilderness in the south of Judah and in areas east of the Jordan River helped preserve the old nomadic way of life. There was a sharp cleavage between the Jewish herdsmen, who lived in patriarchal simplicity like their forefathers, and their settled brothers, who were tillers of the soil, or who lived in towns. There even arose an identifiable group of zealots who refused to follow any but the pastoral way of life. They, consistent worshippers of the Lord, called themselves *Rechabites.* Everything that was noble and good in Jewish society they ascribed to their nomadic existence, which they revered as they did the Mosaic tradition. And all that was evil and corrupt they blamed on the new ways of life, including idol-worship borrowed from the agricultural Canaanites.

The Israelites built their houses of materials at hand. Those in the plains built them of sun-dried brick, held together by a coating of clay. In the hills the houses were of stone. At no time was the country rich in forests, so that only a limited amount of lumber was used in construction.

Almost uniformly the houses of the poor in the towns had flat roofs which served as terraces where the family gathered after the midday heat to enjoy the cool of the evening. In a sense, the roof was also the parlor where the guests were received. For instance, there is the Biblical allusion: "He [Samuel] spoke with Saul on the housetop." All the houses were attached, so that one could promenade along the rooftops and "visit" on the way.

Much more primitive were the houses in the country. These were merely four walls covered with thatch and overlaid with clay mixed with straw. There was only one room, and it was impartially shared by the family and the domestic animals. There was a clay floor and no chimney, so that the smoke from heating or cooking fires had to find its way through the door or the single window, which was usually latticed against thieves.

Furniture was rudimentary, usually a table and one or two stools, and a few straw mats for sitting and for sleeping. Clay vessels, simple in design with little ornamentation, held the family vegetables, the olive and sesame oil, wine and water. More affluent households owned a few metal pans and bowls for kitchen use. Lighting after dark was from a little clay bowl filled with olive oil on which floated a flaxen wick.

By and large, each farming household had to grow its own food, sew its own clothes and fashion its tools and implements. Milk came from goats and cows. The poor ate barley bread; the more affluent made bread out of wheat. There was oil for cooking and for lighting and a jug of wine to drink with the meals. Onions, garlic and cucumbers were the principal vegetables; olives, grapes and figs, the most common fruits.

In his spare time, the farmer carved his light plow out of wood. Its teeth would turn the topsoil in a shallow furrow. He

Excavation of ancient Megiddo.

43

Ancient Palestinian
(1000-586 B.C.E.)
jug and vase.
Metropolitan Museum

Modern Palestinian Arab uses plow virtually unchanged from
ancient times.

made his flail of two pieces of wood with stones tied securely
to the ends and his mill for grinding grain was two small
round stones, one on top of the other.

Most of the work of the household and most of the menial
tasks were done by the women. They ground the grain between the millstones and pounded it into fine flour in a mor-

Ancient Palestinian lamp-filler.   *Jewish Museum*

tar. They baked the bread by laying the kneaded dough in
flat cakes on hot ashes. Some bread was baked in rude ovens
which were only earthenware jars with charcoal burning at
the bottom. They pressed oil from the olives, and made cheese
and butter. They helped gather in the harvest. They carded
the wool, combed the yarn and spindled the thread. They also
wove the cloth and sewed the garments.

Wall-painting on Tomb of Nakht, Egypt, depicting ways of life
similar to those of Israelites in Canaan.

The clothing of the ancient Israelites was generally made
of wool for the poor and linen for the rich. Cotton, which
was imported from Egypt, and silk, from India and China,
were luxuries. The women also dyed the cloth. The most common colors were red, blue, purple and white.

The earliest garment for women was an Egyptian-like apron

Egyptian weavers. (Wooden model.)
Metropolitan Museum

worn around the loins. In time, this developed into an under-
garment—a sleeveless shirt reaching to the knees. Over it was
worn a *sim-lah,* or mantle, usually made of wool for warmth.
It also served farmers as a garment by day and a covering by
night. The Book of Deuteronomy lays down the law to all
creditors: "And if he is a poor man . . . thou shall surely restore to him the pledge when the sun goeth down, that he
may sleep in his garment."

With succeeding generations, when the more democratic
organization of early Israelite society began to make way for
sharper class distinctions, there arose a considerable land-
owner class, which indulged itself in luxuries. This held especially true in the capital cities of Jerusalem and Samaria.
There the upper classes built themselves multi-roomed houses
of hewn stone lined with cedar. The furniture was not only
of better materials but of superior design and workmanship.
Decorative objects were imported from Egypt and Assyria.
The rich boasted an assortment of bronze vessels, wine goblets
and bowls of silver and gold. They wore garments of "purple
stuff" made by the fine weavers of Tyre and of Egyptian
byssus dyed in the most subtle colors. There were also embroideries and all manner of woven materials brought from
Babylonia.

"Ointments and perfumes delight the heart," testified
pleasure-loving King Solomon in *Proverbs.* Perfumes and

scented waters used by both men and women sophisticates were made of frankincense and myrrh, aloes and cassia. Ointments compounded of aromatic spices and olive oil were used after bathing and washing. In emulation of the upper classes everywhere, the rich Jews curled and perfumed their hair and beards according to the prevailing fashion.

The women of the nobility and of the landlord class indulged in every conceivable extravagance. With burning sarcasm, the prophet Isaiah, himself a member of the aristocracy, presented an inventory of the wardrobes of the ladies of fashion in his day ". . . the bravery of their anklets, and the fillets, and the crescents; the pendants, and the bracelets, and the veils; the head-tiaras, and the armlets and the sashes, and the corselets, and the amulets; the rings and the nose-jewels, the aprons and the mantelets, and the cloaks and the girdles;

Egyptian girl musician.

and the gauze robes, and the fine linen and the turbans and the mantles."

Most of these articles came from other countries, for few luxury goods, except during later, more developed periods under Greek and Roman influence, were made in Palestine. The merchants were the Canaanites, Philistines and Phoenicians, all peoples who lived along the seacoast. Through their territories stretched the great caravan route along which passed much of the commerce of the Mediterranean countries. Be-

cause of this direct contact with one of the main streams of world trade the coastal peoples developed a sizable merchant class. It was so important a group that almost all references to merchants in the Bible are to Canaanites, Phoenicians and Ishmaelites. In fact, quite often in ancient Hebrew documents and chronicles the word "Canaanite" also means "merchant."

Perhaps because the ancient Israelites had not developed their luxury crafts to any appreciable degree, the graphic and plastic arts could hardly find the proper cultural, material and technical conditions in which to develop. Painting and sculpture could flourish only in those countries in which commerce was in an active and advanced stage. That is why they thrived in such a significant way in the great commercial centers of Thebes, Memphis, Babylon, Athens and Rome. To be sure, Jews had still another deterrent to the practice of the visual arts: the stern religious prohibition against "graven" images. In fact, although architecture was permitted by the Jewish religion, it did not develop to any point of originality, but imitated Egyptian, Assyrian, Phoenician, Greek and Roman models. This, too, was for the same reason: because of its agricultural economy, the land of Israel lacked the high level of the handicraft skills, the cultural base, and the materials necessary for the cultivation of an original style of architecture.

At all times Jews were great lovers of music. The harvesters in the field sang as they worked, and those who pulled heavy burdens synchronized their movements to the rhythm of their song. At all festivals and on domestic occasions of joy and gladness the people sang and danced and played on musical instruments. When Jephtah, the conquering hero, returned from battle against the Ammonites, ". . . behold, his daughter came out to meet him with timbrels and with dances." Music, poetry and the dance were unified arts in those days, each designed to enhance the effects of the others upon the hearer's senses and emotions. There was processional dancing during the festival pilgrimages to the Temple in Jerusalem. Poems were sung as the strings of the *kinnor* were plucked, and the reedlike *halil* gurgled its liquid notes and the cymbals crashed. The dances were primitive, and sometimes wild and abandoned; the Hebrew word for dance meant "to leap like lambs." The distinctive feature of both the music and the dance was the sharp rhythm.

Ancient Hebrew seals.

ISRAEL BECOMES GREAT

SAUL: THE FIRST KING (about 1030-1011 B.C.E.)

As a result of Samuel's vigorous reforms, the ties of religion were now strong among the tribes of Israel. Perhaps just as effective in drawing them together, although as yet in a half-hearted solidarity, was their desperate need to unite in order to meet the numerous onslaughts of their enemies.

It was generally felt that more centralized controls would make the resistance of Israel more effective, both politically and militarily, and for that reason there were many, probably a majority, who voiced a strong desire for a king vested with absolute powers over all the tribes. In this there was undoubtedly an element of group vanity: since all other peoples had kings, they, too, wished to have one. The Elders of Israel demanded of Samuel: "Give us a king!"

Samuel was taken aback by the popularity of this demand. He himself was a traditionalist, a strong adherent of the tribal democracy established at such cost by Moses. He considered kingship a dangerous precedent for Israel to establish. Like Gideon before him, he recognized only one absolute ruler for the tribes of Israel: the Lord. He warned the people and pleaded with them, but the demand for a king grew even greater.

Samuel went to the Lord, and the Lord bade him: "Make them a king."

The man Samuel singled out to be the first king of the Israelites was Saul, a farmer of the tribe of Benjamin. He was besides "a mighty man of valor," a distinction which seemed

Samuel denounces Saul.

J. S. Copley   *Boston Museum of Fine Arts*

to be his principal qualification for kingship, since he was otherwise cruel and vengeful. However, Samuel had estimated him correctly as a brave and able military commander, a prime requirement for a leader in that troubled age. The physical survival of Israel was at stake, for the Philistines, the principal enemies of Israel, had succeeded in extending their territories beyond the limits of their own coastal plain. They had reached into the mountain country, across the Valley of Jezreel, virtually to the banks of the Jordan.

King Saul succeeded in rousing the tribes from their apathy and defeatism by persuading them that they were facing a common danger. It was either fight or die. Each tribe, therefore, made a contribution to him that he might wage a war of liberation.

Guerrilla Tactics

The first blow, a surprise guerrilla attack, was struck by Saul's son Jonathan. The Philistines pulled back more from surprise than from defeat. They had never expected such belligerence from their cowed Israelite vassals whom they had previously disarmed and kept disarmed. For years they had systematically deprived them of their swords and spears, bows and arrows, slings and battle axes. Also they had carried into bondage all the Israelite blacksmiths to prevent any new arms from being forged.

Saul and Jonathan followed up their initial success by a simple campaign of hit and run, a style of fighting determined by their inferiority in arms and in numbers. By day they lay hidden in their mountain hideouts. But when night fell, they would swoop down on the Philistines, who, for all their well-drilled foot-soldiers, horsemen and chariots, were confused and routed by the Israelites' unorthodox style of attack. Little by little the Israelites forced them back from the hills and finally fought them in the open plains.

King Saul and David

Saul's arrogance increased with his military victories. Samuel could no longer endure him. The Judge's devotion to the people and his determination to keep its religion pure finally led him to tell Saul that he no longer deserved the kingship: "Thou hast rejected the word of the Lord, and the Lord has rejected thee from being king over Israel."

The chronicler records gloomily: "Now the spirit of the Lord had departed from Saul, and an evil spirit from the Lord terrified him." This meant that Saul was insane. His councilors, troubled by his condition, urged him to find a skilled harpist, so that "when the evil spirit from God cometh upon thee, that he shall play with his hand and thou shalt be well."

And so it was that David, a shepherd of Bethlehem, reputed to be an excellent harpist, was summoned.

David and Goliath

David was but a mere youth, "ruddy, and withal of beautiful eyes, and goodly to look upon." Whenever King Saul fell into a melancholy state, he sought consolation in music. So David played for him on his harp and "Saul found relief . . . and the evil spirit departed."

All this time the war with the Philistines was being waged without let-up. The latter had gathered a great force at Socoh for a decisive test of strength with Israel. The two armies faced each other, ready for battle, on opposite hills. For a long time neither side made a move. Then suddenly the celebrated warrior, Goliath of Gath, stepped from the ranks of the Philistines. He was terrible to behold because of his great size, his brute strength and his shining armor.

Goliath taunted the Israelites with being cowards and weaklings. "Choose you a man," he challenged, ". . . and let him come down to me. If he be able to fight with me, and kill me, then will we be your servants; but if I prevail against him and kill him, then shall ye be our servants. . . ."

For forty days Goliath repeated his mockery, but there was no one from the ranks of Israel to accept his challenge.

King Saul and his entire army heard and were dismayed. "And all the men of Israel, when they saw the man, fled from him, and were sore afraid." But the news was brought to King Saul that his young harpist was ready to fight the Philistine giant.

King Saul summoned David to him. He tried to belittle him at first: "Thou art not able to go against this Philistine to fight with him; for thou art but a youth, and he a man of war from his youth. . . ."

Still David was resolute and unafraid. When he saw this, King Saul said to him: "Go, and the Lord shall be with thee."

With his own hands King Saul helped David prepare for the combat. He put on him his own coat of mail, his brass helmet and his great sword. But David was so uncomfortable and hampered by them that he took them off, which displeased Saul.

Instead David took his shepherd's crook, a familiar weapon, and with his sling and five smooth stones from a brook, he ran toward Goliath.

When the giant Philistine, resplendent in his armed might, saw the unarmed shepherd racing toward him, "he disdained him, for he was but a youth." Goliath was furious when he saw David's weapons. "Am I a dog, that thou comest with stones?" he roared, and he flung curses and threats at him. "Come to

me, and I will give thy flesh unto the fowls of the air and to the beasts of the wild."

As David advanced he "put his hand in his bag, and took thence a stone and slung it, and smote the Philistine in his forehead, and he fell upon his face to the earth."

David then drew Goliath's sword from its sheath and cut off his head. This so terrified the Philistines that they fled, the men of Israel and Judah in pursuit.

David brought the head of Goliath to King Saul amidst the rejoicing of the people. On this occasion Jonathan, the king's son, saw the popular hero for the first time, and he pleased him greatly. He "made a covenant with David, because he loved him as his own soul."

Saul recognized that a warrior of such skill, resourcefulness and courage as David could be enormously useful. He therefore gave him his daughter Michal for a wife and appointed him commander of a part of the army, and he sent him on various forays against the Philistines.

David proved uniformly successful. "And it came to pass, when David returned from the slaughter of the Philistines, that the women came out of all the cities of Israel, singing and dancing, to meet King Saul, with timbrels, with joy, and with three-stringed instruments. And the women sang one to another in their play:

Saul hath slain his thousands
And David his ten thousands.

47

Saul Fears David

The people's adulation of David made Saul jealous, and he felt insecure in his power as king. "All he lacketh is the kingdom," he said savagely of him.

From that day on Saul could not keep his mind off David. He hated him with a hatred that devoured his spirit.

King Saul's brooding flung him again into a state of depression. "And it came to pass on the morrow, that an evil spirit

from God came mightily upon Saul, and he raved in the midst of the house."

Day after day David played for him. He hoped that the soothing music would bring Saul back to normal. It was in vain.

One day, as Saul sat toying with his spear and listening to David, a murderous impulse gripped him. He threw the spear at David, who, sensing the mad king's intention, leaped aside and escaped.

David's success on the battlefield continued. Saul was now not only jealous but afraid. "All Israel and Judah loved David," the chronicler reported. King Saul now felt the earth could not hold both him and David. He was resolved to get rid of him. To murder him with his own hand, he craftily considered, would be unwise; David was far too popular an idol with the people. Why not let the Philistines slay him in the natural course of fighting? It would be easy for Saul to keep David constantly involved with the Philistines.

But David seemed to have a charmed life; again and again he returned from the battlefield in triumph. Then Saul spoke openly to his son Jonathan who, he knew, was David's dearest friend.

Jonathan was horrified by his father's proposal and rebuked him. Saul was so chastened by his son's indignation that he took an oath before Jonathan: "As the Lord liveth, he shall not be put to death."

But no sooner had he uttered this vow than his obsession revived again with renewed force. Once again he attempted to transfix David against the wall with his spear, while the youth was playing the harp for him. But this time, too, David was alert to his danger. As the spear came flying at him, he "slipped away out of Saul's presence, and he smote the spear into the wall; and David fled."

This time Saul sent men in pursuit. They had instructions to kill David, but Michal, Saul's own daughter who was David's wife, warned him and he escaped.

The hunt for David was pressed by Saul in an unrelenting passion of hatred. David hid in the cave of Abdullam where he was joined by his father's family-clan, and "everyone that was in debt, and everyone that was discontented, gathered themselves unto him." He welded these elements into an outlaw band which sustained itself by armed raids on neighboring towns.

There were times when David could have done away with Saul, but always he held back. He did not wish, he said, "to put forth my hand against him, seeing he is the Lord's anointed."

Death of King Saul

The manhunt for David, however, came abruptly to an end when Saul learned that the Philistines were gathering a mighty force against him. He summoned all the fighting men of Israel, pitched his tents on Mount Gilboa and waited for the Philistines to attack.

While hiding from King Saul in the mountains of Hebron, David met Abigail, the kind-hearted wife of an enemy chieftain. He fell in love with her and made her his wife.

Rubens   *Detroit Institute of Art*

In the plain of Jezreel the battle was joined. The Israelites fought desperately but in the end they were routed. King Saul and his three sons, including Jonathan, David's bosom friend, were slain.

For all his faults and inconsistencies of character David had the virtues of a great man. Instead of exulting over the death of his relentless enemy he was filled with pity, and he composed a psalm which was a lament and a eulogy for both his friend and his foe:

> Saul and Jonathan, the lovely and the pleasant,
> In their lives, even in their death they were not divided.
> They were swifter than eagles,
> They were stronger than lions . . .
> How are the mighty fallen in the midst of the battle!

DAVID, KING OF JUDAH AND ISRAEL (about 1011-972 B.C.E.)

David was anointed King of Judah in Hebron, where he reigned for seven and a half years. The emergence to power of the tribe of Judah to which David belonged was a signifi-

David anointed king. (After a fresco of the Synagogue at Dura-Europos c. 250 C.E.)   *Courtesy of Yale University Art Gallery*

cant event in the development of Jewish society. By uniting various clans in the south with Bethlehem as their center, David accomplished a great political feat. Thereby he ended the apparent domination of Israel by the tribe of Benjamin of which Saul had been the head.

The rule of David as king of Judah in Hebron proved an uneasy one. The crushing defeat of Saul at Gilboa had made the Philistines undisputed masters of the whole country west of the Jordan. Once again the Israelite tribes, including the kingdom of Judah, became their vassals, and the tribute they were forced to pay was crushing.

There is no orderly record in the Bible of David's life and rule, only a series of unrelated incidents and events. Yet, pieced together, they make a vivid reconstruction of Jewish life in that period. It shows David as consumed with desire to throw off the yoke of the Philistines and to make his people great. To this end he fought the hated enemy from "Dan to Beersheba," and at long last he "smote . . . and subdued them."

At the same time a bitter fratricidal war was going on between David and Saul's heir, Ishbosheth, and other adherents of the House of Saul who had inherited some of Saul's hatred for David. Under the leadership of Saul's former captain, Abner, they fought savagely against the army of Judah led by David's brilliant commander, Joab. In the end, the House of Saul was crushed and Abner was brutally murdered by Joab.

David's conscience became troubled because of what Israelite was doing to Israelite. He lifted up his voice and wept at the grave of Abner.

The civil war, however, did not end until the elders of the other tribes begged David to be king over all Israel, not merely over the tribe of Judah. David consented and was anointed king over all Israel in 1004 B.C.E. in Hebron. But Hebron was too far south to remain the capital city of the united tribes. David accordingly chose Jerusalem, which was then in the hands of the Jebusites. It was farther north, situated high in the hills, and, better yet, was superbly fortified with walls and battlements. David marched against it and took it by storm, a none-too-easy task, and he called it "The City of David."

With the acumen and foresight so characteristic of him, he resolved to make Jerusalem the undisputed center of the religious and political life of the country. For this reason he had the Ark of the Covenant transferred from its sanctuary in Shiloh to Jerusalem.

Once he was firmly settled in the hills of Jerusalem, David systematically wiped out every nest of power the Philistines still held in isolated places. At Raphaim he completely broke

its military backbone. This marked the end of the Philistines as an historic people. "The Lord hath broken my enemies before me, like the breach of waters," exulted David.

David next turned to settle accounts with Moab, Edom, Ammon, Aram and other warlike neighbors. His great general, Joab, crushed them all and exacted tribute from them.

David now reigned as supreme and unchallenged ruler in his part of the world. His kingdom extended as far south as Ezion-geber on the Red Sea and as far northeast as the Euphrates River. It was a relatively large kingdom. In terms of territory, it was the greatest area the Israelites ever held and they did not hold it for long.

The fact should not be overlooked that David was a child of his age and of its moral values. It regarded war as honorable, justified murder if expedient, thought grasping at other people's possessions highly desirable, and accepted the practices of cruelty and deceit as merely ordinary conventions of dog eat dog. Even so, David stood far in advance of the kings in his age. He periodically suffered from a troubled conscience and groped for a moral outlook all his life.

A man of humble origin, a herder of sheep, he had a simple democratic feeling for the people. At all times he was devoted to them and sought to defend their rights. True, he himself was no stranger to corrupt and evil ways, but when he was made aware of his shortcomings, his spirit became sincerely troubled.

That David could be high-handed where the satisfaction of his own personal desires was concerned is nowhere clearer than in the story of his passion for Bathsheba.

David and Bathsheba

One day at dusk, as David was walking on the palace roof, he looked down and saw a woman bathing. Immediately he was smitten with love for her, for she was "very beautiful to look upon." This was Bathsheba, the wife of Uriah, a Hittite soldier in his army.

David sent for Bathsheba. In this instance he showed himself hypocritical as well as cunning. He showered the unsuspecting Uriah with friendliness and personal solicitude. He then wrote a letter to Joab, who was in the field against the Philistines, and sent it to him by Uriah. The letter read: "Set ye Uriah in the forefront of the hottest battle and retire ye from him, that he may be smitten and die."

Joab did as he was instructed and was soon able to report: ". . . thy servant, Uriah the H'ttite, is dead."

David replied to Joab with the cynical message: "Let not

this thing displease thee, for the sword devoureth in one manner or another."

With Uriah conveniently out of the way, David married Bathsheba. She bore him a son, and, quite clearly, he had a genuine love for her.

Nathan the Prophet Rebukes David the King

But the prophet Nathan appeared in Jerusalem. Pointing an accusing finger at David, he asked sternly: "Wherefore hast thou despised the word of the Lord, 'to do that which is evil in My sight?' Uriah the Hittite thou hast smitten with the sword, and his wife thou hast taken to be thy wife."

And the prophet pronounced the judgment of the Lord upon the king: "Now therefore, the sword shall never depart from thy house: because thou hast despised Me, and hast taken the wife of Uriah the Hittite to be thy wife."

This episode illustrates the fact that in the thinking and conduct of Israel the moral law was beginning to supplant the jungle law of the strongest. King as well as subject had become answerable to God for misdeeds toward their fellowmen. An incident drawing to a moral climax such as King David's confrontation by the angry Nathan is not to be found in the annals of other ancient peoples. Never before had a subject dared question the acts of an all-powerful king. To a ruler of ancient times his people were chattels. If they lived and prospered, it was by his benevolence. If they were killed or robbed, it was to satisfy his greed, to suit his convenience, or a mere caprice.

The drama of David's crime and moral punishment achieves genuine poignancy and grandeur when his conscience is violently stirred by the prophet's rebuke. Guiltily he bows his head and agrees with Nathan: "I have sinned against the Lord."

Thereafter, Bathsheba's son died. But in due time she bore him another son, named Solomon, and "the Lord loved him."

Absalom

Perhaps the greatest humiliation King David suffered, the epitome of his personal tragedy, was the rivalry and treacherous conduct of his favorite son, Absalom.

When David was an old man, his guilt and soul-searching because of his sins left him humbled and gentle. He interpreted his conflict with Absalom as a just punishment from the Lord for his sins and his many crimes against his fellowmen.

Vanity seemed to be the driving force behind Absalom's wayward conduct. He longed to sit on his father's throne! He could hardly wait for his father to die. "Oh, that I were made judge in the land!" he declared openly, and what he said was reported to his aged father, who was filled with grief.

Secretly, Absalom laid the groundwork for a revolt. He was not only handsome and clever but a man of extraordinary charm. For reasons both unspecified and hard to understand, he found ready allies among the elders in each of the tribes. The plotters were merely biding their time. When Absalom thought the right moment had come, he told his father that he was leaving on a pilgrimage to Hebron. From Hebron he sent his spies to all the tribes of Israel with the signal for revolt: "As soon as ye hear the sound of the horn, then ye shall say: 'Absalom is king of Hebron.'"

The conspiracy had been planned in a thoroughgoing fashion and was not only strong in numbers but well organized. Armed forces poured into Hebron from every tribe so that Absalom soon found himself commanding a formidable army. When messengers brought the alarming report to David: "The hearts of the men of Israel are after Absalom," he felt betrayed and abandoned. There was no time to lose. Hebron was not far from Jerusalem and the rebels were already approaching Mount Zion. "Arise and let us flee," said David, "or else none of us shall escape from Absalom!"

It was a tearful exodus from Jerusalem. Only a small part of the army had remained loyal to David, but a large number of the city's inhabitants, out of genuine devotion, chose to follow him no matter where he went. A gloom pervaded all: "and all the country wept with a loud voice . . . and as the King passed over the brook Kidron, all the people passed over, toward the way of the wilderness."

David and his band succeeded in escaping over the Jordan, with Absalom in pursuit. But because Absalom was slow to follow up his advantage, David used the precious time to rally around him loyal fighting elements in the country. Now the

roles of father and son were reversed: the pursued became the pursuer. David turned back to meet the rebels. They met at Mahanaim and there the decisive battle was fought.

But before the battle, David called the captains of his army together and instructed them: "Deal gently with Absalom." The rebels were defeated "and there was a great slaughter there." Twenty thousand Israelites lay dead on the field.

But matters turned out somewhat differently from the way David had planned: first to put down the uprising and then to forgive his wayward son. As Absalom galloped across the battlefield he happened to ride under a large terebinth tree. His long hair caught in its branches and he was left hanging in mid-air when his horse ran from under him. David's chief captain, Joab, who was immediately informed of this strange accident, hastened to the spot. No doubt out of loyalty to David, with his own hand he sent three darts through Absalom's heart.

When David was told that Absalom was dead, he "covered his face and cried with a loud voice . . . O my son Absalom, my son, my son Absalom! Would I had died for thee, O Absalom, my son, my son!"

And this grief never left David, and helped bring him to his grave.

Absalom's Tomb. The traditional tomb of Absalom in Jerusalem, whether it is authentic or not, has been looked upon by the pious through the centuries as the sepulchre that David erected for his wayward son's remains. It has been an ancient custom for passersby to fling stones at it in execration of a son who had violated the commandment: "Honor thy father and thy mother."

KING SOLOMON
(about 972-933 B.C.E.)

In the inevitable course of events "David slept with his fathers and was buried in the city of David [Jerusalem] . . . and Solomon sat upon the throne of David his father; and his kingdom was established firmly."

Before he died David had charged Solomon: "I go the way of all the earth; be thou strong therefore, and show thyself a man." David exhorted him to follow God's commandments according to the Law of Moses. Solomon promised faithfully to honor his father's counsel and David's eyes closed forever.

The Wise King: The Judgment of Solomon. (From a Hebrew manuscript of the *Song of Songs,* France, c. 1750.)
Jewish Theological Seminary

Solomon's Wisdom

According to tradition, Solomon started out his reign in humility. In a dream he heard himself say to the Lord: "I am but a little child; I know not how to go out or come in . . . give Thy servant therefore an understanding heart to judge Thy people, that I may discern between good and evil." The Lord replied that since Solomon had shown himself so unselfish, had not clamored, like other grasping men, for long life and riches but only for understanding, so that he might rule in wisdom and justice among the people: Therefore, saith the Lord: "I have given thee a wise and an understanding heart; so that there have been none like thee before thee." Furthermore, since Solomon had not asked anything for his own gain or glory, therefore Heaven's bounty would be showered on him, and honor and good fortune the like of which had never been seen before.

For whatever reasons this tradition of Solomon's great good fortune arose, his reign marked the era of Israel's greatest power and material development. He must have possessed much practical sense and skill both as organizer and administrator. Equally wise was the restraint and tact he showed in dealing with foreign powers. Unlike the headstrong and passionate David, he knew that a nation can prosper only in peace, in unbroken productivity. His rule consequently was unmarred by excessive blood-letting on the battlefield against other nations or in crippling civil strife.

Whereas David had been limited in his outlook by his tribal mentality, Solomon, probably because of the greater opportunities he had found for intellectual development, showed a more worldly, even a cosmopolitan attitude which resulted in a marked cultural advance of the people. He was a broad-minded leader who drew from all the cultures and skills of the world for the aggrandizement of his own power and reputation. But this also worked for the benefit of all the people. They ceased to be a conglomeration of tribes and became a full-grown nation of considerable importance in the world of those days.

It must by no means be assumed that all that Solomon did as king of Israel was meant to serve the best interests of the people. The Biblical chronicler analyzes his motives and his drives, and these do not appear to have been always either selfless or virtuous.

The Queen of Sheba visits Solomon to test his wisdom and to see his magnificence.   *Metropolitan Museum*

Solomon's Glory

For all his reputed wisdom, Solomon is revealed as an inordinately vain monarch who hungered after glory and the world's applause. He indulged himself in every imaginable luxury to enhance his self-esteem and perhaps to reassure himself of his great power. Therein probably lay the canker of his corruption. It was ultimately to spell the doom of so much of his work and to make of him an ironic byword to generations of plain folk who lived after him: "Solomon was the wisest man on earth, yet see how foolishly he lived!" It is noteworthy that, with only one striking exception, the sages of the *Talmud* dwell almost exclusively on his weakness, vices and misrule when they comment upon his life and reign. They use him as an object lesson in the futility of cleverness, power and glory.

Solomon's compulsion to be the equal of all the great rulers of his age led him into great extravagances for display. He poured the nation's wealth freely into private as well as public projects. With skill and foresight, which probably helped make his reign the most peaceful in Israel's troubled history, he established a large standing army, trained and equipped along the most advanced lines of the military science of the age. He had many thousands of horses for his iron chariots and mounts for a force of twelve thousand horsemen. He erected a large number of fortresses in strategic parts of the country, and girded the walls of Jerusalem with nearly impregnable walls.

Perhaps the greatest single act of his brilliant reign was his organization of the civil arm of the government. Even under his father's able guidance the operation of the government had been primitive and inefficient. These shortcomings Solomon, copying the methods of the most advanced nations, quickly remedied.

He divided the land into twelve districts. Over each of these he appointed a governor, who was strictly responsible to a governor-general, who in turn had to answer to the king himself. It was a centralized and efficiently controlled mechanism. The principal function of his governors was to collect taxes and the king's share of the produce of the land.

With tough-minded realism Solomon recognized that the continued existence of the tribes *as* tribes did not work to the best interests of Israel. The tribal system would only keep the people divided as they had been all along. He was determined to weld them into a nation. In establishing the boundaries of his regional districts he purposely ignored the tribal concentrations and thus broke them up. From that time on tribal consciousness and differences began to disappear.

Under Solomon, most of the Canaanites and other non-Israelite tribes were absorbed into the Jewish population by intermarriage. This, too, was of far-reaching importance. It eliminated much of the temptation to worship idols in the very heart of Israel.

Solomon's Temple

Another great unifier of the people, but with greater significance for the Israelites of later times, was the Temple which Solomon built. However, "the wise king" had a far different aim in mind in constructing it than strengthening the worship of the One God among the people. Solomon's vanity and love of grandeur led him into this vast construction program which was evidently intended to rival the Egyptian pharaohs, King Hiram of Tyre and the Assyrian rulers. Besides a grandiose palace and a harem for himself, an armory, an assembly hall and halls of judgment, he planned a sanctuary, a kind of royal chapel, to match the other monarchs in magnificence.

The difficulties were many and not easily surmountable.

52

Underground quarries of King Solomon. These furnished the stone for the Temple.

The land of Israel possessed neither the building materials nor the financial resources for putting up anything as opulent as Solomon's dream-palaces and Temple. Israel was an agricultural country not distinguished for the production of luxury goods or for its fine arts and crafts. Both materials and skills had to be imported from other lands that possessed more advanced cultures. Furthermore, there were few skilled craftsmen among the Israelites. The material conditions of the country had not encouraged in the past either their need or their training. But King Solomon found a way to solve these problems: he entered into a barter contract with King Hiram of Tyre whereby the latter agreed to supply him with all he lacked.

Solomon asked Hiram for a sufficient supply of cedars of Lebanon and cypress trees, also skilled lumbermen, carpenters, fine workers in metal, stone-cutters, masons and jewelers. The King of Tyre agreed to provide all this if Solomon sent him every year a specified amount of wheat and pure oil as payment. In addition, Solomon was to cede to him, upon completion of all the construction work, twenty towns in Galilee which lay adjacent to Tyre.

This should be remembered: it was not voluntary but forced labor which Solomon used to build his palaces and the Temple. Thirty thousand Israelite workers were assigned to assist King Hiram's Phoenician lumbermen in cutting down cedar and cypress trees in Lebanon. The trees were then loaded on barges and shipped by sea from Tyre to Joppa (Jaffa). From there they were transported overland through the Valley of Sharon and up the Hills of Judea to Jerusalem.

The account of how King Solomon forced the non-Israelites in the land who persisted in maintaining their separate identity into a condition of virtual servitude is somewhat reminiscent of the bondage in Egypt. These people worked without pay in the construction of the Temple and other buildings. Seventy thousand of them were laborers and carriers of burdens; an additional eighty thousand were sent into the mountains to quarry stones and prepare them for use. Over this army of workers were thirty-three hundred supervisors, that is, taskmasters.

Solomon started to build the Temple four hundred and eighty years after the Exodus from Egypt, in the fourth year of his reign. It took seven years to complete; the other buildings took thirteen. Joint was made to fit into joint so that "there was neither hammer nor axe nor any tool of iron heard in the house while it was in building."

King Solomon's enterprise extended into other directions as well. Observing that Phoenician Tyre's prosperity was due largely to its maritime and trading activities, he decided to imitate it. He went into a business partnership with King Hiram, but afterwards struck out for himself. He built a fleet of ships, "ships of Tarshish," and harbored them in the Red Sea ports of Ezion-geber and Elath. The captains and the most skilled sailors who manned these ships were Phoenicians borrowed from King Hiram, but they trained many Israelites. Solomon's ships called at every large port from Spain to India with cargoes of grain and stone, gold and silver, ivory, ebony, spices and costly woods. This active barter enriched Solomon's royal treasury greatly. It helped him carry on his vast construction work.

The memory of King Solomon's splendor—a glittering world of gold and silver, emeralds and rubies, onyx and marble, of strutting peacocks and chattering apes in his palace halls—took on a dreamlike fascination for the Jewish people through the ages. But the Biblical chroniclers saw things more soberly. They commented objectively on the king's levies of forced labor, on the fact that his grand style of living taxed the people so oppressively that they were chronically rebellious. Only Solomon's powerful army prevented outright insurrection.

In vain did Abijah, the prophet of Shiloh, warn the king against the oppression of the people by his tax collectors. But Solomon, basking in his glory and immersed in the vices of his brilliant court, turned a deaf ear.

The fierce devotion with which David the king and psalmist gave to his God all his life was hardly duplicated by his pleasure-loving son. Whether for expediency or political effect or whether from personal inclination or cynicism, especially as he advanced in years, Solomon was not at all loyal to the faith of his father.

Somberly the chronicler records the king's apostasy: "Now King Solomon loved many foreign women, besides the daughter of Pharaoh, women of the Moabites, Ammonites, Edomites, Sidonians and Hittites." These were women concerning whom the law of Moses had sternly made warning: "Ye shall not go among them, neither shall they come among you; for surely they will turn away your heart after their gods."

And this is precisely what happened to Solomon. "His wives turned away his heart . . . after other gods." Grief-stricken, the narrator notes: Solomon's heart was not to the Lord "as was the heart of David, his father." He worshipped Ashtoreth, the Ishtar goddess of the Sidonians. He also sacrificed before the Ammonite god, Milcom. He even built "high places" for the Moabite god Chemosh and for Moloch, the child-devouring God of Ammon.

To punish him for all his evil-doing, notes the Book of Kings, the Lord vowed to break his power and to rend his kingdom. As his instrument of retribution the Lord chose Jeroboam, one of the taskmasters Solomon had put over the forced laborers. Jeroboam began to organize a rebellion. When Solomon heard of it he tried to have him killed, but Jeroboam fled to Egypt where he lived under King Shishak's protection until Solomon's death made possible his return.

THE TEMPLE IN JERUSALEM

The further removed in point of time the Temple became, the more glamorous grew its memory. This is easy to explain. The drabness and poverty of Jewish life everywhere in the world, the hazards and misfortunes Jews always had to face, made them look back nostalgically to the time of the Golden Age of the Jewish people when the Temple in Jerusalem still stood. In a larger sense, the undimming memory of the Temple was merely the ache and longing of a disinherited and humiliated people reaching back to the glory of its past for solace.

Objectively speaking, merely as a structure, the Temple was neither as large nor as imposing as, for instance, some of the sanctuaries of the Egyptians, the Assyrians or the Athenians. If we accept the estimate that the Biblical cubit was the equivalent of 21.85 inches, the Temple in Jerusalem must have been a relatively small building. Its dimensions, as noted in the Bible, were in round figures—120 feet long, 40 feet wide and 60 feet high. Since it took seven years for virtually an army of artisans, craftsmen and laborers to build it, one cannot help but assume that its distinction did not lie so much in its elaborateness and magnificence as in its exquisite architectural design and workmanship.

The Temple structure was three stories high, surrounded by a colonnaded porch and by an inner and an outer court. It was built of hewn stone, but its interior walls and ceilings were paneled with cedar overlaid with gold. The floors and the folding doors were of fir; the door posts of olive wood. The whole interior was ornamented with carved figures of cherubim, palm trees, flowers and buds, all of which were overlaid with gold.

The Holy of Holies

The sanctity of every part of the Temple and of its terraces, stairways, gates and courts was well established. Yet there was one spot which was deemed unutterably sacred and inviolable—the Holy of Holies where the Ark holding the Tables of Moses rested. The High Priest alone was allowed, by priestly law, to enter this inner sanctuary, and then only on *Yom Kippur,* the Day of Atonement. Anyone else daring to penetrate its precincts merited death. Death was the pen-

Probably the earliest graphic representation of the façade of the Holy of Holies—believed to have been made before the destruction of the Temple in 70 c.e.—was painted on gold-glass, and was found in the Roman catacombs. The inscription is in Greek.

alty for a non-Jew found in *any* part of the Temple area.

The Holy of Holies was built on a raised platform and was separated from the rest of the sanctuary known as "The Holy Place" by an enormous curtain and by a chain of gold. It was, therefore, more like a sanctuary within a sanctuary, and was built in the form of a perfect cube, each of its dimensions being exactly 20 cubits or about 40 feet. Its ornamentation and the materials employed were identical with the rest of the building. Perhaps its most striking decorative objects were two great carved figures of cherubim modeled after the winged sculpture of the Babylonians. They probably had a human face, the body of an animal, and two spreading wings that, in a later period, became associated pictorially with the artists' conceptions of angels. The two cherubim were carved out of cedarwood and were overlaid with gold. Their wings met in the center of the Holy of Holies in a protecting arch like the hands of the High Priest raised in benediction. From tip to tip they measured about twenty feet. It was underneath these wings, in the Ark of the Covenant where the stone Tablets of Moses were enshrined, that the *Shechinah,* the Divine Radiance of the Lord, was presumed by tradition to dwell.

A seventeenth-century reconstruction of the Temple. (From the Amsterdam *Haggadah,* 1695.)

The leading artist-sculptor of these cherubim, who also designed and wrought the altars, the holy vessels and ritual objects for the Temple, was a half-Jew from Tyre by the name of Hiram.

At the entrance to the Temple interior stood two pillars of bronze that the ingenious Hiram had wrought. These were called Jachin and Boaz. They were about thirty feet high and were crowned by capitals ten feet high. These capitals were embellished with a design of carved lilies. Some archaeologists conjecture that they were hollowed inside, their basins serving as giant braziers where the burnt-offerings were consumed. A large altar of brass was placed nearby. On it were brought the animal sacrifices.

Hiram was also responsible for the huge laver called "the molten sea," for the ten small movable lavers on wheels, the shovels, the basins and the *menorahs*, the seven-branched candlesticks. Besides the *menorah* that Bezalel had made for the Tabernacle centuries before, Hiram had designed ten others for the Temple. Five of them flanked each side of the sanctuary. For the care of these *menorahs* there were tongs and basins, firepans and snuffers, all made of gold. The elaborate Temple service required a great variety of other ritual objects and vessels. There was, for instance, an altar of gold reserved exclusively for offerings of incense, and a golden table ten handbreadths long and five wide. On the golden table were laid the twelve loaves of showbread baked of fine flour. They lay exposed on the table "in the presence" of the Lord for a whole week after which they were eaten ritually by the priests as holy bread.

The "molten sea" was an enormous laver designed for the frequent ablutions of the priests who were required to wash their hands and feet before they entered into the sanctuary. It had a diameter of some twenty feet, its huge basin resting on the backs of twelve oxen cast out of iron. Its rim was circled by a bas-relief of lily buds and open flowers. The ten lavers on wheels were made of bronze and were ornamented with figures in relief of cherubim, lions and palm trees.

Destruction and Reconstruction

The Temple of Solomon, consecrated during the Feast of Tabernacles about 955 B.C.E., was destroyed by Nebuchadnezzar, King of Babylonia, when he captured Jerusalem in 586 B.C.E. He laid the sanctuary in ruins, ransacked the Temple of all its treasures and carried off the flower of the people into captivity. But when the Jewish prince Sheshbazzar returned from Babylonia in 538 B.C.E., leading the first contingent of Israelite exiles, he was given all the sacred Temple vessels and appurtenances by King Cyrus, so that after the sanctuary was rebuilt they could be restored.

The sacred rock of Mount Moriah where, according to tradition, the Temple altar stood. The Mosque of Omar was built over it more than a thousand years ago.

Levite or priest filling *menorah* lamps of Temple with oil. (Illumination from Hebrew Bible c. 1288.)
British Museum

The rebuilding of the Temple began during the reign of the Persian King Darius in 519 B.C.E., and the work was completed in three years. But this time the Holy Ark no longer rested in the inner sanctuary. The *urim* and *thummin*,

A modern Russian synagogue laver, samovar-style, with priest's hands raised in traditional benediction. This is a survival and a modern adaptation of the Temple laver.

those oracular stones worn in the breastplate by the High Priest in former days, also were no longer a part of his sacerdotal dress. They had mysteriously disappeared after the sack of the Temple and there is no hint in the Bible of what had happened to them. The only reference to their loss is found in the *Talmud*, which was written hundreds of years later.

For a second time the Temple was rebuilt. In 20-19 B.C.E. King Herod renovated and rebuilt the centuries-old Temple in order to ingratiate himself with the Jewish population, which was constantly seething with rebellion against his oppressive rule and the overlordship of Judea by Rome. Whatever changes Herod made in the design of the Temple were not fundamental. He followed the general ground-plan and

Probable site of the Temple court and the adjacent temple area.

Left. Substructure of Temple area built by Herod. *Right.* Jewish captives, probably Levites, playing the *kinnor,* with an armed Babylonian guard behind them.

interior arrangement of the Temple of Solomon, but he did make the structure higher and he gave it a Graeco-Roman façade, to conform with the prevailing taste of the times.

In passing, one might mention that of Solomon's Temple nothing is left except the site itself. There are, however, still standing a few remains of Herod's reconstructed sanctuary. The most widely known of these is the outer western wall, popularly known as "The Wailing Wall." It is built of enormous blocks of hewn stone. There is also a massive piece of masonry which was wrongly identified in the past as "Solomon's Stables." Actually it served as the arched support for the pavement above it on the south side of the Temple.

Rites and Ceremonies

Today, only the rites and ceremonies that were observed during the Second Temple, and especially those that were performed in the days of Herod, are remembered. The Rabbinic sages wrote vivid accounts of them in the *Mishna* and in the *Talmud.* Because tradition was always paramount in Jewish religious life, we can therefore assume with some reason that the ceremonial observed in Solomon's Temple was fundamentally the same as that described by the ancient rabbis of later times.

There were two religious orders that served in the Temple: the priests and the Levites. The priests had to be descendants of the House of Aaron. They put the sacrificial sheep and oxen, the first fruits of the soil and the incense on the altars. In addition, they were the teachers of the people. Until the rise of the Rabbinic institution, the House of Study, in a later period, they publicly read passages from the *Torah* and expounded their meanings for the greater understanding of the people who sat or stood about listening That, probably, was the extent of religious education in those days.

The Levites, on the other hand, were the "servants" of the Temple. They did all the required menial and custodial work, took charge of the priestly vestments, guarded the holy vessels and the Temple treasure and policed the sanctuary area. However lowly these tasks may have been, the Levites assumed great dignity when they took part in the Temple rites for which they furnished the sacred music. Their singing and their playing, as the priests sacrificed and intoned invocations, became a golden memory to Jews of later and more desolate days. Especially elaborate was the musical service during the three annual pilgrimage-festivals to Jerusalem: on *Pesach, Shavuoth, and Succoth.*

Not all the Levites were musicians. The calling was hereditary, confined to certain families who cultivated the art.

Music in the Temple

Probably nothing in all the world's religious literature can rank with Hebrew psalmody, which was such an important element in the Temple ritual. About half of the one hundred and fifty poems in the Book of Psalms, which were written to be sung to well-known *modes* or melodies and often to be accompanied by specific musical instruments, are attributed to David, the king, harpist and poet. The remainder of the Psalms are ascribed to other musician-poets connected with the musical life of the Temple. They occupy a unique eminence in the world's great poetry. Their great variety of lyrical and dramatic utterance, their evocation of moods of exaltation, grief, hope or regret, their passionate expressiveness in extolling justice and in hungering after righteousness have all become a part of the cultural heritage of the world.

As among all Eastern peoples, vocalists among the Levites were required to be skillful instrumentalists as well. They often accompanied their own singing on instruments, principally on the harp, psaltery, lyre, reed-pipes and brass cymbals.

It is quite certain that the *magrepha,* or organ, was played during the musical service. The description the *Talmud* gives of it indicates that it was built on the principles of an organ. It was supplied with a bellows and perforated pipes. A much earlier Biblical source, the Book of Samuel, notes that this instrument had ten pipes and that each pipe was punctured with ten holes, which made it capable of producing one hundred different tones.

The question is often asked: why did the organ disappear from the synagogue service since it was played in the Temple? The answer is a simple one: the early Christians, being Jews in the main, adapted much of the synagogue ritual, including the organ, into the church service. In order to emphasize sharply the difference between Jews and Christians, the rabbis of old suspended the use of the organ. It was not until the beginning of the nineteenth century that the organ was reintroduced into the religious service, but only by Jewish Reform congregations.

The principal solo instruments, which were also used by the Levite singers to accompany themselves, were the *kinnor,* the *nebel* and the *halil.* The *kinnor* was a harp or lyre played with a plectrum or pick. It varied in the number of strings: some had three, and others had five, seven or even ten strings. The *nebel,* too, was a stringed instrument with a range of only twelve notes and was plucked with the fingers. The *halil,* often referred to as a flute, was a form of reed-pipe. It was played only on the great festival days.

ROSH HASHANAH AND YOM KIPPUR

Yom Kippur, the Day of Atonement, called for impressive Temple rites. It is a fast-day observed on the tenth day of the seventh month of *Tishri*, which usually coincides with September. It is the last and climactic day in the "Season of Repentance," that consists of ten penitential days, of which the first is *Rosh Hashanah* (New Year).

"The Season of Repentance," by means of introspection, was designed to soften the erring heart of man with contrition for his misdeeds, thus leading him to wholehearted repentance by the time *Yom Kippur* arrived. During this ten-day period, also known as the *Yamim Noraim*, "Days of Awe," the Orthodox rise from sleep in the dark hours of the morning to go to the synagogue for the recitation of *selihot*, supplications for forgiveness. The Jewish doctrine of repentance is predicated on the belief in the perfectibility of the individual, to whom free will and understanding are given to correct himself. The doctrine was elevated into a fundamental ethical principle by the Rabbinic sages: "Greater is the merit of the transgressor who repents than that of the saint who has never sinned." That is why the Jewish Confession of Sins (*Viddui*) was prescribed as much for the High Priest as he entered on the Day of Atonement into the Holy of Holies within the Temple sanctuary as for the common murderer before his execution on the gallows. The reason for this relentless self-examination and purgation was given by the ancient teachers of Israel: "God gave man his soul that he might keep it pure, and in that unsullied condition must man return it to Him, for the soul belongs to God."

New Year's Day

Many are baffled as to why *Rosh Hashanah* is called the Jewish New Year although it takes place in the seventh and not the first month of the Jewish year. Furthermore, confusion deepens because Orthodox Jews in the United States celebrate it for two days instead of one.

Rosh Hashanah, the Jewish New Year, is the first of the Ten Days of Penitence. Jewish tradition holds that God created the world on that day, and although there is no mention in the Bible that it was to serve as New Year's Day, it did specify: "In the seventh month [i. e., *Tishri*], in the first day of the month shall ye have a sabbath, a memorial of blowing of trumpets, an holy convocation." *Rosh Hashanah* is considered the annual Judgment Day, on which all mankind, like sheep before their shepherd, pass in searching review before the all-seeing Eye of God. The Babylonians, who so deeply influenced Jewish beliefs and customs, also considered the first day of the year as their gods' day of judgment upon the destinies of individuals and peoples. The Jews adopted from the Babylonians the custom of observing *Rosh Hashanah* on the first day of the seventh month of *Tishri*, although the real beginning of the Jewish year, counting from the day of the Exodus, was designated by Moses as the first day of *Nisan* (March-April). Actually a number of other peoples belonging to the Semitic language-culture family began their new year at the close of the old harvest year; it was the agricultural-economic demarcation point on their calendar.

In Biblical times in the land of Israel, *Rosh Hashanah* was observed for one day only, but when the Romans had put an end to the Jewish state and its inhabitants were strewn to the winds, the great Talmudic sage, Yohanan ben Zakkai, added a second day. This was done because of the wide time-differential in various parts of the world, and in order to ensure that all Jews would be able to observe together at least one day of *Rosh Hashanah*. Today not only Reform Jews everywhere, but also the Jews in Israel, have returned to the Biblical custom of celebrating only the first day.

Services in the synagogue are marked by a deep solemnity. After an elaborate liturgy, the *shofar*, the ram's horn, is sounded. Its clarion call is, as it were, a summons to the worshippers to look within, to search their consciences, and then to come to sincere repentance. But festal joy follows this introspection; all exchange the encouraging greeting: *Leshanah tobah tikkathebu*, "May you be written down [in the book of life] for a good year!" The belief is that on Yom Kippur, nine days hence, the celestial book of accounts will be closed and judgment reached.

The *shofar's* call to repentance.

Day of Atonement

The Day of Atonement had been instituted originally by Moses during the wandering in the wilderness. It was a fast day to be marked by prayer and contrition as an everlasting reminder to the people that they had worshipped the golden calf. After the Temple of Solomon was dedicated, atonement for the whole people was symbolically made by the High Priest on *Yom Kippur*. Amidst solemn prayer and song he lighted a censer and, immersed in a cloud of burning incense, went into the Holy of Holies. He entered it alone, and alone in the utter darkness he intoned a prayer. He implored that the year be free from care for all Israel, that the Lord protect everyone from misfortune and illness. He prayed that a blessing descend upon the fields and bring sufficient rain, that the dew fall and the sun shine, so that the crops would be plentiful and there would be joy in the land.

As the culmination in this imposing Temple service, the High Priest sacrificed a bullock as a sin-offering for himself, for his household and for the entire priesthood. Then he brought forward two goats that were presented as sin-offerings by the people. One goat, reserved by lot "for the Lord," was sacrificed on the altar, and then the High Priest sprinkled its blood and the blood of the bullock eight times before "the mercy seat" in the Holy of Holies and between the staves of the Ark of the Covenant, in order "to make atonement for the holy place, because of the uncleanliness of the children of Israel, and because of their transgressions. . . ." Then the High Priest solemnly confessed the people's sins before them and placed them in substitution upon the head of the remaining live goat, the so-called "scapegoat" destined for Azazel, the evil demon who infested the wilderness. The animal was then led ceremoniously up a high cliff and flung down the precipice to its death. The instant this was done the great multitudes who thronged the Temple area and all the surrounding hills of Jerusalem received a signal: the waving from the Temple gate of a strip of snow-white wool suggesting purity. When the people saw it, they shouted for joy. They took it as a sign that their sins had been forgiven. It was a signal, too, for the young people to break into song and dance.

Spiritual Repentance

But with the passing of the centuries the earlier tribal form of expiatory atonement, namely, the shedding of the blood of an animal instead of the blood of the sinner who morally deserved death for his misdeeds, underwent a profound change. The conception of atonement had become spiritualized, replete with ethical and social overtones. Prayer, repentance of the heart, fasting, suffering, consecrated *Torah* study and acts of benevolence toward the needy and the unfortunate were regarded as the most potent purifiers and regenerators of the spirit. Furthermore there was no longer any compelling need on the part of the individual for priest or rabbi, prophet or savior, to mediate between himself and the Deity. He had at last established a direct and intimate communion between himself and God his Father.

This new religious outlook is epigrammatically described in the following parable in the *Talmud:* "Human Wisdom was asked: 'What shall be done with the sinners?' It replied: 'Evil pursueth sinners.' [*Proverbs,* 13:21.] Prophecy was asked: 'What shall be done to the sinner?' It replied: 'The soul that sinneth, it shall die.' [*Ezekiel,* 18:4.] The Law was asked: 'What shall be done to the sinner?' It replied: 'Let him bring a guilt-offering and the priest shall atone for him.' [*Leviticus,* 1:4.] Then God was asked: 'What shall be done to the sinner?' The Almighty, blessed be He, replied: 'Let him repent and he will be forgiven.'"

Yom Kippur is considered the holiest day of the Jewish year, reverently called the "Sabbath of Sabbaths." With *Rosh Hashanah* it constitutes the "High Holy Days." Many Jews who do not attend the synagogue the rest of the year join their co-religionists in solemn prayer during these holy days. *Yom Kippur* lasts from sundown to sundown in accordance with the Jewish custom for all festivals and fasts. A ceremony, probably dating back to Gaonic times in Babylonia before the Middle Ages, that of *kapparah*, the sacrifice of atonement, is still practiced by many of the Orthodox. Holding a rooster or hen by its legs, the pious Jew circles the fowl over his head three times as he recites the prayer which designates the blood of the animal soon to be shed by the *shochet,* the slaughterer, as vicarious atonement for his own sins. Nowadays money may be substituted for a hen, and then given to charity.

Still another ritualistic survival from ancient times among Orthodox Jews is the ceremony of *malkut,* or scourging. It takes place informally in the synagogue on the afternoon preceding *Yom Kippur.* The penitents, as they abjectly confess their sins, inflict one on the other thirty-nine expiatory lashes with a strap. Another traditional custom on the day before *Yom Kippur* is for penitents to call on those they may have injured in any way and humbly implore their forgiveness. There are also performed acts of charity and kindness in fulfillment of *Proverbs* 10:2: "*Zedakah* [charity] delivers from death." Visits are paid by the pious to the graves of ancestors, to honor their memory, to offer prayers, and to implore divine pardon for themselves on account of the merits of the sainted departed.

Supplication on the Day of Atonement in a Warsaw synagogue, 19th century.
Painting by Jacob Weinles

On the eve of *Yom Kippur,* the prayer service in the synagogue which is then somberly lighted by candles begins with the singing by the cantor of the celebrated *Kol Nidre* supplication, while the congregation sings after him. In Orthodox congregations the adult male worshippers wear the *kittel,* the traditional white shroud of the pious. This is in order that their thoughts might turn upon man's ultimate dissolution, and thus to lead them to reflect contritely that "there is not a righteous man upon earth that doeth good that sinneth not." Consequently, while there is still time, they must repent of all their misdeeds. Many of the older men stay up all night reciting psalms and intoning prayers. The following day, as well, is dedicated to an elaborate liturgy set in the minor key of grief and regret. The *Sefer Torah* is read from twice during the day. *Yizkor,* the memorial prayer for the souls of all the departed, is recited. Then, during *Neilah,* the concluding service, the worshippers make their final peace with their God and their conscience. Their fate for the year is resolved. As dusk falls in the dimly lit synagogue, the *shofar* sounds a solitary note of comfort and resolution.

DECLINE AND FALL

THE DIVISION OF THE KINGDOM

The instant King Solomon died, the death knell of Israel's power sounded. Forces, both internal and external, were working for its destruction. From without, the King of Egypt, Shishak (Sheshonk) skillfully laid his traps to crush Israel, which stood as an obstacle between him and Syria and Mesopotamia. He, therefore, had offered sanctuary to the rebel Jeroboam whom Solomon had defeated. He lost no time in sending him back to Israel when Solomon died. Shishak supplied him with the means of starting a new revolt against Solomon's successor, Rehoboam, but this time with better chances of success.

From a strategic, political point of view, the position of Israel as a world power was untenable. The extraordinary achievements of David and Solomon in building up the country were bound to be wrecked sooner or later by forces that were beyond their control. To the north lay the formidable new kingdom of Aram with its center in Damascus. During King Solomon's reign the seed for the future harassment of Israel was already being sown there. Even more threatening was the emerging power of Assyria in the Tigris-Euphrates valley. What with Egypt lowering from the south, and the two northern nations insatiably hungry for more territory and power, the land of Israel was caught helplessly between the two great millstones which ground it to pieces in the course of little more than two centuries.

As if these enemies were not threat enough, internal strife and jealousy among the tribes made the doom of Israel as an important kingdom almost inevitable. This national weakness had been even more apparent during Solomon's harsh rule. His levies in forced labor, in taxes and in soldiers for his large standing army had caused misery and discontent among the people. It had provoked Jeroboam's first revolt. Now that Rehoboam, Solomon's son and heir, was oppressing the people even more cruelly than his father had done, Jeroboam's second revolt was certain to succeed.

Jeroboam

Jeroboam separated the ten northern tribes from the tribes of Benjamin and Judah and established them as a separate kingdom—that of Israel—with its capital in Shechem. Rehoboam remained in Jerusalem as ruler of the two tribes loyal to him and to the House of David.

Jeroboam, who had come to power as the champion of the people, misruled the land with no less savagery than Rehoboam. Since he resolved to destroy the house of David in order that he might be master of Judah as well as of Israel, he invited his patron, Pharaoh Shishak, to help him, a call which the King of Egypt heeded eagerly.

In a hieroglyphic inscription in the Temple of Karnak, Pharaoh Shishak records his triumphs against Judah. He reduced many fortified towns to heaps of stones and drove his chariots as far north as the valley of Jezreel. He made sure that he left nothing of value behind, deported a great many Israelites into Egypt, and stripped the Temple and Solomon's palaces of their gold and treasure. Moreover, both the northern and southern kingdoms were obliged to pay him a heavy annual tribute.

From that time on Judah suffered an even worse indignity: it became virtually a vassal of the northern kingdom of Israel and it was fated never again to regain its independence.

Despite the division of the kingdom, the people of Israel continued a united religious and cultural existence with the Temple in Jerusalem as the magnetic center. To put an end to this anomalous situation, King Jeroboam of Israel reopened the old disused sanctuaries of Dan and Bethel in the north and forbade the people of Israel to worship in the Temple in Jerusalem. To make the religious divorce more complete he created a new priesthood.

There was in fact another motive for Israel's "secession," so to speak, from the Temple. In ancient times religion was not merely a matter of private belief or worship. It was an indispensable affair of state which had great economic value. The Temple in Jerusalem, for instance, with its numerous sacrifices, offerings and tithes, was the principal source of revenue for Judah. The vast number of pilgrims who flocked to it, especially during the three great festivals of the year, brought prosperity as well as political importance to Jerusalem. Jeroboam, no doubt, had this in mind when he re-established the sanctuaries in Dan and Bethel. Unfortunately for him, Jerusalem and its Temple already commanded the unwavering loyalty of the people.

Civil War

The subsequent history of the two Israelite kingdoms was marked by incessant warfare against Damascus and by internal strife between the competing contenders for the two thrones. Assassination was a convenient political weapon of kings as well as of their usurpers. The greatest sufferers, naturally, were the people of the two kingdoms.

In time, religious and social life in the northern kingdom deteriorated. The kings of Israel were more concerned with maintaining or extending their power than fostering the Law of Moses among the people. For instance, King Omri (887-76 B.C.E.) who established his dynasty in the strong new fortress city of Samaria in the mountains, never quite resigned himself to be a vassal of the King of Damascus. Like so many of his successors, he was continually hatching plots for revolt.

Left. Jewish captives from Judah before Pharaoh Shishak, c. 930 C.E. (From relief, Temple of Amon, Karnak.) *Right.* Captive from Judah, some scholars think Rehoboam. (From the Karnak sculptures commemorating King Shishak's successes.)

Above. Earthenware figurine of Astarte. Judah (1000-586 B.C.E.)

Right. The Mesha Stele, c. 850 B.C.E., on which Mesha, King of Moab, recorded his triumphs over King Ahab of Israel. This is the oldest historical inscription in any Hebrew dialect.

The Louvre

"I am Mesha, son of Chemosh, king of Moab. . . . My father reigned over Moab for thirty years, and I reigned after my father. And I made this high-place for [the god] Chemosh . . . a high place of salvation, because he had saved me from all assailants, and because he had let me see my pleasure upon all them that hated me. Omri was King of Israel and he afflicted Moab for many days, for Chemosh was being angry with his land [2 Kings 17.18]. And his son [Ahab] succeeded him, and he also said, I will afflict Moab. In my days, said he thus, and I saw my pleasure on him and his house. And Israel perished with an everlasting destruction. . . . Now the men of God had dwelt in the land of Ataroth from of old; and the king of Israel built for himself Ataroth. And I warred against the city and seized it. And I slew all the people of the city, a gazing stock to Chemosh and to Moab. . . . And Chemosh said unto me, 'Go, seize Nebo against Israel.' And I went by night and warred against it from the break of dawn unto noon. And I seized it, and slew all of it, 7,000 men, and male sojourners and women and female sojourners and maidens. . . . And I took thence the vessels of Yahveh and I dragged them before Chemosh. . . ."

For this reason, he thought a military alliance with Tyre would prove valuable. To cement it he arranged a marriage between his son and heir, Ahab, and Jezebel, a daughter of the King of Tyre. These personal and political involvements left the country wide open to the penetrations of Phoenician culture and to *Baal* and *Astarte* worship. These influences, by the force of circumstance, kinship and geography, even

An ivory cherub with wings. (From Ahab's Palace, Samaria.)
Jewish Museum

filtered down into the southern kingdom of Judah. Pagan rites were once more performed in the Temple of Jerusalem.

Ahab

King Ahab (876-855 B.C.E.) was a man of weak character and even weaker principle. He completely succumbed to the wishes of his Phoenician wife. She was determined to introduce into Israel the idolatry of her own people and at the same time to destroy the Mosaic faith. In this aim she was almost successful. At her urging, King Ahab erected a temple for the Phoenician *baal*, Melkart. The Rechabites, firm believers in the Lord and upholders of the nomadic way of life, were outraged but helpless. Despite the persecution they suffered at the hands of the royal house and of the priests of the pagan cult, they clung stubbornly to their faith.

The prophets of the Lord were the special butts of Jezebel's hatred. They were forced to flee into the wilderness and to hide in caves. The most hunted of these prophets was Elijah of Tishbi, "the Thunderer of the Lord." Unmoved by

Elijah rebukes Ahab and Jezebel.

fear, he denounced Ahab and Jezebel to their faces for their crimes against the people. Ahab called him "a troubler of Israel."

"Not I, but thou and thy father's house are the troublers of Israel," retorted the prophet.

Elijah and the Angel in the Wilderness.
Dirk Bouts

60

Elijah, in a fiery chariot on his way to Heaven, bequeaths his prophetic role to his disciple Elisha.
William Blake, Metropolitan Museum

Jewish tribute bearers following King Jehu to his submission before Shalmeneser III. (From the Black Obelisk.)
British Museum

Seal of Shebanian, an official of Uzziah, 8th century B.C.E.

THE MENACE OF ASSYRIA

An ominous shadow over the Near and Middle East was already being cast by the rising Assyrian power. During Ahab's reign Ashurnazirpal (884-59 B.C.E.), the King of Assyria, started knifing systematically into the kingdom of Damascus with his superior military machine. First he captured Byblus, then Tyre and Sidon. It was only a matter of time, of reducing the intervening cities, until the Assyrians would be standing at the gates of Samaria. However, Damascus was far too formidable a power to be easily subdued. The struggle went on inconclusively for a long time, even after the next king of Assyria, Shalmaneser III (859-824 B.C.E.) had subjugated all the Aramean cities. As vassals of Damascus, the Israelites were obliged to join in the fight against the Assyrian invader. At the battle of Karkar in 855 B.C.E., for instance, Ahab's contingent consisted of ten thousand men and two thousand chariots.

Israel finally became a vassal of Assyria in 842 B.C.E. In that year its king, Jehu, journeyed to Nineveh to pay homage and to swear fealty to Shalmaneser III. But when the Assyrian king withdrew his troops from Syria because he needed them elsewhere, it was the signal for the Arameans to take savage revenge on the Israelites. They slaughtered uncounted numbers of them.

Once more Israel became a vassal to Damascus, yet it was

Inscription on an ossuary lid: "Here we brought the bones of Uzziah, king of Judah—do not open!"

King Jehu (842 - 816 B.C.E.) offers his submission to Shalmeneser III. (From the Black Obelisk.)
British Museum

never completely resigned to its humiliating position. It was constantly rising in rebellion under succeeding monarchs, but without avail. Finally, when Tiglath-pileser III (745-728 B.C.E.), the king who was to make Assyria the great world power of that age, succeeded in beating down the Arameans, Israel started paying tribute to him instead of to the king of Damascus.

The history of the two kingdoms henceforth was little more than a bewildering succession of royal plots and murders, of petty wars between Israel and Judah, of invasions by foreign armies and of hopeless rebellions. For only a brief period did the sun shine again for the two unhappy Israelite kingdoms. This took place when Uzziah (780-740 B.C.E.) ruled as king of Judah and Jeroboam II (785-745 B.C.E.) sat on the throne in Samaria. This brief respite from everlasting carnage was known as "The Silver Age." It was made possible because Damascus lay broken as a power and the kings of Assyria had more important military business elsewhere. There was much rebuilding and development of the country. It was the last material blossoming ancient Israel was fated to have.

THE PROPHETS

But this prosperity and peace were temporary. Forces outside and inside the country were at work to fling it again into turmoil. This was clearly foreseen by the major prophets who arose in the people's most desperate hour to warn it of impending tragedy. These prophets were not mere seers like most of their predecessors; they were profound students of the social, economic and political problems of the day. Under the tyrannical rule of the kings the prophets felt a prompting from within, which they declared came from the Lord, to step forward as the champions of the people and of God against social injustice, personal corruption and violation of the Law of Moses.

These prophets—Amos, Hosea, Isaiah, Micah, Jeremiah and Ezekiel—vividly recorded their thoughts and feelings on the burning problems of the day. Their writings became a fundamental part of the Bible and for the Jewish pious have almost as much religious authority as the Five Books of Moses. The prophets saw a profound connection between the crushing blows inflicted on Israel by its external enemies and the equally crushing blows dealt it by its own corrupt kings and aristocracy. Together, these hammer-blows spelled the doom of the Jewish state, the prophets believed.

Even during Solomon's reign there were already discernible those elements of social oppression which were a violation of the democratic society Moses had established. "The Age of Silver" which Jeroboam II's reign had ushered in emphasized this state of affairs even more sharply. This period marked the emergence of a sizable class of landowners who had swallowed up the holdings of a great number of small farmers. Grown affluent, this landed aristocracy indulged in every luxury in the ancient world. In glaring contrast there also appeared a vast new class of expropriated small farmers, town dwellers and artisans, impoverished by the king's ruthless tax collectors.

Amos

The first of the major prophets to indict the corruption of the time, to hold it up before the universal conscience, was the blunt-speaking shepherd, Amos. His prophetic call was touched neither by the taint of professionalism nor by self-interest. "I was no prophet, neither was I a prophet's son," he declared. Because of his love and devotion to the Lord as well as to the people, he was ready to endanger his life by denouncing the tyrannical king, the parasitic nobility, the unscrupulous merchants, the accommodating priests and the lying prophets.

Isaiah

A generation later, perhaps the profoundest, certainly the most eloquent of all the prophets, Isaiah, appeared in Jerusalem. He lived and preached during the reigns of King Ahaz (735-720 B.C.E) and of King Hezekiah (720-692 B.C.E.). Although he belonged to a princely family, he was incensed at the shameless conduct of the whole upper class and he chose to be the spokesman for the people. Pointing an indignant finger at the rulers, he accused:

"It is ye that have eaten up the vineyard; the spoil of the poor is in your houses; what mean ye that ye crush My people and grind the face of the poor?"

It was King Ahaz of Judah in particular against whom Isaiah's attacks were directed. In panic over the alliance between King Pekach of the northern kingdom of Israel and Rezin, King of Damascus, Ahaz called upon the Assyrian king, Tiglath-pileser, for assistance against his fellow Israelites in the north. Isaiah was horrified. He counseled the King of Judah against the step and warned him that his invitation to the King of Assyria was a provocation, a "covenant with death." What profit would it bring the mouse to play with the cat? Assyria was rapacious and its power overwhelming.

THE ASSYRIAN CONQUEST

Isaiah's keen political analysis proved unfortunately only too correct. Tiglath-pileser swooped down on Damascus in 734 B.C.E. He killed Rezin, its king, and reduced the entire country of the Arameans to a province of Assyria. He next descended on Israel. In his annals he recorded later: "Pekach, their king, I killed; Hoshea I placed over them." He then helped himself to the territory of Manasseh in the

Assyrians besieging a fortified city in Palestine. War-relief of Tiglath-pileser III. (From Central Palace, Nimrud.)
British Museum

northern and eastern districts of the kingdom, annexing Galilee and Gilead to the province of Damascus. He also deported a great many inhabitants of Israel into Assyria, how many is not recorded. But this marked the beginning of the strange "disappearance" of the Ten Tribes.

King Ahaz hastily journeyed to Damascus where he groveled in homage before the Assyrian conqueror. To buy Tiglath-pileser's sufferance he plundered not only the people of Judah of its wealth but he robbed the Temple of its treasure. Ahaz also wished to purchase Tiglath-pileser's favor in still another way. He abolished Hebrew as the official language of Judah and substituted Assyrian. He flatteringly introduced the star-worship of the conquerors and corrupted the priesthood to perform its rites in the Temple.

But the Assyrian avalanche continued to roll inexorably over the land of Israel. For three years an Assyrian host under Shalmeneser V besieged the almost impregnable capital city of Samaria. It finally fell in 720 B.C.E. under the hammer-blows of Sargon II.

Sargon's own cuneiform inscription found in his palace at Khorsabad tells the story: "In my first year of reign the people of Samaria to the number of 27,290 . . . I carried away. Fifty chariots for my royal equipment I selected. The

Sargon (left) and an officer. (From Khorsabad Palace.)
British Museum

city I rebuilt. I made it greater than it was before. People of the lands I had conquered I settled therein. My official I placed over them as governor." The deported Israelites were colonized in Media and in other parts of Mesopotamia. To replace them with elements he considered "safe," King Sargon brought into Israel considerable numbers of Babylonians, Arameans and Cutheans. These amalgamated with the people of Israel and in time were absorbed by them.

The kingdom of Israel, renamed "Samaria" by Sargon, which had lasted about two hundred and fifty years, had come to an inglorious end. Although the southern kingdom of Judah was to continue for about one hundred and fifty years more, it was as a weak dependency of Assyria, without a shred of its former political influence. As compensation of worldly power, its holy city, Jerusalem, and the Temple were to command increasing reverence from all Israelites.

THE DESTRUCTION OF THE FIRST TEMPLE

The tragic fate that had befallen the kingdom of Israel humbled the people of Judah. It became gravely thoughtful over what might befall it in turn. Isaiah preached the lesson Judah was to draw from Israel's disaster: Israel had been punished for its sins, and Assyria was nothing less than "the rod of Mine anger, the staff in whose hand is My indignation."

What was the hope for Judah, then? Only one, comforted the prophet. To be saved, it had to emerge out of the current smallness of its political power into the larger but spiritual function of "a light unto the nations," and Jerusalem must be transformed into "a city of justice."

Isaiah gibed at those who were merely formally pious but ignored the ethical precepts of the Law of Moses:

> To what purpose is the multitude of your sacrifices
> unto me?
> Saith the Lord;
> I am full of the burnt-offerings of rams,
> And the fat of fed beasts.

That was not the way to the Lord. The way of salvation for Israel, Isaiah exhorted, lay in personal morality and in social justice:

> Seek justice, relieve the oppressed,
> Judge the fatherless, plead for the widow.

Unfortunately, Isaiah and his younger contemporary, the prophet Micah, exerted little influence on the royal house of Judah. Instead of working for internal reforms of society and to deepen the ethical content of religion, Judah's kings were constantly conspiring with rulers of other countries to break loose from the overlordship of the Assyrians. Of three futile revolts, the third proved the most disastrous. In 701 B.C.E., Sargon's successor, Sennacherib (705-681 B.C.E.), led a punitive expedition against the Phoenician and Judean rebels. He reduced forty-six of the principal cities of Judah, including Lachish, but for some unaccountable reason he raised the siege of Jerusalem. Two hundred thousand Judeans were led into captivity. King Hezekiah, just as Isaiah had foretold, had to put his neck under the foot of the conqueror while Judah lay prostrate. A staggering tribute was exacted from the people and the Temple once again was denuded of its treasure and gold decorations, which were taken to Nineveh.

For the next period, during which Manasseh (692-637 B.C.E) and his son Amon were kings, Judah lay supine and inert under Assyrian overlordship. But during the reign of Josiah (637-607 B.C.E.) an astonishing thing happened.

It was during the invasion by Sennacherib that King Hezekiah ordered the construction of the underground Pool of Siloam (c. 700 B.C.E.). It carried water into the heart of Jerusalem from the river Gihon by way of a subterranean tunnel. It was intended to supply the inhabitants of the city with water during the anticipated long siege by Sennacherib. The inscription, as well as the tunnel, was discovered by archaeologists in 1880. The pool demonstrates what a high level of engineering skill the Israelites had reached, even long before the Greeks.

Deuteronomy Is Discovered

In the year 619 B.C.E. a hitherto unknown "Book of Laws" was discovered in the Temple. While the traditional belief has been that it was the Pentateuch, modern scholars seem to be persuaded that it was but the Book of Deuteronomy. Josiah read it, and when he was through, he was filled with zeal for the reform of religious worship. With great energy he set about purifying the Temple rites of *baal, ashera* and the Queen of Heaven idolatry. He ordered idols and altars pulled down from their high places, and to centralize worship in the Temple, he had all other sanctuaries destroyed.

The rediscovery of the Book of Deuteronomy reveals that for a long time there had been no written *Torah* or Law for the guidance and teaching of the people. Because there was no canon law and the people relied only on oral tradition, it was easier for heathen beliefs to creep into the Jewish faith. The discovery of the Fifth Book of Moses, therefore, was epoch-making in its effect on the future course of the Jewish religion and on the development of the Jews as a people.

Siloam inscription, in the Phoenician-Hebrew script from which the modern alphabets of Europe derive.

Jeremiah

Yet these reforms were considered entirely inadequate by one man, the prophet Jeremiah. To the priests and prophets who had purged the Temple of its unsavory rites he declared that reforms in worship could guarantee neither the redemption of Israel from its Assyrian oppressor nor the preservation of the faith. Rather, it was a purification and a reform of the heart which were desperately required. Not *more* devout worship of God, as the prophets and priests counseled, but

Jeremiah.   *Michelangelo (Sistine Chapel)*

rather more upright action would most effectively sustain them in their national tribulation.

For this reason the hostility of the priestly class was aroused against Jeremiah. But Jeremiah was constantly warning of disaster to come. He foretold the national catastrophe the people feared most to contemplate—the fall of the Temple.

In vain he pleaded with the Israelites in high places who clamored for revolt against the foreign overlords. He warned that it was not so much for love of the people as to increase their own power that they were ready to plunge Israel into war.

When, during the reign of King Zedekiah, the Assyrian dynasts were overthrown and Nebuchadnezzar re-established the Babylonian kingdom, the king of Egypt grew alarmed. He was determined to put as many obstacles as possible in the path of the great power to the north. To this end he sent ambassadors to Jerusalem who plotted with war-minded adventurers to revolt against Nebuchadnezzar. King Zedekiah was inclined to support the conspiracy, but Jeremiah's fierce opposition deterred him. After five years of clamor by the nobility and by the professional prophets, however, Zedekiah gave in.

The princes of the land, who were of the war-party, then petitioned Zedekiah: "Let this man, we pray thee, be put to death: for as much as he weakeneth the hands of the men of war that remain in this city, and the hands of all the people in speaking such words unto them; for this man seeketh not the welfare of this people, but its hurt." They then took Jeremiah and threw him into a pit from which he was rescued by an Ethiopian officer of the guard.

Finally the signal was given and Judah rose in revolt. Nebuchadnezzar promptly brought a besieging army to the walls of Jerusalem. Jeremiah's pleas not to defend the city were without avail. It would be the death of everything the people held precious, he warned. For a short while the approach of a large Egyptian force brought relief to the beleaguered city and Nebuchadnezzar prudently withdrew. But the outbreak of a pestilence in the city, aggravated by hunger, forced the protracted tragedy to a close.

THE FALL OF JERUSALEM

After a year and a half of merciless siege Jerusalem fell. The city was razed; the Temple was destroyed. Zedekiah saw his sons killed. Afterwards his eyes were gouged out and he was carried off in chains to Babylon for public exhibition and humiliation. With him went a vast number of captives, consisting of the best and most educated elements. Only the poorest, the feeblest and the most backward were allowed to remain.

Jeremiah watched in overwhelming grief the fulfillment of his dire prophecies. The Jewish state lay in ruins. The Temple was only a pile of stone rubble, and the people were broken and scattered. No longer did he wish to play the part of a prophet of doom, now that disaster had struck, but that of consoler. He advised the exiles to live at peace among themselves and to cultivate friendly relations with the Babylonians. And he comforted them with the promise that if they kept the faith and dealt justly with one another, the Lord would some day redeem and re-establish them on Mount Zion.

SUFFERING AND REBIRTH

The Jewish exiles who had been carried off to Babylonia were inconsolable: the Captivity rested crushingly upon them. A fierce nationalism and a longing to return to their homeland consumed them. Turning toward Judah, they, in the words of the psalmist, made a stirring vow:

> If I forget thee, O Jerusalem,
> Let my right hand forget her cunning.
> Let my tongue cleave to the roof of my mouth,
> If I remember thee not;
> If I set not Jerusalem
> Above my chiefest joy.

But since men cannot always be the choosers of their lot, the captives tried to make the best of their national misfortune. This adjustment was not too difficult, for the Babylonian rulers were far from harsh or vindictive. A period of great prosperity was being enjoyed by Babylonia, now the greatest power in the world. Not only had they looted the countries they overran of all their wealth, but they had built up a thriving commercial traffic everywhere. Babylon was "The City of Merchants." Untold riches poured into the country. The possession of leisure and the material means stimulated every branch of cultural activity.

It was a period of unusual intellectual advances. A century before, Ashurbanipal had established his great library of ancient cuneiform writings in Nineveh. In but a short time the Jewish captives acquired a considerable degree of Babylonian culture, which in some ways was superior to their own. The researches carried on by the Babylonians into their own past stimulated the Jewish captives to gather and study their own chronicles and sacred writings.

The Jewish captives were allowed a measure of self-rule in their own community life. Because they had been deliberately chosen for deportation on account of their superior education and their skills as artisans, they found a ready field for their talents in the productive life of the country. They thrived as merchants, as farmers and as skilled workers. They were even permitted to acquire property and to keep their wealth. But most significant of all was the freedom they were given to worship their own God in their own way without interference. Also every Jew remembered his family tree. No attempt was made by the Babylonian authorities to break up the clan and tribal groupings headed by their own elders.

Job ("The Just Upright Man is laughed to scorn").

Personal tribulation and national misfortune are merely two aspects of the same problem of existence. The dilemma of "suffering man" is posed searchingly in the *Book of Job*, one of the supreme masterpieces in world literature. Job, a righteous man, is overwhelmed by a variety of misfortunes. In an agony of doubt he raises many disturbing questions: Why do the righteous suffer and the wicked prosper? Why, if there is a just God in heaven, should man be tormented so grievously? And the answer he gets is that human existence has its limitations, and man must learn to accept and to reconcile himself to them, and yet preserve his faith in God and in the good in life.

In this manner the group cohesion and solidarity of the exiles was maintained.

The Faith Is Purified

Communal necessity led them to form assemblies everywhere. Out of these developed the synagogue, that epochmaking institution of the Jewish religion whose forms were later taken over by the church and the mosque. It grew out of the urgent need for religious worship because the Temple no longer existed and they were exiles in a distant land. At one time, there was even a movement started to build a Temple in Babylon, but the prophet Ezekiel opposed it strenuously. He realistically perceived the danger in the proposal: if such a sanctuary were built in exile, the Jews might no longer feel any need of returning to the land of Israel, since all their

Ezekiel's Vision of the Resurrection. (From frescoes in the Dura-Europos Synagogue, Syria, 3rd century C.E.)
Courtesy of Yale University Art Gallery

desires, spiritual and material, would have been satisfied.

At all costs Ezekiel wished to keep the gaze of the exiles fixed on their return to the land of their fathers. Accordingly, he wove a rapturous vision of their eventual restoration. "Thus saith the Lord God: Behold, I will take the children of Israel from among the nations . . . and will gather them on every side, and bring them unto their own land; and I will make them one nation in the land upon the mountains of Israel. . . ."

It is one of the astonishing facts of history that while the Jews were settled as a nation in their own land, while their kings wielded considerable power and their upper classes acquired wealth and lived in luxury, their culture and religion remained backward. The teachings of the great prophets exhorting them to righteousness and social justice had fallen mostly on deaf ears. But suddenly, now, in exile, with their national state at an end, their holy Temple in ruins, their priesthood scattered and their people but a broken reed, there was an intense spiritual and cultural awakening. In adversity, it seems, the Jews had developed a feeling of group solidarity. The teachings of Moses and of the prophets, which they had formerly taken lightly, now took on a soul-stirring significance. They began to question the reasons for the disaster to their national life. Only then did they realize how true were the warnings of the prophets they had despised. They readily accepted their explanation for the blows that had rained upon them—"on account of our sins."

Disillusionment set in: worldly pursuits had proven vain, national power a snare, formal religious worship without righteousness a mockery. A social feeling for one's fellow-men and a desire for the advancement and protection of human rights and well-being, ideals which lay at the heart of the Jewish religion, awakened among the exiles. Henceforth, they resolved, they would cherish only moral and intellectual values. The educated men among them turned enthusiastically to a study of the uncollected Jewish religious writings which they had brought with them into captivity. These they read

The *Book of Jonah* is a diverting allegory with a moral, composed, no doubt, under the duress of the religious fervor which gripped the Jewish exiles in Babylonia. In the story related, God bids Jonah go to Nineveh, the capital of Babylon, to preach the way of righteousness to its inhabitants. But Jonah resists the divine command and tries to escape by sea. When he is thrown overboard by the sailors, a whale swallows him. Promising to preach God's truth to all men, he is released by the whale.

from publicly at their religious assemblies and expounded and emphasized their ethical meanings to the worshippers.

Remarkably enough, this renaissance of the Jewish spirit and intellect took place in a very brief time span—in three or four generations. We are apprised of this historic fact suddenly by the decree, in 538 B.C.E., of King Cyrus, the Persian who had overthrown the Babylonian Empire as the prophet Daniel had warned King Belshazzar he would. This rescript is recorded in the Book of Ezra and reads as follows: "Thus saith Cyrus, King of Persia: the Lord God of heaven hath given me all the kingdoms of the earth and he hath charged me to build him a house at Jerusalem which is in Judah. Who is there among you of all his people? His God be with him, and let him go to Jerusalem, which is in Judah, and build the house of the Lord God of Israel (he is the God) which is in Jerusalem."

Ezekiel. *Michelangelo*

Daniel interpreting the dream of Nebuchadnezzar.

The Handwriting on the Wall: *Mene, Mene, Tekel, Upharsin.* According to the *Book of Daniel*, the prophet Daniel interpreted these mysterious words for King Belshazzar, foretelling the death of the king and the downfall of Babylonia before the superior might of Persia. Later, through a conspiracy, Daniel was thrown into a den of lions, but was unharmed because he prayed and the Lord "shut the lions' mouths."

THE EXILES RETURN

The return of the exiles to their native lands was not limited only to the Jews. It was a part of the general political policy of this truly humane and wise ruler, the very reverse of his Babylonian predecessors and of the Egyptian pharaohs. On a clay cylinder Cyrus noted simply: "I assembled all those nations and I caused them to go back to their own countries."

The first contingent of the returning Jewish exiles numbered 42,360. One-tenth of them were priests and 245 were Levite singers. They left for Jerusalem that same year under the leadership of Sheshbazzar, a royal prince of the House of David. Another band, under the latter's nephew, Zerubbabel, followed in 536 B.C.E.

As they stood at last before the ruins of the Temple they were stricken with grief. Jerusalem had become a desolate city. Even more desolate they found those of their people who had been left behind by the conquerors—"The poor of the land to be wine-dressers and husbandmen." These had intermarried in the meantime with those foreign peoples the Assyrians and the Babylonians had colonized in Samaria in place of the Jews they had deported. Thenceforth, this mixed group became known as Samaritans. Although they considered themselves Jews in every way and wished to join the returned exiles in rebuilding the Temple, Zerubbabel nonetheless declined their offer curtly: "Ye have nothing to do with us to build a house for our God."

During their brief stay in Babylonia the Jewish captives had developed a high degree of group and religious identity, so that they felt little kinship with the Samaritans of mixed stock. Furthermore, many of them had been taken into captivity principally because they had belonged to the upper and educated classes. The broader culture they had acquired in Babylonia only accentuated the great difference between themselves and the backward Samaritans.

This rejection of the Samaritans as brother Jews and equals by the returned exiles had serious consequences, of both a religious and a political nature. The Samaritans kept presenting their grievances to the Persian satrap of the province, who, in turn, forwarded their petitions to the "King of Kings" in Babylonia, with the result that the construction of the Temple edifice was suspended for eight years.

The Temple Is Rebuilt

The rebuilding of the Temple, nevertheless, was resumed. The whole project was carried through in the most democratic manner, in traditional emulation of the way in which the Tabernacle and the Ark of the Covenant had been built during the years of wandering in the wilderness: all the people took part in it. The Temple at last stood completed in 515 B.C.E., seventy-one years after the Temple of Solomon had been destroyed. The feast of dedication was held amidst general rejoicing, and the future smiled tranquilly again for the fledgling society.

It is a curious fact that there is a big gap in known historical and Scriptural references to the fate of Palestine after the dedication of the Temple. The thread of history is not picked up again until the appearance of Ezra the Scribe in 458 B.C.E. in the reign of Artaxerxes.

Ezra was a profound religious thinker. In Babylonia he had made a close study of all the extant sacred Hebrew writings. Suddenly, he found himself empowered by the Persian king to return to the land of his fathers and to serve as its religious head. Accordingly, Ezra, accompanied by fifteen hundred fellow Jews and their families, journeyed to Jerusalem. Ezra found the situation concerning the Samaritans even more aggravated than it had been during the governorship of Zerubbabel. Intermarriage between Samaritans and the returned exiles was widespread. Armed with the authority vested in him by King Artaxerxes, he issued a decree declaring all intermarriages with Samaritans invalid. Furthermore, he forced all Samaritans out of the congregation of Israel.

War with the Samaritans

Naturally, this harsh ruling stirred up great bitterness among the Samaritans as well as among their Israelite mates. A kind of civil war resulted, so that the Persian king in Susa was obliged to send his able Jewish cupbearer, Nehemiah, to Jerusalem on a mission of pacification, armed with full authority. Nehemiah was a vigorous administrator and a man of prudence. He realized that to protect Jerusalem his first task was to rebuild its walls as quickly as possible. With a building tool in one hand and a weapon in the other, the inhabitants of Jerusalem started work on the walls. Many attempts were made by the Samaritans to interrupt the construction, but the Israelites fought off their attacks. In only fifty-two days the walls were completed and the danger to Jerusalem from the embattled Samaritans from the north was averted.

Ezra Compiles the Torah

It was Ezra's firm conviction that what the Israelites needed most to preserve themselves as a religious entity and as a people was a body of Scriptural writings which would best represent the Mosaic and prophetic teachings. In order not to allow later alteration and distortion of the sacred text he wished to make it final, a closed canon. Accordingly, he surrounded himself with a learned company of priests and scribes or *soferim* (singular, *sofer*) like himself. Among them were chroniclers, legal scholars, teachers of ethics and generally men who were familiar with all manner of Jewish sacred writings, traditions, religious rites and ceremonies. They

Left. Ezra(?). (From frescoes in the Dura-Europos Synagogue, Syria, 3rd century c.e.) (*Courtesy of Yale University Art Gallery*) *Right.* Sefer Torah.

helped Ezra compile and edit the *Torah*, the Five Books of Moses. Collectively, these compilers and editors went under the name of the *Men of the Great Assembly.*

The first day of Tishri in the year 444 (some say 445) B.C.E., Ezra designated as the day on which he would promulgate the Book of the Law. That day, all the people congregated in vast numbers in the open place before the Water-Gate of the Temple. "And Ezra the priest brought the Law before the congregation, both men and women. . . . And he read therein . . . and the ears of all the people were attentive unto the Book of the Law."

The Torah Is Consecrated

Ezra stood on a wooden pulpit or reading desk which had been erected for the purpose. "And Ezra opened the book in the sight of all the people—for he was above all the people —and when he opened it, all the people stood up. And Ezra blessed the Lord, the great God. And all the people answered: 'Amen, Amen,' with the lifting up of their hands, and they bowed their heads, and fell down before the Lord with their faces to the ground."

Then certain leading scribes and Levites, presumably the Men of the Great Assembly, went about among the people explaining the *Torah* to them. Under the mighty emotional fervor that gripped it, the people took a solemn oath of consecration read to it by Ezra. It swore "to walk in God's law, which was given by Moses, the servant of God, and to fulfill all the commandments of the Lord."

Yet Ezra was not completely satisfied. He wished to utilize the solemnity of the occasion for still another purpose: to preserve the purity of the stock. He made the Israelites swear "that we would not give our daughters unto the peoples of the land, nor take their daughters for our sons."

Thus the *Torah* was consecrated and accepted by the people of Israel some eight centuries after Moses and the Covenant on Mount Sinai.

THE TORAH

The *Talmud* says about the *Torah*: "It is not the Torah of the Priests, nor the Torah of the Levites, nor the Torah of the

Israelites, but the Torah of Man. Its gates are open to receive the righteous nation which keeps the truth and those who are good and upright in their hearts."

From this it is easy to see that in later Jewish belief and tradition the *Torah* was not considered to be concerned with theology but with humanity and righteousness. It indulged in little special pleading, advanced few dogmas, nor was it often narrowly sectarian. Its gaze embraced the entire vista of life. The fatherhood of God and the brotherhood of man became its fundamental doctrines. To paraphrase the words of the Talmudic sage Hillel, all the rest was commentary.

What is the *Torah?* The Hebrew word *Torah* means "doctrine." However, the Hellenistic Jews of Egypt, who were quite legal-minded, chose to call it "the Law" in their Greek Septuagint translation of the Five Books of Moses made during the third century B.C.E. Actually, this conception of *Torah* is too limited and misleading. The *Torah* is not merely a codex of laws which, in their ancient historic framework, attempted to cover every need of Jewish life of the times— ceremonial, ritual, social and criminal—but a text which teaches, moralizes and exhorts to right conduct. Furthermore, it is a chronicle of events, personalities and traditions.

In its most limited meaning the *Torah* consists of the Five Books of Moses. In Hebrew it is called the "Chumash," but the Greek-speaking Jews called it the "Pentateuch." This was the book of scriptures which Ezra, the scribe, assisted by the Men of the Great Assembly, compiled and edited and promulgated in 444 B.C.E. In time, with the addition of other sacred works, such as the Prophetic writings, the Psalms and the wisdom literature by later assemblies of learned men, the Bible, or, as it is called in Hebrew, *Tanach*, was completed. Gradually, the conception of *Torah* was enlarged to include these writings.

The Mishna

Though the *Soferim*, or scribes, who had collected and edited the Bible, finally declared it a closed canon, religious thinkers and the Jewish people alike remained dissatisfied. This merely emphasizes the fact that at no time did the Jews have a static or frozen philosophy of religion. There was little dogmatism in it, and it grew and changed organically with the development of life itself through the ages.

The Palestinian successors of the *Soferim*, one hundred and forty-eight scholars and teachers called *Tannaim* (singular— *Tanna*) proceeded to compile a so-called "Second Law" which they named the *Mishna* (repetition or doctrine). It consisted of traditional doctrines which had been transmitted orally from generation to generation. It was a code which had developed slowly and took almost five and a half centuries before it was completed. However, it, too, like the Bible, became a closed canon in the third century C.E., when it was compiled and edited by Judah ha-Nasi ("The Prince").

The Talmud (Gemara)

Before long the *Mishna*, too, was found to have obscurities which required elaboration and interpretation. To answer this need the *Gemara* (complement), a discursive commentary on the *Mishna*, came into being. The *Talmud*, consisting of both *Mishna* and *Gemara*, is not just one book, as is commonly believed, but a collection of many books. It is not just the product of one time but of several centuries. It was not created in

Judea alone, but in Babylonia as well. In fact, it took several hundred rabbis, who went under the collective name of *Amoraim* (singular, *Amora*) or "Expounders," to complete what is universally considered to be the *Corpus Juris* of the Jews.

There are actually two *Talmuds*. The more important of the two is called the *Babylonian Talmud* because it was developed in the Rabbinical academies of Babylonia where there was a great settlement of Jews, probably numbering between one and two millions at the time of the destruction of Jerusalem. The work was closed by its Rabbinic editors during the fifth century C.E. The other, called the *Jerusalem Talmud*, had been completed one hundred and fifty years earlier in the year 370.

With the care of practiced legal scholars, the *Amoraim* had examined the *Mishna* text sentence by sentence and phrase by phrase. They tried to trace every source and, in cool objective discussion, sought to reconcile the contradictions they encountered there. It was a rare instance, indeed, when they proceeded to lay down the law dogmatically. Most of the time they merely gave their reasoned opinions and presented their views in the course of the discussion, the dissenting ones side by side with those of the majority. The laws they were trying to interpret and clarify touched on a vast number of subjects, down to the most minute circumstance or problem that might arise. Not just religious belief, rite and custom, but also philosophic problems, personal hygiene, individual and social ethics and other matters of a civil and secular nature were searchingly examined. In this connection it must be kept in mind that ancient Jewish society was theocratic, was centered in its religion, and that, therefore, all secular and civilian as well as religious matters were supervised by the same legal authority.

The Midrash

Finally, there is the *Midrash*. It is a body of popular interpretive literature written by the *Tannaim* and the *Amoraim* simultaneously with their work on the *Mishna* and *Talmud*. Unlike the latter, the writing of the *Midrash* went on continuously. It did not end until the great Talmudic academies in Babylonia were forced to close in 1040. The *Midrash* ("to study," "to investigate") consists of exegetical writings, deeply devotional and ethical in character. By means of elaboration, legalistic and often poetic, and by employing folk legend, parable, fable and wise sayings, it attempts to illuminate the literal text of the Bible, to bring out its inner meaning.

Thus we see that the conception of *Torah* was a constantly widening one. Besides the basic scriptural works, it also included the *Mishna*, the *Gemara* and the *Midrash*. In medieval times and later there were many who were ready to add to it the celebrated commentaries of Rashi and Ibn Ezra.

The Intellectual Tradition of the Talmud

The highest obligation of the religious Jew since those distant centuries has been to devote himself to the constant study of the *Torah*. It was to be a daily exercise in piety, in moral reflection and in search for *chochma*, understanding. This, in the course of the centuries, became a compelling preoccupation of the Jew, in fact, a way of life.

Torah study was meant not only for a learned élite, for scholars, but for all men. It was based on the recognition of the principle that all men are equal and therefore must pursue the same path to virtue and illumination. "The *Torah* is the Bride of the Congregation of Jacob," said the rabbis of old.

The study of the *Torah*, however, meant more than mere religious intellectual activity; it was meant, above all, to be a *moral action*. "On three things the world is based," wrote a Talmudic sage, "on the study of the *Torah*, on worship and on loving-kindness." By the example of their own lives the Talmudic authors wished to set the moral pattern for *Torah* study. One of them counseled: "One should study the *Torah* with self-denial, even at the sacrifice of one's life." Teachers of the *Torah*, like Hanina ben Teradion in the days of Hadrian, fulfilled this precept literally.

Wherein lay the profit of this consecrated study? The *Talmud* gives the answer: "Whosoever labors in the *Torah* for its own sake, merits many things . . . he is called friend, beloved, a lover of God, a lover of mankind; it clothes him in meekness and fear [of God], and fits him to become righteous, pious and upright; it keeps him far from sin, brings him towards the side of virtue and gives him sovereignty and dominion and discerning judgment. To him the secrets of the *Torah* are revealed; he becomes a never-fading fountain, he grows modest and long-suffering, forgives insults and rises above all things."

The Jews' universal devotion to this task, an intellectual-moral phenomenon without parallel in all cultural history, aroused both the admiration and the mockery of their enemies. Many of them understood only too well its significance and its power as a catalyst binding the Jews together. The *Talmud*, in this connection, relates a quaint story. Once the Greek philosopher Oenomaos of Gadara was asked: "How can we make away with this people?" He answered: "Go about and observe their schools and academies. So long as the clear voices of children ring forth from them, you will not be able to touch a hair on their heads."

Since it was obligatory to teach all Jewish boys the *Torah*, religious schools had to be provided by every Jewish community. This was in order that they might fulfill the declaration of God: "The Crown of the Torah is offered to everyone."

Generation followed generation in the unbroken continuity of Jewish life. Also the study of the *Torah* went on like the ceaseless flow of a river. It never stopped and it could never be stopped, neither during periods of bitter persecution, nor during those of flight and expulsion, nor by threats of the torture-rack and the burning stake, nor by the harassments of poverty and hunger. And the reason for this? On *Yom Kippur*, the Day of Atonement, as the day draws to an end and the shadows of night begin to fall, the worshippers in the synagogue raise their voices in declamatory affirmation:

> Our splendor and our glory have departed,
> Our treasures have been snatched from us;
> There remains nothing to us but this *Torah* alone.

The Sefer Torah

The *Sefer Torah*, the Scroll of the Law, which rests in the Ark of the synagogue, consists of the Five Books of Moses. It is a parchment scroll fixed on two wooden rollers. Wrapped in an embroidered mantle and adorned with figured silver ornaments, it reposes in the sanctuary of the Ark of the Law.

The ritual law is uncompromising on the manner in which the *Sefer Torah* is to be written by the *sofer* or scribe: the scroll must be parchment; each page, in preparation for the fine Hebrew calligraphy that is to adorn it, is ruled with a stylus into squares and lines by the *sofer*. In former days it was traditional for the *sofer* to use only the finest goose quills and the best black ink. Furthermore, it was not considered merely a professional service he was performing, but it was also regarded as a sacred rite, and he was exhorted to come to his work in a pure and lofty frame of mind. Into this mood he could be brought only by means of *Torah* study, prayer and pious meditation. He wore his *tallith* (prayer shawl) and his *tefillin* (phylacteries) at work. Moreover, it was forbidden him to write a single word from memory lest he make an error. He always had to hold a correct copy of the Pentateuch before him and, before setting a word down on the parchment, he was required to pronounce it distinctly and with fervor. If he made a mistake, he was permitted to erase it, but if it was God's name, he had to use a new page. This was one way in which the text of the *Torah* was protected against distortion through the ages.

The great reverence and love for the *Sefer Torah* naturally led to its physical beautification. The calligraphy had to be perfect and exquisite. The mantle which covered it, the *paroket*—the curtain before the Ark—and the covering for the reading desk on which the *Torah* would be laid when opened had to be made of the finest velvet, satin, brocade or silk and embroidered with the utmost care and loveliness. Even the wooden handles of the rollers usually had carved ivory ends.

Perhaps the objects on which was lavished the greatest love and which served as an outlet for the repressed sense of visual beauty among Jews were the *Torah* ornaments: the finely patterned crowns of gold or silver, the breastplate hanging by a chain from the rollers, the silver pointer to guide in the reading from the *Sefer Torah*, and the *Rimonim*, those exquisitely towered ornaments for the top of the rollers, jingling with their little bells of silver.

The *Paroket* (curtain before the Ark).

The *sofer* (inscribing the *Sefer Torah*) *Ilya Schor*

"This is the *Torah*." Part of the ceremony of reading the *Torah*.

71

SIMCHAT TORAH

Simchat Torah (Simchas Torah), "Rejoicing over the Torah," is a religious festival to celebrate the completion of the reading of the *Chumash*, the Five Books of Moses. It marks the end of a cycle of weekly readings of Scripture passages from the *Sefer Torah* in the synagogue.

This festival constitutes a sort of adjunct to *Succoth*, of which it might be considered the ninth day. Most definitely it is a day of rejoicing and of merriment in which both old and young take part in a spontaneous, informal manner. In the synagogue it is celebrated by *hakafoth*, processions. Everyone is given a chance to hold the beloved scrolls (the cabalists referred to it as the "Bride of the *Torah*") in his arms, chanting: "Lord save us, Lord prosper us!" The procession makes a circuit of the synagogue, with the children bringing up the rear, holding aloft and waving little paper pennants bearing the words "The Crown of the *Torah*." In former immigrant days in America, apples, sometimes candied red, would be stuck temptingly on the top of the little flagstaffs and tiny candles would be fixed into the apples. Before joining the procession the children would light their candles and on the way home would eat their apples.

The final passage in the *Torah* is read before the congregation with great ceremony. The man so honored is called *Chathan Torah*, "The Bridegroom of the Torah." As he concludes his reading, the congregation chants as with one voice the ancient formula: *"Hazak, hazak, venithhazak"*—"Be strong, be strong! And let us gather new strength [to continue in the service of the *Torah*]."

But since the reading of the *Torah* never really ends, and because it follows in a continuing cycle, without loss of time another worshipper is immediately called to the *Bimah* (reading platform) only to begin all over again with the reading of the timeless story of creation. He is therefore called *Chathan Bereshith*, "The Bridegroom of Genesis."

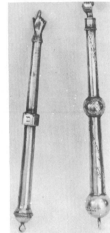

Silver pointers and breastplate (*Torah ornaments*). *Jewish Museum*

Procession on *Simchat Torah*, Amsterdam, 1725. *Bernard Picart*

Torah Crown, Holland, 18th century.

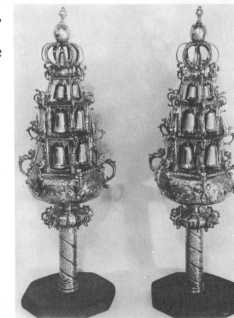

Rimonim, Germany, c. 1700.

THE SABBATH

The modern Jewish philosopher, Ahad ha-Am, observed: "More than the Jews have kept the Sabbath, the Sabbath has kept the Jews." That holy day has been one of the cornerstones of the Jewish faith and people throughout their troubled history.

According to Jewish belief, the Lord blessed and hallowed the Sabbath day (the seventh), the day on which He rested after creating the world. It was to be designated as *Shabbat*, which in Hebrew means "rested."

The observance of the Sabbath was considered to be the supreme requirement for the pious. The hallowing of the day was ordered in the Ten Commandments so that it might serve as part of the Covenant of Israel with the Lord: "Remember the sabbath day, to keep it holy. Six days shalt thou labor, and do all thy work but the seventh day is a sabbath unto the Lord thy God, in it thou shalt not do any manner of work, thou, nor thy son, nor thy daughter, nor thy manservant, nor thy maidservant, nor thy cattle, nor the stranger that is within thy gates."

The Sabbath, as a regular weekly institution, represented the highest expression of social ethics among the ancient Jews. It established the principle that no matter how poor, how downtrodden or how rejected a man may be in the world, on the Sabbath he achieves dignity and human stature. He has natural rights that transcend all property rights, and to obtain and protect these rights the Lord himself steps forward as his champion.

The observance of the Sabbath by the Jews often aroused the ridicule and hostility of their neighbors. This was especially true of the Greeks and the Romans. However, their scorn had an economic basis. Their societies, which boasted such advanced civilizations, were built on the toil of millions of slaves. The mere notion of a day of rest for them filled them with horror or mirth. To them, the rest day indicated that the Jews were "lazy." The Roman satirists made merry at their expense. The Stoic philosopher Seneca, who was deeply concerned with the problem of personal morality, described the Sabbath of the Jews as a form of robbery. It was, said he, stealing one full day's labor from the week.

There is an allegory in the *Talmud* concerning the Sabbath.

Left. Summoning the pious to the communal bathhouse early Friday afternoon, Poland, c. 1750. *Right.* Kiddush cup, Germany, c. 1750.

The six days of the week stood joined together. Only the Sabbath day was left standing solitary and apart. The Sabbath complained: Why was it so discriminated against? The Lord explained: If the Sabbath stood apart from the other days of the week, so did Israel stand isolated in its faith among other peoples of the world. It was meant as a distinction, not as a punishment. Moreover, the Sabbath would never be alone, for it was wedded to Israel, who would treasure it forever.

It was not until the Babylonian Exile that the Sabbath evolved, simultaneously with the synagogue, into a great religious institution. It afforded the captives the opportunity to meet in community worship and to read aloud from the sacred writings. It is noteworthy that by the time of the Maccabees in the second century B.C.E. the observance of the Sabbath bristled with so many ordinances, regulations and prohibitions that Jewish soldiers would not fight on the Sabbath day even in self-defense. This fact was well known to the enemy generals, records Josephus the historian, and they took advantage of it in war with the Jews.

In the later days of the Temple, the advent and departure of the Sabbath was announced by priests blowing on golden trumpets. The Sabbath was then treated as a day of peace and joy, not of solemnity. True enough, the *Mishna* records thirty-nine kinds of tasks that were forbidden on the Sabbath. Among these were the preparation and cooking of food, the carrying of burdens, the lighting of a fire, buying and selling, accepting money and traveling. However, said the ancient Rabbinic sages, these prohibitions were not laid down to afflict man with burdens but to help him keep the Sabbath inviolable and holy for his own spiritual joy and illumination.

The simple fact is that the spirit of the Sabbath was held dearer than all the minutiae of observance. R. Simon ben Menasya, a sage of the *Talmud*, expressed this view: "The Sabbath is given over to you and not you to the Sabbath." The ancient Rabbinic view was that on the Sabbath man becomes transformed from within and from without. He not only bathes and puts on festive raiment to welcome "The Bride of the Sabbath" appropriately but his face begins to shine with an inner light. There was even a popular belief that if every Jew in the world would at the same time keep one Sabbath, it would bring the Messiah.

The observance of the Sabbath is ushered in late on Friday afternoon. Not later than eighteen minutes before sunset the mistress of the home (generally wife or mother) lights the Sabbath candles and recites a benediction. When the father returns from the special synagogue services after dark, he blesses his children and recites *Kiddush* (sanctification) over a goblet of wine. In East European countries the custom was to invite a poor man or a stranger to sit as an honored guest at the Sabbath table. Perhaps the most moving part of the home services is the singing by the head of the household of *Eshes Chayil,* "A Woman of Valor." It is a song culled from the 31st Chapter of the Book of Proverbs, a eulogy to the Jewish wife and mother of whom it conceives in ideal terms. It reveals how much higher, much of the time, the position of the woman was among the Jews than among other peoples.

> Strength and dignity are her clothing . . .
> She openeth her mouth with wisdom;
> And the law of kindness is on her tongue . . .
> Her children rise up, and call her blessed;
> Her husband also, and he praiseth her.

Lighting the candles, Germany, 19th century.

Left. Sabbath lamp, Germany, 18th century. *Right.* Sabbath cover, Germany, 19th century.

In eastern and central European countries certain foods had become traditional for the Sabbath Eve. It was customary to serve braided *challeh,* or white bread, *gefilte* (stuffed) fish, *lokshen* (noodles) in chicken broth, boiled chicken, *helzel* (stuffed neck) and finally *tzimmes* (sweet dessert).

Upon returning from the synagogue the following morning, the family gathered for the Sabbath feast. The main dish this time was usually the traditional *cholent* or *shalet,* which was derived from the French word *chaleur* meaning heat or warmth. *Cholent* consists of potted meat and vegetables, cooked on Friday and allowed to simmer overnight in the oven. Another favorite dish was *kugel,* a noodle or bread pudding baked with chicken fat.

Beginning with ancient Rabbinic times, the afternoon of the Sabbath was traditionally spent by the pious in devotional reading or in group study in the synagogue. This included the reflective reading of *Pirke Abot,* "The Sayings of the Fathers," a work on ethics which forms a part of "The Sea of the *Talmud.*" At home, too, on the Sabbath afternoon fathers would discuss these moral reflections with their children. They would help them draw the right lessons from them. By having this work included in the Sabbath prayers, the Rabbinic sages, the teachers of the people, wished to keep them constantly preoccupied with the problems of ethical conduct.

The womenfolk, beginning with the late sixteenth century, were also supplied with devotional reading for the day. Be-

cause very few were taught Hebrew, a special body of moralistic literature in the vernacular Yiddish was written to answer their needs. The most beloved and universally read of all these writings was the *Teitsch Chumash,* the Yiddish translation of the Pentateuch which was compiled by Isaac Yanova (died 1628 in Prague). It was enriched in its margins with all kinds of Rabbinic anecdotes, moralistic parables, allegories and pious observations. Oddly enough, this unpretentious work proved to be one of the supreme educators of the Jewish

On the Sabbath even the poorest Jew is a king, his wife—a queen, his sons—princes royal.

people. For one thing, it permitted the Jewish woman to share in the religious and cultural life of her people. It taught her Jewish history and ethics. For another, it was a *household* book. For almost four centuries it served as the Jewish mother's guide for training her children in the ethical and religious values of their fathers.

The Sabbath drew to a close at sundown with a genuine feeling of regret to the pious. The life of the Jew was almost always hard, full of unpredictable griefs. Persecution and lack of opportunity made it difficult for him to earn a stable living. The days of the week, from the vantage point of Sabbath serenity, seemed gray and discouraging. It was often with this sharply in mind that the Jew of the ghetto sang the Sabbath song:

> Light and rejoicing to Israel,
> Sabbath, the soother of sorrows,
> Comfort of downtrodden Israel,
> Healing the hearts that were broken.
> Banish despair! Here is hope come!

Study and prayer on the Sabbath.

The Sabbath ends after the *maarib*, or evening service, in the synagogue with the *Habdalah*, or "Separation" ceremony, which is repeated later at home. A candle is lit. Then, filling a goblet to overflowing with wine, the worshipper intones a prayer. After reciting the benedictions, he opens the spice box which is used in the *Habdalah* ceremony. He smells the spices and pronounces a benediction. The smelling of the spices, in which the entire family joins, is a symbolic act, a wishful prayer that the week which lies ahead may be free from care and grief, may be sweet-smelling as the spices and may delight the heart and sustain the spirit.

In his last years, the Hebrew poet Bialik introduced the custom of *Oneg Shabbat*, or taking delight in the Sabbath. Groups of people would gather for cultural and elevated pastimes appropriate to the day, which would be crowned with group-singing of *zemiroth* (religious table-songs) and folk-songs. This custom rapidly spread from Palestine to all other countries. Today *Oneg Shabbat* gatherings are very popular in the United States and Canada.

Cholent ovens, 18th century; lighted on Friday afternoon for keeping the Sabbath food warm. Jewish law (Orthodox) forbids the cooking or warming of foods on Saturday, considering it a form of labor.

PURIM (The Feast of Lots)

Some modern scholars express serious doubt that the personages and events described in the Book of Esther ever really came to pass. They find no corroborative proof of them in the contemporary records of ancient Persia where this Jewish national drama was supposed to have taken place. Furthermore, they point to many contradictions in the text. Yet, however skeptical they may be, and whether they are justified or not in their assumptions, the fact remains that the Festival of *Purim*, which is based on the story of Esther and Mordecai, King Ahasuerus (in Hebrew, Achashverash) and Haman, has been celebrated by Jews every year since the latter days of the Maccabees!

Unlike other festivals, it is secular in character, and only in later centuries did it take on religious features.

The story behind *Purim*, as it is recounted in the *Megillah*, or "Scroll" of the Book of Esther, concerned a plot by the grand vizier Haman to exterminate all the Jews in the Persian

Spice boxes—their designs are myriad, Warsaw, 18th century.

Empire. At first he succeeded in having King Ahasuerus (some historians identify him as Xerxes I [485-465 B.C.E.]; others as Artaxerxes II [404-361 B.C.E.]) issue a decree ordering the massacre of all Jews in the empire. This was to take place on the 14th day of Adar (February-March), this date being decided upon by the casting of lots. That is why the holiday is called the Feast of *Purim* (Feast of Lots).

Habdalah ceremony, Germany, 1850-60.

In his argument for killing the Jews, Haman drew upon all the well-known reasoning of anti-Semites through the ages. "There is a certain people scattered abroad and dispersed among the peoples in all the provinces of thy kingdom; and their laws are diverse from those of every people." Furthermore, he said, they were disloyal and subversive and might prove a menace to the power of the king.

King Ahasuerus was readily won over to Haman's plan because the latter had made it more attractive by suggesting that the Jews being numerous and rich the plunder taken from them would fill the royal coffers. He was even ready to guarantee the king twelve hundred talents of silver.

But before the plan could be carried through, it was frustrated by the Jewish official, Mordecai, who, unbeknown to Ahasuerus, was the uncle of the king's favorite wife, Esther. Through her intercession Haman was exposed and hanged on the very gallows he had built for Mordecai. On the 14th

Megillah, engraved by the Jewish artist Salomon d'Italia, 17th century.

Mordecai's Triumph.   *Rembrandt*

of Adar, the day set for the general massacre, the Jews of the kingdom rose up in arms and assisted the authorities of the land in beating back the attacks of their numerous enemies. In commemoration of that stirring event, the Festival of *Purim* was instituted.

In past centuries the day was unique in the manner of its observance; no Jewish festival approached it in its gay carnival spirit. It was marked by all kinds of mummery and burlesque. Some people drank more than was good for them. That is how the Yiddish folksaying originated—"Everything is allowed on *Purim.*"

Borrowing from the Roman carnival of Renaissance days, Jews introduced into *Purim* the custom of masquerading and buffoonery. The mirth overflowed from the home into the synagogue and from the synagogue into the street.

Children especially loved to masquerade. They went from house to house singing a popular *Purim* jingle, the main point of which was: "Give me a penny!" Even the synagogue became the scene of light-hearted merriment. During the reading aloud of the *Scroll of Esther,* every time the name

of the perfidious Haman was mentioned it was a signal for the children to raise a din with *greggers,* clappers and other noisemakers. Some banged with hammers on a stone, others stamped their feet and hooted.

Purim musicians, Prague, 1741.

Like all festive occasions *Purim,* too, called for conviviality, singing and special food. Beginning with the late sixteenth century in central and eastern European countries there were special *Purim* plays performed in Yiddish. These were of a comic and boisterous character. *Shalachmones,* gifts of food and drink, were exchanged, the poor being especially remembered. There was much merry group singing and traditional Purim delicacies were eaten, principally *Hamantaschen* (Haman-pockets). These are triangular pastries filled with poppy-seed or prunes.

Folk-art picturization of the story of *Purim.*

Purim players, Holland, 1657.

JEWS UNDER THE GREEKS AND ROMANS

Alexander the Great

Almost one hundred years after Ezra and Nehemiah, mastery over Judea changed hands: Alexander the Great, by smashing the Persian Empire, became the overlord of Palestine.

Alexander, the pupil of the philosopher Aristotle, was a man of generous and broad view for the times. He showed friendship for the Jews, and when he established the city of Alexandria in Egypt as a world metropolis in 332 B.C.E.; he invited the Jews of Judea to settle there. Moreover, he set a pattern of civilized tolerance for national minorities within the empire.

The large cities in the vast new Hellenistic Empire had a magnetic attraction for Jews of intellect and initiative. The equal rights and opportunities they could enjoy there, especially in Egypt, siphoned off a large number of Jews from the homeland. The most populated settlements during the next several centuries sprang up in Egypt, Syria and Asia Minor. In smaller numbers they colonized Cyrenaica, Carthage, Abyssinia, Morocco, Mesopotamia, the Crimea, Greece, Bulgaria, Armenia, Arabia and Spain.

This fact should help dispel the myth so widely believed: that the dispersion began with the destruction of Jerusalem in 70 C.E. There is ample evidence that during the last Hellenistic period, for instance, there were some three or four million Jews in Palestine, and even more than that number living in foreign countries! In fact, according to the Jewish philosopher Philo of Alexandria, there were more than a million Jews living in Egypt in his day, two hundred and fifty thousand of them in the city of Alexandria alone. Actually, more Jews lived in that foreign metropolis than in the all-Jewish city of Jerusalem, which had a population of about two hundred thousand!

Jews Become Greeks

The remarkable feature of Hellenism was that it was a cosmopolitan force. It was also a great cultural leveler. By giving the various peoples of the Mediterranean world a common tongue—Greek, a common literature, philosophy, art, music, dress and manners, it broke down many divisive national distinctions.

One of the explanations offered for the extraordinary size of the Jewish communities in foreign lands during that period was the large number of converts to the Jewish religion. This is a fact of extraordinary historic significance. During the Hellenistic period Gentiles joined the Jewish fold in great numbers. Philo was, therefore, led to make the statement that the Laws of Moses "attract and win the attention of all, of barbarians, of Greeks, of dwellers on the mainland and islands, of nations of the east and west, of Europe and Asia, of the whole inhabited world from end to end."

Perhaps one of the reasons for this was that the Greek and Roman societies which had built their state power on the system of slavery, with all its attending evils, had begun to repel ever-increasing numbers of people. They found the gentle and ethical precepts of the Jewish religion very attractive. Jewish democratic institutions, practices of mutual aid and benevolence, concern with spiritual rather than with the material elements of religious practice, proved alluring to them. Rabbis and preachers were constantly moving from one foreign settlement to another. They gave public lectures in the Greek language and everywhere found many attentive non-Jewish hearers. It can hardly be doubted that these Jewish missionary labors made many converts.

Ironically enough, just as other peoples were being assimilated by Jewish life and ideas, Jews, in their turn, whether in Judea itself or in other countries, were rapidly assimilating Greek culture. Except in matters of religion, Jews in almost every other way behaved like Greeks. While in Palestine there were still many who prayed in Hebrew and spoke Aramaic, outside the country almost all Jews had adopted Greek as their language. They wore Greek dress and took Greek names such as Theodotos, Menelaus, Jason and Lysimachus.

A time came when Jews were no longer able to understand Aramaic, nor, for that matter, read Hebrew. That is why the Hebrew Bible had to be translated into Greek (the well-known Septuagint version). As reverently as a latter-day Talmudist of Volozhin would quote from Rashi, so did Philo in his sermons and religious writings cite the classic Greek poets and dramatists, historians and philosophers. It was a period of broad intellectual fusion. And so Jewish writers and scholars became facile practitioners in all the fields of general Greek culture. They were philosophers, poets, historians, rhetoricians and even mural painters.

These Jewish intellectuals tried hard to reconcile Judaism with the current Greek philosophy. Aristobulus (180-146 B.C.E.), the first Jewish philosopher in the Greek sense of the word, even claimed that Jewish *chochma* and Greek wisdom were one and the same thing. For proof, he argued that

Left. Alexander the Great (*Louvre*). *Right.* Ptolemy I, King of Egypt and founder of the Graeco-Egyptian dynasty.

Page from the Vatican manuscript of the Septuagint version of Exodus XIX 14-XX 17.

"Plato followed the laws given to us [i.e., the *Torah*] and had manifestly studied all that is said in them."

However, the real danger to the preservation of the Jewish faith and identity in Hellenistic times did not arise so much from the intellectuals as from the upper classes and those in official positions. The latter elements, especially in Judea during the overlordship of the Syrian Seleucid dynasty of the second century B.C.E., tried very hard to ape their foreign oppressors in every way. Moreover, for the price of being "accepted" by their masters they were willing to act as their agents for the destruction of the Jewish religion and national identity. For instance, in 170 B.C.E., Jason, the High Priest in Jerusalem, in order to curry favor with Antiochus Epiphanes, built a Greek gymnasium adjoining the Temple. There Jews were encouraged to perform in all kinds of sports and athletics, such as wrestling, discus throwing, slinging and archery.

Left. Coin of Antiochus (Epiphanes) IV. *Right*. Ptolemy (Philadelphus) II and his wife Arsinoë, during whose reign the Septuagint was translated.
Kunsthistorisches Museum, Vienna

Many of the pious were horrified by this heathen innovation. They considered it the essence of impiety and a sharp break from the traditional religious-intellectual values. Nonetheless, other religious leaders did not take this extreme view of physical sport.

When the Romans arrived on the scene about a century after the Maccabean revolt, they found assimilationist elements in high places who wished to be even more Roman than the Romans. In place of the Greek gymnasium these "modernists" introduced the circus. Gladiatorial contests were held between Jews and, as in Rome, they often were fought to the death. Resh Lakish, for instance, one of the sages of the *Talmud*, had been a gladiator in his youth. In fact, this "sport" became so popular that the Patriarch Gamaliel II gave it his religious sanction.

Resistance

Yet all this subversion of the earlier Jewish way of life by the aristocrats and the wealthy sophisticates did not take into consideration the great majority of Jews in Judea, settled in farming villages and small towns. There they could hardly enjoy the benefits, real or imagined, of Greek culture. They persisted in their ancient tastes and customs and felt nothing but scorn for those who allowed themselves to be enticed by the Hellenistic fashions. This constituted one of the major Jewish conflicts of the age. It was fought out bitterly between the Hellenistic party and the party of the traditionalists for several centuries.

The crisis was finally resolved. It is described in terse dramatic terms in the first two books of *Maccabees*. The arch villain in the tragedy was Antiochus Epiphanes IV, who ruled over the large Seleucid Empire from Antioch, his capital. A morbid ambition to rule the entire world had sent him on a military expedition against Egypt. On his return journey to Antioch he stopped off in Jerusalem. There he proceeded to destroy the houses, pull down the walls and plunder the Temple.

Antiochus next issued a decree "that all should be one people, and that each should forsake his own laws." Furthermore, he ordered the Jews to suspend their worship in the Temple and to cease their offering of sacrifices. Worse yet, he commanded that all Jews should demonstratively break their religious laws and practices, "should profane the Sabbath and feasts and pollute the Sanctuary . . . that they should build altars and temples and shrines for idols; and should sacrifice swine's flesh . . . and that they should leave their sons uncircumcised." And he who did not obey "the word of the king, he shall die."

On the fifteenth day of the month of Kislev in the year 168 B.C.E. the Temple sanctuary was desecrated. A gigantic statue of Jupiter Olympus was raised on a pedestal behind the altar of sacrifice. And the Temple courts, where formerly the priests had offered sacrifices and the Levites had raised their voices in Hebrew psalmody, became the scene for lewd bacchanalian revels.

A cry of anguish and indignation convulsed the Jews in Judea as well as in the foreign settlements. They could not be bludgeoned into becoming Hellenistic pagans, and refused to obey the king's decrees, come what might. Thousands were slain, thousands fled into the wilderness, into the mountains, or hid in caves. They wandered about, famished and hunted, dressed in skins of sheep and goats, and daring to show their faces only when darkness fell.

The Tradition of Martydom

It was in this time of trial that love of their religion and their people became a patriotic passion among the Jews of Judea. This was the beginning of the tradition of martyrdom, to die *al kiddush ha-Shem* (to sanctify His name). Especially stirring to latter-day Jews was the story of the martyrdom of Hannah and her seven sons who refused to forsake the God of their fathers even if it meant death. In the final agony of her seven sons she recalls to them wistfully in what spirit their late father had raised them: "He sang to us the words of David the Psalmist: 'Many are the afflictions of the just.'"

Out of this fervent religious emotionalism was born a mass

Hannah comforts her sons, who are about to die.

78

movement of the Pious. It was to exert a fundamental transformation in the character of later Jewish society and religion. It was militant, austere and puritanical and, most important of all, consumingly patriotic.

THE MACCABEES

Two years later, this movement flared up in rebellion. Into the town of Modin, not far from Jerusalem, there came the imperial Syrian commissioner Apelles to see that the decrees of Antiochus were carried out. He had an altar erected to Zeus and summoned all the inhabitants before it. "Come forth and do the command of the King," he ordered the aged priest, Mattathias the Hasmonean. But Mattathias refused. When one Jew, in fear of his life, started for the altar Mattathias drew a sword and pierced him through the heart. Then he called out to his fellow townsmen: "Whosoever is zealous for the Law and maintaineth the Covenant, let him come forth after me!"

Mattathias.

This served as the signal for the revolt of the Maccabees. Mattathias and his five sons fled into the mountains. There they were joined by many others, plain folk, poor farmers and sheep herders for the most part. They waged guerrilla warfare from their hiding place. They lay in wait for renegades and betrayers among their own people and killed them. They broke heathen altars, and where parents showed faintheartedness, they even circumcised infant boys by force.

Only one year later, in 167 B.C.E., when Mattathias felt that it was time for him to relinquish his leadership to more vigorous hands, he called together his five sons: John, Simon, Judah, Eleazar and Jonathan. Judah, known henceforth as the Maccabee, or "The Hammer," because of his extraordinary skill as a fighter, was appointed leader of the band. To his brother Simon were entrusted all the political affairs. The old priest then concluded with the exhortation: "And now, my children, be ye zealous of the Law, and give your lives for the Covenant of your fathers!"

And this they did. The band of fighters Judah led was small indeed. They were untrained as soldiers and fought with the most primitive weapons. But in the course of the fighting they picked up arms from the enemy. In time they became formidable warriors, moved to acts of valor by a passion the enemy neither possessed nor understood.

Judah was a brilliant tactician. He was consistently successful in confusing the enemy and in beating him by surprise attacks. Before each battle Judah tried to lift his men into an

exalted mood. First they fasted. Then they prayed. After that he spoke to them. During the decisive battle of Emmaus Judah exhorted his men: "It is better for us to die than to look on the calamities of our people and our Sanctuary." Many died that day, but the Jews won the battle.

Judah Maccabee Pursues the Enemy. _Doré_

The Temple Rededicated

Before long, moved by this fervor, the army of the Jews swept into Jerusalem. They found the Temple profaned and partly in ruins. Its great gates were burned, the chambers for the priests torn down. Angrily they turned on the statue of Zeus and smashed it. The adherents of the Hellenistic party in the capital fled to Syria to escape the vengeance of the people they had betrayed.

The Temple was cleared of all debris. Its courts were swept clean and its sanctuary was purified. New Temple vessels were made, for Antiochus had taken the old ones to Antioch. Priests untainted by Hellenistic sympathies were appointed to officiate at the sacrificial altars.

On the 25th day of the month of Kislev (December) in the year 165 B.C.E., Judah rededicated the Temple during a solemn convocation of the people. He lighted the lamps of the _menorah,_ offered incense on the golden altar and burnt-offerings on the altar of sacrifices.

HANNUKAH

In commemoration of the occasion, he decreed that on that same day every year the Jews were to celebrate _Hannukah,_ the Festival of Dedication, for eight days. They were to burn lights during this period, adding a new light each night. And so Hannukah is known also as the Festival of Lights and the _menorah_ is its outstanding symbol. Since it was a festival of rejoicing, it was proper to celebrate the triumph of the Jewish people in its struggle for freedom with songs of praise and thanksgiving.

A supernatural explanation for lighting eight candles is furnished by the _Talmud._ When the priests made ready for the service of dedication, they discovered that all the holy oil in the Temple had been made impure by the pagan rites which had been carried on there. After a thorough search they found a single cruse of unprofaned oil which bore the seal of the high priest during the days of the prophet Samuel. Although the vessel contained oil sufficient for only one day, it was proclaimed a miracle since it sufficed to light up the Temple for eight days, by which time new holy oil had been prepared by the priests.

And so, every year since then, whether in good or in evil times, _Hannukah_ has been faithfully and joyously celebrated

Hannukah lamps (*left to right*): First three, Palestine—Roman period; Germany, 1814; Poland, 18th century.

wherever Jews have lived. It is a secular holiday and work is permitted. Yet it has also a religious aspect observed both in the synagogue and in the home. The lighting of the *Hannukah* lamp in the home, whether burning waxen candles or oil, is a solemn ceremony performed nightly during the period. Appropriate benedictions are recited and psalms of thanksgiving are sung. The rite is concluded with the singing of *Ma'oz Tzur*, a well-beloved hymn.

Hannukah developed its own special food in East European countries, namely *latkes*, potato pancakes. All kinds of games are played, notably that of the *Hannukah draydl*, which resembles the English game of put-and-take, and gifts are exchanged between friends and family.

To Jews in all ages, the story of *Hannukah* dramatically demonstrated that there was no force in the world that could succeed in crushing the free and dedicated spirit in man.

THE ROMAN OCCUPATION

The Maccabean era lasted seventy-seven years under its Hasmonean princes. They held Judea together and returned it to its Hebraic traditions. The Hellenistic influences began to recede. Then in 63 B.C.E. Judea lost its sovereignty. The Roman legions under Pompey swept into Jerusalem and massacred many thousands.

Under the Romans there was a systematic but legal robbery of the people by means of taxation. Herod (37-4 B.C.E.), a half-Jew, was put on the throne by the Romans because he was both able and pliant. His spendthrift splendor and his vast building program, including the rebuilding of the Temple, were carried out for show. While it increased his glory, it helped ruin the country. He was followed in time by equally rapacious Roman governors who bled the people white and oppressed them without mercy.

Tomb of the *Sanhedrin*, Jerusalem. Early 1st century C.E. The Great *Sanhedrin* (Hebraized from the Greek *synedrion*, "assembly") was, according to the *Talmud*, the supreme court and state council for legislating and interpreting Jewish religious law and tradition. The tribunal, consisting of 71 members, existed from the Maccabean era to 66 C.E.

For this the Romans found willing collaborators from among the Sadducees, Jews who belonged to the aristocratic ruling class. Formerly that element had headed the Hellenistic party in Judea. Now it strove to be more Roman than the Romans and the struggle was on again between traditional Judaism and expedient assimilation.

But these very conditions gave rise to a new patriotic movement whose militant followers, drawn from the ranks of the Pharisees, were called Zealots. They were fiercely opposed to the Romans and to their own Jewish oppressors. They mustered unusual strength among the poor farmers, especially among the landless in Galilee, where, shortly after, Jesus was reported to have found his most numerous followers. They also gained many adherents in the cities and towns among the nearly starving working men, of whom there were a great many. The violent contrast between the condition of the very rich and of the very poor resulted in unhappy questioning in many minds. Revolt was seething everywhere in the land.

The Messiah

It was a period unique in all Jewish religious experience. It marked the peak development of Messianism among Jews. The idea of *saviors* was already well established in the 5th century B.C.E. We find Nehemiah saying: ". . . and in the time of their trouble, when they cried unto Thee, Thou heardest us from heaven; and according to Thy manifold mercies, Thou gavest them saviors who might save them out of the hand of their adversaries." Among these saviors undoubtedly were Moses, David and Elijah.

Because it was a time of acute suffering, much of the Jewish apocalyptic literature of that period was permeated with the expectation of the imminent coming of the Messiah. The prophets Ezekiel and Enoch had spoken awesomely of the drawing near of the Last Judgment and of the Resurrection, both of which had now become associated in the popular mind with the era of the Messiah. It was the tradition among Jews that the Messiah would come when the affliction of the Jewish people became unendurable.

Suffering, insecurity, and the helplessness of the Jews under the iron heel of Rome made them abandon faith in their own strength and efforts. They yearned increasingly for a supernatural redeemer who would have the invincible power to bring the enemies of Israel to justice and who would usher in the era of the Kingdom of God on earth. The prophets, beginning with Isaiah, had articulated this desire and dream, which they expected would bring everlasting peace and happiness not only for the Jewish people but for all of mankind. They had a vision of an ideal ruler who once more would raise up the fallen kingdom of David whose departed glories so haunted and tormented the Jews of later days. It finally became a fixed tradition that the Messiah would be of the stock of David.

The Essenes

The unhappy times gave rise to sects of pietists of all kinds who were preparing themselves for the imminent coming of the Messiah, son of David. Idealistic brotherhoods of the poor and of the socially rejected formed as an escape from the social evils of the day. The best known of these were the Essenes. They fled from the cruelty and corruption of the cities to the peace of the countryside. Philo, who was well acquainted with the Essenes and their mode of life, wrote about them as follows:

"There they live together, organized into corporations, free unions, boarding clubs, and are regularly occupied in various tasks for the community. For none of them wishes to have any property of his own, either a house, or a slave, or land, or herds, or anything else productive of wealth. But rather by joining together everything without exception they all have a common profit from it."

While the Essenes were pacifists who wished to do away with violence, poverty and inequality by setting an example with their own dedicated lives, the Zealots, on the contrary, were men who believed in militant action. It was they who finally rose in rebellion against Rome. Not once, but time after time it required the full armed might of the Roman legions to quell their uprisings.

The Jewish historian Josephus speaks of several contemporary "messiahs" who were the leaders of these armed revolts. Three of them were especially important: Judas of Galilee, who led a rebellion in 6 C.E., Theudas in 44 C.E. and Benjamin "the Egyptian" in 60 C.E.

All these messiahs, when captured by the Romans, were crucified, the customary form of execution for rebels. On one occasion the Romans crucified two thousand of the rebels and sold thousands more into slavery.

Jewish Influences on Christianity

Nothing is known about the life of Jesus of Nazareth, the Messiah according to the Christians and the founder of Christianity, except what is found in the Gospels of the New Testament, which Biblical scholars estimate as having been written in the latter half of the first century C.E.

Judging by the words and actions of Jesus, as recorded in the Gospels, he quite clearly was a teacher of exalted purpose and purity of character who loved people and was ready to lay down his life in serving them. He was very likely an Essene, and the disciples who gathered around him lived in a commune resembling that of the Essenes. Jesus required of his disciples that they pool their property and have a common treasury.

It is clear from Jesus' own assertions, according to the Gospels, that he did not aim to found a new religion: "Think not that I came to destroy the Law [i.e., the *Torah*] of the Prophets: I come not to destroy but to fulfill" (Matt. 5:17). He observed scrupulously all Jewish feasts. Moreover, he taught Jewish doctrines and ethics. The widely held belief that Christianity introduced a new conception of morality into the world is, on the basis of the historic record, an overstated one. Jesus' whole system of ethics, sometimes even down to the very expressions he used, were derived from current Jewish Pharisee teachings. Also, the notion that the Jews believed in a God of Vengeance and that Christianity first projected a God of Love is from an historical point of view equally untenable. Jewish writings *before* and *during* the time of Christ prove this conclusively.

There are innumerable references in Jewish writings, centuries before Jesus, which condemn hatred, cruelty, envy, lying and, conversely, which glorify truth, love of man, gentleness, generosity of spirit and forgiveness. The ethics of Jesus were totally Jewish, and they were derived from the Mosaic commandment: "Love thy neighbor as thyself."

To cite only a few examples: The Book of Proverbs, written many centuries before the Christian movement arose, wished to establish the moral truth that: "The reasonable man is noble, he glories in pardoning injury." In fact, the prayer uttered by pious Jews before lying down at night exalts this virtue for all men and for all time: "Master of the World, I pardon every transgression and every wrong done to my person, to my property, to my honor or to all that I have. Let no one be punished on my account." Moreover, the essence of the Lord's Prayer, the supreme expression of Christian faith, is obviously derived from Jewish religious writings, even using some of the same figures of speech. For instance, Philo, who was not only a Greek philosopher, but also the chief rabbi of Alexandria, exhorted: "If you ask pardon for your sins do you also forgive those who have trespassed against you. For remission is granted for remission."

It was tragically inevitable that Jesus should have suffered the same fate as Judas of Galilee, Theudas and Benjamin the Egyptian, each of whom, incidentally, was also called by his followers "King of the Jews." While the other "messiahs" led armed rebellions against Rome and were crucified for doing so, the preachings of Jesus and the devoted following that clustered around him, although pacifist in nature, were also considered inimical to the security of the Roman state in Judea.

Jesus preached publicly that the Kingdom of God was at hand, and exhorted the people to repent and to make ready for the era of the Messiah—Son of David. (The Hebrew word *Mashiach*, meaning "The Anointed," is *Messiah* in English. The Greek word for Messiah is *Christos*.)

To Roman ears, not used to this mystic conception of a savior, it sounded very much like high treason against the Emperor in Rome. Whatever the title "King of the Jews," by which his followers called him, may have signified to Jesus, to the Romans it probably appeared only that another Judas of Galilee or a Theudas had arisen to challenge the imperial authority. They promptly arrested Jesus and tried him for plotting against the state. He was found guilty and condemned to die in the usual *Roman* way, by crucifixion.

Whose Was the Guilt?

The religious basis for anti-Semitism in the Christian world was derived from the accusation, as it appears in the Christian Gospels, that it was the Jews who really were to blame for the death of Jesus. The epithet "Christ-killer" as a synonym for "Jew" was bandied with unthinking ease by many Christians through the ages. In modern times, Christian historians, including liberal theologians, have begun to re-examine critically the Gospel accounts of the Passion and Crucifixion of Jesus. A number of them have come to the conclusion that, because of the overheated emotionalism with which the story is charged, the Jewish part in the death of Jesus has been greatly exaggerated. True enough, it is quite conceivable that being hailed as the Messiah by his followers must have aroused intense opposition toward him on the part of the Pharisees who upheld the traditional views of Judaism. At his trial, according to one Gospel account, when the High Priest Caiaphas asked Jesus: "Art thou the Messiah?" he unhesitatingly answered: "I am, and ye shall see the Son of Man at the right hand of God."

Jesus' messianic role may have seemed to the rabbis of his day as fraught with the greatest danger to the Jewish people, since it aroused the apprehensions of the Roman authorities. Moreover, the claim of Jesus that he was the Messiah in itself could have been considered unforgivable heresy by the rabbis. Obviously, then, they had to oppose him as they would have any other preacher of heresies they considered inimical to Judaism.

As for the High Priest Caiaphas, who figured in the trial of Jesus, he was a pro-Roman Sadducee. As such he was probably ready at all times to do the will of the Roman authorities, even if it were at the expense of his own people. Actually, point out some New Testament scholars, it would be absurd and unrealistic to believe that there was the slightest possibility that the arrogant and despotic Roman procurator Pontius Pilate would have for one moment considered delegating his own supreme judicial powers to Jews whom he despised. After all, they stress, was it not the Jews with whom he constantly was struggling to keep from rebellion? Where would be the sense then of allowing these very Jews to pass sentence on an alleged "King of the Jews"?

The later Gospel writers, many historians agree, were anxious to placate the Romans, whom they wished to win over as converts to their sect. Since anti-Jewish feeling was widespread among upper-class Romans at this time, because of the constant harassment the Jews were causing them with their rebellions, it was probably advantageous for Christian missionaries to picture Jews in an unflattering way. Conversely, the actions of the Romans in connection with the crucifixion of Jesus were to be put in the most sympathetic light in order to prove that they had no part in it. Therefore, the legal-minded Pilate, after sitting in judgment upon the accused Jesus, is made by the Gospel writer to say to the Jews: "Behold, I bring him forth to you; that ye may know that I find no fault in him."

Although nowhere in Jewish writings is there any mention made of the custom of letting a condemned criminal go free on Passover, the Roman procurator supposedly invokes it. They, "the rabble," are thereupon given the privilege of setting free either Jesus or Barabbas, a common thief. And in order to make the alleged crime of the Jews appear still more heartless, the Gospel writers have them shout for Barabbas' release. This free choice dooms Jesus. He is crucified—*by the Romans....*

THE SYNAGOGUE

It was when the Jews were in Exile and in adversity that the synagogue first came into being. Far from the Temple, which lay in ruins in Jerusalem, the Jews in Babylonia wished

Ruins of Herod's "Street of Columns" in Samaria.

White marble throne of the archisynagogos in the Synagogue of Delos, Greece, 2nd century B.C.E.

Throne of the archisynagogos in the Synagogue of Chorasim Galilee, 2nd century C.E.

Probably the oldest representation of the Star of David, in the Synagogue of Capernaum, Palestine, 2nd century B.C.E.

Menorah motifs in frieze over door of Jewish residence in ancient Nave, Roman Period.

Small synagogue. (Representation from a mosaic of the 5th century, Rome.)

Left. Mosaic representation of Aron-ha-Kodesh in synagogue at Beth-Alpha, Palestine, 6th century C.E.

The Aron-ha-Kodesh of the ancient Peki'in Synagogue, Palestine, said to date from the days of the Second Temple. Has been in use since then without interruption.

to maintain their religious life to whatever extent possible. Since they could no longer offer sacrifices to the Lord in their own sanctuary, "so will we render for bullocks the offering of our lips."

Prayers Instead of Sacrifices

Thus the institution of formal prayer was established and given priority over worship by sacrifice. Even though the synagogue had not formally come into being, Jews who lived in scattered communities throughout the river country of Babylonia congregated on the Sabbath and during the festivals for prayer as well as for public discussion of communal problems. They intoned prayers and sang hymns and psalms in unison. They felt drawn together by the warmth and fervor of common beliefs and rites. In this group life they found an island of safety in a sea of hostility.

The institution of prayer took such a firm hold in time that after the Return and following Ezra's innovations, the popularity of animal sacrifices in the Temple in Jerusalem sharply declined. Often enough, the offering of more agreeable incense was substituted. Implicit with ethical meaning, a more spiritualized conception of divine worship was evolving. No one in ancient Jewry described this substitute for altar sacrifice better than a contemporary of the last days of the Temple, Philo, the philosopher-rabbi of Alexandria. "Though the worshippers bring nothing else, in bringing themselves they offer the best sacrifices, the full and truly perfect oblation of noble living, as they honor with hymns and thanksgivings their Benefactor and Savior, God."

One of the profoundest changes effected by the synagogue was to bring communion with God directly and easily to the worshipper. Whereas before the Jew could only worship Him through the spectacular mediation of the priest and by means of the material sacrifice he could afford to offer, now he was enabled to commune with Him simply and unrestrainedly at all times. It was either with a prayer on his lips or a wordless prayer in his heart. The Jewish priest-caste thus began withering away, and a large class of rabbis and teachers took its place even before the Temple's final fall. By means of common prayer and the study of sacred writings fraternal bonds of an indestructible kind were wrought. The religion of Israel had thus become both spiritual and democratic in the deepest sense of the words. Historically it was an event without parallel.

Many Sanctuaries Instead of One

Thereafter, wherever Jews lived in any community where a *minyan*, or a quorum, of ten male worshippers could be mustered for public prayer, it was obligatory for them to build a synagogue, and so the entire community life of Jews began to center around it. True enough, the pious were still expected to go on pilgrimages to the Holy City during the three great festivals of the year. The Temple, however, had been transformed from the sole sanctuary into a great national religious shrine where the most impressive sacrificial rites were still performed. But the hearts and the minds of the people turned increasingly to the local synagogue. It represented, even if not the most dramatic and spectacular, certainly their most intimate, daily religious experience.

The very word *synagogue* is derived from the Greek *syna-*

Floor mosaic of the Zodiac at Beth-Alpha Synagogue, Palestine, 6th century C.E.

gogé and means "assembly" or congregation. Henceforth, it was the "together-ness" of the Jews which marked their history and their activities. It welded and integrated them by means of a common way of life. The *Torah* and the synagogue thereafter constituted their religious, cultural and psychic center.

All in Israel Are Brothers

The functions of the synagogue after the Destruction were many, and they applied to almost every aspect of Jewish community life. The synagogue was simultaneously a House of Prayer, a House of Study and a House of Assembly. Moreover, it was also a House of Charity and a House of Judgment. It was there that the distribution of clothing to the poor and of *matzohs* and wine to the needy on the day of Passover Eve took place. It was there that societies of the pious were formed and met to take care of every kind of benevolence and mutual aid required within the community. There were societies to visit the sick, to bury the dead, to comfort the sorrowing, to lend money without interest to the needy, to feed and clothe orphans and widows, to provide dowries for penniless girls, to help raise ransom for some afflicted fellow-Jew or Jewish community and to redeem Jewish slaves. This practice of mutual aid in the concrete works of compas-

sion for the suffering and the needy, this identification of the individual Jew with all other Jews led to the coining of the famous saying, "All in Israel are brothers."

When the Jewish people were dispersed and fragmentized it was the institution of the synagogue which not only held the Jews together but gave them the identity and the moral strength to endure. The destruction of one, or even of a hundred, synagogues did not mean the end of everything as it had when the Temple was destroyed. Synagogues could always be replaced by other buildings on the original sites or elsewhere. The original concept of the Temple was deepened, enlarged and universalized.

In the course of several centuries, synagogues sprang up in every city, town and village of Judea. There the children were taught and their elders studied the *Torah* and heard it expounded. In far-away Alexandria, in Persia and the Crimea, in Babylonia and Yemen, in Rome and Greece, in Syria and Asia Minor and wherever else there were Jewish communities Jewish life became centered in the synagogue. Tradition has it that in Jerusalem alone there were 394 synagogues at the time when the Temple was destroyed by Titus.

Architecture of the Synagogue

It may be accepted as a truism that, no matter how segregated Jews were from the rest of the population in whose

Frescoes in Dura-Europos Synagogue, Syria, 3rd century C.E. *Courtesy of Yale University Art Gallery*

Below left. Synagogue at Kfar Birim, Galilee; existed before the destruction of the Second Temple. *Right.* Synagogue at Kfar Nahum (Capernaum), 2nd century B.C.E.

midst they lived, they, nonetheless, were exposed at all times to local cultural influences. The architecture of the synagogue and its interior decoration always reflected local and contemporary styles. In Hellenistic-Roman times Jewish houses of worship bore all the well-known features of Greek and Roman architecture. Later, in medieval Spain under the dominant influence of Islamic architecture, the synagogue was built in classic Moorish style. Subsequently, in other parts of western and southern Europe, the synagogue was designed according to prevailing architectural fashions, Byzantine, Romanesque, Gothic, Renaissance, Baroque, and still later styles in turn. In Russia and Poland, where in later times most of the Jews of the world came to live, the ancient synagogues outwardly resembled the various styles of church architecture current there. This held somewhat less true of the Polish wooden synagogues (seventeenth to eighteenth centuries), which reveal a striking Mongolian "pagoda" style. This may have been due partly to the lingering influence of the refugee Khazar Jews from the East.

Nonetheless, however polyglot and different the styles of synagogue architecture were, they succeeded in preserving certain classic features which were fixed by tradition. The interior, for instance, had to consist of a vestibule, the hall of the synagogue itself and the *Aron ha-Kodesh,* the holy Ark or chest containing the Scrolls of the Law, which was built into a niche in the wall. In these features the synagogue perpetuated the principal architectural elements of the Temple in Jerusalem. Naturally, like the Ark that stood in the Holy of Holies, the Ark in the synagogue also constituted its holiest

spot. In memory of the Temple it was mandatory that it face east, toward Jerusalem. No effort or expense was considered too great to make it beautiful. It was usually flanked by pillars with sculptured lions standing guard before them, and an eight-branched *menorah* in the center. A perpetual lamp glowed like an all-seeing eye before it, and the Tables of the Law, modeled in relief with the Ten Commandments in Hebrew upon them, stood crowned above it. Over the Ark hung a curtain of red silk, brocade or velvet embroidered with decorative religious symbols in gold and silver thread. The Ark was usually carved with flowers, leaves, birds, lions, deer and fanciful arabesques, but no specimen has ever been found bearing any representation of the human face or figure.

Although the *Talmud* attempted to lay down directions for the construction of the synagogue, these proved so vague and even contradictory that they could not be followed except as a general guide. Since nothing created by man remains static, synagogue architecture, too, underwent a gradual development in which non-Jewish national and local influences by no means played an unimportant part. For example, an innovation during the Graeco-Roman period was the erection of the *Bimah,* meaning "stage" in Greek, or as it was later called, *Almemor,* a word derived from the Arabic "alminbar," pulpit.

Until very recent times it was generally assumed that the art of the synagogue rigidly forbade any representation of the human face or figure in sculpture, relief or painting. It was based on the assumption that the Mosaic commandment against the making of images, which was to discourage idol worship, was strictly observed by Jews. However, excavations

Relief from the Synagogue at Priene, Greece, showing *menorah*, and to left, *lulab* and *ethrog*; to right, *shofar* and willow branch.

Jewish catacombs in Beth Shearim, Israel, 3rd century, C.E.

Figures with representation of a *menorah* in the Torlonia Catacombs, Rome.

Cover from a Roman funerary urn of a Jewish actress, Faustina, 1st or 2nd century C.E. Besides the Jewish symbols of *shofar*, *menorah* and *lulab*, the inscription bears the Hebrew word "Shalom" (Peace).

Stone ossuary, or bone-casket, from Judea, c. 1st century C.E.

of ancient synagogues during the last few decades have demonstrated how wrong that belief was. In Beth Alpha, a sixth century C.E. synagogue in Palestine, a remarkable floor mosaic was found. It was of Hellenistic design and workmanship and, startlingly enough, showed human faces! Far from this being considered heretical by the Jews of those days when the *Talmud* was being created, the synagogue carries this enthusiastic memorial in Greek: "Blessed are the creators of this work, Marianus and his son Chanina."

The discovery in 1932 of the synagogue at Dura-Europos in Syria proved even more astonishing. The entire wall surface of this house of worship, built in 245 C.E., was covered with frescoes Graeco-Roman in style and strikingly similar to those found in the Greek temple of Zeus Theos. Each fresco was painted by a different artist, an indication that there were a considerable number of accomplished Jewish painters in that period. The wall-paintings are on such Jewish religious and historic themes as the Temple in Jerusalem; Ezra the Scribe reading from the Scrolls of the *Torah;* the finding of the infant Moses in the bulrushes; David being anointed king and the apocalyptic vision of Ezekiel. To show to what extent Greek culture had infiltrated into Jewish thinking in those days there is even a fresco showing David the harpist in the role of Orpheus, holding animals and beasts in thrall with his music.

During the Renaissance, representations of the human face, although not of the entire body, were sometimes permitted by the more advanced rabbis of Italy and Provence. This we have on the authority of the religious leaders Rabbi Leona da Modena of Venice and Rabbi Profiat Duran of Perpignan.

In the ruins of the most ancient synagogues, even in those of Kfar Nahum, or Capernaum, which existed in the days of the Second Temple, recognizable Jewish religious symbols have been found. Perhaps the most surprising was the *Magen David,* the star of David, found in Kfar Nahum. It was used as a decoration on one of the capitals. This is of special interest because, according to the Christian gospels, Jesus of Nazareth preached there. It is undoubtedly the earliest star of David ever found. It was not until modern times, though, that the *Magen David* became accepted as the universal symbol of the Jewish faith and people. Actually, for more than two thousand years and until modern times, the *menorah* or seven-branched candlestick and the Tables of the Ten Commandments were the principal symbols. They have figured inevitably in the decoration of synagogues and Jewish tombstones since the nineteenth century.

Of course there are a number of other Jewish religious symbols, although of lesser significance. These are the *shofar* (ram's horn), the *lulav* (palm branch), the *ethrog* (citron), the lion of Judah, lavers, shovels, oil jars and other vessels and utensils used in the Temple service, the royal crown of the *Torah,* and the hands of the *cohen* or priest outspread in benediction. Not the least popular of these symbols has been the circular Zodiac with its signs for each lunar month in the Jewish calendar. Since Hellenic times it has graced many a ceiling, and sometimes floor, of the synagogue structure.

THE END OF THE JEWISH STATE

During the early rule of the Romans over Judea, the Jews felt their conqueror's mailed fist on their political and economic life. Yet, in matters purely religious, both the Jews in the homeland and those who lived in foreign colonies of the empire enjoyed considerable freedom. All this changed as the millennium drew to a close.and anti-Jewish feeling began to spread, not only in Rome but in Alexandria and in other places as well.

Persecution Begins

Persecution of the Jews on a systematic basis started during the reign of the Emperor Tiberius. In the year 19 C.E. he ordered the expulsion of all Jews from Rome. From that time on repressive measures were increasingly imposed. The Sanhedrin, the supreme council and tribunal of the land, which was composed of seventy-one leading priests and elders, found itself stripped of many of its legislative and judicial powers. The puppet Jewish kinglets placed over the people were little more than tax collectors and assistants to the Roman procurator in Jerusalem. As we have already seen, the foreign despots found willing tools to help keep the people quiet and in subjection.

In the course of more than a century, there were many abortive revolts aimed at the overthrow of Roman authority. Their frequency and savagery left unhealing wounds on the spirit of the people. Moreover, they caused great material devastation.

The Revolt of 66 C.E.

National pride had been humbled, religious sensibilities had been outraged, the land was seething and a great upheaval was inevitable. This erupted violently in the year 66 C.E. It could not be stopped either by fear of reprisal by the Roman legions or by the pleadings of the quietist Pharisees. It could not even be stopped by the machinations of the aristocratic and high-priestly collaborators of the Romans—the Sadducees.

The pattern of the revolt was bewildering and involved. The Romans found even their military might inadequate for putting it down. The zealots fought with the ferocity of men imbued with the spirit of a sacred cause, like the Maccabees before them. Furthermore, their principal leaders, John of Gischala and Simon bar Giorah, were brilliant tacticians. They were completely dominated by the idea that, by fighting for the freedom of their people, they were fulfilling the will of God.

What the rebels lacked in numbers, in supplies and in weapons, they made up for in consecration. They could muster only some twenty-three thousand fighting men, whom they pitted against some sixty thousand superbly trained and equipped Romans. It was no longer possible, as it had been in the time of Judah the Maccabee, to engage in the hit-and-run type of warfare. The Romans, with their characteristic foresight, had seen to that. They had built excellent military roads throughout the country. The surprise attack, therefore, could no longer be as effective as before, since reinforcements could be brought up quickly.

Adroitly the leaders of the rebellion decided on a different strategy: they concentrated their troops in strongly fortified key positions behind high walls constructed of huge stone blocks that could withstand long siege.

The first surprise blow the Zealots struck was at the Jerusalem garrison. They overpowered it, seized the Temple fortress, and began making preparations for the long siege by the Romans that was inevitable.

The Siege of Jerusalem

That Rome did not consider this uprising of a casual nature is attested by the fact that Emperor Nero eventually was obliged to dispatch Vespasian, his most able general, to quell it. Previous Roman forces had not only been powerless to do so but had been annihilated.

The story of Vespasian's military campaign is long and involved. Confident of the might of his legions and of the endless resources of the Roman Empire, he resigned himself to reducing the rebel fortresses, one by one. The Zealots fought valiantly and well. Their leaders planned to exhaust the Romans with long sieges, but they did not anticipate that treachery within their own ranks would do Vespasian greater military service than his legions.

It was under the most dubious circumstances that the rebel commander of Galilee, Josephus (later the historian), led the Jewish armed forces. Although his treachery was long suspected by the highly intelligent John of Gischala, he, nonetheless, after making a pretense of fierce resistance, was enabled to surrender to the Romans all the strong points under his command. Shortly after, as if to put a seal on his betrayal, Josephus was openly attached to the Roman field staff and helped Vespasian fight against the Jews.

When news came to Vespasian in 69 C.E. during the siege of Jerusalem that the Emperor Nero had died, he relinquished his command to his son Titus and hurried back to Rome where he was made emperor.

Titus rushed to the walls of Jerusalem. He was a man of action and a very wily general. He proceeded to surround himself with Jewish renegades, but relied most heavily for counsel on Josephus, who had a complete knowledge of the rebel movement.

In later years, when Josephus had been ennobled and made "an honorary Roman" by the Romans for his services and had added Flavius to his name, he wrote a detailed but

Vespasian.   Titus.

87

Siege machines of the Romans before Jerusalem.

hardly veracious history of the events in which he had taken such a prominent part.

He wrote of how Titus had sent him close to the walls of the city where, by speaking into some kind of megaphone device, he exhorted the defenders not to throw away their lives uselessly but to surrender. They had scornfully turned down his request.

Titus then decided to become more persuasive by military means. He had brought with him the most formidable and the greatest number of siege engines ever used.

It was the rebels' misfortune that they were split into several rival factions. One group was outrightly terrorist. They thirsted for revenge both against the Romans and their Jewish collaborators and killed without mercy all those they suspected of sympathy or of dealings with the enemy. Another and larger group, under the leadership of John of Gischala, represented the middle-class religious patriots who were interested only in liberating the country. Still another large group, led by Simon bar Giorah, was composed mostly of farm laborers and city workmen who were stirred to rebellion by a special program obviously of Essene character. They strove not only to drive out the Romans but to do away with some of the social evils from which they were suffering. There was constant bickering. The various factions never could decide on a policy until the perilous moment the enemy attacked. Then they had no alternative but to stand together and fight.

It was during the Festival of Passover, "at the time of the singing of the birds," that Titus ordered the siege machines to be drawn up before the outer walls of the city. Each time his soldiers succeeded in putting one up, the rebels, under Simon bar Giorah and John of Gischala, made a fierce sortie from the gates and overwhelmed the Romans. They smashed the engines. As fast as the siege machines, such as banks, catapults and battering-rams, were destroyed, Titus had them repaired. Ultimately the rebels were helpless against them. Within fifteen days Titus had succeeded in breaching the outer walls.

The people, not only the regular soldiers, but even old men and women, fought back savagely. As the Romans climbed ladders to scale the walls, the defenders hurled huge stones on them. The women poured hot oil on their heads. Even the stones which the Romans catapulted over the walls into the city were flung back at them. This delayed the enemy; it did not stop him. The people were forced to retreat yard by yard.

Seventeen days later, with the methodical genius for which they were noted, the Romans had raised their siege structures opposite the Antonine Tower. The desperate situation called for desperate methods. With reckless bravery John of Gischala and Simon bar Giorah led a rebel detachment in a surprise sortie through a secret tunnel under the walls and set the structure on fire.

The farther the Romans advanced into the city, the more stubborn and heroic the resistance became. Josephus thought it a good time to broach again the matter of surrender. His pleas through his megaphone had no effect. All his promises of mercy from the Romans sounded hollow. The rebels soon found out what sort of mercy could be expected from Titus, whom his sycophants had ecstatically dubbed "The Delight of All Mankind." Every day, he would round up the Jewish prisoners, sometimes as many as five hundred, and have them crucified. Occasionally he varied his savagery: he cut off the hands of the prisoners and sent them back into the city in a procession.

These measures, abetted by stark hunger, succeeded at last in frightening many of those who had opposed the war in the first place. They stole out of the city to surrender. When Simon bar Giorah discovered a plot among his men to give themselves up, he took all the ringleaders and, in full view of the Romans, beheaded them.

As the days passed the situation became more desperate. Famine gripped the city. Starving people lay down on the streets to die. Thousands of corpses were strewn everywhere. There was no time to bury them.

Many of the faint-hearted realized that the city was doomed. Quarreling among the various factions only added to the demoralization. Once more Titus offered them the choice of surrender or death. John of Gischala replied that the City of God could not be destroyed and that the rebels were content to place themselves in God's hands. The defenders retreated into the fortress of the Temple area.

Once more the Romans moved up their war engines to the walls that girdled the Temple. Although weakened by hunger and exhaustion the Jews fought back with almost superhuman strength. Yet they knew they were doomed.

The Ninth of Ab

It was on the ninth of Ab that the defenders made their final stand. They made two last-ditch sorties, but both times they were driven back. Then a Roman soldier hurled a firebrand through the Golden Window of the Temple and the great wooden beams inside began to burn.

At the sight of the burning sanctuary the defenders were frantic. A desperate hand-to-hand struggle followed. Rather than fall into the hands of the Romans many chose to die in the flames. Thousands perished that day. The survivors who were identified by informers as rebels were promptly crucified. The flower of the country's youth was sent to work in the Roman mines. Others were sold into slavery, including many women.

Romans looting the Temple of its holy vessels. (Sculptured relief from the Arch of Titus, Rome.)

It was a ghastly procession of prisoners which wound its way in chains through Syria toward Rome. Seventeen thousand died on the way. In every city where he stopped, Titus sent hundreds of his captives into the arena to fight wild beasts, or he forced them to kill one another in gladiatorial contests. When he halted at Caesarea he celebrated his brother Domitian's birthday by such games. Twenty-five hundred Jewish youths died that day.

Roman victory coin: "Judea Captive."

Reading the Book of Lamentations on the Ninth of Ab, in a Polish synagogue, 19th century.

JERUSALEM DESTROYED

Jerusalem was utterly destroyed. It was now a wilderness of burned houses and desolation. According to the Roman historian Tacitus six hundred thousand Jews were killed or had died from starvation and disease during the siege of Jerusalem, which had lasted one year and a half. Almost the same number were led away as captives or slaves to Rome.

For all their scorn of the Jews, the Roman historians had to admit that the war with the Jews was the most fateful and desperate struggle in which the empire had ever engaged. Seven hundred of the leaders of the rebellion, including John of Gischala and Simon bar Giorah, followed Titus' triumphal chariot to Rome in chains.

It was politically expedient for the Romans to keep the Jews humiliated and to do everything in their power to prevent a recurrence of the bloody events which had proved so expensive to the empire. The Sanhedrin was dissolved and the half-shekel tax every Jew used to pay into the Temple treasury for its support was now insultingly diverted to the support of the Temple of Jupiter Capitolinus. Also, the high priesthood was abolished. From now on the religious head of the Jews was called *Nasi*, or Patriarch, but he possessed only limited powers.

Although the Jews were grief-stricken by their losses and by the destruction of their Temple and their state, they could not resign themselves to defeat. During the reign of the Emperor Trajan in 115 c.e. revolts flared up simultaneously in the populous Jewish centers of Egypt, Libya, Cyrenaica and Cyprus.

In the initial stages of this war the Roman legions were routed, but in the end, they managed to crush the uprisings in the Jewish settlements, one by one.

Bar-Kochba.

REVOLT OF BAR-KOCHBA

In 132-135 c.e., under the inspired military leadership of Simon bar-Kochba, rebellion once more broke out. It was Rabbi Akiba, the leading Rabbinic authority of the age, who gave it its motivating force. The expectation of the Messiah's coming was still as strong among the Jewish masses as it had been a century before. That Rabbi Akiba believed in the imminence of the End of Days is attested by the fact that he publicly proclaimed Bar-Kochba as the Messiah.

Left. Hadrian. *Right.* Rabbi Akiba. (From the Mantua *Haggadah*, 1650.)

Like all previous revolts against Rome, this one had specific provocation. The Emperor Hadrian apparently was moved by aims similar to those of Antiochus Epiphanes. He wanted to deprive the Jews of their uniqueness as a people, to force them to adopt the Roman religion, and by this and other methods of cultural assimilation, to end once and for all their inclination to rebel.

The fierce hostility of the Jews to his decrees, which forbade the rite of circumcision, the study of the *Torah* and the observance of the Sabbath and other holy days, finally erupted into open rebellion in 132 c.e. The struggle lasted for three and a half years and cost a staggering number of lives—

Bar-Kochba Coin of Liberation with Temple façade. *Jewish Museum*

580,000 killed, besides many thousands more who died of the pestilence and starvation. When it was over, the Roman writer, Dio Cassius, could say with full justification: "All of Judea became almost a desert."

Bar-Kochba's supreme confidence in final victory may have been due to his own belief, strengthened by the enthusiasm of Rabbi Akiba, that he was the Messiah and, therefore, invincible. The smashing defeats he inflicted on the proud Roman legions must have deepened this conviction. He was, furthermore, so confident in the prowess of his army that he once prayed before battle in the sight of his assembled host: "O Lord, do not help the enemy; as for us, we need no help."

The Pharisee quietists and pacifists among the Jews—those who would let well enough alone—and, of course, those of the pro-Roman faction, argued against the war in the same way the renegade Josephus had argued sixty-five years before: "Are you wealthier than the Gauls, stronger than the Germans, more intelligent than the Greeks, more numerous than all the peoples of the world?" Their plaintive voices were drowned, however, in the patriotic roar of the Jewish people.

The situation of the rebels was not completely hopeless. Bar-Kochba drove the Roman legions out of the country. Some historians believe that had he continued pursuing them instead of stopping at the borders of Syria, he might possibly have roused the entire colonial empire to rebel against Rome, so great was the social turmoil of the times.

Bar-Kochba declared the independence of Judea almost as soon as he had taken over command of the rebel forces. In emulation of the Maccabees, each year he struck special coins, commemorative shekels and half-shekels, with the Hebrew superscriptions, "First year after the liberation of Jerusalem" and "Redemption of Zion."

Hadrian, alarmed by the defeat inflicted on his legions, summoned his best general, Julius Severus, from Britain.

WAR OF ATTRITION

Julius Severus was a resourceful soldier. He realized that it would be folly for him, as it had been for other Roman generals, to engage the Jewish army in open battle. Rather, he decided to cut off their supplies and to starve them out. One by one, he isolated and then took by storm the strongholds of the Jews. Bar-Kochba was finally forced to flee to the last rebel stronghold of Bethar. For several months he held out there and managed to inflict great losses on the Romans, but Bethar fell in 135 C.E. and he with it. Most of the survivors were butchered. The *Talmud* mournfully tells that when Bethar fell, the blood of the murdered women and children flowed for a mile like a turgid stream into the nearby sea.

MARTYRS

Ten Rabbinic heroes, wise and gentle men, died the martyr's death. One of them, Hanina ben Teradion, had been found teaching the *Torah,* and the Romans, fitting the punishment to the crime, they thought, wrapped him in the parchment scroll of the *Sefer Torah* and burned him at the stake. Just as tragic was the end of Rabbi Akiba, the man who had been the "soul" of the rebellion. The Romans imprisoned him in Caesarea, tortured him constantly and tore the flesh off his body with a sharp iron comb. By dying, he said, he had at last found the most exalted way of affirming his belief in God and of fulfilling the commandment, "Thou shalt love the Lord thy God with all thy soul."

A thousand villages and fifty fortress cities lay in ruins. To symbolize the end of Jerusalem, the Romans raised a new city, called Aelia Capitolina, upon its site. In the Temple area they erected temples to their own deities, Venus and Bacchus, and there, where not so long before the sanctuary had stood, they built a temple in honor of Jupiter Capitolinus. For centuries thereafter Jews were not allowed in the city. Only on the ninth of Ab and only after paying heavy bribes were they allowed to visit the Wailing Wall, to grieve over the disaster to their sanctuary and their state. Judea was no more.

The Wailing Wall.

ISRAEL DISPERSED AMONG THE NATIONS

LOVE FOR ZION

The destruction of Jerusalem in 70 c.e. marked the death of the Jewish state. The crushing of the determined revolt of Bar-Kochba in 135 c.e. by Hadrian's legions put an end to the hope of re-establishing it by force. Yet, of course, it did not mark the end of the Jews as a people. If anything, the final Dispersion intensified Jewish consciousness of identity and tightened the bonds of group kinship.

The Jews who remained in Judea proved flexible enough to adjust to their new circumstances. If anything, their preoccupation with the *Torah* became even more consuming. In the hour of their supreme rejection by the world their religious cultural heritage became their principal unifying agent. The *Mishna* and *Gemara* were produced during this period.

To many, however, Jewish life in the country appeared constricted and unattractive. Because of the terrible impoverishment and desolation which had resulted from the wars of liberation against Rome, many emigrated in search of better opportunities to countries such as Babylonia, Syria, Egypt and Italy, where large Jewish settlements were already established.

It has already been noted that the Dispersion was not, as most people believe, an historical consequence of the destruction of Jerusalem by Titus. Actually, more Jews had been living in settlements outside of Judea than in it for several centuries before the end of the Jewish state. The elimination of Palestine as the national and religious-emotional center for the Jewish people only meant that thenceforth they were to consider themselves *exiles* and their separation from Zion as the *Galuth* (the Exile). It is this concept of the *Galuth* which never gave the Jews a moment's peace or resignation. They constantly turned a longing gaze toward their far-off homeland. When they prayed they faced reverently eastward toward Jerusalem, and their passionate love and mourning for Zion desolated pervaded the liturgy of the synagogue. "And to Jerusalem, Thy city, return in mercy . . . rebuild it soon in our days . . ." is a benediction the Jewish worshipper recites daily.

In every way possible the Jews throughout the world gave themselves ceaseless reminders that without Zion they were like children bereaved of their mother. It became the custom for pious Jews when they built a house or a synagogue to leave a square yard unfinished on one of the walls. On it they inscribed in Hebrew the words of the Psalmist: *Zecher La-churban,* "In memory of the Destruction." The Jewish child thus became acutely aware of the grief of his people at a very

"By the waters of Babylon." (Palestinian embroidery, 19th century.)   *Jewish Museum*

early age. It lingered on painfully in his consciousness all the years of his life until the day of his death when a little bag of holy Jerusalem earth was placed under his head to serve as a pillow to rest him until the Day of the Resurrection.

Because he had voluntarily chosen to go into perpetual mourning for the vanished glories of Zion and the Temple, the Jew banished sensory beauty from his world of experience. The *magrepha,* the organ played in the Temple, and the other musical instruments of the Levites were barred both by religious decision and custom from the synagogue service.

The Rabbinic sages, humane fathers of the people as well as down-to-earth rationalists, were greatly troubled by this obsessive grief of the Jews. Rabbi Joshua therefore cautioned: "Not to mourn at all is impossible, because the fatal decree [i.e., the Destruction] has already been enacted. To mourn too much is likewise impossible; it is beyond human endurance."

The Messianic Hope

The pious set themselves to waiting for the day when God, taking pity on the people's suffering, would send the Messiah. With His help they would be able not only to establish the Kingdom of God on earth, but they would be everlastingly re-

The Jewish cemetery in the Valley of Jehoshaphat, Jerusalem.

Above and right. Elijah blows the *shofar* and Messiah comes riding on his white horse to redeem Israel. (From *Haggadahs* of the 15th and 16th centuries.)

stored to their ancient homeland, and the sanctuary in Jerusalem would rise again even more splendidly than before.

This Messianic hope, nourished by despair and insecurity, at various times seemed about to be fulfilled but invariably ended in disappointment. To the religious Jew during the long centuries of the *Galuth,* however, the expectation of the Messiah, who would come riding on his white mount, blowing upon the *Shofar* of the Redemption, was hardly a dream. It was a certainty. He knew it would be fulfilled in God's own time by his ardent striving for self-perfection and righteousness.

Church and Synagogue

The *Galuth,* or Exile, entered into a new and seemingly interminable era with the triumph of Christianity in Europe. After Constantine the Great made the new faith the state religion of the Byzantine Empire, it spread elsewhere on the continent. Then the savage and systematic persecution of the Jews began. Although in his Edict of Toleration issued in Milan in 313 C.E. Constantine had included the sufferance of Jews and Judaism, nonetheless they did not enjoy civil equality with either Christians or pagans. Only two years later he initiated a series of repressive edicts, including those forbidding Jews to seek converts or to intermarry with Christians. His reason for their exclusion from the rest of society was that they were "a nefarious and perverse sect."

Constantine the Great.

Two centuries later, the Emperor Justinian (527-565) issued his celebrated code which laid the legal groundwork for anti-Semitism as a permanent Christian state policy. One clause provided: "They [the Jews] shall enjoy no honors. Their status shall reflect the baseness which in their souls they have elected and desired."

Under those circumstances it was quite natural that the Church Fathers should have wished to purge Christian belief and practice of their original Jewish elements. For example, the Justinian Code, based on the earlier decisions of the Council of Nicaea and the Laws of Constantine, forbade Christians to observe Easter during Passover week. Even the Jewish Messianic doctrine of "The Kingdom of God" *on earth* was fundamentally altered to "The Kingdom of God" *in heaven.* Notwithstanding these efforts to "de-Judaize" itself, the church was modeled on the synagogue in all its principal institutional forms, its congregation, ritual, chanting of prayers, singing of hymns, public reading of Scripture and the homiletic sermon. Even the *Missa Catechumenorum* and the Divine Office of the Catholic Church, for example, were modeled on prototypes in the Jewish ritual. The Milan *Te Deum* was practically a literal translation of the Jewish hymn: "Rejoice O Ye Daughters of Zion." Jewish cantillation of the divine service by the *baal-tefilah,* the leader of prayer, and plain-song chanting of the responses by the congregation laid the musical basis for the later Gregorian chant which exercised such a profound influence on the development of the musical art of Europe.

Judaism and Islam

If Jewish life in Palestine gradually became moribund, in Babylonia, despite the persecution, it continued to blossom. *Mishna* and *Gemara* received their greatest impetus there. Scholars and students from all over the Diaspora flocked to its great academies, especially to those of Sura and Pumbeditha, under the direction of the *Geonim* (Rectors). Thus the Baby-

Emperor Justinian. (From a mosaic at Ravenna.)

lonian community developed Rabbinic learning to its highest flowering.

The foremost social position was held not by the wealthy merchants as elsewhere but by scholars. Study of the *Torah* had become the dominant way of life. Rabbis and Talmudic scholars followed their own injunction not to use the *Torah* "as a spade" with which to earn their living. Instead they worked at various useful trades, including farming, and only in their leisure time studied and taught the *Torah*. Jewish tradition honored productive work because it helped keep people upright.

With the conquest by the Arabs of Palestine in 638 and of Babylonia in 642, Jewish life entered a new cultural phase. There was an inevitable fusion between the Graeco-Arab and Jewish-Babylonian civilizations. Aramaic, which had been the Jewish vernacular since the return of the Exiles, gave way to Arabic, although Hebrew continued to be the language of prayer and religious study.

Like Christianity, the religion of Islam, which Mohammed had founded in the seventh century, was an offshoot of the Jewish religion. Like Jesus, Mohammed, too, did not plan to found a new religion. He had, in fact, announced himself as "a Jewish prophet."

And the mosque, like the church, was modeled on the synagogue. In the matter of prayers, forbidden foods, circumcision, hygiene, marriage and divorce, and the study of sacred Scripture, Mohammed and his successors also followed Jewish models faithfully. This may explain in part why Arabic and Jewish culture during the first centuries of Islam showed such a remarkable affinity and why in Spain, North Africa and Babylonia they went through an almost parallel development.

Whether from conviction or expediency—a motive by no means foreign to him—Mohammed, at the outset of his prophetic career, addressed his preachings almost exclusively to the Jews of Arabia. He borrowed much of the narrative material as well as doctrine for the *Koran* from the *Talmud* and *Midrash,* but in strangely garbled form. In composing his poetic *Suras* he used the well-known Jewish Bible stories of Adam, Abraham, Lot, Joseph, Moses, Saul, David, Solomon, Elijah, Job and Jonah.

Mohammed's confession of faith ran, curiously, as follows: "We believe in God, and in what has been revealed to us, and in what was revealed to Abraham and Ishmael and Isaac and Jacob and the Twelve Tribes, and in what was given to Moses and to Jesus, and what was given to the Prophets by their Lord."

When Mohammed first raised the standard of militant Islam in Mecca, he was persecuted and had to flee. He went to Medina, where he expected that a large part of the Jewish population would accept him as the Prophet of Allah since, as he saw it, their religion was the same as his. He posed as a prophet of Israel and preached to the Jews of Medina in a style he thought rabbinical. Furthermore, at the direction of the Angel Gabriel he made Jerusalem his *Kibla,* the direction in which he turned his face while at prayer.

But when the Jews of Medina, who were well acquainted with their sacred writings, proceeded to expose his brand of *Torah* as a fraud, Mohammed furiously turned away from them after many acrimonious disputes with their rabbis. The Angel Gabriel opportunely paid another visit to Mohammed and ordered him to change his *Kibla* from Jerusalem to Mecca.

He was shortly to avenge the verbal insults of the Jews with fire and sword. Although the Jewish settlements in Arabia

Yiddish or German in Hebrew characters. *Machzor* (prayer-book for the Holy Days), printed at Cracow, 1571.

were numerous and powerfully fortified, he managed to overcome them by a combination of craft and ferocious attack. Thousands were decapitated and mutilated.

The Jewish Languages

Wherever Jews lived they spoke the language of the country. In addition, they used Hebrew in their prayers, in the public reading from the *Torah,* and in their Talmudic studies. But in their complicated history over many centuries Jews evolved a special approach to foreign languages.

In the Middle Ages, at a time when illiteracy was almost general in Europe except for a small class of scholars and priests, most Jews were literate. They knew Hebrew because their religion required it. In medieval Germany, for instance, they began to write German *but with Hebrew characters.* Because of their segregation in the ghettos, the different phonetics of Hebrew, their use of Hebrew words and idioms, and the special requirements of Jewish life, the German of the Jews slowly evolved from a German dialect into a distinctive Germanic language—Yiddish. By the middle of the nineteenth century in Slavic countries, where it gathered Russian and Polish words, Yiddish began to produce a first-class literature, which is only now being accorded the recognition it deserves.

Judeo-Greek had been used in Byzantine and early medieval times. Although like Yiddish, and for the same cultural reasons written in Hebrew characters, it absorbed only a few Hebrew words.

Judeo-Italian, on the other hand, evolved into much more of a "Jewish" language than Judeo-Greek. Because each region of Italy had developed its own *parlate* of Italian, Italian

Italian in Hebrew characters. Jewish prayers printed in Bologna, 1538.

Spanish in Hebrew characters (*Ladino*). Title page of Ibn Pakudah's *Duties of the Heart*.

Arabic in Hebrew characters. Holograph page of *Guide to the Perplexed*, by Maimonides.

Jewish scholars and rabbis during the Renaissance could communicate with other Italian Jews only in Judeo-Italian. Most of the Italian Jews could *not read* Italian although they could speak it and therefore *could* write it in Hebrew characters. They produced Judeo-Italian Bible translations, prayer books and both religious and secular poetry.

The pattern for writing the vernacular of the country in Hebrew characters became world-wide. For example, Saadya Gaon, Maimonides and other medieval writers usually wrote Arabic but with Hebrew characters. After the Expulsion from Spain in 1492, Spanish Jews, who found refuge in North Africa and in the Balkan countries, wrote Spanish with Hebrew characters. In time they enriched this language with all kinds of foreign words: Turkish, Italian, Greek, Arabic and even a few Slavic. This Judeo-Spanish language is called Ladino and sometimes *Spaniolish*.

There is even an ancient Judeo-Persian language spoken in Persia and different dialects of it are used in all of Central Asia. The Jews of Bokhara speak a Tadjik dialect of the Persian language family and have brought into it a number of

Persian in Hebrew letters, 1660.

Aramaic expressions. The Mountain Jews of the Caucasus use *Farsi-Tat*, a Persian dialect enriched with Hebrew words and expressions. They have developed an interesting "Jewish" folk-literature—in *Farsi-Tat*.

THE ROAD OF THE MARTYRS
The Scapegoat

There was hardly a time during the Middle Ages when the Jews were not under harsh attack from feudal king and baron, bishop and "preaching friar." And whenever these attacks were based on religious grounds, the Jews trembled for their lives. It was a sure sign that those in power were casting covetous eyes on their money, their goods and their homes. This greed, of course, was dressed up impressively with pious sentiment and high-sounding legality to make it more palatable.

There are an astonishing number of instances on record in which hatred for the Jews was accompanied by a love of Jewish possessions, and this love was delicately blended with the incense of faith and civic virtue. Thoughtful Jews, turned into sober realists by their enemies, had no illusions about it. A medieval Jewish writer noted ironically: "The princes of Edom [Christendom] are coveters of money. Therefore they flay us alive." The German crusaders, as they descended upon the helpless Jews in the Rhineland towns, cried: "Hab-hab!" In Old German *hab-hab* meant: "Give, give."

Beginning with the First Crusade during the eleventh century, religious hysteria was whipped up against the Jews in Europe. By that time hatred of the Jews had already received official sanction and had been written into the canon law of the Church. It had been made a part of state policy by rulers everywhere. Its general practice centuries later led Martin Luther to gibe: "If it is a mark of a good Christian to hate the Jews, what excellent Christians all of us are."

Hatred of the Jew served as an incendiary torch. It could be employed profitably at all times for the purpose of diverting the attention of the Christian population from the misery of its daily life in feudal society. Jews, therefore, served as convenient scapegoats. The rulers could incite against them the anger of their subjects, which otherwise might have been directed against themselves. Thus every private grief and every public calamity could be charged against the Jews.

There was hardly an imaginable crime in the catalogue of

Ways of executing Jews. (From the Dresden *Sachsenspiegel*, c. 1220.)

Burning of Jews at Trent, 1475. (German woodcut. 15th century.)

human wickedness of which they were not considered guilty. When the Black Death killed off a great part of the population of Europe in 1348-49, the Jews were blamed for it. They were accused of poisoning the wells of the Christians. In Germany alone this charge so inflamed the population that armed mobs in a very short time wiped out physically more than 350 Jewish communities. Tens of thousands of Jews—men, women, and children—were "murdered, drowned, burned, broken on the wheel, hanged, exterminated, strangled, buried alive, and tortured to death." So recounts a contemporary chronicler.

This, and every other type of crime charged against the Jews, such as ritual murder and Host desecration, sprang from some need on the part of the rulers to distract the attention of the people from more pressing matters, or simply to satisfy a naked greed. Scenes of violence always followed such accusations. At the height of the public excitement the authorities, armed with the majesty of the law, and the clergy, fervent with religious devotion, would appear to intervene. They would go through the righteous motions of preserving law and morality. The judges would then put to the torture all Jews charged with anti-Christian crimes.

The property of those Jews put to death was confiscated. Someone usually had the foresight to point the crime against the wealthiest Jews. Staggering fines were laid on the survivors. Sometimes, by almost superhuman effort, Jewish communities succeeded in unlocking dungeon doors with the payment of heavy bribes and ransom money.

The justification for this brutal treatment of the Jews stemmed from the historical invention that their ancestors had killed Jesus. Objective Bible scholars ascribe this harsh view to an uncritical reading by many Christians of the Gospel story of the Crucifixion. For many sincere and devout Christians the subject has been charged with excessive emotion which has led them to an injudicious conclusion. Countless generations of Jews through the ages thus were branded in perpetuity as Christ-killers, made to suffer violence and death for the alleged crime of some of their ancient ancestors.

Job-like sounds the plaint by Benjamin ben Zerah, a religious poet who fled from the Rhineland into the Polish Provinces before the savage mobs of Crusaders: "Am I made of iron? Is my flesh made of steel to bear this burden? I am weary of exile and slavery. I am tired of letting the nations tread me down on all sides. When they jeer at me, 'Where now is the

Rock of your salvation? Why does He not stretch out His arm to support you?' I want to hide my face in the earth."

Challenging as the poet's rebuke was of his God's seeming injustice, the Jew through the ages found the strength to endure in his unyielding faith. A Day of Atonement prayer, composed during the Middle Ages, proclaims his will to triumph in defeat:

"Though maimed and shattered, yet we are Thine."

The Slander of Host Desecration

One of the most persistent accusations leveled at Jews during the Middle Ages was that of Host desecration. This quite obviously stemmed from the tragic fiction that Jews were "Christ-killers." Not only were they blamed for the original crucifixion of Jesus, but also for having an undying hatred of him. This gave them, reasoned their calumniators, a compulsion to continue the act of crucifixion if only in symbolic form, that is by Host desecration. There are hundreds of instances on record, in practically every country in Europe, in which Jews were accused of this anti-Christian crime. In almost every case they were believed to have stolen, or corrupted a Christian to steal for them, consecrated wafers from church altars. Popular hysteria pictured Jews in an orgy of fiendish glee, piercing, burning and defiling these holy wafers. And where else would it take place but in the synagogue—before the Holy Ark. In fact, it was almost generally considered a sacred Jewish rite.

The charge first arose after Pope Innocent III, during the first quarter of the thirteenth century, gave official recognition to the doctrine of "transubstantiation," which meant that the Christian worshipper by drinking the wine of the sacrament was considered to be drinking of the blood of Christ— symbolically, of course; by eating the holy wafer, or Host, he was partaking of the body of Christ.

The usual accusation was that the Jews "pierced" the holy wafer (namely, the body of Christ) by means of knives, needles and other sharp objects. Popular belief had it that every time Jews pierced the holy wafer it miraculously began to bleed as if it were from the very wounds of the crucified Christ. Many of the clergy encouraged belief in this "miracle" and considered it the design of Heaven to bring the secret sacrilege into the open, so that stern punishment might be meted out to the guilty Jews.

Whenever the charge of Host desecration occurred, it aroused mobs to riot, resulted in massacres of the Jews, in burnings and mass expulsions, in the payment of large fines, and in the confiscation of Jewish possessions. But there were always those who had a great deal to gain from these disasters to the Jews, among them the clergy. Quite often, on the site of a destroyed synagogue, a Christian chapel was consecrated to commemorate the "miracle," as in the case of the Ratisbon synagogue. Another instance was the alleged Host desecration of 1337 in Deggensdorf, a town on the Danube where the chapel and shrine of the Holy Sepulcher were erected on the site of the destroyed synagogue. Miraculous cures of the sick, the lame and the halt were constantly reported by visiting pilgrims. Perhaps the most impressive miracle of all was the declaration of the ruling prince, Heinrich of Landshut, which released all Christians from their obligation to pay their debts to Jews. Furthermore, he praised his subjects for "burning and exterminating our Jews of Deggensdorf." He himself pocketed the money of the massacred Jews and seized their possessions as an act of piety.

Probably the charge of Host desecration which resulted in the greatest catastrophe took place in 1298 in the Franconian town of Rotingen where the Jews were accused of stealing a holy wafer and crushing it in a mortar. Led by the master builder, Rindfleisch, who announced that God had elected him to kill all Jews, a mob howled its bloody way through Germany and Austria, gathering recruits as it went. In a period of only six months they wiped out one hundred and forty-six Jewish communities, killing, burning, raping and pillaging. Over one hundred thousand Jews were slain, a staggering number for those days. The authorities did little to stop the massacre. In the end, however, they recognized the danger to themselves in Rindfleisch's growing power, and hanged him.

The Ritual Murder Libel

A "blood relation," so to speak, of the Host desecration myth was the ritual murder libel. It, too, originated from the "Christ-killer" fiction and involved the shedding of blood. Popular conception believed the ritual murder of a Christian child by Jews was a reenactment of the crucifixion of Jesus in the person of one of his most innocent followers. After the alleged murder the Jews supposedly used the blood of the victim in the making of *matzohs* for Passover.

The first case of this kind on record is that of William of Norwich in 1144. The boy had mysteriously disappeared. An alarm was raised. An apostate Jew, Theobald of Cambridge, went before the authorities and charged the Jews with having murdered the boy. He swore that it was an ancient custom to sacrifice a Christian child during the Passover festival, that representatives of the Jews throughout the world had assembled for that very purpose in Narbonne, France. They cast lots, he said, and the "honor" for the ritual murder had fallen to the Jews of Norwich in England. When the boy's body was found there was no evidence of murder, so no one was punished. However, the boy was declared a martyr, made a saint by the church, and a memorial chapel and shrine were erected in his honor in his native town.

Although the ritual murder libel cropped up several times in England after that, it was not until 1255 that an incident occurred in Lincoln which had tremendous consequences. It led, in 1290, to the expulsion of the Jews from England for four centuries, until Oliver Cromwell readmitted them.

The most vivid account of the tragedy is given by the contemporary English chronicler, Matthew Paris, who wrote in his *Historia Major*:

"... about the feast of Peter and Paul, the Jews of Lincoln stole a child called Hugh, being eight years old; and when they had nourished him, in the most secret chamber, with milk and other childish aliments, they sent to almost all the cities of England wherein the Jews lived, that, in contempt and reproach of Jesus Christ, they should be present at their sacrifice at Lincoln. . . . And coming together, they appointed one Lincoln Jew for the Judge, as if it were for Pilate. By whose judgment by the consent of all, the child is afflicted with sundry torments. He is whipped even unto blood and lividness, crowned with thorns, wearied with spitting and strikings . . . and after they had derided him in diverse manners, they crucified him."

Tomb of St. Hugh.

The report of little Hugh's crucifixion let loose an indescribable hysteria among the population. The authorities, to prevent disorders, arrested all Jews. When they found the body of the murdered child in the well of the Jew, Jopin, where it is believed it had been secretly deposited by the real murderers, the Jew was put to the torture. To end his torment, he confessed whatever he was asked to say. Besides Jopin eighteen leading Jews of Lincoln were tortured and forced to confess. They were publicly hanged. Twenty others were imprisoned in the Tower of London. They were freed only after a huge ransom was paid to Henry III, who then confiscated the property of the executed Jews. By an odd coincidence, they happened to be among the richest Jews of the kingdom.

Amidst great pomp and solemnity the body of little Hugh was borne to the cathedral for burial. Shortly after, he was canonized as St. Hugh of Lincoln and a shrine was erected over his tomb in Lincoln Cathedral to which untold thousands came to worship.

One of the earliest ritual murder accusations was brought in Blois, France, in 1171. It resulted in the mass burning alive of all the Jews of the town. They had been offered one avenue of escape—baptism—which they rejected, and died singing the martyr hymn, *Alenu leshabéach*.

The ritual murder myth reached epidemic proportions all over Germany. First it moved through the towns of Franconia, then through Bavaria from where it swept into Austria and other parts of Europe. This troubled some of the authorities and the princes of the Church. Where, they asked, would these bloody excesses lead?

Pope Innocent IV Intervenes

Pope Innocent III and the Fourth Lateran Council of the Church did nothing to stem the outrages. If anything, the measures they took only poured oil upon the flames. It remained for the humane Pope Innocent IV to challenge not only the savagery of the practice but to brand the so-called proof of ritual murder by Jews as a fraud. In answer to what he called "the piteous complaint of the Jews of Germany" he issued a Bull in 1245 in which he made clear his own views. He sternly forbade Christians to bring the blood accusation against any Jew. It was groundless, he declared, a mockery of Christ's teachings, and led only to evil. Pope Gregory X found it necessary to ban the slander in another Bull in 1274.

There were other popes as well who denounced the ritual blood libel in official decrees of the Church. Unfortunately,

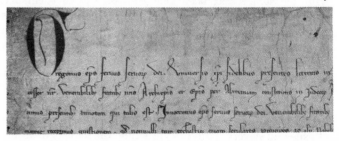

Pope Innocent IV's Bull.

their decrees were not always obeyed and only for brief periods was it possible to stem the outrages against the Jews.

There were few secular rulers who took a firm stand against the ritual murder fever. When they did, it was less on legal or moral grounds and more from fear that the lawlessness which followed riot and bloodshed might weaken their own authority. This was behind the ban against the ritual murder charge issued by the Emperor Frederick II (1194-1250) and by the Emperor Rudolph of Hapsburg (1275).

To those familiar with traditional Jewish ethics and practices which regard life as sacred and the brotherhood of man equal to the love of God, such accusations appeared incredible. On a number of occasions learned Jews debated the matter publicly with Christian theologians, for the most part forced by fanatical priests or designing rulers. During the sixteenth century, for example, the celebrated rabbi, Judah Low of Prague, the cabalist to whom Jewish folklore ascribes the making of the *Golem,* asked for a public disputation with the Dominican priests. He wrote Johann Silvester, the Cardinal of Prague, "I demand justice for my oppressed brothers."

In the archives of the Dominican Order in Prague, it is said, is deposited a record of this public disputation.

The Dominican theologian asked: "According to the *Talmud,* do the Jews need the blood of Christians for their Passover festival?"

Rabbi Judah answered: "The use of blood is forbidden by Holy Scriptures. The *Talmud* neither canceled nor modified this commandment. On the other hand, the *Talmud* made it even stricter. Those sages who have taught: 'Whoever raises his hand against his neighbor even if he does not strike him is an evil-doer' (*Sanhedrin* 58 b) and 'Somewhat greater is the value of human beings, for in order to keep them alive even the commandments of the *Torah* may be suspended' (*Berachat* 19 b), surely could not have authorized the use of human blood especially when even the blood of animals is forbidden."

The Martyrs

There was hardly a year, or a country in Europe, in which the ritual murder libel was not raised, resulting in the impoverishment and death of countless Jews. Though torture brought many "confessions," there were nevertheless many Jews who had the strength and courage to die for the truth. The pious considered that to perish *al kiddush ha-Shem,* "to sanctify the name of God," was to die a holy martyr. Hundreds of thousands chose that course. Of all martyrologies the Jewish is probably the vastest, as well as the most poignant in its record of man's inhumanity to man.

Those Jews who survived did so by hiding, by flight from one place to another, always in fear—and their spirits were deeply bruised. It gave them a feeling of physical insecurity, a deep sense of injustice, and of being unwanted. Jews knew they stood alone, strangers everywhere on earth.

The Pattern of Restriction

During the early Middle Ages, whenever Jews were allowed to live side by side in neighborly relations with Christians and without interference from the state authorities and the Church, they got along in reasonable amity. They could reside in places of their own choosing; the compulsory ghetto enclosure was still unknown. They were even permitted a variety of productive trades and callings. Except for the practices of their religion there was little to differentiate Jews from their Christian neighbors. They wore the same clothes, spoke the same language, and sang the same songs.

It is also true, however, that at no time were Jews free from persecution. Yet, compared with later centuries, life was relatively tolerable and secure for them until the advent of the Crusades, when they were condemned, in 1215, to a living death as social pariahs by Pope Innocent III and the Lateran Council. They were ordered to wear distinctive Jewish hats and identifying arm patches and were incarcerated behind ghetto walls in every town. Every movement and activity was restricted; every aspect of their lives was controlled. This established the basic pattern of the brutal treatment Jews were to suffer until modern times.

One of the chief harassments to which they were subjected was the unceasing effort by the Church to convert them. There were many sincere though fanatical churchmen and princes who believed that in the conversion of the Jews the Church would achieve one of its greatest spiritual triumphs and would thus demonstrate the superiority of the Christian faith. Innocent III declared that "as wanderers ought they to remain upon the earth, until their countenance be filled with shame and they seek the name of Jesus Christ our Lord."

But the more the Church tried to convert them, the more passionately the Jews clung to their own religion. "It is as easy to convert the Jews as the Devil himself," said Martin Luther in exasperation.

There were two principal ways the Church worked for the Jews' conversion. One was by means of public disputation between rabbis and Christian theologians; the other was by conversionist sermons delivered by Christian preachers in synagogues, and sometimes in churches, on which occasions the attendance of all Jews above twelve years of age was compulsory.

Religious Disputations

Characteristic of the age, the disputations were called by the medieval Church "Tournaments for God and Faith." But there was little of the chivalrous element in these so-called "tournaments," the position of the combatants being so flagrantly unequal. Almost always the verdict went against the Jewish debaters, with the direst consequences to the practice

"The Eternal Wanderers." *Alexander Jaray*

97

Disputation between rabbis and priests, 16th century.

of their religion, to themselves and to their fellow-Jews.

In the year 1240 the king of France ordered a public disputation between Nicolas Donin, a learned apostate from Jewish faith, and four eminent rabbis, among whom were the celebrated Talmudist, Rabbi Yechiel of Paris, and Rabbi Moses of Coucy. Present at the disputation were the queen, the archbishops and bishops of the realm, and many theologians and nobles. Vainly Rabbi Yechiel strove to expose Donin's accusations as inventions and slanders. In the end, the *Talmud* was declared to be an evil, lying work and ordered burned in a great public ceremony arranged by the Dominicans.

To leave no loophole for the Jews, Donin persuaded Pope

Edict for burning the *Talmud*. Bull of Pope Julius, May 29, 1554.

Gregory IX to issue a Bull (probably the first of its kind) for the burning of the *Talmud everywhere,* and to establish inquisitions and censors over other Jewish writings, a practice which tormented the Jews for centuries.

Spain, too, instituted these religious disputations at an early period, but without the excessive fanaticism that accompanied such public debates in less enlightened parts of Europe. For example, in June, 1263, Pablo Christiano, a baptized Jew, prevailed upon the King of Aragon to order Nachmanides, the famed Talmudist and philosopher, to dispute with him before the court and clergy in Barcelona. From the report in Hebrew by Nachmanides, it is plain that he was granted full freedom of speech. So courteous and dignified was his bearing, and so sincere his defense that, in presenting him with a gift at the conclusion of the disputation, the king declared that never before had he heard "an unjust cause so nobly defended."

But with the passage of time, the gentle intellectual climate changed in Spain. A fiery Dominican preacher, Vicente Ferrer, arose in Valencia at the turn of the fifteenth century. Upon his urging, the King of Aragon "invited" the most learned rabbis in his kingdom to a public disputation in Tortosa. Leading the Christian theologians was Pope Benedict XIII's own physician, a former rabbi and a convert to Christianity. The twenty-two Jewish defenders counted among them the noted philosopher and Talmudist, Joseph Albo.

This was probably the most remarkable disputation of its kind ever held. It took place in the presence of Pope Benedict, many cardinals and bishops, and a vast audience. It was arranged in sixty-nine sessions and lasted twenty-one months. The principal matter debated was whether the Messiah had already arrived or not.

Naturally, the Jews were declared ignominious losers by the Pope. He ordered them to accept baptism, which they promptly declined to do. Made angry by their refusal, he placed a ban on the study of the *Talmud* by Jews.

Conversionist Sermons

Shortly thereafter, in 1450, Pope Benedict issued a Bull introducing a new method of persuasion, the enforced conversionist sermon. He indicated what the subjects of the sermons were to be: the propositions, that "the true Messiah has already come," "the heresies, vanities, and errors of the *Talmud* prevent their [i.e., the Jews] knowing the truth." Furthermore, that "the destruction of the Temple and the city of Jerusalem, and the perpetuity of their captivity" had been prophesied by Jesus as just punishment for the Jews.

Conversionist sermons to the Jews were delivered in Rome uninterruptedly until early in the nineteenth century.

Jews compelled to listen to a conversionist sermon in Rome.
Basle Museum

ITALY (Medieval)

Since the second century B.C.E., Jews had lived in settled communities in Rome, Naples, Venice, Bologna, Ferrara, Ravenna, Genoa, Milan, Capua, Salerno, Pompeii and in many other places. In imperial Rome, for instance, during the age of Cicero and Seneca, they were concentrated on the right bank of the Tiber where the *Pons Judaeorum (Quattro Capi)*, or

Jews' Bridge, connected the Jewish quarter with the rest of the city. Though under Roman rule, the lot of the Jews was tolerable, with the ascendancy of Christianity as a state religion during the fourth century, persecution of them grew apace.

Yet there were times, for example, during the brief reign of Julian the Apostate and again during the period of Norman rule in Sicily and southern Italy, when a general benevolent policy resulted in a fairly undisturbed, even productive life for the Jews. So many became craftsmen, weavers, dyers, blacksmiths, carpenters, tailors, jewelers and minters that in some places they formed Jewish trade guilds. Where they had their own guilds, it was because they were systematically excluded from the guilds of the Christians. In time, though, the privilege of following whatever trade they chose was sharply curtailed. In most Italian cities during the Middle Ages and the Renaissance, Jews were for the most part allowed to be dealers in old clothes, pawnbrokers, street hawkers, money lenders and changers.

Wedding ring, Italy, 16th century.

To dispose of the popular notion that most Jews during the Middle Ages and the Renaissance were, of their own free will, only merchants, peddlers and money lenders, there is the petition against the expulsion of the Jews from Sicily presented to Ferdinand the Catholic by his worried councilors of state toward the end of the fifteenth century: "Another difficulty is that nearly all the artisans in the realm are Jews. In case all these are expelled at once, we will lack craftsmen capable of supplying mechanical utensils and especially those made of iron—as horseshoes, agricultural implements and equipment for ships and other conveyances."

MONEY LENDING

It was the great misfortune of the Jews of Italy and elsewhere in medieval Christian Europe that, against their will,

they were forced to engage in the despised occupation of money lending. They had fallen heir to this doubtfully profitable calling because the medieval canon law of the Church had forbidden Christians to lend money at "usury," or interest. The irony was that Jewish religious law also frowned on the taking of usury. The *Talmud* compared usurers with murderers. Both, it averred, would be unable to make atonement for their crimes in the world to come. In fact, the *Talmud* makes severe strictures against taking *any interest whatsoever* on loans of any kind. Nonetheless, because the feudal state and Church rulers could not manage their affairs without outside financing, Jews were *compelled* and also encouraged by various inducements to follow the despised calling and to charge an interest rate. This rate was not fixed by the Jew's caprice or by his alleged cupidity but by written agreement with the authorities. The profits from money lending were certainly considerable, but as soon as a fortune was amassed by a Jewish lender it quickly found its way by a variety of confiscatory actions into a well-ordered, descending hierarchy of pockets: first the imperial, then the royal, princely, baronial and clerical. One Christian chronicler realistically described the process as allowing the Jew, like a sponge, to fill up with money, then squeezing him dry.

Of course, lending money at interest no matter how small earned for Jewish money lenders the hatred and often the envy of Christians. Powerful debtors often threw lenders into prison or, more conveniently, murdered them whenever they had the temerity to demand payment. The term "money lender" became so associated with "Jew" that even the saintly Bernard of Clairvaux, the spiritual guide of the First Crusade, thought fit to coin the contemptuous word "judazaire" for it. It is, however, amusing to find that at a somewhat later date the same Bernard accused the Christian money lenders who happened to evade the ecclesiastical ban against money lending of being "more heartless" than the Jews.

At various times in medieval Italy the Church itself, notwithstanding its well-publicized scorn of usury, did a thriving

Bronze medallion. "Benjamin, son of Rabbi Elijah Beer the Physician, long life to him!" Lived in Rome and Ferrara, 15th century.
Jewish Museum

99

money-lending business. When Jews engaged in it, they called it "usury," but when the Church practiced it, it was considered a holy work, *"Monti di Pieta,"* or "Mounts of Piety," they called it. The Tuscan Christian usurers were notorious and those in Padua were dispatched by the poet Dante in *The Inferno* down to the seventh and lowest Purgatory. In some parts of Italy there were so many abuses that in 1409 the Merchants' Guild of Brindisi was forced to petition the authorities to allow the Jewish money lenders to return in order that "the greed of the Christian usurers be checked." In Venice, although the Christian money lenders were permitted to charge as much as forty per cent interest on loans, Jews were forbidden to ask more than five per cent and were severely punished if they did.

Nonetheless, it was these money-lending activities which were the major cause for the popular indignation and slander against the Jews. They led to an interminable series of repressive laws, persecutions, rioting and worse.

Yet at hardly any time was the intensity of anti-Jewish feeling and action in Italy as harsh as it was elsewhere in Europe, possibly because the Italian temperament was gentler and sunnier, possibly because the presence of the emperors and popes in Rome may have had a tempering effect on intended mob violence. For all the tribulations they had to undergo, Italian Jews seem to have succeeded in creating a rich life of their own, which, however, showed the impact of the spirit of the age.

JEWISH CULTURE FLOURISHES

During the ninth century important Talmudic academies had been securely established in southern Italy, especially in Bari and Otranto. No wonder the saying paraphrasing Scripture arose at the time: "From Bari shall go forth the Law and the Word of the Lord from Otranto." It was from this broad intellectual activity that there arose a distinguished line of Hebrew grammarians, Talmudists, mathematicians, astronomers, physicians, philosophers and secular poets who wrote in Hebrew, in medieval Latin and in Italian. Apparently they found a ready acceptance of their work, which in itself implies a high level of culture among the Jews in Italy.

THE PREACHING FRIARS

But tranquillity for the Jews vanished in Italy after the Black Death in 1348-49. There took place, then, continuous attacks on Jewish money lenders, who were the ready pretexts for the massacres and the riots whipped up by Franciscan and Dominican friars. The worst were incited by two Franciscan monks, John of Capistrano (1386-1456), the Papal Inquisitor of the Jews, also known as "The Scourge of the Jews," and Bernardino da Feltre (1439-1494). A contemporary Jewish writer, Joseph Colon, added this observation to his melancholy chronicle: "Thirty years ago, conditions were better until the preachers [i.e., Franciscans] appeared in great numbers. They were a scourge to Israel. They wished to destroy us each day, so that our lives and possessions were in constant jeopardy."

This only followed a well-known pattern of persecution of the Jews by many popes and regional Church councils. The Fourth Lateran Council in 1215, under the fanatic whiplash of Innocent III, had ordered that the yellow badge be worn prominently by Jews to identify them readily and to humiliate them as social pariahs. Even the most illustrious philosopher of the Church during the Middle Ages, "The Angelic Doctor," Thomas Aquinas, recommended that on religious as well as moral grounds Jews be held in perpetual servitude.

With the counterfires the Church lit against the Protestant Reformation during the sixteenth century, the repression of the Jews intensified even more sharply and they were driven unrelentingly into ghettos.

Pope Paul IV (formerly Cardinal Caraffa, the ruthless enemy of the Jews) issued a Bull on July 12, 1555, which decreed ". . . in Rome and all other cities of the Papal States, the Jews shall live entirely separated from the Christians, in a quarter or a street with one entrance and one exit. They shall have but one synagogue, shall build no new synagogue, nor own real estate."

Oddly enough, there were many Jews who considered their ghetto prison not without advantages. For one thing, they said, it helped the Jews keep out of the lawless mob's sight. For another, its strong walls and gates offered some physical protection in time of attack. The Jews of Verona went so far as to commemorate the completion of the walls of their ghetto with an annual feast day.

Tomb of "The Jewish Pope," St. Paul's, Rome. Pope Anacletus II (Cardinal Pietro Pierlioni) was the grandson of a Jewish money-lender of Rome who, seeking a career, had become a Christian. Duly elected by a majority of the cardinals to the papal throne, he ruled at St. Peter's for eight years until his death in 1138. But he had made many enemies among churchmen who, for political and other reasons and especially because of his Jewish descent, had rallied around his defeated rival for the papacy, the man who was later to succeed him, Innocent II. Throughout his rule, he was reviled by his enemies outside of Italy. Bernard of Clairvaux was especially bitter: "To the shame of Christ a man of Jewish origin was come to occupy the chair of St. Peter." In later Church annals he was excoriated and dishonored by the name of "anti-pope" and the most sordid of motives and methods were ascribed to his rise to eminence.

Synagogue, now Church of Saint Anne, Trani. Street still called *"Via Sinagoga"* (built 1247).

Papal censorship of a Hebrew religious work, Venice, 1547.

THE GHETTO

What really was the ghetto? The word "ghetto" was first coined in Italy, but the institution itself, without its compulsory features, was of more ancient origin. During the Byzantine and early medieval period its Latin name was *vicus Judaeorum,* the Jewish quarter. Later it assumed various names in different countries; it was called *Judiaria* in Portugal, *Juiverie* in Northern France and *Carrière des Juifs* in Provence, Jews' Street in England, *Judenviertel* and *Judengasse* in Germany.

Probably the first compulsory ghetto was established in Wroclaw (Breslau) during the thirteenth century. The first ghetto in Italy, however, was established in Venice in 1516 when the Jews were not allowed to live anywhere but on the island of Lunga Spina. Some believe that the name "ghetto" was derived from the fact that the Jewish quarter in Venice was situated near a cannon foundry called *gheta* in Italian. However, there are other speculations concerning the word's origin—that it was derived from the Italian *borghetto,* small burg or quarter; *guitto* or *ghito,* both meaning "dirty"; *gitter,* the German for "bars"; and *get,* Hebrew for "divorce."

lowed to leave the ghetto from dusk to daybreak. Discovered outside the walls, he was subject to the harshest penalties.

Only on rare occasions were the Jews permitted out of the ghetto. When, for instance, a new pope was elected, the Jewish elders of Rome were required to march out in procession through the ruined Gate of Octavian, carrying a *Sefer Torah* resplendent in its finest mantle and shimmering in its silver ornaments. They were obliged to station themselves near the Arch of Titus, the everlasting reminder of their national desolation. When the pontiff was carried by in the procession it was customary for him to pause a moment in front of the Jewish elders, and he would ask them sternly: "What are you doing here?" The *Ordo Romanus* of the Church prescribed the manner of their conduct as well as the protocol of the pope's responses: "And the Jews come with their Law, make obeisance and present to him their Law that he might honor it."

Trade scene, Northern Italy, 13th-14th centuries. (From an illuminated manuscript of Maimonides' *Mishneh-Torah.*)

Whatever its etymology, the physical characteristics of the ghetto were nearly always the same. Its streets were narrow and gloomy, and because of poverty and overcrowding, hopelessly squalid. Its houses were piles of crumbling masonry. Little sunlight ever penetrated there and usually the ghetto was separated from the rest of the city by high walls and a ponderous gate called, in official Italian records, the *Porta Judaeorum.* It was barred and bolted and made additionally secure at night by heavy chains and locks. No Jew was al-

Ark in the Padua Synagogue.

101

Synagogue of Trapani, Sicily, 13th century.

Deputation of Roman Jews offers Emperor Henry VII a scroll of the *Torah* (c. 1312).

While presenting it, the elders recited the well-known formula: "We solicit the grace of offering Your Holiness a copy of our Torah." The pope thereupon touched the *Sefer Torah* lightly with his fingers and replied: "We praise and honor the Law, for it was given your fathers by Almighty God through Moses. But we condemn your religion, and your false interpretation of the Law, for you await the Messiah in vain. The apostolic faith teaches us that our Lord Jesus Christ has already come." At a later date, the popes gave a much briefer and more crushing reply: "Excellent Law—detestable race."

It was also the bizarre custom, rigorously enforced by the authorities, that on the first day of the Carnival in Rome eight Jews should run a footrace, in order that, like their ancestor Samson, they might "make sport" for the populace. Wearing only loin cloths, they were speeded on, whipped, jeered and hooted at by the crowds. For the entire length of the Corso, side by side with donkeys and asses, they were forced to run the gantlet. They were often so brutally beaten, spat upon and kicked that some fell in a faint or even died.

CO-WORKERS IN THE RENAISSANCE

Nonetheless, like a medal, history has two sides always: the forward-moving and the retrogressive. The spirit of the Renais-

Five synagogues in one building, in compliance with the law which permitted only one synagogue structure in Rome.

sance was too powerful a cultural and social force to be suppressed easily by either Church or state. Within the limits of their freedom of choice and action, the Jews of Italy became active co-workers in the Renaissance with Christians. The historic view, so commonly stated, that the ghetto Jews lived in a deteriorating self-enclosed universe, is patently false. Jews, too, profited greatly from the spirit of liberalism and striving after culture that was current in that day. The humanism of the intellectual classes of that period helped divert men's minds a little away from heaven and more toward the mundane affairs of society. Thoughtful people everywhere were avid for knowledge of mankind, and true knowledge is a humanizing agent which helps bring understanding and dispels prejudice. When Christians of education and good will perceived that Jews were human beings like themselves, their artificial defenses against them, often built up by malicious indoctrination and ignorance, broke down.

Jewish Humanists

Many eminent Christian scholars and writers chose learned and cultured Jews as their teachers and companions. Immanuel of Rome (1270-1330), the poet who wrote both Hebrew and Italian verse, was an intimate of Dante and his "Young Italy" circle. Elias del Medigo (1460-1497) taught philosophy and Hebrew studies to the foremost Italian humanist of the age, Pico della Mirandola. The woman poet, Sara Copia Sullam of Venice, was a lifelong friend of the priest-poet, Ansaldo Ceba. Joseph del Medigo, scientist, doctor, philosopher and rabbi, who was touched with real genius, was a pupil in astronomy of Galileo. Elijah Levita, the Yiddish-writing scholar and *Spielmann,* or troubadour, from Germany, lived

Elia de Lates Ebreo, son of Bonet de Lates, physician to Pope Leo X, and his mother Rica (1552).

The most philanthropic of all Jewish women of the Renaissance was Gracia (Beatrice de Luna) Mendes, widow of Francisco Mendes, first of the great Jewish bankers of modern times. A former New Christian, she spent a great part of her fortune helping *Marranos* to escape from Spain. Her daughter married Joseph Nasi whom Suleiman the Magnificent of Turkey made Duke of Naxos.

for thirteen years in intimate friendship with his devoted pupil, Cardinal Egidio of Viterbo, the head of the Augustinian order.

Music and the Dance

Some of the best music conservatories in Italy were conducted by Jews in the ghettos of Venice and Ferrara. Talented Christian musicians, as well as Jewish, received their training there. Jews enjoyed great favor and patronage as composers, singers and instrumentalists, and a number of them were attached to the courts of the popes, kings, cardinals and merchant princes. Raphael found the model for Apollo, the central figure in his famous painting, "Apollo on Mount Parnassus," in the Jewish musician Jacopo Sansecondo.

The latter was lutist to Pope Leo X and had played at the wedding celebration for Lucrezia Borgia. A distinguished colleague of Sansecondo at the papal court was the convert Giovanni Maria, a violinist renowned throughout Europe. At the court of the musical dukes of Gonzaga in Mantua, flatteringly called "The Paradise" by contemporaries, a sizable number of Jewish musicians helped add luster to the concerts.

The most noteworthy of these was Salamone Rossi, composer, singer and violinist. He was musical director at the ducal court of Mantua from 1587 to 1628. During his tenure he invited Claudio Monteverde, the great initiator of the "*ars nova*" of polyphony, to join his musical circle. In his own right as composer, Salamone Rossi was a distinguished pathfinder in the trio-sonata form out of which the sonata evolved in time. He wrote madrigals, canzonets and vocal balletos, for which he achieved renown. Most interesting was his startling application of the new polyphonic style to synagogue music. As cantor in a synagogue in Venice, when his talents at the court in Mantua were not in demand, he composed musical settings in Renaissance style to the Psalms and to prayers for the Sabbath and the Holy Days. In a Hebrew dedication he stated that his aim was "to glorify and beautify the songs of King David according to the rules of music." There was so much orthodox opposition to his bold and unheard of innovation that the rabbi of his synagogue, Leone da Modena, thought it wise to publish a vigorous defense of Rossi's purpose.

In spite of the intense hostility toward the theater among traditionalist Jews, there were many Jews in Italy during the late Renaissance who achieved great renown as actors, playwrights, stage directors and ballet dancers. It is more than odd that the first known theoretical work on the dance was written by a Jew, Guglielmo of Pesaro, who has been called "the father of the ballet."

Facsimile of tenor part in synagogue service, composed in 1622 in Venice by Salamone Rossi.

The Arts

It was inevitable, too, that the influence of Renaissance art should have penetrated the ghetto. Rabbi Leone da Modena (1571-1648), the Chief Rabbi of Venice and a gifted Jewish humanist, was led to comment: "But in Italy there are many who have freed themselves of this restriction [i.e., the Second Commandment, against graven images] and have paintings and portraits in their homes, although they avoid sculpture both in relief and in the round."

Leona da Modena.

If there were only a few minor Jewish painters, sculptors and goldsmiths among the Jews of Italy, perhaps it was because the Jewish population was comparatively small. Moreover, because they were excluded from the Christian artists' guilds, Jewish artists, whatever the degree of their emancipation, found little outlet or encouragement for their creative talents. Nonetheless, the sense of beauty that pervaded the times was carried over into the synagogues, Jewish ritual objects, book making and printing.

Curtain for the Ark, 17th century.

Marriage contract (*ketubah*), Modena, 1677.
Jewish Museum

It is an irony of history that during the so-called Christian "Dark Ages," Jews were among the most cultured and creative elements in Europe. Yet, oddly, at the time of increasing enlightenment among Christians during the sixteenth and seventeenth centuries, the events stemming from the Counter-Reformation, from the Thirty Years' War and from other bloody events led to a sharp cultural deterioration among Jews, including the Jews in Italy.

Coat-of-arms of Italian doctor and rabbi, Abraham Menachem Rapoport (Rapo of Porto), died 1596 in Cremona.

SPAIN (Medieval)

THE GOLDEN AGE: ARAB-JEWISH CULTURE

With the conquest by the African Moors of the south of Spain in 711, the Golden Age of the Jews in that country began. The Jews had enjoyed equal treatment in Arab lands under the enlightened rule of the Mohammedan caliphs. Accordingly, as soon as the Moors had established their first foothold in Spain, the Jews began to arrive in great numbers from all parts of the Islamic world. Every encouragement was given them to develop their own religious communal life.

This held especially true during the tenth century in the reign of the enlightened Omayyad Caliphs, Abd-al-Rahman and his son, Al-Hakim, in Cordova. It was a time marked by liberality of mind and the advancement of the sciences and the arts. Despite Mohammed's attempts to suppress Greek cultural influences among the Arabs, they nonetheless persisted; Greek-Arab civilization reached its most brilliant development during this period. The Jewish intellectuals became enthusiastic co-workers of the learned Arabs in every branch of knowledge and cultural creativity. When the Jews began to emigrate from Spain into southern France, Italy and other Mediterranean countries, they brought with them into those still backward Christian lands elements of the superior Greek-Arab-Hebrew culture. The historical fact seems somewhat paradoxical: the Jews and the Arabs who were nurtured by the Orient were, in a cultural sense, the first Europeans. They planted the intellectual seed of Western civilization on the Continent.

In Arab lands, where there had existed a free intermingling of many cultures, there had blossomed a rich and unique Jewish culture. It had spread to Babylonia after its conquest in 642 by Mohammed in the course of his holy war. In the centuries of Babylonian Jewry's declining preëminence as the world center of Jewish learning, there emerged a galaxy of highly gifted religious philosophers, scholars, poets and scientists whose writings showed the impact of the best of Greek-Arab thinking and literary taste.

The Flowering of Jewish Genius: Saadya Gaon

The most profound of these Jewish intellectuals was Saadya Gaon (892-942). He was the *gaon,* or rector, of the great Talmudic academy that flourished in Sura. Although originally from Egypt, his encyclopedic learning, genius and

Page from a Saadya Gaon holograph ms.

moral probity made him readily acceptable to the Babylonian Jewish community as the ultimate religious authority of the age. This held equally true of the Jews of Spain, with their strong Greek-Arab cultural traditions. A brilliant writer on philosophic and scientific subjects, Saadya Gaon had introduced a new and novel method of Bible study which attempted a rational analysis of the Scriptural text based principally on scientific philology. This was a field in which he was ably followed a century later by the great poet and Bible interpreter, Abraham ibn Ezra. This method, objective and critical at the same time, left an indelible mark on the intellectual religious development not only of the medieval Jews but of both the liberal Christian scholastics and of the Protestant reformers who followed them.

The love of secular learning among the Arabic-speaking religious Jews was even greater than it had ever been among the Jewish Hellenists in Alexandria a thousand years before. In a testament addressed to his son, Hai Gaon (998-1038), the last of the illustrious line of Babylonian religious educators, wrote: "I have provided you, too, with books on all the sciences. . . . I have also made exhausting journeys to distant lands and brought for you a teacher of the secular sciences, counting neither the expense nor the dangers of the journey."

Earliest Hebrew musical notation known, Cairo, 12th-13th century.

It was this religious-secular tradition, more than a thousand years old among the Jews of the Near East and North Africa, which so vividly shaped the character of Jewish culture in Spain and which produced so many learned Jews: poets, philosophers, Biblical exegetes, doctors, astronomers, grammarians and mathematicians. The brilliant era had begun under the enthusiastic patronage of Hasdai ibn Shaprut (915-70), vizier to two caliphs in Cordova. Because he was a genuine scholar and physician in his own right, he used his influential position at court and his wealth to encourage a great number of writers, thinkers and scientists to develop their gifts. It was partly due to his energetic efforts that the chief center of Jewish culture gradually shifted from Sura in Asia to Cordova in Europe. It is no overstatement that Jews were active as humanists in Europe at least four or five centuries before the advent of the more widely known Christian humanists who were their lineal descendants.

During the century that followed, under the further encouragement of another Jewish patron of learning, Samuel ibn Nagdela (Samuel ha-Nagid), himself a scholar and a poet of distinction as well as the vizier to the Moorish king of Granada, there was a renewed flowering of Jewish learning in Spain. The science of Hebrew philology, grammar and lexicography was painstakingly developed by a small army of scholars.

Maimonides (traditional portrait). *Etching by Saul Raskin*

Maimonides

This great age labored and gave birth to a giant—Moses ben Maimon (Maimonides) (1135-1204). He was regarded by worshipful generations of Jews who came after him as the Jewish scholar and thinker par excellence. An Aristotelian, endowed with a balanced mentality and character, he tried to pursue within the practical framework of Jewish ethics the ideal of the Golden Mean in all things, including religion. Besides being one of the greatest of medical scientists and practitioners of his time—he served as court physician to Saladin in Cairo—he was one of the greatest thinkers the Middle Ages produced. The logical method that he developed for reconciling religious faith with reason was eagerly adopted by the leading schoolmen of the Church: Alexander of Halles, Albertus Magnus and Thomas Aquinas, particularly by the latter. This grafting of Maimonides' method of reconciliation onto Christian theology had a significant historical impact on the further development of European thought, far more than has been generally realized.

Maimonides' intellectual independence as an interpreter of the Bible and of Jewish religious belief and law met with a fervent response from the more advanced Jewish thinkers. At the same time, his reliance on philosophy to buttress religious faith was sharply attacked by the traditionalists. They had no desire to see a marriage of convenience between Aristotle and the *Torah* handed down from Mount Sinai. In fact, they saw it as conceivably leading the unwary to heresy. Despite this opposition, the name of Maimonides, whom the Jewish folk

A Guide for the Perplexed. Hand-written and illuminated parchment leaf from Maimonides' celebrated book.

Holograph *responsum* of Maimonides.

reverently call *Rambam* (the Hebrew mnemonic of "Rabbi Moses ben Maimon"), took on with time a legendary aura of greatness. It led to the popular saying: "From Moses our teacher to Moses ben Maimon there was no one like this Moses."

Tomb of Maimonides at Tiberias.

Solomon Ibn Gabirol

Another thinker of striking originality in that period was the Hebrew poet and philosopher, Solomon ibn Gabirol (1021-1070). He was a philosophical poet of the first order, still to be rediscovered by world literature. He is best known to Jews for his deeply emotional liturgical poems which to this day are still chanted by the pious in the synagogues of the world. Ironically enough, the profoundest impact of his genius was on Christian thought. Under the pseudonym of Avicebron there was published in 1150 the *Fons Vitae,* a Latin translation of his philosophical work, *Fountain of Life,* which he had originally written in Hebrew. Leading Christian schoolmen became deeply imbued with its ideas, never suspecting that its author was a rabbi. Its profoundest impression of all was on Duns Scotus, the founder of the Franciscan Order and the great intellectual rival of Thomas Aquinas. The Scottish philosopher adopted Ibn Gabirol's concept of a material substratum (matter and form) to spiritual essences as well as to the universe, an idea which played an important role in the development of scientific thought and of rationalism in Europe.

Yehudah Halevi and the Ibn Ezras

Numerous were the poets, philosophers, scientists and religious writers that the fecund Jewish cultural milieu produced in Spain. Of true genius were the celebrated philosopher-poet, Yehudah Halevi (1085-1140), Moses ibn Ezra (1075-1138), who wrote much secular verse, and Abraham

Synagogue scene. (From a 14th-century Hebrew manuscript.)

ibn Ezra (1110-1180), the lyric poet, liturgist and Biblical commentator whose interpretation of the Scriptural text, in Jewish religious estimation, ranks next to that of Rashi.

Undoubtedly, one of the great services the Jews rendered Western civilization was to make available, beginning with the Middle Ages, translations in Latin of important scholarly and scientific works of every variety that had originally been written in Hebrew, Greek and Arabic. This constituted the raw material out of which much of Christian culture, thought and knowledge was fashioned.

THE MOORISH-CHRISTIAN CONFLICT

All this occurred while the bulk of the Jews of Spain lived in the Mohammedan south, in Cordova, Seville, Toledo, Granada and other cities. But when the Christian kingdoms in the north united their forces under Alfonso VI of Castile to break the power of the Moors and drove them out of Toledo in 1085, the Jews fell on evil days. The Moors then called to their aid the fanatical Berber tribes of the Atlas Mountains, the Almoravides, who defeated the Christian armies the following year and then started a merciless campaign to convert the Jews to Islam. Sixty years later, in 1146, the even more fanatical Berber tribes, the Almohades, wrested power from the Almoravides. Monistic in their religion, the new Mo-

Ferdinand III of Castile was one of the more humane rulers of medieval Spain. In 1247, after he had driven the Moslems out of Seville, he was met at the gates by a procession of Jews who presented him with a key bearing an inscription in both Spanish and Hebrew: "God opens, the King enters." His tombstone bears epitaphs in four languages, one of them Hebrew.

hammedan masters tried to force the Jews at the point of the sword to accept Islam. Many Jews perished. Others, including young Maimonides and his parents, fled to Egypt or to the Christian kingdoms of northern Spain, thinking hopefully to find a refuge there.

For less than a century the Christian rulers acted with restraint. Jewish culture in an Arabic-Hebrew context continued to flourish in Spanish-speaking Aragon, Castile, Navarre and Leon. But with the years, the dominance of the Church over the state power increased. Tensions, encouraged especially by the Dominican Order, accumulated and were finally released in explosions of violence and pillage in the ghettos of Seville, Cordova, Toledo, Barcelona and in some seventy other towns and cities. In these holocausts, countless thousands of Jews were killed and many were forcibly baptized.

In the year 1411 the Dominican friar, Vincent Ferrer, later sainted, swept through Castile at the head of a huge armed mob of fanatics and looters. On the Sabbath, when the Jews were assembled at worship in their synagogues, he would rush into their midst holding a *Sefer Torah* in one hand and brandishing a crucifix like a sword in the other. The choice he offered was very simple: "Baptism or death!" Thousands were slaughtered. Vincent Ferrer boasted that he himself had baptized thirty-five thousand Jews.

THE INQUISITION

The events of the fateful year 1411 marked the catastrophic turning point of Jewish destiny in Spain. There was a continuing and relentless pressure, legal and extra-legal, from both Church and state to bring the reluctant Jews to the baptismal font. The opportunists and the frightened succumbed to the terror and became *conversos*. At first the blandishments of being Christian communicants appeared alluring: all the shining doors of opportunity were opened wide to the apostates. Many of them carved out careers in government, finance, trade and the army. A number became *hidalgos* and even *grandees* of the kingdom. Quite a few who had been schooled in the Talmudic academies found a ready outlet for their religious learning in the service of the Church. One of them, an able Jewish scholar—it is said, a rabbi—was almost elected pope in Avignon. This was Paulus de Santa Maria, formerly Solomon Halevi (1352-1435). He eventually became Archbishop of Burgos, the Primate of the Church of all Spain, and acted as Vincent Ferrer's evil genius, inspiring him to ever greater ferocity in his crusade to convert or exterminate the Jews.

It was to be expected that in an atmosphere charged with violence and intimidation informers, eager for reward or approval, should have risen everywhere to furnish the Church with alleged knowledge of heretical views or actions of the *conversos*. The heresy consisted principally of secret relapses into Jewish religious beliefs and practices. By a treacherous ruse, thousands of *Marranos* (literally "Pigs") or New Christians, who were promised amnesty if they would confess their "Judaizing" sins, stepped forward voluntarily and did confess, only to discover that they had been lured into a trap. Under torture many implicated other *Marranos*, who in turn were stretched on the rack only to implicate still others. It was an ever-widening circle of violence and treachery which cast a deadly pall over Jewish life in Spain.

The Alba Bible. Translated into Spanish by Rabbi Moses Arragel, with extracts from the commentaries of Rashi, Abraham ibn Ezra and Maimonides. Commissioned by Grand Master Don Luis de Guzman, it was presented to him at Toledo in 1430. The illumination shown here depicts Rabbi Moses presenting the finished work to Don Luis, who is shown surrounded by his Knights of the Order of Calatrava. The figures at top represent the deeds of kindness they were sworn to practice, benevolences also cherished by Jews: (left to right) feeding (*comer*), giving drink (*beuer*), giving shoes (*calcar*), and clothing (*vestir*) to the poor, as well as visiting (*visitar*) the sick, comforting (*consolar*) the sorrowful and burying (*entercar*) the dead.

All this time a righteous pretense at legality was kept up. As early as 1237 the Church had armed itself against heretics and relapsers by means of special tribunals of inquisitors, made up exclusively of friars of the Dominican Order. The sole object of these tribunals was to investigate all charges of heresy and unbelief, though they also had the power to punish.

The Golden Tower of Seville where Jews of the city, during the Middle Ages, sought refuge from the mob.

By 1480 the Cortes at Toledo had fervently sanctioned the institution of a similar Inquisition for the entire country. Under the implacable direction of the Dominican Confessor of Queen Isabella, Tomas de Torquemada, the Inquisition, or Holy Office, as it was sometimes called, began to operate on an enormous man-devouring scale. Many thousands of *Marranos* were arrested and flung into dungeons, waiting in agonizing suspense for their turn to be tried by the courts of the Inquisition.

The Inquisition was efficient and legalistically scrupulous. It issued special manuals for the guidance of the inquisitors, and others for the instruction of would-be informers. How, really, was one to tell a heretic among the *conversos*? There

Transito Church of Toledo, originally a synagogue. Note the Hebrew inscriptions.

were a number of recognizable signs of heresy, the manual pointed out helpfully. If a New Christian wore his best clothes on the Sabbath; if he celebrated the *Seder* on Passover; if he was overheard muttering prayers in Hebrew; if he bought wine and meat from a Jew; if he fasted on *Yom Kippur;* if he circumcised his male child—then he was most certainly a "Judaizing heretic."

Home of Samuel Abulafia (1320-60) at Toledo. He was Finance Minister to Pedro the Cruel, who executed him in 1360.

The trials of the *Marranos* were not routine hearings. They were invariably marked by tragedy and a trail of blood. Those who refused to confess were put to the torture, and the ingenuity of sadists was fully taxed to create the most agonizing torments for the crushing of the stubborn. Thousands babbled incoherent confessions they never believed and almost eagerly implicated innocent persons in order to be free at last of the pain they could not endure. Amazingly enough, there were thousands who remained firm under torture. They died in tight-lipped agony in the flames of the *autos-da-fé*.

The *auto-da-fé*, or "act of faith," took on all the theatricality of a religious spectacle and, like the morality play, it was designed by the Church to strengthen the religious fidelity of

Marranos surprised at secret *Seder*.

The Grand Inquisitor Thomas de Torquemada. His grandfather, Alvar Fernandez de Torquemada, had married a recently baptized Jewess, a genealogical fact that throws psychopathologic light on the grandson's ruthlessness toward Jews. He burned 2,000 heretics and imprisoned and ruined 100,000 others, most of them *Marranos*. (Detail from a painting by Pedro Berruquete in the monastery of St. Thomas at Avila.)

The Inquisition's torture chambers, c. 1725.

Bernard Picart

Auto-da-fé, c. 1500.

the crowds who assembled to witness it. Besides, it was also intended as a stern warning to the vacillating and to the unrepentant heretics.

To the churchly sound of chanting priests and amidst the full display of the Church's panoply of power, the relapsed were led into the arena, especially constructed for this purpose, while the assembled thousands watched.

The heretics wore the *sanbenito*, or penitent's tunic of sackcloth, and carried lighted candles in their hands. For the last time the priests came forward and exhorted them to confess their relapses into Judaism, promising the sincere penitents the Church's forgiveness.

Many did confess, and their abject contrition saved them from the stake. But others remained obdurate and refused to confess. What had they to confess? They were innocent! Still others proudly affirmed their unregenerate devotion to the faith of their fathers and tearfully prepared for the end.

The end came on the *Quemadero*, the stake to which they were tied. As the flames licked upwards the faithful expired, reciting the *Shema*: "Hear, O Israel, the Lord our God, the Lord is One!"

Confessing her sins of heresy, the "repentant" woman receives forgiveness. Unbroken in his Jewish faith, the "unrepentant" goes mournfully to the stake.

The first *auto-da-fé* was held on February 6, 1481, when six men and six women, unrepentant of their backsliding, were burned at the stake. During the sixteen years of Torquemada's blood-and-iron rule of the Holy Office a virtual reign of terror gripped Spain. A great number of *Marranos* perished in this theatrical manner, as did many non-Jewish heretics. Many were condemned to rot in the Inquisition's dungeons. Every *converso* was suspected of relapsing into his old faith, and even high Church dignitaries of remote Jewish ancestry were drawn into this spider's web of fear and distrust spun by the Inquisition over the whole country. It even caught a number of *hidalgos*, men prominent at the royal court, who, because of their Jewish descent, had to undergo merciless grilling and torture, and the *Quemadero* burned brightly with their aristocratic bodies, too.

For more than three hundred years the pyres of the Inquisition blazed throughout Europe, especially in Portugal and Portuguese Goa in India, in Provence, in Spain and her Latin-American domains. Despite the forces of enlightenment which were working against it during the seventeenth and eighteenth centuries, the bloody power of the Holy Office remained unbroken. It led the great French thinker, Montesquieu, to remark bitterly in 1738: "If anyone in days to come should ever dare to say that the people of Europe were civilized in the century in which we are now living, you [Holy Office] will be cited as proof that they are barbarians."

109

Portuguese *Marranos* celebrating Passover, but without the *Seder* service. The existence in Portugal of some 10,000 families of *Marranos* was first disclosed to the world in 1919 by a Jewish mining engineer, Samuel Schwarz. Throughout the Inquisition and in the years that followed, these people had lived outwardly as Catholics, but considered themselves as a group apart and secretly practiced curious adaptations of Jewish rites. Since their accidental discovery they have been integrating themselves as a Jewish-conscious community.

EXPULSION

The Grand Inquisitor Torquemada finally came to the conclusion that to suppress the virulent heresy of Judaism among the *Marranos* would be impossible unless the source of the contagion were removed. He therefore appealed to Pope Innocent VIII, a Borgia, that he order the expulsion of the Jews from Spain. The pope, doubting the wisdom of this plan solely on practical grounds, rejected the proposal, but Torquemada was determined to pursue his objective even without papal sanction. As Queen Isabella's confessor he found it easy to make a pliant tool of her. He finally persuaded both her and her husband Ferdinand that the expulsion of the Jews was most urgently necessary for the greater glory of the Church and the Christian religion.

When news of this reached the Jews, dismay was the least of its effects upon them. Most of them were of stock that had lived continuously in Spain for many centuries. The two most prominent Jews who were close to the court, Abraham Senior, the chief tax farmer, who had helped finance the voyage of Columbus which resulted in the discovery of America, and Isaac Abrabanel, the minister of finance to the king and queen, made desperate but futile attempts to intercede. The story, however apocryphal, runs that these two *grandees* sought an audience with Ferdinand and Isabella. They offered to pay an enormous sum of money into the royal treasury provided the order for the expulsion of the Jews were rescinded. In the midst of this proposal, when the royal pair

showed signs of being tempted by the offer—for they were badly in need of money at the time—Torquemada burst into the room waving a crucifix before Ferdinand and Isabella. He cried: "Behold the Savior, whom the wicked Judas sold for thirty pieces of silver! If you approve that deed, then sell Him for a great sum."

The king and queen signed the edict of expulsion on March 31, 1492. The Jews were allowed four months to prepare for their departure. They could take out of the country only their personal effects and were forbidden to have with them any gold, silver or jewels.

The fear of expulsion proved overpowering. It caused the weak to compromise with the harsh reality. They purchased animal safety and residence in the country at the bitter price of baptism. Yet there were hundreds of thousands of others who preferred exile to dishonor.

Isaac Abrabanel (traditional portrait).

In his diary Columbus noted: "In the same month in which Their Majesties issued the edict that all Jews should be driven out of the kingdom and its territories, in the same month they gave me the order to undertake with sufficient men my expedition of discovery to the Indies."

It is related in contemporary chronicles that the roads leading to the port cities of Spain were choked with the mass of departing exiles. Their misery was indescribable.

About one hundred thousand of the expelled sought a haven in neighboring Portugal. But these were merely leaping from the frying pan into the fire. Thousands there were forced into baptism. Many were sold into slavery. Others, out of a despair that could no longer be endured, sought escape in death.

In this manner, the great Jewish community that had wrought a wondrous Golden Age of Jewish civilization in Spain came to a disastrous end.

Torquemada opposes the Jewish plea against expulsion before Ferdinand and Isabella.

THE NETHERLANDS

Seventeenth and Eighteenth Centuries

The shadow of the Inquisition spread like a pall over Europe, drawing one country after another into it. Under its blight the culture of the Renaissance began to wither.

From Spain the Holy Office next moved into Portugal in 1531. Then started its unrelenting persecution of *Marranos* there on charges of relapsing from the Catholic faith and of secretly practicing "the Judaizing heresy."

As time went on the harassment of these new converts became intolerable. Those who possessed the means sought to escape from the country. Unfortunately, the great majority of *Marranos* had become desperately poor. They saw little hope of cutting themselves loose from the fatal net of their double loyalty: as Christians openly, and as Jews secretly. Many resigned themselves to the hopelessness of their lot, and, putting an end to their inner struggle, went over completely to the Church. Others, however, with stronger moral fiber, set themselves to wait resolutely for the day when they might manage to escape from the country to a more tolerant environment where merely to be a Jew would not be considered a major crime punishable by death.

But eventually the power of Spain started to crumble. First came the unexpected successes of the Dutch in their struggle to gain independence from Spanish rule, which was marked by the Union of Utrecht in 1579. This was followed in 1588 by the crushing defeat dealt the Great Armada by the English navy. Spain now lost its long-maintained supremacy as a maritime power.

In all this the *Marranos* of Spain and Portugal saw a new hope for themselves. Many began exploring the possibilities of settling in the Netherlands now that it was a Protestant country.

The first group of Portuguese New Christians arrived in Amsterdam in 1593 under the leadership of Jacob Tirado. When word got back to Portugal that they were not being molested by the Dutch and lived openly as Jews, an even larger group of *Marranos* set sail for Holland nine years later.

They landed in the port town of Emden in the province of Friesland. As they wandered through the streets they came to a house over whose doorway were written several words in Hebrew. They entered and were welcomed by Rabbi Moses Uri Halevi. Overjoyed to find an openly professing rabbi, they begged him to reconvert them to Judaism. He explained regretfully that even under Protestant rule it would be dangerous for all concerned if he brought Christians back into the Jewish fold. However, believing that the authorities in Amsterdam would show greater tolerance in the matter, he led the little band of refugees to that city. There he instructed them in the tenets of their ancestors' faith and declared them to be Jews thenceforth.

Amsterdam

It was this group, in addition to the earlier one led by Tirado, which served as the nucleus for the Jewish community of Amsterdam. In a short time, because of the vital cultural and religious Jewish life that developed there, the city acquired the name of "New Jerusalem" among the Jews of Europe.

At first the Amsterdam Jews had no synagogue. They held prayer services in the home of Samuel Palache, a former *Marrano* acting as consul for Morocco in Amsterdam. Because of the secretive ways to which the Inquisition had habituated them in Portugal, they now held their services in a manner which aroused the suspicions of the Amsterdam authorities. The latter swooped down on them and caught them—deep in the soul-searching prayers of *Yom Kippur*.

Hailed before the magistrates, they were accused of secretly practicing their "Papist" religion which was banned under the new government. Unfortunately, there was not one among the Jews who could make himself understood properly in Dutch, but the imaginative Jacob Tirado by speaking in Latin finally managed to identify his brethren to the magistrates. He pleaded that if the *Marranos* were allowed to stay and practice the Jewish religion freely and openly in Amsterdam they would bring many of their friends and relations from Portugal. These were, he maintained, men of means, education and business ability, who, if allowed full scope to their capabilities and enterprise, would undoubtedly bring commercial and cultural benefits to the city.

Tirado's arguments proved attractive to the practical-minded Dutch. When the magistrates asked for a legal opinion from the noted jurist, Hugo Grotius, he replied in favor of the *Marranos*. Official permission was therefore granted them to settle in Amsterdam in the year 1615. In legal documents they were thenceforth described as "members of the Hebrew nation." The authorities laid down only two restrictions: first, Jews were not to marry Christians, and second, they were not to make any attacks on the state religion.

The Dutch never had occasion to regret the settlement of *Marranos* and Jews in their country. From their activities, prosperity and energy flowed to Amsterdam. With their help the city became one of the principal maritime centers of

Synagogue interior,
Amsterdam.
Rembrandt

Interior of the first Amsterdam synagogue, in which Uriel da Costa and Baruch Spinoza were excommunicated.

Europe. By and large, the *Marranos* were enterprising merchants and traders. They were fluent in many tongues and were thus ideally suited for carrying on international commerce. Moreover, they had world-wide connections with the dispersed communities of Spanish and Portuguese Jews and *Marranos,* especially in the countries of North Africa, in Arab lands, Turkey, Greece, Persia and India. They also established important shipping branches in such strategic trade ports as Livorno, Genoa, Venice and Naples.

Finding a ready and unrestricted field for their energies, the Jews of Amsterdam founded new factories and industries. They also did an effective banking business; at one time they controlled more than a quarter of the stock of the East India Company which played such a decisive role in the history of New York.

The prosperity and the relative freedom they enjoyed in Amsterdam drew more and more Jews and *Marranos* to the city. They came from every part of Europe, but mostly from Spain and Portugal.

Rabbi Saul Levi Morteira, Chief Rabbi of the Synagogue of Amsterdam, who was Spinoza's teacher of Hebrew and the *Talmud.*
Rembrandt

Marrano Culture

As everywhere else they went, the *Marranos* brought with them to Amsterdam their superior culture. It was a worldliness foreign to the ghetto Jews of Germany and Poland. Even under the oppression of the Holy Office they had functioned in Spain and Portugal as doctors, lawyers, scholars, writers, university professors, army officers, manufacturers and even as statesmen, diplomats and landed *hidalgos.* In "New Jerusalem" they picked up the threads of their past callings and many achieved great distinction in them. One has only to consider that two of the most eminent physicians of the age, practicing for many years in Amsterdam, were former Portuguese *Marranos.* One was Abraham Sakut, better known in the history of medicine as Zacutus Lusitanus. He came from Lisbon to Amsterdam in 1625. The other was Isaac Orobio de Castro, the *hidalgo* philosopher-physician who died in Amsterdam in 1684.

In time, many of these former *Marranos* acquired fortunes from their banking, manufacturing and shipping activities. They built imposing homes and raised beautiful synagogues. They helped advance both Jewish and Dutch culture in all branches. With traditional Jewish piety they gave generously of their money for the support of the needy and of Jewish communal institutions.

A surprising number of *Marranos* who escaped to Amsterdam were priests and monks. Some had even achieved con-

House of the da Costa family, Amsterdam; and signature of Uriel da Costa.

siderable eminence in the Church. They, too, wished to be reunited with their Jewish brothers. One of them, Fra Vicente de Rocamora, was a Dominican friar who had served as confessor to the Infanta Maria of Spain who later became Empress of Austria. In 1643 he vanished from the royal court and appeared in Amsterdam. There he returned to the Jewish religion and assumed the name of Isaac. He spent the remainder of his life as a physician practicing in the ghetto.

It was not unnatural for many *Marranos,* who had previously achieved positions of eminence in the Christian world as scientists, writers and scholars, that they should occasionally have differed in their religious views from those Jews with less liberality of mind and worldliness. Their nonconformism, however, did not add to their popularity, and inevitably led to sharp controversies within the Jewish community. The grief, and sometimes tragedy, experienced by such individuals, who had to live within the rigid religious framework of the Amsterdam ghetto, could be laid at the door of the new zealots. It was only the other day, figuratively speaking, that they themselves had been brutally victimized by bigotry in Spain and Portugal. Yet, no sooner had they escaped into a milder religious and community life than they in turn be-

Zacutus Lusitanus, 1642, foremost Jewish doctor in Holland in the days of Rembrandt.

Spinoza's house, Rijnsburg.

came harsh persecutors of those who dissented in any way from their ideas.

They humiliated, excommunicated and drove from their midst as a pariah such a gifted and honest thinker as Uriel da Costa, a young man under the strong influence of the new spirit of scientific inquiry. In order to escape from his position of complete social isolation he recanted his heretical views publicly in the synagogue before the entire congregation. Then, overcome by remorse because of the moral weakness he had shown, he sat up all night writing his last will and testament, reaffirming his heresies, and then shot himself.

Baruch Spinoza.

A similar punishment was meted out by the bigots to another and much more eminent dissenter: Baruch Spinoza, the greatest philosopher the Jewish people have produced. He, too, was charged with heretical views and, after a trial, was excommunicated. Although only twenty-four years old then, and unlike the vacillating Uriel da Costa, he was a man of singular strength of character. Instead of seeking to purchase a doubtful safety with a recantation of the truths he believed in, he voluntarily turned his back on the ghetto. He went out into the world to pursue with a serene spirit and a consistency

Dedication of first-born, 1722.   *Bernard Picart*

the life of reason and virtue which has become so synonymous with his name.

Sephardim and Ashkenazim

Community life in the *Jueden-Bort,* or ghetto, continued to bloom luxuriantly, especially in a religious-cultural sense. During the seventeenth and eighteenth centuries Amsterdam was the principal Jewish intellectual center of Europe. Rabbinical scholars and writers flocked to it from all parts of central and eastern Europe. Many learned and religious works rolled off its busy Hebrew and Yiddish presses. In a limited sense, this represented a minor Renaissance of Jewish religious culture.

After a while, the character of the Jewish community went through a profound transformation. It was only a half century after Jacob Tirado's little band of *Marranos* had come to settle in Amsterdam when Yiddish-speaking Jews from Germany began to arrive. They founded, in 1640, their own little community within the larger Jewish community. For a long time they were separated from the Iberian Jews by differences of language, culture, wealth, manners and religious rites. The Spanish and Portuguese Jews observed the Eastern or *Sephardic* rite and order of prayer in their synagogue services. Therefore they referred to themselves as *Sephardim.* The Yiddish-speaking Jews from Germany, and later from Poland, followed the German or *Ashkenazic* rite, and so they were called *Ashkenazim.* Each group worshipped in its own way and in its own synagogue.

Only eight years later, in 1648, following the massacres by the Cossack Hetman Chmielnicki, a stream of fleeing refugees poured into Amsterdam from Poland, Galicia, the Ukraine and Lithuania. Since the newcomers, alike with the German Jews, spoke Yiddish as their mother-tongue and also observed the same *Ashkenazic* rites and ceremonies, they merged their congregations in 1673 and readily intermarried. This, however, was not the case with the *Sephardim,* who considered them socially and culturally inferior, and so would not intermarry with them. They constituted mostly a wealthy and cultured class, while the *Ashkenazim* were in the main poor Jews who earned their livelihood as peddlers, petty traders, artisans, diamond polishers, jewelry workers and silversmiths.

However, a change came into the strained relations which put both *Sephardim* and *Ashkenazim* on an equal social footing. Poverty was the great leveler. When the English began to dominate the shipping and commercial world in the eighteenth century, thus dealing Dutch trade a severe blow, the "seven fat years" the *Sephardim* had enjoyed for a century or more came to an end. Unwise investments in speculative projects added further to their impoverishment. In fact, many of them had to seek aid from the *Ashkenazim* who ultimately constituted a majority of Amsterdam Jewry. Gradually, the differences that previously divided them began to be less marked, and together they formed a more reasonably united community.

Ceremony of *shofar* blowing, Rosh Hashanah, 1725.
Bernard Picart

FRANCE (Medieval)

Wherever the Romans went, Jews went, too. As subjects of the empire, a number were allowed to settle in Gaul. It is possible that there were several small colonies of Jews in France during the first centuries after the end of the Jewish state. There is evidence in the *Talmud* that the illustrious Rabbi Akiba visited that country some time before the outbreak of Bar-Kochba's revolt in 133 C.E. It is certain, though, that by the sixth century there were compact little communities of Jews in some twenty towns, most of them in the Provence, such as Arles, Narbonne, Orléans, Marseilles, and among those in the north, Paris.

Earliest dated Latin inscription (689 C.E.) relating to the Jews of France. This Narbonne tombstone shows *menorah* upper left and *Shalom al Yisrael* in Hebrew lower right.

Within certain limitations the Jews enjoyed the rights and privileges of the other inhabitants of the land. They could own houses, till the soil and cultivate vineyards. Under the Merovingian kings, Provençal Jews were allowed to be artisans. Many of them became expert spinners and weavers, dyers, tailors, goldsmiths and silversmiths, armorers and ornamental saddlemakers. To be sure, Jews also furnished their quota of mint-masters, tax farmers and collectors, money lenders and cloth merchants. They, however, distinguished themselves most as merchants and carried on an active trade with the Levant, North Africa and the Orient. In medieval history they are referred to as the "Radanites" (from the Latin *Rhodanus,* namely, men of the Rhône valley).

Seal of Kalonymos ben Todros (d. 1194), the "Nasi" (leader of the Jewish community) of Narbonne.

At first, the Church and the rulers were at cross purposes in their policies toward the Jews. Christians and Jews lived side by side in neighborly amity. Popular prejudice had hardly been stirred up yet against the Jews. It was this fear of fraternization with them which led the early Church councils to issue to Christians stern prohibitions against having social relations with Jews, against intermarriage and against priests dining in the homes of Jews. The Church, independently of the state, initiated its own restrictions. For example, it ordered Jews off the streets during Easter Week because "their appearance is an insult to Christianity." There were attempts at forcible conversion of Jews, but this trend did not develop very favorably, due to the strong hand and, relatively speaking, the enlightened policy of the Frankish kings.

UNDER CHARLEMAGNE

The great Frankish Empire had been founded by Charlemagne (742-814). It extended from the Mediterranean to the North Sea and from the Atlantic Ocean to the Elbe River. Charlemagne not only ignored or circumvented many of the more stringent Church decrees, but he prevented violence against the persons and the possessions of the Jews. He employed a number of Jews in high diplomatic and financial capacities at court. When, for instance, he wished to establish relations with Haroun al-Rashid, the Caliph of Bagdad, celebrated in the Arabian Nights stories, he sent the Jew Isaac on the mission.

The Jews of Carolingian times enjoyed almost complete religious freedom. They could live and travel wherever they pleased. The Jewish communities ruled themselves. They dispensed justice through their traditional religious court, the *bet din,* and were free to build synagogues and to establish houses of study. When, at a Council of Bishops, in 829, Agobard, the Bishop of Lyons, vehemently demanded that Jews be completely segregated from Christians, Charlemagne's son, Louis the Debonair, retorted: "Divine Law bids me protect my subjects who share my belief, but it nowhere forbids me to be just towards those who differ from me."

But after Charlemagne's empire broke up a generation later, the Church became ascendant over the state. It introduced a great variety of vexatious laws and harassments against the Jews.

DURING THE CRUSADES

The first Crusade in 1096 marked a startling change in the fortunes of the Jews of France and of all Christian Europe. The call for the Crusade against the Mohammedan "infidels" who then ruled the Holy Land was issued by Pope Urban II

Attitude of the Church toward the Jewish religion, shown in 13th century representations of church, left, and synagogue, right, at Strasbourg Cathedral. The synagogue is depicted as blindfolded without a crown and with a broken staff.

on November 26, 1095, at Clermont. By the following summer a host of some two hundred thousand knights, priests, burghers, peasants and artisans had assembled in France in order to march against the Saracens ruled by Saladin the Great. Under Peter the Hermit's impassioned lashing, the religious hysteria of the Crusaders mounted. He told them that, since Jews were as much infidels as Moslems, a sure way to earn salvation was to kill them. First in France and then

Meeting of rabbinical and lay leaders. (From a 13th-century French ms.)

in England, the Crusaders massacred the Jews. From there the tide of violence rolled on into Germany, Austria and elsewhere across Europe. The Crusaders shouted to the Jews: "Christ-killers, embrace the cross or die!"

Many saved their lives through baptism or flight, but most chose death. Entire communities destroyed themselves in a mass martyrdom. Thousands of others, driven into the synagogues, were burned alive by the Crusaders. Jewish mothers even killed their own children, or, clasping them in their arms, leaped with them into the Rhine to their death.

While the Crusaders accomplished their goriest deeds in the Rhineland, northern France and Lorraine, the towns in Provence largely escaped their fury. During the third Crusade, in part due to the efforts of the renegade Jew, Nicholas Donin of La Rochelle, who had become a Franciscan monk, the Crusaders blazed another bloody trail through Brittany, Poitou and Anjou. In Anjou alone three thousand Jews were killed and five hundred were forced into baptism.

French Jewish costume, 14th century.

This period was also marked by strenuous efforts of the Church to liquidate the Jewish people as a religious entity. The apostate Donin had gone to Rome in 1238, and while there he had convinced Pope Gregory IX that if the Jews hitherto had resisted all efforts to convert them to Christianity it was largely because of their fanatical devotion to the *Talmud.* Pope Gregory, known in Chruch history as "the Great," then ordered all copies of the *Talmud* confiscated. Following this papal action, Saint Louis, king of France, ordered that the Jews in his kingdom surrender their *Talmuds* to the civil authorities on pain of death. The indefatigable Donin, driven on by some insane compulsion to justify his break with the Jewish people and his former faith, also induced the French king to command a disputation between himself and the Christian theologians on the one side, and leading Talmudic scholars, including Yehiel of Paris, Moses of Coucy and Samuel ben Solomon of Chateau-Thierry on the other. The subject of the disputation: that the *Talmud* blasphemed the holy name of Christ and the sacred dogmas of Christianity and sanctioned evil-doing against Christians as a religious requirement. Not only were the king and the nobility present at this verbal "tournament," but also the two famed philosophers of the Church, Albertus Magnus and William of Auvergne.

The verdict was a foregone conclusion: the Jews were forced to surrender their *Talmuds,* which were ceremoniously burned in a huge bonfire.

RASHI

There were two opposing trends evident in the religious life of French and German Jews during the Middle Ages. One was strongly traditionalist. It was dominated by Rashi of Troyes, "The Prince of Bible Commentators" (1040-1105), and his disciples known as "The Tosafists," the continuators of his orthodox method of interpreting Scripture. The other, rationalist and philosophical, was best represented by Levi ben Gerson (1288-1344), one of the most original thinkers of the Middle Ages. While the impact of Rashi's thinking was greatest in the Rhineland, the chief stronghold of French-German orthodoxy, the liberal religious philosophy of Levi ben Gerson, which stemmed from Maimonides, flourished best in Provence, which, contiguous with Spain, shared in much of its culture.

Rashi, the Hebrew mnemonic of Rabbi Solomon ben Isaac, had a far-reaching influence on the Jewish religious thought of Europe, an influence that is still potent today. It is customary to find his Bible commentary printed side by side with the Hebrew text of the *Chumash,* the Five Books of Moses. His other commentary, that on the *Talmud,* has had almost equal authority through the centuries. Unlike Maimonides and Levi ben Gerson, both ardent followers of Aristotle and both rationalists, who believed that the Bible was not to be taken in its strict literal meanings but should be interpreted freely and allegorically, Rashi took a diametrically opposite point of view. He laid down an undeviating rule: "Scripture must be interpreted according to its plain natural sense, each word according to the context. Traditional explanations, however, may also be accepted."

Levi ben Gerson of Perpignan and Avignon in the south, on the other hand, was the brilliant intellectual product of Greek-Arabic thought that streamed from Babylonia, Egypt, Morocco and Spain. Both the content and method of his religious writings were influenced by his training and outlook as mathematician, astronomer and philosopher. The orthodox followers of Rashi were shocked by Levi ben Gerson's daring discussions of religious matters. His principal work, "The Wars of the Lord," they satirically dubbed "The Wars against the Lord."

EPILOGUE

The Jews were expelled from northern France in 1306. Most of them went to live in Provence, Lorraine, the Comtat Venaissin and Savoy. During the seventeenth and eighteenth centuries many *Marranos* came to those parts, where they augmented the Jewish population. Upon the signing of the Peace of Westphalia in 1648, the province of Alsace, where Jewish communities had held on precariously since the twelfth century, was joined to France. From then on French Jewry declined until 1789, when the egalitarian French Revolution ushered in for it a new era of usefulness and importance.

Massacre of Jews. (From *Miracles de Nostre Dame,* by Jean Mielot, 15th century.)

ENGLAND (Medieval)

There is evidence that there were Jews in England in Anglo-Saxon times. But there is no conclusive proof that they had lived there in settled communities before the Norman Conquest.

When William the Conqueror crossed the Channel in 1066, he brought a number of Jews from Rouen. With later arrivals from Normandy, they founded communities in London, Bury St. Edmond, Exeter, York and Norwich. In fact, in less than two centuries there were seventy "Jew Streets" in towns throughout England.

Obviously then, the English Jews of those days were mostly of French ancestry. They spoke French and had French names. In contemporary records there are references to Jewish women bearing such medieval French names as Belaset, Chère, Gentil, Précieuse and Riche, and to men named Amiot, Deulecress, Vives, Copin, etc.

The popular supposition that English Jewish life in the Middle Ages was always cast in gloom and devoid of normal joys and pleasures is false. The medieval Jewish historian, Ibn Verga, related that when the great poet and Bible exegete from Spain, Abraham ibn Ezra, visited London in 1158, he found there nearly two thousand Jewish families. They, like the Jews in all other communities throughout England, were leading an integrated community existence *as Jews.* Although the threats of robbery, torture and death were all too real for them, they only succeeded in uniting them in practices of mutual aid and group benevolence to an extraordinary degree. In the pursuit of these ethical values and in their religious life they found what their enemies could not take from them—the sustaining force for survival.

In all the English cities, but especially in London, there was intense intellectual activity among the Talmudists, Hebrew grammarians, astronomers and doctors. Appointed by the Crown to supervise the communal and religious affairs of the Jews was a rabbinical official called the "Arch Presbyter." The most famous of these presbyters was Rabbi Elhanan ben Isaac, a grandson of Rashi. The Church records referred to Rabbi Elhanan as "Deodatus Episcopus." This office was identical with that of the Hellenistic *Archesynagogos,* the Austrian *Judenmeister,* and the German *Judenbischof.* Probably the most beloved of all the religious leaders was Rabbi Yom-Tob of Joigny, of whom a contemporary Christian scholar wrote: "A certain old man, a most famous Doctor of the Law . . . who, it is said, had come from the parts beyond the sea to teach the English Jews. He was honored by all and was obeyed by all, as if he had been one of the prophets."

Jewish scholars found sympathetic friends in the most advanced intellectual circles. Three of the foremost Christian thinkers of the age, Roger Bacon, Michael Scot and Robert Grosseteste, acquired their knowledge of the Hebrew language and of Jewish philosophical and scientific writings from the learned Jews of England.

THE KING'S CHATTELS

The Jews admitted into the country were obviously selected for their potential usefulness to the Plantagenet kings. They were principally traders, doctors, and money lenders. In time,

however, the great majority of Jews in England consisted of the wretchedly poor.

As everywhere else in feudal society, the Jews in Angevin England were considered *servi camerae,* the chattels of the king. They stood outside the feudal system. Because they were "property," both in their persons and in their possessions, they received a certain measure of protection from the Crown. The pattern for the laws governing them was based on the earlier charter of Charlemagne in which the "chattel" clause was given great prominence. The charter promulgated in the year 1180 made this point very clear: "It should be known that all Jews, wheresoever in the realm they be, ought to be under the guard and protection of the King's liege. Nor ought any of them place himself under any rich man without the King's license; because the Jews themselves and all theirs belong to the King, and if any detain them or their money, let the King, if he will and can, ask it back as if it were his own."

Beginning with the Conqueror, the kings of feudal England required the services of Jewish money lenders to finance their wars and to run the fiscal departments of the government to enable them to remain independent of the barons who were struggling for greater power. A number of Jews were, therefore, allowed, encouraged and even helped, to engage in money lending, an activity forbidden to Christians.

Not only did Jews help finance the Royal Exchequer, but they also engaged in a general banking business with the lesser nobility, the Church and the town councils, but always *as agents of the Crown.* The more money they would make from these transactions the more profitable it would turn out in the end for the kings, who never hesitated to rob them of their profits by special levies or even by outright confiscation.

In an ironic way the Church, too, was made to profit from the activities of the hated Jewish money lenders. For instance, Aaron of Lincoln, the wealthiest Jew of England in his day, financed the construction of nine Cistercian abbeys with the money furnished by his Jewish banking pool. His loans also made possible the erection of Lincoln and Peterborough Cathedrals. It was in connection with the celebrated Church of St. Albans that Aaron is alleged by a Christian contemporary to have boasted that he had built a home for a Christian saint when he was homeless. When Aaron died in 1186, the Royal Exchequer promptly confiscated his wealth and used it for fighting the war against France.

The word "Jew" after a while became synonymous with "money lender." It was mentioned by Christians with revulsion and contumely, because lending money at interest, no matter how small, was considered a form of moral leprosy.

"Starr" of Aaron of Lincoln. Aaron's signature in Hebrew to a Latin receipt (1181) from Richard Malebys, later mob leader in the York Massacre.

The Christian debtors of the Jews also proved a major source of hostility to them. In order to protect the "king's chattels," it was required by law of all borrowers that they give collateral pledges to the Jews. In this manner, the Jewish money lenders were forced against their will and better judgment to accept a great variety of articles and property which they knew beforehand would ultimately bring them ruin and grief. This collateral consisted of houses, suits of armor, baronial estates and even the corn crop. The clergy frequently pledged the Church plate, the holy vessels and sometimes—as in the case of Bishop Nigel of Ely in the twelfth century—the relics of a saint.

All this did not endear the Jews to those in authority, who quickly communicated their hostility to the unthinking, suffering population, which was already inflamed by prejudice against the Jews on religious grounds. Furthermore, the religious hysteria that convulsed England during the Crusades dangerously aggravated the situation. The slanderous accusation against the Jews for the ritual murder of William of Norwich in 1144, followed about a century later by a similar charge involving "Little Hugh" of Lincoln, unleashed mob violence of the most savage kind.

After the bloody riots of 1204 in London, King John felt outraged by what had been done to his Jewish "property," and issued a stern order to the magistrates and the barons of the city to take stricter measures for maintaining the peace: "We say this for our Jews, and for our peace, for if we have granted our peace to anyone, it should be observed inviolably. Henceforth, however, we commit the Jews residing in the City of London to your custody, so that if any attempt to do them harm, you may defend them, coming to their assistance with an armed force."

EXPULSION

With the constant increase of the power of the barons, the situation of the Jews grew progressively worse. When the barons revolted against the king in 1215 they sacked the London Jewish quarter and killed many Jews. In the rebellion of 1264 they massacred some fifteen hundred Jews in the city and a great many in Canterbury and Northampton.

Caricature of Aaron of Colchester, labeled "Aaron, Son of the Devil." Note English form of Jewish badge: tables of the law on saffron taffeta. Cowl indicates he belonged to the professional classes. (From "The Forest Roll," a document in the County of Essex Record Office, 1277.)

Isaac of Norwich depicted in a contemporary caricature, 1233.

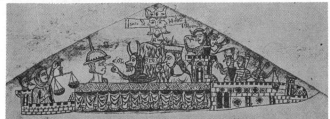

On the extreme right, Aaron of Lincoln's house, considered by many authorities as perhaps the oldest stone house in England.

The kings, too, did not hesitate to harass the Jews with repressive decrees, special taxes, levies, fines and other methods of legal robbery. As a result of this systematic royal mulcting and pillage by the Crusaders, the Jews became utterly impoverished. Furthermore, they had been displaced in the banking field by Christian money lenders, the *Caorsini*, officials who formerly had served as the collectors of the pope's revenue. Therefore, the Royal Exchequer no longer required the services of the Jewish money lenders.

Additional harassment came from the Church which, inspired by missionary zeal, increased its pressures on the Jews to enter its fold.

At first the Jews had been allowed a relatively free exercise of their religion. The chronicler Matthew Paris described a synagogue situated on Threadneedle Street in London as having been more magnificent than any church in the city. That was at a time when there were two thousand Jews living in London. But during the riots of 1263 this house of worship was badly damaged and was taken over as a church by the Brethren of St. Anthony of Vienna. Another synagogue damaged in the riots was situated in the house of Cresse fil Moses. It was closed in 1272 because the "Friars of the Sack" in the church nearby "were not able to take the body of Christ in Quiet [i.e., communion] because of the howling [i.e., praying] of the Jews."

In 1275 the Jews were ordered to cease their moneylending activities. Henceforth they lived in squalor and poverty as artisans and petty merchants. They were permitted to live in towns only and were not allowed to travel. All Jews above the age of seven had to wear a white, and later a yellow, badge called the *tabula*, which obviously was a representation of the tablets of the Ten Commandments.

Church for converted Jews. (From a ms. of Matthew Paris', 1200-1259.)

The end of Jewish life in England came in 1290 with the expulsion of some sixteen thousand Jews. Several thousand perished on the way. Most of the survivors fled to France, while the rest wandered disconsolately over Europe looking for a safe haven.

THE RETURN

Jews were not allowed to return to England until 1656. Again, as in the case of their first admission by William the Conqueror, the fundamental motive was practical. Oliver Cromwell, then Lord Protector of the Commonwealth, was a realist. England found herself in an intense trade competition with Holland, Spain and Portugal, the leading maritime powers. By readmitting the Jews into the country, Cromwell thought he would strengthen England's commercial position.

Another factor which worked in favor of the Jews' readmission to England was that the Puritans, who were then in power, were steeped in the Jewish Scriptures, and for that reason were favorably disposed toward the Jewish people. It was at this juncture that Menasseh ben Israel (1604-1657), the eminent doctor and rabbi of Amsterdam, appeared in London. He sought to convince the Puritan divines of the urgency of allowing Jews to settle in England in order that the Last Judgment might be hastened. He based his plea on the prophecy of Daniel that the Jews had to be first scattered "from one end of the earth to the other before the redemption could be realized." However, he maintained, since there were no Jews in England, the expectation of the End of Days could not be fulfilled until they were readmitted. His mystical argu-

Menasseh ben
Israel.

ments sounded persuasive to many influential Englishmen, including the Lord Protector.

On December 4, 1655, Cromwell called a conference to consider a petition from Menasseh for the readmission of Jews into England. Although no conclusion was reached, the Lord Protector's favorable interest was well known. There seemed to have been a tacit understanding that even without official consent Jews could enter England without fear of molestation.

The first Jewish community since the expulsion of 1290 was founded in London, in March, 1656. It consisted almost entirely of *Marranos* from Spain and Portugal. Other *Sephardim* came later from Germany, France and Italy.

The Crown laws were lenient toward the first Jewish settlers. They were free to build synagogues and to observe their Sabbath and Holy Days. Merchants, especially, received every encouragement to carry on foreign trade. As in Amsterdam, these *Marrano* merchants had valuable Jewish connections throughout the maritime world and were able to establish branch trading agencies everywhere. Although Jews were not yet allowed to engage in retail trade, in the wholesale field as exporters and importers and as brokers on the Royal Exchange beginning in 1657, they gradually achieved positions of influence in the commerce of the country. Some acquired great wealth.

By the middle of the eighteenth century the character of the English Jewish community had changed radically: German and Polish Jews, although inferior in culture and in wealth to their *Sephardic* brothers, arrived in growing numbers.

The claims of Jews for civil equality had at last found many defenders in liberal Christian circles, beginning with John Locke, the philosopher who in 1689 wrote his famous *Letter Concerning Toleration*. Because of this liberalism among English intellectuals as well as for the general advance of civil rights, the Jews of England were emancipated earlier and more quickly than Jews anywhere else.

The wealth of the "Jew brokers" and the merchants of London became proverbial and, among those Christians who envied them, exaggerated. The *Sephardim* who had a high level of culture rapidly assimilated the best of English secular culture. They were not only better educated and more worldly, but also more broad-minded than their German and Polish fellow-Jews. It is indeed remarkable that at a time when Germans Jews were still hemmed in by the grossest features of the ghetto, English Jews had made brilliant careers as writers, actors, doctors, botanists, mathematicians and astronomers. But the price of admission they had to pay to a successful future was indeed high—baptism in the Church of England.

Jewish petition
to Oliver Cromwell.

GERMANY (Medieval)

The first mention of Jews in Germany is found in a set of instructions about them by Constantine the Great in 321, directed to the magistrates of Cologne. But settled Jewish communities first emerged into prominence during the reign of Charlemagne. By the tenth century there were quite a number of them in existence. Besides Cologne, there were Aachen (Aix-la-Chapelle), Mainz, Worms, Speyer, Merseburg, Trèves, Bamberg, Regensburg on the Danube and Metz.

PRIVILEGES AND PROTECTIONS

Under the Carolingian kings the Jews in Germany, as everywhere in the empire, were protected by charters whose chief characteristic was a practical liberality. Jewish merchants were found necessary for the economic development of the empire. They were encouraged to carry on an active trade with the East, bartering textiles, weapons of war and all kinds of implements for fine silks, precious and semi-precious stones, drugs and medicinal herbs, and spices, especially saffron and pepper. During the Middle Ages pepper was considered practically a form of general currency in Europe, and Jews were frequently required to pay part of their taxes and collective fines with pounds of pepper. Saltpeter was another commodity in which Carolingian Jews dealt.

Interior of the old Worms Synagogue, consecrated as a House of Prayer in 1034.

The privileges which the Jews of Germany enjoyed until the Crusades were considerable. They could own land and houses. Quite a number were actually farmers and cultivated vineyards. It was considered sound economic policy then to extend rights and privileges to the Jews.

Bishop Rüdiger of Speyer, for instance, had issued a charter to the Jews in 1048. Its preamble read: "Desiring to make a city out of the village of Speyer, I have admitted the Jews. . . . I have thought to multiply one thousand times the honor of our city by gathering the Jews within its walls." But only twelve years later eleven Jews were slain and mutilated in Speyer—among the first victims of the Crusaders' hysteria.

THE CRUSADES

The Archbishop of Cologne also rejoiced over the acquisition of Jews by his principality. In his charter of 1252 he wrote: "We believe that it will rebound not a little to our prosperity and honor if the Jews who entrust themselves to our support and who—hoping for our protection and our favor —submit to our rule—may actually enjoy this protection." The archbishop, however, made only a half-hearted effort to protect "his Jews" when the Crusaders swarmed over the town, and proceeded to butcher the Jews and to baptize their children forcibly. Many Jewish families preferred a death of their own choice: holding hands, they found courage in their collective love to jump together into the Rhine.

About the same time in Mainz the Jews' Protector, Archbishop Ruthard, allowed them to take refuge in his palace where they were conveniently slaughtered by their enemies. Many elected to stab one another to death, with the *Shema,* the Jewish creed, fervent on their lips.

When the carnage was over, thirteen hundred bodies of Jews were carried out of the archiepiscopal palace.

In vain did Bernard of Clairvaux, shocked by the bestiality of the Crusaders, try to put out the fires he himself had helped light. But his pleas against violence toward the Jews went unheeded. The incitements of his colleagues in muscular Christianity, Peter of Cluny and the monk Rudolph, successfully drowned out his moderating voice.

THE BLACK DEATH CALUMNY

But barely had the Jews of Germany begun to recover from these crushing blows when a reign of terror was again let loose upon them, following the terrible ravages of the Black Death in 1348-49. A wild rumor circulated that the Jews had poisoned the wells and the Rhine and Danube rivers in order to kill off all Christians at one blow.

Mobs raged against the defenseless Jews everywhere in western and central Europe. Some accepted baptism, many were burned at the stake, and others, under more merciful circumstances, were allowed to depart. Bands of roving Christian pietists, who flagellated themselves with scourges studded with sharp nails, thereby earning the name of *Flagellants,* scurried over Europe in breathless urgency calling Christians to the holy massacre of the Jews. Jews were massacred by the thousands. The fortunate succeeded in fleeing eastward to the milder religious climate of the Polish provinces where the Christian Church had only recently established itself. Thousands of them died of disease, starvation and mob violence on the way. A Christian chronicler of the time, who believed in the rumor of the poisoned wells, punned sardonically on the fate that had overcome the Jews: "In truth, it was their own poison that killed the Jews."

The savagery against the Jews alarmed Pope Clement VI. Attempting to calm the public hysteria, he declared that the charge that the Jews had poisoned the wells was a fabrication. But his declaration had little effect on the mobs. The carnage continued.

Rashi Chapel at Worms. Traditional "chair of Rashi" in niche.

The Jews at Worms met their ordeal in the spirit of religious quietism. In a communal council they decided that if it was God's will they should die, then they had to die. But since it would be humiliating to allow themselves to be butchered by their hateful enemies, they themselves set their houses on fire and were burned alive.

But this attitude of non-resistance was scornfully rejected by the Jewish communities of Mainz and Cologne. They took up arms and defended themselves, and continued to fight until they were overwhelmed. In Regensburg a small band of Jews succeeded in holding the mob at bay for a long time outside the city walls. The Jews in Nuremberg were rounded up in the square, later named *Judenbuhe,* and burned alive on December 6, 1349.

Trade between a Jew and a peasant. (From the Dresden *Sachsenspiegel,* 1220.)

CHATTELS OF THE KING

The net result of this carnage was that the Jewish communities of Germany were almost obliterated. The princes, barons, bishops and city councils divided the plunder taken from them and the emperor expediently ignored the lawlessness of his vassals. It was not long, however, before the Jews were asked to return, with promises of protection and privileges. The rulers of Europe had discovered that without them their economy suffered and their income from taxation and levies was sharply curtailed.

When segregation of the Jews in ghettos was ordered by the Fourth Lateran Council in 1215, Jews were given the privilege, granted even to serfs, of owning arms with which to defend themselves. But later they were deprived even of this fundamental feudal right. They were designated as *servi camerae,* "chattels of the king." This status was based on the theological decision rendered for the Church by Thomas Aquinas, who laid down the principle of *servitus Judeorum,* "the servitude of the Jews" to Christians.

Despite the fact that the Jews formed only a tiny part of the population in the imperial domains they were, nonetheless, expected to pay the emperor twelve per cent of all the taxes he received. In addition, they had to pay one fifth of all city and town taxes.

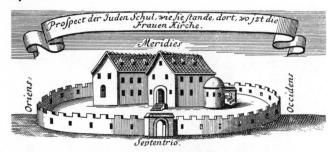

Old Nuremberg synagogue. Built in 13th century.

Left. Costume of German Jews of the 13th century. *Right.* Taking the Jewish oath (*More Judaico*), Augsburg, 1509.

OATH OF HUMILIATION

Whatever rights Jews continued to possess, beginning with the thirteenth century, were either nominal or of trifling importance. An index to their legal position in Christian society is in the *More Judaico* (oath according to the Jews' custom). This humiliating oath recited before a Christian judge had been ordered by the otherwise humane Charlemagne. In some places, before taking this oath, the Jew was required to put a wreath of thorns on his head in damning memory of the crucifixion of Jesus, with which "hereditary crime" he was charged. Standing ankle-deep in water, in pointed contempt of the Christian baptism which he, as a believing Jew, rejected, he was forced to recite aloud: "In the name of the Lord Zebaoth I swear truthfully. . . . But if I swear falsely, may my descendants be cursed, may I grope along the wall like a blind man . . . at the same time, may the earth open up and swallow me as it did Dathan and Abiram."

Even more humiliating were the circumstances under which the oath was taken in Saxony. There the Jew had to stand on the skin of a sow, an animal traditionally forbidden to a pious Jew as the most unclean. In Silesia, they made even more sport of the Jew in court by making him recite the prescribed oath while struggling to keep his balance on a rickety three-legged stool. This he had to do while standing in his bare feet and wearing the obligatory Jew's conical hat and his *tallith,* the prayer shawl.

As his personal "property" the emperor could dispose of the Jews, and did, in any way he saw fit, as a gift, or, in lieu of cash, as payment for some service rendered by a feudal vassal. Sometimes he "sold" them outright or "pawned" them to a princeling or even to a city when he happened to be in need of cash. For the protection they were to receive, at least theoretically, the Jews were obliged to pay, half to the emperor and half to the reigning prince, an annual *opferpfennig,* or penny-offering, which in fact amounted to considerably more than a penny. The pfennig swelled into a gulden for each Jew over twelve years of age. Jews were also required to pay for a special "coronation tax" separately to emperor, king and prince when each ascended his throne.

Onerous was the payment of the so-called "Jewish body tax." Because of the many robber bands that infested the medieval city streets and made them unsafe, Jewish travelers were forced to pay the authorities for supplying the protection of a military escort, as they passed through the city. Even in death the Jew was not free from the tax collectors. His family had to pay not only "escort money" to the cemetery but a special burial tax in the cemetery. It was thus expensive for the Jew to keep alive and equally as expensive to die. Some Jewish communities had to pay "special" imperial taxes in addition to the "regular" taxes. For instance, in Frankfurt-am-Main the local Jews were ordered to supply all the parchment needed by the emperor's chancellory, all the bedding required by the imperial court, all the pots and pans for the kitchen, as well as specified sums to the imperial officials—a form of salary or bonus.

Interior of 13th-century synagogue at Ratisbon (Regensburg). Built 1210, destroyed 1519. *Altdorfer*

Seal of the Jewish community of Augsburg in 1298.

JEWISH CULTURE PERSISTS

Despite these considerable extortions and harassments, despite pillage, persecution and massacre, the Jews of medieval Germany managed, in a religious and cultural sense, to lead a well-integrated group life. That in itself is testimony to the Jews' capacity for adjustment to all manner of conditions of life, a virtuosity in survival acquired from their historic conditioning.

During medieval times the Jewish community was an official institution, and it automatically included *all* Jews: none could stand outside of it. For that reason, it was designated as the *universitas Judeorum*. It was headed by a *Judenbischof* ("Bishop of the Jews"), and its religious-cultural and communal life followed one unified pattern. It centered around the synagogue, the house of study with its public library of Hebrew religious literature, the community house and sometimes the *Tanzhaus* (dance hall) where weddings and other festivities were held.

Hebrew teacher and pupil. (From a 14th-century German Pentateuch.)

To a large extent, religious and civil Jewish law was operative in all strictly Jewish affairs, and only on rare occasions did the Christian authorities attempt to interfere. Talmudic learning, which had established a principal stronghold in the Rhineland, was enriched by an illustrious line of scholars and religious leaders, such as *Rabbenu* Gershom, "The Light of the Exile" (960-1040), the rabbinic Kalonymus family of

Miniature (bride and groom with tree of life) from the 14th-century Leipzig *Machsor* (prayer book for the Holy Days).

121

Mainz, Rabbis Meir of Rothenburg (1220-93) and Asher ben Yehiel (1250-1328) who finally settled in Toledo, Spain. However, Jewish learning in Germany, from celebrated savant to anonymous Talmudic student, remained rigidly orthodox, devoid of those humanistic features that characterized it in the more cultured countries of Spain, Italy and the Provence.

Despite the unyielding piety of the Jews of Germany during the Middle Ages and the Renaissance, they were by no means impervious to outside cultural influences. Jews spoke German, even if they wrote it with Hebrew characters and employed Hebrew phonetics instead of German. By adding Hebrew words and expressions to German, in time they created a distinctive language—Yiddish. In other fundamental ways as well the Jews behaved like Germans: they sang the same songs, danced the same dances, wore the same dress, except for the mandatory Jewish badge and conical hat required for Jewish identification. When the epic lays of chivalry were the rage among Christians, they were equally popular among Jews in the ghettos. They, too, had their own *Spielleute*, their merry-andrew *troubadours* who accompanied themselves on the lute or lyre as they sang and declaimed in heroic cadence. They sang of the incomparable exploits of King Arthur and his Knights of the Round Table, of Bevis of Hampton and of Hildebrandt, of Paris and Vienna and of the lovely Blanche-fleur—but in *Yiddish*, spiced with Scriptural and Talmudic allusions, and quaint with Hebrew expressions and exclamations. There were, in fact, Jewish poets who figured in the composition of these musical epics of chivalry.

Süsskind von Trimberg (about 1250-1300), a Jewish *Minnesinger*, achieved great fame among Christians. He was a poet of distinction whose verses reveal an innate thoughtfulness and a quiet nobility of mood. After the reaction had set in following the edict of the Fourth Lateran Council in 1215, his lot as a Jewish master-singer among Christians became intolerable, and he was filled with that strange melancholy best described as *Judenschmerz*, the grief-consciousness of being a Jew in a hostile world. Süsskind lamented:

> Be silent, then, my lyre,
>   We sing before lords in vain.
> I'll leave the minstrel choir,
>   And roam a Jew again.

Prayer leader (*baal-tefilah*) reading the service in the synagogue, 14th century. (From the Leipzig *Machsor*.)

Note and check in Hebrew and Latin with Hebrew signatures. End of 13th century.

Jew prays before death as executioner stands behind him with poised sword. (From a 15th century *Machsor*)

Left. German Jew, 15th century.
Right. Süsskind von Trimberg.

The Frankfurt Ghetto, early 19th century.

122

The Pope blesses the homage-rendering Jews as they approach him in procession with lighted tapers, during the Council of Constance (1414-18).

CONFLICTS AND CONTESTS

During the first decade of the sixteenth century all Germany was deeply stirred by an intellectual duel between the Christian humanist and champion of the Jews, Johann Reuchlin, and the converted Jew, Pfefferkorn. Pfefferkorn, once a butcher, with only a smattering of Jewish learning, wrote furious diatribes against the Jews. His principal argument was the one Nicholas Donin had used so effectively almost three centuries before: that the principal obstacle keeping Jews from embracing Christianity was the *Talmud*. To provoke action against that basic Jewish religious work, Pfefferkorn charged that it was full of unspeakable blasphemies against Jesus and the Christian religion. His slanders fell on fertile soil. He was empowered by Emperor Maximilian to examine all Jewish books and to destroy those he found sacrilegious. In this heresy hunt he was assisted by the Dominican Inquisitors.

The controversy between Pfefferkorn and Reuchlin became a *cause célèbre* of the age. Pfefferkorn had as allies the faculties of the universities of Paris. Mainz and Erfurt. Supporting Reuchlin in his defense of the Jews and the *Talmud* were the theological faculty of the University of Vienna, the Elector of Saxony and a number of princes of the Church, including

Pfefferkorn and Reuchlin, the latter caricatured as two-tongued (false).

Cardinal Egidio da Viterbo, the friend of Elijah Levita, the Yiddish *Spielmann*. Martin Luther, too, was one of Reuchlin's supporters. The controversy ended in Pfefferkorn's defeat. The Reformation had begun.

A duel of a different kind was being fought in Protestant

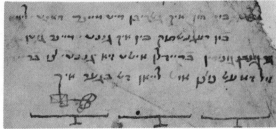

Fragment of the 16th-century Yiddish *Shmuelbuch* (Book of Samuel) written by a Jewish *Spielmann* in the verse style of medieval German epics. It was sung in the synagogues to a musical mode, now forgotten, called "the melody of the Shmuelbuch."

Frankfurt-am-Main in the year 1614. A pastry cook, Vincenz Fettmilch, who called himself jestingly "The New Haman of the Jews," led a mob in a fierce attack on the city's ghetto. Forewarned, the Jews had armed themselves in time. They threw up barricades and fought with desperate determination on the streets. They inflicted severe blows on their attackers, killing and wounding many of them. Due to the great numbers of the mob, the Jews were eventually overwhelmed. A massacre followed. Cartloads of Jewish books were gathered, piled up and burned in great bonfires, thereby setting a precedent for book burnings in Germany.

The massacre in the Frankfurt ghetto had a curious epilogue. Two years later Fettmilch was arrested by order of the

The Fettmilch massacre, Frankfort-am-Main, 1612.

123

Costumes of Nuremberg Jews, 18th century.

emperor and publicly executed as a warning to those who considered themselves above imperial law. In memory of that tragic event and of the identical fate that had overtaken the new as well as the old Haman, the Jews of Frankfurt thereafter celebrated the twentieth day of Adar as a second Purim, which they called *Purim Vinz* (Vincenz).

THE COURT JEW

A unique Jewish figure arose during the Middle Ages, the Court Jew, or as the Jews called him, the *shtadlan*, the intermediary. He was the indispensable minister or agent of caliphs, emperors, popes, kings and princes. Sometimes, as in the case of Hasdai ibn Shaprut, he was also court physician. It was his special personal relation to the sovereign that made it possible for him occasionally to intercede for his fellow-Jews and sometimes even to avert disaster to them.

In Germany there were a number of these Court Jews, or *Hofjuden*, who served the various princelings as financial agents and as civilian quartermasters for their armies. Perhaps the two most noted Court Jews were Jossl of Rosheim (1480-1554) and Joseph (Jud Süss) Oppenheimer (1698-1738).

Jossl of Rosheim was a brilliant financier with influence all over Europe. Whenever danger threatened a Jewish community, he promptly interceded with the Emperor Charles V, or with kings, electors, princes, bishops and provincial Diets. Because of his alleged great wealth he was exposed to the most scurrilous attacks by his enemies and the mobs they incited against him.

Joseph Süss Oppenheimer, financial minister to the Duke of Würtemberg, was so able that he dominated the affairs at court and made many enemies among the nobility. They plotted tirelessly against him and finally succeeded in destroying him in 1738. He was placed in an iron cage suspended from a high beam over the city square for all to see and mock. When the mob tired of the spectacle, Oppenheimer was hanged.

Jewish bridal procession, early 18th century.

Left. Anti-Jewish caricature of the celebrated "Court Jew"—Yossl of Rosheim, financier to the Emperor Charles V. In one hand is a Holy Book, in the other, a money bag. *Right.* Caricature of Jud Süss and the cage in which he was exhibited.

Jewish *kahal* (communal) officials distributing clothing to the poor, early 18th century.

124

VIENNA AND PRAGUE (Medieval)

By the twelfth century small Jewish communities had been established in Vienna, Salzburg, Graz and other places in the Tyrol, Styria and Voralberg. The treatment they received from the Christian rulers there was very much like that of the Jews in Germany. They were restricted in all their movements and activities and enjoyed but a few meager privileges. As everywhere, Court Jews functioned as financial agents and as mint-masters. A Jew by the name of Shlom was given the official title, in 1194, of *super officium monetae*, Superintendent of the Mint. Another distinction was granted the Jews of Vienna by the Emperor Frederick II in 1238. He graciously designated them, for their own good, as *servi camerae nostrae*, "chattels of our chamber."

Gate of the *Judenstadt*, the old ghetto of Vienna.

At any one time there were very few Jews in Vienna, usually only a handful of badly needed money lenders, minters, commercial factors and foreign traders. And even those Jews who were admitted were not left in peace for long. The Viennese archdukes, whenever it served their interests, would cold-

The *Judenmeister* Lesyer, head of the Jewish community in Vienna, before 1389.

bloodedly ruin the local Jews. This they accomplished by canceling all debts of Christians to Jews. They quaintly called this a measure "to kill the Jews' letters."

Periodically, after this sort of legal robbery, orders of expulsion were issued against the Jews of Vienna. Then they were asked to return, lured back by lavish promises of protection and privileges. With the rise to economic power of the burgher class, Jews were forced into intense economic rivalry with Christian merchants and money lenders. This made their position most insecure. They never knew what the next day would bring, or whether there would even be such a thing as the next day. For instance, in 1599 the thirty-one Jewish families in Vienna were taxed the stupendous sum of twenty thousand florins. Unable to raise the money, they were driven out of the city. In 1637 the Christian merchants of Vienna

The *Judenturm* (Jews' Tower) in Vienna where the Jews would seek refuge when danger threatened them.

petitioned Emperor Ferdinand III "to drive out all the Jews, no one excepted, three miles beyond this city, if not from the whole country." The emperor resolved the matter with a compromise. He forbade Jews to trade in the inner city where the Christian merchants' shops and counting-houses were situated. This segregation resulted in the near ruin of the Jewish traders.

Again in 1670 a clamor was raised by the Vienna City Council for the immediate expulsion of the Jews. It charged them with having had secret and treacherous commerce with the enemy Swedes. The mob believed it and, unhindered by the authorities, looted all Jewish homes and shops. In consequence, on March 1, 1670, the emperor complacently signed the decree of expulsion. He went much further than the city authorities had petitioned for: he included in the expulsion all

Jews being publicly humiliated. (From a copper engraving by Peter Fehr, 1715.)

Jews living in Upper and Lower Austria as well. He directed the Jews to be gone from the kingdom before Corpus Christi Day and never to return.

Five years later the city fathers began to repent of their hasty action: their treasury was suffering from a depressed state of finances. They agreed to permit the return of two hundred and fifty Jewish families upon the proviso that they would give the city a friendly "gift" of three hundred thousand florins, and, in addition, pay an annual tax of ten thousand florins. Unfortunately for the City Council, it had exaggerated in its reckonings the wealth of the Jews. There were not two hundred and fifty Jewish families able to muster that huge sum.

Nine years later two court factors, Samson Wertheimer and Samuel Oppenheimer, were induced to become financial agents to the emperor. They furnished the money for Prince Eugene of Savoy's campaigns against the Turks. Other rich Jews followed them, tentatively at first, for they feared that nothing good would come of their settlement in Vienna. And nothing good did! They were constantly being victimized, robbed and squeezed for money, by riots, looting and open blackmail. In the beginning of the eighteenth century Markus and Meir Hirschl accepted the "invitation" to donate one hundred and fifty thousand florins to help build the Church of St. Charles Borromeo.

By the middle of the eighteenth century the Jews of Vienna, numbering only seven hundred, were no better off than those Jews who had lived there many centuries before. They were not allowed to have any synagogue. They could not own houses. True, the wearing of the yellow circle had just been abolished, but Jews had to keep their beards long and untrimmed. The Empress Maria Theresa boasted that she was always seeking how to "diminish the Jews, by no means how to increase them."

No synagogue was allowed to rise up in Catholic Vienna until the year 1811. This would demonstrate that the Middle Ages were a state of mind rather than a chronological period in European history.

PRAGUE

The Jewish communities scattered over Bohemia and Moravia during the Middle Ages were dwarfed by the one in Prague, the chief city of the kingdom of Bohemia. Prague was then a key trade center for Europe and a stopping-off place for the Jewish merchants of Mainz and Worms on their way to countries in the East.

The first reliable evidence of the presence of Jews in Prague is in the year 906. As with the Jews of France under the

The *Meiselgasse* (15th-century houses) in Prague. Left foreground, the old Bassevi House.

Frankish kings, the Jews of early Prague could engage in almost any trade they chose, and they chose many. They were weavers, minters, masons, carpenters and even farmers. They dealt in wine and salt and engaged in barter trade with foreign lands.

Jewish father (15th century) examining his sons in the Scriptural portion of the week on the Sabbath as their mother listens.

As time went on the mildness with which Jews were treated came to an end. The first Crusade exacted its toll of Prague Jews in forced conversions and in dead. By 1269 the Municipal Council of the city specified in its *Codex Juris* that: "A Jew found with an unmarried Christian woman shall be sentenced to death. A Jew found with a married Christian woman shall be impaled at the crossroad." As in other cities of Europe the law in Prague also fixed the rate of usury: "The Jews may take interest at the rate of five pfennig in the mark, six pfennig in the pound and one pfennig in thirty."

During the thirteenth century the Jews of Prague were forced into the ghetto which took on the name of *Judenstadt* (City of the Jews). It was located in the Old City and the quarter was isolated. When the Jewish community grew during the fourteenth century, owing to new arrivals from Germany and Austria, its troubles grew apace. In 1336, in consequence of a ritual murder slander, a number of Jews were burned at the stake. Later, a mob, stirred by a rumor that a great treasure of gold was hidden underneath the foundation of a synagogue, completely destroyed the house of worship. During Easter Week, in 1389, as a Christian religious procession was winding its way through the street it happened to pass close to a street in the ghetto where some Jewish boys were throwing stones at one another. One of the priests in the procession charged that the Host he was carrying had been hit by the stones. That day the churches resounded to the exhortations of the priests calling for Christian reprisal against the Jews for their shameful act of desecration. Led by a priest, a mob descended on the ghetto and massacred 3,000 Jews, almost the entire Jewish population of the city. Part of the ghetto was burned and the rest looted. The surviving Jews had to pay a fine of five tons of silver.

In spite of subsequent persecution and harassment, especially during the sixteenth century, the Jews of Prague persisted in their own mode of life which was rich in content in a religious-cultural sense. It was so rigorously traditional, with a strong inclination toward mysticism, that the city became a center for orthodox Talmudists and Cabalists.

Monument and tomb of Rabbi Judah Löw, died 1609, hero of the Golem legend.

The Legend of the Golem

Especially famous among the Cabalists toward the end of the sixteenth century was "Der Hohe Rabbi Löw" to whom Jewish folk-legend ascribed the fashioning of the *Golem* in the attic of the Gothic-styled *Altneuschul*. He blew the breath of life, Jewish legend avers, into this homunculus of clay by highly secret cabalistic formulae and incantations. He created him in order to provide the much harassed Jews of Prague with an invincible defender against their enemies. It was perhaps no accident that the *Golem* legend should have arisen at a time when the Jews found they could no longer cope with their persecutors by natural means. They looked increasingly for supernatural assistance in the struggle for survival.

Expulsion and Return

The presence of a considerable number of Jewish merchants and artisans in Prague was deeply resented by the rising burgher class, which agitated and finally succeeded in getting repressive measures introduced against them. Expulsions were frequent, but fortunately brief. Finally, when a great many could no longer earn a living, with the eternal hopefulness of children, they emigrated to Poland, most of them going to Galicia.

It did not take long, however, for the tide of emigration to start flowing in reverse. It was from Poland and Russia in 1648 that a stream of refugees, fleeing from the massacres of the Cossack *hetman*, Bogdan Chmielnicki, sought refuge in Prague. They were for the greater part artisans and handicraftsmen who increased enormously the working population

The *Altneuschul,* interior. First half of 19th century.

The *Altneuschul,* 1860.

of the ghetto. They were glaziers, goldsmiths, locksmiths, shoemakers, butchers, saddlemakers, tailors, carpenters, potters, glove makers, embroiderers, mattress makers, furriers and weavers. It is worthy of emphasis that during the first half of the eighteenth century, when the Jewish population of the city numbered about twenty thousand, Jews were engaged in some fifty separate trades, besides being doctors, teachers, rabbis and merchants.

These Jewish artisans formed trade guilds of their own.

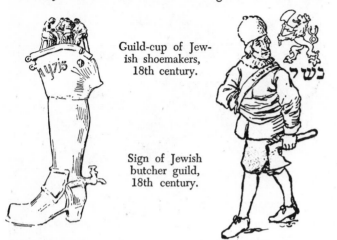

Guild-cup of Jewish shoemakers, 18th century.

Sign of Jewish butcher guild, 18th century.

The Jewish physician Isachar (Baer) Teller ben Yehuda Loeb Satan, c. 1637.

Unlike the Christian artisans, they were restricted by numerous ordinances.

Nevertheless, with that skill at adjustment taught them by pressing necessity, the Jewish artisans managed to keep their heads above water, but barely more than that.

By the middle of the eighteenth century the *Judenstadt* of Prague had become badly overcrowded. Most of its twenty thousand inhabitants lived in insufferably crowded conditions in some three hundred crumbling old houses which seemed to stand piled up one against the other, huge human anthills of stone and squalor which the sun never seemed to penetrate.

in February of that year, a disconsolate and embittered band of wanderers.

The Roman Catholic rector of the University of Prague, as he watched aghast the procession of exiled Jews, was constrained to observe: "Dreadful indeed is the spectacle of these people as they and their children depart in the blistering cold!" The highways were clogged with them and the roadside was lined with the dead and the sick. Thus in one day eight centuries of continuous Jewish community life and of dynamic religious-intellectual striving were wiped out. It was as if they had never been.

By way of an historical footnote: it was only three years later that the Imperial Treasury in Vienna began to feel acutely the financial loss resulting from the expulsion. The empress then regretted her excessive "patriotic" resentment against the Jews. In fact, upon investigation, the Imperial Military Council discovered and announced that there was not a grain of truth in the charge that the Jews of Prague had had treasonable relations with the Prussians.

Jewish guilds of embroiderers and tailors in Prague in the year 1741.

Maria Theresa Expels All Jews

It is indeed odd that the most dramatic expulsion of the Jews from Prague should have taken place not during the so-called Dark Ages but in the year 1745 when the Industrial Age and the modern spirit had already made their appearance in Europe. In that year, during the war of the Austrian Succession after Frederick the Great's Prussian troops had left the city, the Empress Maria Theresa accused the Jews of Prague of having secretly helped them, her most hated enemies. She therefore ordered the expulsion of all Jews. They left Prague

Commemorative medal—Expulsion of the Jews from Prague, 1745.

RUSSIA (Medieval)

HELLENIST JEWS OF THE CRIMEA

There were, probably, Jews living in ancient Tauris, now the Crimean region of Russia, long before they had settled in any European country. It is presumed by vague historical deduction rather than by reliable documentary proof that the Jews had followed the conquering Greeks during the reign of the Ptolemies in Egypt into Asia Minor, and from there with them into Tauris. There is abundant historical evidence that by the time of the destruction of Jerusalem there were securely anchored Jewish communities in the Hellenistic kingdom of Bosporus in the area where the Black Sea and the Sea of Azov flow together.

This is documented by the Greek inscription on a marble tablet dated 80 C.E. It concerns the liberation of a slave whose owner, a Jewish widow, had adopted as her foster son. It reads in part: "I, Chresta, formerly the wife of Drusus, declare in the House of Prayer that my foster son, Herakles, is free once and for all, in accordance with my vow. . . ." For solemn witness to her deed she declared her act of manumission to be "with the participation of the synagogue [in Greek the word "synagogue" also meant "assembly"] of the Jews. . . ."

Jewish gravestones from the Hellenistic period found in the city of Kerch in the Crimea.

Jewish inscriptions on ancient tombstones found in Pantikapoeum (modern Kerch) and in other places in the Crimea bear the traditional religious symbols found in other parts of the Hellenistic Jewish world—the classic seven-branched candlestick, or *menorah;* the *lulav,* or palm branch; the *ethrog,* or citron; and the *shofar,* or ram's horn. From all this we can deduce that, notwithstanding the classic Greek names and the Greek language they had adopted, the ancient Jews of the Crimea seem to have led a close community life centered in the synagogue and in the practices of their religion. The population of the Crimean Jewish communities increased greatly with the centuries as a result of a long series of major and minor revolts by the Jews against Roman rule, not only in

Hebrew inscription on a Jewish gravestone in Kerch, Crimea, from the year 846.

Judea but in their far-flung settlements in Egypt, Syria and Asia Minor. Thousands of Jewish refugees from those parts sought haven in the Bosporus settlements of Kerch, Theodosia, Taman and Anapa. With the rise of the Christian empire of Byzantium the Bosporus settlements, too, fell under its sway. Because Constantinople, the capital of the empire, lay on the opposite shore of the Black Sea, the Crimean Jews carried on a lively trade with it. They prospered and attracted many other Jews to Crimea from other parts of the empire.

By the ninth century the Eastern Church had already adopted a militant policy for the conversion of the Jews. The Patriarch Photius tried to intensify the missionary zeal among his bishops. He wrote to the Bishop of Bosporus: "Were you also to win over the Jews there, securing their obedience to Christ, I should welcome with my whole soul the fruits of such beautiful hopes." Church tradition even has it that during the middle of the ninth century the two celebrated missionaries to the Russian pagans, Cyril and Methodius, learned Hebrew from the Jews and carried on endless religious disputations with them with the object of converting them to Christianity. The Eastern Church chronicle has it that "by prayer and eloquence they bested the Jews and put them to shame."

THE JEWISH KINGDOM OF KHAZARIA

Of all the astonishing experiences of the widely dispersed Jewish people none was more extraordinary than that concerning the Khazars.

The Khazars, during the Byzantine era, were an aggregation of warlike tribes who, it is conjectured, must have sprung from Hun or Turkish stock. They occupied a vast stretch of

A letter in Hebrew from a Khazar Jew, dated 950 C.E., five years prior to the letter received by Hasdai ibn Shaprut, the Jewish Vizier of the Caliph in Spain, from King Joseph of Khazaria. In this letter are recounted the incidents that led to the conversion of the Khazars to Judaism and events that took place in Khazaria during the 10th century.

territory sprawling north of the Caucasus and including the entire Volga region. This area was called the Kingdom of Khazaria. Its geographic position, strategically poised between Persia and Byzantium, gave it great commercial and military importance. The Byzantine emperors respected its fighting power and eagerly sought a military alliance with it against the Sassanid kings of Persia.

With time the Khazars succeeded in establishing themselves firmly in the Crimea. They began then an aggressive war against the Slavonian tribes inhabiting the lands to the west. Finally they subjugated the Russian *boyars* of the principality of Kiev, reduced them to vassalage and forced them to pay annual tribute.

With dramatic suddenness the Khazars entered the orbit of Jewish life. One of their *khagans* (kings), called Bulan, was converted to Judaism about the year 740 C.E. and with him went the Khazar tribes. There was a tradition, believed by the Khazars themselves, that Bulan decided to become a Jew after he had listened to a disputation participated in by an Arab *mullah*, a Christian priest and a rabbi on the relative merits of Islam, Christianity and Judaism. A later *khagan*, Obadiah, who wanted to establish the Jewish faith on firmer doctrinal foundations imported rabbis and Talmudic scholars from either Babylonia or the Crimea. These founded synagogues and religious schools where they taught the *Torah* to the Khazar people.

The noted Arab geographer and traveler, Ibn Khordadbeh, wrote, circa 850, concerning the unusual linguistic abilities of the Jewish merchants of Khazaria, "that they speak Persian, Romanian, Arabic, Frankish, Spanish and Slavonic, and that they travel from the west to the east and from the east to the west, sometimes by land, sometimes by sea. The great overland trade route from Persia led over the mountains of the Caucasus through the country of the Slavs, near the capital of the Khazars."

The probability is that many of the oppressed Jews in Europe, when they heard the well-nigh incredible story of Khazaria as a great and independent Jewish kingdom, decided to go there. But the Khazars left behind them hardly any physical evidence of their history and culture.

Practically all the little that is known about the Khazars is derived from Arabic sources. The indefatigable traveler, Ibn Masudi, gave the following report in 954: "The population of the Khazar capital consists of Moslems, Christians, Jews and pagans. The king, his court and all members of the Khazar tribe profess the Jewish religion, which has been the dominant faith of the country since the time of the Caliph Haroun-al-Rashid. Many Jews who settled among the Khazars came from all the cities of the Moslems and the lands of Byzantium, the reason being that the king of Byzantium persecuted the Jews of his empire in order to force them to adopt Christianity."

It was about Ibn Masudi's time that the power of this unique Jewish kingdom began showing signs of crumbling. This fact is revealed in the strange correspondence between the *khagan* Joseph, the last Jewish king of Khazaria, and Hasdai Ibn Shaprut, the celebrated Jewish vizier to the caliph in southern Spain. In his letter Joseph informed his fellow Jew in Spain: ". . . I live at the mouth of the river [Volga] and with the help of the Almighty I guard its entrance and prevent the Russians who arrive in vessels from passing into the Caspian Sea for the purpose of making their way to the Ishmaelites [Arabs]. In the same manner, I keep these enemies on land from approaching the gates of Bab-al-Abwab. Because of this I am at war with them, and were I to let them pass but once, they would destroy the whole land of the Ishmaelites as far as Bagdad."

Apparently nothing the Jews of Khazaria did was sufficient to restrain the emerging power of the Russians. Only several years after the *khagan* Joseph had written his letter, the Russian princes succeeded in overrunning Ityl, the Khazar capital on the Volga. Under Prince Svyatoslav of Kiev, the Russians raged through all the Jewish towns and cities on the Volga, ravaging and slaughtering their hated enemies and overlords. In 969 the Khazars were driven out of the entire Caspian Sea region and retreated into the Bosporus region of the Black Sea where, in a smaller and more compact area, they were able to stem the advance of the invaders. But even that limited power of Khazaria was fated not to endure for long. The Russians, with the help of Byzantium, finally crushed it in 1016 and thus the Jewish kingdom of Khazaria came to an end.

What happened to the Khazar Jews is an intriguing historic mystery. It is, however, certain that of those who remained in Khazaria most were baptized by force. The rest were dispersed: some of them fled into northern Hungary where in time they, too, were absorbed by the local Christian population. To this very day there are villages in northern Hungary that bear such names as Kozar and Kozardie. It is also widely believed that many Khazar Jews, escaping from baptism, found their way into Poland. There, by inter-group blending, they soon became indistinguishable from other Jews. It is also significant that *Tshagataish*, the language of the Khazar Jews, a Turkish dialect, is still spoken in Poland, Hungary and Lithuania by the Karaites, the Jewish sectarians whose homeland was originally in the Crimea. Even more significant is the fact that *Tshagataish* is spoken by the few surviving Jewish *Krimtchaki* of the Crimea.

KIEV AND MUSCOVY

Driven from Khazaria by the Russians of Kiev, the latter principality became the center of gravity for Khazarian Jews struggling for survival. Since Jews were needed by the Russian princes as traders and as intermediaries between East and West, they were tolerated in Kiev. The priests, however, continually fulminated against them. Abbot Theodosius, during the second half of the eleventh century, issued continuous diatribes against them from his famous monastery at Pechera. He steadfastly urged as a mandatory act of faith the persecution of Jews "who have a crooked religion."

Under those circumstances it could hardly have turned out otherwise: the first Russian pogrom in history took place in the year 1113 in Kiev. Obviously, some manner of segregation was also required for the outcast Jews; by the middle of the twelfth century the Slavonian chroniclers of Kiev made passing note of a "Jewish Gate" in the city.

A brief period of relative quiet was enjoyed by the Jews of Kiev when the Mohammedan Tatars overwhelmed the Christian principalities of Kiev and Muscovy for three years beginning in 1237. Under Tatar rule the Jews of the Crimea found it possible to make close contact with the Jews of Russia, an intercourse which was culturally and religiously profitable to both regions. Together they initiated a brisk trade between Moscow, Kiev and Theodosia.

LITHUANIA

Toward the end of the fourteenth century the Jews of the Crimea were invited by Grand Duke Witovt of Lithuania to settle in his domain for the explicit purpose of developing its commerce. Communities of Jews were established in Lutzk and Troki, in the latter place by the Karaite sectarians. And that is how the great Jewish community of Lithuania first came into being.

About one hundred years later, in 1475, the Turks wrested the Crimea from the Tatars. They held it firmly in their grip until 1783. Jews fared better in Mohammedan countries under Turkish rule than they did in Christian lands. They served as diplomatic and commercial intermediaries between their Turkish rulers and the Muscovite princes. One Crimean Jew of Theodosia, Khoza Kokos, was appointed Muscovite Am-

bassador to the Khan. He successfully consummated a military pact between the Grand Duke Ivan III of Muscovy (1472-75) and the Khan of Crimea. It is exceedingly interesting to note that Khoza Kokos, for reasons of his own, chose to write his diplomatic reports to Ivan III in Hebrew.

There were also other Jews who achieved official positions of distinction at the Court of the Khan. One, an Italian Jew, Zechariah Guizolfo, bore the grandiose title of "Prince of Taman." Oddly enough, he owned outright the entire Taman Peninsula, by virtue of which he had become its ruler, owing fealty only to the Khan. The Grand Duke of Muscovy recognized his value as well and invited him to be his diplomatic representative to the Khan.

THE NOVGOROD "JUDAIZING" HERESY

It was about this time that the curious religio-political disturbance in Novgorod, known as the "Novgorod Judaizing Heresy," started. It was destined to inflame the Christian populace against the Jews for a long time to come. It started when Zechariah Guizolfo, "The Prince of Taman," was charged with having won over to the Jewish faith two noted priests, Denis and Alexius, of the Greek Orthodox Church in Novgorod. These priestly converts went about the country ardently proselytizing for the new religion. They made a number of converts, some of whom even cheerfully submitted to circumcision. In fact, the Jewish religion became quite fashionable in some court circles in Moscow, one of its adherents being the daughter-in-law of the grand duke himself.

The Greek Church hierarchy became alarmed and convoked a special council in 1504. It decreed that all "Judaized heretics" were to be mercilessly hunted down and burned at the stake.

Because of the religious hysteria engendered by this heresy hunt, most Russians, backward and superstitious, who hardly knew any Jews, genuinely began to fear them as magicians and instruments of Satan. This led the Muscovite ambassador in Rome to declare in 1526: "The Muscovite people dread no one more than the Jews, and do not admit them into their borders." This may help explain why there were so few Jews in Russia until relatively modern times.

UNDER THE TSARS

The tsars, who subsequently created the Empire of Muscovy, were just as superstitiously frightened of the Jews as their most ignorant *mouzhiks*. When Tsar Ivan IV (Ivan the

Samuel Eliezer Aidels (*Mah'rsha*).

Shabbethai ben Meir ha-Cohen.

Elijah (*Vilner Gaon*).

Akiba Eger.

Terrible) received a petition from the Polish king in 1550, asking that he permit Jewish merchants from Lithuania to attend the Russian fairs, he replied: "It is not convenient to allow Jews to come to Russia with their goods, since many evils result from them. For they import poisonous herbs into the realm and lead Russians astray from Christianity."

A century later, when Alexis Mikhailovich was Tsar of Muscovy, he unintentionally became ruler over a great many Jews when he annexed Little Russia (Lithuania). These Jews lived not within walled ghettos, as they did in the countries of the West, but in concentrated Jewish quarters in the various towns and cities.

Drunk with victory and left to their own counsel by a tsar who had no clear idea what his policy toward the Jews should be, the Russian soldiers proceeded to exterminate them. They plundered them, and when they had finally tired of the killing and looting they drove out the remaining Jews from Wilno, Moghilev and other cities into the interior of Russia and as far as Siberia. The Jewish problem for the Russian tsars became more complex after they had annexed parts of Poland and the Ukraine which were more densely populated by Jews than Lithuania had been.

PETER THE GREAT

When Tsar Peter the Great ascended the throne he was fired by a practical liberalism for reform in his culturally backward country. But he stopped short of the Jews. He definitely did not like Jews. But neither would he tolerate any brutal mistreatment of them. It is recorded that when he was in Amsterdam in 1698, learning how to build ships, the Christian burgomaster of the city, acting as spokesman for the Jews, petitioned him to allow Jews to settle in Russia. Tsar Peter is reported to have replied: "My dear Witsen, you know the Jews and you know their character and habits; you also know the Russians. I know both, and, believe me, the time has not yet come to unite the two nationalities. Tell the Jews that I am obliged to them for their proposal, and that I realize how advantageous their services would be to me, but that I should have to pity them were they to live in the midst of the Russians."

That Peter was quite sincere in this opinion becomes clear on reading an entry in the communal *pinkas*, or minutes, the Jews kept in Mstislavl, a town in White Russia. It records how in August of 1708 as Tsar Peter and his army stood facing the Swedes just before the famous battle of Lesnaya—"Robbers and murderers from among his people fell upon us without his knowledge, and it almost came to bloodshed. And if the Lord Almighty had not put it into the heart of the tsar to enter our synagogue in his own person, blood would certainly have been shed." The tsar then gave orders, the *kahal* minutes continue, "that thirteen men from among the rioters be hanged, and the land became quiet."

EXPULSION OF JEWS

Jews were ordered expelled in 1727 "immediately from Russia beyond the border" by Peter's successor, the Tsarina Catherine I. But the following year, for practical considerations, she modified her original *ukase*: "The Jews are per-

mitted to visit temporarily the fairs of Little Russia for commercial purposes, but they are only allowed to sell their goods wholesale, and not retail, by ells and in pounds." The same fear of competition from Jews which disturbed Christian shopkeepers all over Europe was at the bottom of this restriction to keep Jews out of the retail trade in Russia.

The Tsarina Elizabeth Petrovna went even further than her predecessor in a *ukase* of 1744, in which she ordered all Jews expelled from the fairs unless "they shall be willing to accept the Christian religion of the Greek persuasion." By 1753 she had expelled thirty-five thousand Jews from Russia.

With the three Polish partitions of 1772, 1793, and 1795 the Tsarina Catherine II found herself even more embarrassed than all her imperial predecessors had been. She had come unexpectedly into possession of nine hundred thousand Jews. Her problem was how to keep them out of Holy Mother Russia!

Tobias Cohen, medical scientist and astronomer, physician to three sultans of Turkey.

Diagram by Tobias Cohen, comparing the human body to a functional structure.

POLAND (Medieval)

JEWS ARE INVITED

The circumstances surrounding the beginnings of Jewish settlement in Poland remain nebulous, though it is more than a surmise that the first Jews must have come from the Crimea. After the fall of the Jewish kingdom of Khazaria they continued to arrive, fleeing from the Russian *boyars* of Kiev who after several centuries of vassalage to the Jewish kings had finally risen in revolt and conquered them. In time, these Khazar Jews blended with the other Jewish elements in Poland and ultimately lost their ethnic group identity. After the Crusades and the massacres which followed the Black Death, thousands of Jewish refugees fleeing Germany and Bohemia settled principally in the cities of Wroclaw (later renamed Breslau), Posen, Cracow and Kalisz.

Polish coins, 12th century, with Hebrew inscriptions. Believed to have been minted by Khazar Jews employed by Polish rulers.

By contrast with the experience of the Jews in other Christian countries, the lot of the Jews in medieval Poland and Lithuania was indeed bearable. The religious animus against them among Christians almost everywhere was relatively weak there. This was because, until the end of the tenth century, Poland was still pagan and Lithuania had not accepted Christianity until the time of King Yaghello (1386-1434), a pagan converted to Christianity, who forced the new religion on his subjects. The early kings of Poland, troubled by the breakdown of their economy and the devastation of their domains by the constant and savage wars they were fighting with the Tatars, were anxious to rebuild their country and to develop it to the economic level of the countries to the west. They therefore "imported" German and Jewish traders and money lenders who were eagerly, almost hospitably, received in Po-

land. Actually, the country then was an empire, including besides Great Poland and Little Poland parts of the Ukraine, Lithuania and Red Russia, the old name of eastern Galicia.

RICH YIDDISH CULTURE

With the mass arrival of Jews from Germany and Bohemia after the middle of the fourteenth century the hitherto Slavonic character of Polish-Jewish culture was rapidly transformed into a Yiddish-speaking one. Polish Jews adopted the *Ashkenazic* rites, liturgy and religious customs of the German Jews as well as their method of *Torah* and *Talmud* study and the use of Yiddish as the language of oral translation and discussion. By the sixteenth century, except for inevitable regional variations, a homogeneous Jewish culture had crystallized. Besides the Hebrew element dominant in the religious life, it was based on a common secular use of Yiddish in speech and in writing. A Yiddish literature, principally of a devotional and moralistic character, evolved among the Jews of Germany, Switzerland, Austria, Bohemia, Lithuania, Galicia, Poland, Russia, Hungary and northern Italy. Yiddish thus became a sort of *lingua franca*, practically an international language that bound together the Jews of eastern and central Europe.

THE STATUTE OF KALISZ

In the year 1264 Boleslaw the Pious issued a charter governing the Jews after their flight from the Crusaders in the West and their hospitable reception in the Polish empire. This became known as the Statute of Kalisz. In this document, promulgated with the consent of the "estates" of nobles and burghers, the king declared his intention of giving equal protection to Jews and Christians. He forbade the desecration of or any physical injury to synagogues, Jewish schools and cemeteries. Full protection was to be given to all Jews and their possessions. They were free to travel anywhere without molestation. If attacked it was the duty of every Christian at hand to come to their aid. Moreover, it was forbidden to charge Jews with ritual murder, which the charter declared to be false and slanderous. However, if such a charge were pressed by Christians, they had to produce at least six reliable witnesses to the alleged crime, three of them Jews!

Casimir the Great (1333-70) even extended the Jewish privileges and rights of the Statute of Kalisz and in 1344 made it operative in every part of his domain. Jews were permitted to rent not only estates but even entire villages from the feudal landowners. They also were granted a greater

Casimir the Great gives his royal protection and privileges to the Jews of all Poland.

Medieval Polish Jews.

measure of communal self-rule. It was Casimir the Great, too, who wrested eastern Galicia, or Red Russia, from the Russian principality of Kiev. From that time on it remained a Polish province whose Jewish community played an historic role in Jewish life for centuries after.

Anti-Jewish convulsions, other than those caused by the Crusades and the Black Death, sent continuing waves of fleeing Jews into Poland and Lithuania from Germany, Austria and Bohemia. They resulted from John of Capistrano's holy tirades, from the rivers of Jewish blood shed by the looters Rindfleisch and Armleder and from the horrors of the Hussite Wars.

THE EPIDEMIC REACHES POLAND

This epidemic of hatred, pietism and violence soon penetrated the Slavic lands, carried there by German traders, the unforgiving business rivals of the Jews. They instigated charges against the Jews for alleged ritual murders and host desecrations. The most disastrous results of these took place in Cracow in 1407 during Easter Week. Incited by German traders and led by a local priest, a mob of looters roared through the ghetto. Only those who accepted baptism were not slain.

By this time conditions for the Jews in Poland had become as bad as they were elsewhere. The regional church councils periodically issued anti-Jewish laws which, for instance, forbade Jews to have any social intercourse with Christians, a prohibition obviously unnecessary if Christians were not reasonably well disposed to Jews. They forced them to pay a special Jews' tax for the support of the churches. To give the matter a pious flavor, as well as to allow wide latitude to the priests in determining the rate of the tax, the law stipulated that they could fix the amount of the tax at a sum equal to the "losses inflicted by them upon the Christians." Furthermore, the Church laws forced Jews into ghettos and obliged them to wear the identifying Jewish badge on their outer garments.

THE FIRST GHETTO

Probably the first compulsory walled ghetto was set up in Poland. "Since the land of Poland is a new acquisition in the body of Christianity," declared the Church Council of Breslau in 1266, "lest perchance the Christian people be, on this account, the more easily infected with the superstition and depraved morals of the Jews dwelling among them . . . we command that the Jews dwelling in this diocese of Gnesen shall not live among the Christians, but shall live apart in houses near or next to one another in some sequestered part of the city or town. The section inhabited by Jews shall be separated from the general dwelling place of the Christians by a hedge, a wall or a ditch."

THE *SHLAKHTA*

A new and complicating factor suddenly entered the already complex life of the Polish, Lithuanian, Galician and Ukrainian Jews: the organized assembly of the nobility called the *Shlakhta*. Like the feudal barons of England, the Polish nobles, too, frequently challenged the king's omnipotence. Because they were well organized, their influence in state policy soon made itself felt—to the injury of the Jews.

On the one hand, the king and a small number of the highest nobility required the services of the Jews as money lenders, as tax and customs farmers, as lessees and operators of the salt mines and as merchants and agents in foreign lands for the sale of surplus stocks of grain, lumber, wool and hides. On the other hand and opposed to them in economic self-interest were extensive sections of the lesser nobility who were excluded from this small all-powerful ruling circle. Accordingly, they organized themselves into the *Shlakhta*, or Assembly of Nobles. They considered themselves the natural allies of the Church, of the disgruntled German business rivals of the Jews, and of the merchant and artisan guilds. It was between these upper and lower millstones of class conflict that the Jews of Poland were caught and crushed.

A test of strength was furnished by King Casimir IV's relatively benign charter of privileges which he gave to the Jews in 1447. He had his self-interest uppermost in mind when, with simple candor, he declared: "We desire that the Jews, whom we wish to protect in our own interest as well as in the interest of the Royal Treasury, should feel comforted in our beneficent reign."

The Church, supported by the *Shlakhta*, was up in arms against the charter and its mild attitude toward the Jews. The Archbishop of Cracow, Oleshnicki, apparently felt strong enough to fling this challenge at the king: "Do not imagine that in matters touching the Christian religion you are at liberty to pass any law you please. No one is great and strong enough to put down all opposition to himself when the interests of the faith are at stake."

The king quickly backed down before such formidable opposition and lamely canceled his charter to the Jews on the grounds that it was "equally opposed to divine right and earthly laws."

EXPULSION FROM LITHUANIA

This policy bore bitter fruit almost immediately. Riots and massacres took place in Cracow, Lwow, Posen and other cities. Under clerical and *Shlakhta* pressure, the Jews were expelled in 1495 from Lithuania where they had established flourishing communities in Grodno, Brest, Pinsk and Troki. Whether or not the example of Ferdinand and Isabella of Spain was the source of inspiration, one thing is certain—the king confiscated the property of the Lithuanian Jews and distributed part of it among the nobility to keep its good will.

Jews' Gate in Lublin.

The "kuna" or communal lock-up in a synagogue in Lwov (Lemberg), 18th century. *Inset.* Photograph of the *kuna* in a Polish synagogue wall, 17th or 18th century.

In spite of this, after six years Jews were once more admitted into Lithuania. Step by step, *Shlakhta*, Church, city authorities, Christian merchant and artisan guilds took discriminatory action against the Jews of Poland. They were permitted to engage in fewer and fewer trades and businesses. Merchants were allowed to sell fewer articles and in fewer places and, worse yet, at fewer fairs. This process of economic strangulation meant that Jewish tradesmen in Lwow, for instance, could sell only cloth, wax, furs and horned cattle. It was from constricting conditions such as these that the wry Yiddish saying may have stemmed: "How does a Jew make a living? He claws his way up the wall."

JEWS TURN TO THE HANDICRAFTS

These prohibitions in commerce during the sixteenth century led many Jewish merchants to turn, however reluctantly, to the handicrafts. This was an event of the greatest historic significance: it diverted Jews from the huckstering into which they had been driven by Christian charity to other more stable occupations. At no time and in no country in Europe were there so many Jewish artisans as in Poland and Lithuania during that period.

Because they were prevented by fear of competition and religious bias from joining the Christian guilds, the Jewish artisans formed their own guilds. They worked as well as they could within the serious limitations and the few opportunities the law provided for them. In some of the larger cities there were at times as many as ten or twelve Jewish guilds, some of which even had their own synagogues, named for the trade of its members, as, for instance, "The Tailors' Synagogue" or "The Butchers' Synagogue." In time, these Jewish guilds became so influential and assertive that communal officials, who usually belonged to the wealthy class, often found themselves at odds with them on issues affecting the interests of the artisans.

From the sixteenth century on, when business opportunities in the ghetto grew increasingly limited, many Jews from Poland hopefully emigrated into the less developed parts of the Ukraine. There they became innkeepers, petty merchants, artisans and quite frequently "stewards" on the estates of the land-owning gentry.

JEWISH SELF-RULE

The Jews everywhere in feudal society stood outside its framework. Even its rigorous laws did not apply to them because they were merely "the King's chattels," and were, therefore, treated as a separate social group. Moreover, their devotion to their religion, their use of a separate language—Yiddish—and their development of a Hebrew religious culture tended to isolate them further from their Christian countrymen. The kings and princes of Poland, with the sanction of the Church, considered it both necessary and expedient to encourage this group isolation to a large degree in order not to "contaminate" Christians with Jewish beliefs and practices. Consequently, the Polish rulers viewed with favor the establishment of the *kahal*, or Jewish community, to serve as the administrative organ of Jewish self-government. Strangely enough, the inhuman walls of the ghetto which immured Jews from the rest of society set up a Jewish city within the heart of the larger Christian city—virtually an island of spiritual safety.

The *kahal*, to an extraordinary degree, was autonomous. It provided for its own religious and communal institutions. It took care of its poor and sick, of the victims of fire and of mob pillage, of dowerless girls and children orphaned by the massacre of their parents. It dispensed justice through the *bet din*, the traditional religio-civil court of the Jews. It also supervised the religious education of the young, regulated the activities of Jews in the handicrafts and commerce, looked after the proper burial of the dead, carried out the orders of the Christian authorities and was responsible for the preservation of the peace within the ghetto. Best of all, from the practical point of view of the rulers, the *kahal* served as an efficient and inexpensive collection agency for the numerous taxes, imposts, levies and fines imposed on the Jews individually and collectively.

Although it was far from the intention of the Polish kings, princes and bishops, the self-governing community life of the Jews, with its devotion to traditional religious values, as well as its cultural separation, had a unifying effect on the Jews of Poland. Thus, paradoxically, Jews compensated themselves for the grief of their pariah-isolation and their persecution by developing independently their own culturally rich group life within the barren, sunless ghetto. One can soberly make the assessment that for all the warping and stagnant features of the Polish and Lithuanian ghetto, its moral and cultural level for centuries was higher than that among the general Christian population of Poland.

With the second half of the sixteenth century the *kahal* achieved a paramount position in Jewish life in Poland. It was governed by a board of *kahal* elders, judges and rabbis elected annually by the community. By this time it had become customary for the *kahals* of entire regions to meet in synodal conventions during the great provincial fairs, especially at the Lublin fair when thousands of Jews gathered for trade. These conventions resolved disputes, judged criminal cases and decided and legislated on a great variety of religious and civil matters exclusively affecting Jewish community interests in various provinces of Poland. Still later they became more centralized: the provincial *kahal* organizations merged into "The

Jewish types, Poland, 18th century.

Council of the Four Lands," i.e., of Great Poland, Little Poland, Red Russia (Eastern Galicia) and Volhynia. The Lithuanian *kahals* had originally belonged to this Council, but in 1623 they seceded and formed their own "Council of the Principal Communities of the Province of Lithuania."

THE COSSACK REVOLT, 1648

Perhaps the nearest approximation in history to Hitler's monstrous project for the extermination of the Jews was initiated in 1648 by the Cossack nationalists of the Ukraine. Aided by the Tatars, the Cossacks rose in armed rebellion against their Polish oppressors, the feudal *Pans* of Poland. The leader of this uprising was the Hetman Bogdan Chmielnicki, an intelligent but brutal Cossack leader who wished not only to wipe out the hated Poles but also the Jews, whom he indirectly associated with the oppression of his people. Judging superficially, he saw many Jews serving as stewards on the estates of the Polish king and of the *Pans*, acting as their financial agents and factors, tax-collectors and money lenders —a class of people he despised. An historian of that melancholy period recorded: "The most terrible cruelty, however, was shown towards the Jews. They were destined to utter annihilation, and the slightest pity shown to them was looked upon as treason. Scrolls of the law were taken out of the synagogues by the Cossacks, who danced on them while drinking whiskey. After this, Jews were laid down upon them and butchered without mercy. Thousands of Jewish infants were thrown into wells or buried alive."

Many Jews fled to the illusory safety of the fortified towns which Polish troops were defending, but instead of safety they found only a ready tomb. Massacres on a vast and frightening scale took place wherever the Ukrainian insurgents went. It is believed that in that year and a half of Cossack terror about one half the total Jewish population of the Ukraine and Galicia perished. The number of the slain has been variously estimated from two to four hundred thousand.

THE POLISH MASSACRES

If the Cossacks, in their despair and ignorance, considered the Jews to be their enemies, working together with their Polish overlords, the Poles, in their turn, accused their alleged "allies," the Jews, of plotting against them with the Swedes.

This happened when the Swedes invaded White Russia and Lithuania in the year 1654. One contemporary chronicler described the plight of the Jew as that of a man who "flees from a lion and is met by a bear." The Polish "patriots" quite obviously had learned a lesson in carnage from the Cossack butchers. They, too, proceeded to exterminate all the Jews they could find. They slew without mercy the Jews of some seven hundred communities, they tortured the old, violated the women and brained the infants.

These horrible experiences at the hands of both Cossacks and Poles left unhealing wounds in the consciousness of the survivors. Their fear and insecurity was carried over into the inner life of succeeding generations of Jews.

From that time on the Jews of Poland, Lithuania, the Ukraine and Galicia felt like strangers and outcasts in the land where they had been born and raised, in which their forefathers had toiled and suffered for so many centuries.

During the first half of the eighteenth century armed bands of rebellious peasants called *Haidamaks*, once more headed by Cossack leaders, rose in revolt. This time they were determined to end their unendurable condition as serfs to the *Pans*. The *Haidamaks* raged with fire and sword through the

1. The haidamak plays the guitar. 2. He drinks vodka. 3. He dances. 4. He makes himself a stew and reflects what to do with the Jew (bearded figure, extreme right). 5. He finally makes up his mind and hangs him feet up, while the horse looks on wonderingly.

same territory which, a hundred years before, Bogdan Chmielnicki had laid desolate. They murdered Jews and *Pans* alike, following a weird formula. They would hang a *Pan*, a Jew and a dog on the same tree. To the tree they would then affix the inscription:

> "Pole, Jew and hound,
> All to the same faith bound."

FORTRESS STONE SYNAGOGUES.

Zolkiew, 17th century.

Cracow, 1350.

Cracow, interior.

At Uman, because it was a fortified and garrisoned city, tens of thousands of Poles and Jews sought refuge from the *Haidamaks*. When the Poles were assured that no *Pans*, only Jews, would be hanged, they treacherously let the *Haidamaks* into the city. Then the carnage began. Three thousand Jews sought the illusion of safety behind the strong stone walls of the synagogue, but after a vain defense they were slain to the last man, woman and child. Thousands of others perished that day in other parts of the city. Ironically, their betrayal of the Jews helped the Poles but little. The *Haidamaks* next turned their murderous attention on them, hunted them through the streets like rabbits and killed them.

All that happened to the Jews subsequently at the hands of the Christians of Poland and Lithuania were only variations of that same bloody theme—oppression, torture, looting and slaughter.

FORTRESS SYNAGOGUES

Styles of architecture always reflect in some measure contemporary historic forces. During the seventeenth century in many parts of Poland an arrestingly new type of synagogue appeared, distinguished by the unique architectural features of stone buttresses and fortresslike superstructures. They were characterized as "Fortress Synagogues," an accurate name as well as descriptive.

It is claimed by some historians that the Polish king, Jan Sobieski, had ordered not only synagogues but churches built that way. The hazards of the times called for well-armored devotion. These synagogues were intended to be fortified places of refuge as well as houses of worship during those trying days when Jewish physical survival was imperiled by the horrible massacres perpetrated by Bogdan Chmielnicki's Cossacks and by the *Haidamaks*.

WOODEN SYNAGOGUES

Although modest and unobtrusive both in their style of architecture and in the kind of materials employed in their construction, the wooden synagogues of Poland, Galicia and the Ukraine are probably the most original contribution Jews ever made to synagogue architecture. They are marked by different features at different times, yet they all present a remarkable esthetic unity which easily distinguishes them from the wooden churches of Poland with which they have a certain kinship.

Bogdan Chmielnicki.

WOODEN SYNAGOGUES.

The four-century-old synagogue in Gumbin.

Jurbarkas synagogue.

"Worms mural" of Mohilev synagogue, 18th century.

Old synagogue of Konskie.

Wolpa, c. 1650.

Holy Arks. *Left*. Vilna. 1593-1633. *Right*. Selwa.

When, exactly, the Jews of Poland first began to build wooden synagogues is unknown and probably will remain so, partly because the life span of wooden structures is short. In consequence, the earliest examples of the wooden synagogues which have survived decay, fire and mob destruction date from the seventeenth century.

There are many theories about the origins and the architectural influences that entered into their building. One view is that they were created for the Jews of Poland by Turkish builders; another that they were introduced into Poland by Jewish emigrants from Silesia. A third and far more plausible conjecture is that the Middle Eastern refugees from the Jewish kingdom of Khazaria introduced them during the Middle Ages when they settled en masse in Poland. The Asiatic characteristics are obvious in the wooden synagogues. Byzantine elements are artfully mingled with Mongolian. The roofs, pagoda style, arranged one upon another and surmounted by vaulted ceilings and cupolas, sometimes create the illusion that one is in central Asia rather than Poland. But these features had largely disappeared by the end of the eighteenth century. The Mongolian pattern gave way before the then current Polish fashion for saddle and mansard roofs, and wooden synagogues were decorated with the ornamental balconies found in Polish manorial houses.

Culturally significant is the fact that the building and decoration of these wooden synagogues encouraged a sizable number of Jews to become architects, craftsmen, fine embroiderers, mural painters, art-metal workers and woodcarvers. One can judge from their beautiful work that there were a number of highly gifted artists among them, although they lacked professional training and learned only by doing. And although sensory beauty had, in large measure, been banished from the synagogue by the interdiction of tradition, it was never quite suppressed. While the human face and figure were rarely portrayed in the art of the synagogue, animals, plants and trees were, and whether they were used within the design of the zodiac or in other decorative patterns, they were nevertheless sanctioned by religious custom.

"Lion" from the decoration in the synagogue of Mohilev, 18th century. (Painted by Isaac Segal, ancestor of Marc Chagall, noted modern painter.)

138

THE *CABALA* AND THE "MESSIAHS"

Like the two sides of a medal, Jewish religious thought has had two major but complementary aspects. One has been that of down-to-earth rationalism represented by the *Talmud* and its vast commentary literature. The other has been that of mysticism embodied in the literature of the *Cabala*. While the Talmudists sought to apprehend God, wisdom and righteousness by means of logic, the cabalists sought the same objectives by means of the "hidden wisdom" and esoteric practices of the visionary.

Interior of the traditional tomb of Rabbi Simeon bar Yochai, the father of the *Cabala*, in the *yeshiva*, or Talmudic academy, at Meron, in Israel. To Rabbi Simeon, a Talmudic sage who flourished during the second century in Palestine, is ascribed the authorship of the mystic work in Hebrew, the *Sefer Yetzirah*, which is the oldest, and except for the *Zohar*, the most venerated work in the entire literature of the Cabala.

For centuries the theosophical beliefs of the *Cabala* wracked Jews like a fever. It is easy to understand the hold of the supernatural on a people as persecuted, as helpless and as overwhelmed by the hostility of the world as were the Jews. Denied the natural means for coping with reality they grasped at the magical. It served as both a snare and a consolation, a crutch to lean on in the frustrations and insecurity of living. At times, excessive preoccupation with the cabalistic mysteries made Jews easy prey for the charlatans and self-deluded mystagogues. Countless thousands were flung into mass-hysteria and activities that led only to disaster and disillusionment.

What is *Cabala?* It is not just one book, but constitutes an entire body of occult knowledge which originated about eighteen hundred years ago at the time when the *Talmud* was being created. The Hebrew word *cabala* means "traditional lore," or "The Hidden Wisdom." Its knowledge could be acquired not by the average man but by the elect of heaven, could be learned not by ordinary reason but by the mystic illumination of the spirit.

THE BOOKS OF *CABALA*

The history of the *Cabala* winds along in a labyrinthine course. It was an intoxicating mystical brew which combined Jewish ethics with primitive occultism, Zoroastrian dualism with Pythagorean numerology, and neo-Platonic emanations with just ordinary mystification. While numerous works collectively constitute the *Cabala*, the two most prized books are the ancient *Sefer Yetzira* (Book of Creation) and the *Zohar* (Book of Splendor). The *Zohar*, which people sometimes erroneously use interchangeably for *Cabala*, was compiled by the Spanish mystic, Moses Shem-Tob de Leon (1230-1305). Besides being an encyclopedia of occult lore, the *Zohar* is also a mystical commentary on the *Torah*. In its own abstruse fashion it deals with astronomy, the creation of the world, with angels and demons, with physiognomy and—perhaps most important—with the mystic "science" of numbers. Applied practically to the *Torah*, the *Zohar* purports to give numerical values to the Hebrew letters in various Scriptural words. Cabalists were fond of arranging the Hebrew Biblical text in squares and in other geometric forms. Sometimes they read the lines vertically, sometime backwards or even upside down. They did this believing that it would unravel for them the hidden meanings of God's words.

Even the anatomy of the human body was given an esoteric interpretation. There were ten bodily *sefirot,* or spheres, which cabalists believed constituted the divine attributes in man. The first three spheres—the head, the brain and the heart—represented the world of thought; the right arm, the left arm and the chest, the world of the spirit; and the right and left legs, the sexual organs and the rest of the body, the material world.

Next to the Bible itself, *Cabala* was generally revered by its devotees and by awestruck superstitious folk above all other sacred Jewish writings. For that reason the *Cabala* fell into greater disrepute among rationalists than it really deserved. Inadequate knowledge of its literature and history made it appear a silly hodge-podge of numerological reckonings, alphabetical abracadabra, childish beliefs, dreams and superstitions fortified by magical amulets and incantations in gibberish.

Actually, the *Cabala* had two fundamental aims, both prompted by social-ethical considerations that have been traditional with Jews. The more obsessive of the two involved the redemption of the suffering Jewish people which the cabalists hoped to achieve by seeking God, and, through a

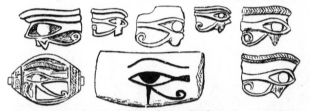

Amulets against the Evil Eye, dating back to ancient Canaan, found by archeologists in Gezer, Palestine.

process of spiritual purification, hasten the coming of the Messiah. The second aim, closely linked to the first, was to overcome the unendurable difficulties Jews suffered in their daily lives and to frustrate the designs both of human enemies and of evil spirits and demons. They expected to accomplish this by the use of practical magic. Superstition, excessive piety, the rapturous discovery of new mystic formulas and delirious cabalistic dreams proved excellent modes of escape, particularly to many idealistic and hypersensitive youths, from the unhappy reality of Jewish life. Paradoxically enough, in trying to lighten the burden of the Jews' existence, the cabalists only succeeded in adding to it. Besides massacre, hunger,

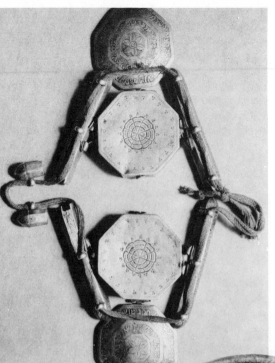

Left. Paper amulet, 17th century. *Right.* Palestine silver amulet, 19th century. (*Jewish Museum*)

epidemics, expulsions and ceaseless persecution, his regular portion in life, the average Jew, except for the rationalists, now had to cope with the terrors of a shadowy world that was haunted by the Evil Eye and populated by transmigrating souls, spectres, ghouls, kobolds and demons. Falling under Christian monastic influence, with its total rejection of the life of the senses, the medieval Jewish cabalists, too, mortified the flesh in order to subjugate it and thereby purify and uplift the spirit. By the power of penance and prayer they strove to break the fatal grip of Satan which kept their spirits earthbound. The desire to hurry the coming of the Messiah, to rescue the Jewish people from the torments that were destroying them was a passion that came close to inspired frenzy. It was a consuming fire in the hearts of the cabalists which robbed them of all peace.

A magic bowl, containing a cabalistic Hebrew incantation against evil spirits, Babylonia c. 1st century C.E.

MEDIEVAL CABALISTS

It is said that the first of the medieval cabalists was Isaac the Blind, who lived in France during the twelfth century. He, in turn, was superseded in his mastery of abstruse knowledge by his disciple, Azriel ben Menahem of Catalonia. Although a student of philosophy, Azriel was more interested in poetic speculations about God and the supramundane world than in the practical application of cabalistic "wisdom." He tried, for instance, to reconcile the Biblical account of the creation with Aristotle's concept of the eternity of the world. There were even "scientific" cabalists, like Isaac ibn Latif, who attempted to bring their mystical ideas into line with the scientific spirit of the age. This proved a highly popular intellectual exercise in the Jewish-Arabic milieu of Spain which

(Left to right.) Mohammedan, Jew and Christian. A symbolic cabalistic representation of the unity of the three religions, from a work in Hebrew by Rabbi Jacob Emden (1697-1776) of Altona, Germany.

was so acutely science-conscious. It even fascinated Christian humanists like Pico della Mirandola and Johann Reuchlin, who studied it under Jewish masters.

The *Cabala* went through a course of development in Germany that was quite different from that in Spain and in Provence. In Germany it was entirely practical, devoid of any philosophic overtones and quite primitive and naïve in its working. It had, however, a moral and emotional motivation lacking in the more intellectual *Cabala* of Spain and Provence.

OUTSTANDING CABALISTS

The outstanding German cabalist was Judah Hasid (Judah the Pious) who died about 1200. His book, *Sefer ha-Hasidim*, the Book of the Pious, achieved an enormous popularity among the plain folk. Its vogue persisted down to modern times. A follower of this tradition, who established a cabalistic school of his own in Safed, Palestine, was Isaac Luria (1533-71), better known as the *Ari*. His cabalistic writing, an odd blend of fervent piety and poetic superstition, had a practical content, too. Though he and his numerous disciples were absorbed by wonder-working, they strove ardently to hasten the Redemption of Israel, that is, to bring the Messiah.

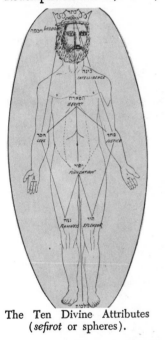

The Ten Divine Attributes (*sefirot* or spheres).

With the social and religious reaction that set in after the Reformation had begun, great areas of Jewish cultural life in Germany, Bohemia, Poland, Galicia, Lithuania and the Ukraine were flung into the darkest shadow. Learning, hitherto one of the most cherished of Jewish traditional values, began to lose its high intellectual standards. Clamped forcibly into their prisonlike ghettos many Jews fell prey to the most superstitious beliefs and practices. Their confinement furnished the perfect intellectual climate for cabalistic charlatans who wandered over Europe calling themselves "wonder-workers."

And they did perform what the ignorant considered "wonders" by means of "supernatural" antics they had learned from cabalistic writings or from fellow charlatans.

MESSIANIC ADVENTURERS

In such depressed circumstances the *Cabala* lent itself naturally to sordid and deceitful uses by professional mystifiers, adventurers, and self-deluded visionaries. One of the self-deceived cabalists was Abraham Abulafia, who lived in the thirteenth century. To impress his followers, he announced himself as the Messiah and openly declared his intention of calling on Pope Nicholas II in Rome and, by means of his cabalistic powers, of converting him to Judaism. When the church authorities got wind of his plan they flung Abulafia unceremoniously into a dungeon.

Another cabalist with Messianic pretensions was Asher Lämmlein who set himself up in the role of Elijah the Prophet. He announced that he was the forerunner of the Messiah who would arrive in 1502. Accordingly, he appointed that time as the "Year of Penitence," and thousands of simple-minded and unhappy Jews believed him. They fasted,

"The *Ari's* Holy Ark" in the old synagogue of Safed, Palestine, called *Beth Knesseth Ari*. According to legend, it was behind this very Ark that the *Ari* learned *Cabala* from the Prophet Elijah.

kept long vigils to mortify the flesh, prayed incessantly and gave away their possessions in expectation of the imminent coming of the Messiah. But when the end of that year came and no Messiah appeared, the disillusionment was so great that many Jews renounced Judaism as a false religion and became Christians.

Only a generation later the cabalists announced that the End of Days was in sight. When Rome was sacked in 1527 they promptly pointed to it as proof that the Last Judgment was not far off. As if by coincidence, there suddenly appeared a self-styled Prince David Reubeni who declared himself to be the ambassador of his brother Joseph, the Jewish king of far-off Khaibar (Habor). He made a series of sensational and dramatic appearances in Europe, and proposed to the pope,

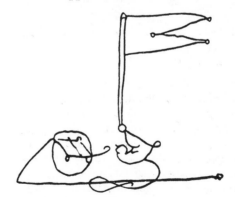

Cabalistic signature of Solomon Molcho, with pennant of Messianic redemption (1527).

to Emperor Charles V, and to King John of Portugal, a military alliance against the Turks on behalf of the Jews of Khaibar. The very theatricality of his appearance led thousands of hopeful Jews to think of him as the Messiah. Although he emphatically denied that exalted distinction, for it could only mean his undoing at the hands of the Church and the Christian rulers, there nevertheless were many who fervently believed that he was the Messiah, notably the brilliant but mentally unstable former *Marrano* intellectual and *Cabala* student,

Solomon Molcho. His activities led to Reubeni's eventual imprisonment and death and to Molcho's own tragic martyrdom.

The Messianic delirium raged on unabated among the more emotionally disturbed. Once again, in 1648, the cabalists triumphantly argued that according to their numerological calculations that year would bring the Redemption. They pointed to the frightful catastrophes that had befallen the Jews that very year as demonstrable proof that the End of Days was approaching. The disastrous Thirty Years' War had just come to an end, and Bogdan Chmielnicki's Cossack and Tatar insurgents were still engaged in the mass slaughter of the Jews of the Ukraine, Poland and Galicia.

All this despair and suffering made the cabalists' revelations appear credible. It was inevitable that someone who considered himself a Messiah should appear at this time to satisfy the burning need of the Jews for divine and immediate help.

The Messiah of Ismir

That someone was a youth of twenty-one and his name was Sabbatai Zevi. He was the son of a wealthy merchant of Ismir (Smyrna) in Turkish Anatolia; he had studied *Cabala* and was well acquainted with the apocalyptic "signs" which mystics asserted would precede the coming of the Messiah.

Sabbatai Zevi is anointed with celestial oil by angels and proclaimed the Messiah.

With supreme self-confidence, this young cabalist announced himself, in 1648, as the Messiah. The Rabbinic Assembly of Smyrna, horrified by what it branded as the most flagrant blasphemy, excommunicated him and ordered him to leave the city. But Sabbatai Zevi's mere announcement excited an indescribable religious hysteria among all the backward elements. The popular excitement was intensified when Sabbatai's Messianic claims were championed by Nathan of Gaza, a cabalist initiate who proclaimed himself to be "the forerunner" of the Messiah, such as the Prophet Elijah was deemed by tradition. He wrote pronouncements and manifestoes which he sent by messengers to all the far-flung Jewish communities of Europe. He exhorted all Jews to confess their sins, to do penance and to prepare themselves for the approaching Day of Wrath, Day of Woe.

After a profitless sojourn in Jerusalem, where Sabbatai Zevi was bitterly denounced by the rabbis as an impostor and swindler, he visited the principal cities and towns of Anatolia,

from Aleppo back to Ismir. Wherever he went great crowds of hysterical men and women paid him homage. Waving palm and myrtle branches they cried: "Hail to our King Messiah!"

The madness was like a forest fire. It swept through the ghettos of Europe and collected thousands of followers among

Nathan of Gaza.

Sephardim of Spanish-Portuguese descent, among Central and East European Jews, Italian and North African Jews, Balkan, Near East and Palestinian Jews. Excited deputations arrived from Jewish communities everywhere with worshipful messages. They presented valuable gifts to the "Messiah" and paid him homage. Entire communities in distant lands started preparing themselves for the day on which Sabbatai Zevi would proclaim the beginning of the Messianic era and would lead them in a triumphal procession to the Holy Land.

Sabbatai Zevi anoints a disciple.

A Ukrainian Christian writer, an eyewitness to some of these extraordinary events, made careful notes: "Some abandoned their houses and property. They refused to do any work whatsoever, claiming that the Messiah would soon arrive and would carry them off in a cloud to Jerusalem. Others fasted for days, denying food even to their little ones. During that severe winter they bathed in ice holes, at the same time reciting a recently composed prayer."

Sabbatai Zevi, following somewhat the curious example of the thirteenth-century "Messiah," Abraham Abulafia, announced in 1665 that in the next year he would go to Adrian-

142

ople and drive the Sultan of Turkey, the ruler of the Holy Land, off the throne. He would then personally lead the dispersed remnants of Israel back to Mount Zion and the life eternal.

Perhaps Sabbatai Zevi overdid his boasting. In any case, he was rash enough to journey to Adrianople in 1666, where the Turkish authorities promptly clapped him in chains and threw him into a dungeon in the fortress of Abydos in the Dardanelles. So great was the faith of his followers, however, that they felt no discouragement because of his imprisonment. On the contrary, they were the more inspired by it. They saw it as the fulfillment of the prophetic description of the Suffering Messiah whom men first would despise and persecute before they would acknowledge him. Moreover, they were

Followers of Sabbatai Zevi doing penance in preparation for the redemption.

confident that the sultan could do no harm to so exalted a person. Instead of lamentations, prayers were recited for him in countless synagogues, and many thousands everywhere readied themselves for the impending climax.

The climax came, but not in the inspiring manner the believers expected. Faced with the alternatives of embracing Islam or decapitation, the practical "Messiah" thought well of

Sabbatai Zevi, a prisoner at Abydos.

his own head and turned Mohammedan. In fact, many of his adherents followed his example, for they were convinced that the ways of the Messiah like the ways of God were inscrutable and beyond mortal man's understanding. The "Messiah" now received a new title of distinction from the Turks, that of "Mehmed Effendi," and in this new role began to preach Islam to the Jews.

The disillusionment among many of his adherents after this betrayal can be imagined. They cursed his name and wished

his memory to be forever blotted out. Nonetheless, so great was the hypnotic effect he had on some that, notwithstanding objective proof of his perfidy, they continued to believe in him. They tried to rationalize his misconduct away by all kinds of mystical exegesis. To this day, in Turkey, the descendants of the Jewish followers that Sabbatai Zevi converted to Islam live as a sect apart. They call themselves *Dönmeh*.

THE FRANKISTS

After Sabbatai Zevi's death in Albania in 1676 the Messianic fires smoldered fitfully. They flared up again during the second half of the eighteenth century when a Polish adventurer and cabalist, Jacob Frank, announced himself as the divinely elected successor to Sabbatai Zevi. Before long he boasted a sizable following whose contributions allowed him to live in luxury. He tried to dazzle the poor and the ignorant with his wealth, his elegant clothes, magnificent equipage and palatial residence. He even called himself "Baron de Frank." The rabbis, alarmed by this resurgence of the Sabbataian heresy and hysteria, excommunicated him and exposed his venality and charlatanism. In spite of that he proceeded to gather many more devoted adherents who lavished on him much money, jewels and other gifts, even after he walked to the baptismal font and became a Catholic missionary to the Jews. With the baffling loyalty of the simple-minded, many of his followers still clung to him. They constituted a strange Christian-Jewish cult.

Sabbatai Zevi's successors, Jacob Frank and his daughter Eva.

During the last years of his life he retired to a baronial castle which he had bought to shelter his old age and kept himself aloof and mysterious except from a handful of Polish nobles and wealthy men. After his death, his attractive daughter Eva continued as leader of the Frankist sect. She artfully combined licentiousness with mysticism to preserve her hold on the minds of her emotionally unstable followers.

THE *HASIDIM*

BAAL-SHEM

The so-called practical *Cabala* of the *Ari* (Isaac Luria) and his school of Safed, Palestine, mystics received a new and powerful impetus toward the middle of the eighteenth century. It came from Israel Baal-Shem (Israel "the Wonder-Worker"—about 1700-60), the founder of the new mystic cult, *Hasidism,* which was to influence profoundly the whole interior course of Jewish life for two centuries. This movement of religious ecstasy was merely a new and heady wine that Israel Baal-Shem poured into the old bottle of *Cabala.* He was directly in the line of the traditional Jewish mystics, but he endowed his cult with a poetic earthiness and a love of life and people which the old ascetic cabalists lacked.

Baal-Shem's synagogue in Miedziboz, the Ukraine.

No knowledge of the *Hasidim* (The Pious) can be complete without some insight into the life of its extraordinary founder. Israel ben Eliezer's place of birth is disputed as having been variously in Galicia, on the Polish-Romanian border and in the Volhynia region of the Ukraine. It strikes one as paradoxical that the future evangelist of the joyful spirit was born and raised in the most depressing circumstances. As a young child he was orphaned and became a community

An inscription on a millstone found at the bottom of the *mikveh* (ritual bath) at Ronsperg in Western Bohemia: "In this spring-well bathed Rabbi Israel Baal-Shem 310 times during the cold days in the year 1744. He said that this spring brings general relief to the sick, and helps childless women. In the year 1814 this house was rebuilt as a *mikveh.*"

charge, the recipient of both its charity and its neglect. Escaping from the wretched reality into daydreams he became, even at an early age, an incorrigible weaver of poetic fancies, a lover of nature in a mystical way.

From the very beginning Israel was a misfit. As a *cheder*-boy he often played truant from religious school and would wander over the countryside, through field and forest, immersed in his own dreams. This rapturous communion with nature strongly influenced his later pantheistic views that all creation was beautiful and holy, that nothing was so lowly that God was not in it. He himself often said that he felt the presence of God in the woods, heard His divine music rustling among the green leaves, perceived His harmonious spirit in the sun-spangled forest lanes, felt the eternity of the world in the recurrence of the seasons and in the myriad shapes, colors, sounds, smells and textures of all things and creatures.

But when he reached the age of ten the communal officials shook him out of his daydreams and made him a "belfer" (*bahelfer*), assistant to the *melamed*, the communal Hebrew teacher of the village. This proved an invaluable experience. As an orphan, without brothers or other kin of his own, he acquired their equivalent in the small boys he was obliged to carry on his back to and from *cheder,* the religious school. Of a warm and gentle nature, he became deeply attached to them. He not only practiced their daily prayers and the recitation of the benedictions with them, but he secretly taught them the words and melodies of hymns he himself composed.

Evidently he was not found entirely satisfactory as a "*belfer*," for when Israel was thirteen the community philanthropists appointed him handy-boy to the *shammes*, the sexton of the synagogue. The story has it that after all the worshippers had left the synagogue at night the boy would secretly study the *Cabala.* But even as assistant to the *shammes* he showed himself a misfit, and so his services were soon dispensed with.

Little is known of his adolescence, but undoubtedly it must have been troubled. He married young and lived with his family in the direst poverty in an obscure village in the Carpathians. He wandered in the beauty and silence of the mountains and found his solace there. The hills, he said, were like songs of praise. They trembled with the Divine Presence: "All the earth is full of His glory." However, he found neither glory nor a livelihood in the lime and clay that, it is claimed, he carted for a living. He then rented an inn in a small town in Galicia, but he was too impractical and temperamentally unsuited to be an innkeeper, so his already overburdened wife had to attend to the customers. Utterly maladjusted, a superfluous man, he spent entire days in a hut in the forest where he prayed, studied *Cabala* and ate dry bread and water because of poverty and not from a desire to mortify the flesh. Israel had, finally, to give up the inn, and because he loved children he became a *melamed,* a teacher in a *cheder,* which was the inevitable profession of so many learned but maladjusted misfits in the ghettos of eastern Europe.

MASTER OF THE NAME

With dramatic suddeness, in his thirty-sixth year, Israel ben Eliezer emerged as a *Baal-Shem* (Master of the Name). Supposedly, he had made himself master of the Secret and Ineffable Name of God, what the cabalists called the *Shem Ha-meforesh* and by whose supernatural means he could perform miracles among men. He journeyed triumphantly through Galicia, Volhynia and Podolia, where, legend has it, by invoking the *Shem Ha-meforesh* he was able to heal the sick, to cast out demons and transmigrating souls (*dybbukim*) and to foretell the future. In his mystic consciousness he heard voices from heaven which communicated to him all the mysteries of creation and of human destiny.

To many of his adherents who flocked to him readily he was little more than a *Baal-Shem*, a holy magician, whose wonder-working was conclusive evidence that he was a prophet. However, the ethical ideals and the warmly human values he preached could be appreciated by only a sensitive and thoughtful minority. The Dark Ages had settled like a starless night upon the Jews of eastern Europe ever since the end of the sixteenth century. Confined in crowded ghettos and deprived of the normal productive outlets for their energies, the great mass of Jews had sought and found a refuge in primitive superstition and in cabalistic abracadabra, in wishful visions and in weird practices. The arid state of Jewish religious culture was largely to blame for this retrogression. Upon the rapid decline of Jewish life in Slavic countries after Chmielnicki's Cossack hordes had devastated it, religious worship had become ever more formalistic. It suffered from a diminishing emotional content. Besides, *Torah* learning, traditionally obligatory for all Jews, had greatly deteriorated. It had become dry-as-dust and concerned principally with legalistic trivialities and Talmudic hairsplitting. At that, only a learned and well-to-do elite were qualified by a knowledge of Hebrew and rabbinic literature to devote themselves to this study. The great majority of Jews were sunk in the most abject poverty and ignorance. Many were barely able to recite their prayers in the sacred tongue, repeating words they did not understand, reciting sentiments which only eluded them. They, therefore, could find neither guidance nor consolation in the Jewish religion.

As if in answer to this universal need of the plain Jews for a comforter, Israel Baal-Shem appeared. He journeyed devotedly, an itinerant preacher, from town to town and from village to village.

EVANGEL OF JOY

Everywhere he went he affirmed the rewards of faith in God and of joy in life. God, he said, was everywhere, in all creation. The universe was only a radiant garment in which He wrapped His majesty! Therefore, everything in creation, including the commonplace, was holy and blessed.

Israel Baal-Shem was an optimist. He was also an ecstatic. He conceived man as being fundamentally good and perceived the world as beautiful. How could it be otherwise, he asked, since God created it and put his divine signature on everything? Not tears and lamentation but a joyful spirit and a cheerful demeanor were, therefore, God's moral requirements of man. To laugh, to sing and to dance with the intention of praising the Almighty, he declared, was the highest form of prayer. He put the heartfelt love of God above all religious worship and even above the study of the *Torah*. To do good among men, he held, was more meritorious than to observe punctiliously the mandatory 613 precepts of the Jewish religion. He contrasted the moving devotion of the heart with the empty casuistry of the intellect. He considered excessive

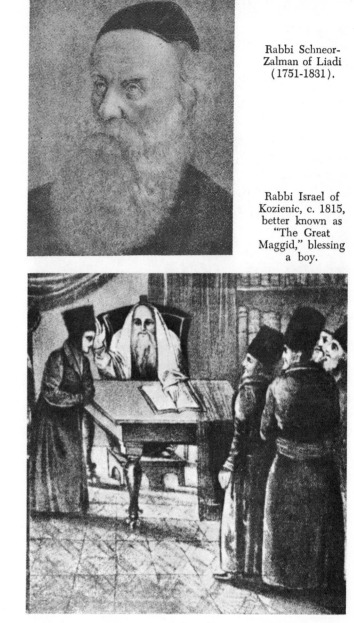

Rabbi Schneor-Zalman of Liadi (1751-1831).

Rabbi Israel of Kozienic, c. 1815, better known as "The Great Maggid," blessing a boy.

rationalism a menace to true religion which basically had to do with sentiment and feeling. Satan could rationalize, too, he argued, thereby ensnaring the clever in a web of falsehood and conceit which led but to the destruction of the soul. This position logically led Israel Baal-Shem to make the daring statement that the learned Talmudist or rabbi who was puffed up with the pride of his *Torah* knowledge and piety had less chance of enjoying the rewards of the World to Come than the humble and the pure in heart, no matter how ignorant, socially despised or lowly.

HASIDIM AND MISNAGDIM

The preaching of the founder of *Hasidism* acted like tinder on dry stubble. It set the whole Slavic Jewish world aflame and alarmed the rabbinic authorities as well as the Talmudic rationalists. These denounced the new sect as heretical, its tenets as sheer lunacy and destructive of the holy fabric of the *Torah*. The ban of excommunication was pronounced by some rabbis against Israel Baal-Shem and all Jews were for-

Invocation. (The *Rebbe* intercedes with God for the childless woman.) *Painting by Max Weber. Collection of Mrs. Rose Gershwin*

bidden to have contact with him. But it was in vain. *Hasidism* rolled on like a tidal wave over Galicia, Poland, the Ukraine, Hungary and Slovakia. Nothing seemed able to stop its advance. In a relatively short time, the sect counted fully half the Jews of eastern Europe. Its rationalist opponents, who called themselves *Misnagdim* (Opponents), fought the so-called "heresy" relentlessly and often unfairly. Only in Lithuania, the citadel of rabbinic rationalism, did *Hasidism* make few inroads. Elsewhere, especially among the suffering poor

Rejoicing. (The highest form of prayer is to praise God with joy and rapture in song, music and the dance. Illustration in beaten copper of the Yiddish folksong: *Der Rebbe Elimelech is gevorn zayr fraylach.* "Rabbi Elimelech became very merry.")

and the rejected, it came to still an emotional and religious hunger for a livable way of life and for a democratic sharing of God.

THE DECAY OF *HASIDISM:* THE *TZADDIK*

Unfortunately, as in the case of so many religious sects, *Hasidism* carried within itself the seed of its own corruption. The purity of belief and practice which characterized it during the lifetime of Israel Baal-Shem and his first great disciples before long showed the taint of institutionalism and even commercialism. By the end of the eighteenth century, a new kind of *Hasidic* rabbi began to emerge. This was the so-called *tzaddik* (holy one) or saint, who acted as intermediary between God's will and man's urgent desires. Therefore, the intimate personal communion between God and man which Israel Baal-Shem had preached became less and less possible for the *Hasid.* The office of *tzaddik* was dynastic. A *tzaddik's* eldest son would inherit not only his father's lofty official position but his lavish income derived from worshipful followers. Hundreds of these self-perpetuating dynasties were founded in eastern Europe. The most famous, as well as the most affluent, were those of Belz in Galicia, of Sadagora in Bukovina, of Ger in Poland and of Lubavitsch in Russia.

The pious *Hasidim* visited the *tzaddik,* or *rebbe,* at least three times a year. Each time they presented him with a *pidyon,* or free-will offering. In addition, the *Hasid* called on his *rebbe* on special occasions or in emergencies which required intercession with the Almighty. Most frequently it was to get the *tzaddik* to bless his wife's barren womb, to implore God to help him in time of illness and to get his advice as to whether or not it would be propitious to begin a business venture. It was a tradition among *Hasidim* to take their sons to the *rebbe* so that he might bless them to grow up to be pious and upright Jews. The *rebbe* gave the sick and the barren wives amulets to wear, inscribed with appropriate protective incantations and cabalistic formulae against Satan, the demons and evil spirits.

Some of these rabbinic wonder-workers, for example, the *Tzaddik* of Sadagora, lived in opulence. When they went out, it was often in an elegant coach and six. They were usually followed by a large household staff in addition to an immense retinue of worshipful adherents. Their homes had all the appointments of minor royal courts, although without the latter's splendor, decorum and ceremony. Hundreds of *Hasidim* ate at their tables, sometimes remaining as guests for days or weeks at a time. Together they worshipped God in fervent song and danced with abandon in the mystic circle. The disciples listened with bated breath to the *rebbe's* cabalistic exposition of the *Torah* and, together with them and in intimate group communion with their fellow-*Hasidim,* took fire from one another and soared to dizzy heights of mystic rapture—the most characteristic feature of their religious movement.

Whatever its backwardness and other undeniable retrogressive features, *Hasidism* as an historic movement created a necessary religious revolution in Jewish life in its time. It revitalized the Jewish spirit, gave it emotional warmth and hope in the future, set for it a practical pattern of ethical group living and, above all, provided it with the inner strength to endure the many ordeals it had to undergo.

JEWS IN SCIENCE

JEWISH TRADITION AND SCIENCE

It was entirely inevitable that the intellectual life of the Jews, so soberly keyed to reality and to rationalism, should have led many of them to take an active interest in the sciences. The scientific attitude was acquired quite early by Jews when they came in cultural contact with Egyptian, Babylonian, Graeco-Roman and Arab practitioners in the sciences. Undoubtedly, the tradition had become fully matured during the closing years of the Jewish Commonwealth at which time Yohanan ben Zakkai, one of the authoritative compilers of the *Mishna*, thus eulogized science: "He who understands astronomy and does not pursue the study of it, of that man it is written: 'But they regard not the work of the Lord, neither do they consider the operation of his hands.'"

However, the scientific enthusiasts were opposed by the school of rabbinic thought which maintained: "He who ponders over the following four things might as well not have been born: what is above, what is below, what is in front and what is behind." This fundamentalist view was motivated principally by a protective desire "to build a fence around the *Torah*," that is, to keep out secularist and alien thought. The conflict between these undeviating adherents of religious tradition and those who adopted the scientific attitude was especially bitter during the Middle Ages. That was a time of searching and testing, of rationalistic dawning. Science and philosophy were considered by their votaries as entirely compatible with and even complementary to rabbinic studies and traditional religious beliefs. This attitude was especially in evidence among the enlightened and worldly rabbis of Spain, Provence and southern Italy.

It was different, though, among the German Jews. The proud boast of Rabbi Asher ben Yehiel, the celebrated thirteenth-century German Talmudist who later became a religious leader in Spain, was: "It is well that I know nothing of profane science. I thank God for this, that he has saved me from it, because philosophic proof leads the people away from the fear and the teaching of God."

As happened in the Christian world as well, the pro-science and anti-science factions never quite declared a truce. With militancy and sincerity they battled the issue until the so-called "Dark Ages" which came into the ghetto with the Counter-Reformation, when the rigorous traditionalists won a victory by default. Interest in science had died of intellectual starvation. It was only to waken again with the fall of the imprisoning ghetto walls.

Astrology and Alchemy

Though astrology was frowned upon as an expression of idolatry in Jewish religious belief, nevertheless its superstitious practice was never successfully suppressed. During the Renaissance it was popular even among rabbis and Talmudic scholars. The slight smattering of astronomy which almost every cultured religious Jew acquired in connection with his use of the Hebrew calendar and the Zodiac no doubt encouraged in some an unhealthy preoccupation with prognosticating future events by reading the stars. The erudite but unstable chief rabbi and humanist of late sixteenth-century Venice, Leone da Modena, had built up for himself a persuasive rationale for it: "God studded the stars into the heavens to rule those on earth, to be the Second Cause. I was positively convinced that nobody could release himself from their influence." Moreover, Rabbi Leone always had the courage of his oscillating convictions: he had his horoscope read often by various astrologers, and with what result? "Until now they, unfortunately, have been invariably correct regarding sad events."

There is little doubt that this superstitious preoccupation of both Christians and Jews with the stars eventually led to a more scientific obsession during the Renaissance of trying to transmute base metals into gold by alchemical means. There were a number of Jewish alchemists. Rabbi Leone, for example, was also an enthusiast of alchemy, but being troubled by the well-known Hebraic conscience, he finally had to confess: "One blows upon the coals, but in doing so one also blows one's soul away, spending money on it and accomplishing nothing. A mighty lust dominates the mind to turn copper into gold, but all that it brings is shame."

From the hindsight advantage possessed by the informed person of today, the alchemists' delirious experiments with metallurgical fortune seem only a little less irrational than nightmares. But here is the surpassing wonder of it: that just as astrology had stimulated the study and development of astronomy, so did the fantastic "cooking in pots" experiments of the alchemists lead to the development of the science of

From a manuscript (1282) of the Latin translation by Farrachius of Rhazes' *Liber Continens*. On the left, Farrachius presents his translation to Charles of Anjou. On the right, Farrachius accepts the Arabic original from an eastern ruler.

147

chemistry. Tradition has it, for instance, that a certain Marie the Jewess, a celebrated but historically unidentified alchemist, had invented the "Bain-Marie," an alchemical bath which was widely used. Also she is reputed to have been the discoverer of hydrochloric acid.

Astronomers and Mathematicians

Jewish scientists and scholars during the Middle Ages stood, so to speak, with one foot in each of two civilizations—the Greek-Arabic-Jewish and that of western Europe. Beginning with the thirteenth century, Jewish intellectuals constituted in large measure the active leaven which made European culture rise. This was because of their erudition in general and their knowledge of many languages in particular. They were the most indefatigable translators into Latin and other languages, as well as interpreters, of the scientific writings of the Greeks, Arabs and Jews. But they were much more than fluent carriers and intermediaries of this culture: they also made significant and original contributions of their own to all branches of science and thought. Abraham bar Hiyya (Abraham Judaeus), for example, has been evaluated by some historians of science as one of the greatest of medieval European mathematicians. He produced one of the most important scientific works of the era, the *Hibbur ha-Meshihah*. In fact, it was the first scientific work ever written in Hebrew and dealt in an original way with practical geometry and with algebra. It was subsequently, in 1145, translated into Latin by the apostate Jewish mathematician, Plato of Tivoli, under the title of *Liber Embodorum* and won the author great renown among Arab and Christian scholars. Perhaps Abraham's greatest distinction, according to some authorities, was that he was the first writer to introduce the scientific method into Europe.

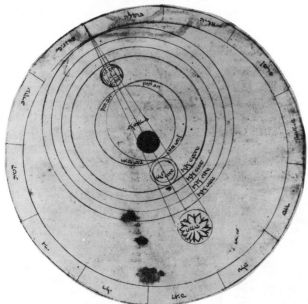

Bonfils' astronomical tables.

Another remarkable rabbinic mathematician and astronomer was Immanuel Bonfils, whose astronomical tables were extensively used by mariners and explorers beginning with the fourteenth century. Recent researches have brought to light the fact that he had invented a decimal system one hundred and fifty years before the first one known in Europe.

The Jewish scholars of the Middle Ages, especially those of Moorish Spain, pursued the well-known Greek pattern of mul-

tiple intellectual interests. They were in a literal sense encyclopedists who avoided being narrow specialists and tried to excel in several fields. Quite often they combined in themselves the varied callings of doctor, rabbi, astronomer, mathematician, grammarian, philosopher, poet and Talmudic commentator. The archetype of this "universal thinker" was Moses ben Maimon (Maimonides).

Levi ben Gerson (1288-1344) of Perpignan, one of the most original of all thinkers of the Middle Ages, was not only a distinguished philosopher and religious writer, not only an eminent astronomer (he influenced Copernicus) and mathematician, but was in a casual way also an inventor of note. He is credited by some writers with the discovery of the *camera oscura*, the first kind of camera known. He also was the first to describe and reputedly was the inventor of the "Jacob's Staff," a quadrant which was used for centuries by navigators, including Columbus, Magellan, Martin Behain and Vasco de Gama, and was displaced in 1731 only when the Englishman Hadley produced his improved quadrant. Another quadrant in general use during the Renaissance was the "quadrans judaicus," invented by the astronomer Jacob ben Makker (died 1308).

The astronomical knowledge possessed by an unusual number of intellectual Jews found a practical outlet in the service of navigation. This occurred especially under the latter-day medieval Spanish and Portuguese kings who, because of their lust for the discovery of new continents to add to their empires, encouraged astronomers, even if they were Jews. The

Zacuto's Almanach.

nūmer⁹ annorūz	Tab eclipſis luminariūz et pꞥmo de ſole								
	nomina menſiūz	dies	digiti	feria	hore	minūt	finis eclipſis hore	minu	
1493	octob	10	9	5	0	0	1	20	
1502	ſeptēb	30	8	6	17	28	19	12	
1506	Julii	20	3	2	1	49	3	3	
1513	martii	7	4	1	23	49	1	9	
1518	Junii	7	10	2	18	22	19	17	
1524	fannaz	23	9	2	3	12	4	6	
	Tabla de eclipſib⁹ lunne								
1494	ſeptēb	14	17	1	17	5	2	33	
1497	fannaz	18	17	4	3	50	7	18	
1500	nouēb	5	13	5	10	17	13	30	
1501	maii	2	19	1	15	33	19	6	
1502	octob	15	14	7	10	15	12	9	

Detail of world map by Cresques.

148

famous "Alfonsine Tables," for instance, in wide use among navigators and by the great astronomers Kepler and Galileo several centuries later, were arranged in 1272 for King Alfonso by the Toledan Jewish astronomers, Judah ben Moses and Isaac ibn Sid, a synagogue cantor. Astronomical tables drawn up by a number of Jews, and principally those by Abraham

Gravestone of David Gans, historian and astronomer, with sign of star (astronomer) and goose (*gans*), 1613. He worked with the celebrated astronomers Johann Keppler and Tycho Brahe in their Prague Observatory.

Zacuto (1450-1510) and his pupil, Joseph Vecinho, the chief astronomers and cartographers to Manuel the Great of Portugal, were carried and consulted by Columbus on his voyage to America.

Other early Jewish inventors, cartographers and astronomers who aided the great explorers in their voyages of discovery were Joseph ben Abraham ibn Wakar, the already mentioned Immanuel Bonfils, and the great Mallorcan cartographer, Yehuda Cresques.

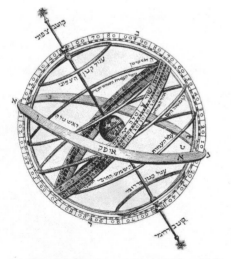

Astrolabe from Tobias Cohen's *Ma'ase Tobia*, 1707.

Physicians

The science of healing has an intensely revered tradition among Jews, with an unbroken continuity of more than two thousand years. It was in evidence twenty-two centuries ago

when the ancient Hebrew "wisdom" writer, Jesus Ben Sira (about 200 B.C.E), admonished his readers: "Honor the physician. His knowledge allows him to walk with raised head, and gains for him the admiration of princes. If you fall ill, cry to the Lord, but also call for the physician, for a sensible man does not neglect the remedies which the earth offers."

As far back as the Alexandria of the Ptolemies, Jews had become prominent as professional healers. Later on, living among the cultured Arabs, the inheritors of classic Greek science and thought, who excelled in the field of medicine above all other peoples, Jews in time achieved an equal celebrity with them as doctors and as medical scientists and writers. When in medieval and Renaissance days the Jews of Europe were being harshly treated, almost the only exceptions made among them for special consideration were the Jewish court doctor and the Jewish court financier. Their personal services to the ruler were so highly valued that they transcended all considerations of creed and greed. Often enough the Jewish court physician would serve, sometimes successfully, as the intercessor for his people whenever it was threatened by anti-Jewish decrees or the murderous acts of its enemies. This gave the Jewish court doctor a supremely important social function far beyond that of healer.

Frontispiece of the translation of Isaac Israeli's medical works, by Ali Abbas and Constantine.

To be a doctor was generally considered among Jews as the most exalted moral and worldly calling a Jew could aspire to. It was lucrative and yet was also a highly respected profession much to be preferred over the despised and compulsory occupations of money lending, huckstering and dealing in junk and old clothes. The doctor could claim great humanitarian and social usefulness—all the more important to a Jew because of the religious belief that alleviation of human suffering is one of the most meritorious pursuits of righteousness.

In any case, the medical profession always had enormous attraction for Jews. Centuries of social idealization have fixed for them its tradition and pattern to this day. They have been producing many more doctors in proportion to their number than any other ethnic or culture group.

One of the great doctors of the Middle Ages was Isaac Israeli (850-950). He was not only a philosopher of originality, but also court physician to two Fatimide caliphs. In addition, he was a medical scientist of consequence. His medical and philosophical works, written in Arabic, were subsequently translated into Latin by the former Jewish doctor, the monk Constantine, and the Jewish doctor Abbas. These writings were carefully studied and admired by such foremost Christian scholastics as Albertus Magnus, Vincent of Beauvais and Thomas Aquinas. His medical ideas, enunciated one thousand

Lecturer and class in medicine, 13th century. (From Avicenna's Codex in Hebrew.)

years ago, sound astonishingly modern. His treatises "On Fever" and "On Diet" remained authoritative for some five hundred years. Without scientific pedantry he always tried to penetrate to the heart of any question in a common-sense way: "The most important problem of the doctor is how to prevent illness. . . . The majority of diseases are cured by the help of Nature without the aid of a doctor. . . . If you can cure a patient by means of diet forbear to prescribe drugs. . . . Hold forth the prospects of recovery to patients, even if you are not sure of them yourself, so that at least you shall second the efforts of Nature to cure them."

For a thousand years Jews were among the most honored healers in Europe. Beginning with the ninth century they helped found the finest medical colleges. Those in Tarentum, Palermo, Salerno and Bari, and, a little later, those in Rome and Montpelier, furnished Europe for centuries with its best doctors. Some of the early Jewish writers on medical subjects, who brought luster to their names, were Meshulam ben Kalonymos, Joseph ben Gorion, Todros of Narbonne and Zedikiah, court physician to the Carolingian kings, Louis the Meek and Charles the Bold. The three greatest figures in tenth-century medicine were Haroun of Cordova, professor of medicine in the Cordova College of Medicine; Yehuda Chaioug of Fez, professor of medicine at Kairouan Medical College in Tunisia; and Amram of Toledo, the most eminent medical scientist of the age.

The study of medicine was introduced as part of the regular curriculum in rabbinic academies about the year 1000. A long and distinguished line of rabbi-physicians were graduated from them and served caliphs and emperors, popes and kings, bishops and princes.

With the possible exception of the redoubtable Isaac Israeli, the foremost physician the Jews produced during all the Middle Ages was the universal genius, Moses ben Maimon (Maimonides). He served as physician to Saladin the Great. He also was a voluminous writer on a wide variety of medical subjects, especially on opthalmology, on poisons and antidotes. In their Latin translations these works were carefully studied by Christian doctors for centuries.

Ranking high on the seemingly endless list of eminent Jewish doctors and medical scientists who flourished in Europe as the modern era approached were Maestro Vidal, Amatus Lusitanus and Rodriquez Lopez. They made significant contributions to medical knowledge and practice.

Bigotry and Medicine

The fruitful epoch of Jews in medicine, which had lasted uninterruptedly for seven or eight centuries, came ingloriously to an end with the severe repression of the Jews that

Left. St. Basil attended by a Jewish physician. (Woodcut from a 13th-century German ms.) *Center.* Amatus Lusitanus, born 1511 in Castel Branco, Portugal, died 1568 in Saloniki. *Right.* Joseph Solomon del Medigo, pupil of Galileo in astronomy and noted medical scientist and Rabbinic author.

was initiated by the Church in Rome during the Counter-Reformation. Pope Gregory XIII issued the Bull, *contra Medicos Hebreos,* on March 30, 1581, which forbade Christians to receive medical treatment from Jewish doctors. The famous Jewish physician, David de Pomis, thereupon presented the Doge and the Senate of Venice with "An Apology for the Jewish Physician." Although they received his defense with sympathetic interest they were powerless to alter the papal decision.

Though Jewish doctors were honored and rewarded when they effected cures, they also risked disgrace, punishment or execution if the patient died. This was especially true of Court doctors, and in a number of instances on record the unhappy consequences of medical failure extended to the entire community of Jews. The classic example is that of the Jewish doctor Lippold who could not save the life of his patient Joachim II, Elector of Brandenburg. When Joachim died in 1573, Lippold was accused of poisoning him. He was tortured to death, as shown in this contemporary engraving, and all the Jews were banished from Berlin and the rest of Brandenburg.

Prayer for Physicians

by MAIMONIDES

"O God, Thou hast formed the body of man with infinite goodness; Thou hast united in him innumerable forces incessantly at work like so many instruments, so as to preserve in its entirety this beautiful house containing his immortal soul, and these forces act with all the order, concord, and harmony imaginable. But if weakness or violent passion disturb this harmony, these forces act against one another and the body returns to the dust whence it came. Thou sendest then to man Thy messengers, the diseases which announce the approach of danger, and bid him prepare to overcome them. The Eternal Providence has appointed me to watch o'er the life and health of Thy creatures. May the love of my art actuate me at all times, may neither avarice, nor miserliness, nor the thirst for glory or a great reputation engage my mind; for, enemies of truth and philanthropy, they could easily deceive me and make me forgetful of my lofty aim of doing good to Thy children. Endow me with strength of heart and mind, so that both may be ready to serve the rich and the poor, the good and the wicked, friend and enemy, and that I may never see in the patient anything else but a fellow creature in pain.

"If physicians more learned than I wish to counsel me, inspire me with confidence in and obedience toward the recognition of them, for the study of science is great. It is not given to one alone to see all that others see. May I be moderate in everything except in the knowledge of this science; so far as it is concerned, may I be insatiable; grant me the strength and opportunity always to correct what I have acquired, always to extend its domain; for knowledge is boundless and the spirit of man can also extend indefinitely, daily to enrich itself with new acquirements. Today he can discover his errors of yesterday, and tomorrow he may obtain new light on what he thinks himself sure of today.

"O God, Thou hast appointed me to watch o'er the life and death of Thy creatures; here am I ready for my vocation!"

MODERN FRANCE

THE FRENCH REVOLUTION FREES THE JEWS

The Jews of Europe had to wait some fifteen hundred years before they were officially accorded equality as human beings. It was the French Revolution, extolling reason above dogma, the rights of man above the property rights of kings and nobles, freedom of conscience above subservience to an authoritarian Church, that liberated the Jews from their ghetto prison.

This new attitude toward the Jews did not happen overnight in France. It was slowly, painfully, even courageously nurtured by a long line of eminent social thinkers and frontiersmen of the modern spirit: Montaigne, Montesquieu, Voltaire, Rousseau, Diderot, Condorcet and many others.

Two years before the Revolution, Count Mirabeau, one of its major architects, had visited Berlin on a diplomatic mission. There he met Moses Mendelssohn, who helped clarify for him the complexities of the Jewish question. Deeply moved by the historic injustice to the Jews, Mirabeau sat down to write a denunciation of their persecutors, coupled with an appeal to the conscience of mankind to redress the wrong by granting them equal rights with all Christians.

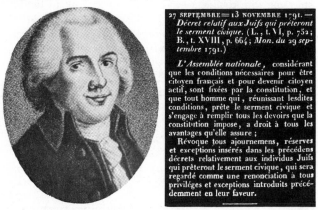

Left. Portrait of Abbé Gregoire. *Right.* Decree of the French National Assembly on September 27, 1791, granting equal rights to Jews.

The Bastille, the last stronghold of reaction, fell before the will of the embattled French people on July 14, 1789. Before long the Protestant churchman and deputy, the Abbé Gregoire, presented to the National Assembly in Paris a delegation of Jews from Alsace-Lorraine, a province of France still steeped in medieval darkness and fanaticism. They pleaded with the deputies to make the ideals of the Revolution more than high-sounding phrases by according ordinary human rights to the Jews. The deputies representing Alsace-Lorraine, aided by other clericalists and Jew-baiters in the Assembly, tried to shout them down. But times had changed: the great leaders of the Revolution were present to safeguard its principles. Mirabeau spoke, as well as the Abbé Gregoire, Clermont-Tonnerre and Robespierre. The clericalist representatives, Abbé Maury, Reubel, and La Fare, the Bishop of Nancy, answered them vehemently. The debate continued indecisively until finally it was decided by pressure from below —from the people. The National Guard of Paris, which consisted of the foot-soldiers of the Revolution, in democratic

fashion took a referendum on the issue. Of the sixty *Arrondissements* in the Paris Commune, fifty-three voted overwhelmingly in favor of complete Jewish emancipation. Tired of the debate, the guardsmen sent their representative, the Abbé Malot, to the National Assembly to demand the prompt granting of citizenship to Jews. The clericalists once more attempted to block action. Furious because of their tactics, the Jacobin Deputy Duport ascended the tribune to challenge them: "I believe that freedom of worship does not permit any distinction to be made in the political rights of citizens on account of their creed. The question of the political existence of the Jews has been postponed. . . . I demand that the motion for postponement be withdrawn and a decree passed that the Jews in France enjoy the privileges of full citizenship."

When, despite this, an opposition deputy arose to oppose the motion, the President of the Assembly, Regnault de Saint-Jean, promptly cut him short. He ruled that to oppose the motion was equivalent to opposing the Constitution of the Republic.

On September 28, 1791, there took place the most momentous event in Jewish history since the loss of their state in 70 C.E. Jews were declared to be equal with all men and free citizens of the Republic of France.

Abraham Furtado.

NAPOLEON AND THE JEWS

To Frenchmen, who were afraid that the Jews would remain alien and unassimilable, Clermont-Tonnerre, one of the champions of the Jews, gave the reassurance that the intention was to make them Frenchmen first and foremost. Jews would not be encouraged to stand apart from the mainstream of French life, except for the practice of their religion, which was a matter of private conscience. He said: "To Jews as human beings—everything; to Jews as a people—nothing!"

The process of becoming Frenchmen for many Jews was so rapid and thoroughgoing that, according to the eminent French-Jewish scholar Reinach, "After 1791 it was no longer proper to speak of 'the Jews of France' but only of 'French citizens professing the Jewish religion.'"

Although the Revolution had officially and legally bestowed full equality on the Jews, its civil struggles for the next several years and its subsequent betrayal by Napoleon prevented genuine implementation of its decisions on behalf of the Jews.

Brilliant opportunist that he was, Napoleon decided to attach the 77,000 Jews of France to his cause. To make himself ruler of the world, as he planned, he required every friend he could make. On May 30, 1806, he issued a call for a convocation of the leading Jews of France and of the German Rhineland, to be known as the Assembly of Notables. Under the presidency of Abraham Furtado, a wealthy Portuguese Jew of Bordeaux, one hundred and twelve Jewish dignitaries met on July 12th to listen to an insolent address by the imperial commissioner, Molé, an undisguised enemy of the Jews. He told them that the emperor would like to know their attitudes on various matters affecting them and on Christian-Jewish relations. He put before them for careful consideration a list of twelve questions.

Though the Napoleonic Code had the practical effect of helping emancipate the Jews of Europe, the emperor's twelve questions appear to have been deliberately insulting and humiliating to the "Notables." Some of the questions were: Were Jews allowed to be polygamists? Was it allowed for a Jewess to marry a Christian? Did French Jews feel any obligation of loyalty to France? Did Jewish law forbid taking usury from Jews but sanctioned it from Christians? Probably the most constructive question the emperor asked was about the need of a plan for "stimulating the Jews of the Empire to take up the practice of arts and crafts, in order that they might learn to substitute dignified callings for the disgraceful occupations to which for generations and centuries they had largely devoted themselves."

The imperial commissioner finished with this gratuitous advice: "The Emperor grants full freedom of counsel, but he desires that you become Frenchmen and that you bear in mind always that you will be deprived of this honor if your

Medal struck
in honor of
Napoleon by
Sanhedrin,
1806.
Jewish Museum
Left. Rabbi
David Sinz-
heim.

actions prove unworthy of it." On September 17th the Assembly of Notables was summoned again. Imperial Commissioner Molé informed it then that the emperor was graciously agreeable to their answers. He wished, however, to give their decisions, for making patriotic and productive Frenchmen of the Jews, the force of religious sanction, so he bade the Notables convoke for this purpose a *Grand Sanhedrin*. It was to be composed of forty-six rabbis and twenty-five laymen.

The *Grand Sanhedrin* assembled in the Hotel de Ville on February 9, 1807, and elected Rabbi David Sinzheim as its president. It readily confirmed the decisions of its parent body. It also issued prohibitions against usury and introduced an innovation: civil marriage for Jews.

It was not long before Napoleon fully revealed his duplicity. He engineered a Jewish decree through his rubber-stamp Chamber of Deputies on March 17, 1808, which was referred to by French liberals at the time as *l'infâme décret* (the infamous decree). It bristled with special restrictions against Jews in all their business affairs. For example, before a Jewish merchant or shopkeeper could engage in trade he had to obtain a license from the local prefect. But before he could get a license he had to present a "guarantee" of his moral character from the Jewish Consistory as well as from the city authorities. The decree also ordered the expulsion of the Jews from the Rhineland unless they consented to become farmers.

Napoleon was more concerned with "using" Jews for his own ends than with freeing them. By imperial decree on March 17, 1808, he ordered the institution of the *Consistoire* (Consistory for Jewish Affairs). There was to be a central consistory for the whole empire in Paris and regional consistories in Jewish communities with a population of at least two thousand. Each consistory was to be run by two rabbis and two laymen, and this system was to be established in France, in the four provinces of the Rhineland, in Westphalia and in Italy—all territories which fell to Napoleon by force of arms. The idea behind the consistory was a practical one: to keep the Jews in line with his purposes and to let it serve as an agency for supplying the army with Jewish recruits.

Sanhedrin in session.

CAREERS FOR THE TALENTED

In spite of the restrictions placed on Jews, France became the freest country on the continent. It attracted all those Jews who felt stifled and uncomfortable in their own lands. One of the ways in which Napoleon had broken with the past was his policy of *carrières aux talents*, careers for gifted men. Jews who until now had been starved for lack of opportunity to use or to develop their gifts were given free rein to do so now. Within two generations a considerable number succeeded in

STATESMEN

Adolphe Crémieux.

Léon Blum.

René Mayer (center).

René Cassin, also noted jurist.

BANKER

MUSICIANS

Isaac Pereire.

Jacques Offenbach.

Jacques Halévy.

Georges Bizet.

THE THEATRE

Jules Janin, drama critic.

Rachel.

Bernhardt at twenty.

Bernhardt at forty.

FILM DIRECTOR

ARTISTS

Jean Benoit-Lévy.

Camille Pissarro.

Rosa Bonheur.

Marc Chagall.

making careers for themselves in almost every calling—in banking and commerce, in government, in the learned professions and in the arts and sciences. French Jews continued to excel in all these fields down to our own times.

Statesmen

With the Revolution of 1848, Jews stepped forward for the first time as political leaders and statesmen. With Victor Hugo and Lamartine, the writer-statesmen, two Jewish statesmen, Michel Goudchaux, Minister of Finance, and Adolphe Crémieux, Minister of Justice, served in the Provisional Revolutionary Government. Crémieux was probably the greatest public figure French Jewry produced. He was a consistent champion of Jewish rights and, while Minister of Justice, initiated two basic social reforms: abolition of Negro slavery in the French colonies and of the death penalty for political dissenters.

Achille Fould also achieved eminence in the field of government, but, unlike Crémieux, was a reactionary monarchist who served as Minister of Finance during the Second Empire. Later French Jewish statesmen were David Raynal, Eduard Millaud, L. S. Klotz, Paul Straus, Maurice Bokanowski, Georges Mandel, Jules Moch, Daniel and René Mayer and others. However, the most influential of all after Crémieux was Léon Blum, several times Prime Minister of France and leader of the Socialist Party.

Bankers

There have been a number of prominent Jewish bankers and industrialists in France, such as Lazard Frères, the French Rothschilds, the fabulous Lowenthal and Osiris. But none equaled Isaac Pereire and his brother Émile in originality or in the scope of their grandiose projects. They founded the *Crédit Foncier* and later the *Crédit Mobilier* and were instrumental in establishing and developing the credit feature as the keystone of the modern banking system. It was their view that easy and increased banking facilities would result in lower interest rates and would therefore increase commerce and better conditions for workers, business men and the entire economy. With their cousin, Olinde Rodrigues, they built the first railway in France in 1835 and in later years, a network of railways throughout France, Switzerland, Spain and southern Russia.

Musicians

As in other countries maintaining a high cultural level, the Jews of France, too, distinguished themselves in the field of music. Outstanding among these were Georges Bizet, the composer of *Carmen;* Offenbach, of *Tales of Hoffman* fame; Halévy, the composer of *La Juive;* Saint-Saens, who wrote the music for *Samson and Delilah;* Paul Dukas, best known for *The Sorcerer's Apprentice;* and Darius Milhaud, one of the group of the modern composers known as "The Six." French instrumentalists well known to America are the Polish-born harpsichordist Wanda Landowska, the orchestral conductors Eduard Colonne and Pierre Monteux, and the pianist-pedagogue Isidor Philippe.

The Theatre

Perhaps in no field of the arts have French Jews distinguished themselves more than in the theatre. Probably the two most illustrious actresses in the history of the French stage were Rachel and Sarah Bernhardt. Each in turn established styles of acting which set the fashion for a long time not only in France but throughout the world. Two other renowned Jewish actresses were Amélie Hirsch and Rosine Bloch.

In the contemporary French theatre there have been a number of notable playwrights and directors: Tristan Bernard, Henry Bernstein, Porto-Riche and Alfred Savoir. Benoit-Lévy is one of the foremost movie directors.

Arts and Artists

Camille Pissarro, world-famous Impressionist master, helped to swell the Jewish contribution to French culture. So did a number of other Jewish artists who, though not born in France, have been identified with the School of Paris and later French art trends: the painters Chaim Soutine, Moise Kisling, Marc Chagall, Zadkine, Léon Zack, Mané Katz and the sculptors Elie Nadelman, Jacques Lipshitz and Chana Orloff. Another native French artist of Jewish descent was Rosa Bonheur, the nineteenth-century academician.

Writers

France has produced many Jewish writers of eminence who represent every school and every style from the most esoteric to the most sensational. The best known are Ludovic Halévy, Catulle Mendes, Gustave Kahn, Marcel Proust (a half-Jew), Fernand Nozière, André Maurois, Jean-Richard Bloch, Bernard Lazare, Georges Duhamel, André Spire, Edmond Fleg, Joseph Kessel, Iwan Goll and Jules Romains.

Philosophers

In the field of philosophy, Jews have occupied an important position in France since the turn of the century. Henri Bergson's mysticism has pervaded much of modern philosophy. His book *Creative Evolution* has been one of the most widely admired philosophic works written during the last fifty years.

Other noted philosophers of Jewish extraction are Léon Brunschvigg, Émile Myerson and Julien Benda.

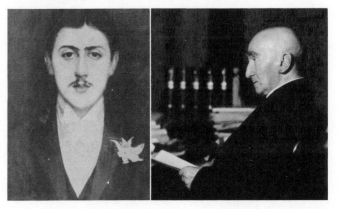

Marcel Proust.   Henri Bergson.

Joseph Kessel.

André Maurois.

Bordeaux Synagogue.

Scientists

Although not so numerous as in Germany, French scientists of Jewish origin have made important contributions in their respective fields. August-Michel Lévy was a foremost geologist. Fernand Isidore Widal did pioneer work on typhoid fever and was the first to propose vaccination against it. Georges Hayem was a brilliant pathologist of the stomach and Alexander Besredka made a significant contribution in the field of immunology. Perhaps the most important of all French physicists was Gabriel Lippman, who was awarded the Nobel Prize in 1908. One of the great mathematicians of France is Jacques Salomon Hadamard, noted for his work in the theory of functions and the theory of numbers. The "Hadamard Theorem" is well known to all students of higher mathematics.

Above. Strasbourg Synagogue. *Below.* The new synagogue in Strasbourg.

Gabriel Lippmann.

Jacques Hadamard.

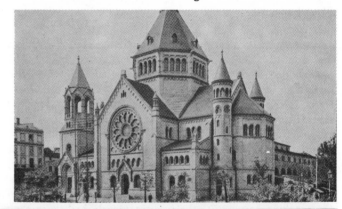

Left. Prayer for Emperor Louis Napoleon at the installation service for the Chief Rabbi of Paris at the Synagogue de la rue Notre Dame de Nazareth. *Center.* Grand-Rabbi Zadok Cahn, late 19th century. *Right.* The *shammes* summons to early morning prayer, Alsace, 19th century.

156

Carpentras Synagogue.

RELIGIOUS LIFE IN FRANCE

Only a few synagogues in France, such as those in Carpentras and Cavaillon, date back to the eighteenth century. The rest were built after the Napoleonic era. There are Liberal temples and Orthodox synagogues, as everywhere else. The citadel of Orthodoxy is still Alsace and that of Reform Judaism is Paris, although a considerable number of Orthodox congregations were established in the French capital by refugees from Poland and Russia who migrated there beginning with the 1880's.

THE DREYFUS CASE

L'Affaire Dreyfus is one of the most celebrated cases in modern legal history. At the time it engulfed the French people in the most violent of partisan emotions. Before long it became a national issue and was fought out not only in the courts but in the ballot boxes of the republic, in the press, the universities, the union halls and on the *terrasses* of the sidewalk cafés. It also captured world interest.

The degradation of Dreyfus.

It began in 1894. Captain Alfred Dreyfus, a sedate and conservative captain of artillery, suddenly found himself pulled out of the ranks and charged with selling military secrets to the Germans. Precipitately he was court-martialed, found guilty and branded a traitor to France. He was degraded, his epaulettes torn from his uniform and his sword

broken. As he was led off to a lifetime of penal servitude on Devil's Island, he cried out: *"Je suis innocent! Vive la France!"*

All France applauded—a traitor had been caught and properly punished. The reactionaries, led by the arch-anti-Semite, Eduard Drumont, made a Roman holiday of the occasion. Dreyfus' conviction proved what they had alleged all along—that the Jews were traitorous by nature, that they dominated the life of France and if their grip were not loosened, they would soon destroy it.

Some time later, and quite by accident, Colonel Picquart, Chief of the Army Intelligence Bureau, examined the document, supposedly in Dreyfus' handwriting, which had incriminated him—the so-called *bordereau*, or list, of the military secrets he had sold to the Germans. He came to the conclusion that it was a forgery and that the handwriting was not that of Dreyfus at all but of a Major Esterhazy, a notoriously debauched officer.

Major Esterhazy.

Picquart, in line of duty, reported his suspicions to the Chief of the Army General Staff, General Boisdeffre, and to the Minister of War, General Billot. He was amazed when they ordered him to drop the matter at once. They told him that besides the *bordereau* there was a secret *dossier* of which Picquart knew nothing, and that it definitely had established Dreyfus' guilt before the court-martial.

Picquart began to suspect the existence of some sort of plot, but exactly what its nature was he could not guess. Nonetheless, in all conscience, he felt it his duty to press for a re-examination of the findings of the court-martial. As if in

Picquart in prison.

Emile Zola.

answer to this pressure, he was immediately removed as Chief of Intelligence and sent to a dangerous outpost in Tunis where there was fierce fighting with rebellious Arab tribesmen. In his place a Colonel Henry was appointed Chief of Intelligence.

Picquart's public statements, in addition to those of friends and relatives of Dreyfus, shocked and aroused many decent people in France, conservatives, liberals and radicals alike. To drown their clamor for the reopening of the case the anti-Semites launched a series of scurrilous attacks. They branded all *Dreyfusards* as traitors to France and enemies of the army. They worked strenuously to build up popular hysteria. They even organized a new political party, the Nationalist Party, which drew into its ranks monarchists, clericalists, militarists and other reactionaries, all of whom fervently declared themselves patriots of France and defenders "of the honor of the Army." A religious order even published a daily newspaper, *La Croix* (The Cross), in which it relentlessly attacked Dreyfus and the Jews.

At first the camp of the *Dreyfusards* was small, made up mostly of writers, professors, journalists, artists and students. But soon broad sections of the people awoke to the full implications of the case. The leader of the Socialists in the Chamber of Deputies, Jean Jaurés, pointed out that the conviction of Dreyfus appeared to him to be the opening move in a far-reaching plot for the overthrow of the republic by a monarchist-military *coup d'état*. This suspicion grew when a leading deputy, on asking the premier to reopen the case, was advised not to press the matter because it was *"une chose jugée"* (a closed incident).

But the clamor increased and something had to be done to silence it. Major Esterhazy was engineered into a widely publicized court-martial, was acquitted unanimously and with enthusiasm. Thereupon Colonel Picquart, the man who had accused Esterhazy of the crime charged to Dreyfus, was promptly arrested and imprisoned.

"I Accuse"

The Nationalists rejoiced over their triumph, but not for long. On January 13, 1898, the great novelist, Émile Zola,

wrote the famous open letter, *J'Accuse*, which he addressed to the President of the Republic. In it he charged the top generals of the army and their eminent civilian associates in the government with having organized a conspiracy against the republic. He accused the military judges of Dreyfus of premeditated fraud. Their verdict he described as "a crime of high treason against humanity." To intimidate and silence other *Dreyfusards* the government immediately arrested Zola. It tried and sentenced him to prison for one year. Zola fled the country and the public excitement was greater than ever.

Vindication

Then the truth came to light. Colonel Henry, Picquart's successor, suddenly committed suicide and Major Esterhazy confessed having written the *bordereau*. The new president, Émile Loubet, ordered the *Cour de Cassation*, the Supreme Court, to review the case, and it acquitted Dreyfus in 1906 with the declaration that, in its opinion, the case was completely constructed out of lies, forgeries, collusion and conspiracy. So, as in all well-ordered romances, Dreyfus was restored to his place in the army. He was promoted to major and awarded the Legion of Honor. Colonel Picquart was made a general and later became War Minister. To many he was the real hero of this astonishing drama. But perhaps the real hero was France itself, the French people, who turned in wrath on the plotters against its liberties and compelled justice to be done and retribution to be made to an innocent Jew.

Dreyfus reinstated.

GERMANY

THE ENLIGHTENMENT

With the industrial revolution in the eighteenth century, Jewish life in Germany entered a new phase. Jews were among the new capitalists in Prussia who built factories, started industries and, in general, acted as entrepreneurs in commerce and as bankers. Some of them became wealthy.

Parallel with this economic development was the overflow into Germany of the social enlightenment, that ferment which soon culminated in the French Revolution. Jews, too, were caught up by the egalitarian ardor of the times. They perceived that in the general spread of freer ideas, laws and institutions, such as the separation of church and state, Jews would be enabled to come into their own on an equal footing with Christians. The most noted of the handful of Jewish apostles of enlightenment in Germany was Moses Mendelssohn (1729-1786). He was the little hunchback philosopher whom the great German philosopher Kant described as a genius "destined to create a new epoch in metaphysics and to establish an altogether new norm of criticism."

It was Moses Mendelssohn who organized the historic movement among Jews, not only to break down the walls of their physical ghettos, symbols of their economic and social strangulation, but also to destroy the equally imprisoning ghetto within—the backwardness, ignorance, cultural stagnation and hopelessness that had been depressing Jewish community life for so many centuries. Mendelssohn rallied round him a group of enthusiastic disciples, among them Hartwig Wessely (1725-1805), a poet who wrote in Hebrew, and David Friedländer (1750-1834), a son-in-law of David Itzig, the foremost Jewish banker in Berlin. By means of the printed word and of the establishment of liberal religious schools in which German was the language of instruction, the *Haskalah*, or Jewish Enlightenment Movement, sought to draw reluctant fellow-Jews out of the ghetto and into the broad light of the world and general culture. Mendelssohn had translated the *Pentateuch* into German and had published it in parallel text with the Hebrew, thus making it possible for thousands of German Jews who knew Hebrew and Yiddish to learn the German language.

David Friedländer.

Hartwig Wessely.

The Ghettos Crumble

The physical ghettos, too, had begun to crumble. A stirring incident took place in 1798 in Bonn, then the city of young Beethoven. In festive procession a great multitude of the Christian inhabitants marched to the ghetto, where several carpenters stepped forward with axes and other tools and broke down the ghetto gates. Jews were drawn to the head of the procession and linked arms with Christians. The parade continued through the city streets, demonstrating for the first time in German history the human equality of Jews with Christians.

This was more than a manifestation against the barbarous institution of the ghetto; it was a signal to the world that in Germany, too, the age of feudalism and fanaticism was passing. Years before this incident, Moses Mendelssohn, aided by his Christian friends, Wilhelm Dohm and the great writer Lessing, had appealed to the conscience of the world for the release of the Jew from his fetters of inequality. To the charge that Jews were parasites and unproductive, Mendelssohn had retorted bitterly: "Our hands are bound, and yet we are blamed for not using them!"

Medal commemorating the emancipation of the Jews of Westphalia in 1808.

But the emancipation of the Jews was to come slowly. At various times in the decades which followed, the granting of Jewish rights was sonorously proclaimed. In 1808, under the pressures of the French Occupation and the Napoleonic Code, the Jews of Westphalia were declared free and equal by Jerome Bonaparte, brother of Napoleon. But this freedom ended with the declaration. In 1812 Prussia officially emancipated its Jews but this, too, was merely a verbal concession to the liberal fashion of the period. The struggle had to go on year in and year out, gaining ground in some parts of Germany and losing it in others. Full equality, at least legally, was achieved only in 1871, following the arduous campaigns waged for it by the champions of Jewish rights—Eduard Lasker, Ludwig Bamberger and Gabriel Riesser.

Some Fruits of Assimilation

Oddly enough, although the Jewish Enlightenment Movement succeeded in secularizing many Jews and in leading them to more modern values, it ultimately defeated its own intention to bind Jews closer to their religious heritage. Many of its most vocal devotees were lured eventually by a hunger for careers and social acceptance among Christians into expediently becoming Christians. In fact, there was a morbid movement to apostasy. It is estimated that at least half of Berlin Jewry was baptized during the first decades of the nineteenth century. The assimilation of German culture by Jews moved faster than the wearer of the proverbial seven-league boots, especially in the wealthy and educated circles.

Henriette Herz.   Rahel von Ense.

It is an ironic commentary on Moses Mendelssohn's strivings for a modernized Judaism that his own two daughters and his son, the father of the composer, Felix, became converts to Christianity. His daughter Dorothea and two other converted women, Rahel von Ense and Henriette Herz, established elegant salons for the famous in which an elite of generals, princes, philosophers, poets, scientists and beautiful women gathered for interminable and elevating discussions and also, of course, to see and to be seen. How far this trend toward submersion of religious and group identity went on among cultured Jews may be gathered from the remarkable proposal made to a Christian clergyman in 1799 by Mendelssohn's principal lieutenant, David Friedländer. The latter announced that he was ready to accept baptism for himself and his entire circle, provided the Church would not oblige them to accept all the "historical" dogmas and doctrines of Christianity, such as the Holy Trinity and the Immaculate Conception. The clergyman berated Friedländer for being a trifler.

SEEKERS OF TRUTH

While some leading Jewish intellectuals became converts to Christianity to escape their pariah status, to pursue some cherished career or just chameleon-like to blend with the rest of the world, others left the Jewish community because they found it too circumscribing. These were often men with bold original minds whose quest for truth led them in directions which were sometimes unpopular.

In the eighteenth century, contemporary with Moses Mendelssohn, there were a handful of such free, inquiring minds: Dr. Markus Eliezer Bloch, the pioneer in the modern science of ichthyology; Solomon Maimon, one of the most eminent German philosophers of his day and the principal critic of Immanuel Kant. Maimon was a prodigy of erudition in the

Talmud. While living in a small Lithuanian town, he became a rabbi at an extremely early age. But his love of learning and his questioning mind gave him no peace. He ran away to Germany from the ghetto which he hated and, despite many hardships, within only ten years made an arresting début in German philosophy.

Markus Bloch.   Solomon Maimon.

Another eminent philosopher and a Hegelian was the physician, Marcus Herz. He was one of the leading lights in the Berlin "Society for the Promotion of Jewish Culture and Science."

Marcus Herz.

Karl Ludwig Boerne.

Heinrich Heine.

Excepting Goethe there were no more illustrious figures in German literature during the first half of the nineteenth century than Karl Ludwig Boerne and Heinrich Heine. Both were apostles of republicanism and of the new literary party of "Young Germany." Both were found unpalatable to the autocrats who ruled Germany at that time. To escape imprisonment they had to flee to Paris where they lived as exiles for many years. Heine, the greatest lyric poet Germany had produced, and Boerne, the ardent champion of an unfettered Germany, were men with a universal vision. Though both fought for Jewish rights, they conceived the fight only as part of the struggle for human rights. Heine expressed it this way: "The greatest task of our times is not merely the emancipation of Irishmen, Greeks, Frankfurt Jews, West Indian Negroes and similarly oppressed peoples, but the emancipation of the whole world that has now found tongue and breaks the iron reins of Privilege."

REFORM JUDAISM

The demolition of the ghetto in Germany also resulted in the partial breakdown of religious orthodoxy. Liberal or Reform Judaism was then born. It was fostered by a considerable class of prosperous Jews who, although eager for secular German culture, yet wished to preserve their Jewish religious identity. They tried to introduce into the synagogue and the home religious ideas, ceremonials and rites which they considered more in consonance with the spirit and practices of the times than the traditional ones. The first practical attempt at Reform Judaism was made in 1815 by Israel Jacobson who introduced the organ into the synagogue service and allowed the Hebrew prayers to be recited in German. This was nothing new, of course. Under Renaissance influence, at the beginning of the seventeenth century, Rabbi Leone da Modena and the composer-cantor, Salamone Rossi, had introduced into the Venetian synagogue service the organ, instrumental and vocal choirs, and sermons delivered in the most literary Italian.

Reform Judaism first took root in Berlin and Cassel, but

especially in Hamburg. From there it spread quickly to other cities. It was not satisfied merely with the "modernization" of the religious service, however. It re-examined the entire corpus of Jewish religious literature from which it eliminated all those beliefs, rites, ceremonies and practices it deemed anachronistic and in disharmony with the spirit of modern thought. Its principal religious-intellectual leaders were Leopold Zunz, Abraham Geiger and Samuel Holdheim.

When the Jewish child was one year old, his father took him to the synagogue for the first time. As a symbolic act of piety he had him touch the *Sefer Torah*—"his destiny" for the rest of his life.

Jewish children "performing" as they made their rounds from house to house during the merry Festival of *Purim.*

Synagogue in Frankfurt-am-Main, middle 19th century.

Synagogue in Glogau.

JEWISH STUDIES

In 1819 a group of intellectuals founded in Berlin the "Society for the Promotion of Jewish Culture and Science." Its initiators were Eduard Gans, the celebrated philosopher of law; Heinrich Heine, then still a fledgling poet; Marcus Herz, the philosopher; and Leopold Zunz, the pioneer of modern Jewish religious scholarship. Their purpose was the presentation of Judaism, first its gradual development and growth from the historical point of view and, then, its essential meaning and thought from the philosophic point of view.

The society soon dissolved because most of its members and officers became converts to Christianity in the most opportunistic manner. Nonetheless, under the guidance of Leopold Zunz, it had successfully initiated the scientific method in the study of Jewish religion, history and culture. The leaders in this field of scholarship were Moritz Steinschneider, Abraham Geiger, Heinrich Graetz and Moritz Lazarus.

Bankers and Industrialists

With the disappearance of the last vestiges of feudalism, the Court Jews went also. Their financial manipulations, which formerly had been of a highly personal nature, made way for the more "respectable," certainly more public, banking system which we know today.

The first of these bankers was Meir Anschel Rothschild of Frankfurt. When he died in 1812 he left behind him a great banking house and five sons to carry on his almost legendary business in branch establishments throughout Europe. The Rothschilds were truly the premier bankers of Europe, and their financial services and counsel to sovereigns, states and private enterprises were vastly important in the commercial development and industrial growth of Europe.

Other leading financiers contemporary with Rothschild were Solomon Oppenheim, the great banker of Cologne, and Daniel Itzig of Berlin. In 1779 a visitor to Berlin noted: "There are very rich Jews in Berlin; Itzig and the Ephraims rank as the wealthiest. Some possess factories, though most of them are in commerce."

With the increase of Jewish rights in Germany, wealthy Jews became active in all kinds of business enterprises. In banking, the important financial houses of Bleichröder, Speyer, Dreyfus, Sulzbach and Warburg emerged. As with everything else Jewish, the anti-Semites greatly exaggerated the wealth as well as the number of Jewish bankers. In 1925, of the 7,500 bankers and brokers active in Germany, only 3.3% were Jewish.

The new industrialism in Germany found its most enterprising pioneers among Jews. The first iron foundry was built in 1840 in Silesia by Moritz Friedländer, Simon Levy and David Löwenfeld, and shortly thereafter they built the first smelting plant. The coke industry was established by the Caro Brothers and Moritz Friedländer. The great railroad builder of north Germany was Bethel Henry Strousberg. The electrical, chemical, shipping and dye industries also owe much to Jews. Albert Ballin created the Hamburg-American Line. Emil Rathenau, father of the statesman Walter Rathenau, organized the Allgemeine Elektrische Gesellschaft (A.E.G.), the great network of electric companies which supplied power to all Germany.

In Germany, as in other countries, Jews were outstanding in the retail trade. Some of the biggest department stores, such as Wertheim and Israel in Berlin and the great Tietz chain of sixty stores, were owned by Jews.

Political Leaders

Immediately after the Congress of Vienna, which ended triumphantly in 1815 with the restoration of all the dynastic princes to the thrones of Europe from which Napoleon had removed them, a harsh political and social reaction set in. Anti-Semitism, already garbed in modern style, made its appearance in Germany. The hopes Jews had entertained for their emancipation were now shattered. An emigrant movement, impelled by a deep yearning for a freer life and more opportunities, began in the 1830's to France, Italy, South Africa, England, Canada, and especially to the United States.

House of Meir Anschel Rothschild in the *Judengasse* at Frankfurt-am-Main where his five sons and successors were born.

It increased greatly after the collapse of the Revolution of 1848.

At no time could it be objectively stated that Jews were of one mind in their political or economic views. Like everybody else in the world they reacted to social, economic and political problems only as individuals, not as a group. One could, therefore, find every conceivable point of view and class interest represented by individual German Jews: monarchists, conservatives, republicans, liberals, social reformers, socialists, trade unionists, communists and philosophical anarchists. A number of prominent statesmen and political leaders were monarchists and conservatives. The banker Bleichröder, for instance, was Prince Bismarck's principal financial adviser. It was he who helped the Iron Chancellor impose the staggering war indemnity on France after its defeat in 1870. In fact, Bismarck seemed to have had an affinity for Jewish counselors. He appointed three Jews to his cabinet: Eduard von Simson, Heinrich Friedberg and Rudolph Friedenthal, founder of the Free Conservative Party.

Undoubtedly, the most able and the most reactionary of these statesmen was Friedrich Julius Stahl. An apostate from Judaism, he possessed an unusual intellectual equipment. He served as Bismarck's principal political adviser. He coined the cynical battle cry of the Junkers: "Not majority—but authority!" He has frequently been described by historians of his epoch as the intellectual father of latter-day Prussianism.

Meir Anschel Rothschild.   Karl Marx.

At the opposite political pole from Stahl stood Karl Marx, whose wealthy father had had him baptized at the age of six in the belief that Karl's course through life would thereby be made smoother. It is generally held, even by his opponents, that no man in modern times has influenced the course of history so profoundly as did Marx with his political-economic philosophy. His theories, based on a materialistic conception of history, were evolved in collaboration with Friedrich Engels, a non-Jew. Applying them to the problems of modern capitalistic economy, he claimed to have discovered the laws that determined its development. His analysis, he said, pointed to its inevitable collapse—the consequence of its own inequitable, inefficient and unworkable character, and especially of the unremitting class struggle. In his book, *Capital*, he elaborated his basic ideas into a socio-economic system which has been variously called "Marxism," "Scientific Social-

ism" and "Communism." He proposed a classless society in which all property and natural resources, all the tools of production and the means of distribution would be owned by all the people which, during the initial phases, would be ruled by a "dictatorship of the proletariat."

Marxism, as a world force, achieved its greatest importance when it became the cornerstone of the social system of the Soviet Union, and, in more recent years, of its communistically oriented allies in Europe and Asia. No system of thought in history has aroused such fierce contention as Marxism.

A contemporary of Marx, who was not a Marxist but a socialist reformer, was Ferdinand Lassalle. He organized, in 1863, the General German Workers Association, the first great trade union movement in the world. From it sprang the Social-Democratic Party which has since played a powerful role in the political and economic affairs of Germany. A prodigy of learning but an incorrigible romanticist, Lassalle was goaded into fighting a duel over a baroness and was killed, thus prematurely ending a brilliant career. Gabriel Riesser was also a liberal and active leader during the first half of the nineteenth century in Germany. A brilliant parliamentary debater, he stood out as a champion of constitutional reforms, including Jewish civil rights. Not only Riesser, but later also the famous liberals, Eduard Lasker, Ludwig Bamberger and Johann Jacoby joined in the struggle for Jewish civil rights. This bitterly fought issue was finally won after the Franco-Prussian War in 1871.

Musicians

It was in Germany that the Jews began to distinguish themselves in every branch of musical art—as composers, instrumentalists, vocalists, conductors, teachers and musicologists. One of the most eminent was Giacomo Meyerbeer, the operatic composer of *The Huguenots, The Prophet* and *The African*. He was the principal target of Richard Wagner's anti-Semitic attack in the scurrilous book, *Judaism in Music*, and his reputation as a composer suffered because of the notoriety. The outstanding Jewish musical talent of the nineteenth century, however, was Felix Bartholdy-Mendelssohn, the baptized grandson of Moses Mendelssohn, the philosopher. The incidental music to Shakespeare's *Midsummer Night's Dream*, the oratorio *Elijah*, the *Songs without Words* for the piano, and the *Violin Concerto in E Minor* are among the most widely performed musical compositions.

Ferdinand David was a lesser composer but a great master on the violin, an instrument for which Jews seem to have a striking partiality. He also served as concertmaster under Mendelssohn at Leipzig. He even collaborated with the latter and helped finish his violin concerto. Another world-famous violin virtuoso was Heinrich Wilhelm Ernst, who was also the composer of a widely played concerto for the violin. Ferdinand Hiller was one of the most popular pianists and conductors of the century. His compositions, especially his choral and chamber works, enjoyed a great vogue in his day. Salomon Jadassohn, one of the leading modern musical theorists and also a composer of note, was greatly admired by Brahms. His overfondness for the canon-form in his own compositions earned for him the punning nickname of "the musical Krupp."

Other celebrated Jewish musicians in Germany were the pianists Karl Tausig, Sigismund Thalberg; the conductors Her-

SCHOLARS IN JEWISH STUDIES

Leopold Zunz.

Moritz Steinschneider.

Heinrich Graetz.

Abraham Geiger.

SCHOLAR

Moritz Lazarus.

RELIGIOUS LEADER

Rabbi Israel Jacobson.

BANKERS

Daniel Itzig.

Solomon Oppenheim.

POLITICAL LEADERS

Friedrich Julius Stahl.

Gabriel Riesser.

Ferdinand Lassalle.

MUSICIAN

Giacomo Meyerbeer.

MUSICIANS

Mendelssohn, aged twelve.

Mendelssohn.

Heinrich W. Ernst.

Ferdinand David.

man Levi, a leading conductor whom Wagner asked to direct the first performance of *Parsifal* at Bayreuth in 1882, Ferruccio Busoni, Alfred Hertz, Bruno Walter, and Otto Klemperer. The most famous of all German-Jewish vocalists was Lilli Lehmann, considered by some critics as the greatest of all German operatic singers. Lotte Lehmann (related to her) is world-famous as a *lieder* singer.

Kurt Weill, who in his last years achieved fame as a composer of American musicals, was one of the most gifted of Arnold Schoenberg's atonalist disciples. His compositions, however, showed the impress of the American jazz idiom and spirit. He was the composer of the *Three-Groschen Opera*, based on the text of *The Beggar's Opera*, by John Gay, a work admired as one of the few successful operas written in the ultra-modern vein.

Journalists and Publishers

For those Jews who were intellectually alert and articulate, the press in Germany was a natural and even necessary outlet for self-expression. It was varied enough to serve all kinds of talents, from the moderate, even gentle, commentaries on life, literature and the drama of Alfred Kerr, Julius Bab and Felix Holländer to the double-edged political satires of Maximilian Harden. Harden, one of the foremost journalists Germany produced, was a contradictory and complex personality. He found it easy to support Bismarck and yet heap ridicule on liberals. Nonetheless, with the years, he turned out to be one of the most formidable and relentless foes of Kaiser Wilhelm, of autocracy and of Prussian militarism. Georg Bernhard (1875-1944), a more balanced mentality, added great prestige to the *Berliner Tageblatt*, one of the great German dailies, edited by Theodor Wolff and founded in 1872 by still another Jew, Rudolph Mosse.

Probably the most spectacular of all the Jewish publishers was Leopold Ullstein. Besides books, he published at one time some one hundred daily newspapers and weekly and monthly magazines. But the great publishing empire he had built came to an inglorious end when the Nazis came to power. Intimidated, as he himself related, he helped finance their campaigns and even Nazified his business for them. In the end, for all his collaboration, he was forced to flee abroad for his life.

Of great importance in the development of news-gathering agencies in Europe were the pioneer efforts of Bernhard Wolff (1811-79). Wolff's Telegraphic Bureau had world-wide news coverage and, with Havas and Reuters, laid the groundwork for later agencies.

Writers and Philosophers

Writers serve always as the sensitive cultural barometers of their age. Ever since Heine and Boerne, Jewish writers in Germany, to a greater extent than many of their non-Jewish colleagues, expressed in their works the *Zeitgeist*, or spirit of the time, which was characterized by liberal and humane aspirations. Writing principally about the humble life of the Black Forest peasants, Berthold Auerbach followed in this tradition along with the Nobel Prize-winning novelist, the half-Jew Paul Heyse and with Clara Viebig, a loyal disciple of Emile Zola's socially conscious naturalism.

With the turn of the twentieth century a veritable renaissance in literature took place in Germany and in Austria—a movement in which Jews greatly distinguished themselves, especially in the novel. Some of the more outstanding novelists were Ludwig Fulda, Jakob Wassermann, Leonhard Frank, Alfred Döblin, Alfred Neumann, Lion Feuchtwanger and Georg Hermann. Notable among playwrights were Ernst Toller, Franz Wedekind and Georg Kaiser.

In the field of philosophy in Germany, Jewish thinkers, although never stars of the first magnitude, occupied positions of great distinction. The leader of the neo-Kantian movement in philosophy was Hermann Cohen, who taught at the University of Marburg. Eduard Husserl was the founder of the phenomenological school of philosophy which stressed the existence of an inner reality in the mind. Ernst Cassirer was concerned primarily with formal logic and the problem of meaning, and has achieved renown as an original thinker.

Actors and Producers

The creative talent of many Jews found an outlet in the theatre where artistic expression combined with practical enterprise in a perfect fusion. This was particularly true in Germany and in other German-speaking countries where from the beginning of the nineteenth century both the art and the business of the theatre were to a large extent considered a special preserve of Jews. Many Jews excelled in all fields that concerned the stage: as playwrights, stage-directors, scenic designers, drama critics, coaches, actors and managers.

An imposing figure on the German stage in the nineteenth century, a pathfinder in the modern theatre of realism and leader of the "literary" school of the drama was Otto Brahm. It was due to his energetic efforts and high standards that *Die Freie Bühne* (Free Theatre) was established in Berlin in the old classical Deutsches Theater. He created memorable productions, the first of their kind, of the plays of Ibsen, Sudermann, Strindberg and Hauptmann.

Although himself a Viennese, Max Reinhardt accomplished most of his creative work in the theatre while in Germany. Under the tutelage and encouragement of Brahm, then at the helm of the Deutsches Theater in Berlin, he blossomed into one of the greatest of modern stage directors. His fame was second only to that of the Russian Stanislavsky. It led him ultimately to America where, however, he became known more as a creator of brilliant dramatic spectacles than of the well-modulated "chamber drama" which was his real contribution to the art of the theatre.

One of the foremost of the classic school of German actors and directors was Ernst von Possart, who was ennobled by the Kaiser. He not only produced and acted in the dramas of Goethe, Shakespeare and Schiller, but at the Prinzregenten Theatre at Munich he was responsible for magnificent productions of the operas of Glück, Mozart and Wagner.

Another molding force in the German theatre was Leopold Jessner, who laid the foundation for the modern school of expressionism of which Germany was the leader. His methods were bold and highly flexible. He was eager for any innovation, in acting, stage sets, lighting or costuming, that he believed would add greater meaning, effectiveness or suggestiveness to his productions.

It was in collaboration with him and with Max Reinhardt that another Jew, Oskar Strnad, created his striking stage sets. He ranks with Gordon Craig among the most original stage designers of modern times.

THE PRESS

Maximilian Harden.

Bernhard Wolff.

WRITERS

Jakob Wassermann.

Ernst Toller.

PHILOSOPHERS

Hermann Cohen.

Ernst Cassirer.

SINGER

Lotte Lehmann.

ARTIST

Max Liebermann.

THE THEATRE

Otto Brahm.

Max Reinhardt.

Rudolf Schildkraut, as Yekel
in Sholem Asch's *God of
Vengeance.*

SCIENTIST

Ludwig Traube.

SCIENTISTS

Paul Ehrlich.

Ferdinand Julius Cohn.

Otto Warburg.

Oscar Liebreich.

Artists

At no time did Jewish artists achieve true greatness in Germany, though there were many gifted men among them from early in the nineteenth century. Some of these were: Philip Veit, a grandson of Moses Mendelssohn, Moritz Oppenheim, Felix Possart, Eduard Bendemann, Carl Jacoby, Hermann Jurger, Max Liebermann, one of the eminent modern German graphic artists, Herman Struck and Lesser Ury.

Modernist art, too, has found its practitioners in Germany among Jews. Two well-known modernists are Franz Marc, the leader of New Secession, and the "primitive" painter, Max Pechstein. Architects who employ "functional" design are Erich Mendelssohn, now in the United States, and Alfred Messel.

Scientists

The Jewish intellectual tradition, nurtured continuously for so many centuries by Talmudic studies and enriched at various periods by fusion with other cultures, received a new impetus with the emancipation of the Jews that followed the French Revolution. Although severely handicapped by the *numerus clausus,* an anti-Semitic device for limiting Jewish students in universities on a percentage quota, Jews nonetheless entered into all fields of study. They distinguished themselves especially in the sciences: in medicine, mathematics, physics and chemistry. While science does not know any racial or national boundaries, since it aims to serve all mankind, in Germany, however, sharp distinctions were often made between Jewish and non-Jewish scientists—to the detriment of science and of Germany.

Doctors

We have already seen how the Jewish doctor figured historically since the early Middle Ages and how the practice of the healing art had become in time a social ideal transformed into a tradition among certain sections of the Jewish people. But during the seventeenth and eighteenth centuries repressive laws kept the Jews from making any great contributions to medical science and practice. This changed, however, after the first quarter of the nineteenth century. Students of medical history have noted, sometimes with surprise, that the many significant achievements by Jewish doctors have been far out of proportion to their relatively small number.

To consider chronologically only the foremost leaders in the field, the first outstanding neurologist in Germany was Moritz Heinrich Romberg. Robert Remak, one of the founders of modern neurology, did pioneer work in embryology and in electro-therapy. Ludwig Traube was the so-called "Father of Experimental Pathology." Jakob Henle has been ranked with Vesalius among the great anatomists and histologists. His studies on the muscles, viscera, ligaments and the vascular nervous systems have been considered of fundamental importance. Rudolph Heidenhain, the great physiologist and toxicologist, first advanced the theory that the chemical processes within the cell itself were responsible for the glandular activity in the body. Gustav Magnus, the physiological chemist, made significant discoveries about body tissues.

Medical thought and practice were revolutionized by the pathologist Julius Cohnheim when he advanced his basic theory of inflammation. Ferdinand Julius Cohn, the great botanist, was a trail-blazer in the new field of bacteriology. He paved the way for Louis Pasteur and Robert Koch, and is generally looked upon as the founder of bacteriology. With Nathaniel Pringsheim he discovered the existence of sexuality in plants, a discovery which revolutionized the entire science of botany. Karl Weigert, the neurologist and microscopist, with his method of differential staining made possible the use of the microscopic slide which led to great advances in the field of neuropathology and neuroanatomy. Paul Ehrlich first expounded the theory of immunity which resulted in the use of serums to combat disease. For his chemical treatment of syphilis, known as "606" (its development required 606 experiments), he was awarded the Nobel Prize. Perhaps less known is the fact that by introducing dyestuffs in his experiments he founded the science for the study of blood cells.

Hugo Kronecker, the physiologist, established "the all-or-none" theory of heart action which holds that either the *entire* heart reacts to stimuli or does not react at all. Another great physiologist, Hermann Munk, was the first to point out the true functions of the brain cortex.

In the field of pediatrics, too, Jews were among the pioneers and leaders. Eduard Heinrich Henoch was the first to describe the blood disease "purpura." Heinrich Finkelstein was a celebrated innovator of the new principles of infant feeding.

Paul Gerson Unna, a distinguished dermatologist, made important contributions to the study of leprosy, syphilis and tuberculosis. He discovered the cause of soft chancre.

Just as in Spain during the Middle Ages, in Germany during the nineteenth century Jewish doctors were greatly attracted to the diseases of the eye and to the problem of vision. Three great ophthalmologists were Julius Hirschberg, Ernst Fuchs and Julius Jacobson.

Oscar Liebreich, the eminent chemist and pharmacologist, introduced chloral. Ismar Boas, the famous clinician, pioneered the specialty of the diseases of the digestive tract. Albert Fränkel was the first to advance the theory of the micrococci of pneumonia. Albert Neisser, a bacteriologist, discovered in 1879 the bacillus of gonorrhea. One of the founders of modern neurophysiology was the pharmacologist, Rudolph Magnus. Two remarkable internists and clinicians, who had a great influence on medical practice throughout the world, were Hermann Senator and James Adolf Israel.

Of far-reaching influence were the contributions to internal medicine and bacteriology by August von Wassermann. His work in immunology was of outstanding importance. However, he is best known to the lay world for his discovery, in 1906, of the so-called "Wassermann Test" for the diagnosis of syphilis.

Biochemists

Biochemistry, a science which embraces both medicine and chemistry, counts a number of German Jews among its leaders. Perhaps the greatest of all biochemists in the world is Richard Willstätter. Although he won the Nobel Prize in chemistry in 1915, he was, like Einstein, the victim of the anti-Semitism which forced him out of the University of Munich in 1925. Nonetheless, his scientific contributions enriched Germany enormously. The preëminence of the German dye industry is to a great extent due to his discoveries. Just as important are his chemical researches on carbon dioxide, chlorophyll, enzymes and ferments. His work with living or-

167

ganisms led to his fundamental studies in cholesterol in relation to longevity.

Two other biochemists of distinction, both Nobel Prize winners, are Otto H. Warburg, whose researches in the metabolism of cancer won for him world renown, and Otto Meyerhoff, who made a significant contribution to medicine with his studies on the chemistry of the muscles.

Chemists

During the second half of the nineteenth century, the German chemical industry made tremendous advances and was without a peer in the world. Jewish chemists contributed much to this. Fundamental, for example, was the success of Adolf Frank in obtaining nitrogen from the air in 1895. His scientific researches led to the founding of the potash industry. He also showed remarkable ingenuity in producing the so-called "by-products" which have become such an important division of industry.

Everyone is familiar with aniline dyes. In Germany the dye trust owed its existence to them, and it received its first great impetus from the industrial chemist, Heinrich Caro. Not only did he himself discover some of these dyes, but by the indirect agency of one of these, methylene blue, he opened up a vast new field for medical research. Another great pioneer in the field of organic chemistry was Adolf von Bayer, the discoverer of artificial indigo and a number of aniline dyes.

A chemist who did fundamental work in many organic fields was Victor Meyer. He was responsible for benzol derivatives, ammonias and gas mixtures. Richard Wolfenstein discovered hydrogen-peroxide in 1894 and a year later, acetone-peroxide.

Two chemists of striking originality were Willy Marckwald and Carl Liebermann.

Otto Wallach, the important organic chemist, won the Nobel Prize in 1910 for his original work in terpenes and camphor.

One of the foremost chemists of modern times was Fritz Haber who, in 1919, was awarded the Nobel Prize for constructing ammonia from hydrogen and nitrogen in the air. However, for all his distinction as a great chemist he has come under severe criticism from many of his scientific colleagues. He is considered the "Father of Poison Gas" which was first used by the Germans during World War I.

Physicists and Mathematicians

From the medieval Jewish astronomers to Albert Einstein, there has been a continuity of the traditional Jewish concern with the material universe. Jews in Germany have distinguished themselves greatly in the field of theoretical physics and mathematics. F. G. M. Eisenstein was a rare mathematical genius. When he died in 1852, at the age of twenty-nine, the great mathematician, Gauss, wrote to Alexander von Humboldt: "Eisenstein belongs to those talents who are born but once in a century." One of the greatest algebraists of all time was Leopold Kronecker. Karl Gustav Jacobi discovered elliptic functions. His brother, Moritz Hermann Jacobi, also a physicist but a practical one, discovered in 1850 that the action of the dynamo was the converse of the motor. His greatest contribution to industry as well as to science was his discovery of galvanoplastry, a method of coating metals by galvanism.

When Heinrich Rudolf Hertz died in 1894, at the age of thirty-seven, his great teacher Helmholtz remarked: "In classical times men would have regarded the untimely death of Hertz as due to the jealousy of the gods." The science of electricity owed much to him. He contributed greatly to the advance of its development, begun by Faraday and Clerk-Maxwell, by successfully demonstrating the presence of electro-magnetic waves of slow frequency, now called Hertzian Waves. These he found could be reflected, refracted and polarized exactly like light waves, but they were much longer. The development of wireless, radio and television stem from the discovery of these Hertzian Waves.

Two eminent physicists who helped develop the theory of the atom, for which they jointly received the Nobel Prize in 1926, were James Franck and Gustav Hertz. Another distinguished researcher in the structure of the atom is Max Born, a co-worker of the great Max Planck. Rudolf Otto Lipschitz won renown as a mathematician in higher analysis and in the function theory. Edmund George Hermann Landau did important work in the theory of numbers.

It is almost a commonplace to state that the most influential physicist of modern times is Albert Einstein. He unfolded to a startled but skeptical scientific world, in 1905, his new theory of space and time, which he named relativity. But when he was awarded the Nobel Prize in 1921 the world was filled with wonder, so daring and incomprehensible was the theory to all except a handful of physicists. Einstein good-

MATHEMATICIANS

C. G. J. Jacobi.

Leopold Kronecker.

PHYSICIST

Heinrich Hertz.

INVENTOR

David Schwarz and his wife Melanie.

Albert Einstein.

humoredly attempted to explain the general idea of his theory in terms simple enough for the layman: "Since the time of the ancient Greeks it has been well known that in describing the motion of a body we must refer to another body. The motion of a railway train is described with reference to the ground, of a planet with reference to the total assemblage of visible fixed stars. In physics the bodies to which motions are spatially referred are termed systems of coordinates. The laws of mechanics of Galileo and Newton can be formulated only by using a system of coordinates."

Portion of manuscript of Einstein's theory of relativity.

Anti-Semitism in Germany had not only prevented Einstein from pursuing an academic career but even from finding employment. So he went to Switzerland where, while employed as an examiner of patents in the Federal Patent Office in Bern, in his spare time he developed his special theory of relativity. After the spectacular fame that he did not desire was pressed upon him, even the German anti-Semites were eager to claim him. With the rueful irony of a Heine, Einstein then jested: "By an application of the theory of relativity to the taste of readers, today in Germany I am called a German man of science, and in England I am represented as a Swiss Jew. If I come to be regarded as a *bête noir*, the description

will be reversed, and I shall become a Swiss Jew for the Germans and a German man of science for the English!"

In the early 1920's Einstein came to the United States, where he became a naturalized citizen and worked and taught at the Institute of Advanced Studies at Princeton University.

Einstein's Mass-Energy equation, the keystone of the science of nuclear physics and atomic energy, is probably the most important scientific discovery of our time.

Inventors

There have been a number of gifted inventors of Jewish origin in Germany, although none of the first rank.

Joseph Poppner discovered the way to transmit electric power. Peter Ries invented the electric thermometer. Hermann Aron made the electrometer.

The dirigible airship, whose invention commercial ballyhoo has ascribed to Count Zeppelin, actually was the work of an obscure Jewish inventor, David Schwarz, in 1892. He died before he could make his trial flight. Count Zeppelin bought the patents for it from his widow and the contract is deposited in the archives of the Hebrew University in Jerusalem.

A pioneer inventor of the flying machine, from whose experiments the Wright brothers profited, was Otto Lilienthal, who crashed to his death in 1896.

TWO WARS

The Franco-Prussian War

In the years between the Revolution of 1848 and the Franco-Prussian War of 1870, industrial growth in Germany showed tremendous advances. During this interval, the Germany of Prince Bismarck began to give evidence of a muscular type of nationalism, aggressive enough to challenge the supremacy of France as the political economic power on the

Yom Kippur service at a farmhouse in Alsace during the Franco-Prussian War.

continent. The Franco-Prussian War and the temporary engulfment of the French nation were the results. The hunger for territory was partially satisfied when the Germans swallowed up the French provinces of Alsace and Lorraine and, as Anatole France quipped, also stole and "carried off to Germany all of the French town clocks." Seven thousand Jews served in Bismarck's Imperial Army against the French.

169

World War I

The development of Prussian militarism, which had been fed assiduously for four decades by a rampant chauvinism highly spiced with Jew-baiting, led inexorably to World War I. Germany's theme on the cultural battlefield had become German *Kultur,* in the political arena, *"Deutschland Über Alles."* Most Jews in Germany, too, took up this cry, because they considered themselves fervently patriotic Germans, and laid down their lives gladly for Kaiser and Reich. Their recognition *as Germans* was still to come—from Hitler.

1915: Yom Kippur service for German troops in the synagogue at Brussels.

Political Leaders of the Republic

Jews took an active part in the political life of the country when Germany became a republic after World War I. They belonged to the various political parties and represented ideologies from Right to Left. Among the leaders of the Provisional Government of the Reich were the two Jewish commissioners, Hugo Haase and Otto Landsberg, members of the Social Democratic Party. For years the Reichstag debates were enlivened by the participation of the Socialist intellectuals, Eduard Bernstein, Karl Kautsky and Paul Singer. It is noteworthy that the Weimar Constitution, the pet but synthetic phobia of Hitler and the Nazis who railed at it as "The Jewish Constitution," was drafted by Hugo Preuss, a former professor of public law at the University of Berlin, when he was first Minister of the Interior after the Revolution in 1918.

Walther Rathenau.   Hugo Preuss.

Both conservative and radical Jewish and Catholic political leaders were marked for assassination by the Junker reactionaries and the nationalist anti-Semites through their secret terrorist organization known as the *Fehme.* The *Fehme* had the same diversionary intention as the anti-*Dreyfusards* in France and the Black Hundreds in Russia. It aimed first to discredit and then to overthrow the republic by using the Jews as the scapegoat. The most shocking political murder of the period was that of the conservative Jewish statesman, Walter Rathenau. Rathenau was a great industrialist and a distinguished intellectual besides. He served as Foreign Minister of Germany. Both his liberal policies in foreign affairs and his humanitarian views in general earned him the enmity of the Junkers. His murder in cold blood was intended as a demonstration of their power. He was shot by two members of the fascist Eberhard Brigade whose political slogan, set to raucous music, was: "Only a German shall a German leader be." Naturally, they did not consider Jews as Germans.

Rosa Luxemburg.

Another political assassination by the *Fehme* was that of Rosa Luxemburg, a militant Socialist member of the Reichstag. Together with her close associate, the non-Jew Karl Liebknecht, she was shot by the police for an alleged attempt to escape from their custody on her way to prison. The real motive for her murder was established only years later when some of the secret activities of the *Fehme* accidentally came to light.

Both of these political murders of Jews took on added significance because they foreshadowed the tidal wave of Nazism which was rolling on soon to engulf six million Jews and to dehumanize many more Germans.

AUSTRIA

After the three partitions of Poland, in 1772, 1793 and 1796, in the course of which that country was sliced up like a melon among Prussia, Russia and Austria, the Hapsburg Empire consisted of a patchwork of unrelated national groups who had little in common with one another because of tradition, customs, culture or even religion. The dominant culture was, of course, that of the ruling national group, the Germanic, which attempted through the years, by a variety of means, to impose the German language and culture on the other national groups, including the Jews, but without too striking a success. Of all the minorities, the Jews resisted most stubbornly the enticements of this *Kultur*, even though it was spiced with ingratiating Austrian *gemütlichkeit*. A great number of them persisted in talking Yiddish. They wore their gabardines and *payyes* long, left their beards piously untrimmed and pursued their ancient religious culture with unswerving fidelity.

Under the reign of the Spanish-born Empress Maria Theresa there was little *lebensraum* allowed the Jews, except, of course, those who were ready to step to the baptismal font. To the converts, full pardon was extended for the alleged original sin of their people toward the founder of Christianity, and they were even permitted to climb the ladder of worldly success to the topmost rung. All other Jews were treated like social outcasts. They were hemmed in on every side by discriminatory decrees and statutes, by prohibitions and regulations, by the poll tax and the body tax, by a tax for candles and a tax for kosher meat, by a tax on arriving and a tax on departing, by a tax on being born, being married and finally buried—in short, by a vast variety of legalized extortions.

What was the choice that faced the Jew? He could either flounder helplessly in the quicksands of the ghetto—be a peddler of notions, a dealer of old clo', a hated money lender—or he could become an "honorary Christian" and have the gates of opportunity opened wide for him.

Illustrative of one solution to this moral dilemma was the career of *Freiherr* Joseph von Sonnenfels. The grandson of an old-fashioned rabbi, he came originally from the ghetto of Nikolsburg, an ancient town in Moravia. His conversion to

"Old clo'," or
junk man.

Catholicism proved the open sesame to success. It is no overstatement that he was the most influential figure in the literary, academic and theatrical world of eighteenth-century Vienna. Everybody admired him, from the Empress Maria Theresa and her successor, Joseph II, to Goethe and Lessing. He basked in their esteem and was glad of the profusion of honors showered on him.

Joseph
von Sonnenfels.

It was Sonnenfels who established the German National Theatre in Vienna long before the Germans in Germany thought of it. Besides being a professor of political science at the University of Vienna, he was President of the Royal Academy of Arts and, by special imperial appointment, the absolute monarch of education, literature, the press and the arts in the Austrian Empire. He was also a brilliant writer, and, if we are to accept the testimony of Lessing, a great contemporary, he was an honest thinker as well.

"A LOVER OF MANKIND"

"I love humanity without limitations," said Joseph II when he mounted the throne of Austria in 1780.

All Europe was astonished, just as it had been when Frederick the Great had first dazzled the populace in the shining armor of his liberal pose. Joseph II had read the French *Politiques*, and had, figuratively, sat at the feet of John Locke, the English radical thinker. Fired by his new democratic vision he had, while still Crown Prince, remonstrated with his pious mother because of her implacable hatred for the Jews.

One year after his coronation Joseph II issued his Edict of Toleration (October 13, 1781) in which he promised the Jews a number of privileges they had never before enjoyed. Though these fell far short of the rights the French Revolution was to grant the Jews only a few years later, the edict, nevertheless, allowed them to travel and to live wherever they pleased in the empire. But as if to take back with one hand what he gave so generously with the other, the Jews were told that they could neither own nor build houses. Even the titled and wealthy Baron Rothschild, who had served the emperor so devotedly with his cash, had to live in a rented house. To compound the housing problem, prejudice, as well as legal restrictions, deterred Christians from renting apartments to Jews. This may help explain why there were so few Jews

Turkish Jews in Vienna, end of 18th century. The Jewish community of Vienna, which was the center for all Jewry in the Austrian empire, was composed of colorful and variegated elements. They hailed from everywhere in Europe—from Germany, Hungary, Bohemia, Moravia, Galicia and even from Turkey. The settlement of Turkish Jews in the capital began in 1736. They carried on a lively commerce with Turkey and the Balkan countries. As subjects of the Ottoman Sultan, they enjoyed a more privileged position than most other Jews in Vienna. They were prosperous and very pious, and in 1887 they built a handsome synagogue along Turkish architectural lines.

Joseph II.

living in Vienna in the late eighteenth century. They simply had no roof for their heads.

Another hollow privilege granted the Jews with a magnanimous flourish was the freedom to engage in all the handicrafts, trades and arts. But since the law did not allow Jews to be either burghers or masters they could not belong to the guilds. Consequently they found little opportunity for employment.

Baron Salomon Rothschild.

"THE KAISER JEWS"

It was to Joseph's imperial self-interest to lean on the financial help of a handful of Jewish bankers and industrialists. They guaranteed his income with their loans and provided part of the money with which to run his government. He and his successors were, therefore, personally very friendly to them, and some of these privileged Jews were even granted titles of nobility and allowed coats-of-arms on their carriages. Plain Jews who could not look forward to such distinctions ironically nicknamed these illustrious personages *Kaiserjuden* (the Emperor's Jews). Some of the best known of these were Baron von Arnstein, *Ritter* von Hofmannsthal, *Ritter* Hönig von Hönigsberg, Joseph *Ritter* von Wertheimer, Biedermann, Eskeles and Figdor.

Left. Josef *Ritter* von Wertheimer. *Right.* Michael Lazar Biedermann, Court jeweler and financier.

The Austrian emperors found dependable allies in these *Kaiserjuden*. In times of crisis, for instance, when they wanted to wage war the Jewish bankers not only loaned their own money for the cause, but as leaders of the Jewish community, they obliged all other Jews to come forward with their "contributions."

The Jews collect funds to help finance Austria's war
(April 14, 1797).

Here, too, as with the upper-class Jews in Germany, the acquisition of wealth was followed by the desire for social recognition and distinction. Jewish *salonières* began to appear in Vienna, too, at the turn of the nineteenth century. Especially brilliant was the aristocratic-political *salon* conducted during the Congress of Vienna (1814-15) by the Baroness Fanny von Arnstein, the daughter of Itzig, the Berlin banker. She had reached her eminence via the baptismal font. It was considered *de rigueur* by foreign diplomats and statesmen, who took part in the Congress, to make their appearance at the Arnstein *salon*.

172

EARLY NINETEENTH CENTURY JUDAISM

For one or two generations Jewish group life in Austria was reasonably satisfactory. The spirit of the times was relatively tolerant. The assimilation and conversion contagion which was then "decimating" the Jewish middle-class population of Germany on the pretext of "enlightenment" was also epidemic in Austria, especially in the elegant Vienna circles. At the same time the other and more positive aspect of enlightenment, the Hebrew *Haskalah,* was making headway in Vienna, in Prague and in the cities of Galicia. Hebrew printing presses were established, curiously enough, under imperial patronage, which profited from their output financially. For decades these presses supplied millions of Jews in Russia, Poland, Bohemia, Hungary, Turkey and other Balkan countries with Hebrew and Yiddish religious and devotional books of every description, and therefore had an important effect on the development and spread of Jewish culture during the nineteenth century.

Left. Jewish street in Vienna, end of 18th century. *Right.* Where the first modern "Betstube" was established in 1811.

Despite all the talk about freedom of worship and the imperial pronouncements concerning it, realistically speaking, the first Jewish place of public worship in Vienna was established in 1811, and only by poetic license could the tiny *Betstube* (prayer-room), in an apartment house on the Katzensteig, be called a synagogue.

The first real synagogue, the *Stadt-Tempel* (City Temple), had a Reform orientation. The Jewish bankers and industrialists of Vienna engaged Kornhäusel, the noted Christian archi-

The Vienna City Temple.

Left. Salomon Sulzer. *Right.* Rabbi Mannheimer.

tect, to build their house of prayer. He designed it in the elegant Empire style for which he was famous. It was dedicated on April 9, 1826, and Rabbi I. N. Mannheimer, its first religious leader, who was imported from Copenhagen, preached the sermon *in German.* The famous cantor-composer, Salomon Sulzer, a friend of Franz Schubert, sang the musical service which, incidentally, had been composed especially for the occasion by Drechsler, a Christian. Originally, Beethoven had been invited to write the music. He had made a study of Jewish traditional modes and musical idioms in preparation for this task. Why he never carried out the project remains a mystery.

Leopoldstadt (Vienna) Synagogue, built 1858.

EMANCIPATION IN 1848

The Congress of Vienna in 1814-15 wound up its deliberations under Prince Metternich's reactionary whip-cracking by robbing the Jews of Europe of most of the rights and privileges they had previously enjoyed. Revolution and counter-revolution followed each other in quick succession until the successful liberal Revolution in 1848, which led to the establishment of the constitutional monarchy in Austria and culminated in the convocation of the first parliament. Jews joined with Christians in all these insurrections against absolutism. In fact, two of the principal liberal revolutionary leaders in Vienna, Adolph Fischhof, a young physician, and Ignaz Kuranda, a brilliant political journalist from Prague, were Jews. Fischhof served as chairman of the Committee of Security, the governing body of the revolution; Kuranda served as the first president of the new parliament.

An interesting footnote to the relationship between the emperor and his "Kaiser-Jews" in Vienna is furnished by the "loyal" conduct of Baron Salomon Rothschild during the Rev-

Left. Adolph Fischhof. *Right.* Ignaz Kuranda.

olution of 1848. He helped Prince Metternich, architect of official reaction and anti-Semitism of the day, to escape from the city and from the anger of the populace. Rothschild even financed Metternich's exile abroad.

The Revolution of 1848 granted the Jews full civil equality. Joseph Unger, a baptized Jew, who later became an imperial minister under the first constitutional monarchy of Franz Joseph I, expressed himself in this paradox: "I came into the world in 1817, but only in 1848 did I see the light of the world." For the first time the Jews were allowed to live in those parts of the empire which had been forbidden to them. But it was not until 1867 that Jewish emancipation was made permanent by law.

Medal, struck in 1860 by Austrian Jews in honor of Emperor Franz Joseph I, to commemorate his granting them the right to own real estate.

Literature

It is difficult to evaluate properly Jewish cultural contributions in central Europe by national group, chiefly because there was a constant cultural exchange between the German-speaking peoples of Austria, Germany, Bohemia, Hungary, Galicia, Switzerland, Denmark and Holland. The Hungarian writer, Moritz Saphir, for example, founded a new style of literary humor in Vienna, while the Viennese stage-director, Max Reinhardt, helped establish the modern realistic theatre in Berlin and Munich. Franz Werfel, although a native of Prague, was as much esteemed as a German writer in Vienna and Berlin. Actually these new and countless other creators in the arts belonged to the cultural constellation of the

German-speaking world, and it is within this frame of reference that their work should be considered.

The influence of literary men of Jewish origin in those lands which once constituted the Austro-Hungarian Empire is considerable and the roster is impressive: Moritz Hartmann, Moritz Saphir, Ludwig August Frankl, Karl Emil Franzos, Arthur Schnitzler, Hugo von Hofmannsthal, Richard Beer-Hoffman, Peter Altenberg, Ottokar Fischer, Frantisek Langer, Stefan Zweig, Arnold Zweig, Ferenc Molnar, Lajos Biro, Ludwig Hatvany, Melchior Lengyel, Erno Vajda, Jenö Heltai, Ferenc Körmendi, Laszlo Bus-Fekete, Felix Salten, Karl Kraus, Sacher-Masoch, Franz Kafka, Max Brod, Franz Werfel and that half-Jew of poetic genius, Rainer Maria Rilke.

The Stage

From the time of Sonnenfels, the founder of the national theatre of Austria during the days of the Empress Maria Theresa, Jews figured prominently in all branches of the stage and opera in the empire. They were also distinguished dramatists.

Perhaps the greatest actor the German stage produced during the nineteenth century was Adolph Sonnenthal, a Viennese who dominated not only the classical theatre of Austria but of Germany as well. He received a title of nobility from the Emperor Franz Joseph for his services to the Austrian theatre. Other actors who achieved fame on the Viennese stage were Ludwig Barnay, Rudolf Schildkraut, originally of the Yiddish stage, Max Pallenberg, Lucie Mannheim and Fritz Kortner. Elisabeth Bergner and Luise Rainer became internationally known movie stars.

Music

Diverse as the cultural currents were within the Austro-Hungarian Empire, they produced a remarkable aggregation of composers, conductors and instrumentalists who were Jews. Gustav Mahler and his pupil, Arnold Schoenberg, were probably the most potent musical influences in Austria after Brahms. Other composers of note were Karl Goldmark, Erich W. Korngold, Jaromir Weinberger, Egon Wellesz and Alexander von Zemlinsky.

One of the titans of the keyboard during the first half of the nineteenth century was Ignaz Moscheles whom Beethoven considered his truest interpreter. Unquestionably, the musical artist most admired by the cognoscenti of his generation was the violinist, Joseph Joachim. The nineteenth century was an age of dazzle and brilliance, and the number of those Jewish virtuosi, who were the musical ornaments of the empire, were too numerous to list. The first half of the twentieth century produced a number of distinguished interpreters. To mention only a few: Heinrich Grünwald, David Popper and Feuermann—cellists; Moritz Rosenthal, Artur Schnabel and Carl Friedberg—pianists; Bronislaw Hubermann, Erika Morini and Josef Szigeti—violinists; Bruno Walter and Artur Bodanzky—orchestral conductors.

One of the outstanding music critics of the nineteenth century in central Europe was Eduard Hanslick, foremost champion of Brahms' music, which he defended stoutly against Wagner's derogation. In turn, Wagner took his revenge on Hanslick by caricaturing him as Beckmesser in *Die Meistersinger.*

WRITERS

Moritz Saphir.

Hugo von Hofmannsthal.

Arthur Schnitzler.

Stefan Zweig.

WRITERS   PLAYWRIGHT   ACTOR

Franz Kafka.

Franz Werfel.

Ferenc Molnar.

Adolf Sonnenthal as
Nathan the Wise.

MUSICIANS

Ignaz Moscheles.

Joseph Joachim.

Carl Goldmark.

Gustav Mahler.

MUSICIANS

Moritz Rosenthal.

Arnold Schoenberg.

Bronsilaw Hubermann
as *wunderkind*.

Bruno Walter.

There have been quite a number of excellent musicologists, musical theorists and historians among Austrian Jews; some of the best-known of recent years are Guido Adler, Paul Nettl, Kurt Sachs and Heinrich Schenker.

Medicine

Within the advanced cultural context of Austrian life in which the sciences occupied an important place, Jews, too, proved outstanding. This held especially true in the field of medicine. The fame of Vienna as a world medical center was in great part due to its Jewish medical scientists and clinicians.

Left. Wilhelm Winternitz. *Right.* Karl Landsteiner.

Some of the most noted doctors were Fleischl von Marxow, the physiologist; Leopold Oser, the internist; Emil Zuckerkandl, the anatomist; Hermann Zeissl and Isidor Neumann, dermatologists; Wilhelm Winternitz, the founder of scientific hydrotherapy; the otologists Politzer and Robert Barany. Ba-

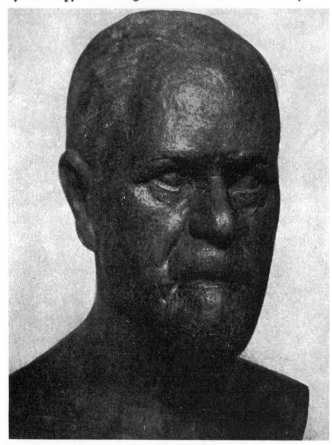

Sigmund Freud.

rany was awarded the Nobel Prize for his investigations in physiology and in methods of diagnosis. Another Nobel prize-winner was Karl Landsteiner, the physiologist, who discovered that there are four main types of human blood. Salomon Stricker, a pioneer pathologist, discovered the use of cocaine as an anaesthetic. Noted as a physiologist was Julius Wiesner who received a title of nobility from the emperor for his scientific work and was appointed Rector of the University of Vienna in 1898. A well-known pathologist was Samuel Basch, physician to the Emperor Maximilian of Mexico. Moritz Benedict was a pioneer in electro-therapy and in nervous pathology. An original investigator into hysteria was Joseph Breuer in whose work the young Sigmund Freud collaborated. It was Freud, however, who gave an entirely new direction to mental therapy with his theory of the unconscious and his development of the technique of psychoanalysis. One of his principal followers who struck out into a psycho-analytic bypath of his own was Alfred Adler. He advanced the theory of inferiority caused by an organic inadequacy.

Science

Among Jewish physicists and inventors of prominence in Austria were Joseph Popper-Lynkeus, noted for his pioneer experiments on the transmutation of electric power and for the invention of a turbine in 1867; Robert von Lieben, whose inventions contributed to the realization of radio, television and the sound-film; Siegfried Marcus who devised, in 1875, a vehicle driven by benzine. Interestingly enough, it was an amateur scientist, Abraham Schreiner, a Galician Jew from Boryslav, who first discovered, in 1853, the use of petroleum, and later established his own distillation plant.

Armin Vambery, noted 19th century Hungarian-born explorer, traveler and ethnologist in Central Asia.

WORLD WAR I

On the heels of the reaction which stemmed from the Congress of Vienna, an aggressive Teutonomania set in for Germany and Austria. All that was noble, creative and significant was ascribed exclusively to the German national genius. The Austrian nationalists despised Czechs and Slovaks, Poles and Magyars as inferior, but they treated the Jews as lowest of all. Jews were declared spiritually incapable of holding "German ideals" and were stigmatized as unassimilable enemy-aliens. Under this withering fire quite a number of Jews of the upper and middle classes found it expedient to turn Christian.

In addition to Teutonomania, the Jews were also exposed to the consequences of Magyar-mania, Polonia-mania, Czechomania and lesser assertions of national pride stimulated by the German assumption of superiority. The Jew was at the bottom of the ladder and all chauvinists aimed at keeping him down. The mumbo-jumbo of ritual murder was revived. In 1882, for example, a Christian girl in Tisza-Eszlar disappeared. With a great display of legal evidence, fifteen Jews were charged with her murder, perpetrated, it was stated, for ritual purposes. The case, which was exposed as a fabrication, became the *cause célèbre* of the generation in Hungary.

Free public kitchen in the Vienna ghetto, World War I.

A number of ritual-murder scandals cropped up also in Bohemia and Slovakia. In 1889 a Jew by the name of Hilsner was condemned to a life sentence in prison on a charge of ritual murder. It was only after the Revolution of 1918 that he was set free, but he was then already old and broken.

Nonetheless, whatever anti-Semitic pressures were exerted on Jews, especially in Hungary and Galicia, they were kept within bounds by the Imperial Austrian government. It was the boast of the Emperor Franz Joseph that, unlike the Tsar of Russia, he would not countenance any pogroms in his domain. He recognized that any violent disorders in the empire, which was composed of conflicting elements and ethnic groups, would threaten the security of the state.

Retired Jewish officers of Imperial Army and officers of Republican Army honoring the fallen dead in the Vienna Jewish cemetery.

Although the majority of the two million Jews in the empire lived in poverty and insecurity, quite a number of them, especially in the big cities of Budapest, Lemberg and Prague, did find it possible to prosper. In Vienna, for instance, the Jews had managed to anchor themselves firmly in the economic and cultural life of the nation—in business, in politics, in the professions and in the arts and sciences. The future looked bright for them. But the outbreak of the war in 1914 marked the be-

ginning of the end of the golden age for the Jews in Vienna, and unleashed social and political forces which, within three decades, succeeded in obliterating almost all vestiges of organized Jewish life there.

The devastation and tragedy which the first World War brought to all of Europe struck Austrian Jews hardest. The bloodiest fighting during the first year took place in the border regions where the German, Austrian and Russian empires joined. Four million Jews were trapped in this geographic pocket. Terrible atrocities were committed against them, especially in Galicia and Bukovina, on the one hand by the Russian enemy and on the other by their Polish countrymen. Densely settled in these regions, they were literally blown out of their homes. Thousands took to the road and fled in every direction, not only from the dangers of the battlefield where their homes were but from the mobs of pogromists who surrounded them. Vienna alone sheltered 36,000 of these refugees who lived in the most abject misery, in cellars mostly, until the end of the war in 1918.

One result of the world conflict was that the empire was dismembered. This created enormous economic and social dislocations in all its previous component territories. Galicia became part of the Polish Republic, and the Galician Jews began to understand what the Polish Jews meant when they talked of "Polish fraternal love."

Muscular anti-Semitism once again revived everywhere in eastern and central Europe, and the Jews again began serving their tiresome historic role as scapegoats. In Vienna, General Ludendorff, the darling of the Kaiser and of the Pan-German reactionaries, inspired the clericalist party of Christian Socialists to organized street brawls and riots against the Jews. It was his violent and demagogic inflammation of the public mind against the Jews which inspired his great admirer, Adolf Hitler. In the years which followed, with the blessings of the Church and under the rule of the Christian Socialists led by the Chancellor, Monsignor Seipel, and later under the clerico-fascists directed by Prince Starhemberg and Chancellor Dollfuss, a "pious" and "patriotic" cold pogrom was waged against the Jews in public life, in business and in the professions. The halls of the universities in Vienna and Graz resounded to the hootings of the anti-Semitic students as they set upon their Jewish professors and fellow students with clubs, swords, knives and firearms. That was several years before Hitler came actively to the attention of the world.

In Hungary, too, there was an upsurge of organized, terroristic anti-Semitism. It was led by the reactionary monarchist Admiral Horthy who battled his way to power leading his shock-troops of the so-called "Awakening Magyars." They "awakened" by beating and murdering Jews on trains, on the streets and in public parks. They threw Jewish passers-by into the Danube and flung Jewish students bodily out of the universities and colleges. The Hungarian Jewish communities were completely terrorized. There was no one to whom they could turn for help.

The principal opposition to the anti-Semitic movement in Austria came from the Social Democratic Party, founded by the Jew, Viktor Adler. It headed the federal government during the first years after World War I. Later, it was pushed from power by the anti-Semitic Christian Socialist Party. Although it continued to control the Vienna City Council, it offered only feeble resistance to the tidal wave of anti-Semitism which swept over the country.

177

Viktor Adler.

THE JEWS OF HUNGARY

It is thought that ever since the fall of the Jewish kingdom of Khazaria in 970 c.e., when the Jews from that country sought refuge in the north of Hungary, there has been an unbroken continuity of Jewish life in Hungary. In Hungary, as in other lands, the inevitable ebb and flow of migrations, expulsions and flights from massacres changed the national composition of the Jewish population. During the Crusades and after the Black Death, there were many emigrants to Hungary from Germany and Bohemia. By the sixteenth century there were four thousand Jews living in thirteen communities, the largest in Buda Ofen and Pressburg. During the first half of the nineteenth century there was a powerful migration from Galicia, and as a consequence, by 1850 there were several hundred thousand Jews in Hungary.

To a large extent the destinies of Hungarian and Austrian Jews were linked. Both suffered in common under the Hapsburg tyranny. Understandably enough, when Hungarian liberal patriots led by Louis Kossuth revolted against Austrian domination in 1848, there were 20,000 Jews among the 180,000 insurgents. With the revolution triumphant, at Kossuth's urging, the National Assembly legislated full equality for the Jews of Hungary in July, 1849. But with the reaction, which set in simultaneously throughout the empire after the republicans were overthrown, the Jews quickly lost their rights. They regained them only after the Constitution was promulgated in Vienna in 1867. For all that, the Jewish reli-

gion was not legally recognized as equal with Christianity until 1895.

There seemed to be shaping up a polarity in the cultural life of the Jews of Hungary. On the one hand, the large number of emigrants from Galicia had transplanted into the Jewish communities of the country the traditionalist and *Hasidic* ways of life. On the other hand, there took place an opposite drive toward assimilation, and even amalgamation, among the wealthy and educated Jews as a consequence of the liberalism of the times. As in Vienna, here, too, mixed marriages were becoming a matter of course. Reform Judaism began to play an increasingly important role. Orthodoxy and Reform Judaism were irreconcilably opposed. The breach between them widened with the years. Even linguistically there was separation: the Orthodox preferred Yiddish for daily speech and Hebrew for religious studies; the Reform and assimilationist, German and Hungarian.

By 1910 there were a million Jews in Hungary, 200,000 of them in Budapest.

Synagogue *Kahal Adath Jeshurun* in Budapest.

Rabbi Moses Sofer (1762-1839) of Pressburg, a famous Talmudic scholar.

THE JEWS OF CZECHOSLOVAKIA

There was less assimilation apparent among the Jews in Czechoslovakia than among those in Hungary. In large measure this may have been due to the fact that the old Jewish communities such as Prague and Pressburg had a traditionalist

Jewish deputation presenting Burggraf Palffy the "Jews' Tax," Pressburg, 18th century.

religious base, and the constant flow of new arrivals into them was from lands where orthodoxy and *Hasidism* were dominant. A case in point were the emigrants from Galicia toward the end of the eighteenth century. They turned Munkac, Huszt and Ungvar into citadels of piety. After the pogroms of 1881 in Tsarist Russia there was another stream of refugees from there. This helps explain the dominance in Czechoslovakia of East European rather than Austrian or German culture. Until World War II there were still thousands of *Hasidim* everywhere in Czechoslovakia who were grouped around *tzaddikim*, or wonder-working rabbis.

The majority of the Jews of Czechoslovakia were poor. About half were petty merchants engaged precariously in the

retail trade; another 20% were industrial workers and artisans. Surprisingly enough, there were more Jews in Czechoslovakia trying to scratch out a livelihood from the land than in any other country of Europe. There was actually a Jewish peasantry. In 1921 in Slovakia 10.7% of the Jewish population was engaged in agriculture. In the Carpathian Mountain region, the percentage of Jewish farmers was 26.9%. At best it was a subsistence kind of farming they were attempting: they worked a tiny plot of ground, owned a cow or two, perhaps a goat for milk, a dozen chickens and a few ducks and geese.

At the time of the founding of the republic by Thomas Masaryk after World War I, the census showed that there were 354,342 Jews in the country: 135,918 in Slovakia, 93,341 in the Carpathian region and the rest in Bohemia. Prague, one of the great historic centers of the Jews, had only about thirty-five to forty thousand Jews at the outbreak

Left. "Synagogue Street," Olmütz. *Right.* Interior of Prague temple.

Left. A tanner. *Right.* Farmer, Carpathian Mountains.

Petty tradesmen in the markets.

Yiddish theatrical troupe.

Bratislava
Hasidim.

Jewish peasant girls in a Czechoslovak village.

of World War II. Despite their small number, because of the high cultural standards and opportunities prevailing in the capital, Jews distinguished themselves in the various arts, sciences and professions to an impressive degree.

179

MODERN ENGLAND

GRADUAL EMANCIPATION

Whatever the privileges wealthy Jews in England could buy for themselves with money, they still did not possess equal rights with Christians. In more than one way they felt at a disadvantage in business dealings, in litigation and in social relationships with non-Jews. And it was worse for the large majority of Jews who were either poor or whose means were moderate. There were several futile attempts during the eighteenth century to emancipate the Jews of England. The first serious move was made in 1753 when the Jewish Naturalization Act, commonly known as "The Jew Bill," was passed in Parliament. It had disastrous results. The liberal proponents and defenders of the bill were mobbed on the streets. Obscene broadsheets, defaming caricatures and offensive jingles about both the Bill and the Jews were circulated. The government, becoming alarmed by the disturbances and the unfavorable agitation, ate humble-pie and repealed the law.

As the years passed, a small number of Jews acquired public influence and wealth because of their usefulness to the Crown, and began to demand equal rights once more. Among these were Isaac Lyon Goldsmid, Nathan M. Rothschild, David Salomons and Moses Montefiore—all financiers. In 1830 they supported Robert Grant's Bill "For the Repeal of the Civil Disabilities of the Jews." Once more the proposal let loose a torrent of abuse from various anti-Jewish groups, and the measure was defeated. Undismayed, the liberal Parliamentary friends of the Jews tried again three years later. On that occasion Lord Macaulay made his maiden speech in Parliament on the moral necessity of granting equality to the Jews. This time the bill passed Commons, but the House of Lords threw it out.

It finally dawned on many Jews in England that, to become free, they had to fight with whatever weapons the laws of England already allowed them. Leading Jews offered themselves as candidates for public office. They did this knowing perfectly well that even if elected they could not take office on account of the Oath of Allegiance they were required to take "on the true faith of a Christian." These election campaigns, superficially examined, would appear to have been to no practical purpose. Actually, they succeeded in focusing attention on the problem and on civil injustice. With it came a growing awareness that denying the franchise to Jews was a social evil which concerned all England, not only the Jews.

For eleven years the question of Jewish rights was debated furiously in England, even though the number of Jews in the country was relatively small, probably no more than 20,000. This was because the issue had been seized upon by the liberals of England as a rallying point in their battle against the Tories. Finally, through Benjamin Disraeli's intercession (he himself, converted in childhood by his father, had taken his seat in Parliament "on the true faith of a Christian"), the objectionable phrase was dropped from the Oath of Allegiance in 1855. From that time on Jews began to enter public life.

Until the complete emancipation of the Jews of England, preferment in any career was given to converted Jews. And a number of them did reach high places, notably the Schomberg family, several of whose members, trained as naval officers, were knighted and reached the rank of admiral. The first of these, Sir Alexander Schomberg, fought as a naval commander off the shores of Canada in the war against France.

In connection with the early role of the Jews in the culture of England it must be remembered that until the first decades of the nineteenth century the Jewish community of England consisted predominantly of *Sephardim,* Jews of Spanish and Portuguese stock. Their intellectual conditioning was weighted on the secular side by former *Marranos,* or New Christians, who had brought with them, as they re-entered the Jewish fold, a knowledge and a love of literature, music, science and art.

Perhaps the first cultured baptized Jew in England to make a name for himself was the popular playwright of comedies, Moses Mendes. A coffee-house friend of Dr. Samuel Johnson, he died in 1748. His ballet-opera, "The Double Disappointment," was produced with great success at the Drury Lane Theatre in 1746.

Early Notables

The stage seemed to draw to it many gifted Jews. This was, perhaps, because of its informal atmosphere it was easier to enter it professionally. Furthermore, in those days "play actors" were considered as standing outside the boundaries of respectability. Therefore, few objected to Jews on the stage as "entertainers." In the first performance of Sheridan's comic opera, *The Duenna,* the principal role of Don Carlos was played by the famous singer Leoni. Leoni's real name was Meyer Levin, which he had first anglicized to Lyon and then, following the Italianate fashion among opera singers, he adopted the name of Leoni. Yet, oddly enough, all his life he remained cantor of the Bevis Marks Synagogue. In fact, his uncompromising orthodox scruples were given special consideration, perhaps because of his importance and financial value as an artist. The management of every company in which he was a member kept the theatre dark on Friday nights to give Leoni, as plain *Hazzan* Meyer Levin, a chance to sing the Sabbath service in his synagogue.

Leoni had a choir boy who sang alto at the synagogue. His name was Abraham. When he grew to manhood he dropped the A and became John Braham. Under that name he became the most famous singer of that generation in Europe. Some of the foremost operatic composers of the day, the Italian Cimarosa and the German Karl Maria von Weber, composed music

John Braham.

especially for him. He sang the principal roles at the first performances of Weber's *Freischütz* in 1821 and in *Oberon* five years later under Weber's personal direction. Possibly he won his most enduring fame for his composition, *Death of Nelson*, which he wrote in 1811 and which became one of the most popular of English patriotic songs.

A colleague of Braham's was Isaac Nathan, a composer of lesser stature. Originally he had been intended for the rabbinate and he always remained a pious Jew. He taught music to the Princess Charlotte and was appointed Musical Historian to George IV. His fame, however, rests as the composer of the music to Byron's *Hebrew Melodies*. He once sent *"motsos"* to Byron as a *Pesach* gift. The poet answered, ". . . the *motsos* shall be to me a charm against the destroying angel."

Long before anyone had even dreamed of founding a Yiddish theatre, not to speak of a literary Yiddish theatre, a Shakespearean Jewish actor by the name of Sherenbeck, jocularly known as "The Rochester Israelite," directed a performance, in 1817, of *The Merchant of Venice,* in which he played the role of Shylock and *in Yiddish.*

Edmund Kean.

Isaac d'Israeli

One of the greatest of all actors who is said to have been of Jewish extraction was Edmund Kean. He made his first appearance in the role of Shylock at the Drury Lane in 1814. His success was so spectacular that it led to a tour of the United States.

There were several Jewish literary men, too. Although not exactly belonging among the masters they were nonetheless polished writers. Lewis Goldsmith, for example, wrote enthusiastically in defense of the French Revolution.

A writer of note, a colleague of Scott, Wordsworth and Coleridge, was Isaac d'Israeli, the father of the novelist-statesman, Benjamin Disraeli. His *Curiosities of Literature* has remained in its small way an English classic.

On a far higher intellectual plane—that of genius—stood the astronomer William Herschel. In his field there had been no one quite like him since Galileo. His discoveries made astronomical history. Original was his method of measuring the relative distance from one star to another, and, in turn, the relative distance from the stars to the sun. This led him irresistibly to his discovery of the circulation of the stars around one another. It proved to him conclusively that even the most distant areas of the universe were subject to the same mechanical laws that determined the motions of our own solar system. His son, Sir John Herschel, was also among the foremost astronomers of the nineteenth century.

Sir William
Herschel.

Sir John Herschel.

The eminence of David Ricardo as a political economist of the first rank is universally recognized. Son of a wealthy London "Jew broker," he was converted to Christianity. He married a Christian "lady of quality" and was elected to the House of Commons. When this happened, his pious father Abraham sat *shiva* for him and recited the prayers for the dead. Nonetheless, David prospered. He amassed a fortune in only a few years by his shrewd transactions on the stock exchange. During the Napoleonic Wars he made huge loans to the English Crown, but unlike many other bankers he was no money-grubber. A public-spirited and amiable man, his philanthropies became proverbial. However, his most valuable

David Ricardo.

bequest to posterity was his theory of the "Iron Law of Wages" which he propounded in his *Principles of Political Economy*. His conclusion led him to recognize as a social evil "the inadequacy of wages to support the laboring classes." With Adam Smith and Jeremy Bentham he championed the economics of *laissez-faire*, which at that time stood for the most radical form of liberal capitalism.

By the middle of the eighteenth century, Jews were beginning to arrive in London from Poland and Russia. The Reverend Isaac Polack was one of them. He was better known in his native Poland as *Reb* Itzig *Chazzan*. In London he officiated as chief cantor in the Great Synagogue. In the assimilationist atmosphere of London the Orthodox *Chazzan* quickly discarded kaftan, beard and side-curls and donned powdered wig and English dress with the white cravat as a proper Church of England touch.

Champions of the Jews

With the emergence of some English Jews to positions of public influence and wealth, a poisonous anti-Jewish campaign was let loose. One of the lethal weapons in the arsenal of satire for which the English were always famous was the art of the caricature. It was now used against the Jews with a sportsmanship hardly reckoned as proudly English. London was literally flooded with graphic obscenities. It finally got so that Jews were physically molested and beaten on the streets and in public places by both rowdies and "gentlemen." As if in answer to this outrage there appeared, in 1780, a champion of his people whose mighty fists were as powerful as battering-rams. This was Daniel Mendoza, an East End Jew of Portuguese ancestry. He was a true champion, and according to some historians of the ring, it was he who transformed pugilistics from crude slugging into the science of boxing.

Mendoza's spectacular success fired a number of the younger and hardier generation of East End Jews to try to become "champions of their people." The hardest-punching fighter of the generation was Samuel Elias, who was known

"Humphreys and Mendoza fighting at Odiham in Hampshire on Wednesday, January 9, 1788." (5. Mendoza 6. Humphreys)

as "Dutch Sam" because originally he had come from Amsterdam. He was a contender in many famous bouts from 1801 to 1814, and is said to have invented the "upper-cut." Other noted fighters early in the nineteenth century were "Young Dutch Sam," Isaac Bittoon, Abraham Belasco and Barney Aron, celebrated as "The Star of the East."

"Dutch Sam," sometimes credited with originating the "upper-cut."

Political Leaders

The abolition of the "on the true faith of a Christian" declaration from the Oath of Allegiance, which English officials were obliged to take, launched a number of Jews on prominent political careers. Lionel de Rothschild, who had been prevented by the Oath from taking his seat in Parliament to which he had been elected in 1847, was admitted readily in 1858. There were a number of Jewish Lord Mayors elected in some of the principal cities in England. Serving as Lord Mayors in London were Sir David Salomons, Sir Benjamin Phillips, Sir Henry Isaacs, Sir George Faudel-Phillips and Sir Marcus Samuel (later Viscount Bearsted).

The great figure in the political life of modern England was Benjamin Disraeli, better known as the Earl of Beaconsfield. Baptized into the Church of England at twelve years of age, he had no difficulty taking his place as a member of Parliament in 1837. Shrewd, resourceful and with a driving will to power, he threw in his lot with the Tory Protectionist squires in 1846. He forthwith became the real founder and leader of the Conservative Party.

First as Chancellor of the Exchequer and then twice as Prime Minister, he made himself the dominant personality in English public life. He initiated the new era of bellicose imperialist policy and earned for it the gratitude of Queen Victoria, whom he proclaimed "Empress of India." His liberal opponents coined the word "jingo" especially for him. It was lifted from a popular song which presumed to describe his political creed:

> We don't want to fight, but, by *jingo*, if we do,
> We've got the ships, we've got the men, we've got
> the money, too.

Benjamin Disraeli.

After the outbreak of the bloody Afghan and Zulu Wars, many in England began to have misgivings about the political morality as well as the practicality of his "jingo" maneuvers. But he, nevertheless, found enthusiastic supporters in the upper and middle classes. These had grown prosperous from the exploitation of England's vast colonial empire, or had obtained secure jobs in the vast civil service it created.

A less brilliant contemporary of Disraeli's, but more widely esteemed for character, was Sir Moses Montefiore, Sheriff of London and financial adviser to Queen Victoria. He was a great banker and a pioneer in the industrial development of Great Britain. London streets were first lit up by the illuminating gas furnished by the Imperial Continental Gas Association he formed. Several leading banking institutions counted him among their founders. His initiative, for example, created

The Berlin Congress, 1878. Disraeli in conference with Prince Gortschakoff (left foreground).

the Provincial Bank of Ireland. Montefiore had not only the rare gift of making money but the even rarer gift of knowing how to spend it. Unostentatiously he poured his wealth into innumerable philanthropies, and in a variety of other ways worked to alleviate the hard lot of his persecuted people everywhere. Whenever its human rights were denied or outraged, he stepped boldly to the defense. His name thus became a byword for rectitude and selfless devotion to the Jews of the world.

When the ritual-murder libel was leveled at the Jews of Damascus in 1840 and infuriated mobs were ravaging and murdering in the Jewish quarter of the city, Montefiore, together with Adolphe Crémieux, the Jewish humanitarian of France, personally interceded with the Sultan of Turkey, Mehemet Ali, to stop the carnage. Their efforts resulted in the promulgation for the first time in the Ottoman Empire of a law which established the physical inviolability of Jews and their possessions. Six years later, when the persecution of the Jews by Tsar Nicholas I resulted in heart-rending appeals to the outside world, Montefiore hurried to St. Petersburg. There he strove, unavailingly, to use his wealth and prestige to soften the Romanov tyrant's cruelty to the Jews. Although he failed, the gratitude of the Jews of Russia knew no bounds. In countless homes engraved portraits of him were hung, a spontaneous expression of recognition.

Sir George Jessel (1824-83) was the first Jew to become a judge in England and, moreover, to earn recognition as the most learned legal authority of his day. He was the real founder of the modern Chancery Court of England, and served as Solicitor-General and Master of the Rolls.

Sir Rufus Isaacs was Lord Chief Justice of England from 1913 to 1921. He was then elevated to the peerage and as the Marquis of Reading was Viceroy of India until 1926.

Sir Herbert Samuel, later Viscount Samuel, was not only an industrial magnate but an accomplished philosopher as well. He was both leader of the Liberal Party and Home Secretary in the Coalition Government after World War I. He became the first British High Commissioner for Palestine in 1920.

Sir Alfred Mond, later Lord Melchett, the foremost chemical industrialist of England during World War I, served as the first Commissioner of Works from 1916 to 1921, and more than anyone else was credited with the high production of military supplies for the British Army in the field. He was chairman of Imperial Chemical Industries. He died in 1931.

Harold Laski, elected chairman of the National Executive Committee of the Labour Party, was a brilliant political writer and economist.

Leslie Hore-Belisha, Conservative, filled the post of War Minister during the first part of the war against the Nazis and was succeeded by another Jew, the Labourite leader, Emanuel Shinwell.

Music and Art

The middle of the nineteenth century found many Jews active in the musical life of England in popular, light operatic, grand operatic and serious concert music, but none of them achieved any real eminence.

A popular composer who had a great vogue in his generation was Henry Russell. He wrote the famous English military song, "Cheer, Boys, Cheer!" and "A Life on the Ocean Waves," which was written in the back room of a New York music store. John Barnett, a cousin of the composer Meyerbeer, was well known in London during the 1830's as a concert singer and as a composer.

Sir George Henschel, famous conductor and singer, founded and led the London Symphony Orchestra and served as the first conductor of the Boston Symphony Orchestra (1881-84). There were a number of other well-known English Jewish conductors: Sir Julius Benedict, a pupil of the German composer Karl Maria von Weber, Sir Michael Costa and Sir Landon Ronald.

The most successful operatic impresario in England during the middle of the nineteenth century was Benjamin Lumley (Levy).

POLITICAL LEADERS

Sir Moses Montefiore.

Sir Henry Isaacs, caricatured by "Spy."

Sir George Jessel.

Lord Reading.

POLITICAL LEADERS

Viscount Herbert Samuel.

Sir Alfred Mond.

Harold Laski.

Leslie Hore-Belisha.

CONDUCTOR   SCULPTOR   SCIENTIST   PHILOSOPHER

Sir George Henschel.

Jacob Epstein.

James Joseph Sylvester.

Prof. Samuel Alexander.

WRITERS

Israel Zangwill.

Sir Max Beerbohm.

G. B. Stern.

Philip Guedalla.

The best-known contemporary virtuosi have been, curiously enough, all pianists: the Anglo-Russian Benno Moiseiwitch, Mark Hambourg, Harriet Cohen, Harold Samuel, Myra Hess and a number of lesser lights.

One of the foremost English ballet dancers is Alicia Markova.

Artists and architects of Jewish origin became prominent in England early in the nineteenth century. Noted were Solomon Bennett (born in Russia before 1780); Solomon Hart, the first Jew elected to the Royal Academy; Abraham and Rebecca Solomon; Simeon Solomon, who although one of the most gifted and admired of the Pre-Raphaelite artists at the beginning of his career has been practically forgotten; Solomon J. Solomons and Sir William Rothenstein. The painter Alfred Wolmark is widely known today.

Sir Charles Walston, one of the leading English historians of art, was for many years Slade Professor of Art at Cambridge.

The first Jewish architect of prominence was George Basevi, a cousin of Benjamin Disraeli. He designed the Fitzwilliam Museum at Cambridge and a number of the fine houses still standing on Belgrave Square. The first London skyscrapers were created by Delissa Joseph. The architects of Shell-Max House, Woburn House and the Prudential Building were Ernest and Charles Joseph.

One of the most impressive sculptors of the modern era is Jacob Epstein. A product of New York's lower East Side, where he received his art training at the Educational Alliance, he has spent most of his creative life in London. Because of his bold and unconventional conceptions he has been the *enfant terrible* of the British art world for several decades.

Science

James Joseph Sylvester was the first Jew allowed to matriculate in Cambridge University. That was in 1831. Because of the anti-Jewish restrictions, he was not allowed to take his degree until 1872, when he was clearly established as one of the leading English mathematicians.

A chemist of great eminence was Raphael Meldolo. He made significant contributions in photo-chemistry and in the field of triphenyl methane dyes. In 1879 he produced the first oxazine dyestuff known as "Meldolo's blue."

Ludwig Mond, the father of Lord Melchett, was a top-ranking chemist, and above all a great industrial organizer. Of immense importance was his discovery that a metal could exist in the form of gas. He produced nickel with his new process, which helped to revolutionize industry. Equally ingenious were the economical processes he discovered for making soda, soap, paper and glass.

Meyer Kopplaus of Leeds invented the signal apparatus for iceberg detection now carried by all ships.

Best known to the world among English Jewish scientists was Chaim Weizmann, who became the first President of the State of Israel in 1948. Born in Russia, he became a naturalized British subject in 1910. During World War I he made an important contribution to the British war effort: in 1915 when there was a critical shortage of acetone for explosives, he developed a process for manufacturing it synthetically. This contribution undoubtedly helped make the English government more receptive to the negotiations, with Weizmann and other leaders in the World Zionist movement, for a Jewish homeland in Palestine. It probably was a factor in the issuance of the Balfour Declaration in 1917.

Dr. Selig Brodetsky is a leading authority in thermodynamics. He was President of the Hebrew University in Jerusalem. An outstanding mathematician and philosopher of science in England today is Professor Hyman Levy.

Julius Reuter, founder of Reuter's News Agency.

Literature

There have been a great many writers of Jewish extraction who have attained distinction, popularity, or both, in England. These have belonged to every literary school and taste. To mention but the best known: Benjamin Disraeli, Grace Aguilar, Arthur Pinero, Alfred Sutro, Israel Zangwill, Amy Levy, Leonard Merrick, Gilbert Frankau, W. L. George, Arthur Waley, Stephen Hudson, Isaac Rosenberg, Humbert Wolfe, G. B. Stern, Siegfried Sassoon, Philip Guedalla, Naomi Jacob, Louis Golding, Gerald Kersh and, not least—Max Beerbohm.

Probably the two foremost Shakespearean scholars were Sir Sidney Lee and Sir Israel Gollancz. The most celebrated anthology of English poetry, *The Golden Treasury*, was the work of Sir Francis Turner Palgrave, whose earlier name was Cohen.

LATER IMMIGRANTS

During the early 1880's when hundreds of thousands of Russian and Polish Jews were fleeing from pogroms and hunger, quite a number emigrated to England. There was a noticeable rise in the London Jewish population. In 1883 there were 47,000 Jews living in the city, many of them the descendants of late eighteenth-century Polish immigrants. By

Chief Rabbi Nathan Marcus Adler, the religious leader of English Jewry throughout the long Victorian era.

1902 the number had more than tripled, to a total of 150,000. Strangely enough, although many of the immigrants from Poland, Lithuania and Russia had come to join relatives, there were many who had no intention of settling in England. America, "the Golden Land," was the magnet which drew most of them, but, too poor to buy even steerage passage to New York for themselves and their families, they considered London as a sort of stopping-off station. As soon as they could save enough shillings to buy steamship tickets, they planned to move on to New York. But as they stayed on—either they got used to English life, or they liked it. Possibly the lure of America began to dim with time, or, more poignantly, poverty and the fear of the unknown made them cling the more tenaciously to what they had and understood. Whatever the reason, two or three native-born generations of English Jews of East European stock grew out of this immigration wave. In 1951 there were about 450,000 Jews in England, some 275,000 in London, 50,000 in Manchester, 30,000 in Leeds and 10,000 in Birmingham.

Manchester Synagogue, 1858.

ORTHODOX TRADITION

The orthodox tradition, established by the first *Sephardic* settlers in London in the days when Cromwell allowed Jews to return to England, remained continuous and dominant in Anglo-Jewish life. Although new cultural variations arose out of the specific nature of Jewish community life in London, the basic Jewish traditional forms remained unchanged.

Scene in the 250-year-old Great Synagogue of London, during the *Blitz*. Note steel-helmeted air-raid wardens.

The Nazi *Blitz* wrecked the Great Synagogue. However, as a symbolic act of faith, the synagogue was reconsecrated as a house of worship while still standing in ruins. Its reconstruction was promptly begun by public subscription.

WHITECHAPEL

Whitechapel, the famous Jewish quarter of London, was established during the eighteenth century. It is in the East End of the city and has depressing resemblances to other large slums, such as New York's lower East Side, the pre-Hitler Warsaw ghetto, and the Amsterdam ghetto, with the same overcrowding, the same restless activity and the same poverty.

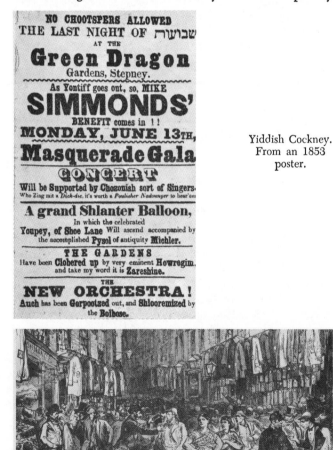

Yiddish Cockney. From an 1853 poster.

Petticoat Lane (Whitechapel) in 1870.

CANADA

EARLY PIONEERS

The Jewish community of Canada today is relatively small, 201,000. Its history, too, is quite brief. It begins a century later than the first Jewish settlement in the American Colonies.

Captain (later Admiral) Sir Alexander Schomberg who fought with distinction against the French in the naval battles of Canada. (From a portrait by Hogarth.)

Probably the first identifiable Jew in Canada was Abraham Gradis, from France. The merchandise he stored in the warehouses he established in 1758 in Quebec was a principal source of supplies for General Montcalm's French army, then contending with the British for the Canadian provinces. The civilian commissary officer who sailed from London with the English army to South Canada was also a Jew, Aaron Hart (1724-1800). He was the first English merchant to establish himself in Canadian commerce. The important Indian trading post he founded at Three Rivers did much for the early economic development and expansion of Canada. Aaron Hart literally founded at Three Rivers a family dynasty which owned large tracts of land. (Only a generation after he died his grandson Samuel, apparently feeling the need of social as well as financial prominence, took on the title of Seigneur de Bésancourt.)

Aaron Hart's son Ezekiel stood for election in Three Rivers and won a seat in the Quebec Assembly in 1807. But since he could not take the Oath of Allegiance "on the true faith of a Christian," a declaration having equal force in Canada as in the mother country, he was expelled from the Assembly. He ran again and was re-elected. Once more he declined to utter the objectionable phrase in the Oath and was rejected. He then lost heart and resigned himself to being a banker with his brothers Alexander and Moses at Three Rivers.

After the Bill of Rights granting Jews full equality was finally passed in 1831, Ezekiel Hart's son, the Seigneur de Bésancourt, who had been elected to the Assembly from Three Rivers, was permitted to take his seat "on the true faith of a Jew."

Facsimile of note issued by Hart's Bank.

Other Jews were influential in the early life of Canada. Most of these came from the American Colonies or directly from London. They were almost exclusively *Sephardim* of Spanish-Portuguese stock who quite naturally considered themselves a group apart from the German and Polish Jews who started coming after 1825. Thus, from the very first, two religious camps and social-cultural groupings arose among the Jews of Canada. The wealthy *Sephardim*, as the earlier settlers, considered themselves an elite. They established the Congregation *Shearith Israel* in Montreal, in 1768, which obtained its first religious leader, Rabbi Jacob Raphael Cohen, in 1778. This congregation was modeled after the congregation of the same name on Mill Street in colonial New York. There were, in fact, close links between the two congregations: a number of Jewish worthies from colonial America were active at various times in Canada. One of these was Colonel David Salisbury Franks.

Jews in Canada's early days were active traders with the Indians. Levi Solomons founded a trading post at Mackinac on the northern shore of Lake Huron before 1776. When Pontiac, the Indian chieftain, led a massacre of the English garrison at the post, Levi Solomons miraculously escaped scalping. Another well-known trader with the Indians was Jacob

Aaron Hart.

Ezekiel Hart.

Moses Hart.

82   C. 56-57.   Anno Primo Gulielmi IV.   A. D. 1831.

Public Act.   VIII. And be it further enacted by the authority aforesaid, that this Act shall be taken and deemed to be a public Act, and as such shall be judicially taken notice of by all Judges, Justices of the Peace, and all others whom it shall concern without being specially pleaded.

CAP. LVII.

An Act to declare persons professing the Jewish Religion intitled to all the rights and privileges of the other subjects of His Majesty in this Province.

31st March, 1831—Presented for His Majesty's Assent and reserved "for the 'signification of His Majesty's pleasure thereon."
12th April, 1832,—Assented to by His Majesty in His Council.
5th June, 1832,—The Royal Assent signified by the proclamation of His Excellency the Governor in Chief.

Preamble.   WHEREAS doubts have arisen whether persons professing the Jewish Religion are by law entitled to many of the privileges enjoyed by the other subjects of His Majesty within this Province: Be it therefore declared and enacted by the King's Most Excellent Majesty, by and with the advice and consent of the Legislative Council and Assembly of the Province of Lower Canada, constituted and assembled by virtue of and under the authority of an Act passed in the Parliament of Great Britain, intituled, "An Act to repeal certain parts of an Act passed in "the fourteenth year of His Majesty's Reign, intituled, "An Act for making "more effectual provision for the Government of the Province of Quebec, in North "America," and to make further provision for the Government of the said "Province of Quebec in North America." And it is hereby declared and enacted by the authority aforesaid, that all persons professing the Jewish Religion being natural born British subjects inhabiting and residing in this Province, are entitled and shall be deemed, adjudged and taken to be entitled to the full rights

The section of Canada's Bill of Rights granting equal rights to Jews.

Franks, who, in 1794, started the trading post which grew to be Green Bay, Wisconsin.

An important place in the economic history of early Canada is held by Henry Joseph. He operated large fleets of canoes and big boats on the Great Lakes and on the St. Lawrence River, and because of this is considered a founder of the Merchant Marine of Canada. His son, Jesse Joseph, greatly expanded his father's shipping interests. Early in the nineteenth century he operated a line of ships between Montreal and Antwerp. In later years, he started the first street railway in Montreal, and, with Jacob Henry Joseph, was a pioneer of Canada's telegraph system. They jointly established the Montreal Telegraph Company and laid the first trans-Atlantic cable line from Canada.

Moses Judah Hays, Montreal's chief of police for sixteen years, was responsible for the city's first water system.

Extensive fisheries were developed by William Hyman and his sons, beginning in 1842. Simon Leiser operated a whaling

The Stanley Street Synagogue (*Shearith Israel*) in Montreal.

and sealing company from Victoria. Sigismund Mohr established the first telephone system in Quebec. In later years he put the first electric light system in Canada into operation.

All this becomes even more significant when it is taken into account that in the year 1846 there were only 200 Jews in Canada.

LATER PIONEERS

In the year of the Gold Rush, in 1858, the German and Polish immigrants were numerous enough to erect a synagogue of their own in Montreal. This was the Congregation *Shaar Hashomayim*. As in the United States during that melodramatic year, the lure of gold irresistibly drew Canadian easterners, including some Jews, to British Columbia on the Pacific Coast. Whether they found gold there or not, their pioneering efforts were considerable and constructive. The ubiquitous Jewish storekeeper brought the amenities of civilization into the isolated settlements of British Columbia. There was little religious prejudice against Jews in those parts. In fact, the first member to represent British Columbia in the Dominion Parliament in 1871 was the Jew, Henry Nathan. Another highly respected political leader of the Province was David Oppenheimer. He served four terms as Mayor of Vancouver.

A new type of Jewish pioneer began to enter Canada after the pogroms of 1881 in Russia. This inflow of immigration soon reached mass proportions, although on a far smaller scale than in the United States. Most of the new arrivals chose to remain in the cities of eastern Canada. They preferred city life and felt happiest where they could feel the reassurance and warmth of their own Jewish community life.

The immigrants from eastern Europe later introduced into Canada the mass production of clothing, a system previously established by fellow-Jews in the garment industry in the United States. Many also engaged in the fur trade, in the processing of tobacco and in the manufacture of cigars.

Farmers

The early Zionist movement in Poland and Russia received its greatest impetus from the harsh persecution of the Jews under the Tsars. Many nurtured romantic dreams of a return to the soil. Hundreds of newcomers during the eighties and nineties, a number of them belonging to the *Am Olam* (Eternal People) organization, were attracted by the Canadian wilderness and the open spaces of the central plain. As early as 1874 Jews had made determined attempts to settle on the

David Oppenheimer.

land. Some of them were back-to-the-land romantic idealists with little conception of the material reality and no farming experience of any kind. Not only were they too urban in their tastes and habits but they were far too intellectual for rustification. There were too many conflicting philosophies and points of view represented in these idealistic colonies. Much precious time was wasted in heated discussion and contention. A number of the agricultural ventures eventually proved economically untenable. Others, worked by doughtier and more enduring elements, have continued to this day. Several of the best known Jewish farming settlements were in the province of Saskatchewan: Wapella (1888), Oxbow (1890), Lipton (1901), Edenbridge (commonly called *Yidnbrik*, 1906), Sonnenfeld (1906), and Hoffer (early 1900's). Today the Jewish settlements have a farm population of 2,200.

Frontier Shopkeepers

There was still another group of Jewish pioneers—the enterprising small businessmen from East European countries. They opened little shops in widely separated and still undeveloped towns in the West and Midwest. As these towns grew, the number of Jewish tradesmen increased. In 1882 there was a sufficient number of Jews in Winnipeg to establish the first congregation there.

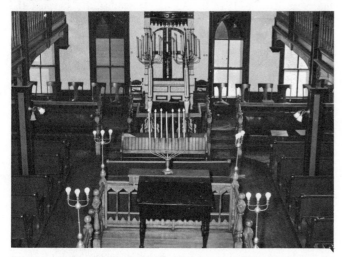

Interior of the old *Rosh Pinah* Synagogue in Winnipeg. Among its founders in 1892 was "Fetter" Nissel, uncle of Sholom Aleichem, the great Yiddish humorist.

The three Coblentz brothers founded the first Jewish community in Winnipeg. The first Jewish settlers in Calgary came in 1889, and in Edmonton, in 1891.

Anti-Semitism, though not very great in Canada, caused most anxiety in the Catholic province of Quebec. This hostility, restrained at first, became marked with the first arrivals of the Russian and Polish immigrants in the 1880's. Not only the practice of their religion but also their dress and their language, Yiddish, set them apart and exposed them to the unreasoning suspicion and hostility so often accorded the stranger. During the turbulent events which stemmed from the Dreyfus case, the inhabitants of Quebec, being of French descent and speaking French, reacted violently. The mark of Cain, which had been placed upon the brow of the Jew Dreyfus by the reactionaries and clericalists of France, was by association also put upon the little Russian and Polish shopkeepers and country customer-peddlers by the clericalists and the reactionaries of Quebec.

After World War I, the determined stand taken by organized Jewish groups against the intolerable treatment of Jewish children in the public schools in Montreal and Quebec aroused further resentment in certain Catholic circles. It all resulted from the determined opposition by the Catholic Church to the establishment of a public school system. Jews had no choice but to send their children to either Catholic or

The American circuit riders carried the word of God to the pioneers of the Middle and Far West. So did the *shochtim*, the Jewish ritual slaughterers, carry on their labors to perpetuate Jewish identity in the remote settlements of Manitoba at the turn of the century. Because of a lack of trained rabbis, the *shochtim*, all learned and pious men, dedicated themselves to the task of circumcising every Jewish male child in the province no matter how long the distance or how hard the journey. The picture above shows the chief orthodox rabbi of Winnipeg flanked by seven *shochtim*, his so-called "sub-rabbis."

Protestant parochial schools. This caused great mental anguish to religious Jews. To add insult to the injury, they were obliged to pay school taxes like everyone else yet had no voice in the education of their children.

The character of Canadian Jewish life is almost identical with that in the United States. It conforms to the same institutional and organizational patterns. The two largest Jewish

The pupils of the Winnipeg *Talmud Torah* in the 1890's.

centers are Montreal (80,000) and Toronto (65,000). Lesser communities are found in Edmonton, Vancouver, Winnipeg, Ottawa, Victoria, St. John, Halifax and other cities. The preponderant number of Canadian Jews are Orthodox, a large segment is Conservative, and there are several Reform congregations in Montreal, Toronto, Edmonton and Hamilton.

About one-third of the gainfully employed Jewish population is engaged in retail merchandising. More than one-third work at skilled and semi-skilled trades in the large cities. About 2% are employed in the basic industries, on farms, in mines and logging camps. More than 10% are white-collar workers; 5% are engaged in the professions.

Shaaray Zion Synagogue, built in Montreal by Jews of East European stock.

189

SOUTH AFRICA

Jews started coming to Cape Colony, South Africa, in 1806. Then, when the English Government sent four thousand settlers to the Cape in 1820, there were a number of Jewish families among them. In time, some of these, the Nordens, Nortons, Simms and Slomans, were to play a leading role in South African Jewish affairs. Some of these newcomers were enterprising men. Because of the unlimited opportunities they found in this new world with its still untapped natural riches, they acquired wealth and prominence quickly.

Aaron and Daniel de Pass, for instance, engaged in whaling, fishing and sealing and became prominently associated with Cape shipping interests. Daniel de Pass not only established the first ice factory in South Africa, but he was also one of the first sugar planters in Natal. The discovery of coal deposits in the Transvaal was made by the German Jew Michaelis. Jews were also among the pioneer ostrich farmers. Jonas Bergtheil ran one of the first cotton plantations in Natal.

Trading with the Zulus proved, perhaps, the most spectacular test of Jewish commercial enterprise. Nathaniel Isaacs (1808-40) so ingratiated himself with the Zulu King Tchaka that he was designated as his-principal chief in the territory of Natal. The best known of the "Zulu traders," however, was Benjamin Norden. He had an agreement with Dingaan, King of the Zulus, which allowed him to lead a trading expedition into Matabeleland. It led to the opening up of the copper fields in Mamaqualand.

A generation later Albert Beit helped Cecil Rhodes carve out a colonial empire. Together, these two financial adventurers acquired from Lobengula, the King of Matabele, exclusive rights to all metals and minerals found in the country. Furthermore, they were empowered to keep out of Matabele "all persons seeking land, metals, minerals and mining rights herein." Rhodes and Beit then formed the British South African Company, of which Beit was the principal director. The

syndicate, with a jurisdiction over four hundred and fifty thousand square miles, also had other Jewish directors—Sir Ernest Oppenheimer, Barons Frederic and Emile D'Erlanger and Sir Edmund Davis. They drew fabulous fortunes out of the minerals, the gold and the coal of the Matabele earth.

First sale to farmers of angora rams brought to Graaf Reinet from the Near East in 1857 by Adolph Mosenthal. It launched the mohair industry of South Africa which has provided the bulk of the world's supply.

When the diamond fields were opened up in 1871, followed by the discovery of gold fields in the Transvaal in 1875-85, there started a new flow of Jewish immigrants from Lithuania, Galicia and Poland. However, these humble newcomers, having neither money nor a knowledge of English, played but a secondary role in the big business world of South Africa. Only the descendants of the first settlers and later-arriving English Jews figured prominently in it. Most East European Jews opened little retail shops in the various towns and cities. They pioneered in only modest areas of the economy.

Jews, too, were among the first to mine diamonds, platinum, gold, copper and salt. Solomon Barnato Joel controlled the North Rhodesian copper fields. Barney I. Barnato, who as a lad in Whitechapel had worked in the fish-and-chips emporium of an aunt, became the fabulous "diamond king" of South Africa. By the time the mass immigration from Russia and Poland was in full swing, the golden era of opportunity had come to a close in the entire region.

In 1951 the Jewish population in the Union of South Africa was about 110,000 or five per cent of the population. It included some 15,000 German refugees. The city with the largest Jewish population was Johannesburg, with 50,000 Jews. In 1943 there were in South Africa more than two hundred Jewish communities.

Ever since the first congregation, *Tikvath Israel* (Hope of Israel), was founded in 1841 in Cape Town, traditional religious life has been sustained by the Jews of South Africa. It has also been a leading Zionist stronghold since the pre-Herzl days when *Chovevei Zion* (Lovers of Zion) societies were established in a number of cities by Russian immigrants.

Saul Solomon, sheriff and "Merchant King" of St. Helena, and his nephew, also named Saul Solomon (1816-92). The elder Solomon was an early Cape Colony settler (1806). He tried to help Napoleon escape from St. Helena but the plot was discovered and frustrated. His nephew was known as the "Disraeli of South Africa." Leader of the Liberal Party in the Cape Parliament, he declined several offers to serve as Prime Minister. His sons and grandsons, too, figured prominently in Cape politics. Sir Richard Solomon became Attorney-General, Sir William Henry Solomon was Chief Justice and Saul Solomon (grandson) was a judge of the Supreme Court. There have been a number of other Jews prominent in South African public life. Sir Matthew Nathan served as Governor of Natal (1907-10); Max Danziger acted as Finance Minister for South Rhodesia (1941); Justice Leopold Greenberg is currently Judge-President for the Transvaal. Other leading jurists are Judge Manfred Nathan and Justice Philip Millin, husband of Sara Gertrude Millin, the popular novelist. Jews have been mayors of all leading cities—Cape Town, Johannesburg, Durban, Pretoria, etc. They have also sat in all the Provincial Parliaments of the Union.

Left. Suasso de Lima (1791-1858), first South African bookseller and poet. *Center.* Barney I. Barnato, "Diamond King" of South Africa. *Right.* Albert Beit.

190

AUSTRALIA

Although small in numbers, the Jewish community of Australia has made impressive contributions to the national life of the country. Out of the general population of some seven million there were only about 52,000 Jews in 1951.

The first Jews came to Sydney in 1817. But the first congregation was not established until 1833 when there were enough Jews to hold religious services. Despite the considerable lapse of time and the growth of the city, there were only 18,500 Jews living there in 1951. The second largest city, Melbourne, could not in 1839 muster even a *minyan,* the quorum of ten required for holding religious services. It had to wait until 1853 to establish a congregation. In 1951 this city also counted 18,500 Jewish inhabitants. That same year the capital of South Australia, Adelaide, had some 1,500 Jews; Brisbane, 1,500; and Perth, a few more than 2,500.

Because of the need for developing its vast virgin territories and for extending its frontiers, Australia eagerly welcomed all comers as pioneers during most of its early history. Little anti-Semitism, official or unofficial, has been in evidence at any time, which has made it possible for Jews to take an active part in the life of the country.

Most of the early Jewish settlers came from England, and the later arrivals from Russia and Poland. The latter groups engaged mostly in small manufacturing and in the retail trade. They also established two agricultural settlements in Victoria, which specialized in fruit growing and in raising sheep. A number of Jews, primarily those of English origin, achieved prominence in government, literature, the sciences and the arts. As early as 1828, the London theatrical director, Barnet Levy, brought over from London the first company of actors. He built the first theater in Australia, the "Theatre Royal" of Sydney. A number of artists achieved prominence, among them the painter E. P. Fox.

NEW ZEALAND

In 1951 there were only 4,000 Jews in New Zealand's population of three million. Ninety per cent of them resided in the cities. The largest Jewish community of 1,500 was in Auckland. Most were of Polish and Russian extraction.

Only a few years after English rule was established over New Zealand in 1840, Jewish community life made its appearance, tentative at first but waxing stronger with the years.

Left. Jacob Montefiore, brother of Sir Moses Montefiore. An early pioneer, he was appointed a Commissioner for the Colonization of Australia. *Right.* V. L. Solomon of Adelaide. He explored for the government the large Northern Territory which elected him to represent it in the Parliament of the Commonwealth.

Sir Isaac Isaacs, first Attorney-General, then a Justice of the High Court, and finally Governor-General of Australia in 1931.

Congregations were formed in 1843 in Wellington, in 1859 in Auckland and in 1862 in Dunedin.

The early arrivals, principally traders, followed the bush tracks into the unexplored interior, carrying goods for barter with the aborigines. One of these was Joseph E. Nathan, who started his adventurous business in the wilds in 1840, but concluded his career years later as the leader of the dairy-food industry. About 1950, of the gainfully employed Jews in the country, thirty-five per cent were in commerce, twenty-three per cent in industry, nine per cent in the professions and two per cent in farming.

Sir Julian
Salomons,
Chief Justice.

A number of individual Jews achieved high positions in government service. Sir Julius Vogel was Prime Minister in 1873. Sir Arthur M. Myers was Mayor of Auckland from 1905; he also held Cabinet posts during World War I, including that of Minister of Munitions. Sir Michael Myers became Chief Justice in 1929.

Lieutenant-General Sir John Monash, one of Australia's greatest soldiers. Son of a Polish immigrant Jew, he was a noted construction engineer until the outbreak of war in 1914 when he was given command of a brigade, with the rank of colonel. He won several promotions, and as commander of the "Anzacs" he led the great Allied assault on the Hindenburg Line in 1918 which he broke with five Australian, two British and two American divisions.

THE LOWLANDS

HOLLAND

Many Jews in eighteenth-century Holland shared with their forward-looking countrymen the hope for a democratic republic. It had been kindled by the success of the French Revolution in 1789 and by the earlier triumph of libertarian ideals in the American colonies. In 1790 a group of Jewish intellectuals in Amsterdam formed the *Felix Libertate Club* which devoted itself to the single objective of securing the privileges of the "Rights of Man" for the Jews of Holland. Five years later the members of the club, under the leadership of Moses Solomon Asser, held a public celebration which was climaxed by the planting of a "Liberty Tree" in a public square.

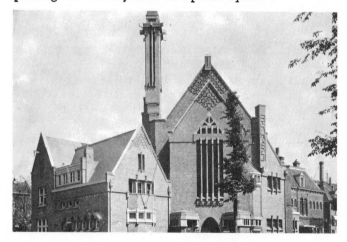

The synagogue in East Amsterdam.

The French Revolutionary Army had invested Holland in 1795, ending the rule of the royal House of Orange. Holland was renamed "Batavia." When the Republican National Convention of Batavia assembled on September 2, 1796, it issued a proclamation: "No Jew shall be excluded from rights or advantages which are associated with citizenship in the Batavian Republic and which he may desire to enjoy." Along with

A *mikveh* (Jewish ritual bath) in Amsterdam, early 19th century.

Christian churches, beginning with 1799, the synagogues were given subventions by the republic. Two Jews, De Lemon and Bromet, were elected deputies to the National Assembly of 1797. In 1798 Moses Asser, the leader of the Batavian Jewish Republicans, was elected to the Legislative Council of the

Assembly. With full equality assured them, Dutch Jews emerged from the segregation of the ghetto into the national life of their country.

Napoleon's subsequent seizure of power in the *coup d'état* of November 9, 1799, and the implementation of his opportunist policies hardly benefited Dutch Jewry. In 1806 he had turned Batavia back into a monarchy and placed his brother Louis Bonaparte on the throne. The early promise of full equality that had been given Jews by the revolution faded rapidly. Amidst a royal fanfare of magnanimity they were ordered to establish their religious *Consistoire*, an institution modeled along French lines.

The Jewish market in Amsterdam.

Like the one in Paris, the *Consistoire* turned out to be little more than a military recruiting agency for Napoleon's *Grande Armée*. It organized an exclusively Jewish regiment for King Louis Bonaparte in Batavia in 1809. This unit fought in the Battle of Waterloo, where it lost thirty-five of its officers and several times that many men from the ranks.

Perhaps even costlier for Dutch Jewry were the consequences of Napoleon's adroit plans for driving English trade out of the Netherlands. The Jewish exporters and importers of Amsterdam, most of them of Spanish and Portuguese stock, whose skill and initiative had so largely brought Amsterdam to the fore as a commercial center of Europe, were now ruined. Many of them became petty traders and shopkeepers, while others were pauperized. In later years the diamond industry once more opened up to Jews opportunities as wholesale and retail dealers and as diamond cutters, setters and polishers. But the majority of Dutch Jews, especially of Amsterdam, lived in poverty and squalor, earning their livelihood as street vendors, as handicraftsmen and as petty shopkeepers.

Beginning with the first quarter of the nineteenth century the educated Jews of Holland, too, distinguished themselves in many fields. There were two ministers of justice: Michael Hendrik Godefroi and Van Raalte. Henri Pollack was among

Jewish diamond cutter.

Josef Israels.

the founders of the Dutch trade unions. Perhaps the most eminent of all Jews in public life was neither a politician nor a statesman, but an idealist and a scholar, Tobias Michael Carel Asser, who had, however, been a member of the Dutch council of state and in 1904 a minister of state. As the foremost Dutch authority on international law since the eminent Hugo Grotius, and an ardent exponent of international comity and of military disarmament, he was co-recipient with A. H. Fried, the Austrian Jew, of the Nobel Prize for Peace in 1911.

A number of Jews have figured with distinction in the national literature of Holland, probably the foremost ones being the poet Isaac Costa and the dramatist and short-story writer Herman Heijermans. Other writers of note have been Israel Querido, Maurits Dekker and the woman novelist Carry von Bruggen de Haan. Louis Browmeester, one of the most gifted actors the stage in Holland has produced, is a Jew.

Tobias M. C. Asser.

Jewish graphic artists and sculptors also have figured prominently in modern Dutch art. The most widely known of these was the painter Josef Israels. Other painters have been Isaac Israels, Martin Monnickendam, Maurits de Groot, Benjamin Prins, Marinus van Raalte and Joseph Teixeira de Mattos. Noted as sculptors have been Joseph Mendes da Costa and Joap Kass. Two architects of prominence were De Klerk and Harry Ete.

Until the Hitlerian era cast its shadow over Holland, there were 156,817 Jews living there, with the largest number, 65,858, in Amsterdam. They were predominantly Orthodox and mostly of German and East European stock. Smaller Jewish communities were at The Hague, Rotterdam, Gröningen

and Arnhem. By 1951, however, after the holocaust, there remained only 27,000 Jews in all the Netherlands, including its overseas possessions.

BELGIUM

During the Middle Ages, Jews had formed tiny though insecure communities in the Belgian cities of Brussels, Ghent, Mons, Tournay and Louvain. But with the Black Death atrocities, Jewish life in Belgium came to an end. Two hundred years later *Marranos* started to trickle into Antwerp from Portugal and continued to arrive in small numbers from Amsterdam in the seventeenth and eighteenth centuries. It was not, however, until the first decades of the nineteenth century that the Belgian Jewish communities first began to show real signs of life.

The Dutch synagogue, Antwerp.

Jews did not enjoy religious freedom to any degree until 1830 when Belgium achieved its national independence and established its own monarchy. Jews were allowed their own communal self-rule, French *Consistoire* style. They even received a subvention from the government for the support of their religious institutions. Brussels, where the Grand Rabbi lived, was the official seat of the United Jewish Communities. Yet, for all this outward demonstration of self-government in religious matters, separate Jewish cemeteries, bizarrely enough, were never allowed. If a Jew died, his family had the choice of burying him either in a Catholic cemetery, or, if it had sufficient means, of having his body conveyed into neighboring Holland for burial in consecrated Jewish ground.

Paul Hymans, Premier of Belgium and first president of the League of Nations. He was the son of a Christian mother and the Jewish poet and scholar, Louis Hymans, who wrote the Belgian national anthem.

The majority of Belgian Jews today are of East European extraction. Either they or their near ancestors were born in Russia, Poland, Galicia, Romania or Hungary. In 1940, until the Nazi *Blitz*, there were more than 75,000 Jews in the kingdom, half of them in Antwerp. There were smaller communities in Brussels, Charleroi, Liège and Ghent.

Before World War II, a sizable section of the Jewish population was engaged in the diamond and jewelry industry—as diamond dealers and brokers, as cutters and polishers, goldsmiths and jewelers. The fancy leather and the garment trades employed more than three thousand Jewish workers. There were even a number of Jewish miners, engineers and technicians, a rare occurrence elsewhere, employed in the mines of the Charleroi district. Originally from the German Ruhr, where they had done the same kind of work, they started emigrating to Belgium beginning in 1923.

ANTWERP GHETTO

As everywhere else, the poor Jews of Antwerp have grouped for the greater comfort of religious and cultural unity in a quarter of their own. The Rue de Pelican is its best known street. It runs through the heart of the ghetto and is world-famous, for the diamond market and exchange are situated on it. Jewish traders and workers predominate in this

industry of Antwerp, which is second only to the diamond industry of Amsterdam. Many of the Antwerp diamond traders and workers came originally from Amsterdam and preserved their Dutch cultural ties and traditions. They even built their own synagogue.

Jewish quarter, Antwerp.

Most Belgian Jews were intensely interested in Zionism. On July 18, 1937, thousands of Antwerp Jews paraded through the Jewish quarter of Antwerp, then assembled before the memorial to the soldiers killed in the First World War and protested against the British Partition Plan for Palestine.

Chief Rabbi
Abraham A. Wolff.

Chief Rabbi
David Simonsen.

Mendel L. Nathanson,
writer and economist.

Herman Trier, Speaker and,
later, Vice-President of
Danish Parliament.

DENMARK

When the King of Denmark consented to admit Jews into his kingdom in 1657, a small number of them, of Spanish and Portuguese descent, began to arrive. The growth of the Danish Jewish community was slow. There were altogether only nineteen Jews in Copenhagen in 1682. And religious life on a legal basis did not begin until two years later when the two Jewish court jewelers, Meyer Goldschmidt and Israel David, petitioned King Christian V for the privilege of holding divine services. Out of a reluctant consideration for the petitioners the king allowed them to assemble for "morning and evening prayers on condition that these devotional exercises take place behind closed doors and without any sermon, so as not to cause any offense."

Not long afterwards the *Sephardic* community was greatly increased by the settlement of German, Dutch and Polish Jews who arrived overland by way of Schleswig-Holstein or by boat from Hamburg. The first synagogue in Denmark was dedicated in Copenhagen, in 1729, and Rabbi Abraham ben Solomon became the community's first spiritual leader. Linked to such a large extent, both by geography and by culture, with German Jewry, Danish Jewish life followed a somewhat parallel course, especially in its acceptance of the *Haskalah,* or Jewish Enlightenment Movement, at the end of the eighteenth century. Tiny as the Danish community was, it nevertheless counted among its leaders several of Moses Mendelssohn's closest intellectual collaborators, including Hartwig Wessely and Isaac Euchel.

There was no "Jewish problem" in Denmark. That was because there were too few Jews living there to arouse either envy or hostility. Furthermore, the religious tolerance of the Danish Protestants allowed them to meet some Jews socially and culturally on a basis of relative equality. Full citizenship and equality were granted the Jews by decree on March 29, 1814. Unlike those in other countries the schools and universities imposed no restrictions on Jewish students, and there was no *numerus clausus.* Secular education, therefore, became very attractive to Jews who possessed the means for acquiring it.

Just the same, the fundamental question of religion stuck like a bone in the throat of those Jews who were ambitious for careers in public life and in the liberal professions. As in Berlin and Vienna, membership in the church, in this case the state-established Lutheran Church, was the passport to greater opportunities, to a more secure future, and to more complete acceptance socially. During the first decades of the nineteenth century there was a strong opportunistic trend in Denmark, as elsewhere in central Europe, toward assimilation and apostasy from the Jewish faith. Although as late as 1902 there were only 3,500 Jews in Denmark, yet the number of those who had attained prominence in various walks of life was unusually large.

Check to Assimilation

When the new synagogue of Copenhagen was dedicated in 1833 a vigorous and determined man mounted its pulpit. That was Abraham Alexander Wolff, who combined considerable secular learning and worldliness with competent Talmudic scholarship. He clearly grasped the essential problem facing the Jews of Denmark—that of group and religious survival under the pressure of assimilation. Although a religious traditionalist at heart, Wolff was nonetheless under the influence of German Reform Judaism. With the intention of attracting young people he introduced a number of "modernizing" innovations in the synagogue service, including a choir and the sermon in Danish. These mild reforms were considered dangerously modern by the Orthodox, and too Orthodox by the youth moving toward assimilation and apostasy. Nevertheless, Wolff is credited with having had some success in checking the conversionist epidemic.

The Copenhagen Synagogue.

Meir Aron Goldschmidt.

Georg Brandes.

Literature, Music and Art

Jews have occupied a prominent position in the literature of Denmark. They have been distinguished as novelists, short-story writers, dramatists, poets, literary critics and historians. During the nineteenth century the most eminent of these were the poet Henrik Hertz and the novelist and short-story writer Meir A. Goldschmidt. Georg Brandes (Morris Cohen) was one of the most influential of modern literary historians and critics.

Other writers of note were Mendel Levin Nathanson, Nicolai L. Abrahams, C. A. H. Kalkar, Ragnild Goldschmidt, Oskar Siesbye, Israel S. Levin, E. J. Trier, Julius Ree, J. A. Fridericia and Paul Levin. Some Jewish writers today are Henri Nathansen, Louis Levy, Simon Koch and Rosalie Jacobson.

Painters, graphic artists and sculptors of Jewish extraction, also well known in Denmark in the nineteenth century, were Ernst Meyer, David Monies, Geskel Saloman and Joel Ballin. Contemporaries are Siegfried and Olga Wagner, Albert Gottschalk, Georg Seligman, Sally Philipsen and Ernst Goldschmidt.

Composers, conductors, musicologists and concert artists of note were Siegfried Saloman, Anton Ree, Eduard Lassen, Otto J. E. Bendix, Leopold Rosenfeldt, Fritz E. Bendix and Victor Bendix. Two contemporaries are Rudolf Simonsen and Charles Senderowitz.

Scientists

Danish Jewish scientists who achieved international reputations were Ludwig Levin Jacobson, the anatomist; Nathanael Wulff Wallich, the botanist; Seligman M. Trier, the clinician; Adolph Hannover, the physiologist; and Niels Bohr, celebrated nuclear physicist and Nobel Prize winner in 1922.

Others prominent in various fields of science and medicine were Mortiz M. Levy, Ludwig I. Brandes, Nota Saloman, Carl L. Salomonsen, H. I. Hannover and Harald Hirschprung. Contemporaries are Louis Fridericia, Edgar Rubin, Max Melchior, Kirstine Meyer, Lis Jacobsen and Harald Bohr.

Niels Bohr.

SWEDEN

It was on an individual's impulse of the moment and under purely accidental circumstances that the first Jewish community in Sweden was established. It happened in 1774. Aron Isak, a trader living in Mecklenburg, Germany, near the Polish border, had bought a herd of fine goats, he thought. But on the way home they all died. Distressed by his loss, he resolved to go to Sweden as a pioneer and thus became the first Jew to settle in that country.

King Gustav III was so pleased with him that he made him his Court Jew and even told him that he was free to worship God in any way he chose. "In that case," replied the nimble-witted Aron Isak, "I need nine more Jews to worship in accordance with the Jewish rite." The king consented, and that is how the first *minyan*, the quorum of ten required for Jewish public prayer, was assembled in Sweden. The newcomers arrived from Mecklenburg and other parts of Germany. Five years later the Swedish Parliament passed a law authorizing the settlement of Jews in the cities of Gotebörg and Norrköping.

The Swedish Jewish community, however, did not grow. In 1870 there were only twenty Jewish families in Stockholm, but despite their small number they built an imposing synagogue structure that year. They also imported a rabbi from Mecklenburg. But this represented, in a manner of speaking, only one side of the medal. As in Denmark, in Sweden, too, there was discernible a headlong trend toward assimilation and intermarriage, mostly among Jews of German origin.

With the years, the ethnic character of the Jewish population changed greatly. Jews of German extraction were gradually outnumbered by Yiddish-speaking arrivals from Poland, Lithuania and Russia, who settled in Stockholm and Goteörg after 1903, following the Kishinev pogrom. Today there are some 8,000 Jews in the entire country, distributed principally among the larger Jewish communities of Stockholm, Goteörg, Malmo and Norrköping.

Nathanael W. Wallich
(1785-1854).

Adolph Hannover
(1814-1894).

Left. Aron Isak. *Right.* Marcus Ehrenpreis was the Chief Rabbi of Sweden beginning with 1914. Due to his efforts the so-called *Protocols of the Elders of Zion* were exposed as a forgery before a Swiss court.

Artists and Musicians

Best known among Swedish Jewish painters were Geskel Saloman, Eva Bonnier, Sigrid Hjerten Grünewald and Isaac Hirsch Grünewald. But the finest of these artists, a leading figure in modern Swedish painting, was Ernst Abraham Josephson, a forerunner of the expressionist school.

There have been a number of Swedish Jews who have devoted themselves to music. Probably none of them achieved the world celebrity of the operatic singer Henriette Nissen. A composer of some note during the third quarter of the nineteenth century was Jakob Axel Josephson.

Writers and Scientists

Three Jews have been among the literary critics and historians who constitute the "Big Eighteen," the committee of the Royal Academy of Sweden which awards the Nobel Prizes: Professor Henrik Emil Schück, who served as President of the Nobel Foundation for several decades from 1918; Professor Karl Johan Warburg and Martin Lamm.

There have been other writers of note. Ludwig Oscar Josephson, the dramatic critic, playwright and theatrical producer, was among the first to champion the cause of Ibsen and Strindberg against the "Philistines" in the theatre. Oscar Ivor Levertin was one of the foremost Swedish poets and novelists. Ragnar Josephson was an eminent art historian; Hugo Moritz Valentin, an historian of Sweden, and Rosa Warrens, a leading authority on Swedish folklore. The Bonnier family established the most prominent book publishing house in the country, and created a fund for the assistance of Swedish authors.

There have been several Jewish scientists of eminence in Sweden. One was Robert Rubenson, the meteorologist, another was Elias Heyman, the hygienist, but perhaps the best known of all was Sven Hedin, the famous explorer of Tibet, a descendant of Aron Isak, the first Jew to settle in Sweden.

Karl Otto Bonnier.

NORWAY

The Jews in Norway have always been negligible in number. In 1951 there were only some 1,200, most of them living in Oslo and Trondheim. As had occurred in Sweden, the first Jews, Portuguese *Sephardim* from Holland, had to become Christians before they were permitted to enter Norway in 1734. Jews who refused to be baptized were not allowed into the country until 1851, and only after many gallant battles had been fought on their behalf by the noted Christian writer, Henrik Wergenland, and Sören Sörenson, the liberal President of Parliament. Although the first congregation had been functioning in Oslo in 1892, it was not until 1920 that the first synagogue in the country was built.

FINLAND

In 1808, a quarter of a century before Finland was taken from Sweden by the Russian Tsar Alexander I, there were already some 2,000 Jews living there. Where they came from originally and how they got there is not clear. Suffice it to say they were not allowed to build a synagogue. In 1858, when the Russian government issued a decree which granted former Russian soldiers and sailors the privilege of settling in Finland with their families, this right also was extended to Jewish veterans, many of whom went to live in the principal cities of Finland—in Wiborg, Abbo, Helsingfors and Tamersfors. In 1930 the Jewish population of Finland was about 1,700.

ARTIST

Ernst Abraham Josephson.

Henrik Schuck.

WRITERS

Karl Johan Warburg.

Oscar Levertin.

197

MODERN ITALY

When the victorious *Grande Armée* of Napoleon overran Italy in 1796, the political rule of the Church was temporarily shattered. In each city enthusiastic crowds of Republicans put up a "Liberty Tree." Wearing French tri-colored cockades, they clasped hands and sang the *Carmagnole* of revolutionary France as they danced around the tree. The proclamation issued during the summer of 1796 by the city of Modena was typical of the contemporary recognition of the new status of full equality for the Jews. "Every man is born and remains free, and should fully enjoy all rights. The Jews are citizens, and must be recognized as such in society."

The enthusiasm of the Jews of Italy for the new state of affairs knew no bounds. Everywhere, at all Republican demonstrations, they paid eloquent tribute to the moral meaning of the revolution and to its ideals—liberty, equality and fraternity. Now, for the first time, they were being accepted as the fellow-Italians of their Christian countrymen. A rabbi, for instance, was thenceforth addressed as "citizen rabbi" and even a humble *shamash* (sexton) was respectfully called "citizen *shamash*." Jews were received in all walks of life with open arms. Just as once they had been excluded, now they were welcomed into the Civic Guard in many towns and cities.

Liberation by the French

Wherever the liberating French Army went it singled out the Jewish community for a symbolic demonstration of the concrete meaning of the revolution's ideals. When the French General Robert led his troops into Ferrara, one of his first official acts was to order the Jews of the city to tear off their yellow badges of shame which the Lateran Council had ordered them to wear in 1215. He also directed that the gates of the ghetto be opened wide and that they stay open henceforth. General Berthier took similar action when he declared the city of Rome a republic on February 15, 1798, and requested the Jews to tear off their yellow badges. Two days later, celebrating their liberation, they festooned the ghetto and illuminated it with torchlight. Amidst general rejoicing, they raised up a "Liberty Tree." On February 21, the day after Pope Pius VII had been led a captive from Rome, they again assembled in the heart of the ghetto. They wore tri-colored French cockades and waved Republican flags. Then General Berthier rode up, followed by his staff, and read Napoleon's Proclamation to the Jews granting them full and equal rights.

Even the little town of Rovigo renamed its dismal Jew Street "Free Street." In Venice, as in many large Italian cities, the inhabitants, Christians and Jews alike, celebrated their liberation by destroying the gates and walls of the ghetto.

But the restless and overconfident Napoleon suddenly decided to abandon the campaign in Italy in favor of the conquest of Egypt. The last French soldier had hardly departed before the enemies of the republic emerged to avenge themselves on the Jews for their lyrical support of the Republican cause. All the ghettos were attacked. Rioting and the pillaging of Jewish houses and shops become the patriotic order of the day. Large fines were imposed by a number of municipalities on their Jewish communities. In Siena, as in other places, the "Liberty Trees" were hacked down.

Frustrated in his plan for the conquest of Egypt, Napoleon made a hasty return to Italy in 1800, and once again the "Liberty Trees" went up.

For the next fourteen years the Jews of Italy enjoyed peace and a large measure of equality. Napoleon extended to the Italian Jews the privileges he was planning for the Jews of France. Four leading Italian rabbis were invited to sit in the *Sanhedrin* he ordered convoked in 1807 in Paris: Abraham Vita de Cologna, the Chief Rabbi of Italy; Isaac Benzion Segre, Rabbi of Vercelli; Graziadio Nappi, a doctor rabbi of Cento; and Jacob Israel Karme, Rabbi of Reggio.

Abraham de Cologna, Chief Rabbi of Italy, early 19th century.

Napoleon's crushing defeat at Waterloo, however, proved almost fatal to the Jews of Italy. Pius VII triumphantly returned to Rome and reintroduced the Holy Inquisition. He drove the Jews back into their ghettos in all the Papal States, and stripped them of the civil rights and liberties granted them by the city-republics. Once again, as during the Middle Ages, the Jews were forced to go to church to listen to conversionist sermons, and once more were made to feel the pressures of intimidation that were intended to make them desert their ancient identity.

Attack on the Roman ghetto, early 19th century.

The *Risorgimento*

But new hope blossomed for the Jews of Italy after 1831 when Guiseppe Mazzini launched his *Risorgimento* (Resurrection) movement of liberation. He attracted many young Jews, especially among the educated, to the banner of "Young Italy." His leading propagandists in Piedmont, for example, were a bookseller and a sausage-maker, both Jews. When he led his unsuccessful expedition from Switzerland into Savoy in 1833, the total expenses for the campaign were paid by the wealthy Jew, Todros of Turin. In fact, the poet of the patriotic movement was David Levi, a liberal-minded banker, who composed its famous hymn, dubbed "The *Marseillaise* of the *Risorgimento.*"

The humane spirit of the times aided the struggle, not only for human rights in general but for Jewish rights as well. When Pius IX, whose views were diametrically opposite to those of Pius VII, mounted the throne of Saint Peter's in 1846, he generously recognized the prevailing democratic trends in Europe and rescinded some of the more obnoxious laws and restrictions in force against the Jews. Although he was far from granting them equal rights with Christians, nonetheless, he abolished the compulsory conversionist sermons. He also forbade the degrading practice of forcing Jews to run the gantlet of blows and curses along the Corso during the Roman Carnival.

The lasting effects of their brief experience with Republicanism were clearly discernible among the Italian people. That very Passover Eve, as the Jews of Rome were celebrating the *Seder* commemorating Israel's liberation from the bondage in Egypt, a loud hammering and chopping was heard at the ghetto gates. Many were frightened; they thought it was an attack on the Jewish quarter. It was only a crowd of Republicans beating down the gates. When they learned from their leader, Ciceruacchio, that *Pesach* was a festival of freedom, they decided to help the Jews celebrate it—but in their own way. They formed ranks and paraded to the ghetto. There they battered down the gates which for centuries had turned the quarter into a prison for their Jewish fellow-Italians. The gates never went up again.

Once more the fires of Republican revolution blazed through Italy and through other countries of Europe, sparked by the fall of the French monarchy in 1848. This time the revolt in Italy was transformed into a patriotic struggle of the people to throw off the yoke of the Austrian Hapsburgs. The fervor for the independence of Italy was almost general among Jews. In some communities the rabbis preached recruiting sermons. There was hardly an area of the conflict in which Jews did not figure actively. One of the leaders of the street fighting in Milan during the epic "Five Days" (March 18-22) was the fifteen-year-old Jewish boy, Ciro Finzi. His acts of bravery stirred all Italy. Another Finzi (Giuseppe) was a close associate of Mazzini and one of his principal military commanders.

Another popular leader of the 1848 Revolution was Daniel Manin, commander of the Republican forces in Venice and subsequently head of its first government. Jews fought in the National Guard of Venice, both as officers and as privates. In the Manin Provisional Government there were two Jewish ministers: Leone Pincherle, Minister of Agriculture and Commerce, and Isaac Pesaro Maurogonato, Minister of Finance. When, after the republic's fall, the haughty Austrian general was looking through Maurogonato's precise accounts he exclaimed incredulously: "I could not have believed that this Republican scum would be so competent."

The Republic Is Doomed

When the republic was again proclaimed in Rome by Mazzini and Garibaldi on February 9, 1849, Jews streamed into the city from all over Italy. Jews sat on the City Council.

Hundreds of them joined the National Guard. Mazzini sent a number of Jews in his entourage on important diplomatic missions to various parts of the country and abroad. Several were appointed to command posts in the defense of threatened areas. All efforts, however, proved unavailing. The doom of the republic was sealed the moment the reactionary French government sent strong contingents of Zouaves to help the Pope overthrow the republic. When Garibaldi retreated northward with his hard-pressed troops, Jewish soldiers followed him into his peril. Among the almost legendary "One Thousand" there were eight Jews.

Once more Jews were victims of mob vengeance. For the part they had played in the short-lived republic, they were severely punished. In fact, rabble rousers pointed to them as the principal instigators of the revolution. The formerly liberal Pius IX ordered them back into the ghetto. But the times were more advanced than either the Pope or the reactionaries realized. It was no longer possible to rebuild the walls around the ghetto or to raise up its rusting gates. Except in Rome where papal rule continued to be oppressive to the Jews, in those parts of Italy which had been united under King Victor Emmanuel II's constitutional monarchy in 1859, Jews were accorded considerable equality. Even the papal power in Rome had finally to give way before the popular onslaught against special privilege. Restrictions were abolished on September 20, 1870, and then Roman Jews began to breathe freely.

OPPORTUNITY

It may sound paradoxical that whenever persecution ceased and the Jews enjoyed equal rights they showed a marked tendency toward assimilation. Religious ties proved increasingly less binding, group identity less urgent and a desire to amalgamate with non-Jews more alluring. That is what happened when the doors of opportunity were opened for the Jews of Italy. The incidence of intermarriage became very high, especially in Rome, Florence, Livorno, Milan and other cities. Sometimes mixed marriages outnumbered marriages between Jews. Jews also turned intensely nationalistic, even chauvinistic, as Italians. Local patriotism, for example, induced many Jews to enter the Fiume Legion of the poet-swashbuckler, Gabriele d'Annunzio.

Civil equality was the spring which released the pent-up Jewish intellectual bent in Italy. Jewish youths studied at the universities and many entered the academic and professional fields as scientists, writers, scholars, statesmen, lawyers, doctors and engineers. The number of notable men and women of Jewish origin was disproportionately large for the size of the Jewish population. There were only some forty thousand Jews in Italy when Mussolini seized power.

Explorers

A number of Italian Jews have distinguished themselves as explorers. Baron Franchetti, a relative of the composer, has been one of the principal explorers in the interior of Central Africa. Angelo Castelbolognese explored the Sudan. Eduardo Foa successfully traced the Zambezi River to its source. Aldo Pontremoli was with Nobile on his flight to the North Pole, in 1929, when they both lost their lives.

Scientists

One of the greatest mathematicians and theoretical physicists of modern times was Tullio Levi-Civita. His principal contribution was an absolute differential calculus which proved of fundamental help to Einstein in the development of his theory of relativity. In addition, his studies in geometry, in mechanics and in electrodynamics are considered of enduring value.

Vito Volterra, physicist and mathematician, was noted for his studies on permutable and integro-differential functions.

Other eminent mathematicians were Luigi Cremona and Guido Castelnuovo, whose work in calculus and probability drew wide attention.

Perhaps only a trifle in itself, but a great convenience to all mankind, was the invention of the safety match by Samson Valolera.

Césare Lombroso was noted as a psychiatrist and criminologist.

Writers

There have been a number of gifted literary men of Jewish origin in Italy. Salamone Fiorentino was official Court Poet to the Grand Duke Ferdinand III. Prominent among the writers of the *Risorgimento* were Giuseppe Revere, Tullo Massarani, Eugenio Camerini and Sabatino Lopez. Italo Svevo, especially admired among the older generation of writers, was sometimes called "the Proust of Italian literature."

Perhaps best known outside Italy are the contemporary novelists Alberto Moravia (Pincherle) and Carlo Levi. Other novelists, poets and critics of note are Alberto Cantoni, Angiolo Orvieto, Guido da Verona Pittigrilli, Annie Vivanti, Ida Finzi, Enrico Rocca, Arturo Foa, Cesare Levi and Paolo Milano.

Musicians

The Italian grand opera, as a form of mass entertainment in the theatre, blossomed during the first half of the nineteenth century. Their partial emancipation afforded Jews the normal opportunities for a musical education and for professional careers on the concert and operatic stages and as teachers in the conservatories and universities. However, the Jewish contribution to music in Italy during this period was practically limited to vocalists. One of the greatest singers of the age was the soprano Giuditta Pasta. Donizetti composed *Anna Bolena*

for her in 1830, and Bellini created *Sonnambula* and *Norma* especially for her in 1831. The sisters, Giuditta Grisi and Giulia Grisi, were the chief adornments of the Italian opera stage in their time. Giulia was considered the foremost soprano of her generation, and was greatly admired by Rossini, Bellini and Donizetti. When she made her début in Paris in 1843 in Bellini's *Norma,* an emotional music critic reported that the audience "did not applaud, but wept, sobbed, groaned, trembled, cried out and barely was able to breathe from delight and grief."

There have been a number of minor Jewish composers in recent times, of whom the best known is Baron Alberto Franchetti, a member of the Rothschild banking family. He is the composer of the successful operas *Germania* and *Christoforo Columbo.* Frederico Consolo, a famous violinist and a pupil of Franz Liszt in composition, wrote several violin concerti and the *Hebrew Melodies* for the violin.

One of the most talented of contemporary Italian composers is Mario Castelnuovo-Tedesco, who has written a considerable amount of music on Jewish themes employing traditional Jewish idioms.

Artists

While the continuity of the great Renaissance tradition in Italian art was broken during the nineteenth century, there has been a minor resurgence on the part of several Jewish artists in recent times. Jewish painters, for example, have been largely responsible for the modern trend in Italian art. Serafino de Tivoli is known as the founder of Italian impressionism. Most creative and original of all Italian modernists was the painter Amadeo Modigliani. A foremost exponent of the art of the School of Paris, he died young and in the direst poverty in Paris. Although Enrico Glicenstein was born in Poland and died in the United States, his most fruitful period as a sculptor and graphic artist was during his long residence in Italy. Arrigo Minerbi was another sculptor of distinction.

Statesmen

Ever since the *Risorgimento* the Jews of Italy have had important roles in the government. Cavour's secretary, Isaac Artom, was not only his closest co-worker in the struggle for a united Italy but the first Jew to become a senator. Sansone d'Ancona was Minister of Finance and Public Works, Gabriele Pincherle served as chairman of the "Council of State." Leone Wollemberg, who established the first rural savings banks in Italy, served as Finance Minister from 1900 to 1903. General Giuseppe Ottolenghi, a veteran of Garibaldi's campaign of liberation, occupied the War Ministry from 1902 to 1903.

Undoubtedly, the outstanding Italian statesman since Cavour was Luigi Luzzatti. A noted economist and writer, he was a liberal in his social views and strongly believed in co-operatives and people's banks to improve the living standards of the poor. He founded the *Banco Populare* in Milan and opened the first cooperative store in Italy. The poet D'Annunzio grandiloquently remarked that with the founding of the people's banks, Luzzatti had succeeded in "spiritualizing" the base power of gold. Luzzatti was Finance Minister five times, Minister of Agriculture once, and Prime Minister from 1909 to 1911.

Sidney Sonnino, a half-Jew and a conservative in his poli-

SCIENTISTS

Vito Volterra.

Césare Lombroso.

WRITER

Carlo Levi.

BALLERINA

Carlotta Grisi.

SINGERS

Giuditta Grisi.

Giuditta Pasta.

ARTIST

Amedeo Modigliani.

JURIST

Ludovico Mortara.

JURIST

Vittorio Polacco.

Luigi Luzzatti.

STATESMEN

Gen. Giuseppe Ottolenghi.

Ernesto Nathan.

tics, was twice Prime Minister, in 1906 and in 1909-10. In 1915-19 he headed the Foreign Ministry.

Ernesto Nathan, a liberal and a Mason, was one of the most popular and respected mayors modern Catholic Rome ever had. He filled that office for six years beginning in 1907.

Ludovico Mortara, the son of a rabbi, was an eminent jurist who systematized civil law procedure in Italy. He was President of the Italian Supreme Court and also served as Minister of Justice.

Another celebrated Italian jurist was Vittorio Polacco, an authority on civil law and rector of the University of Padua.

In the fateful year Mussolini led the Fascists' march on Rome, Carlo Schanzer was Foreign Minister in the liberal Facta government. There were, besides, ten senators and eleven deputies who were Jewish. Until Mussolini took over Hitler's anti-Semitic and racist policy in July, 1938, he had a number of close collaborators among the Jews and some were prominent in the Fascist Party. The official political journal of Fascismo, *Gerarchia,* was edited by Margheritta Sarfatti.

Guido Jung, who had served at the Versailles Peace Conference in 1919 as financial adviser to the Italian delegation, later joined the Fascist Party. He took part in the march on Rome and served as Italian Minister of Finance in 1932-35. With Hitler's ascendancy in Italian affairs he was dismissed by Mussolini.

Scholars

To scholarship as well, Italian Jews have made basic contributions. A classic writer on Italian literature, the theatre and popular poetry was Alessandro d'Ancona. Salomone Morpurgo, curator of the National Library in Florence, was an authority on medieval Italian literature. Emilio Morpurgo was the rector of the University of Padua. Samuel Romanin was the foremost historian of Venice. I. B. Supino was a specialist on medieval sculpture. One of the most respected Italian philologists and a keen student of dialects was Graziadio Isaia Ascoli.

201

JEWISH LIFE

Although legally the compulsory ghetto had been abolished some time before, the habit and tradition of living together continued unbroken for thousands of Jews in the large cities of Italy. Living in close proximity they found it easier to perpetuate their religious customs and traditional ways of life.

MUSSOLINI AND THE JEWS

The most cynical example in modern history of the employment of anti-Semitism as a political weapon of expediency was furnished by Benito Mussolini. Il Duce, insecure in

The ark, synagogue
in Rome.

Pulpit and reading-desk
of the Florence
Synagogue.

his dictatorship, was in need of the help he hoped he might receive from the Jews. Accordingly, when some leaders of his Fascist Party started their inflammatory anti-Semitic agitation and the Jews of Italy showed signs of alarm, he gave an official audience to Chief Rabbi Angelo Sacerdoti of Rome. After the audience, he issued the following communiqué: "Professor Angelo Sacerdoti brought to the attention of His Excellency, Benito Mussolini, the fact that the anti-Semitic parties abroad seek in some manner to find a greater force in their anti-Semitic policy. To accomplish this end they point to a pretended anti-Jewish attitude in Italian Fascism upon which they would like to model themselves. In reply to this, the head of the government formally declared to Professor Angelo Sacerdoti that Italian Fascism has never sought to follow an anti-Semitic policy. In fact, he deplored that anti-Jewish organizations should in such a manner exploit the influence of the Fascist idea."

Not long after, on October 30, 1930, Mussolini promulgated by royal decree a law merging all the Jewish communities of Italy into a Fascist "corporation." It was a compulsory union which represented, without a single exception, all Italians of

Jewish extraction. In this way it became an official agency of the Fascist government. Article 35 of the law which implemented this Jewish corporation made it plain that Mussolini desired the Jews to serve as his unpaid political propagandists and "ambassadors of good will" for Fascism. It required spe-

Jewish market in Rome.

cifically that the "Union of Jewish Communities of Italy" take part in the "general religious and social activity of world Jewry . . . and maintain spiritual and cultural contacts with Jewish communities abroad, especially with those which have close traditional relations with Italian Jewry and with Italy."

When the Nazis seized power in Germany in 1933 and Hitler translated his notorious racial theories against the Jews into law, Mussolini mocked at him in a speech at Bari in September, 1934: "Thirty centuries of existence allow the Italians to look with some pity on certain doctrines which are preached beyond the Alps by those who were illiterate when we had Caesar, Virgil and Augustus."

Only several years later, when Mussolini invaded Abyssinia, he discovered that he required Hitler's help in overcoming the

Mussolini inaugurates the Palestine Pavilion at the Bari Fair
in 1934.

"inferior" Ethiopians. He then turned chameleon, flatteringly tried to imitate the demagoguery of his stronger fellow-dictator, and took on his ghoulish brand of anti-Semitism. Now the proud descendant of Caesar, Virgil and Augustus began to sing the same strident tune that was being sung "beyond the Alps" with a synthetic hatred and abuse of the Jews. With equal opportunism he next wooed the Arab countries, hoping that they would join him in a holy crusade against England. To this end, too, he used his melodramatic excoriation of the Jews as a siren song. Mussolini introduced into Italy the racist Nuremberg Laws of Hitler. With his overthrow these laws were nullified, and the Jews of Italy were restored to their free and equal status.

SWITZERLAND

As *servi camerae* to the Holy Roman emperors, Jews were settled in their own communities in Switzerland: in Basle (1213), Bern (1259), St. Gall (1268), Zurich (1273) and Lucerne (1299). Jews paid the emperor their "golden *pfennig*" for protection, they wore the sugar-loaf *Judenhut* and lived on separate streets in the towns and cities. Principally money lenders, they brought down upon themselves the dislike of the populace. Untold miseries were their lot during the bloody aftermath of the Black Plague. Many lost their lives in consequence of ritual murder accusations.

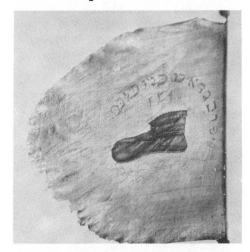

Banner of the shoemakers' guild of Bern, with Hebrew inscription, 1540.

Jews were expelled from various cities of Switzerland during the fifteenth and sixteenth centuries, so that, finally, by 1622, there were none left in the country. It was only during the first half of the nineteenth century that Jews started returning to Switzerland, most of them coming from France, Belgium and Germany. They enjoyed few rights at first, emancipation coming only in 1874. Nonetheless, a non-

Burial in the Jewish cemetery between Laengnau and Endinger, 1768.

violent anti-Semitism has existed in Switzerland. *Shechitah* (Jewish ritual slaughtering of animals) was considered unlawful until very recent years. When there was a marked inflow of Jews from East European countries after World War I, they received some discriminatory treatment, restrictive legislation against them having been introduced in 1921.

During the Nazi agitation and rise to power there was an upsurge of violent anti-Semitism in Switzerland, but it failed of its objective because of the firm stand taken against it by the Swiss government. This was demonstrated during the trial of the twenty-six-year-old medical student, David Frankfurter, who in February, 1936, had shot and killed Wilhelm Gustloff, the Swiss Nazi *führer*. The German government, as well as the local Nazis, demanded the death sentence, but despite all threats and pressures the Swiss court sentenced the Jewish student to eighteen years in prison.

Trial of David Frankfurter.

Thousands of Jewish refugees began arriving from Nazi Germany. The German government clamored for their extradition, but the Swiss stood firm on the rights of asylum traditional in their country. In 1939 and 1940 additional thousands of Jews belonging to the French and Polish armies found a temporary refuge in Switzerland.

There are some twenty thousand Jews today in Switzerland, about a third of them living in Zurich. Other Jewish communities are in Geneva, Basle, Bern, Waadt and St. Gall. Jews are active in industry and commerce, especially in textiles, silk, watches and embroideries. A number have also been eminent in the universities, in journalism, literature and the sciences. Camill Guggenheim was elected to the *Bundesgericht* (Supreme Court) in 1929. Of Jewish descent are the two eminent scientists, both Nobel Prize winners, Wolfgang Pauli (1945), physicist, and Tadeus Reichstein (1950), medical researcher.

THE BALKANS

ROMANIA

The Jewish Community

We can only infer that there were Jews in Romania (ancient Dacia) during the one hundred sixty-seven years of Roman rule which began with Emperor Trajan's conquest. There are some historians who even assert that during the eighth century C. E. Moldavia and Wallachia, which were then separate kingdoms but which later constituted Romania, were vassals of the Jewish kingdom of Khazaria.

The history of the Jews in Romania is indeed nebulous until the fifteenth century when the Turkish sultans became their overlords. Jewish communities, however, became legally permissible only beginning with the middle of the seventeenth century. Since the social system of Romania greatly resembled that of the primitive feudal society of Russia, the Jews of Romania were faced with the same problems as their fellow-Jews in the neighboring country. There ruled over them "a *Staroste* of the Jews," a Christian official whose sole responsibility was to see that his charges paid all their taxes. However, in strictly religious and communal matters, each *kahal* (Jewish community) was allowed its own self-government.

When, in 1648, Bogdan Chmielnicki led a Cossack uprising for independence aganst Poland, his tidal wave of atrocities against the Jews in the Ukraine overflowed into Romania. The eighteenth century and the first half of the nineteenth witnessed many bloody clashes between the Russians and the Turks. Especially bitter were those of 1769-74 and 1806-12, which brought much suffering to the Jews of the two Romanian principalities.

Jewish communities were already well established during the middle of the eighteenth century in Bucharest, Galatz, Berlad, Jassy, Roman and Bacau, when the Jews of Russian Poland were invited to settle in Moldavia. They were expected to found new towns and to quicken the economic development of the country. Unusual inducements were offered them: land

Scene in the Jewish farm colony "Alexandren" in Bessarabia, Romania, before World War II.

on which to build their synagogues, religious schools and ritual bathhouses, free cemetery plots, and above all, several years' exemption from all taxes. Lured by these promises, thousands of enterprising Russian and Polish Jews came to settle among the Romanians. In Moldavia alone they founded sixty-three towns and villages.

These Russian Jews formed the yeast in the dough of economic progress in Romania. The peasants and small townspeople found them indispensable, because the Jewish merchants and shopkeepers provided them with the prime necessities of living. They sold them spun cotton, all kinds of iron utensils, rope, earthenware, leather boots, pipe tobacco and snuff, salt and rice. Enterprising Jewish manufacturers initiated small-scale industries. Unfortunately for the Jews, their prominence in the retail trade, for which they had been especially courted, proved in the end a source of infinite grief to them. These shopkeepers were conveniently used by the feudal *voivods* (princes) and lesser nobles as scapegoats to divert from themselves the antagonism of the rebellious peasants who, as in Russia and Poland, were still under the yoke of serfdom. There were excesses against the Jews in 1801. In Bucharest one hundred twenty-eight Jews were killed. Synagogues were ordered closed by the authorities. Repressions of every kind took place.

Hope burgeoned for the Jews after liberal revolutions broke out all over Europe in 1848. In Romania an egalitarian rebellion was launched by the Bratianu brothers who had been personally influenced by the French liberal revolutionaries, Lamartine and Louis Blanc. Among the catch-all slogans they threw out to win the support of the people was "the emancipation of the Jews and the granting of citizenship rights to all compatriots whatever faith they may profess." Ion Bratianu's so-called "liberal" ideals were shown in their true colors when he became Prime Minister. Addressing the Romanian Parliament in 1866, he abused the Jews as "that leprosy" and "social wound" on the body of Romania, an affliction which called for drastic measures.

The Galatz Incident

That same year there occurred in the city of Galatz an incident which dramatized for the whole world the medievalism of the political program of the Bratianu government. Juridi-

Survivors around the bier of one of the victims at Galatz.

cally, the Jews of Romania were never considered as Romanians but as aliens, notwithstanding the fact that they had lived in the country for centuries. The organic law of 1834 stipulated that all Jews who were either "vagabonds" or "who have no useful trade" should be expelled from the country. The elasticity of the wording of the law gave the authorities all the loopholes they needed to rid themselves of whatever Jews they did not like.

In 1866, for example, the city officials of Galatz designated certain Jewish inhabitants as "vagabonds." They then forced them into a boat which carried them to the Turkish shore across the Danube. The Turks promptly sent the Jews back. And so they were being ferried from one river bank to the other until, finally, the Romanian officials lost patience. They issued the order: "Out with the Jews into the heathen land of the Turks—or else into the water with them!" When once again the Turks sent them back, this order was carried out to the letter. The "vagabonds" were flung into the river, but seeing their plight, the "heathen" Turks took pity on them and pulled them out of the water. But two had drowned.

This inhuman action of the Romanians aroused wide indignation throughout Europe and led to the fall of the Bratianu government.

Boys of Kishinev being taught locksmithing in a trade school operated by ORT, before World War II.

Jew-Baiting a State Policy

Ostensibly, the Congress of Berlin in 1878 had granted Jews equal rights. Instead of rights, the Romanian government bombarded its Jews with a bewildering number of discriminatory laws. Some two hundred laws were enacted to keep Jews out of various trades, businesses and professions. Jews could no longer live in the villages but were forced into the overcrowded ghettos in the cities. It was the terror of starvation which drove some 125,000 to emigrate, most of them to the United States. By 1904 there were only 70,000 left in Romania.

A lack of opportunity for cultural pursuits led many Romanian Jews to emigrate. One of these who achieved international repute as painter and draftsman was Jules Pascin. In his style he was a product of the School of Paris. (Portrait bust by Benno Elkan, 1910.)

Once again the barbarous treatment of the Jews of Romania became dramatized for the world in 1900. Four thousand starving Jews organized themselves into a great emigrant band. They were formed into groups, each bearing an identifying name. One group called itself "The Wandering Jew," a second, "The Despairing," a third, "The Walkers." They trudged on foot from Moldavia across all of Europe to the port city of Hamburg where, with the help of Jewish relief organizations, they embarked for the United States. Their

wretchedness, their emaciated appearance and ragged clothes aroused compassion and indignation everywhere they went.

Abraham Goldfaden, the "Father" of the modern Yiddish theatre. Although an Ukrainian who spent his last years in the United States, he established the first professional Yiddish theatre in Romania with a troupe made up of Romanian Jews.

In the United States the incident drew many protests. Public meetings were held in New York, Philadelphia and other cities, denouncing the Romanian government. On August 11, 1902, John Hay, the Secretary of State, addressed a diplomatic note to all the powers who had signed the Berlin Treaty of 1878. He accused Romania of violating every provision of the Treaty by its persecution of the Jews. The Treaty powers, however, discreetly ignored the protest.

In 1919, upon the conclusion of the World War, the Peace Treaty of Versailles, to which Romania was also a signatory, stipulated: "Romania undertakes to recognize as fully privileged Romanian subjects and without any formality the Jews who live in all the Romanian territories and who have no other nationality."

Anti-Semitism, however, feeding on the severe economic crisis which had been brought on by the war, became a vast political movement throughout Europe by 1920. The National Christian League of Students, led by the notorious demagogues Professor Alexander Cuza and Octavian Goga, was established in 1921 in Romania. Another rabble-rouser, Codreanu, later an intimate of Hitler, organized the Iron Guard, a military action group modeled on the Nazi Storm Troops. With the sanction of King Carol and the blessing of the Church, anti-Semitism in Romania became a legal and patriotic movement.

The years that followed were turbulent with bloody anti-Semitic riots on the streets. Jewish students and professors were flung bodily out of the classrooms, shopkeepers were beaten and killed, homes were burned and synagogues were desecrated. Trains and trolley-cars were regularly boarded by Iron Guardists who severely beat Jewish passengers.

It was under such circumstances that more than 750,000 Jews managed to stay alive until they were engulfed by the Nazi deluge.

BULGARIA

Long Sojourn

Except for Greece and the Aegean Islands, the earliest settlement of Jews in the Balkans was in Bulgaria, whose ancient name was Moesia. Josephus mentions it as one of the places which in his day had Jewish settlements. Probably the first Jewish community was founded at Nicopolis (modern Nikopol) in the Roman Emperor Trajan's time. Upon the collapse of the Jewish Kingdom of Khazaria during the tenth century c. e., many Jews fled for refuge to Bulgaria. When the latter country was absorbed by the Byzantine Empire in 967, there was an additional influx of new Jewish arrivals from the other parts of the empire. They established communities in Nikopolis, Vidin, Sofia and Silistria. Two centuries later Jewish merchants from Italy were already plying an active trade between Bulgaria and Venice. They opened trading posts in several Bulgarian cities, most of all in Vidin. Jewish refugees, banished from Hungary in 1367, swelled the Jewish population in Vidin, Nicopolis, Plevna and Trnovo. Finally, when the Turks made themselves masters of the country in 1396, because of their milder Mohammedan rule, thousands of Jews flocked to Bulgaria from all the Balkan principalities.

The migratory movements of the Jews in the Mediterranean area have been little short of fantastic. They present a pattern bewildering in its complexities. After the expulsion of the

In the year 1335 a Jewess named Sarah became the wife of Tsar Ivan Alexander of Bulgaria. Before she mounted the throne she went through the rite of baptism and had her name changed to Theodora. Her royal title was "Newly Enlightened Tsarina and Sole Support of All the Bulgarians and Greeks." Her daughter Tamar became the wife of the Sultan Murad I of Turkey. Her son, Tsar Ivan Chichman, succeeded his father to part of the kingdom. Like his father, he, too, was very friendly to the Jews and was solicitous for the refugees from Hungary. (Painting, in Byzantine style, of the Tsarina Theodora, her husband, Tsar Ivan Alexander, and their two children.)

Jews from Spain in 1492 and later from Portugal, the identifiable Jewish strains in Bulgaria, and similarly in other Balkan countries, were: Greek, Turkish, Italian, French, Russian, German, Austrian, Bohemian, Polish, Romanian, Crimean, Khazarian and, of course, Spanish and Portuguese.

Depressed Status of Bulgarian Jews

When the Russo-Turkish War broke out in 1877, the Jews of Sofia organized a volunteer corps to defend the city against Turkish bands of irregulars. Their part in the defense of the capital won them high praise from the general community. Eight years later, during the Serbian-Bulgarian clash, the bravery the Bulgarian Jews displayed on the battlefield

The Great Synagogue in Sofia.

earned for them in a royal proclamation the compliment that they had deported themselves, in defense of their country, as "true descendants of the ancient Maccabeans."

The emptiness of this praise became apparent in the alarming increase of Jew-baiting that traveled in epidemic force from neighboring Russia into Bulgaria. This came in the wake of the anti-Semitic May Laws decreed by Tsar Alexander III in 1881. Bulgarian Jews soon began to lose their civil rights and their jobs. Ritual murder charges became commonplace. Mob riots began in 1884 and did not cease until 1904. By 1890 Jews no longer could maintain themselves. The liberally phrased Constitution of 1879 had been full of high-sounding assurances to the Jews that they would enjoy the fullest equality in the new independent Kingdom of Bulgaria. But so virulent was the harassment of both official and unofficial anti-Semitism that many Jews emigrated, mostly to Anatolia in Asiatic Turkey.

The Synagogue in Samacoff, with its unusual feature—the two women's galleries.

Matters did not improve any after World War I. The Home Guard, nakedly murderous in its proclaimed intentions toward the Jews, started its Jew-baiting campaign in 1925. It abused the Jews as being aliens, and demanded their expulsion from the country. This agitation kept pace with the growth of Hitlerism in Germany.

In the 1940 census, out of Bulgaria's 6,100,000 total population, there were 48,000 Jews: 29,000 in Sofia, 7,000 in Philipopolis and 5,000 in Rustchuk. There were smaller communities in Vidin, Yambol, Tatar-Bazarjik, Dubnitza, Kustendil and Shumla.

The assimilation of the Jews in Bulgaria was never encour-

Jewish Home for the Aged (*Sephardic*) in Sofia.

aged by the Bulgarian government at any time. In consequence, their economic level was never high. About three-quarters were shopkeepers, jobbers and small manufacturers, mostly in the garment, leather and furniture trade. A third of the Jewish laboring population was employed in the clothing industry.

In the cultural field as well, the Jews of Bulgaria made hardly any advances. Ninety-seven per cent, in a recent census, gave as their mother-tongue *Giudezmo*, or "Jewish." By "Jewish" they mean Judeo-Spanish or *Ladino*. Forty per cent *also* spoke Bulgarian. A small number claimed some proficiency in Hebrew and in French. This would indicate that a majority of Bulgarian Jews were forced to live in linguistic and cultural isolation from the rest of the nation.

Communities

At the helm of the spiritual affairs of the Jewish community stood the Grand Rabbi in Sofia. In Philipopolis was the headquarters of the Central Jewish Consistory which looked after all the communal interest of Bulgarian Jewry. The Grand Rabbi was elected by the thirty-three Jewish communities of the country and was confirmed by royal ukase.

Grand Rabbi
David Pipano.

YUGOSLAVIA

Medieval Times

The settlement of the Jews in Yugoslavia, the country of the Serbs, Croats and Slovenes, had already taken place in antiquity. They are known to have been in the province of Illyria in late Roman times, because archaeologists some years ago unearthed in the vicinity of Spalato in Dalmatia a Jewish cemetery which dates back to the third century C.E.

In any case, by the Middle Ages Jewish communities were well rooted in this region. The community in Zagreb, which had been founded during the thirteenth century, won a number of proselytes among Christians. There were Jews in Slavonia during the twelfth century, and there is an extant record from the year 1213 when the Jews of Ljubljana rebuilt the synagogue which their enemies had burned to the ground.

The principal Jewish settlement in medieval times was in Maribor (Marburg). There the Jews lived in their own quarter, provided with all the dismal trappings of the medieval

The old Belgrade Synagogue.

ghetto: walls, a gate, a Jews' tower in which to retreat in time of attack, and the inevitable *Judenmeister* (Elder). Nevertheless, the Talmudic scholars—Israel Isserlein, Amschel of Marburg and Isaac Sarffati—flourished there.

There was, furthermore, a considerable increase of Jewish settlement in Serbia after the Turks conquered Belgrade in

Interior of Zagreb Synagogue, destroyed by Fascists in 1941.

1521. Many exiles from Spain and Portugal found a haven in the towns of Serbia and Bosnia. Before long, speaking centers of Spanish-Portuguese *Sephardic* Jews arose in Monastir, Dubrovnik, Sarajevo, Travnik, Belgrade and other towns.

The Jewish community in Belgrade was founded in 1546 by the Jewish Duke of Naxos. As refugees from Germany, and especially from nearby Hungary, flocked there, the Belgrade

Sarajevo Synagogue.

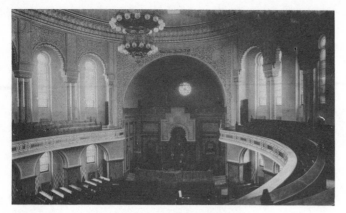

Interior of the Sarajevo Synagogue.

community began to figure prominently in the Jewish world.

Ashkenazic Yiddish-speaking Jews from central and eastern Europe went to Belgrade only after it had been conquered by Prince Eugene of Savoy. With the peace of 1718, Belgrade was returned to Turkey. Oddly enough, Saloniki always remained the chief center for the Jews in the countries of the southern Slavs.

Old graves of rabbis in the cemetery of Spalato in Dalmatia.

Emancipation

The emancipation of the Jews of Yugoslavia was legally provided for by the Peace Treaty of Berlin in 1878. But, like most treaties, its provisions remained largely unfulfilled. Nevertheless, the Jews of the region were treated less harshly than in other Slavic countries. It was as late as December, 1918, that the Kingdom of Yugoslavia was created by the union of Serbia, Montenegro, Croatia, Dalmatia, Bosnia, Herzegovina and the Hungarian district of Banat. Its constitution

Joseph Weissmann, the chief cantor and a professor of music in Zagreb, was murdered by the Nazis, together with 60,000 other Jews of Yugoslavia during World War II. Of the small number of survivors, the majority settled in Israel; about 3,500 Jews remained, of whom almost 2,000 live in Belgrade.

fervidly granted Jews full and equal rights. Some of these rights never materialized.

In 1931 the Jewish population of Yugoslavia was 76,654. The largest number, 12,315, lived in Zagreb; 8,389 in Belgrade; Sarajevo had 8,090; and Subotica, 5,060. Altogether, there were 117 organized Jewish communities in the country. The majority of Jews engaged in trade and commerce, as shopkeepers, clerks, small manufacturers and factors. Jews were well represented in the professions and in government service, and there was a sizable number of factory workers as well as some farmers. Here, as almost everywhere else, they were self-consciously Jewish and active in the Zionist movement. They maintained all the well-known features of East European Jewish community life.

Moshe Pijade, Vice-President of the Presidium of the Yugoslav government, which came into power under Marshal Tito after World War II. Theoretician of the Yugoslav Communist Party, he had a large share in severing connections with the Soviet Union and the Cominform and tying up Yugoslavia with the West.

GREECE

Jews were living in Athens three centuries before the Common Era, and in Epirus, uninterruptedly as a community for almost two thousand years. Philo, who lived two generations before the destruction of the Second Temple, mentioned that there were Jewish communities worshipping in synagogues in the kingdoms of Macedonia, Thessaly and Corinth. Although Jewish life flourished in those places under the Greeks and the Romans, it received a severe setback when Byzantium embraced Christianity. Thousands of Jews were then forcibly converted to the new religion.

The tides of fortune changed again when the Turks captured Constantinople in 1453 and established the Ottoman Empire in the Balkans, including Greece. Attracted by the mildness of Mohammedan rule, Jews who were persecuted in Christian countries came to settle in Greece. After the expulsion from Spain, in 1492, a great many Jews from that country found havens of refuge in Saloniki, Larissa and other places. During the early nineteenth century a sizable community of Italian Jews settled in Corfu, where they still speak more Italian than Greek. In Thrace and Macedonia, however, *Ladino,* or Judeo-Spanish, is the vernacular. In Athens and in Crete, Jews prefer Greek.

The Greek Wars of Liberation, which began in 1821, finally led to the overthrow of Ottoman rule. Yet, while the liberation was very precious to the Christian Greeks, it brought mistreatment and misunderstanding for those Greeks who were Jews. For example, when the Turkish janizaries were putting down the revolt of the Greeks, they killed the Patriarch Gregory in cold blood. They then forced several Jews to throw the body into the sea. When the news of this outrage reached the Greeks of Morea, it was not the Turks but the Jews who were blamed and massacred almost to the last man. This blood-letting marked the beginning of anti-Jewish excesses that have not yet come to an end in Greece and have led to the emigration of thousands of Jews.

Saloniki

The Peace Treaty of Versailles, after World War I, gave Saloniki to Greece. With it went the city's 60,000 Jews, thus raising the Jewish population of the country to 125,000. Even while Saloniki still belonged to Turkey, there was constant rioting on the streets between Jews and Greeks. The ritual-murder slander was monotonously brought up.

These provocative acts were not accidental. The Greek Nationalist movement, which had been initiated by Prime Minister Venizelos, had adopted as its battlecry: "Greece for the Greeks!" The fact that Jews had been living for more than two thousand years in Greece apparently did not earn them the right to be considered Greeks. Petty harassments were carried on by the authorities with the purpose of publicly

A view of the Saloniki ghetto from off-shore in the harbor. The Jews of Saloniki follow trades unlike those taken up by Jews in other communities. They are principally occupied with the maritime trade as ship-builders and chandlers, as dock and harbor workers, and as sailors, pilots, etc. This explains why the Jewish quarter lies along the quays of the harbor.

emphasizing the distinction between Greek Christians and Greek Jews. For example, Jews were forbidden to wear the *fez* or *tarboush*—the national headgear—and their cemeteries were ordered destroyed, including the grave of Amatus Lusitanus, the most celebrated physician of his day in Europe.

Dr. Koretz, the Chief Rabbi of Greece, addressing Jewish soldiers in the Greek Army.

Jewish celebration in Thessalonika in 1926, with a Greek-Orthodox churchman as guest of honor.

The return of one and a half million Greeks to the mainland, beginning in 1922, had a depressing effect on the economic situation of the Jews of Saloniki. Competition in commerce and in the trades became so severe that thousands of Jews, already harassed by petty official discriminations, found themselves deprived of their means of livelihood. The rate of impoverishment among them was so great that in 1935 the Jewish community was obliged to provide 11,000 Jews, twenty per cent of its members, with *matzohs* for Passover. This explains why, until the outbreak of World War II, there was a steady exodus of Jews from Saloniki and from other Greek cities to the United States, Latin America, Palestine, Italy and France.

TURKEY

There were colonies of Jews under the Christian Byzantine emperors, during the first centuries c. e., in Constantinople, Thrace and Asia Minor. With the advent of the Mohammedan Turks during the fourteenth century, the lot of the Jew, hitherto full of tribulation, greatly improved, especially under the benign rule of Suleiman the Magnificent. Jews were encouraged to settle everywhere in the empire, especially in Anatolia and in Brussa. Thousands of merchants and traders were induced to come when Bayazid II (1481-1512) was sultan, since he was anxious to develop the economy of his domain and to keep Turkish culture abreast of that of the rest of Europe.

A Jewish physician in 16th-century Turkey.

The new immigrants came from many countries, but mostly from Spain and the Crimea. The sultan had issued very cordial invitations to former *Marranos* from Spain. As new Christians they had risen to high military rank in the Spanish army, and the sultan, therefore, was eager to engage them to teach advanced military science to his officers. The *Marranos* also introduced into Turkey the use of gunpowder and the manufacture of cannon.

Left. Merchant, Turkey, 16th century. *Right.* A police officer, 1890's.

The Jewish Duke of Naxos

Some of these Jews rose to eminence in the affairs of Turkey. Suleiman the Magnificent had many Jewish advisers.

A Grand Vizier. During the 19th century a small number of Jews prospered in the service of the Sultans of Turkey. One of these was Kiamil Pasha. He became Grand Vizier to Abdul Hamid but at the price of becoming a Mohammedan.

Prominent among them were the court physician Hamon and Solomon Ashkenazi, the brilliant financial expert and Jewish leader. There was also a Jewish woman, Esther Kiera, upon whose counsel the sultan leaned. The Jew whose fortunes prospered most was the able banker and administrator, Don

Rahlo Jammele, a well-known Jewish dancer of Constantinople in the 1890's.

Joseph Nassi, a former *Marrano* from Portugal. The sultan rewarded him for his personal services with a gift of a strip of land, along the sea of Tiberias in Palestine, which included the town of Tiberias. He told Don Joseph he was free to colonize the area with as many Jews as he liked and to govern them as he pleased. When Suleiman died in 1566, his successor Selim II elevated Don Joseph to the rank of Duke of Naxos and of the Cyclade Islands. Thenceforth, Don Joseph opened his decrees with the formula: "We, Duke of the Aegean Sea, Lord of Naxos."

Until Saloniki was transferred to Greece it served as the chief Jewish center in the Ottoman Empire. Its Jewish population then was approximately 60,000. In 1904 the Jewish community of Constantinople counted some 65,000 Jews, Smyrna (Ismir) 25,000 and Adrianople, 17,000. As late as 1914, there were more than 400,000 Jews in the empire. Yet only thirteen years later this number had dwindled to 80,000, a decline which was caused by the growth of a virulent form of nationalism under the leadership of Kemal Ataturk. Jews, along with other ethnic and religious minority groups in Turkey, were persecuted and the Zionist movement was outlawed and suppressed. This led to a mass-migration of Jews. The 1927 census revealed that only 55,592 Jews remained in European Turkey; Asia Minor was left with 26,280.

Chief Rabbi Haim Nahum, elected to his post in 1909. The religious head of the Jews of Turkey is known as the *Chacham Bashi* (Chief Sage).

LATIN AMERICA

MEXICO

The records of the Inquisition in Mexico reveal that more than nine hundred trials for the "Judaizing heresy" were brought against *Marranos* in that country during the sixteenth and seventeenth centuries. This would clearly prove that there was a large *Marrano* population in Mexico during that period. It is known that one *Marrano*, the shipbuilder Hernando Alonso who came in the train of Cortez, was rewarded by Cortez with a large grant of land for his part in the conquest of Mexico City in 1521. But only seven years later, he was charged with practicing Judaism in secret and was burned in an *auto-da-fé*.

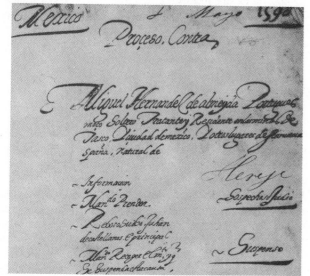

Record of the trial of Miguel Hernandez de Almeida by the Inquisition in Mexico, 1590.

The most noted of all the Mexican *Marranos* was the Conquistador Luis de Carvajal, to whom King Philip II of Spain had given patents to explore and govern an area which today would extend from Tampico in Mexico to San Antonio in

Mariana de Carabajal, accused of the "Judaising heresy," burned in an *auto-da-fé* in Mexico City, 1601.

Texas. Accused, finally, of the secret practice of Judaism, he was tried and exiled in 1590. His nephew, bearing the same name, was burned at the stake in an *auto-da-fé* in 1596. More than a hundred other *Marranos* met a similar fate at the hands of the Inquisition during that decade. Incredibly

Three leaders of the Institute for Mexican-Israeli Cultural Relations. *Left to right*: Alfonso Francisco Ramirez, a justice of the Supreme Court of Mexico; Dr. Adolfo Fastlicht, a representative of the Jewish Agency for Israel; Vincente Donoso, President of the Pro-Palestine Committee of Bolivia.

enough, there are some 3,000 Indians in Mexico today who claim descent from those early *Marranos*.

In 1910 there were 10,000 Jews in Mexico, largely of German, Austrian and Levantine stock. There was also a sizable number of American Jews engaged in various business enterprises. After World War I, when the United States established its quota restrictions, Mexico proved a hospitable haven to immigrants from Poland and Mediterranean countries.

There are some 25,000 Jews in Mexico today. Four-fifths (many of them German refugees) live in Mexico City. There are smaller communities in Guadalajara and Monterey, and scattered groups in other cities.

BRAZIL

Jewish association with the destiny of Brazil has been intimate. Figuring in the very discovery of the land was a baptized Polish Jew who, under his assumed name of Gaspar de Gama (given him in India by his patron, the explorer Vasco de Gama), served both as pilot and interpreter for Pedro Alvares de Cabral when the latter first sighted Brazil in the year 1500. In 1503 a curious flotilla of six tiny vessels filled with *Marranos* arrived in a Brazilian harbor. They were escaping to the New World from the Inquisition and their leader was the *Marrano* navigator, Fernando de Noronha, after whom the island of Fernando de Noronha is named.

Further evidence that Jews figured prominently in Brazil's early history is furnished by a map of 1525 which shows the Guanabana River under its old Jewish name—Rio de los Judios. In fact, one of the principal founders of the cities of São Paulo and Santos, in 1531, was the shipwrecked *Marrano* Joao Rimalho who married the daughter of the local Indian chief Tybirici. In this connection, there have been persistent reports of *Marrano* and Indian communities (in the inaccessible interior of Brazil) which cling to certain religious practices and customs that seem to be Jewish.

The *Marrano* newcomers were highly regarded in Brazil and had a large share in its initial economic development. They were among the first to exploit the natural resources of the country. They introduced the new cultivation of sugar cane from the island of Madeira. They helped establish the tobacco industry, and were among the first to lay out rice and cotton plantations. By the end of the sixteenth century they operated some 200 sugar mills. An important *Marrano* community was already established in Bahia.

Most dramatic was an incident which took place in connection with the Dutch conquest of the land in 1624. When the Dutch fleet entered Bahia and the Portuguese departed, the *Marranos* openly declared themselves as Jews. But only eleven months later, the Portuguese returned and in their turn drove out the Dutch. The Inquisition immediately set to work with torture and faggot on the disloyal New Christians. From then on most of them disappeared from historic view.

Once again the Dutch returned to the attack in February, 1630. They conquered the entire area around the town of Recife (Pernambuco) and renamed it "New Holland." A few of the *Marrano* survivors now re-emerged as Jews. Attractive inducements were offered to the Jews of Amsterdam to settle in New Holland. Because so many of its stockholders were Jewish, the Dutch West India Company, in its proclamation of December 26, 1634, guaranteed to Jewish settlers complete religious freedom and equal rights before the law. Several thousand Jews then sailed from Holland and established themselves in Recife. The Jewish community of New Holland considered itself an offshoot of Amsterdam Jewry and followed the same religious-cultural pattern. It invited two rabbis from the parent-city to settle in Brazil. Besides continuing as plantation owners, as manufacturers and dealers in such staples as sugar cane, tobacco and cotton, Jews also carried on a brisk export trade with Europe in medical herbs, reptile skins and dried fruits.

But once again the Portuguese returned, in 1654, and threw out the Dutch. In mortal danger from the Inquisition, those Jews who were able to escape fled across the sea on sixteen ships, with Amsterdam as their destination. Several months later the Jewish community of New York was founded in the most accidental way by a group of twenty-six of these refugees.

The Holy Office completely blotted out what little remained of Jewish life in Brazil. It ruthlessly hunted down every obstinate Jew and relapsing New Christian. Thus, in 1739, it returned the *Marrano* playright Antonio José da

Synagogue in Sao Paulo.

Silva, known in the history of literature as the "Portuguese Molière," to Lisbon to die in an *auto-da-fé* for his secret practice of the Jewish religion. In 1822, when Brazil finally managed to throw off its Portuguese yoke, a number of seemingly devout Brazilian Catholics announced themselves as Jews!

In the course of the nineteenth century the northern part of Brazil received Jewish immigrants from Turkey, North Africa and Near Eastern countries. A later trickle flowed from France, Germany and Austria. After the Kishinev pogrom in 1903, the Jewish Colonization Association (ICA) helped Russian immigrants to establish the farm colony of Philippson, and some years later, the colony of *Quatro Irmaos* in Rio Grande da Sul.

When World War I ended, Brazil became the focal point of Jewish immigration from eastern Europe. But when refugees from Hitlerism began to arrive in 1934, the agitation of local German Nazis led to drastic restrictions against their admission. Nonetheless, a considerable number did manage to obtain entry. This may be seen in the fact that although in 1934 there were 50,000 Jews in Brazil their number had increased

Protest by the States General of Holland to the King of Spain against mistreatment of Brazilian Jewish refugees (1659). This is the first public document concerning the Jews in the Americas. *Jewish Historical Society of America*

212

to 120,000 by 1951. The largest Jewish communities are to be found in Rio de Janeiro, São Paulo and Porto Alegre.

BOLIVIA

Ever since the settlement of Bolivia in 1531, there have always been some Jews there. At first they were *Marranos* who had traveled overland from Argentina and whose descendants managed to survive the persecution of four centuries. Because the fires of the Inquisition started burning in Bolivia in 1570, other Jews avoided coming there. Hostility toward the Jews fostered by the Church remained endemic with the Christian population even after Bolivia had become a republic in 1825. Jews prudently stayed away. Before 1933 there were only 200 Jewish families in the whole country, most of them from Poland and Lithuania. But when the government offered free homesteads to settlers in 1938, some 6,000 German refugees entered. Several hundred families were established in all-Jewish agricultural colonies in Villa Sacaba and in other places.

The leader of the Jewish jungle colony, "Makkabi," Riegler (*left*), with Indian workers who helped the settlers clear the jungle for cultivation.

CHILE

As in almost every other country in Latin America, the first Jews to enter Chile did so as *Marranos* toward the end of the sixteenth century. They crossed the mountains from Peru and settled in Santiago. Most of them were merchants and traders.

The *Circulo Israelite*, the principal Jewish community center in Santiago, Chile.

Some played a prominent part in the development of local shipping. If no Jewish community materialized, it was entirely because the Holy Inquisition made Chile unsafe for Jews after 1570. In fact, hatred for the Jew had become so traditional with the native population that in 1852, when the

Entrance to the Jewish communal cemetery in Santiago, Chile.

famous Hungarian Jewish concert violinist, Miska Hauser, gave a recital in Santiago, he was accused in the local press of "conspiring diabolically to ruin Christian folk with his hellish art."

The modern Jewish community of Chile is of relatively late origin. It began in 1810 with the arrival of a group of immi-

Benjamin Cohen, leading Chilean diplomat and Assistant Secretary General of the Department of Public Information of the United Nations.

grants from Argentina after Chile had won her independence. In 1914 there were only 3,000 Jews, mostly of German and Near Eastern stock. But during 1933-39 there was an influx of 12,000 refugees from Germany. Today there are some 40,000 Jews, concentrated principally in the cities of Santiago, Valparaiso and Osorno.

Called *Sabatarias* because they are distinguished from other Chileans by their strict observance of the Sabbath, these *Marranos* of Concepcion, in the province of Bio Bio, have preserved the memory of their Jewish identity.

ARGENTINA

One learns of the presence of the first Jews in Argentina from the records of the Inquisition. Inferentially, they point to the settlement of large numbers of *Marranos* during the sixteenth and seventeenth centuries in Buenos Aires, Tucuman, Rosario and Cordoba.

Before 1890 Jewish community life in Argentina was virtually nonexistent. Tiny groups of German, English and Alsatian Jews, totaling less than 1,000, lived in various cities throughout the country. But in 1891 a new and fruitful period began with the arrival of the first Jews from the south of Russia.

Horsemen of Moises Ville, one of the oldest Jewish colonies.

These were largely idealists, not seekers of fortune. They were strongly permeated with the spirit of Zionism and were motivated by the principles of the back-to-the-land agitation. Both of these movements had been precipitated by the economic rootlessness of the Jews in Russia as well as by the numerous pogroms there during 1881-82. The great philanthropist, Baron Maurice de Hirsch, had founded, in 1891, the Jewish Colonization Association (ICA) in London for the purpose of establishing Jews upon the land in Argentina. They were settled in fifteen agricultural colonies which today have a farming population of more than 30,000. Nine of the colonies are in Entrerios Province; Moises Ville and Montefiore are in Santa Fé Province; Maurizio and Baron de Hirsch in Buenos Aires Province; Narcisse Levin in the Central Pampas; and Dora in Santiago del Estero. The colonies own one and a half million acres, most of it grazing land for large-scale cattle raising. Besides dairying, the colonists raise wheat and flax. One-third of them are private landowners and are fairly well off. The remainder are either farm workers, artisans or village shopkeepers.

Baron de Hirsch Library in Moises Ville.

It was quite natural for the Jewish colonies to have experienced a constant turnover in their population. That was because most of the settlers had originally been city or town dwellers. The hardships and the isolation of frontier life drove many back to the cities. The communal character of these agricultural colonies logically called for the establishment of cooperatives. The need for them became especially urgent

The *Templo Libertad,* one of the two most important synagogues in Buenos Aires.

when financial assistance from the Baron de Hirsch Fund ended. Then they found that their only hope for survival lay in the practice of well-organized mutual aid. To answer that need, the cooperative loan-office emerged as a characteristic institution in the Jewish farm colonies of Argentina.

Simultaneous with the settlement on the land, there was a far larger flow of Jewish immigrants into the cities and towns. After World War I some 6,500 Jews on the average arrived each year, most of them from Poland, Lithuania, Romania, Turkey, Syria, and, in later years, from Germany. The majority remained in Buenos Aires (there are about 250,000 Jews there today); the remainder were absorbed by the smaller Jewish communities in Rosario, La Plata, Cordoba, Santa Fé and Bahia Blanca.

The pattern of community development in Buenos Aires, for instance, seemed to be similar to that of other large Jewish centers in the world. Although there was no longer any compulsion for living within a ghetto, the immigrants, nonetheless, choose to concentrate in a special Jewish quarter. There traditional religious, cultural and linguistic bonds made possible a fuller Jewish group life.

It has been estimated that more than half the Argentine Jews are engaged in commerce and more than twenty-six per

Yiddish cultural leaders of Argentine standing in front of the Yiddish-language Sholom Aleichem School under construction in Buenos Aires.

cent in the handicrafts. The rest are professionals, workers and farmers. As everywhere else, the colleges and universities of Argentina draw an unusually large proportion of Jewish students.

The Jewish community in Argentina, being younger than that in the United States, has preserved closer ties with the traditional forms of the Yiddish culture which remains a strik-

A Jewish bank in Buenos Aires.

ing feature of Jewish life in the country. There are two Yiddish dailies, as well as a number of weekly and monthly periodicals, in Buenos Aires. Next to Spanish and Italian, the sound of Yiddish is that most heard in the capital city. Yiddish

Argentine Jewish crowds welcome Tsur, the Israeli ambassador.

theatrical companies play to packed houses. Yiddish schools, bookshops and libraries, including the one maintained by the Yiddish Scientific Institute (YIVO), are found everywhere. There is remarkable activity taking place today in the publishing of Yiddish books in Buenos Aires.

Israeli and Argentine officials signing a commercial treaty in Buenos Aires. Standing at the rear, second and third from the right, are President Juan Peron and his wife, the late Eva Peron.

Whether they speak Yiddish, Spanish or Hebrew, the majority of the Jews of Argentina are motivated in greater or lesser degree by Zionist sympathies and Jewish cultural interest. The *Sociedad Hebraica Argentina* has several thousand

members. It publishes Hebrew books, maintains a large Hebrew library and schools for the teaching of the Hebrew language and literature.

PERU

The prominent role of *Marranos* in the foreign trade of Peru led, in 1569, to the establishment of the Inquisition there. The fires of numerous *autos-da-fé* burned for the "Judaizing heretics." In the great *auto* of 1639 fifty-six *Marranos* perished, among them Manuel Batista Perez, reputedly the wealthiest man in the country. Another victim was Francisco Maldonado da Silva, noted philosopher-poet and surgeon. Upon the payment of 200,000 ducats to Condé de Chinchon, the Spanish governor of the country, six thousand Jews were allowed to remain. It is said that the trade of the city of Lima was concentrated in their hands "from brocade to sackcloth, and from diamonds to cumin-seed."

Today there are little more than two thousand Jews among the seven million Peruvians, the majority of them in Lima, where they engage in commerce, manufacturing and in the professions. They are of mixed national origins: late in the nineteenth century they started to arrive from Turkey, Alsace, Poland, Romania, and also from Argentina and Brazil. In most recent years several hundred refugees from Germany have made their home there.

URUGUAY

There was only a handful of Jews in Uruguay before World War I. However, when Argentina imposed restrictions on immigration, in 1919, part of the flow toward it was diverted into Uruguay. Some 8,000 refugees were admitted in later years. Of the 40,000 Jews in the country today, three-quarters have created an impressive Jewish community life in Montivideo. That capital city is a stronghold of Zionism in the Western Hemisphere and is also a center of Yiddish culture. Despite its relatively small population, the Jewish community of Montevideo supports a permanent Yiddish theatre, two daily Yiddish newspapers and a Hebrew periodical. In addition, it publishes a sizable number of literary works in Yiddish.

CURAÇAO

Jodenwyk (Jews' Town) was the name of the settlement established, with the sanction of the Dutch West India Company, by some fifty *Sephardic* Jewish families in 1650 on the

The Old and the New. The old is the 17th-century Jewish cemetery near Emmastad, containing some of the most venerable graves in the Western Hemisphere. The new are the oil refineries.

The old synagogue in Kniperstraat, Willemstad.

West Indies island of Curaçao. Their descendants have lived there continuously under the rule of Holland for more than 300 years. Although at the time of the American Revolution there were 2,000 Jews in Curaçao, today there are only about 1,000. Much of the island's thriving business is in their hands.

The majority of Jews are still of *Sephardic* stock. Among themselves, many still speak Spanish, although the language generally in use on the island is Dutch.

SURINAM

The first Jews to settle in Surinam, or Dutch Guiana, which lies along the Caribbean Sea, were *Marranos* of Portuguese stock. They made their home in Paramaribo in 1639. Some

Jews' Street in Paramaribo, which leads to the *Ashkenazic* synagogue.

The *Joden Savanne*. (From an early 19th-century engraving.)

years later they were joined by other *Marranos* fleeing from Brazil where, upon the defeat of the Dutch, the Inquisition had been introduced. Together with Jews from Cayenne, the refugees from Brazil, who had experience with tropical agriculture, established in 1669 the *Joden Savanne* (The Jews' Savannah). This was a thriving community whose inhabitants engaged chiefly in the cultivation of sugar cane and in the manufacture of sugar. Besides a large synagogue, the settlement also boasted a well-constructed fort, with ample stores for defense, manned by a Jewish militia unit. It successfully resisted a French attempt to seize the colony. But what the French could not effect, the elements did: the *Joden Savanne* was almost entirely destroyed by fire on September 10, 1832. It was never rebuilt.

Today there are fewer than 1,000 Jews in Surinam.

Sephardic synagogue in Charlotte Amalie on St. Thomas, Virgin Islands.

CUBA

Among the very first to set foot on San Salvador in the New World (October 12, 1492), and a short while later in Cuba, was the *Marrano* linguist, Luis de Torres. He was the interpreter Columbus had taken along on his first voyage. It is noteworthy that among the *Marranos* who settled on the island of Cuba at various times, one, Hernando de Castro, introduced the cultivation of sugar cane, a crop which became the principal economic asset of the country.

Today there are perhaps 10,000 Jews in the Republic of Cuba, half of them in Havana. German, United States, Turkish and East European Jews compose the principal ethnic groups. Because the Inquisition was not abolished in Cuba until 1823, the popular hostility toward Jews persisted longer; therefore, it was not until 1881 that they were permitted to settle there. Moreover, it was not until after the end of Spanish rule in Cuba, in 1898, that they were even granted the right to hold public worship and to build synagogues.

Students' sign (May, 1948) at the University of Havana calling for the establishment of diplomatic and commercial relations between Cuba and the new State of Israel.

"LOST TRIBES" AND REMOTE COMMUNITIES

It is remarkable that after the lapse of some twenty-five hundred years remnants of the so-called "Lost Tribes" are still being rediscovered. To be sure, there is no absolute certainty that any of these Jewish ethnic groups actually are what their ancient traditions claim for them—"Lost Tribes." But historians and ethnologists are being increasingly persuaded that it is reasonably likely, in spite of the many wild theories and speculations concerning them.

The history of the Lost Tribes reads like pure romance. It began when the Assyrian kings, Tiglath-pileser III (745-28 B.C.E.) and Sargon II (722-05 B.C.E.), for political and military reasons, deported many thousands of Jews from the Northern Kingdom of Israel to other parts of the empire. There were also later deportations and resettlements after Nebuchadnezzar's destruction of Jerusalem in 586 B.C.E. Later, Jewish colonies were founded throughout the vast Hellenic world and on the Arabian peninsula. The climax was reached when the Jewish Commonwealth came to a disastrous end, followed by futile rebellions against Roman rule. That started a vast and continuous exodus of Jews from Judea to the foreign Jewish settlements.

It was then that the Lost Tribes almost literally were lost. They simply vanished.

Josephus Flavius, already preoccupied with the mystery during the first century C.E., noted that in his day the generally accepted view was that the Ten Lost Tribes lived in lands beyond the banks of the Euphrates. That assumption was probably correct. Conceivably, the deportees belonging to the Ten Tribes from the Northern Kingdom of Israel had remained living for a long time in the places where they had been resettled by their Assyrian conquerors. But the movement of populations on the continent of Asia, driven by war, hunger or persecution, was always extremely complex and fluid. It is likely then that, in the course of time, some groups of these Jews either wandered off, were driven off, or were again carried away as captives from these Jewish settlements into other and perhaps even more remote parts of the world.

It was during the ninth century that the unknown fate of these lost remnants of Israel first began to arouse speculation among Jews. The subject was brought forward dramatically by Eldad ben Mahli Ha-Dani, a merchant and scholar. He visited all the important Jewish communities in Babylonia, North Africa and Spain, and everywhere he went he announced himself as a member of the long-lost tribe of Dan, from which he derived his name Ha-Dani (the Danite). He claimed that he was a subject of an independent Jewish kingdom situated in East Africa, that his country was inhabited only by Jews and that these were the Lost Tribes of Asher, Gad, Naphtali and Dan. Curiously enough, no one in Eldad's day, and later, doubted the truth of his claims. Even the celebrated Talmudist, Rashi, was convinced of their authenticity. Nonetheless, the sceptical Spanish philosopher-poet, Abraham Ibn Ezra, and Rabbi Meir of Rothenburg considered Eldad Ha-Dani a swindler and an adventurer.

Interest in Eldad's revelations spread to learned Christians. It inspired the apocryphal letter by the semi-legendary, medieval priest-ruler, Prester John, in which he described the manner of life of several lost Jewish tribes who allegedly lived in a fabulous land beyond the River Sambatyon in Ethiopia.

From that time on, the subject of the Lost Tribes and the mythical Sambatyon River held Jewish folk spellbound.

A remarkable incident touching on the Lost Tribes was related by Matthew Paris, the medieval chronicler of England. In his account of the contemporary struggle of the Crusaders with the Tatars and Cumanians, he noted: "During all this time, members of the Jews on the Continent, and especially those belonging to the Empire, thought that these Tatars and Cumanians were a portion of their race whom God had, at the prayers of Alexander the Great, shut up in the Caspian mountains."

Several centuries later, after Manasseh ben Israel, the noted rabbi of Amsterdam, had listened to the report of the *Marrano* Jew Montezinus who claimed that he had met some Jews of the Lost Tribes among the Indians in South America, he wrote to John Drury, the Puritan divine, on December 23, 1649: ". . . I thinke that the Ten Tribes live not onely there [i.e. America], but also in other lands scattered everywhere; these never did come backe to the Second Temple, and they keep till this day still the Jewish Religion. . . ."

There are quite a number of peoples today who cling to the ancient tradition that they are descended from the Jewish Lost Tribes: the tribesmen of Afghanistan, the Mohammedan Berbers of West Africa, and the six million Christian Ibo people of Nigeria. Unquestionably, they all practice certain ancient Hebraic customs and beliefs, which lends some credibility to their fantastic-sounding claims.

BAGDAD

Jews have been living in Mesopotamia, the seat of the Assyrian and Babylonian Empires, ever since the first deportations of the "Ten Tribes" living in the Northern Kingdom of Israel during the eighth century B.C.E. The Babylonian Jewish population was greatly augmented after the destruction of the

Soferim, or *Torah*-scribes, at the traditional Tomb of Ezekiel near the site of the ancient city of Babylon.

First Temple by Nebuchadnezzar in 586 B.C.E. when he carried off the cream of the Jewish youth into captivity. Later refugees further enlarged the Jewish community, especially after Judea, under the hammer-blows of Vespasian and Titus in 70 C.E., ceased being an independent state, and after the Bar-Kochba revolt in 135 C.E. was crushed by Severus.

Because Jews lived under more tolerable conditions in Babylonia than almost anywhere else in the Mediterranean world, they flourished there and at the time of the fall of the

Second Temple numbered more than one million. As a community it was culturally more advanced than even the homeland Judea. The Babylonian *Talmud* (in contradistinction to the Jerusalem *Talmud*) was created there and was taught in the famous Jewish academies of Sura, Pumbeditha and Nehardea to countless generations of Jews. Under its lay leaders, the *exilarchs,* and under its religious-intellectual heads, the *geonim,* the influence of Babylonian Jewry dominated all of the Jewish world down to the middle of the eleventh century when it went into its eclipse. Wars, invasions and increasing persecution drove countless thousands in flight to Jewish communities in other lands.

Homes of wealthy Jews on the banks of the Tigris River in North Bagdad.

When a French traveler, in 1632, visited Bagdad, the foremost Jewish center in the Mesopotamian area, he found only 15,000 Jews. What had happened to the descendants of the more than one million Jews who had lived there in the latter days of the Second Temple we do not know. We can only surmise and speculate.

From the beginning of the eighteenth century Jewish life in Bagdad and throughout Mesopotamia became more and more constricted and was increasingly exposed to harassment by the Mohammedan rulers. Many Jews left to settle in India and China at the start of the nineteenth century. Others, possessing the means, emigrated to the Western Hemisphere. Before the mass emigration to Israel started in 1951, in consequence of the anti-Jewish disturbances, there were some 150,000 Arabic-speaking Jews in Iraq. Of this number, almost half lived in Bagdad. Their cultural level was scarcely above that of their Mohammedan neighbors: together they had been held back by their Moslem feudal rulers.

IRAN

Certainly, some elements of the so-called Lost Tribes must have been colonized in Azerbaidjan and Persia (Iran), although recorded Jewish history there began only with the rule of Cyrus the Great in 539 B.C.E. The Jews of the city of Ispahan have perpetuated a tradition that they are the direct descendants of the exiles brought from Judea by King Nebuchadnezzar in 586 B.C.E. When the Arabs captured the city during the seventh century C.E., they gave the Jews the choice of Islam or expulsion. The great majority elected to remain Jews and to leave. The synagogues were then turned into mosques.

What happened to those Jews who departed? No one knows. At a later period a considerable number of Jews came from other parts of Mesopotamia to Ispahan. As one of the great trading centers between Europe and India, the city offered more opportunities for Jewish merchants than the other cities of old Persia.

A marked decline in the fortunes of the Jews of Persia took place during the fourteenth century when Timur, or Tamerlane, drenched the country in blood and left it devastated. The finishing blows to Jewish life were dealt by the bigoted Mohammedan sectarian Shiite rulers. Adopting the pattern of the caste system in India, they declared Jews to be an "unclean" sect. They segregated them in ghettos, made them wear an identifying red patch of cloth on their breasts, and declared all Mohammedan homes forbidden to them.

In 1952 there were some 80,000 Jews in Iran, 30,000 in Teheran. There were smaller communities in Hamadan, Ispahan and Shiraz. They speak a Judeo-Persian dialect which they write in Hebrew characters. They also follow "the Persian rite," which is observed throughout the entire East, in their religious service. For centuries the Jews of Iran have been noted as handicraftsmen. They have been following the same family trades for centuries—as glassmakers, silk-weavers, silversmiths, workers in brass, masons, tailors and shoemakers. In recent years there has been a mass emigration to Israel.

Jewish blacksmith of Persia.

KURDISTAN

Although Kurdistan has been a part of Persia, the Jews there regard themselves as a group apart and as a remnant of one of the Lost Tribes. Some of them believe that their ancestors first settled in Kurdistan when they were brought

The teachers of the Jewish school, in Seneh, Kurdistan, run by the *Alliance Israelite Universelle*—posing with their armed guard (1908).

there as captives by Nebuchadnezzar; others that their community was founded a little later at the time when Ezra and Nehemiah ruled over the returned exiles in Judea.

The Jews of Kurdistan today are largely city-dwellers. But some are also found in isolated mountain villages. Before World War I there were perhaps 18,000 Jews in the towns,

218

principally in Mosul, the great oil center, and in Arbil and Kirkuk.

The Kurdish Jews speak Aramaic, a dialect which resembles the ancient Aramaic in which the Babylonian *Talmud* was written. But tradition has preserved for them through the

A Jew from Kurdistan who fled to Teheran after the bloody riots that broke out in his region in 1951.

centuries only a few fundamental customs of Jewish religious life: circumcision, observance of the Sabbath and the eating of kosher food. Their poverty and isolation have been bitter in recent centuries. They have only one *chacham*, or rabbi, an itinerant preacher who travels from village to village, to circumcise, to marry, to bury and to preach the word of God. The Jews of Kurdistan are very superstitious: they believe in demons and spirits and in the efficacy of cabalistic amulets. Most of them engage in manual labor: as silversmiths, workers in brass, weavers, dyers, porters, peddlers and petty tradesmen. A number are farmers who either cultivate their own vineyards or work as farm laborers and sheep herders for Kurdish landowners.

The lot of the Kurdish Jews has never been a happy one. Beginning with the last decade of the nineteenth century they started emigrating to Palestine. By 1933 there were 5,000 settled there. This number increased in 1951 after the anti-Jewish riots made Kurdistan unsafe.

YEMEN

Probably the Lost Tribe remnant best known in the West today are the Jews of Yemen, an Arab kingdom in the southern part of Arabia. This is largely due to the fact that their resettlement in Palestine was accomplished in dramatic fashion. The man most responsible for their return to the Jewish homeland was the Palestinian labor leader and scholar, Yavnieli, who has devoted his life to the restoration of the Yemenites to the main body of the Jewish people.

The widespread outbreaks of anti-Jewish violence that took place in Arab lands, in 1949, came in part as a consequence of the defeat suffered by the invading armies of the seven Arab states at the hands of the armed forces of Israel. These excesses were particularly ominous for the Jews of Yemen. Therefore, with funds provided by the United Jewish Appeal, the Joint Distribution Committee arranged for their transportation to Israel. Thousands of Yemenite Jews began a disheartening 200-mile trek from the remote hill-villages in the interior to Aden and safety by the air-lift somewhat spectacularly named "Operation Magic Carpet." By 1952 there were only about 3,000 Jews left in all Yemen.

In 1926 it was estimated there were 8,000 Jewish families (about 35,000 people) living in several hundred towns and villages in Yemen. In Sanaa there was a community of 7,000 and in Sada, one of 2,000. Most of the Yemenite Jews were artisans: potters, weavers, tailors, silversmiths, masons, bricklayers, joiners and tobacco workers. They were desperately

"Operation Magic Carpet," the airlift which in 1949-50 brought 45,000 Yemenite Jews to Israel from Aden.

poor and had been severely persecuted by the despotic kings of Yemen. Nonetheless they persevered through the centuries in a remarkable devotion to their religious culture. They produced many fine Talmudic scholars, especially during the Middle Ages, some of whom corresponded with Maimonides during the twelfth century. Perhaps more than any other ethnic group of Arabic-speaking Jews, they preserved their own synagogue chants and melodies which are of striking originality and beauty. This folk-religious music has been grafting itself significantly on the musical culture of Israel today.

Lighting the Sabbath candles.

The Yemenite Jews believe that their forefathers had come to live in Yemen before the destruction of the First Temple. Their tradition has it that forty-two years before the Babylonian Exile an army of 75,000 Jewish soldiers, accompanied by many priests and Levites, had gone on an expedition into Yemen (Teman). They captured the city of Sanaa and remained there under their own rulers. Later, when Ezra ruled over the returned exiles in Jerusalem, he sent a messenger to them asking them to return to their homeland. This the Yemenite Jews refused to do, with the contention by their religious leaders that the time of the Messianic Era had not yet arrived. When the Moslem Ommiad caliph, Omar II (717-20 C.E.), annexed Yemen and imposed on it the religion of Mohammed, he placed all non-believers, including the Jews, in

Jewish quarter in Aden.

an inferior position socially and economically. From that time on, the life of the Jews in Yemen became increasingly difficult. In attempted flight from the unhappy reality, they took refuge in cabalistic beliefs and Messianic expectations which continuously racked their community like a fever.

GEORGIA (Russia)

There are today perhaps 10,000 Jews in the Transcaucasian Socialist Republic of Georgia. They, too, believe they are sprung from the Lost Tribes and that their ancestors were settled in the country in Biblical times. They call themselves "Hebraeli" or "Israeli." They live in settled communities in the western part of the country near the Black Sea, and speak

Transcaucasian Jews of Georgia, about 1900.

Georgian. Early Christian chronicles make numerous references to them, but the first Jewish mention of them dates from the fourth century C.E. It is an inscription in Aramaic.

There was unquestionably a Jewish community already firmly established in the city of Tiflis during the tenth century. When Marco Polo visited it, in 1272, he found carpet-weaving the principal occupation of the Jews.

Until the middle of the nineteenth century the Georgian Jews held the status of chattels. They belonged, like so much merchandise, to the Orthodox Church and to the local princes. Those who dwelled in the villages were bought and sold, like all other serfs in Russia. When serfdom was finally abolished, Jews became petty tradesmen, gardeners and workers in the vineyards. Many were peddlers, and trudged from village to village carrying in the packs on their backs the usual assortment of notions and knicknacks for the Georgian Christian peasants. Until the Revolution of 1917, urban Jews were to be found principally in Tiflis, Batum and Kutais.

Jewish women of Bokhara.

BOKHARA

In all the centuries until the nineteenth, the Jews of Bokhara remained apart from other Jews. They have a tradition that they are descendants of one of the Lost Tribes. The first historical trace of them goes back to the days of the Samanid kings who had made Bokhara their capital. When Timur (Tamerlane) ruled his vast empire from Samarkand in the fourteenth century, there were some 50,000 Jews settled in the city. In the dreary wake of countless massacres and persecution they were joined by Jews from Afghanistan, from Khiva and Khorasa.

Judeo-Persian (Tadjik Persian written with Hebrew characters) in their language and culture, they created, in the course of centuries, a literature of their own. One of their poets, Moses ben David, who flourished toward the end of the fifteenth century, also wrote in the Persian language. He was greatly admired by the Persians of his time.

Bokhara Jews at their Talmudic studies—a 2,000-year-old practice.

Like all national minorities in Russia, the Jews of Bokhara suffered bitter oppression under the Tsars. Culturally as well as socially, they were tied hand and foot by anti-Jewish laws and restrictions. Consequently, in 1893, many Jews turned hopefully toward Palestine. They established a large colony in Jerusalem, where they have been worshipping in their own synagogues and are trying to preserve their old customs.

After the Bolshevik Revolution in Russia, Bokhara became a part of the newly established Uzbek Socialist Republic. Today these Jews live not only in Bokhara but in some twenty other communities in that region, principally in Samarkand, Tashkent, Khiva, Alma-Ata and Kokand.

HADHRAMAUT

Close by the Yemenites, along the southern edge of the Arabian Peninsula, live the Arabic-speaking Jews of Hadhramaut. While they resemble the Yemenite Jews in some ways, they are dissimilar in others. Who they are and when they first came to Hadhramaut remain unanswered questions. They greatly resemble their Mohammedan countrymen who are nomad Bedouins and camel-breeders. Since the twelfth century B.C.E., Hadhramaut has been an important stopping-off place for caravans on their way to India.

The Hadhrami Jews, numbering no more than several thousand, live in extraordinary "skyscraper" buildings, constructed fortress-like for defense. When the State of Israel was established in 1948 a number of Jews of Hadhramaut settled there.

Left. A Hadhrami Jewish woman. *Right.* A Hadhrami Jew behind the plow.

MOUNTAIN JEWS

Isolated for centuries in remote Daghestan villages that nestle on rocky ledges in the Caucasus or lie on the plains fringing the western shore of the Caspian Sea, the Mountain Jews claim an ancestry that goes back to the destruction of the First Temple. In later centuries, the Jewish rulers of Khazaria held sway over Daghestan. But what happened to the Mountain Jews from then on until the seventeenth century, when they formed a large community in the coastal city of Derbent, remains obscure.

Today there are some 30,000 Mountain Jews in Daghestan, Ossetia and Nalchik. Their principal settlements are in Derbent, the oil center Baku, Makhach-Kala and Kuba which they once called "The Second Jerusalem." They were known in years past for their skillful rug-making and fine leather work. Like their neighbors, until the Russian Revolution in 1917, they were culturally backward. They believed in talismans and amulets as protection against evil spirits and demons, and practiced such primitive Islamic customs as marriage by capture and purchase, polygamy, and the blood feud. They excelled as horsemen and as folk dancers and musicians.

This remarkable photograph of Mountain Jews was taken in 1890 by the Russian Tsar's court photographer.

The language of the Mountain Jews is known as *Tat,* in which a Jewish literature was created. It is Persian spiced with Turkish and Hebrew words and idioms, but is written in Hebrew characters. For the past two decades, however, following the pattern of other Soviet national groups, the Mountain Jews have adopted the Latin alphabet.

In earlier times they followed the religious and cultural lead of the Jewish community in Bagdad. But beginning with the nineteenth century their rabbis were educated in the fa-

mous Lithuanian *yeshivot* (rabbinical seminaries) of Volozhin and Kovno. Until the revolution, most of the Mountain Jews had worked as handicraftsmen, itinerant peddlers in the villages, gardeners and grape-growers. By 1942 the majority worked either on collective farms or in the huge oil industry in Baku. Many of the younger generation of Mountain Jews turned away from the Jewish religion as they did elsewhere in the Soviet Union. Synagogues in Derbent and other towns were converted into workers' clubs, nurseries and schoolhouses. A crop of young intellectuals and professionals sprang up in the regional universities: writers, scholars, actors, musicians, engineers, doctors and agriculturists. The life of the Mountain Jews was completely transformed. Under the new conditions of Soviet life their survival as Jews is doubtful.

AFGHANISTAN

The Tribesmen of Afghanistan, who observe a number of ancient Biblical customs, hold that they are of Jewish origin and of the tribe of Benjamin. They claim that Afghana, their legendary founder, was a son of King Saul, and they trace their genealogy thirty-seven generations from him to Kais, the first apostle of Islam in Afghanistan. Their account runs that the Jewish descendants of Afghana, who were settled in Damascus at the time of the destruction of the First Temple, were transplanted into Afghanistan by Nebuchadnezzar.

There are 3,500 Afghans today who call themselves "Bani-Israil" (Sons of Israel). They are bona fide practicing Jews. Anti-Jewish feelings has frequently led to many restrictions as well as excesses against them. The tribal law of Afghanistan requires them to wear black turbans in public. In 1934 they were expelled from the villages, and two thousand of them wandered homeless in the wilderness. Unlike their ancestors they had no Moses to lead them to the Promised Land.

Most of them now live in Kabul, but there are smaller groups in Herat, Kandahar and Ghasni, north of the Hindu Kush mountains. Because they have been shut off from the rest of the world by towering mountains, they have managed to live throughout their whole long history in virtual isolation from the rest of the Jewish world. They are very poor and speak an Indo-Iranian dialect.

BENE-ISRAEL

It is estimated that there are today some 10,000 "Bene-

The Byculla Synagogue of the Bagdad Jews in Bombay. There are several thousand Bagdadi Jews in Bombay, Calcutta and Poona.

Israel" (Sons of Israel) Jews in India, several hundred of whom have emigrated and settled in Israel since 1951. Their name intriguingly recalls the fact that the Mohammedan Afghans, who also claim Jewish descent, bear a similar name—"Bani-Israil." They all live in the Bombay Presidency, 5,000 of them in the city of Bombay. They wear Indian clothes, speak the vernacular of the country—Mahratti—and bear Mahratti names. But they *know* that they are Jews. Within the limits of their knowledge of the Jewish religion they scrupulously observe Jewish customs, rites and ceremonies. Because they do not engage in any work on the Sabbath but attend services in the synagogue, their fellow-Indians call them *Shanwar Teles*, or "Saturday oilmen." (A great many of the Bene-Israel are employed as oil-pressers.)

The Bene-Israel claim their descent from Jews who had fled from Judea during the atrocities by Antiochus Epiphanes, immediately before the Maccabean revolt in 175 B.C.E. They had journeyed by sea to India, but a storm arose shipwrecking them on the Konkan coast thirty miles south of Bombay. In the excitement they lost their *Sefer Torah*, a loss they considered the major misfortune of their historic experience, for they remained in ignorance of the Hebrew language and of the written law for many centuries.

Bene-Israel Jews.

As time went on, many of the Jewish rites, customs and prayers began to fade from their memory. Of the liturgy all they could remember was the *Shema*, the Jewish creed: "Hear, O Israel, the Lord our God, the Lord is One!" To this affirmation they clung desperately through the centuries, reciting it in Hebrew on every religious occasion, whether during the rite of circumcision, at weddings or at funerals.

Their claim—that their ancestors left Judea before the destruction of the Second Temple—had some historical validity and may be judged from the Biblical character of some of their religious customs. For instance, their offerings of frankincense in the synagogue service recalls the same rite that was observed in the Temple in Jerusalem. It is perhaps of considerable significance that the Bene-Israel, until modern times, remained ignorant of *Hannukah*, the Festival of Lights, which had been introduced by Judah Maccabee upon the reconsecration of the Temple in 168 B.C.E. The Bene-Israel also were unaware of the destruction of the Second Temple by Titus in 70 C.E. After the passage of centuries—some Bene-Israelites say five, others say nine—a half-legendary character by the name of David Rahabi appeared and taught them some of the tenets of Judaism.

It was but natural that in the caste-ridden society of India, group distinctions and separations should have appeared within the tiny Jewish community of the Bene-Israel. There are two classes among them: one, called "Gora-Israel" (White), regards itself as "the real" Bene-Israel; the other, called "Kala-Israel" (Black), probably consists of Indian proselytes. The Gora-Israelites consider themselves socially superior and are pridefully determined to preserve their group "purity." Naturally, the groups do not intermarry.

In recent times, with the awakening among the lower castes of India to the social injustice of their inferior status, the Kala-Israel group, too, has shown its indignation against the racial snobbery of the "White" Jews.

A Black and a White Jew of Cochin.

COCHIN

The Jews of Cochin, a region which lies on the southwestern Malabar coast of India, number few more than 1,200. Like the Bene-Israel, they, too, follow the divisive caste system of India. Only a mere handful themselves, yet they are socially stratified into three castes: the "superior" caste is "White," the intermediary is "Brown," the lowest caste is "Black."

The Black Jews ascribe their color to the tropical sun rather than to a different racial strain, but the White Jews consider them the descendants of slaves once owned by Jews. Black Jews are more numerous than the White and Brown

Ancient Jewish cemetery in Cochin.

Jews combined and wear different dress. The color line forbids them, however, to worship together with the White and the Brown Jews, so they have seven "segregated" synagogues of their own in which they worship the same God with the same prayers.

The Cochin Jews speak Malayalam, which is the language of the Dravidians, the aboriginal inhabitants of India. But in their religious life they use Hebrew, which they teach their children to read. They are strong traditionalists in their customs and rigorously try to follow the 613 precepts of Orthodox Judaism.

The Cochin Jews believe that their ancestors, members of the tribe of Mannaseh, arrived in Malabar in the years following the destruction of the Second Temple. Their earliest written record, however, is an inscription on copper plates, which had been presented as patents of nobility to the Jew Joseph Rabban in 1020 by the Rajah Bhaskira Ravivarman. They gave Rabban the principality of Anjuvannam and granted him the privilege of riding on an elephant, of being carried in a litter and of being shielded from the sun by a state umbrella. It specified, too, that whenever he ventured out in public he was to be preceded ceremoniously by drummers and trumpeters.

CHINA

In K'aifeng, an ancient city on the Yellow River and the capital of Honan Province, live a handful of Jews who cannot be distinguished in any superficial way from the Chinese. Yet

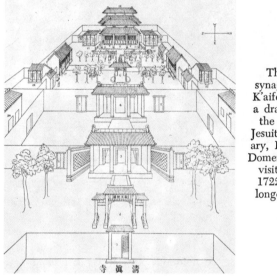

The old synagogue at K'aifeng, from a drawing by the French Jesuit missionary, Pére Jean Domenge, who visited it in 1722. It no longer exists.

what marks them out as a unique ethnic group is their devotion to the Jewish religion. Their synagogue, now relinquished, was beautiful and elaborate, with exquisitely designed courtyards and chapels in the style of a Chinese temple. On one of the stone tablets in the compound of the syna-

A *Sefer Torah* case and its Ark, which formerly belonged to the K'aifeng Synagogue.
Jewish Museum

gogue was an inscription in Chinese characters. It read: "Adam was the first man, Abraham was the founder of our religion, then came Moses and gave us the Law and the Holy Scriptures. . . ."

Now, even without a house of worship they, nevertheless, cling to the Law that Moses gave them. The few traditional clans that they make up, Chinese fashion, desperately hold together in a common identity.

Jews of K'aifeng, 1919.

Some historians speculate that the Jews of K'aifeng are partly descended from Jewish stock that had been previously settled in Persia. Unknown events probably had obliged them to seek refuge in China in the days of the Maccabees, a period which coincided with that of the Han Dynasty.

There is little doubt that the K'aifeng Jews, both in numbers and in influence, must have formed at one time an important element in the community. The Chinese emperors of the T'ang Dynasty (seventh century C.E.) set a mandarin over them to look after their welfare. Once a year this princely official would enter the synagogue at K'aifeng and, in the name of the emperor whom he represented, would burn incense before the altar. The Chinese emperors granted the Jews full protection and accorded them courteous treatment. It is an interesting commentary on the varying social philosophies of peoples that at the very time that the Crusaders were savagely exterminating hundreds of Jewish communities in Europe, a Chinese emperor welcomed the Jews with these words: "You have come to our China; revere and preserve the customs of your ancestors." He even helped them build their synagogue.

There were many migrations of Jews into Honan during the centuries. Their numbers must have been quite formidable to deserve the frequent official mention made of them in imperial records. The Jewish newcomers resembled the Chinese in so many ways as to make them readily acceptable: their gentleness, their scholarly predilections, their devoted study of religious writings, and not the least—their great reverence for tradition and for their ancestors. This may explain why it is that in time Jews began to disappear from Chinese life, though they were neither killed off nor forcibly converted. They were probably absorbed biologically and culturally in a slow but inexorable process. Today only enough of them are left—barely a few hundred—to serve, so to speak, as ethnological museum specimens.

EGYPT

There have been Jews in Egypt since prehistoric times. Under the Greeks, following Alexander the Great's conquest of the country, a great and influential Jewish community had flourished there for many centuries. It had created, first, a Hellenistic Jewish culture and, later, an Arabic-Jewish culture. But, with the passing of time, the Egyptian Jewish community declined greatly. Most of the more than a million Jews who

Ancient synagogue in Cairo, Egypt.

had lived there at the time of Jerusalem's fall, emigrated elsewhere or disappeared from Jewish life through intermarriage. Of the former high culture of the Jews of Egypt, there is not a single trace left.

Of the 50,000 Jews in Egypt in 1951 there were four principal groupings: Arabic-speaking Jews of old Egyptian ancestry, Berber Jews, *Sephardim* of Spanish-Portuguese stock, and *Ashkenazim*, or central and eastern European Jews, the latter mostly from Saloniki, Adrianople and Smyrna. Due to the anti-Jewish agitation which partly stemmed from the military defeats suffered by Egypt in the war with Israel, many Jews emigrated to the Jewish homeland.

ALGERIA

The Jews of Algeria, dating back to ancient times, constitute an amalgam of diverse Jewish ethnic strains—African, Asian and European. The main pattern of their religious and community life as it exists today was laid down many centuries ago by Spanish *Sephardim* who fled the massacres and forced conversions in their country carried out by the Holy Inquisition and Vincent Ferrer in 1391. Under Turkish rule

Interior of a synagogue in the Algiers *mellah*, or ghetto, which was built under the Turks in 1518. Today there are 19 synagogues there—6 public and 13 private. Religious life is intense and follows medieval traditional lines.

(1518-1830) the Jews of Algeria were segregated from the rest of the population. They were obliged to wear distinguishing attire: a black skullcap, a gray cloak with a hood and shoes without heels. When French rule was imposed on the country, in 1870, there was a marked process of European-

ization among the Jews. However, they retained some of the old Arab ways of life and culture.

There were some 140,000 Jews in Algeria in 1952, most of them in the cities. A considerable number were petty merchants, traders, handicraftsmen and itinerant peddlers. The peddlers roamed over the countryside, riding on pack-laden donkeys, with all kinds of household goods for the Algerian peasantry. But the majority of Jews were workers in the cities—jewelers, smiths, painters, carpenters, watch and cigarette makers.

The depressed economic condition of Algerian Jewry today is matched by the squalor and overcrowding in the *mellahs,* or ghettos, which exist in the cities of Algiers, Oran, Constantine, Setif and Tlemsen. A survey in Constantine showed that there was one room to a family for most of the city's 877 families, which averaged six people each. Conditions were so critical during the 1920's that fully two-thirds of the Jews of Algiers were forced to apply to the Jewish *Consistoire* for poor-relief.

Jewish women of Algiers, 1836.   *Delacroix*

While the Jews were declared free and equal citizens of France after the conquest of Algeria in 1870, they also fell heir to the virulent anti-Semitism with which Continental France was being rent. When the Dreyfus Case exploded sensationally in 1897, the notorious leader of the French anti-Semites, Drumont, with the help of the Jesuits in Algeria, inflamed the Moslems against the Jews. Thus the seeds of prejudice that were carefully sown grew into widespread excesses against the Jews in Constantine and several other cities in 1934. The situation became worse when the Arab League declared a *jihad,* "holy war," against the Jews. Thousands fled to Israel as soon as that state was established.

MOROCCO

Morocco, or Mauretania, as it was known in ancient times, had provided a hospitable home to Jews both from Judea and from neighboring North African regions long before it became a Roman province in 42 c.e. The Church Father Saint Jerome made note of early Christians living in the Jewish communities of Mauretania. Like the Jews of Egypt, those in Mauretania had fallen under the molding influence of Hellenism and were accorded equal rights with all other inhabitants until the fifth century when the Vandals made themselves masters of the country.

In the coastal cities of the Mediterranean, Jewish merchants flourished in the shipping and maritime trades and had commercial relations with foreign countries. In the interior the Jews were hardly distinguishable from the Moors. They earned their livelihood as farmers, vintners and wine merchants.

Christian Byzantium swallowed up the land in 534 c.e., and persecution on religious grounds drove thousands of Jews into the remote fastnesses of the Atlas Mountains. There were many Berber tribes who, as the old Arab chroniclers noted, lived openly as Jews. In fact, during the seventh century c.e. they dominated the entire country. At one time, when the Arabs invaded from the East brandishing the missionary sword of Islam, the Berber tribes united under a Jewish tribal queen called the *Cahina*. She led them into battle against the Moslems, displaying great tactical skill and bravery. The Berbers, however, were finally defeated and their *Cahina* was slain. This decisive struggle was followed by the conversion of the Berber tribes to Islam, which took place only at the point of the sword.

In the unremitting struggle with the Mohammedan invaders everywhere in North Africa, an appalling number of Jews were slain. It marked the end of the independent power of the Jews in the entire region. But even today the Mohammedan Berbers still cling to a number of Jewish customs and religious beliefs.

The street of the Jewish gold and silver smiths in the Fez *mellah*.

In 1952, in both the French and Spanish parts of Morocco, including the internationalized city of Tangiers, there were 260,000 Jews, the largest group of Jews on the continent of Africa. The great majority lived in French Morocco, their principal centers in Casablanca, Marrakesh, Fez, Mogador and Rabat. Most Jews speak the same Arabic dialect as the Moors. However, they write Arabic with Hebrew characters just as Maimonides did one thousand years ago. In the coastal cities are found sizable communities of Spanish-speaking *Sephardim* and also a considerable number of French Jews. The Berber Jews in the Atlas Mountains speak the Arabic dialect of the Mohammedan Berbers.

An ancient-style religious school in the Casablanca *mellah*, in which 90,000 Jews lived in 1952. Living conditions are so unhealthy that 50% of the children die before they reach adolescence.

In the *mellahs*, or ghettos of the cities, where most of the Arabic-speaking Jews of ancient stock live, conditions today are reminiscent of those that must have prevailed there during the Middle Ages. The Jews live in narrow streets and in

ramshackle buildings so tall that they keep out the sunlight. Overcrowding and unsanitary conditions have been the cause of an appallingly high death-rate. Many of the petty merchants may be seen today patiently squatting in their little shops just as their forefathers did centuries ago. A number of others earn their livelihood as peddlers or as artisans, especially in the making of leather and metal goods.

Thousands, helped by the Jewish Agency and the Joint Distribution Committee, settled in Israel beginning in 1949.

LIBYA

Libya, a country in North Africa which is made up of Cyrenaica and Tripolitania, lies between Egypt and Tunisia. In both regions Jews have figured prominently since ancient

Libyan cave dweller.

times. Several centuries before the final destruction of Jerusalem, a great Jewish settlement, estimated at one million, had been established in Cyrenaica. A highly developed Hebrew-Hellenistic civilization flourished there and produced a number of cultured and gifted Jews. The best known of them was the historian Jason, famous as the author of the Second Book of Maccabees.

When the Jews of Judea, during the first century c.e., rose in revolt against the Romans and were crushed, the Jews of Cyrene, especially those in the cities of Ola, Sabratha and Leptis Magna, picked up the fallen standard of Jewish resistance, led by the flaming Jonathan the Zealot. Though defeated after a vast number had been slain, they nevertheless renewed their revolt in 115 c.e. After the Roman General Marcus Turbo had vanquished them in battle, he slaughtered them by the tens of thousands. Those who were able fled the country. Few remained after that to pick up the fragile thread of Jewish life.

In Upper Libya, Jews have been continuously settled ever since Ptolemy I of Egypt in 320 c.e. manned with Jewish garrisons the string of fortresses he maintained on that frontier. These Jewish soldiers formed permanent settlements there and, because of their military power, enjoyed a large measure of autonomy.

The modern city of Tripoli is the ancient Oea. The majority of its Jewish inhabitants are descendants of forgotten Jewish ancestral stock but have preserved many traditions of an ancient Jewish origin. A number of Spanish Jews joined them after 1551 when the benevolent Sultan Suleiman the Magnificent made himself master of Tripoli. In 1943 there were 15,000 Jews crowded into the ghetto of Tripoli, called "Al-Hara." Small as their number was, they maintained eighteen synagogues, eleven *Talmud Torahs* and two modern trade schools established by the *Alliance Israelite Universelle*. The majority today are petty shopkeepers, traders and peddlers, though there are also a considerable number of mechanics who have been trained by the *Alliance* schools.

In all of Libya in 1952 there were only 12,000 Jews left; about twice that number had already emigrated to Israel a few years previously.

TUNISIA

While there is archaeological proof that a Jewish community existed in the city of Tunis at the dawn of Christianity, Tunisian Jews claim an even more ancient origin for other Jewish settlements in the country. They maintain that their

Tunisian rabbi.

Jewish quarter in Tunis.

first Palestinian ancestors had arrived in the period before the Babylonian Captivity in 586 B.C.E. Whether or not this tradition is true, there are contemporary writings which refer to the arrival of many Jews in the existing Jewish settlements in Tunisia after the Second Temple's destruction in 70 C.E.

During the seventh century C.E. the bitter persecution of the Jews of Spain by their Visigothic kings forced large numbers of them to cross the Mediterranean Sea to seek refuge in Tunisia. Many intermarried with the pagan Berbers. In fact, a number of Berber tribes subsequently embraced the Jewish religion. To this day, the Moslem Berbers show the influences of Jewish religious customs and beliefs.

For centuries thereafter, Tunisian Jewry flourished under the Caliphate of Bagdad, until the fanatical Almohade caliph seized power in 1146. It was difficult for the Jews after that. Under threat of death many became Mohammedans, but the majority remained loyal to their faith. Turkish rule, which followed in the sixteenth century, proved less oppressive and Jews were not hindered in the practice of their religion. Nevertheless, in order to isolate them from the rest of the community, the Jews were forced to wear identifying garments: a sleeveless blue shirt, black pantaloons and slippers, and a black skullcap. Jews were allowed to wear stockings only in winter and could not use a saddle when riding a mule or donkey. It was only when Tunisia became a French Protectorate in 1881 that its Jewish inhabitants were able to throw off some of their medieval restrictions.

There are two major divisions in Tunisian Jewry: the *Touensa*, those of ancient Jewish stock, and the *Grana*, the descendants of seventeenth-century Portuguese and Italian settlers. With the exception of a small class of prosperous merchants, traders and professionals, most of the *Touensa* are wretchedly poor—petty shopkeepers, peddlers, tailors, shoemakers, wood-workers and jewelers

The latest population estimate has 105,000 Jews living in Tunisia, about half of them in the city of Tunis. There are sizable communities in Sousse, Sfax, Gabes, Gafsa, Bizerte, Kairouan and the island of Djerba.

DJERBA

The Jewish communities on the small island of Djerba, which lies off the coast of Tunisia, have been known to the world since the tenth century C.E. Maimonides had lived with them for some time, and in his letters, written in 1163, he was somewhat caustic about them.

Walking home, after Sabbath services, from the Ghriba Synagogue, situated outside Hara Srira.

So long as they were under Arab rule, the Jews of Djerba were relatively undisturbed. But when the Spaniards conquered the island during the sixteenth century the Jews were driven out. Later, when the Turks came and drove out the Spaniards, the Jews returned and re-established their communities. Ever since 1880, with the French conquest of Tunisia, the Jews of Djerba have declined in number. When immigration to Israel started, 1,700 out of the total Jewish population of 3,500 left for the Jewish homeland. The rest continue living in their two villages, Hara Kebira and Hara Srira.

Worshippers sitting barefoot—Arab fashion—in the Ghriba Synagogue. The chants, melodies and cantillations of these Jews have aroused great interest among musicologists who speculate that they might have an ancient Judean origin.

Although they claim that their ancestors had settled in Djerba following the destruction of the Second Temple in Jerusalem, there is little to tell Jews apart from the Arabs. Many of them cultivate vineyards, operate wine-presses, or trade in wine. Jewish women are as superstitious as their Arab neighbors: they wear the hand of Fathma as an amulet against evil spirits, and are loaded down with strings of colored stones and fish-bones as protection against diseases.

THE SAHARA

Jews live in the stony wilderness which juts into the Sahara. The area is part of the giant Atlas range of mountains that lies sprawling, congealed and bare, over hundreds of miles across Tripolitania and Tunisia. Along the flanks of these mountains, camel caravans wind their course between the coastal cities and the Sudan interior. Strangely enough, there are small Jewish villages in this forbidding region. They nestle in the hollows or are perched high like eagles' nests on top of steep crags. Some of these inaccessible villages have as many as 2,000 Jews. Their houses are constructed of slabs of grayish red stone, cut out of the cliffsides. Chameleon-like, they can hardly be distinguished at a distance from the rest of the terrain. For more than 2,000 years the Jews in these villages have stubbornly resisted the encroachments of nature and of hostile tribes.

Jews and Arabs live peacefully together in the oasis-settlement of Ouarzazate, southeast of the Atlas Mountains in French Morocco. Their houses are made of baked mud; their diet consists mainly of dates and vegetable roots.

Jews are also found in settlements in the oases which dot the wilderness at roughly fifty-mile intervals. They live there in amity with their semi-nomadic Berber neighbors from whom, except for the difference in religion, they are hardly distinguishable. They have been wandering traders throughout the Sahara region ever since Biblical times, have trekked into the most remote parts of the African interior as far south as Somaliland. At one time, before the Christian missionaries arrived to convert entire tribes and peoples en masse, the Jews of the Sahara were more numerous than they are today. In 1600 the famous geographer, Leo Africanus, wrote: "The Abyssinians claim that a numerous people of Jewish origin is found living on the shores of the Nile towards the West under a mighty king. Some of our newer geographers located an unknown mountainous region at the Equator between the Congo and Abassia which they call 'The Land of the Hebrews.' Jews also live in an inaccessible place in the mountains in a northerly direction from the Kingdom of Goiame and south of the Kingdom of Gorhan. They are powerful and independent."

Even in their isolation the Berber Jews of the Sahara have much in common with believing fellow-Jews elsewhere. They have a most touching rite upon completing their fast on *Tisha b'Ab*, which commemorates the destruction of the First and Second Temples in Jerusalem. They march in procession into the desert in search of caravan traces which they hope will lead them to the Messiah.

Some ethnologists are of the opinion that, because the Daggatun tribesmen, who live between Timbuctoo and the Sudan, observe certain Biblical customs and hold to Jewish traditions, they, too, may have been originally Jews.

CAVE DWELLERS

Closely related culturally and historically to the Jews of the Sahara are their troglodyte, or cave-dwelling, brothers. Their settlements are found in the various stony ranges that form part of the Atlas Mountains south of Tripolitania and Tunisia. It taxes credulity how under the forbidding physical conditions of this region, which is considered one of the most desolate in the whole world, it is possible for human beings not only to adapt themselves to their surroundings but even to lead lives in community *as Jews!*

Mud and stone superstructures of Jewish cave dwellers of Medenine in the Atlas Mountains of the Sahara.

Some inhabit caves in mountain summits. The majority, however, live in a series of crater holes or stone labyrinths which are common in this volcanic region. The various cave chambers have been connected by winding underground passageways and galleries by the people who live in them. A number of troglodyte communities have built on top of these cave dwellings superstructures made of baked earth reinforced by stone.

Two villages totally inhabited by Jewish cave dwellers lie along the caravan route that winds from Tripolitania through the mountain pass of Djebel Gharian into the Sudan. These are Beni Abbas and Yehud Abbas. Several hundred Jews live in each of these communities, and each has its own synagogue and *chacham*, or rabbi. Three and a half hours' journey by camel from there lies Tigrena. This is an underground community of 4,700 inhabitants who live by sheep herding. From the wool they obtain they weave the well-known Tigrena carpets.

One day's journey by camel from Tigrena is the Djebel Iffren range of the Atlas Mountains, where three Jewish villages cluster with most of their houses barely rising above the surface of the ground. In the Djebel Nefusa range are also found several villages of Jewish troglodytes. They are very old, for in each of them is found an ancient stone synagogue and a cemetery almost crumbled to the ground. The Djebel Matmata range of southern Tunisia conceals the cave villages of Fum Tatahuina, Hadesh and Matmata. These are not exclusively Jewish communities, but in them Jews and Berbers live in complete amity.

The cave dwellers believe that their ancestors had been

Rabbi of Matmata, in the Djebel Matmata range, Atlas Mountains, with his family before their cave dwelling.

brought as captives from Judea to the Atlas Mountains by Titus after 70 C.E. Their isolation from the mainstream of Jewish life adds poignancy to their longing for the redemption of Israel and for their own return to the land of their forefathers. They have an odd custom of cutting out little paper boats with which they decorate their synagogues. Then they pray fervently: "May a boat soon come and carry us to Jerusalem!"

THE FALASHAS

The early history of the Falashas, the Negro Jewish tribesmen who inhabit some of the regions north of Lake Tana in Abyssinia (Ethiopia), remains shrouded in legend. Their own tradition, dim with primeval memory, is that they had come as triumphant settlers some 3,000 years ago from Jerusalem in the train of Menelik, the royal issue of the Queen of Sheba's visit to King Solomon. Ethnologists and historians, however, prefer their own widely differing speculations concerning the

Falasha synagogue, or *mesjid*. It is quite similar to other Falasha houses. *Courtesy of Dr. Wolf Leslau*

origin of the Falashas. Quite a few theorize that they are descendants of the ancient Jewish community of Upper Egypt that had been founded before the Babylonian Captivity. The circumstantial proof for this is that although the Falashas observe many of the Jewish festivals, they have no knowledge of *Tisha b'Ab,* the Fast of the Ninth of Ab, which commemo-

Left. Falasha *kahens,* or priests. The one on the left carries a drum, a type usually played with wrist and fingers. *Right.* Falasha women. *Courtesy of Dr. Wolf Leslau*

rates the destruction of both the First and Second Temples, of the Festival of *Purim* with its late imperial setting in the Persia of Artaxerxes, and of *Hannukah*, the Festival of Lights, inaugurated by Judah Maccabee two centuries before the end of the Jewish state. They also know nothing of the *Mishna*, or Oral Law, nor of its related body of literature, the *Gemara.*

However, one thing is clear—in their features, hair and color-

ing the Falashas are not to be distinguished from either the Ethiopians or from the Ibo tribes in neighboring Nigeria. This simple fact, on cold genetic reasoning, would lead one to suspect that even though some of the Falashas' ancient forebears might have come originally from Palestine, as tradition claims, their basic strain is nevertheless African Negro. At what period they were converted, or what Jews converted them, is open to speculation. One theory has it that Yemenite Jews, who had only to cross the narrow divide of the Red Sea from their country into Ethiopia, initiated them into the Jewish religion.

There can be no doubt that the Falashas consider themselves Jews. They call themselves *beta Isra'el* (House of Israel). The name Falasha, which in Ethiopic means "emigrant," was given them by the Christian Abyssinians. They know no Hebrew, and the Bible version they use was translated during the seventh century by Christian missionaries from the Greek Septuagint into Gheez, Old Ethiopic. Today, only the priests of the Falashas can read Gheez; the Falashas of central Abyssinia speak the vernacular Amharic; those in the north speak Tigrinya. However, there is an interesting Jewish literature extant in Gheez which is believed to have been created between the fifth and the seventeenth century.

The most recent estimate is that there are no more than fifteen to twenty thousand Falashas.

THE SAMARITANS

Fourteen miles north of Jerusalem is the ancient city of Shechem (Nablus). Almost totally an Arab town, it lies in the shadow of Mount Gerizim. In its most wretched quarter, clustering around their ancient little synagogue, stand the houses of the Samaritans.

Samaritan High Priest kissing the *Sefer Torah* on Mount Gerizim at dawn on the first day of Passover. *The Matson Photo Service*

It is an irony of history that today, when the Jews have been restored to their homeland, the Samaritans, during the past twenty-four centuries their most stubborn rivals to the claim of being "the real Jews," have practically vanished. There are probably no more than two hundred of them left. As if to point up this irony, ever since Israel's war with the seven Arab States, in 1948, Nablus has belonged to the Kingdom of Jordan. And so the separation of the Samaritans from the Jews is now not only religious but physical.

Who are the Samaritans? They may best be described as

dissident Jews who have believed in the revealed truth of the *Torah* but have rejected all oral tradition. Their millennial separation from the Jewish people who first rejected them in the days of Ezra the Scribe constitutes, in human terms, a great tragedy.

Following their conquest of the Northern Kingdom of Israel, the Babylonians carried out a number of mass deportations of Jews whom they colonized in widely separated parts of their far-flung empire. This was in line with their master-plan for breaking up large concentrations of potential enemies among the peoples they subjugated. Equally a part of this state policy was the colonization of other ethnic groups among the Jews in Israel—"men from Babylon and from Cuthah, and from Arva and from Hanath and Sepharvaim."

Only two centuries later, when Ezra the Scribe returned with a band of exiles to Jerusalem to re-establish the ancient religious life of Israel, he found that many Jews who had been left behind by the Babylonians had in the meantime married with the transplanted non-Jewish groups. These intermarried people were thereafter referred to as the *Shomronim*, or Samaritans, because their home was in Samaria. The fact that they considered themselves to be Jews is evidenced by the offer they made to the returned exiles from Babylon when they began rebuilding the Temple on Mount Zion: "Let us build with you, for we seek your God as you do."

Instead of accepting their help, Ezra spurned it. Because they had intermarried, he declared them and their mixed progeny not a part of the Congregation of Israel. From that time there was bitter enmity between the Samaritans and the Jews.

The Samaritans in turn just as stubbornly rejected the Jews. They built a rival Temple on Mount Gerizim in the days of Ezra and declared it to be the only lawful site commanded by God for His House. Every Passover Eve through the many centuries since then the Samaritans have ascended to the summit of Mount Gerizim. On the site of their ancient Temple, long ago destroyed, they pitch their tents to commemorate in a realistic manner the Exodus of the Children of Israel from the Land of Bondage. They sacrifice seven sheep and roast the meat over an open fire. Then, with wanderer's staff in hand, they eat in haste both the flesh with bitter herbs and the unleavened bread, just as it is prescribed in the Bible.

KARAITES

Among the most curious Jewish sectarians are the Karaites. Because of some of their customs and rites which were derived from Islam, but particularly on account of their fierce opposition to the *Talmud*, Orthodox Jews in Russia and Poland placed them on the same level of contumely with free-thinkers and apostates. The Karaites were, therefore, obliged to live in tiny ghettos of their own in the midst of the larger ghettos of Jewry. All contact with them was sternly forbidden by the Rabbinic authorities in order to prevent the inroads of heresy.

How many Karaites were left after the Nazi slaughter of the Jews of Europe is not possible to estimate. In 1932 there were throughout the world only 12,000. Of this number, about 10,000 lived in the Crimea where they had been settled since early medieval times. The remainder were scattered in the

Karaite merchants of the Crimea, 1862. The belief is sometimes advanced that the Karaites are descendants of the Khazars whose vast Jewish kingdom also embraced the Crimea beginning with the 8th century.

Lithuanian towns of Troki, Lutzk and Vilna, in Istanbul, Cairo and Jerusalem, in Hit on the Euphrates and in the Galician town of Halicz. Yet there was a time when the Karaites were very numerous and influential, especially in the Crimea.

The Karaites, or as they are called in Hebrew, *Karaim* (People of the Bible), hold that their sect originated before the destruction of the First Temple. However, the first historic evidence of their existence appeared only in the ninth century C.E. within the Babylonian Jewish community. The movement found its original impulse in a small group of religious dissenters headed by Anan ben David. These were religious literalists who wished to guard the pristine purity of the Bible against the rationalistic additions of Rabbinic literature, i.e., the *Talmud*. Their guiding principle was Anan ben David's personal dictum: "I will search diligently in the *Torah* and will not rely on my own opinion." Anan ben David himself was full of opinions. He and his scholarly followers did precisely what they criticized the Talmudists for. They tried by every manner of reasoning and sophistry to make everything in the *Torah* conform to their beliefs.

The Karaites have their own liturgy and their own body of religious scholarship in Hebrew. Although, like the Samaritans, they had been rejected by the Congregation of Israel, they persisted, nonetheless, in considering themselves not only Jews but "the only true Jews." They produced a number of brilliant *Torah* scholars who possessed so wide a culture that they had considerable familiarity with the natural sciences. During the first quarter of the seventeenth century when Joseph del Medigo, the noted Italian rabbi-scientist, lived in Vilna as court physician to Prince Radziwill, the only scholars with whom he could share his intellectual interests were despised Karaites. By comparison with them, he said, the local *Ashkenazic* Talmudists were a superstitious and pedantic lot, preoccupied with trivia and hair-splitting.

It is interesting that in the United States today there are about one hundred Karaite families. They lead their own miniature community existence in Chicago, New York, St. Louis and several cities in California. They are mainly prosperous—manufacturers of furniture, realtors, doctors, lawyers and engineers—and are devoted to the Karaite colonies in the rest of the world, to whom they give material assistance.

TSARIST RUSSIA

JEWISH LEGION, 1794

It was not in Russia proper but in its Polish provinces that the first stirrings of the modern spirit among Jews were heard. For the first time since the revolt of Bar-Kochba, Jews had awakened to the realization that in order to become free they themselves had to help break their chains. This idea was forcibly brought home to them by two contemporary historic events that had shaken the peoples of Europe to their depths: the triumph of the two libertarian revolutions—in the American Colonies in 1776 and in feudalistic France in 1789. Carriers of this heady excitement of freedom and equality for the Jews were the Christian Polish officers who had fought for American independence in the Continental Army. On returning to Poland they felt a charity-begins-at-home compulsion to continue the struggle for freedom. The leader of this movement was General Tadeusz Kosciuszko, a hero of the American Revolution. In 1794 he thought it propitious to issue a call for a popular uprising of the Polish people against its two oppressors—the Russian Tsar and the King of Prussia.

Although the Jews of Poland were suffering at the hands of the feudal *Pans,* their Polish masters, they, too, responded to the people's urgent desire for liberty. Jewish committees to aid the revolution were organized in Vilna and Grodno. A natural military leader appeared in the person of Berek Joselowicz. He was the Jewish steward of Prince Nassalski, the Archbishop of Vilna. Having had occasion to make a number of

Berek
Joselowicz.

business trips to Paris with the archbishop, he had quickly fallen under the spell of the French Revolution's ideals of liberty, fraternity and equality. It was to him and to another Jew, Josef Aronowicz, that Kosciuszko gave authority to organize a Jewish legion.

Five hundred volunteers responded to the stirring call to arms which was printed in Yiddish. The majority of them were poor youths with no military knowledge—tailors, butchers, wagoners and blacksmiths. The Jews of Warsaw supplied most of the funds for the necessary equipment. Although poorly armed and trained, the Jewish Legion nonetheless held its ground stubbornly against the overwhelming assault of the Russian regulars led by the redoubtable General Suvarov on Praga, the Jewish quarter of Warsaw. There were only some twenty Jewish survivors in the carnage which followed, among them the unit's commander, Berek Joselowicz.

THE REVOLT OF 1830-31

Once again, in 1830, the Polish patriots raised the standard of revolt against Russia. When the Jews petitioned the leader of the insurrection, General Chlopicki, for permission to form a regiment of their own, he replied in a withering marginal note: "It is not fitting that Jewish blood should mingle with noble Polish blood." Nonetheless, the need for fighting men was so great that Jews were finally allowed to join the National Guard. Their presence aroused the resentment of the anti-Semitic Polish officers, and at their demand, General Chlopicki agreed to their expulsion. He then authorized Josef Berkowicz, son of the famous Berek, to organize a wholly

"Beardlings."

Jewish unit of the 850 who had been expelled. Because they were pious and wore beards, the soldiers of the Jewish regiment became known as "The Beardlings." They prayed thrice daily, ate only kosher food and on the Sabbath they rested. They distinguished themselves in battle by such outstanding bravery that General Ostrovsky, the commander of the National Guard, declared in a proclamation: "The sight of the Jewish militiamen and the sacrifices they made for Poland should convince everyone how much we have sinned against the Jews."

But there was no opportunity for the Poles to repent of their Jew-baiting: the revolt was quickly suppressed by the Russians.

THE REVOLT OF 1860-63

Again, in 1860, the embittered Polish patriots challenged the rule of the Russian Tsars, and again Jews stepped forward to make common cause with the rebels. The Chief Rabbi of Warsaw, Dov Berish Meisels, was elected to a committee which early in 1861 addressed a petition to the Tsar asking him to institute urgent reforms for Poland. A few days later popular demonstrations took place in Warsaw. The Russian

Rabbi Dov
Berish Meisels.

garrison there was ordered to fire into the crowds. Many Jews, along with Christians, fell that day.

Public funerals were held, and became gigantic demonstrations of indignation. With the other clergy officiating at one mass funeral were the Orthodox Chief Rabbi Meisels and the Reform Rabbi Marcus Jastrow, later of Philadelphia. So intense was the feeling of outrage among the Christian Poles against the Russians, and so appreciative were they of the Jewish blood that had been mingled with theirs on behalf of a free Poland, that they insisted on marching arm-in-arm with the Jews in the huge funeral procession. On this memorable occasion, tragically infrequent in the history of Poland, the Christian Poles declared that they and the Jewish Poles were "children of one mother—Poland."

Interfaith funeral service for slain Polish partriots. On extreme left, among the officiating Christian clergy, are Rabbi Meisels and the Reverend Marcus Jastrow.

THE JEWISH PALE

A forbidding though invisible wall began to rise all around the Jewish communities of Russia, the Ukraine and Poland, beginning with 1772. Jews were forbidden residence in any place outside of the communities they were already living in. This geographic restriction became known as the *Jewish Pale of Settlement* and was more precisely delimited by statute in 1804. It was, in a manner of speaking, a gigantic ghetto. Those Jews who dared venture beyond its confines were arrested and punished unless protected by special travel and residence permits.

"THE LIBERATOR"

When Alexander I (1801-25) became Tsar of Russia the hopes of the Jews soared high that he would abolish the Pale

WESTERN RUSSIA
and the
JEWISH PALE
within shaded areas

of Settlement and grant them some measure of equality. At least verbally he was aflame with humane and liberal sentiments which he had acquired from his tutor, the French philosopher, La Harpe.

On December 9, 1802, the Tsar appointed a commission to investigate the conditions of the Jews in the empire, with the object of improving them. Its findings led to the law of December 9, 1804, which, in effect, constituted a startling Bill of Rights for Jews. It gave them the right to own land and to till the soil, to establish factories and to follow whatever trades they wished. They were also eligible to attend schools and universities on the same footing with other Russians.

Medal struck for the Jews of Russia, commemorating Tsar Alexander I's "emancipation" of the Jews.

A new and brilliant era for the Jews of Russia, Poland and also Lithuania (which had been annexed in 1795 with the Third Partition of Poland) seemed to have been inaugurated by this liberal Tsar. Jews leaped with enthusiasm to the opportunities opened up to them. Those who had already fallen under the spell of Moses Mendelssohn and his Enlightenment Movement flocked into the *gymnasia* (high schools) and the universities. Quite a few Jews became merchants, brokers, bankers, manufacturers, doctors, teachers, journalists and government contractors. They, and especially their children, became quickly Russianized. Quite a number, following the chameleon pattern of some of the enlightened Jews in Germany, went to the baptismal font.

Expulsion from the Villages

But eventually Tsar Alexander I became frightened by his own liberalism. He began to wonder whether after all it might not lead to revolution and to his own overthrow. He, therefore, nullified all his reforms, including those for the Jews, and constricted the Pale of Settlement even more. He issued an ukase ordering Jews to liquidate their affairs as tavern and inn keepers in all the villages and along the roadsides. As Jews they would no longer be permitted to live anywhere but in the cities and towns. This decree dealt a shattering blow to 60,000 Jewish families.

Alexander's successor, Nicholas I, continued this policy of uprooting the Jews, and even extended its operation into parts hitherto unaffected. In 1827 he ordered Jews driven out of the villages in the District of Grodno, in 1829 from those along the shores of the Baltic and Black Seas, and in 1830 from all the villages in the Kiev area.

Prince N. Golitsyn described the expulsion: "In the dead of winter, half-naked Jews were driven from their homes into the towns. Many were crowded together in quarters that gave them no breathing space. The others, ill-sheltered, were left exposed to the bitter cold."

Many could not find any place at all for themselves. The overcrowding in the towns was indescribable. All Jewish communal resources for feeding and relief had been exhausted. An extraordinary and tragic kind of mass-wandering ensued. Thousands took to the road, trudged from one town to another, starving, confused and utterly despairing. Many died of hunger, exposure and illness.

The Spider Web

When the hordes of refugees flooded the towns within the Jewish Pale they caused frightful overcrowding and near panic conditions. The new difficult circumstances, aggravated by existing anti-Jewish restrictions in commerce and in the trades, resulted in intolerable competition and widespread unemployment. A vast army of unskilled, shiftless and maladjusted elements quickly sprang up. These were people who could follow neither trade nor calling and, in the mad scramble for physical survival, were found inadequate. They became superfluous men.

Many well-established merchants were ruined. Whatever commercial life had quickened in the ghetto almost ground to

Luftmenschen ready for any chance to earn a few *kopeks*.

a standstill now. Out of this economic near paralysis arose a petty-tradesman type who became unhappily well known in Russia, Poland and Lithuania—the *luftmensch* or "air man." He was an incorrigible optimist who literally tried to draw his sustenance, as if by a miracle, from the air. He frittered away his life loitering around the market place or railroad station, looking hopefully for the deal that would bring, if not exactly a fortune, at least the wherewithal to buy bread for his wife and children. In the classic story of "Mendel the Pack-Peddler," by Mendele Mocher Sforim, the "grandfather" of modern Yiddish literature, the *luftmensch* is described as selling Hebrew Bibles, prayer books, fringes for prayer shawls, amulets for pregnant women, *shofars, mezuzas,* wolf's teeth for good luck, children's patent leather shoes, *yarmulkas,* and an assortment of copper pots and pans. And on the collective strength of all these "staples" he remained a pauper.

Jewish traders of Odessa, 1862.

Despite the general poverty of the Jews the taxes imposed on them were onerous. A bewildering number of articles of consumption, as well as activities, were taxed. The traditional Jewish community organization, the *Kahal*, was degraded into a tax-collecting agency for the government. With the punishing Tsarist whip-cracking over them, the *Kahal* Elders were often forced to take harsh, and sometimes inhuman, action against their pauperized charges. For non-payment of taxes, for instance, they would seize the Sabbath candlesticks, the brass mortar and pestle and other heirlooms. They would even take away the bed pillows.

Market-scene in Cracow, 1869.

The Little Cantonists

In 1827 Tsar Nicholas I established a compulsory armed service period of twenty-five years for Jewish recruits. It inaugurated a new system of military levies for boys from twelve to eighteen years old, who were to be known as "Cantonists" and were to be delivered to the army by the *Kahal* officials in each Jewish community.

The reasoning behind this unprecedented type of military recruitment was simple: the Tsar and his advisers aimed to tear away the Jewish boys from their Jewish environment at an impressionable age. They figured that by keeping them for

Tsar Nicholas I, cracking a whip over the Jews whom he robs. (From the caricature by Daumier, 1855.)

twenty-five years in the army, stationed in parts of the country far removed from Jewish influences, they would be able to Russify them thoroughly. Not the least among the imperial considerations was the pious hope that an entire generation of male Jews could be gradually weaned from their religion and be led to accept the creed of the Orthodox Russian Church.

Kahal officials everywhere were flung into a tragic quandary, since they were expected to obey the law to the letter. But the order had struck terror in the hearts of Jewish parents. Pressures and influences of all kinds were naturally exerted, by those able to bring them, in order to get exemptions for their boys. As a result, the children of the poor and the weak were the easiest to recruit. Half-crazed parents concealed their boys and would not bring them voluntarily to the communal officials. In consequence, a new and nightmarish type of Jewish communal official arose to meet the situation. This was the *chapper* (snatcher or kidnapper). The people's memory of the *chapper's* ghoulish deeds was immortalized in many dirgeful Yiddish folksongs. The *chapper* would prowl through the streets and literally "snatch" Jewish children and carry them off.

Sir Moses Montefiore intercedes with Tsar Nicholas I for the Jews of Russia in 1846 in St. Petersburg.

Although twelve was the legal minimum age for Cantonists, some of the frightened *Kahal* officials, in order to fill their quotas, allowed the *chappers* to kidnap children seven and even six years old.

When reports about the Cantonists spread abroad, they stirred up great indignation. Sir Moses Montefiore, in his privileged position as financial adviser to Queen Victoria of England, journeyed to Russia in 1846 in order to intercede with the Tsar for more humane treatment of the Jews. Nicholas I listened to him coldly and continued to persecute the Jews as he always had. It was not until the coronation of Alexander II, on August 26, 1855, that the Cantonist system was ordered abolished.

"THE GREAT REFORMS"

Tsar Alexander II (1855-81), like the first Tsar Alexander, started his reign with a great fanfare of liberalism. He instituted what was euphemistically referred to as the era of "Great Reforms."

In 1861 he freed the serfs. This meant the liberation of the great bulk of the Russian people. The Jews of Russia rejoiced in the good fortune of the liberated *muzhiks,* but this was soon followed by the rise of a militant Russian nationalism which had dire consequences for the Jews. The philosophy of this Slavophile movement was expressed in the terse slogan: "One Russia, One Creed, One Tsar." Naturally, in such a program the Jews had to be made "one" with the rest of the Russians, and this could be done, the authorities decided, only by conversion. As in Berlin during the first quarter of the nineteenth century, quite a number of educated Jews, lured by the promise of careers, joined the Orthodox Russian Church.

Those Jews who did not accept conversion suffered oppression and all the pains and penalties of being unwanted, unprivileged aliens to a greater degree than before. In addition, the economic effects of the liberation worked new hardships on the Jews. Since the Tsar had made the serfs free but had given them no land, it resulted in the dislocation of the existing pattern of Jewish livelihood. Many of the liberated serfs entered small-scale commerce in competition with the Jews, or displaced Jews from jobs and thus reduced the number of gainful occupations open to them. These economic difficulties were even further aggravated by Russia's belated attempts to industrialize; the introduction of machinery worked the severest hardships on Jewish artisans.

Every time the peasants suffered from drought, famine, war, pestilence and higher taxes, the Russian government tried to divert their discontent and anger from itself to the Jews, who were blamed for everything.

The mortality rate among the Jews was twice as great as among the Christians who lived in the same area. The Jews subsisted on a sub-marginal level, although the Russian people also suffered under the terrible economic and political conditions. They, too, felt the crushing weight of the Tsar's tyranny.

It was not surprising that among the six revolutionaries who were sentenced to be hanged for the assassination of Alexander II, on March 1, 1881, was the Jewish girl Khasia Helfman. Her death sentence was later commuted to hard labor for life in the Petropavlovsk Fortress.

When oppression by the autocratic Tsarist government became unendurable for most of the Russian people, many young Jews, too, especially among the better informed, joined the struggle for liberation. A number of them were shot, died on the gallows, were left to languish in prisons or exiled to the frozen tundras of Siberia.

"HOLY MOTHER RUSSIA"

Pogroms

The first pogrom, government approved, took place in Odessa in 1871. It was fired by the incendiary agitation of the reactionaries among the nobility. Ten years later, when Alexander III (1881-96) succeeded to the throne of his father who had been assassinated, the battlecry of the anti-Semites rang out again, but this time more insistently and sharper. The new Tsar, frightened by the fate his father had met at the hands of the nihilists, began his rule with a calculated campaign of terror.

After the pogrom.

Especially marked for imperial retribution were the Jews. Despotic and weak-minded, Alexander III allowed himself to become the tool of Pobiedonostsev, the aristocratic Procurator of the Holy Synod, who had formerly been his tutor. Pobiedonostsev served as the spokesman for the Slavophiles, the religious chauvinists whose political faith was centered in the concept of "Holy Mother Russia." He regarded the modern democratic spirit and all intellectual enlightenment as leprous diseases with which "the vulgar" new middle classes were infecting society. And the worst of these bourgeois elements, he was convinced, were the Jews.

The Jews did not have to wait long to reap the bitter fruit of his policy. Immediately after Alexander III's coronation, during Easter Week of 1881, a pogrom broke out in Elizavetgrad. From there it spread fanwise into Kiev and Odessa. In the Kiev district alone there were pogroms in forty-eight towns. From there, the epidemic of violence and bloodshed moved into the districts of Volhynia, Podolia, Chernigov and Poltava, where it raged all of that year. There was also a massacre in Warsaw. Everywhere, a feeling of hopelessness and helplessness set in. The conviction grew increasingly that these outrages had been carefully engineered by the imperial government and sanctioned by the Orthodox Church. As was to be expected, the Tsar and his ministers piously disclaimed responsibility for the programs. The Jews, they said, had only themselves to blame for their misfortunes because of the way they "preyed" on the Russian people.

Leading personalities in the government, especially Count Ignatiev, the Minister of the Interior, publicly demanded that the Jews be kept strictly segregated and under surveillance in order to protect the Holy Russian People from their nefarious activities. Slavophile journalists kept up a lively agitation in the press, maintaining that the Jews, despite their long sojourn in the country, were not to be considered Russians but an alien, inferior minority. Accordingly, on May 3, 1882, the government promulgated the so-called "May Laws." These, constituting a pogrom by law, burdened the Jews with even harsher restrictions than ever before. These laws were intended to bring a quick and total solution to the troublesome Jewish problem. The formula Pobiedonostsev worked out for the liquidation of the Jews in the Russian Empire was arithmetically neat: one-third by conversion, one-third by emigration and one-third by starvation.

Mass Emigration

As soon as the Jews began to feel the pain of these hammer blows, panic seized them. They wanted to flee the country while there was still time. When the imperial government opened the gates to emigration, the mass-exodus began. Those who did not have the passage money to America compromised on emigration to England, Germany, France and other European countries.

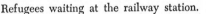

Refugees waiting at the railway station.

However, the lodestone that drew most of the emigrants was the United States, with its promise of economic opportunity and equal rights. Of the 700,000 Jews who fled Russia and Poland during the period 1884-1903, 500,000 went to the United States. In the next fifteen years another 600,000 departed. Many more would have emigrated had they been able to scrape together the passage money.

The emigrants.

The 1880's saw the economic and social noose tightening around the neck of Russian Jewry. In the most brutal manner, accomplished by sudden police raids, arrests and beatings, 14,000 Jewish artisans were expelled from Moscow. Although that city lay outside the Jewish Pale of Settlement, these skilled workers had been allowed privileged residence there only because of a practical need for them. Driven back with them into the cities inside the Pale were other thousands of privileged Jews from Novgorod, Tula, Kaluga, Riga and Yalta.

With the arrival of these refugees, the economic conditions in the ghettos grew even worse. In 1892 the Belgian historian, Errerra, observed: "There are in Russia only ten to fifteen thousand Jews who possess any certain means of existence. As to the masses, they have nothing." Conditions had grown so critical that to maintain themselves and their families, workers had to labor from fifteen to twenty hours daily and were forced to live on a diet consisting principally of bread and water, a few potatoes and a herring, "the poor Jew's chicken."

During the four pogrom years beginning with 1903 —the year of the Kishinev slaughter—410,098 Jews left Russia for the United States. This cartoon, which appeared in a German periodical in 1903, shows the bewildered Russian Jew. He wants desperately to emigrate but he is being pulled apart by his friends: England wants him to settle in the Uganda in Africa; Baron Rothschild, the ardent Zionist colonizer, points to Palestine as a haven; Baron de Hirsch, a prime mover in the back-to-the-soil movement, wishes him to settle in the farm colonies he founded in Argentina. Finally there is Uncle Sam, who pulls him toward the United States. In answer to this profusion of offers, the Jew cries out: "Blessings on that Russian Haman for having led me to this crossroad! If they'll all keep their promises, I'm a made man!"

Tsar Nicholas II (1896-1918) continued the repressive policy of Alexander III, and like his predecessor, was constantly in fear of revolution. The well-established policy of blaming everything on the Jews also proved expedient for him and his ministers. Ritual-murder charges against the Jews, with their circus distraction for the unthinking, were brought with increasing frequency during his reign. And when these expedients were found insufficient, there was cynical recourse to the pogrom. The Jews despised Nicholas II.

Left. Tsar Nicholas II. *Right.* Count Plehve, who was held responsible for the pogroms carried out by the Slavophile *Black Hundreds,* was later assassinated by revolutionaries.

Count Plehve, the Tsar's Minister of the Interior who was in charge of the police, stage-directed the infamous Kishinev and Homel pogroms in 1903. The police not only did not protect the Jews in those cities but even aided the pogromists. The mobs were well organized and seemingly acted without fear of official action against them. In fact, the pogroms were used by the authorities as a threat and warning to the Jews to stay away from the revolutionary movement.

In 1904 the government staged another massacre of Jews in Zhitomir. It did not do this openly but through the government-sponsored Slavophile "League of the Russian People," better known as the infamous *Black Hundreds.* In the diary of the conscience-stricken Prime Minister, Count Witte, was found this remarkable entry: "The Tsar especially loves the so-called *Black Hundreds.* He openly glorifies them as the first men of the Russian Empire, as exemplars of patriotism. . . . The aims of the *Black Hundreds* are usually selfish and of the lowest character. . . . They are typical murderers from dark alleys. . . . Naturally, one's record is still better if one can present evidence of having killed or at least mutilated a few peaceful *Zhidi* [an offensive Russian word applied to Jews]."

Christian Defenders

News of the pogroms shocked the world. Mass meetings were held everywhere. Street demonstrations took place in London's Whitechapel and on New York's Lower East Side.

Leo Tolstoy.   Maxim Gorky.

The press seethed with universal outrage. The indignation was equally strong in liberal Russian circles. Leo Tolstoy wrote a blistering attack on the pogromists in a letter to a Russian newspaper, but it was suppressed by the censor. He branded the Tsarist government "as the real culprit . . . which stupefies our people and makes bigots of them." After the debacle of the Revolution of 1905, when the *Black Hundreds* raged unhindered through the ghettos, intent on exterminating all Jews, Tolstoy appealed to the conscience of Russia to put an end to the savagery. The foremost literary men of Russia joined Tolstoy—Korolenko, Sologub, Andreyev and Maxim Gorky. Gorky especially made the cause of Jewish misfortune his own. From the time of the Kishinev pogrom in 1903 he had fought tirelessly against the *Black Hundreds* and the slanderous anti-Semitic press.

MENDEL BEILIS

The Tsarist government was in constant need of diversionary excitement to siphon off the revolutionary restlessness among the people. The *Black Hundreds* pounced upon a fortuitous incident that occurred in 1911. On March 25th of that year, Andrei Yushinsky, a twelve-year-old Christian boy, was found brutally murdered in a cave on the outskirts of Kiev, with forty-seven knife wounds in his body. Several days before the body had even been discovered there were sinister rumors that the Jews had committed a ritual murder upon the missing boy. An autopsy made later upon the body, according to official records, purportedly revealed that all the blood had been drained from the victim's veins.

At this juncture, the leading newspaper of the *Black Hundreds* in St. Petersburg entered the affair. It charged the *Hasidim* with the ritual murder of Andrei Yushinsky. Its cry of religious outrage was picked up by the reactionaries in the *Duma*, the quasi-Parliament of Tsarist Russia. The crime, so to speak, had been providentially committed just at the time when the Slavophiles could use it as a cudgel with which to beat the liberals who were waging a determined battle in the Duma to abolish the Jewish Pale of Settlement. But, remarkably enough, as in the Dreyfus case, the Chief of the Secret Police of Kiev, Mitschuk, was an incorruptible official. Upon thorough investigation of the crime he had come to the conclusion that it was no ritual murder at all. In his opinion a band of criminals had tortured the Yushinsky boy to death because he had gone to the police and informed against them.

Agents of the *Black Hundreds* lost no time and pinned the crime on Mendel Beilis, a superintendent of a brick kiln in a suburb of Kiev. Two habitual drunkards were brought forward to testify that they had seen "a man with a black beard" kidnap the boy on the street. They promptly identified Beilis.

In protest against this conspiracy the Chief of the Secret Police resigned his post and publicly presented proof of the innocence of Mendel Beilis, charging the actual criminals with the murder. Arrested for "fabricating evidence," he was sentenced to prison for one year. When news of the case reached the outside world, its full implications were recognized by some of the very people who had fought for the freedom of Dreyfus. Protests to Nicholas II were sent by the famous French writers Anatole France and Henri de Regnier, by the German dramatist Gerhart Hauptmann, and from America by Cardinal Farley for the Roman Catholic Church and by Bishop David H. Greer for the Protestant Episcopal Church.

Mendel Beilis.

For thirty-four days Beilis' trial dragged on in Kiev. The life of the defendant hung by a hair, not only because he was at the mercy of an hysterical and arbitrary court but because he was in constant danger from threatening mobs. On one occasion he was almost killed by a bomb. Another time the trolley car in which the police were bringing him to court was savagely set upon by the mob and Beilis barely escaped with his life.

The dénouement of this amazing melodrama was almost as incredible as its origin. Under the withering cross-examination by Beilis' defense counsel, celebrated liberal lawyers who had

volunteered their services, the accusing witnesses broke down on the stand and retracted their charges. Later, the leader of the gang, Vera Cheberiak, confessed her guilt. Under the circumstances the jury and the judges were forced to acquit Beilis. Nonetheless, they brought in the verdict that some "unknown Jews" had committed a ritual murder. This was a sop to the *Black Hundreds* and the government.

Jewish political prisoners from Bialystok in Yakutsk, Siberia, 1897. They are posing with their Russian military guards.

World War I

The case of Mendel Beilis was a straw in the wind: indicating that with the ascendancy of the Slavophile *Black Hundreds* the destruction of Jewish life in Russia was inevitable.

At the outbreak of World War I there were 6,946,000 Jews in the Russian Empire, including Poland, Lithuania and the other Baltic countries. In Poland alone there were 2,000,000 Jews. There were 300,000 Jewish soldiers in the Russian Army. Their lot was indeed wretched, but hardly comparable to the brutal treatment inflicted on their civilian brothers and sisters.

First group of refugees from Kovno, a few of the many thousands of Jews who were expelled from the city by order of Grand Duke Nicolai Nicolaevitch.

The sinister influence of the *Black Hundreds* followed the Russian armies and plagued the Jews wherever they went. The catastrophic defeats suffered by the imperial armies made matters even worse, and quite often the Jews were made the scapegoats for the errors and frustrations of the Russian generals. Jews were charged with pro-German sympathies, with a treasonable hatred for the Tsar. Many were accused of being spies for the German Army and were summarily shot. A number of rabbis and Jewish communal leaders were held as hostages to insure the loyal behavior of the Jewish population.

The Commander-in-Chief, the Grand Duke Nicolai Nicolaevitch, ordered the evacuation of hundreds of thousands of Jews from the battle zones. An interminable stream of refugees tramped the highways into the interior—80,000 to Warsaw alone. The full irony of the Russian government's charges that the Jews were pro-German was made plain when the Germans finally occupied Polish territory. They not only plundered the Jews but forced them into labor battalions.

A group of abandoned and hungry Jewish children roaming through the streets of Vilna during the time of the German occupation.

THE GOLDEN CHAIN

It should be emphasized that for all its miseries and griefs Jewish life in Russia had many normal and even joyous features. The impulse toward a wholesome existence and the will-to-happiness were drives that even the Jew's most implacable enemies never succeeded in suppressing. Moreover, in the course of thousands of years of the most insistent persecution, the Jewish people had acquired what might be described as a talent for adaptation. They possessed in their group, religious and cultural life an integrating force, a reserve strength, enabling them to survive even catastrophic blows.

For many centuries Jewish existence had adjusted itself to the barely changing rhythms of an interior life. It was immersed in the study of the *Torah* and the *Talmud*, in prayer and in ethical introspection, in the ceremonials of faith and in the ritual of observance. It was a dedication of the individual Jew to God and to his people. It began at birth and it ended with death. From this rich inner existence, regardless of the stagnancy of its flow at times, there emerged a unique body of literature and thought in both Hebrew and Yiddish.

In the synagogue, Galicia, 19th century.   *Isidor Kaufmann*

Grandfather teaching his grandson to put on *teffilin* (phylacteries). Fathers and grandfathers handed down the Jewish religious and cultural heritage to their children. This instruction was considered a holy task, a symbolic act performed in the Jewish drama of eternal renewal.

Tashlich prayers recited beside a stream in a small Lithuanian town.

Great Synagogue in Warsaw.

Will-to-Joy

If grief endured longer in the ghetto, joy was the deeper for it. Every opportunity for rejoicing was savored to the full. The merriest and longest-remembered occasions were weddings. They were no staid affairs, but joyous celebrations which lasted, among the well-to-do, for several days, sometimes even

Wedding guests arriving from another town. They are gaily welcomed with spirited tunes played by the little band of *klezmer*, or *klezmorim* (folk instrumentalists).

237

for a week. They afforded all kinsmen and friends living at a distance the welcome opportunity of meeting again in an atmosphere exuding patriarchal family warmth and piety. Moreover, many of the Jews of the town had a share in the rejoicing, for there was close communal living. Each Jew often felt that he was a kinsman to every other Jew in the little town ghetto and was delighted to have a share in his joys. Townsman became almost synonymous with kinsman.

Relatives of the bride and groom dancing the traditional *machitonim tanz* (kinsfolk's wedding dance).

Left. A Warsaw Jew and his wife on a festive occasion, mid-19th century. *Below.* A ghetto custom, dating back to medieval times in Germany, required a *marshalik* (*badchan*), or folk-bard, to improvise in rhyme a half-song half-speech for the bride. He intoned it in a dirgeful minor key. It recalled to her and to all her tearful female relations that her carefree girlhood days were over. Now a new life weighted with grave responsibilities as wife and mother were about to begin. This custom was called *bazingen di kaleh* (singing over the bride).

Singers of Zion

Much of the musical life of the ghetto was concentrated in the synagogue where on the Sabbath and on the holy days the *chazzan,* or cantor, would sing the service. Beginning with the nineteenth century, under the influence of grand opera and oratorio, his singing was supported by a trained choir. Nevertheless, in the smaller towns Jews continued to sing congregationally in the "plain chant" manner without any musical frills. They blended their singing unrestrainedly with that of the *baal-tefillah,* the prayer-leader. The musical modes and tunes they sang were of ancient origin and traditional.

The professional cantor, as he is known today, did not make his appearance in Jewish life until the nineteenth century. Often enough he possessed a fine voice, an innate musicality and a gift for interpretation—of illuminating the Hebrew text with his singing. But he never received any formal training—in the general musical art sense. He acquired his skill in long apprenticeship as a choir singer to one or more experienced cantors. Some of them attained almost legendary fame and built up an adulatory following.

A patriarchal family of *klezmer* in Tsarist Russia. Beginning with the later Middle Ages there were Jewish *spielleute,* or merry andrew troubadours, who sang, danced and played on musical instruments. They declaimed and sang epics of chivalry and Biblical paraphrases in Yiddish metric verse according to specified musical melodies or modes that were well known to Jews. In later centuries, appeared a new type of folk-musicians, called *klezmer* or *klezmorim,* a word derived from the Hebrew *kle zemer* (musical instruments). These were little bands of professionals who played Jewish folk-tunes by ear. They performed at weddings and at special festivities in the synagogue on

Hannukah and on *Purim,* or played marching in procession when a new *Sefer Torah* was being dedicated. Usually these *klezmer* came in dynasties: it was an inherited skill they cultivated. Although untrained in any formal sense, many were extremely gifted men. They were among those anonymous creators of Jewish folksongs and dances dearly beloved among the people. So superior was the playing of many of these *klezmer* bands that Polish nobles often engaged them. It is related that when Johann Sebastian Bach was serving as organist-cantor at the St. Thomas Church in Leipzig he would often trudge to a nearby Jewish village in order to hear the *klezmer* there play their "pretty little tunes."

Yoel-David Strashinsky (1816-1850) was celebrated as the "Vilner Baalhabessil." At thirteen he was appointed city *chazzan* of Vilna, because his singing and his genius for interpretation were so amazing. In 1839 the Polish composer, Stanislaus Moniuszko took him as a pupil. But as soon as the "Vilner Baalhabessil" became acquainted with the music of the masters, cantorial music lost much of its charm for him. He then went to Warsaw where he made concert appearances and caused a sensation. Then tragedy overwhelmed him: he fell in love with a Polish woman. This led him into a conscience struggle, for not only was he already married but he was a devoutly pious Jew. Although still in his twenties, he stopped singing and wandered on foot as a penitent from town to town throughout Poland, grieving and mentally ill. He died at 34 in a Warsaw mental institution.

Old-style Ukrainian *chazzan* of Bershad, with his wife. He was famous as cantor of the town synagogue for several decades.

Sirota, the celebrated *chazzan* of the Great Synagogue in Warsaw (about 1900). His *tenor robusto* voice was often compared with that of Enrico Caruso.

Haskalah

The *Haskalah,* or Enlightenment movement, which Moses Mendelssohn had founded in Berlin during the latter half of the eighteenth century, spread in the decades following to Galicia and from there into Poland, Lithuania and Russia. Lithuania was an especially fertile field. For several genera-

tions before, the Jews of that country had been notable for their cultivation of Talmudic learning. They had established the leading *yeshivot,* or Talmudic colleges. Above all, they had shown a marked preference for rationalism over mysticism. While emotional *Hasidism* swept over other East European Jewish centers, it never quite mustered any popular support in Lithuania, but instead met with the determined opposition of the "Vilner Gaon." The *Haskalah,* naturally, won many devotees there.

Leaders of the Russian Haskalah Movement. *Left.* Isaac Ber Levinsohn. *Right.* Moses Leib Lilienblum.

In a relatively short period of time, throughout the Russian Empire, there emerged a considerable number of Jewish novelists, poets and journalists who wrote on non-religious themes in Russian, Hebrew and Yiddish. The new secular "heresy" was especially attractive to the *yeshiva* students who already possessed an intellectual equipment and had a curiosity about the world. They secretly studied languages, particularly Russian, German and Polish—keys with which to unlock the doors of the Gentiles' knowledge. Before long, some of them entered into the broader field of general culture. A few even gave up being Jews. But many preferred to follow the dualistic credo formulated by Leon Gordon (1830-92), the foremost Hebrew writer of the day: "Be a man on the street and a Jew at home."

Hebrew vs. Yiddish

To the intellectual followers of the Hebrew *Haskalah,* who were known as *Maskilim* (Enlightened Men), Yiddish represented not only the language of the Jew's social inferiority but also the stagnation of Jewish culture in the ghetto. They fought it determinedly. Isaac Ber Levinsohn (1788-1860), the leader of the Enlightenment in Russia, dismissed Yiddish as "an ugly mish-mash of Biblical, Polish, German, Russian and other words. Being poor and little developed it is not suitable for expressing fine feelings and serious abstract thoughts."

By its very nature and program, the Jewish Enlightenment movement could not be democratic because it made its appeal only to the educated classes. Unlettered and unable to speak any other language but their *mama-loshen* (mother tongue), Yiddish, the great majority of Jews remained cold to the blandishments of Enlightenment. There were a small number of *Maskilim,* however, who, although they personally preferred Hebrew as a literary language, stubbornly defended Yiddish as the most necessary language medium of communication with more than three-quarters of the world's Jews.

Mendele Mocher S'forim.

Sholom Aleichem.

Peretz, Asch, Zhitlowsky, Nomberg.

S. Ansky.

Mendele Mocher S'forim ("Mendele the Bookseller"—the pseudonym of Solomon Abramovich, 1836-1917) was affectionately known as *Der Zaydeh*, "The Grandfather," of modern Yiddish literature. He served as literary guide and influence for an entire generation of Yiddish writers, including Sholom Aleichem and I. L. Peretz. Sholom Aleichem (Peace to you!) was the quaint nom-de-plume of Sholem Rabinovitch (1859-1916). As a satirist-humorist he has been ranked with Cervantes, Gogol, Dickens and Mark Twain. Yitzchok Leibush Peretz (1851-1915) was a literary master who exerted on Yiddish literature an influence greater even than that of Mendele Mocher S'forim and Sholom Aleichem.

Without a doubt, the Enlightenment movement, although it showed eager preference for Hebrew, also gave a tremendous impetus to the development of Yiddish as a medium for literary creation. This unfolded in rich measure during the second half of the nineteenth century.

Bankers and Railroad Builders

The rulers of Russia suppressed their hostility toward Jews whenever they could make practical use of them. Under Tsar Alexander II especially, a number of wealthy Jews were in high favor at Court. Some were bankers, others were railroad builders or founders of new industries. Most favored of all these bankers was Samuel Poliakov (1836-88). He was known as the "Railroad King" of Russia. With his two brothers he built several large railroad lines, and for this service he

Peretz drew his raw materials from the life and folkways of the Jewish people. He was both mystic and rationalist, naive and sophisticated, steeped in Jewish tradition and yet a social reformer. The foremost writers in Yiddish were his disciples, among them: Sholem Asch, David Pinski, Abraham Reisen, Yehoash, L. Shapiro, Dinesohn, Spektor, Jacob Gordin, Weissenberg, Yoinah Rosenfeld, H. D. Nomberg, S. Niger, Dr. Chaim Zhitlowsky, Peretz Hirschbein, Leivick and others. S. Ansky (Shloima Zanvil Rapoport, 1863-1920), a well-known Yiddish short story writer, playwright and folklorist, is best known for his drama, *Dybbuk*, which has been produced on the leading stages of the world.

was elevated to the nobility by the Tsar. Another Court favorite was Baron Günzburg, who financed the imperial government with funds borrowed from banks abroad. Other highly regarded Jewish financiers were Abraham Zack of St. Petersburg and the famed Brodsky family which pioneered the sugar industry in Russia.

Music

Music was always considered the "royal" art in Imperial Russia. It was in the feudal tradition for musicians of all kinds to add to the brilliance and diversion of Court life. Consequently, the usual discrimination toward Jews was often omitted where it concerned great Jewish musicians at Court, especially after the middle of the nineteenth century when Jews began to play a leading part in the musical life of Russia.

PHILANTHROPISTS

Berek and Temerl Szmulowicz.

Reb Nochemke.

Jean de Bloch.

Berek and Temerl Szmulowicz were the foremost Jewish philanthropists of Poland during the early 19th century. Berek was the son of Szmul Zbytkower whose extraordinary beneficence to the Jews of Warsaw during the War of Liberation in 1794 has been immortalized in folksong and story. Among his grandsons was Henri Bergson, the celebrated French philosopher. Almost legendary in his self-effacement and acts of kindness to the needy was *Reb* Nochemke of Grodno. Poor himself, he was only the *shammes* of the Great Synagogue of Grodno. Still he was the most redoubtable benefactor of the poor in his city during the middle of the 19th century. Ivan Blioch, better known as Jean de Bloch

(1836-1901), the most eminent figure in public life produced by the Jews of Russia under the Tsars, was a leading banker and railroad builder. He was also a thinker of distinction and courage. Like Sir Moses Montefiore, he had a broad humanitarian outlook and was a champion of social reform and of Jewish emancipation. His monumental work on international peace in 1898 helped bring about the first conference for International Peace the next year at the Hague. It was considered so epochal an event that he was awarded, in 1901, the first Nobel Prize for Peace. Although Jean de Bloch was a convert to Christianity, his last will and testament opened with the words: "All my life I have been a Jew and I die as a Jew."

Anton Rubinstein.   Henri Wieniawski.

Leopold Auer.   Wanda Landowska.

Two of the most important men in Russian music were the brothers Rubinstein, Anton (1829-94) and Nicolai (1835-81). Anton was considered a titan among the pianists of his day and the principal rival of Liszt. In 1862 he founded the great conservatory of music at St. Petersburg. Four years later, his brother Nicolai established the equally famous Moscow Conservatory. Despite the fact that he had been baptized as a child, Anton Rubinstein suffered from anti-Semitism. After Alexander III had bestowed the honorary title of "Excellency" on him, he wrote to his mother in a mood of bitter sobriety: "I have a presentiment that I shall need this *Excellency* some day against the very powers that gave it to me. For all your baptism at Berditchev we are Jews, you and I and sister Sophie!"

Henri Wieniawski (1835-1888), a teacher at the St. Petersburg Conservatory in the 1860's, was described by Anton Rubinstein as "without doubt, the greatest violinist of our time." His violin compositions are in the repertories of most violinists. Joseph Wieniawski (1835-1880), a brother, was almost equally celebrated as a violinist and teacher at the Moscow Conservatory. Leopold Auer, Court violinist to Tsar Alexander III, was successor to Henri Wieniawski at the St. Petersburg Conservatory. During his fifty years of teaching, the last years at the Institute of Musical Art in New York, some of his pupils were Mischa Elman, Efrem Zimbalist, Jascha Heifetz and a number of others who became well-known concert violinists. Wanda Landowska is a celebrated harpsichordist and pianist.

Science

For the young Jew with intellectual ambitions the Russian Empire proved to be nothing but a swamp of discouragement. The more he struggled for an education and a career in his special field, the deeper he sank into hopelessness. He was largely shut out from higher education by the *numerus clausus* which fixed the percentage of Jewish students to be admitted into the universities. The rigid laws governing the Pale of Settlement kept him out of the cultural centers of Russia.

The almost unscalable wall of religious bias, except for the apostate Jew, stood between him and an academic or professional career. Consequently, the serious Jewish student who found the means went abroad for his education and never came back. Among these intellectual *émigrés* who won world renown were the mathematicians Georg and Moritz Cantor, the microbiologists Eli Metchnikoff and Waldemar Mordecai

Haffkine, the endocrinologist Oscar Minkowski, and the cerebral anatomist Mirczyslav Minkowski.

Waldemar Mordecai Haffkine (1860-1930), an associate of Pasteur, Ehrlich and Metchnikoff in Paris, discovered a new vaccine with attenuated virus which proved very effective against cholera. Countless lives were saved with this vaccine when the cholera epidemic ravaged India in 1893. Three years later he discovered a new method of inoculation against the bubonic plague which reduced fatalities by eighty to ninety per cent.

The endocrinologist Oscar Minkowski, a Lithuanian Jew, found scope for his scientific talents in Germany. With Josef von Mering he discovered the direct connection between the pancreas and diabetes which led to the discovery of insulin.

Mirczyslav Minkowski, a Polish Jew, became the foremost cerebral anatomist in Germany. He was noted for his studies of the central nervous system of the human foetus.

ARTISTS   INVENTOR   SCIENTISTS

Mark Antokolsky.   Isaac Levitan.   Abraham Stern.   Georg Cantor.   Ilya Metchnikoff.

Mark Antokolsky (1842-1902) was born in the Vilna ghetto. He refused to follow fame at the sacrifice of his Jewish identity. The art critic, Stassov, for instance, wrote in 1883: "He is the greatest sculptor of our age!" Isaac Levitan (1860-1900) was one of the most admired landscape painters of the late 19th century in Russia. Other well-known Jewish painters were Leonid Pasternak and Leon Bakst.

Abraham Stern (late 19th century) invented an adding machine. An Orthodox Jew and Talmudic scholar, he had no opportunity to develop his mathematical and mechanical bent in the Warsaw ghetto. About Georg Cantor (1845-1918), one of the

greatest mathematicians of all time, Bertrand Russell, the English mathematician-philosopher, said: "In mathematics my chief obligations, as is indeed evident, are to Georg Cantor." Like so many other Jews who rose to eminence as a result of their fortunate departure from Russia and Poland, Georg Cantor found an outlet for his genius in Germany. His brother, Moritz Cantor, also a noted mathematician, is regarded as the foremost historian of mathematics. Ilya Metchnikoff first found an outlet for his biological researches when he went to Paris and worked with Louis Pasteur. For his study of the bacteria in the human alimentary canal, he shared the Nobel Prize for medicine in 1908 with Paul Ehrlich.

THE POLISH REPUBLIC

Many Jews fought in General Josef Pilsudski's Polish Legion of Liberation during World War I. They counted on his promise that when Poland threw off the yoke of the Tsars, Jews would enjoy absolute equality with Poles. Although on seizing power by a *coup d'etat* in 1926 he had formally abolished all anti-Jewish laws, he gave little more than lip service to the positive granting of Jewish rights. As economic conditions

The center of the historic ghetto of Vilna (Wilno). After World War I, Vilna and other parts of Lithuania were annexed to the newly established Republic of Poland.

grew worse in Poland, he accommodated himself to the virulent Jew-baiting in which both government authorities and political leaders engaged. The economic crisis made expedient the maltreatment of the Jews—the traditional scapegoats.

A street in the Vilna ghetto.

The new anti-Semitism in Poland proved most aggressive in the professions, in the universities, in government departments and in business and commerce. Major factors in this virulent agitation during the middle 1930's were the ENDEKS (Na-

Small-town Jews of Polish Lithuania.

tional Democrats) and the NARAS (National Radicals). A well-organized "cold" pogrom, later copied by Nazi Germany, began to operate in all fields, and led to privation and ruin for many of the 3,000,000 Jews of the country. Jews were excluded almost entirely from government service. They were not employed in any of the huge government-operated monopolies in salt, tobacco, alcohol and lumber. Hardest hit were the Jewish shopkeepers, the middlemen and the small manufacturers against whom, particularly, the cold pogrom raged. The argument against them was the ancient characteristic slogan: Jews were not Poles but aliens! If a livelihood was to be had out of trade and commerce, did it not rightfully belong to Poles?

A Jewish street in a small Polish town.

The elimination of the Jews from the economic life of Poland was now turned into a patriotic and religious cause. Although there were official pleas against the use of physical violence, the government and the Church, nevertheless, sanctioned the crusade. The government-owned radio constantly blared forth its appeals to the Polish people to boycott Jewish business establishments. Moscicki, the president of the republic, and Marshal Smigly-Rydz militantly led the campaign against the Jews. Leaders from most political parties made demagogic and slanderous attacks on the Jews from the rostrum of the *Sejm* (Parliament). A concerted campaign of legal and financial restrictions was introduced. To aggravate

Small-town Jewish traders waiting in the market square for a lucky break.

the situation further, the small Jewish shopkeeper found it almost impossible to compete with the new consumer cooperatives that had made their appearance in a vast chain of establishments throughout the country. The anti-Jewish hysteria, so artificially whipped up, soon overflowed into the schools and into all fields of cultural life. "Ghetto benches" were legalized in all the classrooms by the Minister of Education.

The impoverishment of the Jewish population of Poland grew like a fungus disease. Again, as during the Middle Ages, it was hardly possible for a Jew to obtain employment outside of enterprises owned by Jews. In large industrial centers, espe-

Famous Jewish food market in Warsaw, patronized by both Jewish and Gentile customers.

Jobless Jews on the "Koiler-Gass," a street in Kutno made famous in Yiddish literature by Sholem Asch, one of the town's native sons.

cially in the textile city of Lodz, the condition of the Jewish population became intolerable. Almost half of all urban Jews applied for assistance to the Jewish community relief agencies, which could hardly meet their obligations to all the needy. Only small groups of businessmen and professionals still managed to maintain themselves. Most of the 3,000,000 Jews of Poland were facing the grim prospect of starvation. During 1918-1934, 404,000 Polish Jews left the land of their birth. They emigrated to all parts of the world, especially to Palestine, the United States, Latin America and South Africa. Hundreds of thousands more were anxious to leave, too, but they either lacked the means to escape or found the gates barred to them.

The Way of the Pious

Whatever tribulation was the lot of the deeply religious Jew in the Polish ghetto, he found emotional warmth and comfort in his traditional way of life. The daily pursuit of the Tal-

Left. Feivele *Wasser-tray-ger* (water - carrier), who supplied all the Jews of Staszow with water. *Below.* A Jewish countryman stopping along the road to rest his old nag. This type, common in all of Eastern Europe, was immortalized by the famous Yiddish humorist, Sholom Aleichem, in his story of *Tevya der Milchiger* (Tevya the Dairyman).

Nothing better to do, Jews of Lublin gather to settle some of the world's knottiest problems.

CHARACTERS AND MISFITS

The economic swamp into which the Jews of Poland were forced spawned many misfits. Lack of productive employment and involuntary idleness turned many into unstable pipe-dreamers and feverish improvisers. The Jewish town had its full quota of odd characters and "superfluous" men who, nonetheless, maintained

a defensive cheerfulness to help them survive. *From left to right*: *Reb* Mordchi, the town wit of Staszow. An elderly carpenter of Vilna. Deranged by the buffetings of fate, he was called Mashiach (Messiah) because he announced himself as his forerunner. Mordchi Bitter, a celebrated *fresser,* a perpetually hungry man. Kalman *Naar* (fool), the town fool.

243

From left to right: Leading rabbis of Warsaw—Orthodox, Conservative and Liberal—in procession, during the Pilsudski period. Jews of Pinczow on their way to the synagogue. (Practically everybody went, old and young. The Orthodox close-knit character of Jewish community life in the small town made it hard for non-

conformists, "heretics," agnostics or free-thinkers to flourish. These usually gravitated to the big cities which they found more congenial and "progressive.") *Reb* Yekeles of Strij, an old type of Rabbinic scholar. On the table are the inevitable tools of a Talmudist—a sacred book and a box of snuff.

mudic culture he cherished gave him a feeling of timelessness and the reassurance of continuity. For both young and old—and this held especially true in the small-town Jewish communities with their totally conforming pattern—life had an unchanging rhythm. The procession of the festivals and fasts, the rites of the synagogue and the folk-customs—all were facets of a well-defined group culture. It united parents and children in a community of interests, activities and traditions which were handed down from generation to generation like the most precious heirlooms.

The Modern Spirit

The strong tide of progress in Europe at the turn of the twentieth century dashed against the physical as well as cultural isolation of the Jews in Poland and washed away much of the medievalism and stagnation of ghetto life. While the traditional forms of Jewish religious culture continued unaltered, the modern secular spirit became more and more evident among the youth. Within the limits of their meager opportunities for education and self-development, Polish Jews made remarkable advances in every direction. In the field of Polish literature, stated the noted literary critic Wilhelm Feldmann, himself a Jew, perhaps twenty per cent of all

After taking part in a circumcision celebration in Polenitz, four youthful Hasidim from Warsaw are waiting for their train back.

writers were Jews. Antoni Slonimski and Julian Tuvim are the two most admired modern poets of Poland. The latter, born in 1894, has been called "the Polish Pushkin." Joseph Wittlin, now in the United States, was a foremost novelist.

Simon Askenazi, the eminent Polish historian, served as Poland's representative in the League of Nations during 1920-21. Julian Klaczko was a noted writer on the history of culture. Rafael Taubenschlag was an expert on Roman law. Ludwig Gumplowicz was renowned as a sociologist.

The well-known Jewish affinity for music, never allowed more than partial exercise in anti-Semitic Poland, nonetheless

gave rise to a number of first-class musicians. Some of the best known have been the pianists Ignaz Friedmann and Artur Rubinstein, the *lieder* singer Marya Freund, the harpsi-

Zionist sport club, "Bar Kochba," meeting in the Liberal Synagogue in Poznan, Poland.

chordist Wanda Landowska and the composer Alexander Tansmann.

Jewish community life in the cities of Poland had far greater variety and a more progressive character than some would imagine. While the *Kahal*, the traditional Jewish community organization, continued under the Polish republic as the official administrative organ for Jewish religious affairs and institutions, a vast cultural and educational activity went on outside its framework. There were a variety of Jewish political parties and social and cultural organizations with diverse philosophies and employing different language media: Polish, Hebrew or Yiddish. Each propagated its own views and values through its special educational and cultural facilities. Since the Polish government discouraged the education of Jewish children, the various Jewish organizations established their own elementary and even high school systems.

Besides the ubiquitous old style *cheder*, the traditional Orthodox school, and the more modern and nearly as Orthodox *Talmud Torah*, there were a considerable number of Jewish nationalist, non-religious schools in Poland. Of these the most numerous and best supported were the "Tarbut" Zionist schools which emphasized the study of the modern Hebrew language and literature. Next in importance were the secular Labor-Zionist and Socialist schools with Yiddish as their language of instruction.

There were extensive adult cultural activities centered around both the new Hebrew and modern Yiddish literatures: newspapers, periodicals, books, theatres, lecture courses, etc. Important in the cultural advancement of the former was the Institute of Hebrew Studies in Warsaw; of the latter, the Yiddish Scientific Institute (YIVO) founded in Vilna in 1925.

UNDER THE SOVIETS

THE TSAR IS OVERTHROWN

On March 12, 1917, the Tsar's government was overthrown by workers in a general strike assisted by troops that had just returned from the demoralized war front. One of the first acts of the Provisional Government was to abolish the Pale of Settlement by legal decree on March 20, 1917. Although the principle of full equality for all national minorities was officially declared, nothing was done to implement it until after the Bolshevik Revolution on October 25 (November 7, Western Calendar), 1917.

Only a few days after the Soviets seized power, they issued the *Declaration of the Rights of the Peoples of Russia*, which announced the "abolition of all national and national-religious privileges and restrictions, and the full development of national minorities and ethnic groups." Two years later the Soviet government abolished the *Kahal*, or self-governing organization of the Jewish community. The latter was declared to be in disharmony with the social character of the dictatorship of the proletariat. Thus the first significant step was effected for Russian Jewry in its break with the traditional Jewish past.

On the eve of the revolution there were less than 3,000,000 Jews in Russia. Their sudden liberation from the Tsarist yoke left them both breathless and rejoicing at the prospect of enjoying full equality with other Russians. With the exception of the middle-class parties: Jewish People's Group, Zionist Party, National Democratic Party and *Agudath Israel*, as well as of the Socialist *Bund*, and the United Jewish Socialist Labor Party, which belonged in the Menshevik opposition to the Bolsheviks, most other Jews were apolitical. They looked with hope to the future.

THE REVOLUTION

The chief opposition to the revolutionary Soviets came from the "White Guards," who represented substantial elements of the still-undefeated Tsarist forces. They were led by monarchist officers, priests of the Orthodox Church, and aristocrats who had formerly been intimately associated with the Slavophile *Black Hundreds*. An important item of their stock-in-trade was anti-Semitism, which they employed skillfully as an emotional rallying point for many Russians who were opposed to the new regime.

Upon the eruption of the Civil War, reports soon reached Moscow of large-scale massacres of Jews by White Guardists in many cities, especially in the border regions. The "Whites" were energetically spreading the fiction that the Soviet government was a "Jewish government" which was set upon destroying "Holy Mother Russia." They built this fiction upon the fact that several of the prominent leaders of the Bolshevik Revolution were Jews: Sverdlov, Trotsky, Kamenev and Zinoviev. From all this the Soviet government concluded that the anti-Semitic warfare was leveled as much against itself as against the Jews. It branded anti-Semitism as an aggressive weapon of the counter-revolution.

On August 9, 1918, under the signature of Nicolai Lenin, the Council of People's Commissars issued a decree in which it declared: "Any kind of hatred against any nation is inadmissible and shameful. . . . The Council of People's Commissars instructs all Soviet deputies to take uncompromising measures to tear out the anti-Semitic movement by the roots. Pogromists and pogrom-agitators are outside the law."

The Commissariat of War and the Department of Propaganda then took counter measures to weed out anti-Jewish manifestations in the Red Army and among the civilian population. But this task was far from easy, because for centuries the Russian people had been nurtured on the poison of hatred for the Jews.

The Soviet government then initiated a large-scale program of education among the people against anti-Semitism in the press, in the factories and in the schools. Maxim Gorky, the foremost Russian author, wrote a stirring indictment of it. At first, it seemed as if all these efforts were doomed to failure. As the Civil War dragged on, it grew increasingly bitter and bloody, and with it the "Whites" directed a mounting savagery against the Jews. Thousands of anti-Bolshevik Jews, for instance, who had fled for a haven into anti-Soviet Siberia, were butchered by their "protectors," the White Guardist commanders, Admiral Kolchak and General Wrangel.

Funeral procession, led by the Jewish Self-Defense of the town, for the 30-year old Jewish physician Weinfeld of Bershad, the Ukraine (1919). He had been killed in a skirmish between the Jewish Self-Defense of Bershad, to which he belonged, and elements of Petlura's bandit-nationalists.

Infinitely more calamitous was the experience of the Jews of the Ukraine during the Civil War years. They were preyed upon ceaselessly by the troops of the White Guardist General Denikin and by the large bands of marauding nationalist insurgents of the "Ukraine Directory," commanded by the Generals Petlura, Skoropadsky and Makhno. It was a continuous see-saw game: the "Reds" would take a town one day; the "Whites" would retake it the next, and their first act would be to initiate a pogrom, accusing the Jews of sympathy for the "Reds." But Jews no longer were pacifists waiting for the slaughter as they had done in former years. In 1921, the Jewish Self-Defense as a quasi-military organization stepped up its activities in the cities and towns of the Ukraine. Unfortunately, they were neither adequately armed nor numerous enough to contend successfully with the large and well-trained armies of the "Whites" and the Nationalists.

No one really knows how many were slain of the total Ukrainian Jewish population of about 1,250,000. But it is widely conjectured that perhaps 200,000 perished. Several hundred thousand Jewish children were left orphaned. The savagery finally ended in 1922. Although, thenceforth, Jews were given full protection by the Soviet government and even anti-Semitic remarks were made punishable by law, the nightmarish experiences which they had undergone filled many

Ukrainian regulars under the Cossack bandit-leader, the *Ataman* Zelioni, posing with the *tallis*-wrapped Jews they had massacred only a little while before on the road between Bohuslav and Tarastcha, August 10, 1919.

Jews with disquietude for the future. Consequently, there was an extensive emigration of Jews from the Ukraine in the early twenties. Thousands went as *chalutzim* to Palestine. Others sailed for the United States, Latin America, Australia and South Africa.

Schwarzbard, (in witness-box) testifying at his trial. In front of him is his counsel, the celebrated French Jewish trial lawyer, Maître Henri Torres. At the left, for the prosecution, is the equally famous Maître Campinchi who is cross-examining the accused. A dramatic footnote to the Ukrainian massacres was written with a revolver on the boulevards of Paris in 1927. A young Ukrainian Jew, Samuel Schwarzbard, started out for the French capital with the sole purpose of avenging the murder of his father and mother and of 200,000 other Jews. He had heard that after Petlura's flight before the Red Army he had gone to Paris. For days he stalked his prey like a hunter. Then he confronted him and shot him dead. Schwarzbard surrendered voluntarily to the police. Charged with murder, he was tried in the Court of Assizes. Amid scenes of great public excitement and emotionalism, the court unanimously acquitted Schwarzbard.

The Jewish Pattern

A number of special social and economic problems confronted the Jews, despite the Declaration of Rights for them. Due to systematic repression for centuries they had become estranged from the land. There consequently were relatively few tillers of the soil among them. While there had been a large number of Jewish workers in the cities of the Pale even under the Tsars, nevertheless, the largest elements comprised shopkeepers and petty tradesmen, unstable entrepreneurs and commercial will-o'-the-wisps. There were, too, a considerable number who followed the traditional religious callings—rabbis, Hebrew teachers, cantors, sextons, *Torah* scribes, slaughterers, etc.

It is significant that of the fewer than 3,000,000 Jews in Russia at the time of the revolution, perhaps 1,000,000 were classified as non-workers. Their lot was indeed wretched and seemed hopeless under the new conditions, since the Soviet economy was based on the principle that all able-bodied citizens had to be productive. The slogan was: "He who does not work shall not eat." It was fixed into law some years later: "From each according to his ability, to each according to his work."

The question, soberly put, was: what "ability" did a former Jewish middleman have which could be found useful in a socialist economy? What, for example, could a Talmudic scholar contribute to the communistic educational system? True enough, the majority, especially the malleable young people, adjusted themselves without undue hardship to the new economic system. Tens of thousands were taught skills in government trade-schools. The former artisans, of course, found it relatively easy to secure employment in the various industries for which their training fitted them—in heavy industry, machine shops, mines, iron works, etc., jobs which had been closed to them in Tsarist times. Many middle-class Jews and professionals even managed to find places for themselves in the factories, in transportation, in the social services and in government offices, or they underwent retraining for new skills. Nonetheless, large segments of the former middle classes remained expropriated, *déclassé* and in a desperate condition. They found it very hard to fit into the new scheme of things, since they did not have the will, the training nor the psychological elasticity for a break with the past. They made no attempt to learn a manual trade.

This inability to "belong" led many to take a hostile stand toward the Soviet regime, either openly or covertly. Many were punished as "class-enemies." Others, embittered by their hopeless situation, sank into a state of apathetic wretchedness. Both as "class-enemies" and as non-productive individuals they were not allowed to enjoy the worker-consumer's privileges which made the difference between a tolerable and an intolerable existence. They were also disqualified for the privileges relating to travel, entertainment, culture and health which other Soviet citizens were allowed. Their food rations, too, were skimpier. But, worst of all, their doubtful status worked great harm emotionally and practically upon their children, who were excluded from higher institutions of learning and technical schools. This added another link to the chain of group bitterness and frustration.

A reprieve came to the Jewish maladjusted but it was of brief duration. Early in 1921 Lenin introduced his much discussed New Economic Policy (NEP) in order to help forestall a crisis in the Soviet economy. This allowed small-scale manufacturing and retail trade to return to private enterprise. The "old experts" in these areas of capitalistic economy among the Jews came to life again and their establishments mushroomed in profusion. They opened retail shops and artisan enterprises everywhere. In 1924 Jews owned at least one-third of all the retail shops in Moscow. But this reconciliation of the Soviet government with capitalism was a "tactical retreat" and only temporary. After a few years private enterprise was more and more restricted and ended officially in July, 1928. Once more there was a fluid class of shiftless, unabsorbed Jews who looked wistfully into the unpromising future.

With the years, the number of Jews not absorbed into the economic fabric of Soviet life became proportionately smaller. The new conditions and new opportunities opened up by the Five Year Plan resulted in a different kind of vocational distribution. While the white-collar occupations and the professions continued to attract Jews as before (a 1941 statistical study revealed that they included about half of all the gainfully employed Jews of the Soviet Union), there was also a

246

remarkable increase in the number of industrial workers and in the variety of their trades and technical skills.

The historical conditioning of the Jew had made him essentially a city-dweller. This preference he continued to exercise even under Soviet life. For one thing, his traditional attachment to learning and culture found readier channelizing in the cities. Furthermore, his emotional attachment to Jewish group life, although growing weaker in ratio to its assimilation into Soviet life, persisted nonetheless. On the eve of the Nazi invasion of the Soviet Union, more than forty per cent of the Jews were concentrated in Moscow (430,000), Leningrad (275,000), Kiev (200,000), Kharkov, Odessa and Dnepropetrovsk.

The traditional preference many Jews showed for intellectual pursuits and the learned professions found a new impetus from their unrestricted exercise in Soviet Russia. An interesting Soviet study of the distribution of Jewish cultural workers in 1941, the latest available, showed 87,000 engineers, architects, agronomists and technicians; 52,000 doctors, dentists, nurses, etc.: 46,000 teachers; 7,000 scientists and academic scholars; 17,000 artists and writers; and 30,000 journalists, librarians and miscellaneous culture specialists.

With anti-Semitism outlawed and its propagation made punishable as a crime against the state, many Jews found an outlet in the government for their organizing and administrative gifts. Even under the Provisional Government headed by Kerensky, there were several important Jewish statesmen: Isaac N. Steinberg was Minister of Justice; M. Winaver, leader of the Cadet Party, was Minister for Foreign Affairs in the anti-Bolshevik Crimean Republic. From the very first, Lenin chose some of his closest collaborators from among Communists of Jewish origin. Yakov M. Sverdlov (after whom the city of Sverdlovsk was named) was the chairman of the all-important Central Executive Committee after the October Revolution of 1917. Leo Kamenev, chairman of the Moscow Soviet, was Vice Premier and President of the Council of Labor and Defense. And, of course, Leon Trotsky, first as chairman of the Petrograd Soviet, then as Commissar for Foreign Affairs, and finally as Commissar for Defense, was one of the foremost leaders of the October Revolution.

Leon Trotsky as Soviet Commissar for Defense, addressing a gathering before his ouster in 1925.

There were, besides, such prominent leaders as Zinoviev, later President of the Communist International, the diplomat Adolph Joffe, and Ryazanov and Uritzky. Some years later, younger men of Jewish origin stepped into important government posts: Grigory V. Sokolnikov, Commissar for Finance (1925); Aaron L. Scheinman, his successor (1926-28);

Maxim Litvinov, Soviet Commissar for Foreign Affairs, addressing the League of Nations.

Maxim M. Litvinov, Commissar for Foreign Affairs (1930-39); Arkady P. Rosenholz, Commissar for Foreign Trade (1931-36); Moisei I. Kalmanovich, Commissar for Grain and Livestock Farms (1934-35); Abram L. Gilinsky, Commissar for the Food Industry (1938); I. Y. Weitzer, Commissar for Home Trade (1935-36); Moisei L. Rukhimovich, Commissar for the Defense Industry (1936); Lazar M. Kaganovich, Commissar of Land Transport (1936), of Heavy Industry (1938-39), and of Railroads (1940-41); his brother, Mikhail M. Kaganovich, Commissar for the Defense Industry (1938); Semyon Ginsberg, Commissar for Construction (1941); and Lev Z. Mekhlis, Commissar for State Control (1941-50).

Madame Molotova, wife of Soviet Vice Premier V. I. Molotov, visiting a children's home. For a time she served as Commissar of the Cosmetics Industry.

Beginning with the late twenties, a number of these top leaders were removed from their posts. This took place during the *chistkas,* or Communist Party "cleansings," better known in the West as "purges." Several of them, Zinoviev, Kamenev, Sokolnikov and Rosenholz, following highly sensational trials in Moscow, pleaded guilty to the charge of conspiring with foreign powers to overthrow the Soviet government and were

Left. Karl Radek, foremost Soviet political journalist of his day, testifying as a defendant in the "Trotzkyist" conspiracy trial held in Moscow, January 27-30, 1937. He was found guilty of treason and sentenced to ten years at hard labor. *Right.* Lazar Kaganovich, member of the Soviet *Politburo* and reputedly Stalin's brother-in-law, directing the construction of the Moscow subway. As Commissar for Heavy Industry and, later, of Railroads, he earned a considerable reputation as organizer and administrator. After Stalin's death he became a Vice-Premier.

executed. Both the trials and the confessions let loose a storm of disbelief and protest among non-Communists. The man whom the Soviet authorities accused of being the chief plotter, Leon Trotsky, had previously been banished from the country. He, however, perished in 1940 in Mexico City at the hands of an assassin.

Jewish Farmers

At the start of the nineteenth century, during the reign of the "liberal" Tsar Alexander I, there were several Jewish agricultural settlements in Russia. His successor, Nicholas I, tried to make the rustication of the Jews a vital part of his program for assimilating them. In this way, he figured, they would be absorbed by the *muzhiks* and would cease being

Cutting hay on a South Russian Jewish collective farm in 1925.

Jews. To this end the decree of 1847 allowed and even encouraged Jews to be farmers. This was a cause for jubilation among those devotees of Enlightenment who dared dream that their people would eventually be allowed to leave behind them the hopelessness of the ghetto. In little more than a decade, forty-five exclusively Jewish farming villages sprang

Jewish workers in a collective settlement.

up in the Kiev district, fourteen in Kherson, fourteen in Ekaterinoslav and a number scattered throughout Bessarabia, Lithuania and White Russia. The total population of these villages was 65,000.

Unfortunately, many of these farming communities were not resting on firm foundations. For one thing, Jews had been city people for many centuries. They formed a closely knit ethnic group habituated to their own religious life and culture. They, therefore, felt isolated in the country and suffered from an overpowering sense of loneliness in the middle of a sea of unfriendly Russian peasants whom the officials and priests often incited against them. In the end the Tsarist government lost interest in the Jewish settlements and stopped giving them the material aid they required to become established.

Left. A former cobbler-glazier (1940) turned sheep-breeder in the collective farm *Nai Leben* (New Life), one of 86 Jewish collective farms founded in the steppes of the Crimea. *Below.* Concert by artists from the Kiev Regional Philharmonic in the Jewish collective farm, "Kirov," in the Kiev district, the Ukraine.

A revival of official interest in the return of the Jews to the soil first took place some years after the revolution. The economic condition of the maladjusted Jewish middle class had reached a critical point in the 1920's when the New Economic Policy (NEP) was abandoned gradually by the government, beginning in 1924. Soviet leaders, especially the peasant president, Mikhail Kalinin, expressed interest in plans for transplanting a substantial part of the uprooted Jewish population from the city to the land. This, they thought, would help the maladjusted sink their roots into a productive and stable area of Soviet economic life. The opportunity for becoming farmers was especially welcome to those declassed elements who had not been able to find gainful occupations. They expected that by working on the land they would attain full equality as citizens and would enjoy at least a respected social status. The greatest inducement, however, was the prospect that their sons and daughters would thenceforth be given greater opportunities for education and advancement.

The proposal for the resettlement of the Jews on the land was made part of the first Five Year Plan. Because it was a period of financial stringency, the Soviet government readily accepted the material and technical assistance offered by the Chicago philanthropist, Julius Rosenwald, through the American Agro-Joint (JDC) in collaboration with the Jewish Colonization Association (ICA) of London.

To implement the plan the Soviet government established an official bureau, the *Komzet* (Committee for the Settlement of Jews on the Land). Hundreds of collective farms were founded, principally in the Ukraine, White Russia and the Crimea. By 1931 there were about 250,000 Jews living on the land. But in the years that followed, there was so marked a decline in the Jewish agricultural population, that the *Komzet* was ordered liquidated by the government in 1938. The Jewish relief organizations from abroad were also asked to suspend their activities.

What had happened to encourage this decline? Principally, that the young people in the Jewish farming communities had become restless. The big cities held greater attractions for them, with their opportunities for more interesting jobs, better education and the enjoyment of social and cultural advantages not available in rural areas.

Biro-bidjan

Tsarist Russia was once described as "a prison-house of nations." The empire comprised an astonishing number of national minorities and ethnic groups who were looked down upon and were oppressed by the ruling Great Russian Slavs.

Street scene in the small city of Biro-bidjan during its construction.

After the revolution the declared policy of the Soviet government was to grant national autonomy to minority groups in whatever region they formed the majority of the population. Morover, the government encouraged the development of national cultures among these minorities to add to their group self-esteem and to give them a feeling of equality with all other peoples.

Young Jewish railway workers in the Biro-bidjan depot.

Unfortunately, at no time did the Jews in Russia occupy a territory of their own, as did the Armenians or the Georgians, for instance. As a widely dispersed and fragmentized people, they usually constituted a small minority group in the province, region, district, city or town where they lived. Consequently, the minorities program blueprinted by the Soviet government for other national groups could not be applied to the Russian Jews.

With this territorial lack in mind, the Soviet government decided in 1928 to establish a national *okrug* (district) in Biro-bidjan for the Jews. In 1934, six years after its founding, the All-Union Central Committee of the U.S.S.R. advanced Biro-bidjan from a district to a region (*oblast*). It stated then: "Soviet Jewish statehood is being developed and consolidated in forms corresponding to the national and traditional conditions of the Jewish people."

Biro-bidjan consists of 14,200 square miles of primeval *taiga* land, situated in the southernmost bend of the Amur River in eastern Siberia on the Manchurian border. Its first Jewish settlers, who came from the Ukraine and White Russia, had to face great physical hardships. Although they found the country rich in its soil, waterways and natural resources, Biro-bidjan was an undeveloped district. It had few roads and was ravaged by frequent floods. The soil, too, was hard to work, never having been cultivated before. For the new settlers, who for the most part had worked as cobblers, tailors, shopkeepers and peddlers in the towns and cities, the task of adjustment to a pioneer existence proved hard. In spite of the difficulties they built houses and laid roads, established collective and state farms and founded a number of industrial enterprises. They even raised a small modern city, Biro-bidjan, which served as the capital for the entire Jewish Autonomous Region.

A staff member of the Biro-bidjan Ethnography Museum explaining the exhibits in Yiddish to a group of children.

The Jews of Biro-bidjan followed the intensive cultural pattern characteristic of all Soviet Jewry. Although, according to a survey in 1941, the total population of Biro-bidjan was only 113,930, of whom Jews probably constituted less than a third, nevertheless, Jewish cultural institutions and enterprises at the time were proportionately numerous. In the several towns and in the twenty-seven collective and state farms there was a total of one hundred and thirty-two schools of all kinds. The language of instruction was largely Yiddish, an official language of the Region. These institutions included, besides one hundred and eight elementary and four high schools, a railroad academy, a medical school, a music school, a pedagogic institute, several vocational schools and a wide variety of courses in adult education.

The Kaganovich State Theatre in the city of Biro-bidjan was devoted to the production of plays in Yiddish. The Sholom Aleichem Library, with a collection, in Yiddish and Russian, of 110,000 titles, was established in the capital. In addition, there were forty-four reading rooms distributed throughout the Region. Besides a general Regional museum, there was also the Biro-bidjan Museum for Jewish culture. A daily newspaper and a number of periodicals were published in Yiddish.

The response of the Jews in the Soviet Union to the government's invitation to settle in Biro-bidjan was far less than had been anticipated. The optimistic expectation had been that at least 500,000 Jews would eventually make their homes there and would thereby make it possible for the Region to be designated a full-fledged republic. Most Jews, however, felt no compulsion to pioneer in that remote and primitive region.

The Struggle for Minds

Marx's dictum, "Religion is the opium of the people," expresses succinctly the Communist attitude toward religion. The principles of Marxism, which are based on a materialistic philosophy of history, reject all aspects of theology and the supernatural.

From its inception, the Soviet government was determined to neutralize the political influence of organized religion in Russia. The Tsars had vested in themselves absolute power over both Church and State. With the establishment of the Communist regime, the Tsar was eliminated, but the Russian Orthodox Church, one of the twin columns on which his power had rested, still stood. Its continued existence was both a challenge and a threat to the Soviet rule, which was based on the dictatorship of the proletariat. Since the Church exercised political as well as religious influence, it, too, had to go. The need to be rid of it was deemed especially urgent during the early turbulent period. This was at a time when the War of Allied Intervention and the Naval Blockade, the Civil War against the "Whites" and the armed conflict with Poland were making the Bolsheviks' grasp on the reins of government seem most precarious. The Orthodox Church, headed by the Patriarch Tikhon, was waging a determined and open struggle for the overthrow of the new "Godless" society. Its ancient hold on the people was still so firm that the Soviet government was determined to pry it loose. Consequently, it encouraged a nationwide campaign, not only against the Orthodox Church, but against all organized religious denominations—Protestants, Roman Catholics, Mohammedans, Buddhists and Jews.

The weapon the Soviet government chose for this campaign was "The League of Militant Atheists," a vastly ramified organization sponsored by the *Comsomols* (Young Communists). Juridicially, the anti-religious crusade was based on the general principle later incorporated as Article 4 in the 1925 Constitution: "For the purpose of assuring real liberty of conscience to the workers, the church is separated from the state, and the school from the church; and the right of all citizens to practice freely any religious belief or to engage in anti-religious propaganda remains inviolate."

To wage ideological war against the Jewish religion the Jewish *Comsomols* organized their own agitational unit, "The League of Militant Jewish Atheists." It was especially combative during the 1921-23 period when Jews were drifting back into private trade permitted under the temporary NEP policy. In a literal sense, however, freedom of religious worship remained unaffected, nor were any of the congregations molested or suppressed. But the activities of Jewish religious bodies were limited to prayer services and to the observance of traditional rites and ceremonies.

It became clear as time went on that one of the primary objectives of the anti-religious campaign was to wean the youth from religion and to draw it closer to the Communist movement. With this in mind, all religious groups were forbidden to give institutional religious instruction to anyone under eighteen years old. Nevertheless, instruction was allowed to individuals in this age-group provided it was given at home, either by the parents or by a private teacher.

It was hard for the Jewish religious community in the Soviet Union to reconcile itself to such a narrowing scope of activity. It ran counter to all its cultural and historical conditioning during three thousand years. To the pious Jew, the religious education of the young was considered the most sacred of all religious trusts and obligations. On it he pinned his hope for the survival of the Jewish religion and, in large measure, for the continuity of his Jewish identity. The separation of "the school from the church" led to the abolition of all parochial schools on the grounds that they were incompatible with the principles of "socialist education" in Soviet society. For the Orthodox Jews it meant the end of the traditional *cheder* and the *Talmud Torah*, with all the implications attendant on such a loss to them. A large number were determined to resist what they considered a fundamental encroachment on their way of life. The outlawed *cheder* began to operate clandestinely, despite the grief it brought to its initiators. The stream of Jewish religious life continued to flow, for the most part erratically, much of it in the open with official sanction, but some of it subterranean and illegal.

The synagogue buildings, alike with church edifices, were expropriated and turned into workers' clubs, libraries and "houses of culture." However, it was the loss of the majority of its youth to Communism that struck the Jewish community of the Soviet Union its most mortal blow.

Hostility to Religion

The general attitude of religious Jews toward Soviet power was summed up at the time of the revolution by Dr. Pasmanik, the leader of Russian Zionists: "Judaism cannot be reconciled with Bolshevism." There was a hard core of opposition to the Soviet government among religious Jews. It was especially strong in the long-established Jewish organizations, such as the Zionist Party, the Socialist *Bund* and the ultra-Orthodox *Agudath Israel*. These, in varying degrees, were either religious or Jewish-nationalist in outlook, but all were united in their insistence upon complete religious-cultural autonomy for the Jews. Their expectations, however, suffered a severe blow when the *Kahal*, the traditional administrative organ of Jewish self-rule in the old ghetto, was dissolved by order of the Soviet government as a survival of feudal Tsarism and as entirely superfluous in a Socialist society. One of the major functions of the *Kahal*, for instance, had been to collect communal taxes from the Jews for the support of Jewish religious, educational and charitable institutions. The giving of charity had ever been regarded as a paramount duty in the social-religious practice of the Jews. Now it was declared by the government to be no longer necessary, since the function had been taken over by the state welfare services.

An interesting footnote to this conflict was furnished by the *Bund*, the Jewish labor organization of pre-revolution days which was militantly allied with the Socialist Menshevik opposition to the Bolsheviks. The *Bund* went underground in 1919, but a section of it resigned itself as early as 1920 to the futility of the unequal struggle against the Soviet government. It declared that "the demand for national cultural autonomy loses all meaning in a Socialist revolution."

Not so the Orthodox Jews and Labor Zionists, who remained bitterly opposed to Communism and the Soviet government. The great majority of them had come from the middle and lower-middle classes. The social and economic program advanced by the Bolsheviks to win over the proletariat and the peasantry could not waken any enthusiastic response from them, and many deeply resented the government's anti-religious campaign.

Still another cause for widespread Jewish opposition was the Soviet government's relentless hostility to Zionism. As early as 1913, four years before the revolution, Joseph Stalin had expressed the Communist attitude on Zionism with unmistakable clarity. He characterized it as "a reactionary and nationalist movement recruiting its followers from among the Jewish petty and middle bourgeoisie, business employees, artisans, and the more backward sections of the Jewish workers. Its aim is to organize a Jewish bourgeois state in Palestine and it endeavors to isolate the Jewish working-class masses from the general struggle of the proletariat."

The Soviet government openly accused the Zionist movement of counter-revolutionary intentions and declared it both anti-state and a covert agent of British imperialism with which it allegedly was linked under the Palestine Mandate. All Zionist activity and agitation were therefore forbidden. During the first years following the revolution, the Zionist leaders stubbornly maintained their Jewish nationalist position. It has been said that a large number were imprisoned or exiled to remote parts of the country and that several were executed as counter-revolutionaries.

Nahum Zemach in the role of the "Wandering Jew" in David Pinski's drama, *The Eternal Jew*, produced by *Habimah*, the Hebrew Theatre, in Moscow in the early 1920's.

The Hebrew language and literature, too, were casualties in the class war. In the first years they were considered perfectly legitimate, a part of universal culture. In fact, the famous Hebrew *Habimah* Theatre had been founded in Moscow shortly after the revolution. It gave its performances in modern Hebrew before enthralled Jewish and non-Jewish audiences. But in 1924 it, too, was swept away by the changed ideological current, on the grounds that Hebrew was the language of political Zionism, the bourgeois nationalism of the Jews, and, as such, was antithetical to socialist principles of culture.

When the political status of Zionism had changed after World War II and the Zionists began to wage a "war of liberation" against "British imperialism," they received encouragement from the Soviet government, and arms from the Communist government of Czechoslovakia. In fact, the first country to give *de jure* diplomatic recognition to the newly founded State of Israel was the U.S.S.R. This benevolent Soviet attitude continued for some time, as long as the Israeli government observed a "neutralist" position in the conflict between East and West. However, no sooner did the government of Israel begin to abandon this policy for one of closer collaboration with the West, and especially with the United States, than the old war against Zionists and Zionism was re-

sumed by the Soviet government, but this time with greater intensity.

Little of a verifiable nature is known as to what actually took place. There appeared increasingly uncomplimentary references in the Russian newspapers and periodicals to those Soviet Jews still under the influence of "Jewish bourgeois nationalism," "Zionism," and of "cosmopolitanism." In the words expressed at a later date by the Israeli newspaper *Haaretz*, the Soviet authorities began to discover that "despite all the pressure of the last twenty-five years, Russian Jewry has retained its collective consciousness." Early in 1949 the Jewish Anti-Fascist Committee, formed during World War II to unite all Jews in the struggle against the Nazis, was dissolved. In quick order, it was reported, there followed the closing down of a variety of Jewish educational and cultural institutions: the Yiddish state publishing houses, the Yiddish language newspapers, periodicals, schools, theatres, clubs, etc. Yiddish writers, well known outside the Soviet Union, such as David Bergelson, Itzig Feffer and Der Nister, became completely silent.

In 1952 the Jews of the world became deeply alarmed when the government of Czechoslovakia arrested and brought to trial on charges of high treason fourteen important Communist leaders, of whom eleven were Jews, including Deputy Premier Rudolf Slansky, the Secretary-General of the Communist Party. In open court the defendants confessed their conspiratorial activities, reminiscent of the confessions of the Trotskyists and "Right Deviationists" at the Moscow trials in the late 1930's. The Czech State Prosecutor, touching on the confessions, charged: "It is no accident that of the fourteen accused, eleven are the products of Zionist organizations. The danger of Zionism has increased with the foundation of the State of Israel by the Americans." In connection with the Jewish defendants, the Zionist movement, the State of Israel, and the Jewish Agency were specifically accused of serving as agents of Western espionage and sabotage in a widespread plot to overthrow the Communist government.

Jews everywhere were greatly incensed by the charges, the trial, the confessions, and finally by the execution of eight of the eleven Jewish defendants in the trial. Berl Locker, chairman of the Jewish Agency, issued an indignant statement: "We have heard with profound shock of the trial proceedings in Prague. It is for the first time at such a trial that both the indictment and evidence project allegations against the Zionist movement, the Jewish Agency for Palestine and the Israeli Government, and that a note of hostility has been introduced against the defendants as Jews that is bound to fan ominous anti-Semitic instincts."

An event, even more sensational than the Prague trial because of its explosive potentialities, occurred on January 14, 1953. The Soviet press accused nine prominent doctors, most of them Jewish, of having murdered by medical means two members of the *Politburo*, A. A. Zhdanov and A. S. Scherbakov; they were also charged with planning a similar fate for "the military leaders of the country." The official statement charged that all the doctors confessed their crimes, that they admitted secret connection with an "international Jewish bourgeois nationalist organization," i.e., "Joint" (Joint Distribution Committee), which, under the guise of relief activities, allegedly conducted "espionage, terrorism and underground activity in the Soviet Union and other countries." As a principal agent of "Joint" was mentioned "the well-known Jewish bourgeois-nationalist, Solomon Mikhoels" (the now deceased Yiddish actor-director of the Jewish State Theatre in Moscow).

In Israel these allegations aroused the most widespread indignation, and resentment against the Soviet Union ran high. Terrorists bombed the Soviet embassy in Tel-Aviv, and the U.S.S.R. promptly severed diplomatic relations with Israel on February 12, 1953.

On March 5, 1953, Stalin died. Under the new government headed by Malenkov, the Ministry of Internal Affairs announced on April 4, 1953, the release of the arrested doctors. It stated that the charges and testimony against them and against the Jewish actor Mikhoels had been fabricated by the highest officials of the Ministry of State Security, who were then arrested and, according to the statement, were brought "to criminal responsibility." Two days later, as reported in the *New York Times, Pravda* declared in its official editorial that, by these acts, the Soviet security officials had "attempted to inflame in the Soviet society . . . feelings of national antagonism." This was widely interpreted abroad as a public admission that the arrests and charges had been motivated by anti-Semitism. It was felt in the Western world that, in taking this step, the U.S.S.R. was turning from its previous policy of severe antagonism to one more friendly toward the State of Israel and the Jews. The Ben-Gurion government issued a statement declaring: "The Government of Israel hopes that redress of injustice will be completed by the termination of the anti-Jewish campaign, and will welcome resumption of normal relations between the Soviet Union and Israel."

This expectation of a rapprochement was realized with the renewal of Soviet-Israeli diplomatic relations agreed upon on July 15, 1953.

Yiddish Culture

With Hebrew proscribed in 1924 by the Soviet government as the language of "Jewish bourgeois nationalism" and as the "Church Latin" of the religious Jews, Yiddish was readily accepted as the language of the Jewish working class. And since the vast majority of the Jews in the first census in the U.S.S.R. named Yiddish as their mother-tongue, it was made one of the sixty-odd official languages of the country. In places where Jews formed the majority of the local population they were allowed to organize their own soviets and transact the official business in Yiddish. Their local courts, too, were held in Yiddish: judges, prosecutors, witnesses—all were obliged to participate in the proceedings, using Yiddish. In

place of the traditional *cheder* and the *Talmud Torah* a great number of Yiddish secular elementary schools were established. These were integrated into the state-supported general school system. Attendance at these Yiddish language schools was not, however, obligatory. Jewish parents exercised the right of free choice between them and the general Russian-language schools. Nonetheless, a Jewish child living in a predominantly Jewish locality would normally begin its education in schools employing the Yiddish language.

During 1931-32 in the Ukraine alone, where there was the greatest single concentration of Jews in the U.S.S.R., almost 160,000 pupils, or about one-half of all Jewish school children in the republic, attended some 700 state-supported schools. In these schools Yiddish was the language of instruction and special textbooks were prepared in Yiddish for the teaching of physics, astronomy, mathematics, chemistry, biology, art and other subjects.

Yiddish also served as the language of instruction in higher institutions of learning. Associated at one time with the State University at Kharkov, for instance, were several Yiddish-language colleges which included two normal schools for teachers and an agricultural institute. There was, besides, a special institute devoted to research in Jewish history, literature, art, folklore and economics. Yiddish was granted the status of a graduate study in several leading universities. Special Yiddish faculties were established at the Universities of Moscow, Leningrad and Kiev and in the White Russian Academy of Science at Minsk.

On the popular level of culture, there were published more than thirty Yiddish newspapers and magazines, including a number of children's periodicals. To satisfy the insatiable hunger of Jewish readers for books, a number of Yiddish state publishing houses were established by the government in the cities of Moscow, Kiev, Minsk and Biro-bidjan. The publishing houses in Moscow and Kiev each printed on the average of one Yiddish title a day. It was officially computed that during the period of 1918-35 about 5,000 books were published in Yiddish in editions totaling 18,000,000 copies. In 1940, the year before the Nazi flood inundated that part of the Soviet Union where most Jews lived, 5,000,000 copies of Yiddish books were turned out by the state publishing houses, 3,000,000 of this number, it is claimed, were works of Sholom Aleichem, the master humorist. It has been estimated that there were then more than 5,000 Yiddish

From left to right: M. Botvinnik; David Oistrakh; Dr. Lina Stern; Abram F. Joffe. Botvinnik is one of the foremost chess players of the world. Jews seem always to have had a special gift for chess playing. Perhaps the two greatest chess masters of modern times were Zuckertort and Lasker. There are a number of other Jewish chess masters of international renown. David Oistrakh is a foremost Soviet violinist. Other well-known young concert artists are Liza and Emil Hilels, Mischa Fichtenholz and Busya Goldstein. Dr. Stern is a famous Soviet physiologist, founder and director of the Institute of Physiology of the Academy of Sciences in the

U.S.S.R. Among the Soviet scientists of Jewish descent, Abram F. Joffe is perhaps the best known to the Western world. In his early years as a physicist he had been assistant to Roentgen, the discoverer of X-ray. Another physicist of front rank is Grigory Sheyn, director of the important Astro-Physical Observatory in the Crimea. In 1950 he discovered the existence of heavy isotopes of carbon in the atmosphere of some stars. Considered as among the most gifted of the Soviet's physical chemists is A. Frumkin. Top rank in his own field, that of polar exploration, is held by Rudolph Samoilowitsch.

From left to right: Solomon Mikhoels; Sergei Eisenstein; David Bergelson; Ilya Ehrenburg. Mikhoels was a well-known actor and director of the Jewish State Theatre in Moscow which presented literary plays in Yiddish. Eisenstein was the most noted figure in the Soviet motion-picture world. His pictures *Alexander Nevsky* and *Ivan the Terrible* have been universally acclaimed. Soviet Jews have figured prominently in the making of motion pictures, as directors and script writers. David Bergelson is the foremost Yiddish novelist.

writers, editors, journalists, scholars, librarians, actors and radio announcers.

The foremost Yiddish writers in the Soviet Union, a group of very talented men, were David Bergelson, Peretz Markish, Der Nister (Kacyzna), L. Kvitko, Itzik Feffer, I. Kushnerov, D. Hoffstein and O. Schvartzman.

The theatre, a traditionally popular medium in Russia for mass entertainment and political agitation, became an important cultural institution among Soviet Yiddish-speaking Jews. As early as 1919, the Commissar for Education, Lunacharsky, asked A. M. Granovsky, a gifted stage director who had worked with Max Reinhardt in Berlin, to found a Yiddish Dramatic School in Leningrad. Under his direction the school raised a new generation of Yiddish actors trained in the high standards of modern realism and theatrical art for which Russia has always been famous. It was these actors who made possible the ten state-subsidized Yiddish theatres and the two Yiddish drama schools. It has been observed by foreign students of the theatre that the Jewish State Theatre of Moscow, under the leadership of Solomon Mikhoels, the actor-director, was one of the most distinguished institutions of the Soviet theatre. Essentially an art theatre, its repertory extended all the way from the Yiddish folk-operas of Abraham Goldfaden and the folk-plays by Mendele Mocher Sforim, Peretz and Sholom Aleichem, to Shakespeare, Pushkin and Gorky.

Yet, for all this unprecedented, large-scale Yiddish cultural activity, its decline was already in evidence at the very time of its flowering. Although hundreds of thousands of Soviet Jewish youth had been raised in Yiddish-language schools, the political and cultural pressures from without proved well nigh irresistible. The Russification of the whole vast country, with its numerous peoples and mosaic of languages and cultures, was required politically by the Soviet government for the greater unity of the U.S.S.R. Whatever national language an individual of any minority people spoke, it was imperative for practical reasons that he learn and use Russian.

In time, there was a sharp decline in the attendance of the Yiddish-language schools. In the Ukraine, where Yiddish culture had been entrenched most strongly, it began to lose ground markedly when the government-sponsored campaign was started to have all Jewish workers learn Ukrainian. Elsewhere, too, the youth turned more and more to reading Russian newspapers, periodicals and books. In a late census, before the Nazi attack on Russia, more Jews claimed Russian than Yiddish as their mother-tongue. Furthermore, with the process of cultural fusion, with the weakening of religious ties, and with the enjoyment of full equality, intermarriage for Jews was not only inevitable but was considered by some even desirable. This was based on the Communist principle which rejects the socio-biologic separation of races and peoples. It is precisely this process of cultural assimilation and biological amalgamation which largely accounts for the steady disintegration of Jewish group life, culture and identity in the U.S.S.R.

Arts and Sciences

The tradition of Jews in Russian music, laid down by the Rubinstein brothers during the nineteenth century, was continued under the Soviets. Best known of the Jewish composers have been Michael Gniessin, Alexander Kreyn and Alexander Veprik.

In the Soviet Union many citizens of Jewish stock do not make a point of their Jewish origin. They regard themselves as Soviet citizens and are accepted as such by non-Jews. Therefore, it is not always possible to determine who among the prominent are Jewish. Nonetheless, the Jewish identity of many individuals in public life has been ascertained.

The mere statistical figure of 7,000 Soviet scientists who, just before the outbreak of World War II, voluntarily described themselves as being Jews, may be an index to the important role Jews have been playing in Soviet scientific research.

While there were writers of Jewish origin in Russia before the advent of Communism, such as the popular poet Nadson and the playwright-novelist Semion Yushkevitch, they were all of minor stature. After the revolution, with unlimited opportunities to acquire education and to pursue literary careers, Jews began to play an increasingly important role in Soviet letters. The first poet of the new times was Alexander Blok, the author of the famous poem "The Twelve." Among the best known of late Soviet poets have been Bagritzky, Pasternak, Mandelstamm, Selvinsky and the very popular Bezymensky. There have also emerged a number of gifted and even brilliant novelists and short story writers. The best known of these are Isaac Babel, Ilya Ehrenburg, Veniamin Kaverin, Kozakov, Libedinsky, Ilya Ilf, Vassili Grossman and Samuel Marshak. One of the best known among the literary critics is Victor Shklovsky. The foremost political journalist on international affairs in the Soviet Union today is David Zaslavsky, successor to Karl Radek in the columns of *Pravda*. He started his career as a writer in Yiddish.

253

HITLER OVER EUROPE

THE MASTER PLAN

Almost a decade has passed since the end of the Nazi regime. Nevertheless it is still difficult to discuss dispassionately this nightmarish chapter in contemporary history, especially where it concerns the Jews. Nor is it possible as yet to assess objectively all the consequences to mankind of the flood of evil and calamity let loose by the Nazis under Hitler. They engulfed the world in its most devastating war, and caused the death of 25,000,000 people of whom 6,000,000 were Jews. They undermined civilization and set in motion a series of disruptive forces.

In the eyes of the world it was one man alone, Adolf Hitler, who generated the Nazi movement. But this, of course, is historically inaccurate. At first Hitler was only a marionette who ranted, strutted and grimaced while the German General Staff, the *Junker* barons and the great Ruhr industrialists pulled the political strings.

While still a corporal in the defeated German Army after World War I, Hitler had served as the creature of a gigantic conspiracy that had been hatched by the revenge-thirsty *Reichswehr* generals. They were determined to wipe out the humiliation of Germany's military defeat and of the punitive provisions of the Versailles Peace Treaty. In fact, they were plotting to overthrow the republic by a *putsch* and to seize power themselves.

Hitler in 1936.

As the first step in their carefully laid plans, they revived the secret terrorist group, the *Fehme,* whose members murdered some three hundred prominent Jews, liberals, Catholics, Socialists and Communists, allegedly for having caused Germany's downfall. At the same time, however, the *Reichswehr* generals proceeded to the organization of a popular mass-movement which was to serve them as the political weapon for regaining power. In July, 1919, Adolf Hitler, an obscure but highly articulate corporal in an army unit stationed in Munich, was assigned by unidentified higher-ups to help in the organization of the German Workers' Party. This political group served as the nucleus for the National Socialist Party (Nazi Party), which was secretly subsidized by leading German industrialists upon the recommendation of the *Reichswehr* generals.

But this is a Jewish, not a German history. Therefore, we must direct our attention to the impact of the Nazis on the Jews.

From the very beginning Jews were given a suspicious prominence in the rabble-rousing of the Nazis. Seven out of the twenty-five points in the program of the National Socialist Party dealt exclusively with Jews. It nakedly proclaimed its racist objective: " . . . no Jew can be considered a fellow countryman."

Munich became the chief center for Nazi activities in the Reich. The city was flooded with anti-Semitic leaflets, posters and stickers. Well-organized Nazi mobs roamed through the streets shouting, *"Juda, verrecke!"* ("Perish, Judah!") Each day the uniformed Brown Shirts would march out from the Nazi headquarters in the Brown House, goose-stepping and singing at the top of their voices.

The contagion spread swiftly. On November 7, 1923, the *Berliner Tageblatt* took note of some recent occurrences in the capital: "Not only have Jewish shops been plundered and Jews sought out in their homes, but some of them have had their clothes torn from their backs and have been chased naked through the streets while a jeering mob ran after them and beat them."

Nazis jeering as Jewish parents escort their children from school.

The authorities remained benevolent to the Nazi bands of hoodlums. Prime Minister Kahr of Bavaria and the Chief of Police of Munich openly protected them. The Bavarian courts were also accommodating and cooperative. Everywhere the same pattern was followed: the Jews served as the principal target of the Nazis for their abuse, threats and acts of vio-

Nazis making sport of a young Polish Jew. One is trying to tear out his beard with a pair of pliers.

254

lence. Many thoughtful Germans were quite mystified. They could not grasp the demagogic intention of the Nazis for selecting the Jews as "the enemy." Yet, all the while, the official pronouncements of Hitler and other Nazis openly stated their motive. A pamphlet that was issued at the time, *Hitler's Official Program,* declared with cynical frankness: "Anti-Semitism is, in a sense, the emotional foundation of our movement." Hitler beat on all the drums of hate. He directed his siren song to everybody. To the gutter-mob he held out the bright prospect of looting the Jews of their "gold" and possessions. To those who smarted under the disgrace of national defeat he kept repeating that if Germany lost the war it was only because the "Marxian-democratic-liberal-capitalistic Jews" had stabbed it in the back in order to aid the country's enemies. In fact, in a speech he delivered in April, 1923, he charged the Jews with having caused the World War in the first place. They had brought it on, he said, because they were diabolically determined to destroy all of Aryan civilization. With that end in mind the Jews had invented Democracy and also the Weimar Constitution (the German Minister of Justice, Hugo Preuss, a Jewish legal scholar, had drawn it up). "What are the Jewish aims? To spread their invisible State as a supreme tyranny over all the other states in the whole world."

The Betrayal

When the *Reichswehr* generals, the Ruhr industrialists and the *Junker* class of Germany were persuaded that the time was ripe for it, they brought Hitler and the Nazi Party to power on January 30, 1933. They accomplished this with the complaisance of the titular figurehead of the Weimar Republic, the national hero von Hindenburg.

A tidal wave of organized brutality then rolled over Germany. It was Hitler's aim, by employing police terror and the armed might of the Nazi state, to destroy all organized opposition. This meant the inevitable dissolution of all political parties, social institutions, trade unions and fraternal and veteran organizations. It also called for the suppression of the churches, but first and foremost, the Jews. In the course of thirteen years of furious and benumbing propaganda, the Nazis had already succeeded in making anti-Semitism "respectable," "patriotic" and persuasive to millions of frustrated and embittered Germans. Having supplanted Marshal von Hindenburg as the idol of the nation, Hitler's very word was now law. He encountered little difficulty in making his program acceptable. Those Germans, and undoubtedly they were numerous at first, who felt revulsion for him and the Nazi terror were intimidated into silence and finally into acquiescence.

As soon as the Nazis came to power, their campaign of suppression, repeated several years later in all the countries they occupied, followed a well-defined pattern. Jews were systematically expelled from all public places: from theatres, concert halls, museums and parks. They were also strictly forbidden to have any social contact with Gentiles. Infringement of these orders by Jews was punishable by imprisonment. To make sure that they were obeyed, police and Storm Troopers would raid cafés, theatres and parks in search of Jews.

On April 1, 1933, the boycott of Jewish business establishments began officially. Even before they came to power, the Nazis had posted signs and placards on Jewish shops reading:

"Don't buy from Jews!" Or, with even more informality, they would rudely daub with paint upon doors and windows the one word *Jud* (Jew). But now, with the Nazis in the saddle, the Storm Troopers, the specially selected and trained "strong arm" of the Nazis, efficiently picketed all stores, plants and offices owned by Jews. They carried signs reading: "It is forbidden to buy in this Jewish establishment." Jewish doctors, dentists and lawyers found posted on their doors the official warning: "*Achtung!* A Jew! Visits are prohibited!" Germans who disobeyed were harshly punished. Many were severely beaten, some were given prison sentences, others lost their jobs. Buying from a Jew was considered ample legal grounds for obtaining a divorce.

A Jewish passer-by is ordered by a policeman to scrub the pavement.

East European Jews were the objects of hoodlum attacks on the streets of Berlin by Nazi soldiers and Storm Troopers.

To degrade the Jews, and thus publicly to symbolize their rejection as Germans, the police were ordered occasionally to stop Jewish passers-by and force them to clean the streets.

In April, 1935, the Nazi government ordered all Jewish children expelled from the schools of Germany.

The Man-Hunt Begins

Step by step, with micrometer precision, the Nazis proceeded to eliminate the Jews from every area of German economic and cultural activity. It could not have been made more clear that the government was determined to destroy the Jewish people, both physically and morally. In an interview with a London journalist on July 7, 1935, the Minister of Propaganda, Dr. Joseph Goebbels, put the matter quite bluntly: "'Jewry must perish!' has been our battlecry for the last fourteen years. Then let it perish at last." Dr. Alfred Rosenberg, the Nazis' foremost Jewish "specialist," showed his impatience over the delay in carrying out his blueprint for the liquidation of the Jewish problem. He proposed: "On each telephone pole from Munich to Berlin we must display the head of a prominent Jew!"

Hitler, however, although he showed himself a master at whipping up mass-hysteria among the German people, himself remained emotionally cold and deliberate in his calculations. He considered the Jews an indispensable prop for his melodramatic showmanship. "My Jews are a valuable hostage," he once confided to Herman Rauschning, the Danzig Nazi who later deserted his camp. He did not feel that Nazi power was as yet sufficiently consolidated to defy world public opinion. Especially did he have to consider at first the reactions of large segments of the German people who had been conditioned by their training to observe a great respect for law and order. With an eye in their direction, Hitler therefore ordered the promulgation on September 15, 1935, of the so-called "Nuremberg Racial Laws." These laws established that anyone who was more than one-quarter Jewish in his descent was not to be considered a German nor was he to be entitled to the privilege of German citizenship.

High in Hitler's scheme for world conquest was the preparatory need of tempering his followers in hardness by brutality. He therefore encouraged them to acts of sadism, torture and cruelty. The man-hunt for Jews was diligently pursued. They were baited on the streets and invaded in their homes. They were degraded, tortured, imprisoned and murdered. There were few courageous Germans left to dare raise their voices in their behalf. There was no appeal for the victims, no redress at law.

Protest or Submission?

Too many German Jews took exceptional pride in that they were Germans first and Jews afterwards. Several hundred of the foremost Jews in Germany in a paid advertisement in the press declared: "We regard ourselves, along with the overwhelming majority of German Jews, as members of the German, not of the Jewish people."

Leading Jews congregate in the New Synagogue in Berlin (1937) to honor the memory of German Jewish soldiers of World War I.

Dr. Leo Baeck, Reform rabbi and foremost religious leader of German Jewry after World War I, acted as its consoler during the Nazi period. Because he was a pacifist, he preached non-resistance.

Not all Jews reacted the same way to the Nazi attack on them. A great many saw the handwriting on the wall and while there was still time emigrated. The upstanding ones who raised their voices in protest were silenced in the *Gestapo* torture chambers or were thrown into concentration camps from which they never emerged. But many adopted, at least outwardly, a policy of submission. Their leaders advised them: "Don't protest . . . don't resist . . . that will only inflame the Nazis against us the more!"

Those who thought that the chauvinistic Nazis were interested only in "Germany for the Germans" were quickly disenchanted. They literally wanted *Deutschland über Alles!* As the triumphant Nazi youth goosestepped throughout the land,

they sang confidently: "Today Germany is ours—tomorrow the world!" With this objective in mind, Hitler and his associates were resolved to make of anti-Semitism an effective weapon for world conquest. The *Führer* boasted to Herman Rauschning: "You will see how little time we shall need in order to upset the ideas and criteria of the whole world, simply and purely by attacking Judaism."

The Nazis let loose a steady propaganda barrage over short-wave radio beamed to every country in the world. Also, by means of motion pictures, newsletters, periodicals, books and millions of leaflets, which they fed free to all foreign sympathizers and anti-Semitic organizations, they obtained a firm foothold in many countries. By pounding tirelessly away on the single synthetic theme of "the Jewish Bolshevist-capitalistic menace," they made a great part of the Western World racist-conscious. The image of the Jew they were building up on a vast global scale was that of a monster of evil, plotting in each country to poison the well of national life.

But the most telling propaganda effect of the Nazis abroad was the brutal example they were setting at home. Anti-Semitic movements, indigenous to each country and "inspired" by the Nazis' easy rise to power, wishfully saw themselves pursuing the same triumphant course. In this objective they were amply supported with funds furnished by the Hitler government through Nazi organizations formed expressly for that purpose.

The plague of Jew-baiting that swept the world after 1933 soon reached epidemic proportions. In Norway, as early as 1933, the Nazis induced their sympathizer, Vidkun Quisling, whose name subsequently became synonymous with traitor and collaborator with the enemy, to organize the National Union Party. Flatteringly, he imitated his hero, Hitler, in every conceivable act of brutality, demagoguery and terrorism. In other countries, the story was similar: the Nazis found ardent imitators among the local reactionaries, political adventurers, the frustrated, and the criminal population. In England, the British Union of Fascists, led by Sir Oswald Mosley, caused riots and disturbances. In Quebec Province in Canada, during 1933-35, more than twenty anti-Semitic organizations leaped to life under the stimulation of Germany. Their chief ornament was Adrien Arcand, who headed the *Parti National Social Chrétien* (National Social Christian Party) which tried to carry through a boycott against Jews with the slogan: *Achat chez nous!* (Buy from our own!)

The Fascists of South Africa, under the leadership of Dr. Daniel Malan, later Prime Minister, were fired to pursue the same triumphant course to power as the Nazis. Dr. Malan threatened: "We are not race-haters, but anti-Semites. We shall follow the same policy as Germany, Austria and Italy and we shall deal with the Jews in South Africa as the above-mentioned countries." In 1948 Malan assured a Jewish deputation that his government would not discriminate against any white population.

In recent years there has been no persecution of Jews in South Africa.

In France, whose Popular Front Government was headed by Léon Blum in the early 1930's, the Nazi sympathizers, monarchists, ultra-clericalists and other assorted anti-Semites were shrill in their castigation of "Jewish Bolshevism" that allegedly was dishonoring France.

In Hungary, the anti-Semitic pattern established by Admiral Horthy was expanded and became more violent under his successors during the Hitler era.

Most powerful was the Nazi influence in Romania. There anti-Semitism triumphed in the winter of 1937. King Carol, himself pro-Nazi, made Octavian Goga, the leader of the Fascist Iron Guard, head of the government. During his brief stay in power, Goga and the Iron Guard followed the Nazi anti-Semitic blueprint in almost every detail. Goga's successor, Miron Christea, the Patriarch of the Romanian Orthodox Church, declared piously in 1938: "The Jews are sucking the marrow from the bones of the nation." His ultra-clericalist government completed the legal, economic and cultural strangulation of Romanian Jewry, then numbering more than 800,000.

The anti-Semites of Poland, who were sitting in the saddle of power and who long before the Nazis had shown themselves past masters in the art of Jew-baiting, required neither mentoring nor inspiration from the Germans on how to deal with "their Jews." Jubilantly the Polish government, which saw eye to eye with the German government, established fraternal relations with it through Foreign Minister Josef Beck, a "Pilsudski Colonel." The cold pogrom which had been in operation in Poland for years soon threatened to become hot. Incidents of violence against Jews flared up everywhere, permitted and even encouraged by the authorities. The Church looked on with approval and gave its religious sanction to the economic and cultural expulsion of the Jews from Polish life. In his pastoral letter of 1936, the Primate of Poland, Cardinal Hlond, advised all Catholics: "It is also true that the Jews are committing frauds, practicing usury and dealing in white slavery . . . one does well to prefer his own kind in commercial dealings and to avoid Jewish stores and Jewish stalls in the markets."

Hitler in America

The Nazi tentacles reached out into the United States as well. Although there were a number of adventurist anti-Semitic organizations which tried to capitalize on the post-war disillusionment and economic crisis in the United States, the advent of the boom years in the late 1920's and the national prosperity which followed deprived their propaganda of its economic appeal. But with the depression years, shortly after 1929, matters began to look up for them once more. Their appeal was especially directed to struggling small businessmen and shopkeepers, to the unemployed and to the emotionally unstable and the ignorant. With the triumph of the Nazis in Germany, an alarming number of anti-Semitic organizations became active from coast to coast. Their programs and their methods were very much alike. Some of the best known were the "Silver Shirts," the "Black Legion," the "Christian Crusaders," the "Knights of the Camellia," the "Christian Front," "Defenders of the Christian Faith," "Christian Mobilizers," and "American Vigilantes." They flooded the country with their provocative, often libelous and obscene periodicals, leaflets, posters and stickers in which the Jew was hideously caricatured and maligned. Many of these groups had close propaganda connections with the Nazis through the agency of the *Fichte Bund* in Hamburg and the *Welt-Dienst* in Erfurt. A closer Nazi agency at hand, the *Bund,* the American branch of the Nazi Party of Germany, often acted as coordinator and advisor for anti-Semitic propaganda.

The rank and file membership of these organizations consisted largely of embittered "little" men and women who brooded neurotically on their personal frustrations in the eco-

Left. Most formidable of anti-Semitic demagogues in the 1930's was the Rev. Charles E. Coughlin, head of the *Christian Front.* His weekly harangues over the radio won him a vast following throughout the country. The *Christian Front* had close ties with the German-American Bund which distributed for it the notoriously anti-Semitic journal, *Social Justice.* Cardinal Mundelein of Chicago repudiated Father Coughlin for preaching doctrines opposed to the teaching of the Church. *Right.* Joe McWilliams, leader of the hoodlum *Christian Mobilizers.*

nomic crisis. But less publicized were a group of highly placed, wealthy individuals who, like their German counterparts among the Ruhr industrialists, were eager to emulate the Nazis by whipping up anti-Jewish hysteria in America in the hope of getting the reactionary government they desired. Unfortunately for them, the great majority of the American people, conditioned by humane and democratic traditions, rejected their program. Justice Frank Murphy of the United States Supreme Court called upon the American people "to recognize and combat hateful propaganda against American

Fritz Kuhn, *führer* of the German - American Bund, addressing a Nazi "picnic" gathering in one of its New Jersey camps. During World War II he was tried and convicted on the charge of embezzlement and was imprisoned. Upon his release after the war he was deported to Germany where he died in 1952.

citizens of Jewish descent as a powerful secret Nazi weapon— powerful because it has been deliberately spread to this continent where no Nazi invading force has been able to set foot, and secret because victims so inoculated are often unconscious of the source from which it comes."

American Jews did not remain quiescent in the face of this threat to them and to the American people. They fought back with the principal weapon at their command—public enlightenment. The Anti-Defamation League, for instance, the Jewish defense arm of the B'nai B'rith, carried out a spirited educational campaign throughout the United States against the local anti-Semites and the Nazi propaganda. Similarly, the American Jewish Congress through its numerous affiliated organizations and chapters, the influential American Jewish Committee, the Jewish War Veterans of America, the National Council of Jewish Women, the Jewish labor unions, and hundreds of other religious and fraternal groups.

So long as Hitler and the Nazis appeared triumphant, the dream of power soared high among fascist demagogues in the United States. But with the military defeat of the Nazis and the world-wide rejection of their ideas and practices, they lost much of their influence, for the time being.

The Blitz

Der Tag, the "great day" for German reckoning, had arrived. "Tomorrow the world!" had now become "today." With the precision of a train schedule, Nazi Germany had blueprinted its battle course. Austria had been annexed on March 11, 1938. Later, Britain and France agreed at Munich to the Nazi seizure of Czechoslovakia. In August, 1939, Germany and the U.S.S.R. signed a mutual non-aggression treaty. Then Hitler was ready for the *Blitz*.

On September 1, 1939, the German Army invaded Poland. England and France thereupon declared war on Germany. The Polish Army, in which thousands of Jews fought and died, offered desperate but ineffective resistance and seemed to melt away before the overwhelming might of the *Wehrmacht*.

Then there was a partition of Poland, with Germany and the U.S.S.R. dividing the country. Hitler next turned his attention in the spring of 1940 to Belgium, Holland and France. Their governments adopted a fatalistic resignation before the alleged invincibility of the German *Blitz*. Their strength already undermined by influential collaborationists in their midst, they quickly succumbed. After that it was like a house of cards collapsing—Greece, Yugoslavia, Bulgaria, Denmark and Norway fell away. Romania and Hungary, enthusiastically fascist, did not need to be persuaded; they joined the Axis voluntarily. Only England remained unconquered, engaging the Nazi *Luftwaffe* in the skies in the epic "Battle of Britain."

General Jacob Smushkevich, the 44-year-old Commander-in-Chief of the Soviet Air Force. He insisted on leading his airmen personally into battle at the outbreak of World War II and was shot down and killed several months later while in action against the enemy. The Nazi invasion of the Soviet Union brought an estimated 600,000 Jewish youth, including women, into the armed services of their country.

Then suddenly the German Army invaded the Soviet Union on June 22, 1941. Unable to stem the *Blitz*, the Red Army began a general retreat toward Moscow. There were more than 2,000,000 Jews living in Soviet territory in the path of the victorious Nazi advance. The Soviet government evacuated many of these Jews into the interior. Estimates vary from 800,000 to 1,500,000. The rest fled, perished or were captured by the Nazis. The evacuated Jews, including several hundred thousand Polish Jews who had already fled to Polish-Soviet territory as the Nazis advanced, were taken beyond the Urals to Uzbekistan, Kazakhstan and Tadjikistan in Central Asia. There, many additional thousands died during the war years. They could not survive the hardships they had to suffer.

The Jews Rise to Fight

If hatred for the Nazis and for their social crimes inspired millions of people in all nations to oppose them, the Jews of the world had an additional incentive—to avenge the martyrdom of their people.

Religious services conducted by a Jewish chaplain, U.S. Army. There were 550,000 Jews, including women, who fought in the armed forces of the United States during World War II. Eight thousand were killed and many times that number, wounded. More than 25,000 decorations for valor, including the Congressional Medal of Honor, were given Jewish servicemen.

Left. Major-General Maurice Rose, Commanding General of the 3rd Armored Division, one of the most gallant soldiers in the war against the Nazis, who died treacherously at the hands of one of them. *Right.* Sgt. Meyer Levin who launched the bombs that sank the Japanese battleship *Haruna* off the Philippines on December 10, 1941. He lost his life later while trying to save his crewmates, when the Flying Fortress on which he served crashed in a storm off New Guinea.

There were many thousands of Jewish servicemen in the English Army. Their number was almost doubled by Palestinian volunteers who fought under the British flag.

"The Jewish Brigade" of the British Army with its commander, Brigadier Ernest Frank Benjamin.

Lev Dovator.

Frederick Kisch.

General Lev Dovator, Jewish Cossack commander, who was undoubtedly the most colorful Jewish figure in the war. By smashing the German army at Rostov, he stalled the entire Nazi offensive, but not before he himself had been killed in a cavalry charge. Other Russian Jews who won fame in the fighting were Colonel-General Leo Mekhlis, General Samuel Rogachevsky, Lieut.-Gen.

K. P. Podlas, Major-General L. S. Berezinski and the three tank generals, Jacob Kraizer, Mikhail Rabinovich and Abraham Khasin. The noted English Zionist leader, Brigadier Frederick Kisch, was Chief Engineer of the 8th Army. *Left.* An American admiral awarding the U. S. Navy Cross to the Soviet Jewish submarine commander, I. Fisanovich, for sinking 13 German ships.

Throughout the world, Jews of all ages and all callings rallied to the fight. They enlisted in whatever armies they could, they formed their own legions, they joined and organized resistance movements, open and underground. In all armies, they volunteered for dangerous tasks and proved themselves valiant in battle.

The *Gouvernement-General*

After the Nazis had *blitzed* into Poland in September, 1939, they began concentrating the Jews of Poland as well as those from other countries of Europe into a confined area in central Poland. This territorial prison they innocently designated as the *Gouvernement-General*. The concentration was designed to facilitate the employment of Jewish slave-labor for the German war industries. It was also to enable the Nazis to carry out more efficiently their program for the total extermination of the Jewish people. Many of the Jews were confined in forty-five Polish ghetto towns, but the vast majority was herded into the ghettos of thirteen large cities, Warsaw, Lodz (Litzmannstadt), Cracow, Lwov (Lemberg) and Vilna, among others. After the Nazi invasion of Soviet Russia in the summer of 1941, Jews were forced into ghettos in Minsk, Riga, Kharkov, Kiev, Odessa and other Russian cities.

Genocide

At no time, even during the years before they were in power, had the Nazis attempted to conceal their ultimate

intention of exterminating all the Jews in the world. The speeches of Hitler and of his "Jewish specialists," Dr. Alfred Rosenberg and Julius Streicher, were shrill with that murderous decision. Even the Storm Trooper songs in the early 1920's were crazed paeans to the prospect of Jewish blood gushing in rivers, a sort of sadists' "Walpurgis Night" to celebrate the ascendancy of the Aryan-German master-race. But only a sober few in non-Jewish circles took these threats seriously. Even after the retaliatory pogroms in Germany, which followed the assassination of a minor Nazi embassy official in Paris by seventeen-year-old Herschel Grynszpan on November 7, 1938, the Allied world still did not believe Hitler's intentions toward the Jews were so murderous and so far-reaching. Even after the victorious Nazi Army invaded Soviet Russia and massacred, during the summer and fall of 1941, some 200,000 Jews in Minsk, Vitebsk, Grodno, Bialystok, Brest-Litovsk, Berditchev and other cities, as well as another 250,-000 in Kiev, Kharkov and other towns and cities of the Ukraine, there were still many people who scoffed at the notion that Hitler would carry out any genocide plan. In fact, these skeptics did not believe it even after Hitler himself formally declared it as his state policy in a speech before the National Socialist Party on January 30, 1942.

The World Jewish Congress had been informed in advance of the ghastly plan of annihilation already being executed by special units of the Nazi Security Police in the occupied regions of the Soviet Union. It had become plain to all informed people that there were terrible developments afoot when, in September, 1941, there began the systematic deportation of Jews into concentration and labor camps in Poland and in Nazi-occupied Soviet territory. Repeatedly, the World Jewish Congress brought the matter to the attention of the Allied authorities in London and in Washington, but without noticeable effect.

Some of the doomed Jews of Paris assembled in the Vélodrome d'Hiver in July, 1942. In all countries occupied by the Nazis, the dragnet to trap the Jews operated in the same efficient manner. In simultaneous police raids, all Jews were assembled for distribution among the concentration camps.

In his diary Henry Morgenthau, Jr., then Secretary of the Treasury of the United States, bitterly accused certain high unnamed government officials of having "even suppressed information about atrocities in order to prevent an outraged public opinion from forcing their hand . . . the horrors of Dachau or Buchenwald were beyond their conception." Countless thousands of Jewish lives could have been saved, it has been charged, had not most of the efforts on their behalf been torpedoed by cynical officials after eight months of protracted negotiations. Again the Morgenthau *Diaries* somberly record: "But the worst was still to come. On December 17, 1943, the State Department received a cable from

London. . . . The Foreign Office, this letter said, is concerned with the difficulty of disposing of any considerable number of Jews should they be released from enemy territory. For this reason they are reluctant even to approve of the preliminary financial arrangements."

The "financial arrangements" in this matter involved only an official license permitting the World Jewish Congress to spend one hundred million Romanian *leis* for the rescue of many thousands of Jewish children in France and Romania.

And while the bureaucratic statesmen fiddled, millions of Jews were being burned to ashes.

The Nightmare

During the 1930's, the preparatory period of the "cold pogrom," concentration camps in Buchenwald, Dachau, Sachsenhausen and Oranienburg were used principally to house native political opponents of the Nazi regime, such as Catholics, Communists, Liberals and Socialists. But after the war had extended the Nazi grip over most of Europe, Hitler and his *Gestapo* Chief Heinrich Himmler decided, with the bulk of the Jews of Europe in their hands, to proceed with their extermination. With the genius for organization and precision for which the German people are famous, the Nazis embarked on this grisly project as if they were establishing smelting plants and coke ovens in the industrial Ruhr.

While large-scale killings had gone on before in the concentration camps, they had not yet taken on the character of the mass-production of corpses. For various reasons, Hitler and his advisers thought it both prudent and efficient to establish most of the death factories for the Jews in out-of-the-way Poland—in Oswiecim, Birkenau, Maidanek, Treblinka, Belsen and many other places. The "raw material" for these plants arrived by trainloads and truck convoys, packed to suffocation with dazed Jewish humanity gathered from all parts of the Nazi empire.

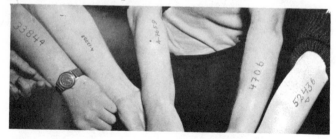

Women slave laborers showing tattooed identification numbers branded on them by the Nazis.

So nightmarish and shocking in its details was the program of extermination carried out by the German government against the Jews that it will suffice perhaps to read from the official indictment that was presented before the International Tribunal for Nazi War Criminals in Nuremberg in October, 1945:

"The murders and ill-treatment were carried out by diverse means, including shooting, hanging, gassing, starvation, gross overcrowding, systematic under-nutrition, systematic imposition of labor tasks beyond the strength of those ordered to carry them out, inadequate provision of surgical and medical services, kickings, beatings, brutality and torture of all kinds. . . . Along with adults, the Nazi conspirators mercilessly destroyed even children. They killed them with their parents, in groups and alone. They killed them in children's homes

Elderly Polish Jews, guarded by armed German soldiers, are forced to dig their own graves before their execution.

A pious Jew in a Galician town, standing beside the bodies of his murdered fellow-Jews, is allowed by the "humorous" Germans a moment's grace to recite the prayer before death for himself and for those already slain.

An eleven-year-old slave laborer, Fogal Abrahams, of Bialystok, shows American war correspondent, Martin A. Bursten, the Buchenwald crematorium ovens in which his father and mother perished.

After the U. S. Army captured Nordhausen, they found the camp strewn with thousands of corpses.

and hospitals, burying the living in the graves, throwing them into flames, stabbing them with bayonets, poisoning them, conducting experiments upon them, extracting their blood for the use of the German army, throwing them into prison and *Gestapo* torture chambers and concentration camps, where the children died from hunger, torture and epidemic diseases."

Living skeletons in the Buchenwald death camp after the Germans were driven out. As the war progressed, German technologists decided it was cheaper to starve Jews to death than to use badly needed ammunition or chemicals on them. As Field Marshal von Rundstedt said: "Malnutrition is better than machine-guns."

In the *Vernichtungslager* (Extermination Camp) in Chmelno, 1,135,000 Jews were slaughtered; in the Maidanek Camp in Lublin, 750,000 Jews; in Oswiecim and its subsidiary plants, almost 4,000,000 Jewish lives were snuffed out. The register of the slain in the electric crematoria of the Oswiecim subsidiary, Birkenau, reads like a carefully itemized account of a business house. The plant first gassed, then burned 6,000 Jews daily.

A Yugoslav Jew is forced by *Ustachi* collaborationists of the Germans to surrender his gold wedding ring before his execution. The final verdict of the International Military Tribunal at Nuremberg, issued on October 1, 1946, charged the leaders of the German Government with the crime of ghoulish robbery: "Hair of the women victims was cut off before they were killed, to be used in the production of mattresses. Clothes, money and valuables were sent to the appropriate agencies for disposition. Gold teeth and fillings were taken from the heads of corpses and sent to the Reichsbank. After cremation the ashes were used for fertilizer and, in some instances, attempts were made to utilize the fat from the bodies of victims in the commercial manufacture of soap."

The tragedy of an individual human being becomes understandable to another only in personal terms of identification with him. But how is one to grasp the total tragedy of 6,000,000 murdered Jews? It is a grief so vast that it leaves one appalled, stunned and self-protectingly cold. The normal imagination cannot assimilate, cannot focus on the reality of criminal acts on such an astronomical scale. This reaction was officially expressed by the English General Sir Douglas Brownrigg when he visited the Breedonck Death Camp in Belgium after the Nazis had fled: "It is difficult to make a normal per-

son believe that such abnormalities could exist today in so-called civilized Europe. I almost wonder whether I should not have been a little skeptical had I not seen things for myself."

The Victims of Birkenau Came From...
April 1942-April 1944

THE WARSAW GHETTO

In Warsaw the *Gestapo* systematically corralled the Jews of the city and its suburbs into a new compulsory ghetto which was carved out of the old one and sealed tight with a high brick wall which was heavily guarded. The man-hunt went on for a long time before the Germans were able to ferret out the Jews who were in hiding.

The last Jews were finally brought into the Warsaw ghetto. On November 15, 1939, the round-up operation was declared officially completed. A population count at that time showed there were 433,000 men, women and children concentrated

A meeting of the *Judenrat* of Litzmannstadt (Lodz) into whose ghetto 200,000 Jews were crowded. The *Judenrat* here and in other ghettos served as a tool for the Nazis to keep the Jews misinformed, confused and submissive. There were in it, however, some selfless men who sacrificed their own lives to save their fellow-Jews. This was not the case with the President of the *Judenrat* of Lodz (bespectacled, gray-haired Rumkowski, second from right, front row). He served the Nazis by deceiving the Jews in his charge and delivering them to the gas chambers. But he, too, ended up in a death camp.

in the small area of the ghetto. Disease, resulting from indescribable overcrowding, killed off hundreds daily. Hunger, organized along the well-known German scientific lines, was employed as the first deadly weapon of extermination. The Nazi governor of the city announced without ceremony: "We will destroy this tribe! They will disappear from hunger and wretchedness." But this was not all. He inaugurated a reign of terror which raged day after day. It had a cumulative psychological effect on the inhabitants of the ghetto. It was calculated to create an atmosphere of general hysteria which would discourage any thought of organized resistance.

The task was made much easier for the Nazis by the cowed and pliant *Judenrat* (Jewish Council), some of whose members had been appointed by the *Gestapo* itself from among

Winter scene, the Litz-
mannstadt (Lodz)
Ghetto.

official report pointed out gleefully: "Forty per cent of the 500,000 Jewish population consists of skilled artisans, tailors, leather workers, tile-makers and joiners." German manufacturers were accordingly urged to make use of this pool of qualified skills by establishing factories in the Warsaw ghetto.

A Jew tearfully protests to a *Judenrat* employee against accepting an iron shovel-head with which he is ordered to dig his own grave before being shot.

the well-known and wealthy Jews of Warsaw. Tragically, the *Judenrat* of Warsaw, by means of intimidation and harsh repression, sought to keep the Jewish population of the ghetto "in order" for the *Gestapo*, sometimes employing the most

An old Jew trapped by a Nazi police dragnet in Warsaw early in the winter of 1940.

bare-faced deceptions. It supplied the Nazis with the required slave-labor gangs and fulfilled the quotas of deportees. Thus it earned for itself the fear and hatred of the Jews it presumably represented. There were, of course, a few *Judenrat*

Nazi guards escorting a column of Jews through the streets of Warsaw to do forced labor, winter of 1940.

leaders who sincerely desired to use their official position for the protection of the Jews. Others developed conscience qualms. When, for instance, the President of the *Judenrat* could no longer endure playing toady and shepherd dog to the murderers of his people, he took his own life.

Bondage in Warsaw

To alleviate the severe shortage of skilled workmen in German war industries, the *Gestapo* drew on the large number of Jewish workers trapped in the Warsaw ghetto. An

The Great Deception

The first deportation to the death camps of Treblinka, Oswiecim, Maidanek and Belsen took place toward the end of July, 1942. A proclamation was posted on the street corners in the ghetto, ordering all Jews, except those working in war plants, to register for immediate and happier resettlement in another part of the country. Few suspected the true nature of their destination. Old people and children were shipped out first, in daily contingents of 2,000. That number was soon stepped up to 10,000 and finally to 20,000 a day. Many of the aged, the sick and the weak were brutally shot on the spot, since they did not merit "resettlement." The grief and panic which followed beggars description. To quiet the apprehensions of those remaining in the ghetto, the German authorities went through the pretense of organizing them into labor camps according to their separate trades.

A contingent of deportees leaving the ghetto for the extermination center at Maidanek in the days preceding the uprising.

When there was a brief pause in the "resettlement" operation, hope burgeoned again. It was generally believed that the practical Nazis merely wanted to get rid of the non-productive Jews but that those with industrial skills would be spared. Yet hundreds of Jews were still being shot every day on the streets of Warsaw by the Nazi soldiers and the *Januks*, the collaborationist Lithuanian and Ukrainian guards. The corpses were taken away in carts and buried in unmarked mass graves, like carrion.

Prelude to Revolt

From the very first days after the Nazis had marched into Warsaw, the groundwork for an uprising had been quietly laid by various groups of Jewish militant youth. They had drawn the proper inferences from the Nazi actions. It was neither despair nor a hunger for martyrdom which led them to prepare for an uprising. It was a calculated and carefully planned act of retribution. At first, because of sharp political and religious differences, the groups failed to unite their forces to carry out a coordinated underground effort. But when the first blood-curdling accounts of the wholesale extermination of the Jews in the death camps were brought to the ghetto by Polish and Jewish underground fighters, they had a sobering as well as a unifying effect on the bickering combat units.

An informer points to the grave of a newly buried Polish collaborationist soldier in Warsaw in which a Jewish underground unit had concealed arms.

They held a hurried conference and chose Mordecai Anielewicz as their commander-in-chief. Then they started making preparations for the rebellion.

It was not easy to acquire arms and ammunition, nor for that matter to conceal them. The *Gestapo* and the ghetto police, aided by informers and spies, seemed to be everywhere. Yet supplies of arms were secured by the most ingenious means. Under severe hazards they were smuggled into the ghetto by Jewish and sympathetic Polish underground fighters. Some arms were acquired also by purchase, by bribery and by theft from the *Gestapo*.

Warsaw Jews, under orders from the German Security Police, dig up heavy and light machine guns, automatic pistols, ammunition cases and belts which they had buried in a grave.

The First Clash

On January 18, 1943, several companies of Nazi S.S. troops marched into the ghetto to enforce a second deportation action. By this time it had become common knowledge among the Warsaw Jews that the so-called "labor camps" in Lublin, to which the Germans were announcing they were taking them, were in reality the *Vernichtungslagern* (extermination camps) of Maidanek. They also had learned that *Gestapo* Chief Heinrich Himmler had ordered the vast area between the Oder and Dniester Rivers made absolutely *Judenrein* ("clean of Jews") within three months. This bit of news turned the Warsaw ghetto into an emotional inferno.

Therefore, that day, as the *Schutzstaffel* companies were proceeding through the streets of the ghetto, they were ambushed by Jewish combat units. For three days the street battle raged. So determined and reckless were the attackers that the Germans were forced to retreat from the ghetto for the time being.

Nevertheless, the deportations continued. The Jewish fighting units were not yet ready for a final showdown. Feverishly they hurried their preparations. They constructed bunkers in cellars and in attics. They also established a maze of connecting passages between house and house and street and street. And at the greatest risk they maintained contact with the Jewish and Polish guerrilla fighters hiding in the forest outside the city.

BATTLE OF THE WARSAW GHETTO

"Tens of thousands will perish, but thousands will get through."
—Motto of the Jewish Fighting Units in the Warsaw Ghetto

The Contenders

There are few conflicts on record comparable to the fantastically unequal struggle which characterized the Battle of the Warsaw Ghetto. On one side were drawn up the unlimited *panzered* might of the German Army, the *Gestapo* and the collaborationists. Pitted against them stood the last remnants of Warsaw's starving Jews—40,000 emaciated and physically exhausted civilians led by the Jewish Fighting Organization

Itzchak Zuckerman, known to the Warsaw ghetto fighters as "Antek," was the commander during the final phase of the Battle of the Warsaw Ghetto. Later, in Israel, he tried to rebuild his life as a farmer and tractor driver.

made up of only several thousand men and women. Food supplies to the ghetto had been cut off. The Jews were wretchedly armed. Worse yet, since they were confined in a small area within the ghetto, they were unable to maneuver. Nevertheless, they held the Nazis at bay for forty-two days. Although most of them perished, like their blinded ancestor Samson, they brought down with them in death some 5,000 of the hated enemy.

The Battle Begins

The leaders of the Fighting Organization assembled early in the spring of 1943. They then decided that, whatever the outcome, the uprising would have to be "now or never." The alert was given. All combat groups stood by.

A shot on Nalewki Street at six o'clock in the morning on April 19, 1943, was the signal for revolt. The fighting units, concealed in nearby bunkers, in attics and cellars, poured out into the streets and engaged the Nazi patrols. The Germans hurriedly retreated. Immediately after, protected by tanks and using flame-throwers and bombers, they returned to the attack. Armed only with light machine guns, rifles, gasoline bottles and hand grenades, but attacking with the heroism born of desperation, the ghetto fighters nevertheless forced the Nazis to withdraw once more.

Gestapo General Jurgen Stroop, who was in charge of the ghetto liquidation operation, then personally led a full-scale

Round-up of members of the Jewish Fighting Organization during the Battle of the Warsaw Ghetto. The words in German (below picture) read: "These bandits defended themselves with weapons." This sentence was written on the photograph by *Gestapo* General Jurgen Stroop, who was hanged as a war criminal several years later.

attack. But so fierce was the resistance that on the second day of the fighting the Germans were again forced out of the ghetto. The Nazi commander then drew up his batteries of heavy artillery. He was going to level the ghetto, building by building, and bury the Jews in the debris. But the fighting units continued their offensive action, and their heroic example roused the timid, who joined them by the hundreds. The whole area became ablaze with the fighting. Yet no one was really deceived. Each in his heart knew that it was an unequal struggle, that the odds were heavily weighted against the ghetto fighters. Yet they hoped against hope. Nothing, the leaders argued, was irrevocably lost so long as they could stand up and fight.

Ghetto fighters, men and women, shot out of a bunker by the Nazis during the last days of the battle of Warsaw Ghetto.

As the days passed, the situation for the rebels became increasingly desperate. Ammunition, water and food were fast giving out. The artillery barrages, bombings and the flame-throwers were rapidly wiping out the 40,000 remaining Jews. The best fighters had already fallen. One by one, the defense posts were destroyed. The commander-in-chief, Anielewicz, with his entire staff perished at the G.H.Q. on 18 Mila Street, a place now immortalized in the memories of Jews. No one surrendered. All fought until they fell.

On May 16, General Stroop proudly reported to his superior: "There *was* a Jewish section, but it no longer exists. Today at 20:16, the *Grossaktion* [principal operation] came to an end." General Stroop was boasting. For weeks thereafter small suicide groups calling themselves "rubble fighters" savagely battled the Nazis from behind the debris and wreckage —all that remained of what only a few years before stood as the principal center of Jewish life in Europe.

Nemesis works in strange and unpredictable ways. Although the Germans were certain that not one Jew had escaped from the ghetto, several hundred, by crawling for twenty hours neck-deep through the sewers, succeeded in making their way to the "Aryan" side of Warsaw. Most of them joined guerrilla bands in the forests. In the end it was their depositions that rose to haunt and to help condemn the Nazi murderers of the *Gouvernement-General* when they were brought to trial in Warsaw after the war.

Wasteland—after the Battle of the Warsaw Ghetto.

GUERRILLA COMMANDOS

Guerrilla bands, since time immemorial, have served as a supplementary force to field armies. They became especially active in the Nazi-occupied territories of Europe. Because of their deadly hatred of the Nazis, Jews in particular distinguished themselves in this hazardous type of warfare in which courage, resourcefulness and absolute loyalty to the group were considered essential qualifications. They were in all the underground resistance movements in France, Poland, Greece, Yugoslavia, White Russia and the Ukraine.

Perhaps best known to Jews were the daring exploits of a small group of underground fighters in Palestine. They had been trained in commando tactics and in military sabotage by the famed General Wingate of the British Army. The Royal Air Force of Britain flew them into various Nazi occupation zones where they were dropped by parachute and left to their own ingenuity and the risk of being discovered. Their principal task was to make contact with the Jews in concentration camps and to rescue as many of them as possible.

Of almost legendary fame among these guerrilla rescuers was the student Hannah Senesch. She was parachuted into her native Hungary where she was eventually captured and tortured to death. Another was the Italian Jew, Enzo Sereni, who was dropped behind the German lines in Italy. Caught by the Nazis in his rescue work, he was sent to the Dachau death camp from which he never emerged.

Just as famous in another sector of the underground was Lido Chaikin, a leader of a guerrilla band in the Soviet Union, who constantly eluded his enemies. Time after time he communicated with the Red Army by short-wave radio from the very center of the Nazi lines. Trapped at last, he was put to the torture by the Germans but died refusing to talk. Wherever they operated, the guerrilla fighters, armed principally with carbines, hand grenades, mines and bottles of gasoline, the so-called "Molotov cocktails," were assigned to derail Nazi troop-trains and to blow up ammunition dumps, communication lines and power plants.

REVOLT AGAINST DEATH

The widespread notion that all of the 6,000,000 Jews who perished in the death factories of the Germans went to their destruction unresisting is not based on fact. There is abundant evidence now available which reveals that armed group resistance did take place against the Nazis not only in Warsaw but in many other places. It occurred despite the fact that arms were virtually impossible to obtain. Even the most guarded attempt to plan an uprising was extremely hazardous because of the constant surveillance by the Germans and the presence of informers among the prisoners. Nevertheless, uprisings of the most heroic character did take place in the death camps of Sobibor, Trawniki, Poniatowka and Treblinka. In Treblinka, where 750,000 Jewish lives had been snuffed out, the final vengeance of a small band of slave-laborers proved total and epic.

On August 2, 1943, the Jewish slave-laborers of Treblinka, although weakened by systematic starvation and overwork, launched a series of coolly calculated attacks on the key points of the Nazi defense system within the camp. So perfectly synchronized and swift was their operation, so fearless their conduct, that they quickly overpowered and slew all the German S.S. guards. After burning the entire camp to the ground, they fled into the woods, knowing they would be pursued relentlessly. Only a few escaped recapture and joined guerrilla bands.

There probably would have been many more uprisings had but the bewildered and disorganized millions of the trapped in the ghettos given more credence to the persistent reports of the certain death awaiting them and of the fiendish ways it was to be accomplished.

Armed uprisings, aided by Jewish and Gentile guerrilla fighters from the outside, took place in the ghettos of Warsaw, Vilna, Bialystok, Lwov (Lemberg), Cracow, Tarnopol, Stryj, Czestochowa, Bendin, Riga and many other cities. They were fought fiercely, skillfully and with the courage of desperation. But besides these large-scale engagements, there were innumerable incidents in which individual Jews, women as well as men, fulfilled an heroic destiny while marching to their death. With arms secreted on their persons—a stolen hand-grenade or a revolver—at the very moment of entering the gas chambers they would suddenly fling themselves upon their Nazi murderers and take as many as possible with them into the Great Silence.

Uprising in Vilna

On the day the Jews of Vilna and its environs were driven into the ghetto by the Nazis they began planning their revolt. It erupted on September 1, 1943, after the Germans had surrounded the ghetto with machine-guns in preparation for a general massacre. The bloody but unequal struggle, marked by acts of self-sacrifice and heroism on the part of the ghetto fighters, raged for one week. Then the survivors were slaughtered.

Nazi officers at the gate of the Vilna Ghetto, sorting Jews for the massacre.

A. Sutzkever, noted Yiddish poet and a guerrilla leader during the revolt in the Vilna Ghetto, was sheltered by the Gentile woman, Yanova Bartashowitz.

Bodies of Vilna Jews on pyre in Esthonia.

LIBERATION

The glory of German *Kultur* was revealed in all its hideous nakedness as the war ground to a climax. The advancing Red Army from the east and the Allied Armies from the west, as they liberated the Nazi-occupied towns and cities in their victorious drive to Berlin, stumbled upon the concentration camps and the crematoria, still smoking and reeking with burning human flesh. The hundreds of thousands of survivors, half dead from starvation and disease, were almost apathetic in the hour of their liberation. So much had they suffered, so many horrors had they seen—life could never be quite the same for them.

Hungarian Jews marching out of a concentration camp after release in 1945.

REHABILITATION

Hundreds of thousands of survivors of the death camps, thenceforth referred to as Displaced Persons (D.P.'s) were established in separate camps. The principal problem was re-

Prisoners of a liberated concentration camp in Germany on their way to an UNRRA Displaced Persons' camp. With the final surrender of the German armies, the care of Jewish survivors was taken over by the United Nations Relief and Rehabilitation Administration (UNRRA), and later by the International Refugee Organization (IRO).

storing them to physical and mental health. They had to be rehabilitated and prepared for re-entry into normal life. Those who already had industrial and cultural skills required retraining because of long years of disuse. Even more important was the vocational training of a large number without trades, mostly young middle-class elements.

In this vast rehabilitation program a number of Jewish organizations were involved. The foremost among them were: the Joint Distribution Committee (JDC), the World Jewish Congress, the American Jewish Conference, the Jewish Agency

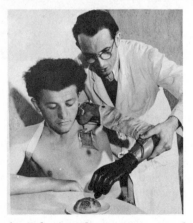

Youth who lost his arm in a concentration camp being trained to use the artificial limb provided by the Joint Distribution Committee.

for Palestine, the American Jewish Committee, the Organization for the Protection of the Health of the Jews (OSE) and ORT. These organizations, especially the Joint Distribution

Orphans of the death camps being fed by the Joint Distribution Committee.

Committee upon whom the principal burden of rehabilitation devolved, accomplished extraordinary results in salvaging broken lives and in providing some of the practical tools for survival. It is probably no overstatement to say that their collective services to the D.P.'s far exceeded the assistance of all governmental and international bodies.

A class for dental technicians supported by OSE in Paris.

Into the World Again

Most of the Displaced Persons, or D.P.'s, had no desire to return to the lands of their origin to face once more the nightmare of anti-Semitism. Those places were too full of tragic memories for them. Especially now after the holocaust there was the tormenting void of missing children, fathers and mothers, wives and husbands, brothers and sisters, friends and neighbors. There was also the physical desolation: of homes no longer theirs, of cherished Jewish landmarks that had vanished completely, of the old Jewish way of life they had known so well wiped out. Not even the smallest Jewish community had been left intact. The survivors figured that it was

Polish Jewish survivors on the way to an UNRRA camp in Austria, gathered in the yard of an emergency reception station in Bratislava, Slovakia.

'to a world in ruins they would be returning. Most of them were determined not to go back.

The new governments of the East European countries understood this state of mind and agreed to consider them officially as a non-repatriable group. Jews were told that they were free to go wherever they chose, including Palestine. A great many wished to go to the United States, where they had relations and friends, but the immigration quotas permitted only a fraction of the applicants to enter. Tens of thousands were willing to emigrate to almost any country that would allow them entry. But the postwar years found governments as well as individuals calloused to the suffering of the death camp survivors. A number of countries closed their gates to them entirely. In the more humane countries only a trickle of some thousands was allowed to settle in the course of a number of years.

The voluntary choice of the majority of the D.P.'s was Palestine. This was because of the predominant Zionist sentiment of the Jews in some East European countries. Despite the unyielding hostility of the British government, the Jewish Agency for Palestine persisted in organizing, as fast as its means allowed, the transfer of the D.P.'s from their wretched camps to the land of Israel.

A contingent of the *Youth Aliyah,* on the way to Palestine, dancing the *hora,* the national dance of Israel. Many thousands of children, orphaned by the Nazis, were brought to Palestine by *Youth Aliyah,* a children's immigration movement first begun in Germany in 1935 by the Jewish Agency with the financial aid of *Hadassah* and other Zionist women's organizations. Fully 60,-000 boys and girls were saved.

The Scattered Reunited

So traditionally close are Jewish family ties that rather than be separated most families in the concentration camps had chosen to meet death together. Nevertheless, after the war there were several hundred thousand survivors who went wistfully in search of near relatives from whom they had been separated in the milling chaos of the Nazi roundups. Location

After a five-year separation in different concentration camps, two brothers unexpectedly meet in the UNRRA Camp for Displaced Persons in Bari, Italy.

services were set up by the World Jewish Congress, by the Hebrew Immigrant Aid Society (HIAS) and by the Jewish Agency for Palestine. This heart-rending but efficient tracing process resulted in the reunion of a great number of widely scattered relatives. The Location Service of the American Jewish Congress, for example, in cooperation with other organizations, successfully traced 85,000 survivors and reunited 50,000 individuals with their families in all parts of the world.

BROTHERHOOD OF MAN

The tidal wave of savagery and murder that swept across Europe with the Nazis left large areas of society unstained and even defiant. In all the countries across which the Nazis

Catholic priest in Namur, Belgium, with a group of Jewish children he concealed from the Nazis throughout the Occupation, thus saving their lives.

goose-stepped in triumph the Jews found some staunch defenders and allies among anti-fascist Gentiles, many of whom risked or lost their lives to conceal or protect them. Belgian priests in monasteries, Dutch university professors, peasants in the Ukraine, underground fighters in France, guerrillas in Poland—all these and innumerable others affirmed their brotherhood with Jews.

On February 23, 1950, the Jews of Amsterdam unveiled the "Monument of Jewish Gratitude" in honor of the Dutch people. It bears the inscription: "To the protectors of the Netherlands Jews in the occupation years, 1940-1945."

It is said that one out of every five Belgian Jews was saved, when the Nazis came, through the courageous efforts of Gentiles. To show their scorn for the "master-race," many Christian citizens of Antwerp demonstratively put on the yellow armbands with the Star of David which Jews were forced to wear. In fact, on *Simchat Torah,* during the first year of the Nazi occupation, the Jews who were still left in Antwerp heard, to their amazement, the carillon of the cathedral peal forth the strains of *Hatikvah.* It was literally meant to be a song of hope to them. Memorable, too, was a rescue operation on a dark night after the Nazis had invaded Denmark: hundreds of Danes helped 7,000 Jews escape in small fishing boats to safety in Sweden.

RETRIBUTION

In October, 1945, the twenty-four foremost figures in the Nazi German Government were indicted as war criminals by an International Military Tribunal set up by the United States, the Soviet Union, France and England. Adolf Hitler, Dr. Joseph Goebbels and the chief executioner of 6,000,000 Jews, *Gestapo* head Heinrich Himmler, had escaped certain retribution by taking their own lives before they could be apprehended. Most of the rest were condemned to die on the gallows in a verdict handed down on October 1, 1946.

Leading Nazi war criminals at their trial in Nuremberg before the International Military Tribunal: (*behind partition, left to right, front row*) Goering, Ribbentrop, Keitel, Rosenberg; (*rear row*) Doenitz, Raeder, Schirach, Sauckel, Jodl.

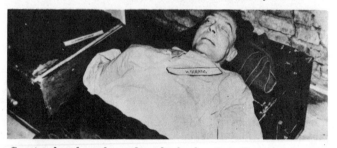

Convicted and condemned to die by hanging, Hermann Goering, most important Nazi next to Hitler, committed suicide by swallowing poison in his prison cell.

Robert Ley, a foremost Nazi and notorious leader of the German Labor Front, after being caught by two American Army privates.

THE AFTERMATH

The Jewish population in the East European countries where most of the murdered six million Jews had lived was truly decimated at the end of the war. It was increased somewhat by the thousands returning from the concentration and D.P. camps in other parts of Europe, but their plight was pitiable. Besides enduring the horrors of the death camps, the ravages of the war and its aftermath, of unemployment and hunger, most of them found themselves economically uprooted. A considerable measure of relief was brought them by Jewish organizations from abroad: the JDC, OSE and ORT, and by the IRO and UNRRA.

A direct result of World War II was the emergence of Communist governments in all the countries of eastern Europe. They became closely aligned with the Soviet Union, not only in their foreign policy but in their social, economic and cultural pattern as well. Their attitude toward the Jewish population, the survivors of the Nazi genocide program, became identical with that prevailing in the U.S.S.R. Jews were not considered or treated *as Jews* but as ordinary citizens of the country. Anti-Semitism was outlawed and hostile acts against Jews were punishable by imprisonment. Nonetheless, such a persistent social disease as anti-Semitism—which had infected these backward populations for centuries and which had been fanned into hysteria by the Nazis' campaign of hatred when they occupied these regions—could not be legislated out of existence. It also required the prophylaxis of mass enlightenment, which takes a long time to show any marked effect.

In consequence of the conditions that prevailed in Poland, Hungary and Romania, where anti-Semitism had been endemic for hundreds of years, many Jews in those countries felt physically insecure and emotionally disturbed. This was especially true during the first year after the war when there occurred quite a number of anti-Jewish outrages. The one which most alarmed the Jews of Poland was an attack by pogromists on Jews who had returned to their old homes in Kielce. Some of them were murdered. Although the Polish

Israel-bound D.P. immigrants receiving medical attention in one of the fifteen centers for transients established by the Joint Distribution Committee in the Marseilles area.

government took prompt action to punish the criminals and promised to take steps to prevent any further incidents of that nature, many Jews remained uneasy. They were anxious to emigrate, chiefly to Palestine. Soon thousands began leaving Poland, Romania, Hungary, Bulgaria, Yugoslavia and Czechoslovakia, with the aid of the Jewish Agency for Palestine, the Joint Distribution Committee and other Jewish organizations.

Until 1951, the flow of immigrants from these countries to Israel was relatively unimpeded. Middle-class Jews unalterably opposed to Communism were the most anxious to emigrate. But when the orientation of the Jewish State turned toward the West, the hostility toward Zionism and Israel on the part of all East European governments except that of Yugoslavia grew marked. Exit permits became difficult to obtain. This erratic but certain exodus further reduced the small Jewish populations in the Communist countries.

The population figures are an indication of this steady decline. Poland, which in 1950 had 65,000 Jews, a year later had 45,000; Romania, which had 335,000 Jews in 1950, registered only 280,000 in 1951. By 1951 only 3,500 Jews were left in Yugoslavia; 6,500 in Bulgaria; 155,000 in Hungary and 17,000 in Czechoslovakia.

In the East European countries there were thousands of Jews of working-class origin who were converted to Commu-

From left to right: Ana Pauker; Matyas Rakosi, Premier of Hungary; Dr. Julius Katz-Suchy, a leading Polish spokesman at the United Nations; Hilary Minc. Ana Pauker, former Foreign Minister of the Romanian People's Republic, daughter of a rabbi now in Israel, was accused early in 1952 by the Communist Party of Romania of open Zionist sympathies and of having encouraged Jewish emigration to Israel from her country. She was reprimanded and removed from office. Hilary Minc, Jewish Vice-Premier of Poland, and a noted economist, is shown here officiating at the opening ceremony of the International Fair at Poznan, April 23, 1949.

nism and freely cast in their lot with the dominant non-Jewish Communist population. While Zionist and Jewish religious culture was taboo in the Marxist atmosphere, Jewish culture in Yiddish was encouraged so long as it had a socialist and working-class content and was in harmony with governmental policy. There were, and presumably still are, newspapers, periodicals and books printed in Yiddish. There are state schools where the language of instruction is Yiddish and state theatres in which plays are performed in Yiddish. However, as in the Soviet Union, the social and economic pressures, international political developments and especially the ideological trends have been working strongly for cultural assimilation. As a result, the traditional features of Jewish life are rapidly disappearing in these countries.

Yiddish elementary school in Bucharest.

Rabbi Stephen S. Wise of the United States addresses the first post-war conference of the World Jewish Congress held in Montreux, Switzerland, in December, 1948. Delegates from East European countries also participated.

THE UNITED STATES OF AMERICA

FIRST JEWS IN AMERICA

From the day Columbus discovered the Western Hemisphere, Jews have been intimately bound up with its destiny. But it was not until 1654 that the first Jewish settlement in North America was established in the Dutch colony of Nieuw Amsterdam.

The first openly avowed Jew to arrive there was Jacob Barsimson. An intrepid spirit, going where no Jew had trod before, he came as a passenger on the Dutch West India Company boat *The Pear Tree* on August 22, 1654. One month later the French naval bark, the *St. Charles,* brought twenty-three Jews, former residents of Holland who had settled in Brazil. They were refugees fleeing from the Inquisition that had been instituted that year in Recife (Pernambuco) by the Portuguese after they had dislodged the Dutch from that territory. The Jews had been robbed on the way and could, therefore, pay only part of their passage money. And so the Dutch magistrates of Nieuw Amsterdam gave permission to the captain of the *St. Charles,* Jacques de la Motthe, to hold two of the Jewish passengers, Abram Israel and Judic de Mereda, as hostages against possible insufficient proceeds from an auction sale of all the Jews' possessions. In this rather inauspicious manner the greatest Jewish community in the modern world was founded.

From the day of their arrival the tiny community of impoverished Jews had to contend with the aggressive hostility of Peter Stuyvesant, the governor of the colony. He harassed them in every way imaginable, hoping that he would succeed in driving them away. On September 22, 1654, he reported to the Board of Directors of the Dutch West India Company, the owners of the colony, that he had asked the Jews "in a friendly way to depart" but they were stubborn and refused to go. He, therefore, petitioned ". . . of your worships, that the deceitful race, such hateful enemies and blasphemers of the name of Christ, be not allowed to infest and trouble this new colony. . . ." The directors of the Company replied on April 26, 1655, informing the choleric governor that they had no choice in the matter and that the Jews could not be ejected, "because of the large amount of capital which they [i.e., the Jews of Amsterdam] have invested in the shares of this Company." However, they did instruct him to deprive the Jews of "exercising their religion in a synagogue or a gathering."

Stuyvesant, however, had not counted on the upstanding character of these Jews. They had already tasted a measure of freedom, first in Amsterdam and later in Brazil, and now they fought boldly for their rights. On November 5, 1665, Asser Levy, one of the *St. Charles* passengers, in conjunction with Jacob Barsimson, the first Jewish settler in North America, petitioned the Nieuw Amsterdam Council that they "be permitted to keep guard with other burghers, or be free from the tax which others of their nation pay, as they must earn their living by manual labor." The Town Council replied curtly to the petition that the Jews were free "to depart whenever and whither it pleases them." But the petitioners appealed to the directors of the Dutch West India Company, who confirmed their stand. And so, thenceforth, together with their fellow-citizens, Jewish guards, too, manned the stockades against Indian attacks along Wall Street.

One advance led to another. Two years later, the irrepressible Asser Levy again appeared before the magistrates of Nieuw Amsterdam. The official record subsequently noted: "Asser Levy, a Jew, appears in Court; requests to be admitted a Burgher; claims that such ought not to be refused him as he keeps watch and ward like other Burghers showing a Burgher certificate from the City of Amsterdam that the Jew is a Burgher there."

Since the weight of the law and of the Jewish investments in the Dutch West India Company were again on Asser Levy's side, he forthwith became the first Jewish citizen in America on April 21, 1657. Yet this privilege was long denied to other Jews. Not until 1727, when the Oath of Allegiance to the King of England was revised to eliminate for Jews the insurmountable obstacle "upon the true faith of a Christian," could they at last become naturalized in New York. In other English colonies, naturalization for Jews did not come into effect until the Act of 1740.

The First Synagogue

Every right the Jews of Nieuw Amsterdam achieved they earned dearly by invoking the law and justice. They had to fight for the privilege of owning houses, of trading with the Indians, of engaging in the retail trade and, not least, of worshipping their God in the manner they were taught by their fathers. This struggle went on unceasingly, even after Nieuw

The first synagogue in America, destroyed in 1817, was erected in 1730 in New York on Old Mill Street (subsequently known as "Jews' Alley") by the Spanish-Portuguese Congregation *Shearith Israel* (Remnant of Israel). It was situated on what today is South William Street in downtown Manhattan. The congregation, which had been in existence ever since 1655 and owned a burial ground on the New Bowery, had not been permitted to hold public worship until 1728.

Amsterdam had become New York in 1664 and English values of law and right supplanted those of the Dutch. When in 1685 the Jews of New York petitioned the English governor to permit them to construct a synagogue, he coldly replied: ". . . none are allowed by an act of assembly so to worship but such as profess a faith in Christ." It was not until 1728 that the Jews of New York at last received permission to build a synagogue and to assemble in public worship without fear of molestation.

Colonial Merchants

By 1750 the *Ashkenazic* Jews formed the majority among the 2,500 Jews in the Colonies. These were Yiddish-speaking Jews who had come from Holland, Germany, Poland and England. Yet, because the *Sephardim,* or Spanish-Portuguese

Moses Levy, of *Marrano* ancestry, had been a successful merchant in London. He became a ship-owner and "engaged in the trade with the north of Africa." He settled in New York in 1705 where he became a leader of the Jewish community. For several years he served as *Parnass,* lay head of Congregation *Shearith Israel.*

Jews, had been earlier arrivals in the New World and were by and large better educated, they constituted financially, culturally and socially the "upper class" among the Jews. They remained the dominant group in Jewish communal affairs for a long time.

Jacob Franks, one of the wealthiest Jews of Colonial New York, born in England of German parents, served as the British Crown's sole fiscal agent for the Northern Colonies. His name as civilian commissary was prominently mentioned during the French and Indian Wars in military correspondence and reports of English generals. He built what was then considered the most elegant mansion in New York, later converted into Fraunces Tavern, the site of Washington's memorable "Farewell Address" to the officers of the Continental Army.

Some of them prospered as merchants and discount brokers. They traded with the Indians, were importers of badly needed finished consumer goods from England and the Continent and of such staples as coffee, sugar, cotton, tobacco, molasses and rum from the West Indies. Moreover, Jews generally engaged in a small but brisk inter-colonial trade, which, although hum-

Aaron Lopez was one of the most important shipowners and importers in Colonial times. Before the Revolution he owned a fleet of more than 30 ships. Upon his death, the Rev. Ezra Stiles, President of Yale College, wrote of him: "He was a merchant of the first eminence; without a single enemy and the most universally beloved by an extensive acquaintance of any man I ever knew."

ble, helped greatly in the development of early American life. Deplorably enough, along with respected Christian "merchants," some Jews were active in the slave-trade then universally sanctioned.

Actually, there were only few more than three hundred

Jews in New York before the revolution began in 1776. Yet the sizable number of well-to-do Jewish merchants and traders was noteworthy, although the majority were small shopkeepers, peddlers and artisans.

Jews of Newport

The second Jewish settlement in the American colonies was founded in Newport, Rhode Island. This could not have taken place but for that trail-blazer of religious liberty—Roger Williams. When he established his Colony of Rhode Island in 1636 the charter he drew up provided that no one living in the colony was to be in "any wise molested, punished, disquieted or called in question for any difference in opinion."

Interior of Newport Synagogue, *Jeshuath Israel* (Salvation of Israel). Dedicated on December 2, 1763, this house of worship, one of the finest examples of New England Colonial architecture, saw its first service conducted by the Rev. Isaac Touro, father of the famous Judah Touro, a *Sephardic hazzan* from Jamaica. The synagogue has been declared a national shrine by the U. S. Government.

Rabbi Raphael Haym Karigal, a *Sephardic* rabbi from Hebron, Palestine, had been sent to the Colonies as a *meshulach,* "messenger," to collect funds for the support of Jewish religious institutions in the Holy Land. His sermons in the Newport synagogue won wide acclaim in 1772. The Rev. Ezra Stiles, President of Yale College, a great admirer of his, studied Hebrew and the Bible with him. Rabbi Karigal had an undoubted influence on the course of Hebraic studies at Yale.

By this example he had set the precedent for the fundamental American principle which one hundred and fifty years later was adopted as the First Amendment to the Constitution providing for the separation of Church and State.

Under this benign democracy, *Sephardic* Jews became firmly rooted in Newport during the second half of the seventeenth century. The town was then a more important commercial port than New York and was surpassed only by Boston and Philadelphia. In reality, the Jews of Newport at first were only a small community of some sixty families, most of whom had emigrated from Surinam, Curaçao and Holland. Exporters

271

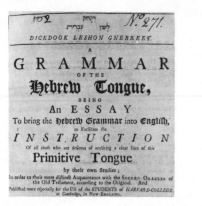

and importers in the main, they plied an energetic trade with Holland, but principally with the West Indies where they had numerous family and business connections. Best known among its merchants and traders were the Rivera and Lopez families. Jacob Rodriguez Rivera was the initiator and principal dealer in sperm oil (for candles and lamps) in the Colonies. His commercial effort helped in the development of whaling as an important industry in New England.

Jews in Other Colonies

Unfortunately, the Puritans, despite their democratic practices among themselves, were bigots who would not tolerate dissenters living in their midst. In consequence, Jews were late in settling in Massachusetts where Puritans held sway.

The situation was far different in Pennsylvania, where the Jews were sincerely welcomed. Although William Penn in his charter did not go so far as Roger Williams in defense of all non-conformists, he, nonetheless, guaranteed freedom of worship to all who "acknowledged one Almighty and Eternal God to be the Creator, Upholder and Ruler of the World." And so Jews founded settlements and established congregations in Philadelphia, Lancaster and Easton. There they lived tolerably in peace, though they did not enjoy full civil rights with Christians. The Quakers were far in advance of other Christian sects in the Colonies in their humanitarian and liberal attitude toward the Jews. This was stirringly epitomized in the inscription from Leviticus that a Quaker traced on the great bell (later the famed Liberty Bell) in Philadelphia in 1753: "Proclaim liberty throughout the land, unto all the inhabitants thereof."

In the Carolinas, too, there was shown a human respect for Jews. When the great English thinker, John Locke, was commissioned to draw up the Constitution for that Colony, he advanced the cause of universal freedom by providing equal toleration to all inhabitants, including "Jews, heathens and dissenters." For that reason Jews were encouraged to settle in the city of Charleston where on *Rosh Hashanah,* in 1750, they dedicated the third synagogue in America—*Beth Elohim* (House of the Lord). It was organized by Spanish-Portuguese Jews from Savannah who were joined later by immigrants from England and Germany. By 1800 it was the largest congregation in the United States.

Whig Jews

The Jewish religion and its ethical traditions had trained Jews in the ideals of human liberty and equality. That is why, from the very beginning, when the agitation arose in the American Colonies for rebellion against British royal tyranny and for supplanting it with a republican form of government, Jews were among its firmest supporters. Not only principle but enlightened self-interest motivated them. Some joined the secret societies, "Sons of Liberty" and the "Committees of Correspondence," which spread the agitation for rebellion among the population. Others helped with money, food and military supplies. When the weapon of economic boycott against England was decided upon by the rebels and the Non-Importation Agreement was drawn up and signed by 375 Philadelphia merchants on October 25, 1765, the small Jewish community of the city was represented by nine signatories who undertook "to be frugal in their use and consumption of all manufactures excepting those of America." Jewish merchants in New York and Newport took similar action. Nevertheless, there were a small number of Jews, especially among the assimilationist rich, who remained loyal Tories throughout the conflict and for that called down upon themselves the scorn of their fellow-Jews. The best known of these loyalists was the wealthy lawyer-merchant of Philadelphia, David Franks, who was the son of Jacob Franks. He had expediently turned Christian in 1743 and served the British Crown faithfully. His socially ambitious daughter Rebecca, a belle of Philadelphia "society," married General Sir Henry Johnson and after the war went to live in England.

It is hardly an overstatement that the financial sacrifices and the personal devotion shown by a small number of wealthy Jews to the cause of the American Revolution made its road to independence much easier to follow. One who is usually ranked with Robert Morris as among the most important financiers serving the cause of the revolution was Haym Salomon of Philadelphia. He was an immigrant who had come from Poland only about four years before the war began. His official title was: "Broker to the Office of Finance." With reckless but modest unconcern for his own interests, he personally endorsed the almost valueless Bills of Exchange issued by the Continental Congress. He died bankrupt and a pauper but admired by all who knew of his devotion to the American nation. When the Bills of Credit were issued in 1776, among their most substantial subscribers were Joseph Simon and Aaron Levy of Lancaster, Pa., Benjamin Jacobs of New York, and Benjamin Levy, Hyman Levy and Isaac Moses of Philadelphia. In the darkest hours of the struggle, Isaac Moses almost ruined himself by subscribing three thousand pounds to buy food for the half-starved Continental Army. In Georgia, Philip Minis advanced seven thousand dollars to feed the rebel troops in Virginia and North Carolina. Jacob Hart furnished a large sum of money to General Lafayette. Michael Gratz gave money to James Madison and to George Rogers Clark to make the Western Campaign possible. Generous to an unusual degree was Mordecai Sheftall, an immigrant from Germany. During the war, until he and his son were imprisoned by the British, he served in Savannah as the Deputy Commissary-General of Issues for the Southern Department of the Continental Army. Later, he was appointed a member of the General Staff. When he fell into the hands of the English after they captured Savannah, they officially denounced him as a "very great rebel."

Soldiers of the Revolution

Jews served in every Colonial militia during the long War for Independence. The rolls of the Continental Army itself

272

Haym Salomon (*right*) with George Washington (*center*) and Robert Morris (*left*). Statue located on Wacker Drive, Chicago.

carry the names of more than forty soldiers and officers who were Jewish. Unusual was the action of twenty-six Jews who lived on King Street in Charleston, S. C. They joined the local militia unit under Captain Lushington, and thus it acquired the name of "The Jews' Company." It took part in the Battle of Beaufort under General Moultrie.

There were a number of Jews who acquitted themselves well in the fighting. Some rose to high rank—Colonel Isaac Franks, Colonel David Salisbury Franks and Major Benjamin Nones, all of the Continental Army. There were also several officers in the militia, including Lieut.-Colonel Solomon Bush and Major Lewis Bush of the Pennsylvania Militia.

Probably the most spirited, certainly the most gallant officer among the Jews, was the Frenchman, Major Benjamin Nones, who served as staff-officer to Generals De Kalb, Lafayette and George Washington. Because of his strong republican convictions, he had come to Philadelphia from Bordeaux, France, to help Americans win their fight for freedom. As a private, so ran the official commendation, the "acts of the said Nones gained in his favor the esteem of General Pulaski as well as that of all the officers who witnessed his daring conduct." David Emanuel's bravery during the siege of Savannah was remembered later in Georgia's election campaigns. He became

Governor of Georgia in 1801 and in his honor its largest county was named "Emanuel."

Unusual and promising was the career, cut short by his untimely death, of Francis Salvador. A wealthy young plantation owner of twenty-nine, who had but recently arrived from his native England, he stepped forward as an ardent proponent of American independence. He was elected to the Provincial Congress of South Carolina on December 19, 1774, and later to the General Assembly. Thus he was the first Jew to hold public office in the Colonies. Early in August, 1776, while leading a night attack of militiamen against hostile Cherokees, Salvador was wounded three times and died after being scalped.

Religious and Civil Liberty

Upon the ratification of the Constitution of the United States in 1788, five thousand citizens of Philadelphia, the capital of the new American Republic, paraded through the streets in a joyous procession. As if to emphasize the fact that the republic was being built on a foundation of religious freedom and civil equality, the Rev. Gershom Seixas, then *Hazzan* of the *Mikveh Israel* (Hope of Israel) Congregation, marched

273

Left. Col. David Salisbury Franks, a nephew of the Tory apostate David Franks of Philadelphia, espoused the Republican cause of America while still living in Canada. There he had already fallen into difficulties with the authorities because of his outspoken libertarian views. When the Continental Army sent a military expedition into Canada, he joined it and saw action against General Burgoyne. As a major he became private secretary to General Benedict Arnold. When the latter was tried for treason, Franks applied to General Washington asking for a Court of Inquiry to clear himself. Arnold, however, cleared Franks in a statement to General Washington: "In Justice to the gentlemen of my family, Colonel Varick and Major Franks, I think myself bound to declare that they . . . are totally Ignorant of any transactions of mine that they had reason to believe were Injurious to the Public." Franks was cleared and subsequently promoted and sent on important diplomatic missions to France. *Right.* Portrait of Colonel Isaac Franks by Gilbert Stuart. Franks enlisted when he was seventeen with a New York regiment and rose rapidly as an officer. It is claimed by some historians that he was one of George Washington's *aides-de-camp*. When the yellow fever epidemic raged in Philadelphia, then the capital of the United States, President Washington lived in Franks' house at Germantown.

Left. Letter addressed to President George Washington by the Hebrew Congregation of Newport, Rhode Island, August 17, 1790, which thanks the President for the civil and religious liberty its members are enjoying under his administration. *Right.* Washington's reply. In it he rejoices with all citizens of the

between two Christian ministers. This was an unprecedented occurrence in the annals of Jewish history.

Yet the achievement they were celebrating that day had not come about easily. Behind it lay a bitter struggle that had gone on for years in the Colonies. Furthermore, the libertarian principles, even though they were legally recognized, were still to be implemented. This applied especially to the First Constitutional Amendment which established the separation between Church and State: "Congress shall make no law respecting an establishment of religion or prohibiting the exercise thereof." However, a number of states refused to recognize this principle.

The whole question of religious freedom was dramatically projected in a controversy which raged for six years in Virginia. On the side of "separation" staunchly stood Thomas Jefferson and his disciple, James Madison. The spokesman for "state religion" was Patrick Henry. He and his partisans insisted that the Episcopal Church continue as the official religion of Virginia. In the end, the liberals triumphed. The law of Virginia on separation of Church and State, which Jefferson wrote, was later adopted by the leaders of the French Revolution. While New York drew up its own religious liberty provision in 1777, remarkably enough, it took the state of New Hampshire until 1877 to enact one.

Notable was the struggle waged in 1809 by Jacob Henry to take his seat in the State Legislature of North Carolina, to which he had been elected. This occurred in the face of a stipulation made in the State Constitution of 1776 that no one was to hold office who "shall deny the being of God or the truth of the Protestant religion or the Divine authority, either of the Old or New Testament. . . ." Henry then delivered an impassioned indictment of bigotry before the Legislature. His theme was this: "Nothing is more easy to demonstrate than that conduct alone is the subject of human laws, and that man

United States—"For happily the Government of the United States, which gives to bigotry no sanction, to persecution no assistance, requires only that they who live under its protection should demean themselves as good citizens. . . ."

ought to suffer civil disqualifications for what he does, and not for what he thinks." Yet so intense was its bigotry that the North Carolina Legislature refused to admit Jacob Henry to the legislative chamber. Ironically enough, it was not until 1868, long after Jacob Henry had died, that this provision of the law was expunged from the State Constitution.

The most memorable battle for Jewish religious freedom in America was fought, not by Jews, but by Thomas Kennedy, a Scotch Presbyterian member of the Legislature of the state of Maryland. A decade after the Federal Constitution had been ratified, Solomon Etting, Barnard Gratz (for whom George Washington had once surveyed land) and several other Maryland citizens petitioned the State Legislature that "they are a set of people called Jews and that they are thereby deprived of many of the invaluable rights of citizenship, and praying that they be placed upon the same footing with other good citizens." Their "prayer," however, went unheeded.

But a generation later, Thomas Kennedy entered the lists against the bigots. He introduced what his opponents derisively dubbed "The Jew Bill." In defense of it he argued: "There are no Jews in the country from which I come, nor have I the slightest acquaintance with any Jew in the world. . . . There are few Jews in the United States; in Maryland there are very few, but if there were only one, to that one we ought to do justice." It is perhaps an indication of the slow evolution of progressive ideas that the "Jew Bill" was defeated. Although defeated at the polls, Kennedy, nevertheless, remained in the political arena, tirelessly agitating for the cause of equal rights for the Jews. Before long he translated defeat into victory. Returned by an aroused electorate to the Legislature, he saw all religious and civil inequalities finally abolished in 1826.

Unbroken Continuity

From the day in September, 1654, when the twenty-three "Jewish Pilgrim Fathers," escaping from the Inquisition's clutches in Brazil, set foot in Nieuw Amsterdam, there has never been a break in the continuity of Jewish community life in the United States. The religious link always remained the strongest in Jewish group identity. Yet American Jews at no time stayed aloof from the general life of the country. As pioneers they helped in its development since early times; as citizens they took an active part in all its affairs.

IMMIGRANT TIDE FROM GERMANY

Pioneers and Frontiersmen

As the country grew, the Jewish communities in the young republic kept pace with it in their development. When the Napoleonic Wars had ended, hundreds of poor Jews in quest of freedom or bread, or both, began to arrive, principally from Germany. The more adventurous struck out westward into the wilderness as the frontier was being extended beyond the Alleghenies. There they founded new outposts of Jewish group life: in Cincinnati, Ohio (1824); Louisville, Ky. (1832); New Orleans, La. (1833); Chicago, Ill. (1837); St. Louis, Mo. (1839); Cleveland, Ohio (1839); also in Newark, N. J. (1852) and in a number of other places.

Most of these newcomers were poor but ready to work hard and, being thrifty, managed to put by a little money with which to take advantage of new opportunities when they came along. The first Jew to arrive in Cincinnati, for instance, was an enterprising watchmaker from England, Joseph Jonas. When he heard the glowing reports in New York about the opening of the Western territories, he set out for the wilds in 1817. It took him two strenuous as well as hazardous months to make the journey from New York to Ohio. It also took him an additional two years to persuade his brothers and two other English Jews to join him there.

On *Rosh Hashanah*, 1819, an extraordinary first religious service was celebrated by the tiny group of Jewish frontiersmen. They constituted themselves, although only five in number, into a rump kind of *minyan*. For the first time the unfamiliar sound of Hebrew prayers rang out in the hushed wilderness.

Peddlers and Millionaires

Some of the best-known and most ample Jewish fortunes in the United States were founded literally in a peddler's pack. Many were the Jewish immigrants from Germany who with packs on their backs trudged hopefully from one remote settlement to another. Lazarus Straus, the founder of the Straus

Isaac W. Bernheim, as a peddler in Pennsylvania in 1867. Five years later he founded the Bernheim Distilling Company in Louisville, Kentucky. It became one of the largest in the United States and is now an important unit of Schenley Distillers.

fortune, and the father of the illustrious Isidor, Oscar and Nathan, started as an itinerant peddler. He drove a horse and wagon through Georgia upon his arrival, in 1852, as a poor immigrant from Bavaria. After a while, he opened a little shop in the town of Talbottom. It took him two years of hard work and much scrimping and saving before he was able to send passage money to his family in Bavaria. But even though it was a period full of hazards and hardships for immigrants, it was also fabulously rich in opportunities. Out of Straus's modest beginning in Georgia were eventually born two great department stores—R. H. Macy's in New York and Abraham and Straus (A. & S.) in Brooklyn. Adam Gimbel, the founder of the Gimbel chain of department stores, starting in Vincennes, Indiana, had a career almost parallel with Lazarus Straus's. However, theirs were unusual cases. The majority of Jewish peddlers remained peddlers, and most shopkeepers kept shop as long as they lived.

The Gold Rush

When the Gold Rush fever began in 1849, Jews, too, were shaken by it. By covered wagon or boat they, too, journeyed

The Rev. Gershom Mendes Seixas, minister of the Spanish-Portuguese Congregation *Shearith Israel* in New York. During the Revolutionary War, when the British General Howe invested New York, the Reverend Seixas led an exodus of New York Jews, who were overwhelmingly for American independence, into voluntary exile and privation. Some went to Philadelphia, the rest to Stratford, Connecticut. Reverend Seixas was a trustee of Columbia College of which he was also an incorporator.

Versatile and popular, "Major" Mordecai Noah was elected High Sheriff of New York in 1822. He was also prominent as playwright, journalist and publisher. As editor of the *National Advocate* in 1816, publisher of the *Evening Star* in 1834 and founder of the influential weekly, the *Sunday Times and Messenger*, he helped raise the cultural standards of American journalism. In 1820 he announced his plan for establishing a haven for persecuted Jews on land he had purchased on Grand Island near Buffalo. Nothing came of the project.

Rabbi David de Sola Pool, historian and present religious leader of *Shearith Israel*, standing beside the grave of the Rev. Gershom Mendes Seixas in one of the oldest burial grounds in the New World, situated in the New Bowery. In it lie some of the 23 "Jewish Pilgrim Fathers" who had settled in Nieuw Amsterdam in 1654.

Lorenzo da Ponte.   Uriah P. Levy.

The famous Italian poet of Jewish parentage, Lorenzo da Ponte, was Imperial Court Poet to Emperor Joseph II and Mozart's librettist for *The Magic Flute*, *Don Giovanni* and *Cosi Fan Tutte*. He also wrote the libretto for Gluck's *Iphigenia in Tauris*. In the course of his stay in New York, da Ponte introduced Mozart's *Don Giovanni* with the great Manuel Garcia and Madame Malibran. But falling on hard times, he opened a bookshop opposite St. Mark's Church and taught Greek, Latin, and the Italian language and literature at Columbia College. Captain Uriah P. Levy fought in the War of 1812 and was instrumental in having flogging in the Navy abolished.

Portrait by Rembrandt Peale of Judge Moses Levy of Philadelphia. Active in the struggle for American independence, he was perhaps the most distinguished Jew during the opening years of the Republic. An able lawyer and a liberal Whig in politics he served as Recorder of Philadelphia (1802-22) and as Presiding Judge of the District Court of Philadelphia after that. He was a trustee of the University of Pennsylvania and a founder of the Pennsylvania Academy of Fine Arts. In 1804, in a letter to Albert Gallatin, President Thomas Jefferson wrote that he was seriously considering "Mr. Levy of Philadelphia" for the post of Attorney General in his Cabinet. The appointment did not materialize.

Mordecai Myers.   Alfred Mordecai.

Captain Mordecai Myers of New York led a victorious charge against the British during the War of 1812 at Chrysler's Farm near Williamsburg, Virginia. Other Jews also distinguished themselves for gallantry during that war. Midshipman Joseph B. Nones, son of the Major Nones of Revolutionary fame, was on Decatur's staff on the *Guerrière*, and later served as private secretary to Henry Clay at the Peace Conference in Ghent. Manuel Phillips served as a naval surgeon throughout the war. In the army were Colonel Nathan Myers, who commanded a brigade; Major Alfred Mordecai, the military expert; Captains Etting, Meyer Moses, Chapman Levy and the Captains Abraham, Moses B. and Solomon Seixas. Bernard Hart of New York, grandfather of the writer Bret Harte, served as a divisional quartermaster.

Judah Touro migrated from Newport to New Orleans in 1802 where he founded the Jewish community. He grew wealthy as merchant, exporter and importer, and his benefactions to both Jews and Gentiles were large.

to California, lured possibly as much by adventure and excitement as by gold. Most of them, however, did not prospect for the elusive metal, but with the ancient sobriety and realism of their people became small shopkeepers and dealers in necessities to the prospectors. It is recorded that the first Jewish religious services ever to take place in California was on *Yom Kippur* of that first mad year of the Gold Rush. It was held in a tent in San Francisco. In at least a dozen of the mining camps there were improvised rough-and-ready congregations which tenaciously held onto their religious and group identity even under the most discouraging circumstances.

Ascendancy of the German Jews

While many of the immigrants from Germany plunged into the expanding frontier of the West, others preferred to remain behind to enjoy the advantages of city life. The latter joined the substantial Jewish communities already in existence in Philadelphia, New York, Newport, Savannah, Charleston, Richmond, Baltimore, Boston and New Haven. Jewish life in these cities, as well as American life generally, became enriched in a cultural and political sense when, upon the collapse of the revolutions of 1848 in Germany, Austria, Hungary and France, a considerable number of educated and public-spirited Jews fled to this country for asylum. One man who best represented this superior class of immigrants popularly known as the "Forty-Eighters" was the eminent physician, Dr. Abraham Jacobi.

B'nai Jeshurun Synagogue in 1825, at 119 Elm Street in lower Manhattan.

Portrait of Israel Baer Kursheedt by C. G. Thompson. A young German merchant of Richmond, Va., and later of New York City, he had studied at the *Yeshiva* in Frankfort-am-Main. He married the daughter of the Reverend Gershom Mendes Seixas, and in later years served as *Parnass*, or President, of the Spanish-Portuguese Congregation *Shearith Israel*. When the secession movement started among the German Jews, he was one of its leaders and subsequently a founder of the *B'nai Jeshurun* congregation.

The German Jewish immigrants first became conscious of their group strength in 1825, and began to assert it more and more. Until then, although they had constituted for a long time the majority of Jews in the United States, they, nevertheless, had accepted the religious, cultural and social domination of the better-educated and wealthier Jews of Spanish-

Portuguese stock. But in 1825, Orthodox German Jews, who belonged to the *Sephardic* Congregation *Shearith Israel*, seceded and formed their own religious society which they called *B'nai Jeshurun*. They bought an imposing edifice from the First Colored Presbyterian Church at 119 Elm Street in lower Manhattan and converted it into a synagogue where they conducted services according to the *Ashkenazic*, or Ger-

Consecration on September 12, 1860, of the new house of worship on West 19th Street near Fifth Avenue, New York, built by the Spanish-Portuguese Congregation *Shearith Israel*. This was the third synagogue building of the congregation.

man, rite. In 1833 the congregation constructed a *mikveh*, or ritual bath. From that time on, with the steady increase of immigrants, congregations formed exclusively of German-speaking Jews from the countries of central Europe were established everywhere. Their rabbis regularly delivered sermons in German.

Ohabei Shalom Synagogue in Boston. Organized by German immigrants in 1843, this Orthodox house of worship, the first in Boston, was built in 1852.

Reform Judaism

The seed of Reform Judaism had been carried by young immigrants from Germany into the United States almost immediately after it had originated in Hamburg and Berlin. Perhaps almost as much as in Germany, the general emancipation of the Jews in the United States, the liberal spirit of the times and, moreover, a strong compulsion among better-educated and well-to-do Jews to assimilate with their environment encouraged the growth of this movement.

The first organized effort for religious reform was made in 1824 by a group of dissidents in Congregation *Beth Elohim* in Charleston, S. C. They petitioned the trustees of the congregation to introduce certain innovations in the synagogue

277

The "Hebrew Synagogue" (*Beth Elohim*) of Charleston, S. C.

service. They asked for a reduction in what they considered its inordinate length. They wanted some of the prayers recited in English translation. Most revolutionary of all was their demand that the sermon on the Sabbath be delivered in English so that everyone might understand what the preacher was saying.

The Orthodox trustees indignantly rejected the petition, and so the dissidents, about fifty members of the congregation, withdrew and, under the leadership of Isaac Harby, formed their own religious fraternity which they named "Reformed Society of Israelites." But due to the hostility of the parent congregation and a variety of other reasons, it disintegrated after eight years of hesitant existence. Nonetheless, its very presence in Charleston, no matter how brief, exercised an imponderable pressure for change on the Orthodox Congregation *Beth Elohim*.

Signs of this influence became noticeable in 1838, after the old synagogue had burned down and a new one was being planned. The new preacher-cantor, the Rev. Gustav Poznanski, a Polish Jew who had been exposed to Reform during a sojourn in Hamburg, proposed that a pipe organ be installed in the new house of worship. When a majority of the congregation sanctioned this innovation, the more Orthodox element indignantly withdrew and formed its own synagogue. This controversy in Charleston was by no means exceptional. It was typical of the strains and stresses in American Jewish life which emerged under the impact of new influences.

The real founder of Reform Judaism in America, who gave it leadership, a distinctive ritual and a religious program, was the Rev. Isaac M. Wise (1819-1900), a German-speaking immigrant from Bohemia. After a tentative start in Albany, he finally established in Cincinnati, Ohio, in 1854, the first Reform congregation in the United States. With the oncoming

Rabbi Isaac Mayer Wise of Cincinnati, Ohio, founder of Reform Judaism in the United States.

thousands of Jewish immigrants from Germany, Austria, Hungary and Bohemia—all speaking German and, in varying degree, products of German-Jewish culture—this liberal religious movement took firm root in all the large Jewish communities

Sketch by Vernon Howe Bailey (1948) of part of the campus of the Hebrew Union College in Cincinnati, Ohio. This is the oldest rabbinical school in the United States, founded by Rabbi Isaac M. Wise in 1875. In the beginning it had only nine students and the faculty consisted of Rabbi Wise and a single assistant. The first four rabbis were graduated in 1883. In later years the institution added a Graduate School for Jewish Studies. The library of the college owns one of the largest and finest Judaica collections in the world. In 1950 the institution merged with the Jewish Institute of Religion in New York which had been founded in 1922 by Rabbi Stephen S. Wise. The combined institutions are now run under the presidency of the well-known archaeologist, Dr. Nelson Glueck. Their main financial support is derived from the Union of American Hebrew Congregations which the indefatigable Isaac M. Wise had organized in 1873. In 1889 he had also founded the Central Conference of American Rabbis.

in the United States. Reform congregations prospered mostly among well-to-do German Jews under the leadership of an exceptionally able group of rabbis, the most prominent of whom were David Einhorn, Bernard Felsenthal, Max Lilienthal, Samuel Hirsch and Samuel Adler.

The Reverend Dr. Kaufmann Kohler, third president of the Hebrew Union College (1903-22). Under his intellectual leadership the institution acquired both scholarly stature and a philosophy of religion which set the course for Reform Judaism in the United States. Dr. Kohler stressed the ethical and universal aspects of Judaism.

THE SLAVERY ISSUE

When slavery became the heated issue of the day in the United States, the sentiment of American Jews in the North, where the great majority lived, was overwhelmingly behind Abolition. Jews were active in the anti-slavery movement from the beginning. An associate of the Abolitionist leaders in the North—Garrison, Wendell Phillips and Geritt Smith—was the Jewish "Forty-Eighter" from Germany, Moritz Pinner. In 1858 he established in Kansas City the *Kansas Post*, a fiercely anti-slavery periodical.

Then, too, there was the Rev. Dr. David Einhorn (1809-79), the intellectual leader of American Reform Judaism. He had come to Baltimore in 1855 to take over the pulpit of *Har Sinai* (Mt. Sinai) Congregation. An Abolitionist in principle, he advocated it in the English-Jewish periodical *Sinai* which he edited. When the Republican Party declared its unalterable opposition to slavery, Rabbi Einhorn lauded the action from the pulpit, to the dismay of the conservatives in his congregation. Baltimore being a slave-center, his life was constantly threatened by the pro-slavery rabble-rousers. Unperturbed by the clamor, Rabbi Einhorn continued to attack the institution of slavery. The trustees of his congregation finally prevailed upon him to go to Philadelphia until the disturbance died

Rabbi David Einhorn.

down. When called back several weeks later, on condition that he would never touch upon the subject of slavery, Rabbi Einhorn resigned his post. Among other Jewish anti-slavery preachers were the Rev. D. Liebman Adler and the Rev. Dr. Bernard Felsenthal. Both in English and in German, they preached Abolition before their immigrant congregations.

The brothers Joseph and Isaac Friedman, who lived in the Deep South, participated in the Underground Railway and, at great personal risk to themselves, helped runaway slaves escape to the North. Leopold Blumberg, a respected Baltimore resident, because of his outspoken opposition to slavery was almost lynched by a mob. As soon as the Civil War broke out, he led in the organization of the 5th Regiment of Maryland Infantry. Severely wounded at the Battle of Antietam, his gallant conduct during the fighting led to his promotion as Brevet Brigadier General.

Plain Jews, too, did their share for Abolition and in defense of the Union. One little-known but dramatic incident involved three Jewish immigrants, partners in a general store at Osawatomie, Kansas—August Bondy, Theodore Wiener and Jacob Benjamin. Because they were fearlessly outspoken in their opposition to slavery, the "Border Ruffians" burned their store to the ground. The partners barely managed to escape with their lives. Instead of being frightened, they joined the "Kansas Regulars" which John Brown had organized. August Bondy's account of that experience is one of the most memorable chronicles written by a Jew about the Civil War.

By and large, the Jews in the South were also carried away by the fierce partisan passions and social pressures generated by the times. The majority were for the continuation of the slavery system, yet because of the traditional Jewish aversion to slavery, they were perhaps a little less enthusiastic for it than other Southerners. Certainly, the more recent immigrants from Germany, Austria, Hungary and Poland had no great love for the Southern slaveocracy. Many, especially the liberal "Forty-Eighters," secretly sympathized with the aims of Abolition.

A comparable situation existed in the North. Although the great majority of Jews stood firmly for putting an end to slavery, there were quite a few, especially among the wealthy with business connections in the South, who openly took a pro-slavery stand. Prominent among the latter was Rabbi Morris Jacob Raphall who had come, in 1849, to Congregation *B'nai Jeshurun* in New York from a fashionable London pulpit. He soon became the recognized spokesman for the small pro-slavery faction among the Jews in the United States. A man of pronounced Royalist views—his father had been court-banker to the King of Sweden—Rabbi Raphall set out to prove that the Bible unequivocally sanctioned slavery.

Just before the Secession he preached a sermon, at *B'nai Jeshurun*, which he called "Bible View of Slavery." It was, so to speak, a theological brief bristling with citations from the Hebrew Scriptures which purportedly supported slavery on moral and religious grounds. Human bondage, concluded Rabbi Raphall, was a divine institution created "through the providential allotment of the Divine Being." The Gentile pro-slavery partisans in New York were so delighted with the sermon that they had it printed as a pamphlet and distributed it widely among Christians as well as Jews. It precipitated a bitter controversy.

Many Jews were dismayed when the Rev. Isaac M. Wise, the leader of Reform Judaism, and Rabbi Isaac Leeser, the spokesman for the Orthodox community, approved the sermon. Rabbi David Einhorn was stung to retort indignantly: "Can that Book [i.e., the Bible] mean to raise the whip and forge chains which proclaims, with flaming words, in the name of God: 'Break the bonds of oppression, let the oppressed go free and tear every yoke!'" The New York *Tribune* also leaped to the attack. In two angry editorials it castigated Rabbi Raphall for trying to drag religion into unholy places. A few days later, on January 15, 1861, it printed a long article by Michael Heilprin: "*Slavery and the Hebrew Scriptures:* A reply to the Rabbi Raphall." Michael Heilprin, a Hungarian poet and scholar and an associate of Louis Kossuth in the Revolution of 1848 in Hungary, had come to the United States in 1856 where he became well known as a liberal journalist and as an editor of Appleton's *American Dictionary of Biography*. His refutation of Rabbi Raphall was widely acclaimed.

Michael M. Allen, although not an ordained rabbi, was appointed the first Jewish chaplain for Union soldiers. He was attached to the Cameron Dragoons, which had a large number of Jews among its officers and men. There was some heated controversy subsequently because of an act of Congress with the delimiting proviso "of a Christian denomination." which disqualified ordained rabbis from serving as chaplains. Finally, Congress passed a law in 1862 which corrected the inequity.

War

War between the States appeared inevitable, but when it erupted the whole nation was dismayed. Rabbis in the North preached fiery sermons calling upon Jews to volunteer for the army and to support the Union against the Secessionists. Rabbis in the South with perhaps equal fervor applauded Secession and justified it with citations from book, chapter and verse in Holy Writ. In the North, 6,000 Jewish volunteers answered the stirring call to arms. Of these, 2,000 were recruited in New York and about 1,000 in Illinois. There were a surprising number of officers among them; most, however, were promoted from the ranks as the fighting continued. When the conflict ceased there were nine Jewish generals, eighteen colonels, eight lieutenant-colonels, forty majors, two hundred and five captains, three hundred and twenty-five lieutenants, forty-eight adjutants and twenty-five surgeons.

Lieut.-Col. Israel Moses, prominent in the early medical annals of Mt. Sinai Hospital, New York, proposed during the Civil War a new treatment for gun-shot wounds which saved many lives in the Union Army. (*From the Blanche Moses Collection, courtesy American Jewish Historical Society*)

There were about 1,200 Jews in the Confederate Army, among them twenty-three staff officers and several naval officers. Commodore Levi Myers Harby, who had resigned from the U. S. Navy when the war began, took a leading part in the Galveston defense during which he commanded the *Neptune*. Commander Julius Hartstein, a baptized Jew from South Carolina, was Naval Commander in Charleston in 1861 and in Savannah the following two years. The number of Jews in leading positions in the Confederate Government and in the Confederate Army was impressive. David de Leon served as Assistant Surgeon-General, A. C. Meyers as Quartermaster-General and J. Randolph Mordecai as Assistant Adjutant-General. In the United States Senate, before the break, a leading defender of slavery and secession was David Yulee of Florida.

Judah P. Benjamin.

Perhaps the most important civilian in the Confederate Government besides Jefferson Davis was Judah P. Benjamin. One of the most brilliant and successful lawyers of the day, he has been called "the brains of the Confederacy." He drew national attention when, as U. S. Senator from Louisiana in 1853 and again in 1859, he delivered his pro-slavery orations in which he described Abolitionists as "insane fanatics." He served the Confederate Government successively as Attorney-General, Secretary of War and, finally, as Secretary of State. Upon the collapse of the Confederacy he fled to England where he assumed English citizenship and became a leading lawyer.

WEALTH AND PHILANTHROPY

Bankers

By the time of the Civil War several important Jewish banking houses were flourishing in the United States. They had been established by enterprising immigrants from Germany: August Belmont, who was American agent for the House of Rothschild; Speyer & Co. (1837); and J. and W. Seligman & Co. (1857). Several decades later other Jewish banking firms were formed: Kuhn-Loeb and Co. (1865); Lehman Brothers (1868); J. S. Bache and Co.; Ladenburg, Thalmann and Co.; and Goldman, Sachs and Co.

The Union Army and the United States Government leaned heavily on the Jewish bankers for financial assistance during the war. Especially distinguished in its devotion and helpfulness to the Northern cause was the house of Seligman which was run by seven liberal-minded brothers. For decades after the Civil War the firm continued to act as the official fiscal agent for the United States Government and the Navy Department. On the other hand, the firm of Lehman Brothers, headed by Mayer and Emanuel Lehman, which had been established in Montgomery, Alabama, during the Civil War, worked for the Confederacy and Jefferson Davis.

Despite their public prominence, Jewish banks at all times constituted only a small fraction of the international banking institutions in the United States. For instance, a survey before World War II revealed that only nine per cent of all international loans floated by American financial firms were negotiated through the Jewish-owned banks which, by that time, probably had almost as many Gentile partners as Jewish ones.

Merchants and Industrialists

Besides the few successful bankers, a larger number of Jewish immigrants, or sons of immigrants, played an important role in the economic and commercial development of America. These were department store owners, leading wholesalers and distributors, textile manufacturers, mine owners and railroad magnates.

Julius Rosenwald (1862-1932) started his business career as an apprentice in the clothing store owned by an uncle in New York. Nine years later he was vice-president and one-fourth owner of Sears, Roebuck and Company. That mail-order house had a spectacular development and Rosenwald accumulated a great fortune. A large portion of it he devoted, through the Julius Rosenwald Fund, to providing manual, agricultural and educational aid to the Negroes of America.

The most spectacular business career among immigrant Jews was that of Meyer Guggenheim and his seven sons. He emigrated from Switzerland and began life in America inauspiciously at the age of nineteen as a horse-and-buggy peddler in a coal mining and farming region in Pennsylvania.

He started making money by manufacturing lye and stove polish. Later he imported machine embroideries from his native Switzerland. A fortunate investment in a silver lead mine in Colorado in 1890 started him on a course which made him the world's foremost producer and smelter of copper, silver and other basic metals.

Art Patrons and Philanthropists

While there have been quite a number of wealthy Jews in America, whatever distinction some of them may have earned has rested not so much on how much money they accumulated but on how much they gave away, and for what. Philanthropy has always been a cardinal practice in Jewish life, considered as much a social obligation as a religious duty. The

Rebecca Gratz (1781-1869), a member of the wealthy Gratz family of Philadelphia, whose benefactions and personal ministrations were directed especially to women and children of all faiths. She was founder of the Philadelphia Orphan Asylum. She also started the first Jewish Sunday School in America. When her friend, Washington Irving, described her personality and character to Sir Walter Scott, that historical novelist made her the model for Rebecca in *Ivanhoe*.

Hebrew word for *charity* is *zedakah,* which really means *justice.* Jewish tradition frowns upon that magnanimity, condescension and vanity which often accompany the giving and the distribution of *charity.*

Jacob H. Schiff (1847-1920) was born in Frankfurt, Germany. In New York he became head of Kuhn-Loeb and Company in 1885. Eminently successful as a financier, in 1897 he carried through the reorganization of the Union Pacific Railroad and its merger with the Southern Pacific and other lines. Nonetheless, he never considered profit as the sole end of his transactions. His hatred of the Tsarist Russian Government for its persecution of the Jews was so intense that, without consideration of any return to himself, he floated a $200,000,000 bond issue to aid the Japanese Government (1904-05) during the Russo-Japanese War. His philanthropies were numerous, liberal and non-sectarian.

This philosophy of assistance to the needy, which extends as much respect to the one who receives as it lends dignity to the giver, was best exemplified in American life by such modest and generous givers as the bankers Jacob H. Schiff, Felix M. Warburg and Otto Kahn, and the great merchants Nathan Straus, Benjamin Altman, Julius Rosenwald and Joseph Fels.

Otto Kahn, a foremost patron of music and the arts in the United States, kept alive many worthy musical and theatrical ventures with his unannounced subsidies. As chairman of the Board of the Metropolitan Opera House he steadily made up its annual deficits. In his quiet way he enriched American culture by underwriting the American tours of Diaghilev's

Ballet Russe (1918), The Moscow Art Theatre under Stanislavsky (1923) and Max Reinhardt's stage productions in German (1928).

There were other art and music patrons who made munificent gifts for the cultural enjoyment of the American public. Benjamin Altman presented his priceless collection of old masters to the Metropolitan Museum of Art. Solomon Guggenheim established, in 1937, his Foundation and the Museum for Non-Objective Art. Another member of the family founded

Felix M. Warburg (1871-1937) was born in Hamburg, Germany. As Jacob Schiff's son-in-law he joined the banking firm of Kuhn-Loeb and Company in New York. But his interests lay more in the promotion of education, music and art than in finance. In the last period of his life especially, he became closely associated with the leadership of Jewish philanthropies.

the John Simon Guggenheim Memorial Foundation to assist a sizable number of gifted artists, scientists and scholars with fellowships. Lucius Littauer's foundation greatly enriched Harvard University. Adolph Lewisohn, who donated the Lewisohn Stadium in New York, and his brother Sam, the famed collector of modern art, became nationally prominent for their public support of music and the fine arts. There have been, of course, many other Jewish philanthropists, too numerous to mention, who have lent their support to almost every branch of culture in America.

However, the philanthropist par excellence, perhaps the most widely beloved America has ever produced, was Nathan Straus. He was one of the owners of the Macy Department Store empire. He himself, an immigrant boy from Germany, had been raised amidst struggle and poverty in Talbottom, Georgia. Significantly, it was not primarily how much he gave away for philanthrophy as the way he gave it that endeared him to people. Opposed to handing out largesse and "charity," he sold his benefices as a commodity to those who needed them. For example, during the panic-winter of 1893-4, when many were in dire need, Nathan Straus went into "a new line of business." He opened depots for selling food and coal to those who could afford to pay five cents a package. He also opened lodging houses where, for five cents, he provided clean beds and warm breakfasts to many thousands. Again during the winter of 1914, when unemployment and hunger caused great distress to thousands, he opened milk stations. For just one cent he furnished milk and sandwiches. Nathan Straus had an equally passionate interest in fighting disease and keeping people healthy. Hadassah's "Nathan Straus Health Center" in Jerusalem probably is the finest example of this warm-hearted concern.

PUBLIC LIFE

The end of the Civil War marked the emergence of the German element as the dominant group in the American Jewish community. However, immigration from Germany declined sharply after 1871 when the Jews there were granted civil and political equality. Nevertheless, Jews from Germany maintained, and to a large extent still do, their position of leadership among American Jews who in 1880 totaled about 230,000. Although most of them had a humble start in the

New World, their practical intelligence and hard work eventually won them a secure place in the economic life of the country.

With the acquisition of means, immigrant parents, who for the most part had only a rudimentary education themselves, were eager to send their children to college. Many immigrant boys entered the professions. Equipped thus for a larger participation in the life of the country many lawyers, for instance, embarked on political and diplomatic careers. A number achieved eminence as Cabinet members, governors, federal, state and municipal legislators, mayors, judges, diplomats, and as heads of Federal bureaus and agencies.

Oscar S. Straus (1850-1926) was the most respected Jewish personality of his time in American public life. Four presidents of the United States—Cleveland, McKinley, Roosevelt and Taft — appointed him to high office: as ambassador to Turkey in 1887 and later as a member of Theodore Roosevelt's Cabinet.

Benjamin N. Cardozo, appointed in 1932 by President Herbert Hoover as an Associate Justice of the U. S. Supreme Court.

Felix Frankfurter was appointed Associate Justice of the Supreme Court by President Franklin D. Roosevelt in 1939. Before that he had been prominent as a professor at the Harvard Law School. He has been widely considered one of the principal architects of Franklin D. Roosevelt's "New Deal" policies.

The Marshall Studio

INFLUX FROM EASTERN EUROPE

The stated policy of the Tsarist government in 1881 was to "solve" the Jewish problem in Russia by starving a third of its Jews to death, forcing another third to emigrate and absorbing the remainder by conversion to the Orthodox Church. An epidemic of pogroms was encouraged by the authorities. The passage of the infamous "May Laws," to further hamper Jews from making a living, marked a turning point in the modern history of the Jewish people. Gripped not only by a fear for their lives but also by a sober appraisal of the realities, tens of thousands, if they possessed only the barest means for the journey, fled the country. As the years went by, the stream of emigration turned into a flood. Not since the expulsion of the Jews from Spain in 1492 had there been such a mass exodus. Between eighty to eighty-five per cent of those who left Russia, Lithuania and Poland crossed the Atlantic to the United States.

Although accurate figures are not available until the year 1899, it is conservatively estimated that during the period 1881-1914 almost two million Jewish immigrants had found

STATESMEN

Pach Bros.   *Blackstone Studios*

From left to right: Herbert H. Lehman; Bernard Baruch; Joseph Pulitzer; Adolph S. Ochs. Herbert H. Lehman, as Democratic Governor of New York for four terms beginning in 1928, drew wide attention with his liberal policies and reforms. A supporter of the New Deal program of the Roosevelt Administration, he served as Director of UNRRA during World War II. Later he was elected a United States Senator from New York. He has always been prominent in Jewish philanthropic and social affairs. Bernard Baruch is known as the foremost unofficial presidential adviser in United States history. His counsel was sought on major political and economic problems by presidents from Woodrow Wilson to Dwight D. Eisenhower. He laid down the blue-

PUBLISHERS

New York Times Studio

print for economic controls during World War I when he served as Chairman of the War Industries Board. He has also been considered the author of the Truman Administration's policy on the control of atomic energy. Joseph Pulitzer is shown here in a portrait by John Singer Sargent. Founder of the *New York World* and the *St. Louis Post-Dispatch*, he was a major figure in American journalism and was largely responsible for its higher standards during the first decades of the 20th century. He endowed the Pulitzer School of Journalism. Adolph S. Ochs was the publisher of the *New York Times* from 1896 to 1935. During the years he directed the daily, it became the outstanding newspaper of the country.

An immigrant Jew about to be inspected by the authorities at Ellis Island in New York Harbor before being allowed entry into the United States. (*Photograph by Lewis W. Hine, 1905*) The processing of the new arrivals at the port of New York took place at first in Castle Garden, later converted into the Aquarium. But in 1890, Ellis Island became the Immigration Station where until 1914 almost 1,000,000 immigrants from everywhere in the world passed through every year. However, although the overwhelming majority of Jewish immigrants disembarked in New York, a sizable number entered by way of Philadelphia (60,000 during 1882-1904), Boston, Baltimore and Galveston.

a haven in the United States. During the later Russian pogrom years of 1903-06 the annual influx greatly exceeded that of previous years: in 1903—77,544; 1904—92,388; 1905—125,-234; 1907—114,932. However, not all these immigrants came from Russia (including Russian Poland and Lithuania). From 1899 to 1914, some 300,000 Jewish immigrants came from Austria-Hungary, most of them from Galicia, with about 75,000 from Hungary. During the same span of years 62,813 arrived from Romania. Hunger and persecution, or both, had brought them from those countries to begin new lives in the United States.

Jewish immigrants in Bremen in 1906, waiting to board the North German-Lloyd liner S. S. *Cassel* which was to take them to Galveston, Texas. Jewish community leaders and immigrant aid organizations, alarmed because the overwhelming number of immigrants chose to settle on New York's East Side, made deliberate efforts to siphon off as many as possible of the arriving immigrants into other cities in the United States. This maneuver was only partially successful. Jewish immigrants did, however, land at ports other than New York and were thus diverted to other communities, especially to Philadelphia, Boston, Chicago, St. Louis and San Francisco.

East Side

Three-quarters of all East European Jews who arrived during the flood-tide of Jewish immigration lived for a while on the lower East Side in New York. Here they found a ready-made ghetto to crowd into. By the time of the Civil War the locality, a fashionable neighborhood earlier in the century, had in its decline become unofficially the "ghetto" of the metropolis. Its poor Jewish residents then were principally immigrant families of German and Hungarian extrac-

tion. However, there were other though lesser "islands" of Jewish life in the city: in Brownsville and Williamsburgh in Brooklyn, and in Yorkville and lower Harlem in Manhattan.

When the new arrivals started moving into the East Side that locality had already become a decaying slum. Its tenements were distinguished then, as they still are today, by a bewildering number of "railroad" and "dumbbell" flats and by narrow sunless air-shafts. The overcrowding, the uncleanliness and malnutrition, typical of all city slums, bred much illness and disease, especially tuberculosis and rheumatic heart ailments.

But apart from all other considerations, it was cheaper to live on the East Side. Rents and other living costs were lower there. The majority of the Jewish immigrants came almost penniless to the United States. The statisticians of the U. S. Immigration Department computed that the average Jew brought with him into the country a capital of about eight dollars. This sum was about half the initial wealth of the average poor Gentile immigrant. Were it not that mutual aid, an ancient and honored practice among Jews, was observed to an unusual extent among the immigrants themselves, many would have suffered even greater hardships than they did. It was characteristic of these Jews that not until they had exhausted all other resources did they think of applying for aid to the Jewish charity and immigrant aid societies. Actually, to the astonishment of philanthropic agencies and social workers, only a small number of Jewish immigrants asked for any but the most temporary assistance to tide them over until they could find work. Parasitic poverty was relatively infrequent among Jews at all times.

A phenomenon of Jewish life, one still flourishing today, was the extraordinary number of fraternal lodges, of mutual aid, benevolent, sick-and-benefit, burial and free loan societies that were formed by the immigrants themselves. Organized charity played but a secondary role in ministering to the sick and the needy of the East Side in those days. The mutual aid society not only helped preserve the pride and dignity of its individual members when they fell into difficulties, but it also gave them a comforting feeling of "belonging" to a respected group. Besides these organizations there were hundreds of big and little *chevras*, Orthodox congregations, that mushroomed up on every block in their own little buildings and even in cellars, stores and small factory lofts. The pious banded together not only for devotions, Talmudic study, and to preserve the continuity of their inner lives, but also to provide burial facilities and to render other forms of assistance to their sick and needy.

But this was not all. It was also customary for most immigrants to join together in an organization with their *landsleit*, their fellow-townsmen from the old country. This was in order to preserve the cherished old ties in the New World, to be convivial together and to render assistance to those requiring it. By 1900 these organizations, known as *landsmanschaften* (societies of fellow-townspeople), exceeded 1,000 in New York; by 1935 there were 3,000 or more.

Undoubtedly, there were still other reasons why so many tens of thousands of Jews kept pouring into the pestilential slums that were the East Side, Brownsville, East Harlem and elsewhere. Living there among their own people somehow assuaged the immigrant Jews' chronic feeling of anxiety, for in Tsarist Russia their lives had been molded in physical and emotional insecurity. To the timid there is an imaginary

Marketing for the Sabbath on Hester Street on a Friday morning in 1898.

A night class in English in the middle 1930's at the Educational Alliance, the famous settlement house on East Broadway which for decades played an important role in the Americanization of East Side immigrants. Thousands of adult "greenhorns" attended night school on the East Side to learn English and to become American citizens as soon as possible. In many a crowded tenement home tired sweatshop workers and pushcart peddlers pored over lesson books, struggling desperately to keep awake in order to learn the language of their adopted country.

strength in numbers. On the East Side the immigrants found a plenitude of near and distant relatives, old friends, and *landsleit*. These people with comfortably familiar faces spoke their own language, recited the same prayers in the same synagogues, practiced the same customs, enjoyed the same foods and clung to the same traditional values. Like water, human beings, too, have a drive to seek their own level.

Jewish children of the Hamilton Fish Park area standing outside P. S. 22, Stanton Street, New York City, 1898.

Bread and Adjustment

Barely had the immigrant landed when he was faced with the urgent need of engaging in some work or business which would immediately earn bread for himself and his family. While there were many thousands of skilled workers and artisans among the Russian and Polish Jews, the majority had been petty tradesmen in the old country. In the New World,

A recent photograph of Yonah Shimmel's Knishery on the lower East side. In 1910, Yonah Shimmel, an unsuccessful *melamed*, teacher of Hebrew, had experimentally Americanized the East European *kasha* and potato *knishe*, or dumpling. He not only earned the title "King of the Knishes," but unexpectedly launched a nationwide industry in this inexpensive "delicacy."

without capital or knowledge of a remunerative trade, they were forced into all kinds of makeshift occupations. Since buying and selling had been part of their accustomed activity in the old country, they turned to peddling as a matter of course. Basket or pushcart peddling, especially in food, dry goods and notions, became the most common occupation of the new arrivals. The East Side, and other parts of the city

Open-air second-hand clothes market on the East Side. Although this photograph was taken in 1935, this activity differed in no essential way from the earlier days. Note the baked potato man's wagon to the right, a familiar institution on the lower East Side for many decades. It is the East Side poor man's equivalent of London Whitechapel's "fish-'n-chips."

as well, were literally flooded with them. Loaded down with every conceivable type of cheap merchandise, they formed an invading army of venders struggling with baskets on their arms or trundling pushcarts hopefully before them into every street and alleyway. Peddling had one positive virtue: although the profits were small, the capital investment was slight and the turnover quick. By imposing on themselves hardships and self-denial many of the peddlers managed to put aside coin by coin until they had saved the barest minimum with which to advance themselves to the more dignified and stable position of storekeeper. The ubiquitous "candystore" virtually became a Jewish monopoly and has continued so to this day.

Pawnbroker's shop in Nashville, Tennessee. (*Photograph by Lewis W. Hine*) It is hard to break the pattern of centuries. The medieval old-clo' man, the money-lender and the peddler persisted in the modern New World. But here they became Americanized. Almost every town and city in the United States had its quota of Jewish street and customer peddlers, old-clo' men, junk dealers and pawnshop "uncles."

But there were still other occupations and businesses that could be improvised with some knowledge, a little skill and even less capital. There was, for instance, a small army of Jewish religious and quasi-communal functionaries: rabbis, cantors, sextons, Hebrew teachers, charity-collectors, ritual slaughterers, *Torah* scribes, religious goods and book dealers, marriage-brokers, supervisors of *kashruth* and marriage-performing "reverends." These occupations at best were tenuous. They afforded only an uneasy kind of hand-to-mouth existence.

Old man selling Yiddish newspapers. (*Photograph by Lewis W. Hine*) Life was hard for the immigrants on the East Side. To add to the meager family income, Grandpa, too, had to do his bit. Newspaper vending was one of the less strenuous means of earning a few pennies. Moreover, by tradition, the old type of Jew who had been a provider all his life resented being turned into a helpless dependent in his old age.

Sweatshops

The most fortunate among the Russian immigrants were those who had come to the United States fortified by some trade or skill, such as carpentry, shoemaking, baking, masonry and the like. These readily found work and became tolerably well adjusted. Many thousands had been garment workers in the old country. In New York, with some adaptation to the new American methods of work and production, they, too,

New York clothing "sweatshop." (*Photograph by Lewis W. Hine, 1910*)

were able to find employment. Oddly enough, the American clothing industry, which was based on factory-made, ready-to-wear clothes at moderate prices, had been initiated in the 1870's by Hungarian and German Jews. They were delighted with the oncoming horde of "greeners" from Russia, Galicia and Romania, who were a plentiful and cheap, skilled but non-unionized labor reservoir. Many who were not skilled in garment work were eager to learn. Strangers in the country, unable to speak English and afraid to assert themselves at first, they proved easy prey for the unscrupulous element among the clothing employers. Soon thousands of unsanitary, dark firetraps became their workshops. There the immigrants toiled six days of the week as much as twelve to eighteen hours each day at near-starvation wages.

These dens were realistically called "sweatshops." Their mere existence aroused widespread protests and indignation, which eventually led to legislation curbing them in New York, Boston, Philadelphia and Rochester, the chief centers of the needle trades. The new labor laws, however, helped but little, because they were too loosely drawn and were not strictly enforced.

Immigrant family engaged in home work on suspenders. (*Photograph by Lewis W. Hine*)

What made these sweatshops possible was the peculiar organization of the clothing industry. Factory owners found it easier and cheaper to farm out much of their work to contractors. These in turn often distributed it to sub-contractors. The latter assumed, sometimes reluctantly, the unenviable preying role of "sweaters" in their anxiety to make even a minimum profit from their workers. Especially brutal was the effect of the sweatshop on young girls and children, for child labor was still legal. An appalling incidence of tuberculosis, malnutrition and other occupational diseases resulted from the intolerable working conditions and the low wages in the sweatshops.

A statistical study in 1900 in New York revealed that in the men's clothing line the average weekly wage for men during the work season was $12.26; for women, $6.34; for children, $2.94. The wages in the women's apparel trade were about the same. And since the slack season was practically as long as the work season, the plight of the clothing workers was indeed desperate. "Homework" became a pressing necessity to keep the family alive. The 1900 Census showed that 53% of all male East European workers and 77% of all female East European Jewish workers were engaged in the needle trades. In New York State alone there were 4,000 clothing manufacturing establishments, most of them in New York City. Except for the large factories, they were nearly all sweatshops.

Orthodox Jewish worker at his steam press in one of the better clothing factories in New York. (*Photograph by Lewis W. Hine*) Side by side with the great number of "sweatshops" were a small number of large bona-fide clothing factories in which better working conditions, shorter hours and higher wages prevailed. These, such as Hart, Schaffner and Marx Company, were the first in the industry to be unionized.

Unions

In 1881, the very year that the Jewish mass immigration from Russia began, the first national labor movement in America was launched. Led by Samuel Gompers, a Jewish immigrant cigar-maker from London, a federation of existing trade unions was formed. It resulted, during the following year, in the founding of the American Federation of Labor. Gompers,

Samuel Gompers, toward the end of his life.

who headed it for four decades, was a conservative. He not only opposed compulsory collective bargaining but was the chief and triumphant advocate of the "craft" versus the "industrial" principle which the radicals in the Federation

Bodies of several of the victims of the Triangle fire. While the needle-trade unions steadfastly fought the evils of the sweatshop system by means of strikes, protests and public education, they found an unexpected ally in tragedy. On March 25, 1911, a blaze broke out in the loft of the Triangle Waist Company in New York. Trapped on the seventh floor in the ramshackle building, some young girls leaped to their death. This disaster focused general public attention on the sweatshop system. It resulted in more effective state laws for insuring better working conditions.

supported. The consensus is that he was the most powerful and influential figure in the history of the American labor movement.

It was inevitable that sooner or later the successful example set by American workers in other industries in winning better working conditions, higher wages and shorter hours through their trade unions would be followed by the organization of labor unions among the Jewish workers in the needle trades.

Mass meeting in Union Square, New York, during the "general" strike of 1910. Of historic significance in the annals of the clothing industry was the bitter two-month strike which began on July 7, 1910. It was not a general strike in the usual sense but was rather a strike of *all* trades in the industry. Sixty thousand members of the International Ladies' Garment Workers' Union took part in it. The so-called "Protocol of Peace" negotiated between employers and union by the impartial chairman, Louis D. Brandeis, laid the basis for a significant new approach to labor conflicts. It set up, for the first time in American labor history, machinery for negotiation, for presenting grievances and for arbitrating disputes.

As soon as the "greeners" became a little Americanized and found out what was going on around them, they organized little independent unions in the various trades in New York, Philadelphia and Chicago. This was especially true in the men's clothing industry.

The Jewish immigrant workers took part in several strikes, in the early nineties, led by the United Garment Workers of America. They were also involved in the famous labor battles of 1910 in Chicago and of 1913 in New York. The latter strike resulted in the consolidation of the Union's strength and in the organization of the Amalgamated Clothing Workers of America. It was formed by rebellious locals who had seceded from the United Garment Workers of America under the leadership of Sidney Hillman and Joseph Schlossberg.

Left. David Dubinsky, President of the International Ladies' Garment Workers' Union, A. F. of L. *Right.* Sidney Hillman, late President of the Amalgamated Clothing Workers of America, C.I.O.

Another great union in the needle trades, numerically even larger than the Amalgamated Clothing Workers' Union, was the International Ladies' Garment Workers' Union. It was founded in 1900 as a result of the merger of seven small unions with a total membership of only 2,000 cloakmakers and pressers in New York, Newark, Philadelphia and Balti-

One of several cooperative housing developments erected by the Amalgamated Clothing Workers Union to provide low-cost apartments for its members. Perhaps more than any other of the American unions, the International Ladies' Garment Workers' Union and the Amalgamated Clothing Workers of America divert a substantial part of their activities and funds for education, culture, recreation, medical aid and health. The ILGWU founded a Health Center for its members in 1913, operates Unity House at Forest Park, Pennsylvania, as a resort, and carries on a great many cultural and social projects. The Amalgamated, which runs its extra-trade union activities along similar lines, established the Amalgamated Bank in New York and the Amalgamated Trust and Savings Bank in Chicago. Like its sister union, it has contributed large sums of money for relief and other public causes.

more. This organization came into being during the darkest period of the clothing industry when sweatshops and home-shops were creating an evil reputation for the trade. It was against these evils that the newly organized Jewish workers took the field.

FARMERS

In the United States, where Jews were free to turn their hands to the plow if they wished, there was evidence among some of the immigrants of a romantic yet often practical urge to return to the soil. The first attempt of this kind on record took place in 1837. About a dozen German immigrant families, who had grown unhappy in their New York confinement, banded together and bought 500 acres of land in the foothills of the Catskills at Wawarsing in Ulster County. The name they gave their colony epitomized their expectation: they called it *Sholem*, meaning "peace." With strong cultural interests, these "farmers" were more preoccupied with establishing a library and holding concerts and literary discussions than with clearing the brush. The colony ceased to exist in 1847.

With Russian immigrants pouring by the thousands into the United States in 1881, a colonization movement started almost immediately, and within two or three years, some sixteen farming colonies were under way. But almost all of them failed, not always because of any real fault of the settlers. For example, the settlement on Sicily Island, Louisiana (1881), was completely washed out by a Mississippi River flood the following spring. Another colony, founded in 1882 in Arkansas, was abandoned several months later because of the intense heat, the torrential rains and the widespread incidence of malaria and yellow fever. Similarly with pioneer colonies in the Dakotas, Kansas, Oregon and Colorado. There, on the desolate frontier, the homesteaders met with discouragement and hardship at every hand. They suffered from drought and hail, from the intense cold, mounting debt, incompetent leadership and inexperience as farmers. But perhaps worst of all they suffered from the intense loneliness pioneers have always

felt in isolated places. In some cases, for a while at least, the colonists hung on with grim determination. These were the idealists, the majority of whom were imbued with the Zionist ideal which encouraged Jews to return to the wholesome life on the land in preparation for their final settlement as farmers in the land of Israel. They belonged to the organized groups of *Am Olam* (The Eternal People) and *New Odessa*.

Baron Maurice de Hirsch (1831-96). This great Continental railroad builder, saddened by the economically rootless life of the ghetto Jews, especially of Russia, spent his entire fortune, more than $100,000,000, helping Jews to emigrate and in "establishing colonies in various parts of North and South America and other countries." Oscar Straus called him "The Napoleon of the Great Exodus" from Russia. Although never himself in the United States, his lavish benefactions made him an important builder of Jewish life in America.

In 1891 the situation took a more encouraging turn. With the aid of the Baron de Hirsch Fund, successful farming-industrial communities were founded at Woodbine and Vineland, N. J., and in Colchester, Conn. The Baron de Hirsch Agricultural School was opened at Woodbine, N. J., for the scientific training of young farmers. The Jewish Agricultural Society helped hundreds of farmers take firm root in the soil, with technical advice, farm loans and continuous guidance by agricultural experts. Since then, scores of Jewish farming communities have sprung up in various parts of the country. A survey in 1940 revealed that from 1,000 Jews on farms in 1900 the number had swelled to over 100,000.

Modern Jewish dirt farmers baling hay.

YIDDISH CULTURE

The Jewish immigrants who came from the various countries and regions of eastern Europe transplanted into Jewish life in America certain facets characteristic of their former group life. *Litvak, Galitzianer, Poilisher, Romainer, Ukrainer* and *Bukowiner*—presented a remarkable mosaic of culture patterns. In the leveling-off process through the years, these groups fused culturally as well as biologically, and thus a new design emerged: a distinctive American Jewish culture.

Besides their common religious heritage to whose values and practices most of them held firmly, the immigrants brought with them certain cherished cultural and social interests. Those they continued to cultivate in America, though with striking modifications from the new environment.

For perhaps three decades, more Yiddish was spoken on the East Side of New York than in any other single locality in the world. By 1900 six large all-Yiddish daily newspapers and a host of weekly and monthly periodicals were flourishing in New York. To hundreds of thousands of readers these became, in a manner of speaking, popular universities. The Yiddish dailies and periodicals, fully responsive to the needs of their readers for self-education, because most of them had had no opportunity for it in the old country, carried popular informative articles on geography, American history and civics, literature, health, music, science and economic and social problems. Publications directed toward religious readers also provided elaborations on various aspects of religious life and Rabbinic culture.

Yehoash (Solomon Bloomgarden), eminent Yiddish poet and translator of the Bible into Yiddish.

A large Yiddish-speaking intelligentsia was created partly by this means and partly through the educational efforts of the *Poale Zion* and the Jewish labor movement which were anchored in the Yiddish language and culture and thus dedicated to their preservation. The groundwork for many a useful career in the arts, sciences, professions and public life was laid in this humble fashion. A fine Yiddish literature, woven of the life-experiences of the immigrants, was also being created. A few among the host of very gifted writers of Yiddish *belles-lettres* were the poets Morris Rosenfeld, Morris Wintchevsky, David Edelstadt, Abraham Reisen, Yehoash, Leivick, Mani Leib and M. L. Halperin. Some playwrights, novelists and short-story writers were Mordecai Spektor, Sholem Asch, David Pinski, Peretz Hirschbein, Moishe Nadir, Isaac Raboy, Ossip Dymov and Joseph Opatoshu. Among the most widely admired critics and commentators on Yiddish literature were Abraham Liessin, Dr. Abraham Coralnik, Moissaye Olgin, Dr. Chaim Zhitlovsky and S. Niger.

The Theatre

The professional Yiddish theatre was only in its infancy when the so-called "Russian phase" in American Jewry began in 1881. Abraham Goldfaden, the highly talented and self-taught Yiddish folk-poet and composer, had founded the first Yiddish theatre only a few years before in Romania. Sensing the unusual opportunities that had suddenly opened up in America with the mass immigration of Yiddish-speaking Jews, a number of enterprising young actors hurried to the New York scene.

Some of these actors and actresses literally became institutions. Each one developed an enthusiastic, worshipful following who went by the picturesque name of *patrioten* (patriots). Foremost among the theatrical idols was Jacob P. Adler, who scored a novel and sensational success in 1893 at the New York Academy of Music when he played the role of Shylock in Yiddish with a distinguished supporting cast of Gentile Shakespearean actors who performed in English. Popular, too, in an extraordinary way, was Sigmund Mogulesco, a comic actor who also was a composer and lyricist, business manager and stage director. He had unusual natural gifts for the stage and began his American career, strangely enough, in Offenbach's *opera comique, Bluebeard,* in 1882. His East Side audience, unaccustomed to such sophisticated fare, was left cold and disappointed. Several years later, when he began to talk the theatrical language the East Side understood and relished—entertainment with "dance, music and song" in the Jewish folk-idiom—he became a popular idol.

At the turn of the century there was an infusion of new blood into the Yiddish theatre. There was David Kessler, the remarkable actor-manager who started an art repertory theatre but owing to his uncompromisingly high standards failed to attract adequate popular support. Other well-known actors of the period were Boris Thomashefsky, Leon Blank and Morris

Jacob Gordin (1853-1909) came to the U. S. toward the end of the 19th century. With the 75 "literary" plays he wrote or adapted, he helped raise the level and taste of the Yiddish stage, the dramatic standards of which had not been very high. However, he died a frustrated and broken-hearted man because the Yiddish theatre resisted reformation.

Moscovitch. Moscovitch years later became one of the most distinguished Shakespearean actors in English on the London stage. Women stars were Kenny Liptzin, Bertha Kalich and Esther Rachel Kaminsky. A decade or two later saw the emergence of new and more Americanized acting talent in Ludwig Satz, Samuel Goldinburg, Jacob Ben-Ami, Muni Weisenfreund (Paul Muni), Jenny Goldstein, Molly Picon, Menasha Skulnik and Joseph Buloff. A courageous attempt to raise the theatrical standards of the Yiddish Theatre was made by Maurice Schwartz when he founded the Yiddish Art Theatre in the 1920's. It was a repertory theatre devoted to the production of "literary" plays of both Jewish and non-Jewish authorship. His ensemble struggled desperately on until 1950 when it was finally forced to disband because of lack of public support. Its passing, perhaps regretfully, marked the close of an era to those who cherished the serious Yiddish theatre.

When the quota system in the U. S. immigration laws was introduced in 1924, it virtually halted the inflow of Jews from East European countries and marked the decline of Jewish culture in Yiddish. Despite the sustained efforts of a number of Jewish cultural organizations and institutions to keep Yiddish flourishing as a living tongue, to the great majority of the American descendants of East European immigrant stock Yiddish has ceased being the mother tongue. This, in great part, explains why there has been such a rapid decline in the number of readers of Yiddish newspapers, periodicals and books. In step with this process of cultural change, the Yiddish theatre, too, has been rapidly disintegrating, so that today, a predominant part of the Yiddish stage has returned to the tastes and standards of the early theatre, brought up to date by influences from Broadway vaudeville and Hollywood musicals.

Boris Thomashefsky.

Jacob P. Adler.

Bertha Kalich.

Paul Muni.

ZIONISM IN AMERICA

The Zionist dream was already stirring in the United States as far back as 1824 when the dynamic "Major Noah" had promised: "We will return to Zion as we went forth, bringing back the faith we carried away with us." When mass immigration from Russia started, the new arrivals transplanted the *Hovevei Zion* (Lovers of Zion) movement to the soil of their adopted country. Joseph I. Bluestone established its first society in 1882 in New York. The Zion Society was founded in Chicago in 1895, and after Theodor Herzl had convoked

Louis Lipsky, a foremost leader of the Zionist Organization of America for almost four decades. He was a close associate of Dr. Chaim Weizmann and his political policies. Other important Zionist leaders have been Rabbis Stephen S. Wise, Max Heller, Judah L. Magnes, Max Raisin, Cyrus Sulzberger, Israel Goldstein and Irving Miller, Dr. Harry Friedenwald, Judge Julian W. Mack, Dr. Emanuel Neumann, Abraham Goldberg, Morris Rothenberg and others.

the First Zionist Congress in Basle, Switzerland, a state-wide organization, fancifully calling itself "Knights of Zion," was formed in Illinois. These and similar groups, in conjunction with the Federation of American Zionists which was established in 1898 under the leadership of Prof. Richard Gottheil, formed the solid base for the future Zionist Organization of America.

Rabbi Abba Hillel Silver, the most influential Zionist leader today. He led the opposition in the Zionist Organization against hinging Zionist policy on British political interest. In 1946 he obtained the active support of the United States Government for the establishment of the Jewish homeland. It was United States pressure, it is said, which helped induce England to drop the Mandate over Palestine.

Until World War I, Zionism in America did not assume the character of a mass-movement. The immigrants were either too busy trying to adjust themselves to American life or they had become immunized against Zionist ideas by the secularist internationalism which had motivated the labor and socialist movements in the old country.

But with the Balfour Declaration in 1917 calling for the establishment of a Jewish homeland in Palestine, a fire was kindled in the American Jewish consciousness. The dream was taking on the outlines of an achievable reality for many. When Justice Louis D. Brandeis was converted to Zionism and assumed leadership of the Zionist Organization of America, thousands of new members were brought into its fold. Yet the wealthy and influential Jews of German stock remained aloof and even hostile. In its well-known "Pittsburgh Platform" of 1885, repudiated by it several decades later, the Central Conference of American Rabbis (Reform) had taken a defiant stand against Zionism: "We consider ourselves no longer a nation but a religious community." However, opinions, too, follow their own laws of change. In August, 1929, the non-Zionists of the United States, represented by Louis Marshall, head of the American Jewish Committee, entered into an agreement with Dr. Chaim Weizmann, then President of the World Zionist Organization, to form together the Jewish Agency for Palestine in order to advance through it the economic and cultural upbuilding of the Jewish homeland.

Rabbi Meir Berlin, American President of the Orthodox *Mizrachi* World Organization, chatting with *Histadrut* leader, later Premier of Israel, David Ben-Gurion, at a Zionist conference.

It was but natural and inevitable that the Zionist movement should be fragmentized by a variety of organizations espousing differing religious, economic and political views. By 1930 there were nine national Zionist groups in the United States with a total membership of about 100,000 besides additional hundreds of thousands of sympathizers. After the State of

Israel was founded in 1948, this number of Zionists could have been multiplied many times over. The Zionist Organization of America and its affiliates—Hadassah, Young Judea, *Histadrut Ivrit,* Sons of Zion, *IZFA,* etc.—form the solid backbone of the Zionist movement in America. They consist largely of conservative middle-class people who uphold the free enterprise system for Palestine. Another important Zionist group comprises the pro-labor *Poale Zion and Zeire Zion* with their affiliated groups: Pioneer Women, *Habonim* (the national youth organization) and the Jewish National Workers Alliance. These are closely linked with Israel's laborite *Mapai* Party and the labor federation *Histadrut.* The religious Zionists are centered principally in the *Mizrachi* organization and its affiliates—Mizrachi Women of America and *Hapoel Hamizrachi* (religious workers group). Then there is the militant and dissident faction of Zionist Revisionists, or New Zionists, closely associated with the *Irgun* and the *Herut* Party in Israel. Finally, there is the leftist Zionist organization, *Hashomer Hatzair* and the ultra-Orthodox *Agudath Israel* with its affiliate *Poale Agudath Israel* (ultra-Orthodox labor group).

Nevertheless, in practical matters, for example, in fundraising, most Zionist organizations have submerged their differences and run a combined campaign. Formerly, this was accomplished mainly by the *Keren Hayesod* (Palestine Foundation Fund), the *Keren Kayemeth* (Jewish National Fund), United Palestine Appeal, and, later, United Israel Appeal. In recent years it has been the United Jewish Appeal which has raised the funds for most of the Zionist and relief organizations in the United States.

Religion and Education

There are three major religious groupings among American Jews: Orthodox, Conservative and Reform. Their differences in religious philosophy and in ritual were created by the special circumstances of modern life. But the degree and intensity of division is not as accentuated among them as it is, for instance, among some of the Christian denominations. This is probably due to the fact that the Jewish religion has been less burdened by dogma and theology than some other faiths. In consequence, the Jewish congregations of varying views have found little difficulty in working together on major issues affecting Jewish life, culture and interests. This is best typified by the Synagogue Council of America, an organization which brings together all Jewish religious groups.

Yet Orthodox, Conservative and Reform congregations lead their own separate existence and have their own organiza-

Professor Louis Ginzberg (at left), a foremost authority on Talmudic literature and Jewish folklore, who teaches at the Jewish Theological Seminary of America; Dr. Louis Finkelstein, Chancellor of the Jewish Theological Seminary of America since 1940, and a noted scholar of Rabbinic culture.

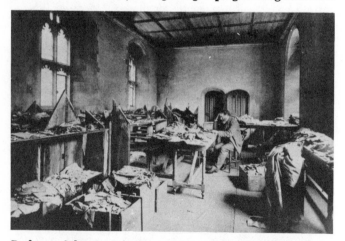

Professor Solomon Schechter (1850-1915), at first Reader in Rabbinics at Cambridge University in England and later President of the Jewish Theological Seminary of America. He is seen here in a Cambridge University attic amidst his invaluable collection of *genizah* fragments—discarded but piously preserved medieval Hebrew manuscript pages which he had accidentally discovered in the *genizah* (storeroom) of the ancient Cairo Synagogue in Egypt in 1897. Dr. Schechter's eminence as a scholar and teacher in Hebrew studies prompted the Jewish Theological Seminary in New York, which had been founded in 1887 by the Rev. Sabato Morais, to invite him in 1902 to become its President. Under his intellectual leadership the seminary not only trained rabbis and religious teachers but became the dynamic center of Conservative Judaism in the United States. Behind it organizationally is the United Synagogues of America, formed by Conservative Jews in 1913. Its principal aim: "To assert and establish loyalty to the *Torah* and its historical exposition."

The main building of Yeshiva University in New York City. Yeshiva had its beginnings in the Rabbi Isaac Elchanan Theological Seminary which had been established as a school for Orthodox rabbis in 1897 on the lower East Side in New York. Under Dr. Bernard Revel's 25-year presidency, which ended in 1940, the institution expanded to include a teachers' institute, the first Jewish college of arts and science (Yeshiva College), a graduate school and, finally, the Albert Einstein School of Medicine. The institution first received the status of a university in 1945 under Dr. Samuel Belkin's presidency. This university is the foremost educational institution of Orthodox Judaism in the United States.

Left. Dr. Samuel Belkin, President of Yeshiva University. Right. Dr. Mordecai Kaplan, founder and leader of the Jewish Reconstruction movement, which advances the concepts of Judaism as a civilization and Jewish "peoplehood" as an integrating identity.

tions. They maintain separate educational and cultural institutions, from kindergartens, Sunday schools and *Talmud Torahs* to Yeshivas, theological seminaries and other higher institutions of learning.

AMERICAN CULTURE

Rapid Americanization drove the Jewish immigrant out of his self-isolating ghetto and into the main stream of American life. Nor did he find his Jewish identity in any way incompatible with his obligations as an American. Opportunities for

"The Castle," one of the 18 major buildings on Brandeis University's 190-acre campus. The University (non-sectarian), named in honor of the late Justice Louis D. Brandeis, was founded at Waltham, Massachusetts, in 1948 with the object of merging the two cultural streams that the great jurist cherished: the liberal traditions of America and the enlightened values of the Jewish cultural heritage.

self-development and advancement were greater in the United States than elsewhere. Therefore, in the relatively short time span of perhaps two or three generations, a large number of Jews, of German as well of East European antecedents, became eminent in all fields of culture, in the professions and in public life. Of perhaps equal significance was the collective contribution of the so-to-speak anonymous Jewish foot soldiers in the army of American culture, the many thousands of ordinary teachers, engineers, artists, doctors, musicians, scientists, writers and chemists. With their colleagues of other ethnic stock, they helped collectively in the advance of material and cultural progress in America.

Chemists and Biologists

In the technological world of today the scientist has become the *beau idéal* of the age. Along with other American scientists of non-Jewish extraction, Jews have collaborated in all branches of science and quite a number have made impressive contributions in their particular fields.

The contributions of Jews in the fields of biology, chemistry and biochemistry have been noteworthy.

One of the greatest figures in modern biological science was Jacques Loeb of the Rockefeller Institute. In 1889 he advanced his famous theory of "tropisms," in which his main conclusion derived from many experiments was that all life is conditioned by physical and chemical processes. That same year he won world acclaim for his successful experiment in fertilizing the eggs of the sea urchin by treating them with salt and sugar, thus proving his tropism theory.

Two biochemists who did outstanding pioneer work in the new science of vitamins and nutrition were Casimir Funk, who originated the word *vitamin* in 1912, and Lafayette B. Mendel, famous nutritionist connected with Yale University.

Other biochemists, chemists and biologists of great distinction have been Jacob G. Lipman, a pioneer soil chemist and bacteriologist whose researches did much to advance scientific farming in the United States; Herman J. Muller, who was awarded the Nobel Prize in medicine in 1946 for his studies on artificial transmutation of genes through X-ray; Selman

The first graduate of Brandeis University, June, 1952, receiving her diploma from Trustee Chairman George Alpert. In the center is Dr. Abram L. Sachar, historian and President of the University, formerly both founder and director of the Hillel Foundation, a cultural institution aiming at instilling the Jewish student on the American college campus with a knowledge and respect for the Jewish cultural heritage.

Waxman, a Nobel laureate in 1952 for his discovery of streptomycin; Carl Neuberg, Carl L. Alsberg, Richard B. Goldschmidt, A. J. Goldforb, Gregory Pincus, Phil Rau, I. Newton Kugelmass and Victor Emanuel Levine. Still others have been Julius Oscar Stieglitz, Henry Arnstein, Morris Loeb, Albert E. Woolf, Moses Gomberg, Phoebus A. Levine and Casimir Fajans.

Physicists and Mathematicians

Albert A. Michelson, who during his lifetime earned the rare distinction of being hailed as "the foremost scientist of America," was awarded the Nobel Prize for Physics in 1907. Early in the 1880's he had invented the interferometer, an instrument with which he was able to make precise measurements of distance according to the length of light waves. The celebrated Michelson-Morley experiment, carried out in 1887 to determine whether the velocity of the earth through the ether would show any effects on the velocity of light, served as the starting point for Albert Einstein's later theory of relativity.

291

Dr. Albert Michelson.   Emil Berliner.

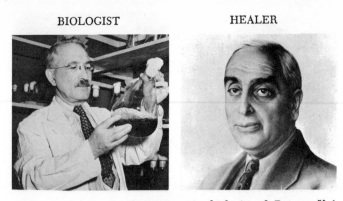

Left. Dr. Selman A. Waksman, microbiologist of Rutgers University, examining a bottle of streptomycin culture. This discovery, which proved an effective aid in checking many virus diseases, won him the Nobel award in 1952. During his youth in Russia, Dr. Waksman was a *Yeshiva* student; he still reads Yiddish and Hebrew books and periodicals. *Right.* Dr. Bela Schick, who in 1913 devised the Schick Test to identify diphtheria.

In the field of nuclear physics and in the making of the atomic bomb, quite a number of Jewish scientists figured very prominently. To mention only the leaders: Isidor I. Rabi, who was awarded the Nobel Prize for Physics in 1944 for his studies in the magnetic properties of molecules, atoms and atomic nuclei; Samuel A. Goudsmith, a foremost atomic scientist at Brookhaven National Laboratory; Edward Teller, atomic scientist at the University of Chicago; Paul Wigner, Hungarian-born specialist on atomic fission; Leo Szilard, another Hungarian-born physicist who, with Enrico Fermi, the noted physicist of Italy, developed the chain-reaction system which made the atomic bomb practicable. Other noted nuclear scientists are Victor F. Weisskopf of the Massachusetts Institute of Technology, Gregory Breit, P. H. Abelson, K. Cohen of Columbia University, Robert Oppenheimer of the Institute of Advanced Studies at Princeton University, Kurt Bloch, who was awarded the Nobel Prize for Physics in 1952, and Otto Stern, the Austrian-born scientist who became a Nobel laureate in 1943.

Augmented by eminent mathematicians, refugees from Nazi Germany and Austria, Jewish specialists in this field of science in America provide an impressive list: O. Zarisky and Richard von Mises (Harvard); Solomon Lefshetz (Princeton); N. Jacobson (Yale); Hans Lewy and A. Seidenberg (University of California); I. Kaplansky and A. A. Albert (University of Chicago); J. S. Cohen (University of Pennsylvania); Edward Kasner, Joseph R. Ritt and S. Eilenberg (Columbia University); Leo Zippin (Queens College); W. Prager and H. Federer (Brown University); Norbert Wiener and Withold Hurewicz (MIT); Fabian Franklin, Abraham Cohen, Aurel Wintner and Leonard M. Blumenthal (Princeton and Missouri); Jacob D. Tamarken (Brown University) and Wallie A. Hurwitz and M. Kac (Cornell University).

Noted throughout the world as an astronomer was Frank Schlessinger, for many years Director of the Yale University Observatory.

Inventors

American Jews have been active in the field of invention since Colonial times. The first on record is Jacob Isaacs (died 1798) who invented a process for transforming salt water into fresh water. Thomas Jefferson gave the matter some serious consideration. Louis Edward Levy, an early typographer and photo-engraver, invented the popular *Levytype* in 1875. With his brother Max, he later invented an etched glass screen for making half-tone engravings for reproduction. An electrical engineer-inventor of stature was Elias E. Riess. Among his two hundred inventions perhaps the most outstanding was the converter for alternating current which made possible the electrification of railroads. In 1923 he invented the device for adding sound to film, which he sold to Lee DeForest.

Emil Berliner, whose numerous important inventions have been ranked second only to Thomas A. Edison's, made the Bell Telephone possible by inventing, in 1877, a microphone which was used as a telephone receiver. It, too, was the forerunner of the modern radio microphone. In 1887 he invented the gramophone, or disc phonograph, which subsequently became the Victor Talking Machine. Captain (later Vice-Admiral) Hyman G. Rickover, U.S.N., designed and supervised the construction of the first atomic-powered submarine, *Nautilus,* early in 1953.

Great Healers

It was the unusual privilege of Jewish doctors to have been the first in their profession to be associated with the American continent. Accompanying Christopher Columbus on his first voyage of discovery were five *Marrano* Jews, among them Maistre Bernal, the official doctor of the expedition, and Marco, the surgeon. One of the first doctors to practice in the American colonies was "ye Jew doctor," Jacob Lumbrozo, who settled in Maryland in 1656. Not finding the practice of medicine lucrative enough, he traded with the Indians on the side.

Many Jews gained eminence as medical scientists and practitioners in the United States, beginning with the German phase of Jewish immigration in the 1840's. Abraham Jacobi, a fighting liberal and intimate of Carl Schurz who had fled Germany upon the collapse of the 1848 Revolution, became one of America's most eminent doctors after he had settled in New York in 1853. He invented the laryngoscope in 1854. In 1862 he established the first pediatrics clinic in the country. His scientific contributions on infant feeding were substantial.

Landmarks of no little significance in the history of medicine in the United States were the following inventions, innovations and discoveries: Carl Koller, in 1884, was the first doctor ever to have used cocaine as a local anaesthetic in his specialty, eye surgery; in 1887 W. Meyer introduced cystoscopy; Max Einhorn (1862-1922), the famous diagnostician, invented a number of instruments for the diagnosis of gastrointestinal disorders. Solomon Solis-Cohen fixed for the first time the syndrome of vasomotor ataxia. Dr. Simon Flexner of the Rockefeller Foundation made experimental studies of diphtheria toxin and in 1899 isolated the bacillus of "Flexner

Emma Lazarus.

Gertrude Stein.

Irwin Shaw.

Ludwig Lewisohn.

B. Dysentery." He was noted for his serum treatment of spinal meningitis. Leo Buerger described and gave his name to "Buerger's Disease" in 1908. The "scratch method" in the study of allergy was initiated by O. M. Schloss in 1912. A pathfinder in the relatively new field of public health was Milton Joseph Rosenau, Director of the School of Public Health at Harvard University. Distinguished as a medical educator was Milton Charles Winternitz, who was Dean of the Yale University Medical School (1920-35). Bernard Sachs headed the Neurological Institute at New York Medical Center for many years. Albert A. Berg was a celebrated surgeon. Leo Davidoff is a foremost neuro-surgeon today. The list of distinguished medical educators and practitioners could be many pages long.

Joseph Goldberger deserves notable mention for his genius, courage and selflessness. He entered the U. S. Public Health Service in 1899 and, using himself as a guinea pig, almost died of his experiments with malaria and typhus. Until the time of Goldberger it was universally assumed that the dread disease, pellagra, was contagious. In 1914 he made an intensive study of poor Southern whites and Negroes. He soon discovered that pellagra was a poor man's disease, the result of malnutrition, in the case of the Southern whites and Negroes, caused by a diet consisting principally of sugar, syrup, cornbread, coffee and sweet potatoes. More than anyone else in the world Goldberger laid the basis for the science of nutrition which calls for a balanced diet for the preservation of health.

Two Nobel Prize awards for their contributions to medical science went to Otto Loewi (1936) and to Joseph Erlanger (1944).

Literature

From the year 1805, when the first Jewish writer in the United States, the dramatic critic of Charleston, S. C., Isaac Harby, wrote the neo-classic drama *Alexander Severus,* there has been a continuous literary activity by Jews. They have written in every medium and in every style. They have belonged to every literary school and followed every fashion. It is impossible to do more than catalogue here the names of a number of the most gifted and the most popular: Edna Ferber, Dorothy Parker (also noted for her poetry), Ludwig Lewisohn, Waldo Frank, Gertrude Stein, Albert Halper, Meyer Levin, Maurice Samuel, Irving Fineman, Robert Nathan, Michael Blankfort, George Sklar, Manuel Komroff, Albert Maltz, Irwin Shaw, Norman Mailer, Herman Wouk, Irving Stone, Samuel Ornitz, Henry Roth, Budd Schulberg,

Howard Fast, Laura Z. Hobson, Ben Field, Leonard Ehrlich, Michael Gold, Stefan Heym, and Matthew Josephson.

Popular fiction writers with a vast book and magazine audience are: Ben Hecht, Jerome Weidman, Konrad Bercovici, Fannie Hurst, Octavius Roy Cohen, MacKinlay Kantor, Thyra Samter Winslow, S. J. Perelman, and Arthur Kober.

Among poets were Emma Lazarus, protegé of Ralph Waldo Emerson and friend of Walt Whitman; James Oppenheim, Louis Untermeyer, Joseph Auslander, Arthur Guiterman, Jean Starr Untermeyer, Muriel Rukeyser, Babette Deutsch, Karl Shapiro and Delmore Schwartz.

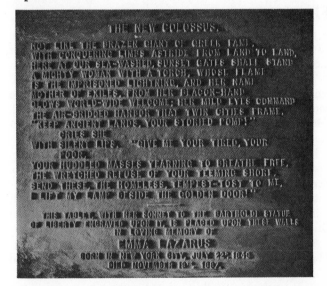

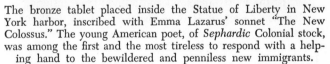

The bronze tablet placed inside the Statue of Liberty in New York harbor, inscribed with Emma Lazarus' sonnet "The New Colossus." The young American poet, of *Sephardic* Colonial stock, was among the first and the most tireless to respond with a helping hand to the bewildered and penniless new immigrants.

Scholarship

Although relatively few in number, Jewish thinkers and scholars have left their profound impression on higher learning in the United States. In philosophy, especially distinguished and original have been Morris Raphael Cohen and Harry Austryn Wolfson. Among other Jewish philosophers of note are Irwin Edman, Ernest Nagel and Paul Weiss.

In political science and economics two of the most distinguished names are those of Frank W. Taussig and Edwin R. A. Seligman. An illustrious figure in the field of psychology was Hugo Munsterberg who taught at Harvard for twenty years. Otto Klineberg has done important work in social

Left. Dr. Abraham Flexner, a leader in academic research and the first director of the Institute for Advanced Studies at Princeton with which Einstein has been associated. *Right.* Franz Boas.

Left. Max Weber, eminent American painter, a leader of the modern school for many years. *Right.* Ben Shahn at work. Both these artists have employed themes of specific Jewish content in many of their canvases.

psychology. Nelson Glueck has been prominent in Near Eastern archaeology. Arthur Schlesinger, Jr., Louis Hacker, Oscar Handlin, Salo Baron and J. Salwyn Schapiro have done valuable historical writing.

Franz Boas, the great American anthropologist who received his early training in his native Germany, became the founder of the modern social school of anthropology.

Boas trained a number of Jewish anthropologists of note, among them Robert Lowie, Alexander Goldenweiser, Paul Radin, Harry Shapiro, Edward Sapir and Melville Herskowits.

Fine Arts

Jews are recent arrivals in the world of the graphic arts, but their number is growing, and their achievements are not inconsiderable.

The following are only a small number of those Jewish painters, sculptors, etchers and engravers who have made contributions to American art. They have belonged to all schools: academic, impressionist, post-impressionist, modern-realist, expressionist, abstractionist and surrealist.

Painters: Jonas Lie, Ernest C. Peixotto, Maurice Sterne, Leon Kroll, Morris Kantor, Louis Kronberg, Joseph Hirsch, Ben Shahn, Ivan Olinsky, Jerome Meyers, Abraham Walkowitz, Albert Sterner, Robert Brackman, Max Weber, Walt Kuhn, Ben Koppman, Peter Blume, Jack Levine, William Gropper, Raphael Soyer, Moses Soyer and Bernard Karfiol.

Sculptors: Jo Davidson, William Zorach, Nat Werner, Ahron ben Shmuel, Saul Baizerman, Minna Harkavy and Chaim Gross.

Perhaps the most influential and authoritative historian of the Renaissance art of Italy in the world today is Bernard Berenson.

Music

The musical culture of America has, to an unusual degree, been created by foreign-born musicians. Not the least significant contribution has been made by Americans of Jewish descent. The influx during the last few decades of a small army of both greater and lesser Jewish musical luminaries from central European countries has helped make the United States the great music center of the world. These newcomers have included conductors, concert artists, composers, teachers, musicologists, orchestral and chamber instrumentalists. They have participated in the musical life of virtually every town, city and educational institution in the United States.

The poet Walt Whitman sang of Americans as "a nation of many nations." It was, therefore, only natural that different

streams of cultural influence, of musical styles, harmonic systems and folk-idioms should have been poured into the crucible of American music-making. There have been composers of Jewish extraction in every area of serious and popular music. A number have written on Jewish themes, employing Jewish idioms and traditional melodies in their own stylistic manner. Their attitude toward this borrowing from their people's cultural heritage was most strikingly expressed by Ernest Bloch, one of the most individual of contemporary composers: "I am a Jew. I aspire to write Jewish music, not for the sake of self-advertisement but because it is the only way in which I can produce music of ability and significance—if I can do such a thing at all!" Among American composers who have consciously tried to draw inspiration from traditional Jewish musical materials have been: Lazare Saminsky, Jacob Weinberg, Joseph Achron, Isidor Freed, David Diamond, Frederick Jacobi, Leonard Bernstein and George Gershwin.

Composers whose work has not been directly affected by traditional Jewish music are: Louis Gruenberg, Rubin Goldmark, and Leo Ornstein, the son of a famous Russian cantor.

Perhaps even more remarkable, and culturally more influential because it is part of grass-roots American life, has been the activity of Jewish composers in popular music. It is no exaggeration to say that in this field they have been a dominant factor in the United States for the past generation. They have not only written some of the most famous popular songs but they have also been responsible for a great many of the musical productions on Broadway and in Hollywood. In the very top rank among these composers are: Irving Berlin, George Gershwin, Richard Rodgers, Sigmund Romberg, Otto Harbach, Arthur Schwartz, Jerome Kern, Harold Rome and Irving Caesar.

The Jewish virtuoso, the instrumentalist par excellence, has been accorded ample recognition on the American concert stage. Many, European-born and trained, decided to make their permanent home in the United States, where they became naturalized citizens. Among the most eminent of these artists have been the following:

Pianists: Ossip Gabrilowitsch, Harold Bauer, Josef Lhevinne, Leopold Godowsky, Vladimir Horowitz, Alexander Brailowsky, Carl Friedberg, Artur Rubinstein, Sascha Gorodnitzki and William Kappell.

Violinists: Mischa Elman, Efrem Zimbalist, Jascha Heifetz, Michel Piastro, Max Rosen, Joseph Fuchs, Nathan Milstein, Isaac Stern and Yehudi Menuhin.

Cellists: Gregor Piatigorsky, Emanuel Feuermann and Raya Garbousova.

Albert Kahn.

Ernest Bloch.

George Gershwin.

Irving Berlin.

Albert Kahn was one of the most famous of all industrial architects and designed some of the world's biggest plants. Perhaps the best-known Jewish architect today is Ely Jacques Kahn. George Gershwin, genius of popular American music, also achieved high rank as a serious composer with such notable works as *Rhapsody*

Singers: Alma Gluck, Sophie Breslau, Hulda Lashanska, Jenny Tourel, Rosa Raisa, Alexander Kipnis, Jan Peerce, Richard Tucker and Robert Merrill.

The Theatre Arts

Like their fellow-Jews in other countries, American Jews have displayed a striking affinity for the stage and its associated fields—the movies, radio and television. Jewish singers, actors, playwrights, composers, stage directors, designers, producers and managers have found a ready outlet for their talents. Their achievements in all forms of theatrical entertainment have left an indelible mark on this branch of popular American culture.

The history of the American theatre could not possibly be written without recording the primary importance of Jewish producers and their productions of literary plays, popular comedies, musicals and almost all other types of entertainment.

This is not the place to mention all of them, but several do bear almost legendary names in the American theatre: Abraham Erlanger and Marc Klaw, for several decades beginning in 1888, managed theatrical companies, produced a

in Blue, Piano Concerto in F, An American in Paris and the notable folk-opera *Porgy and Bess.* Irving Berlin, the most famous composer of popular American songs, gave American ragtime and jazz their significant direction during the decade before World War I. His *Alexander's Ragtime Band* was a landmark in this development.

great number of famous plays and finally organized a syndicate that controlled most of the important legitimate theatres of the country. Perhaps most active and effective of all American theatrical producers were the three brothers, Gustave, Charles and Daniel Frohman. They mounted 400 plays in the United States and 125 in London through the 1890's and until World War I.

Lee, Sam S. and J. J. Shubert managed and owned a great number of theatres in the United States, especially in New York. They also produced many successful plays and musical comedies. David Belasco was probably the most important figure of his time in the American theatre. Other noted producers have been Morris Gest, Sam H. Harris, Edgar Selwyn, Jed Harris, Herman Shumlin, Max Gordon, Oscar Serlin, Arthur Hammerstein, Schwab and Mandel, Charles Friedman, Richard Rodgers and Oscar Hammerstein II, Alfred Bloomingdale, Kermit Bloomgarden and Walter Fried.

Among the major influences in the American theatre have been the Theatre Guild and the now defunct Group Theatre. In both these repertory institutions, Jews figured prominently. Theresa Helburn and Lawrence Langner have been the leading directors of the Theatre Guild and Lee Simonson and Aline Bernstein have been among its best designers. Abe

Serge Koussevitzky.

Benny Goodman.

Oscar Hammerstein.

David Belasco.

Serge Koussevitzky was the noted conductor of the Boston Symphony Orchestra. Orchestral conductors of Jewish origin have been prominent in the United States for several generations. Several of the best known have been Leopold Damrosch of the New York Symphony Society which he organized; Alfred Hertz and Pierre Monteux of the San Francisco Symphony Orchestra; Artur Bodanzky of the Metropolitan Opera and the Friends of Music; Vladimir Golschmann of the St. Louis Symphony; Bruno Walter of the New York Philharmonic; Fritz Reiner of the Cleveland Symphony Orchestra and Ossip Gabrilowitsch of the Detroit Symphony Orchestra. Benny Goodman, a serious and gifted musician who

turned to jazz, became a sensational success during the late 1930's. The "swing" band he led and his virtuoso playing on the clarinet made his name a household word in America. Oscar Hammerstein, the most enterprising and influential promoter of grand opera in America, carried on a spirited rivalry with the conservative Metropolitan Opera House. In 1906 he opened in New York his Manhattan Opera House on whose stage he produced contemporary works in the most brilliant manner. He caused such devastation to the reputation, as well as to the box-office receipts of his powerful competitor that in 1910 the Metropolitan Opera Company paid him $2,000,000 to get out of business.

Mischa Elman.

Jascha Heifetz.

Yehudi Menuhin.

Artur Rubinstein.

Feder has done outstanding work in stage lighting. Prominent among the directors of the Group Theatre were Harold Clurman and Lee Strassberg, with Mordecai Gorelick as the principal designer of its decor and stage sets.

While the plays of the early Jewish dramatists who wrote for the American theatre at the turn of the twentieth century were not distinguished for their profundity, they did enjoy great popularity. Among the leading playwrights of that period were David Belasco, Charles Klein, Max Marcin, Samuel Shipman and Montague Glass.

Among the better contemporary playwrights are: S. N. Behrman, George S. Kaufman, Lillian Hellman, Arthur Miller, Moss Hart, Elmer Rice, Clifford Odets, Rose Franken, John Howard Lawson, Garson Kanin, John Wexley, Samson Raphaelson, Leopold Atlas, Sidney Kingsley, Samuel and Bella Spewack, Rita Weiman, Irwin Shaw and Arthur Laurents.

Among the foremost writers for radio have been Norman Corwin, Morton Wishengrad and Arch Oboler.

Actors

Actors and movie stars rarely identify themselves by their ethnic stock or religion. However, living like fish in glass bowls, very little about them is left in the dark for long. There have been American actors of Jewish extraction since early in the nineteenth century. But it was not until 1890 that one of them achieved great distinction. This was David Warfield, who became a leading figure on the American stage

with his performances in *The Auctioneer* (1900), *The Music Master* (1903) and *The Return of Peter Grimm* (1911). Alla Nazimova, originally a Russian actress, starred on Broadway for many seasons in Ibsen plays, beginning in 1905. Lina Abarbanell was one of the famed actresses and singers in musical comedy of her generation. Bertha Kalich, although originally on the Yiddish stage in New York, soon became a distinguished actress in English. Florence Reed was a well-known performer on the legitimate stage and in the movies after World War I; her most admired role was in *Shanghai Gesture*. Other talented actors are: Joseph Schildkraut, Stella, Celia, Julia and Luther Adler—all four children of the famous Yiddish tragedian, Jacob P. Adler, Edward G. Robinson, Joan Blondell, Kitty Carlisle, Edward Arnold, Sam Levene, John Garfield, Sanford Meisner, Francine Larrimore, Edward Bromberg, Lee J. Cobb, Morris Carnovsky, Sylvia Sidney, Judy Holliday and Melvyn Douglas.

Hollywood Producers

Since the early days, Jews have continued to play major roles in the business, management and executive producing ends of the movie industry. Among the pioneer producers of films were an impressive number of Jews: Sigmund Lubin, Carl Laemmle, the four Warner brothers, William Fox, Marcus Loew, Adolph Zukor, Jack and Harry Cohn, Louis B. Mayer, Jesse Lasky, Samuel Goldwyn, Louis J. Selznick, Nicholas and Joseph M. Schenck and others.

PLAYWRIGHTS

ACTOR

Lillian Hellman.

Arthur Miller.

S. N. Behrman.

David Warfield.

Marcus Loew.

Louis B. Mayer.

Harry Houdini became famous in 1900 as "The World's Greatest Magician." His specialty was sensational "escapes." Here, on top of a moving train, he is freeing himself from a police strait-jacket (1910).

Brigadier - General David Sarnoff, board chairman of Radio Corporation of America (RCA). A pioneer in the field of wireless, he was a leader in the development of radio and television. Another leader in these fields is William S. Paley, president of the Columbia Broadcasting System (CBS).

Sports

Not since Hellenistic times, when they excelled in classic Greek sports—in chariot-racing, marathon running, discus-throwing and even as gladiators in the arena—have Jews taken such an interest and active part in athletics and sports as in the United States today. Their integration into American life had led them gradually to share the enthusiasm of other Americans for every kind of sport and skill—baseball, football, tennis, golf, boxing, fencing, wrestling, swimming, bowling, handball, track meets, hockey, basketball, etc. Out of the activities of American Jews in all sports, able amateur and professional athletes and players were bound to emerge.

Entertainers

Vaudeville and musical comedy, with their inevitable translation from the stage into the media of the movies, radio and television, have attracted a great number of gifted Jewish popular singers and comedians. Perhaps the earliest to win fame in vaudeville was the comic team of Joe Weber and Lew Fields, starting in 1877. Al Jolson, who began as an end-man in Dockstader's Minstrel Show, rose quickly to be the most admired popular singer of his day.

A singer-comedian, who came later but earned perhaps as great popularity, is Eddie Cantor. Other vaudevillians who have virtually become household intimates by their performances on radio and television are George Jessel, Ed Wynn, Lou Holtz, Milton Berle, Sid Silvers, Fannie Brice, Phil Baker, George Burns, Danny Kaye, the Marx Brothers, Sid Caesar and Sam Levenson.

Among popular women singers are: Sophie Tucker, Belle Baker, Vivienne Segal and Dinah Shore.

BASEBALL	BASKETBALL

Henry "Hank" Greenberg.

Nat Holman.

Benny Leonard, retired and undefeated lightweight champion of the world (1917-24), fought 210 bouts of which he lost only two. He was considered by many experts as the most skillful and scientific boxer in modern pugilism. There were other famous Jewish fighters. Joe Choynski, a famous heavyweight (1884-1904), defeated Jack Johnson and fought Jim Jeffries to a draw in 20 rounds. Abe Attell was world featherweight champion (1908-12). Al McCoy (Albert Rudolph) was world welterweight champion (1914-17). "Battling" Levinsky was world light-heavyweight champion (1916-20). Barney Ross held three world titles in 1934: lightweight, junior welterweight and welterweight. Maxie Rosenbloom held the world light-heavyweight title (1930-34). Al Singer was lightweight champion (1930). Max Baer ruled briefly as heavyweight king (1934). Three popular lightweight fighters who enjoyed great popularity although they never won the prize titles were: Leach Cross (about 1910), Sid Terris and Lou Tendler.

Eddie Cantor.

Al Jolson.

WAR AND PEACE

More than 250,000 Jews, the equivalent of eight regular divisions, saw service in the United States armed forces during World War I. Of this number, 10,000 were commissioned officers. About 40% of the famous 77th Division of New York were Jews. Killed in action were 3,500; 12,000 were wounded and crippled. Decorations, honors, citations: six Congressional Medals and two hundred Distinguished Service Crosses, the usual quota symbolic of bravery that was characteristic of all Americans fighting in the war.

Louis Marshall (1856-1929), eminent constitutional lawyer and American Jewish community leader. As founder and chairman of the American Jewish Committee, he took a prominent part in the work of the Jewish delegation to the Versailles Peace Conference in 1919, and led in Jewish defense work against anti-Semitism.

The end of the blood-letting in 1918 witnessed an unusual stirring of a feeling of group solidarity among Jews of the whole world. This was expressed in a practical and organizational way by the Jews in every country. They were resolved to take common action on all matters affecting Jewish interests and rights, and for the relief of war and pogrom sufferers everywhere. These activities were no longer to be carried on sporadically, in an improvised manner, but in a united and organized fashion. From that time on, Jewish organizations both in the United States and in other countries entered a new phase of growth and influence.

AS JEWS AND AS AMERICANS

World War I had a profound impact on Jewish life in the United States. There was a marked awakening of Jewish consciousness among thousands who hitherto had stood aloof from their Jewish identity. As had happened after every social cataclysm in the past, there also took place among Jews a religious revival best sounded by the well-known English writer, Israel Zangwill, with his clarion call of "Back to the Sabbath candles!" Community feeling surged up spontaneously in the middle 1920's and led to the rapid development of Jewish national organizations active in religion, Jewish education, community service, philanthropy at home and relief abroad, Zionism and the building of Palestine, and, not least—defense against anti-Jewish prejudice and discrimination. All over the country, through the initiative and supervision of the Jewish Welfare Board, there sprang up hundreds of Jewish community centers and "Y's." They provided Jewish youth with guided activities which were centered in the Jewish tradition and culture. They resulted in the strengthening of Jewish identity and group-cohesion, but within the context of general American life and citizenship.

Other national Jewish organizations made striking advances in membership and in the scope and intensity of their activities. Spectacular growth, for instance, was registered by the B'nai B'rith organization, with its numerous lodges in almost every city and sizable town. Its defense arm, the Anti-Defamation League, took strong counter-measures to offset the agitation of the Anti-Semites and the Nazis; and its Hillel Foundation, working through chapters on American college campuses, guided and stimulated Jewish students to explore and to appreciate their Jewish religious and cultural heritage.

Simultaneous with this revival, and no doubt one of its precipitating causes, was the flare-up of anti-Jewish bias beginning in 1920. It was generated by political demagogues, psychopaths and adventurers who found the frustrated and the unthinking ready for their racist ideas and anti-Semitic libels. The war's end had brought about an acute economic crisis which was acerbated by a bellicose nationalism and a disillusionment in law and society that sought relief in aggressive action against weak minorities.

Most prominent in this vigilante hate movement was the Ku Klux Klan. Henry Ford's *Dearborn Independent* did much to spread the myth of the "International Jew" and widely disseminated the slanders of the *Protocols of the Elders of Zion*, a proven forgery. (Some years before his death, Henry Ford, realizing his error, issued a public apology to the Jews for the damage he had done them.) This agitation had some regrettable effects and contaminated certain areas of American business, educational and social life. Most telling of all was the increased discrimination against Jews in employment and an undisguised effort, headed by President Lowell of Harvard, to restrict the admission of Jewish students into colleges, especially medical schools, by means of the percentage norm, the *numerus clausus*. Joining with nine other national Jewish organizations, including the B'nai B'rith and the American Jewish Congress, the American Jewish Committee, led by Louis Marshall, counter-attacked. They succeeded in exposing the *Protocols* as a fraud and aroused many Americans to the danger of anti-Semitism as a divisive and anti-social force in the life of the nation. Numerous Christians, including President Woodrow Wilson and his predecessor, William Howard Taft, denounced the agitation as disruptive of the American traditions of racial and religious equality. The Federal Council of Churches of Christ condemned the anti-Semitic movement as anti-Christian and evil. Thus the American people both in places of influence and at the grass-roots rejected the hysteria of hatred that was being whipped up so synthetically by a vociferous minority of bigots and adventurers. No small part in the recession of aggressive anti-Semitism was played by the era of prosperity that came in the mid-1920's and lasted for a few brief years until 1929.

Yet the agitation had left its indelible marks. In 1921, and again in 1924, a pliant Congress, responding to the clamor of certain anti-Semitic legislators and the pressures of the Ku Klux Klan and the more respectable "protectionists" among business interests, labor unions and chauvinists who disliked the foreign-born, enacted harsh immigration laws based on quota restrictions. This legislation virtually put an end to immigration, more particularly Jewish immigration from eastern Europe. Nonetheless, the emergency created by Hitlerism in Europe led to the temporary easing of these quota laws. From 1934 to 1952 about 300,000 Jews were permitted to enter the United States. They came in two distinct waves: first, refugees from Nazi Germany; then, after World War II, "Displaced Persons" (D.P.'s) who could not or would not return to the lands of their origin. These elements, formidable in culture and in professional and business skills, left their constructive mark on the national life. Yet they also aroused, inadvertently, the enmity of the bigots and the political rabble-rousers. The passage of the McCarran-Walters Immigration and Nationality Act in 1952, bristling in its regulations with open hostility and discrimination toward Italians, Jews and Asiatics, aroused widespread criticism and demands for its repeal.

At no time since the end of World War I have those Jewish organizations representing broad sections of the Jews of the United States been guided by a narrow sectarian policy in matters affecting self-defense against anti-Semitism. By and large they have recognized the principle that the threat to the civil rights of any minority group, whether of the foreign-born or of Negroes, also poses a danger to the Jews of America, since the privileges and safeguards in a democratic society either work for all without exception or for none at all. Therein lies the reason most of the national Jewish organizations have given their active support to the passage of the Fair Employment Practices Act (F.E.P.C.), have worked for the end of racial segregation and for the repeal of the McCarran-Walters Act. Moreover, they have felt the need of achieving unity and common action by American Jewry. This has given rise to the American Jewish Conference, to which all but two of the influential national Jewish organizations belong.

Left to right: Nathan Straus, the philanthropist, Justice Louis D. Brandeis of the U. S. Supreme Court, and Rabbi Stephen S. Wise, President of the American Jewish Congress, on their way to attend the Versailles Peace Conference as members of the Jewish delegation. The Jews of the United States, under the auspices of the American Jewish Congress and with the assistance of the American Jewish Committee, sent a delegation of twelve to represent them at the Versailles Peace Conference in 1919. This group joined with Jewish delegations from other countries in forming the International *Comité des Délégations Juives auprês de la Conférence de la Paix*. This united effort succeeded in having included in the peace treaties the so-called "minority clauses" which made mandatory the protection and full equality of all national groups in the countries of the signatories.

ISRAEL

THE BEGINNING OF ZIONISM

The seeds of the Zionist movement were sown when the first grieving captives departed from Jerusalem for Babylon in 586 B.C.E. The Psalmist poet's ringing cry—"If I forget thee, O Jerusalem, let my right hand forget its cunning!"—was echoed down the ages by every pious Jew of every generation. Thenceforth, the thoughts, dreams and prayers of the persecuted ended with the yearning and consoling words: "Next year in Jerusalem!"

The very concept of the Messiah and the prophetic expectation that his coming would signalize the climactic "ingathering" of all the wanderers of Israel was an intense form of Zionism expressed in terms of the supernatural and the religious.

This was the emotional nourishment upon which the bruised consciousness of the Jew fed through the centuries. It gave him solace in his dark hours, buoying him up with the hope of eventual restoration to the ancient land of his fathers. This expectation reached unendurable climaxes of tension among the plain people with the appearance of such Messianic adventurers as David Alroy, Prince David Reubeni and Sabbatai Zevi. Even the disillusionment that followed these will-o'-the-wisps of the Jewish redemption intensified the emotional need for it.

It was the secularist spirit of the nineteenth century, seeking social solutions in practical terms, that saw the rise of the modern Zionist movement. The doctrine of the Rights of Man, proclaimed by the French Revolution to the whole world, also gave the Jews a sense of their own group worth and dignity. The leaders of the Jewish Enlightenment in Russia, for example, ever since the days of Tsar Alexander I, had had the confident belief that if only Jews succeeded in becoming as Russian as the Russians the Tsarist government would promptly grant them full equality, and the Jewish problem would be solved once for all. Their advice was: "We must prepare ourselves for this golden future and take advantage of the opportunities offered us. We must come out of our shell, obtain a secular education, acquire Russian culture! Then all else will follow."

But when, in May, 1881, the Tsarist government decreed its harsh anti-Jewish laws and initiated a series of shocking pogroms throughout the empire, the hope of the assimilationist *Haskalah* evaporated overnight. Zionist ideas, although vague and romantic at first, now found a fertile field among disenchanted Jews throughout the world.

Rabbi Kalischer

There were a number of proposals made during the first half of the nineteenth century to acquire Palestine as a homeland for the Jews. But all these plans were of a utopian character. Nothing was ever done to realize them. The first concrete Zionist effort was made by Rabbi Zvi Hirsch Kalischer (1795-1870) who wrote pamphlets in which he called for a return to the soil in *Eretz Yisrael*. Beginning in 1836 he tried to interest wealthy Jews, the Rothschilds and Moses Montefiore among others, to finance his colonization project. Only

Montefiore showed interest. He bought an orange grove in Palestine in 1841, the first Jew to acquire one. The majority of religious Jews to whom Rabbi Kalischer addressed himself considered his plan blasphemous, since they assumed that the

Rabbi Zvi Hirsch Kalischer.

return of Israel to Zion was within the province of the Messiah only. The first practical result of his agitation was that he aroused the interest of the noted French-Jewish philanthropist, Karl Netter, who established in 1870 through the *Alliance Israelite Universelle* an agricultural school for young colonists at *Mikveh Israel* near Jaffa. The school trained its students in scientific methods of farming and helped make possible the first modern settlements of Jewish farmers in the country. This marked the historic turning point in the building of Palestine.

Moses Hess (1812-1875). Distinguished as a Socialist thinker and a friend of Marx and Engels, his awakening as a Jewish nationalist soon made him part company with them. The political reaction, and with it the increased anti-Semitism which followed the collapse of the Revolutions of 1848 in Europe, led Hess to abandon his belief that the Jews would be able to achieve permanent and equal rights as a minority group anywhere. He called (in his book, *Rome and Jerusalem*, 1862) for a return of the Jewish people to Palestine and to its settlement on the land in a "spiritual center" of their own.

Lovers of Zion

Rabbi Samuel Mohilever (1824-1898), a Talmudic scholar and one of the leading Orthodox rabbis of eastern Europe, was so deeply stirred by the tragedies resulting from the pogroms which convulsed Russia and Poland in 1881 that he issued a call for a mass meeting in Warsaw where the first association of *Hovevei Zion* (Lovers of Zion) was founded. This was the first Zionist body in history and preceded the World Zionist Organization founded by Theodor Herzl by sixteen years. Rabbi Mohilever is regarded as the real founder of the religious Zionist party, *Mizrachi*.

Rabbi Samuel Mohilever.

Pinsker's Auto-Emancipation: *Bilu*

Leo Pinsker, a leader of the Enlightenment and a believer in assimilation, after he had witnessed the pogrom in Odessa in 1881 came to the conclusion that Jews could rely only on themselves for their emancipation. His pamphlet *Auto-Emancipation* (1882) became the fervent platform for the

Leo Pinsker.

Hovevei Zion Organization. His motto—quoting Rabbi Hillel, the sage of the *Mishna*—"If I am not for myself who is for me?" became the battle-cry of all the "Lovers of Zion." In the organized settlement of the Jewish people on the land in Palestine they saw the single hope for its survival.

The first agricultural settlements of East European Jews in Palestine were founded by a *Hovevei Zion* group known as *Bilu*, a Hebrew mnemonic formed by the line from II Isaiah —"Come, O house of Jacob, let us go up." *Bilu*-ite settlements included *Rehoboth, Rosh Pinah, Rishon-le-Zion, Zichron Ya-'akov, Ekron* and *Gederah*. During the period 1882-1903

First settlers of Zichron Ya'akov, at a reunion in later years.

about 25,000 settlers arrived from Russia and Romania. Their life on the land was hard and frustrating. They had to contend with the hostility of the Turkish authorities and with Arab attacks and depredations. Moreover, they had come into a semi-wilderness where at first they had to wrestle not only with malaria and dysentery but with the ungenerous soil and different climatic conditions. In addition, they found themselves at odds with the old established Jewish community of Palestine. This consisted principally of some 20,000 pious people who had gone to the Holy Land either to die and be buried in sacred soil, or to devote themselves to prayer and study and thereby hasten the coming of the Messiah. A large number of these people had been receiving support from charitable contributions made by Jews throughout the world. The new settlers, with their modern secular ideas, their vigor and enthusiasm for work, threatened to undermine their livelihood as well as their philosophy of the Jewish redemption. Therefore, they rose up against the *Biluim*, although they fought them only with religious and communal weapons.

Eliezer Ben Yehudah

A *Bilu*-ite who had great impact on the cultural development of the new Jewish settlers in Palestine was Eliezer Ben Yehudah. As early as 1879 he had written of his belief that only Jewish toil on the land in Palestine could redeem the

Eliezer Ben Yehudah.

collective life of the Jews. But being a philologist and lexicographer, he had pointed also to the necessity of modernizing Hebrew and of making it a living tongue for the new settlers. He went to Palestine in 1882 with the *Biluim* and insisted with a holy fanaticism on speaking only Hebrew. Moreover, he proceeded to adapt and increase the number of Hebrew words and expressions for modern use. These he collected in the Hebrew *Thesaurus* (1910). It was his fanaticism, aided by a combination of fortunate circumstances, which finally made a reality of his dream. If modern Hebrew became a living tongue with time it was partly because of his efforts.

Theodor Herzl

The founder of World Zionism was Theodor Herzl. In January, 1895, while covering the trial of Captain Alfred Dreyfus in Paris as foreign correspondent of the Viennese *Neue Freie Presse*, he was present at that Jewish officer's degradation on January 5, 1895. This proved the turning point in his life. An assimilationist until then, he experienced a painful emotional crisis when he heard the anti-Semitic mob hooting at the unfortunate Dreyfus: "Death to the Jews!" He gave much thought to the question: "Why should we not help one another and leave this unhappy exile and build for ourselves a free Jewish state?" He sat down in a mood of inner agitation to write his essay, *Der Judenstaat* (The Jewish State)

Theodor Herzl.

in which he presented his well-known program of political Zionism.

For the next two years he literally burned himself out trying to enlist support for a Jewish State in Palestine from prominent and wealthy Jews such as the London Rothschilds and Baron de Hirsch. When they proved unsympathetic he sought by personal contact to influence various rulers and ministers of state. Again he was frustrated. "Whom do you represent?" they asked him. Profiting from this experience, he threw himself vigorously into the work of creating a Zionist mass movement among the Jews of the world.

In 1897 he convoked the First Zionist Congress, held August 29-31, 1897, in Basle, Switzerland.

Theodor Herzl greets Max Nordau at the First Zionist Congress.

First Zionist Congress

While the *Hovevei Zion* movement had held a World Congress of all Zionist groups before—the Kattowitz Conference in 1885—it had no practical issue. However, when Theodor Herzl convoked his First Zionist Congress it took on the

character in miniature of a world parliament of Jews. Strongly represented was the *Hovevei Zion* movement. Herzl addressed himself especially to its delegation when he declared that no reliance was to be placed on the agricultural resettlement of Palestine by insignificant piecemeal methods. He then proposed the so-called "Basle Program" as the objective of a revitalized and greatly extended Zionist movement. It stated: "The aim of Zionism is to create for the Jewish people a home in Palestine secured by public law."

The enthusiasm of the delegates knew no bounds. The World Zionist Organization and its financial arm, the Jewish Colonial Trust, were established before the Congress adjourned.

Theodor Herzl then noted in his diary: "In Basle I established a Jewish State. If I were to say that aloud today, universal laughter would be the response. Maybe in five years, certainly in fifty, everybody will recognize it." The Jewish State was founded exactly fifty-one years later.

The First Zionist Congress established a broad democratic base for its operations. It made it easy for Jews, most of whom were poor, to become *bona fide* members of the Zionist movement. All it required was adherence to the Basle Program and the annual purchase of a *shekel* (about twenty-five cents) from the Zionist Organization.

The *shekel*, symbol of membership in the Zionist Organization. It was an exact replica of the *shekel* of "liberation" minted in Judea in the days of Bar-Kochba's last stand against the Romans.

The Revival of Hebrew

Side by side with the growth of the Zionist movement, in fact an integral part of it, was the revival of the Hebrew language as a living tongue. Periodicals in Hebrew began to appear in Russia and Poland, fed by a generation of talented writers who helped create a distinguished body of literature. Its pioneers included the poet Judah Leib Gordon; Peretz Smolenskin, the proponent of a Jewish national spirit; the philosopher of cultural Zionism, Ahad Ha-Am; Nahum Sokolow and Reuben Brainin, two noted Hebrew editors and journalists who were also among the foremost political leaders of world Zionism; Micah Joseph Berdychevsky; S. J. Agnon; Zalman Schneour; Joseph Klausner and David Frischman. All these writers were East Europeans, cultural products of the Hebrew *Haskalah* movement.

Two writers of *belles-lettres*, however, stood out above the rest—the poets, Chaim Nachman Bialik and Saul Tchernichovsky. Tchernichovsky was a poet of affirmation, bubbling over with joy and an earthy love for nature and the life of man. Bialik, the more profound of the two, was an introspective misanthrope. He devoted himself to themes of bitterness and grief over the national humiliation of the Jew and his abject resignation to suffer defeat everlastingly. Both these great poets helped shape the thought and feeling of several

Chaim Nachman Bialik.   Saul Tchernichovsky.   Ahad Ha-Am.

generations of thoughtful Jewish nationalists in Europe and in the Americas, but especially in Palestine.

The young *Poale Zion* intelligentsia from Russia, the pioneers of the "Second Aliyah" in the settlements and towns of *Eretz Yisrael*, followed the lead of the uncompromising philologist-lexicographer Eliezer Ben Yehudah, and persisted in speaking and writing *only in Hebrew.* By these determined means, sustained through the years, Hebrew eventually became a living tongue in Palestine. In a matter of years it was spoken by the child in the nursery, the farmer in the field, the student at the university and the scientist in the laboratory.

Dissension

Theodor Herzl never abandoned his conviction that the best way to achieve the Jewish state was by means of personal diplomacy. It was with an all-consuming passion that he set himself the task of reaching important people—the Pope, kings, ministers of state, bankers and philanthropists. He ruined his health and impoverished his family traveling from one capital to another, trying to win support for his plan among the influential. These efforts were directed to but one end—to obtain a legal charter for a Jewish State in Palestine from Sultan Abdul Hamid II, then the Turkish ruler of Palestine.

Twice in 1898 Herzl had audiences with Kaiser Wilhelm II of Germany. He pleaded with him to use his influence with the sultan for a Jewish State. He even journeyed to St. Petersburg after the Kishinev pogrom in 1903 to urge the Russian Imperial Government, which was at the time anxious to get rid of its Jews, to bring pressure upon the Sublime Porte in Constantinople to allow the Jews to establish a homeland in Palestine.

In the meantime, so great had grown the tension and despair among the Jews of Russia and Romania, because of the intolerable persecution to which they were subjected, that rumblings of revolt began to be heard against Herzl's personal diplomacy, which thus far had brought no results. A sharp division in the Zionist ranks took place between the "Politicals" who supported Herzl and the "Practicals" who clamored for step-by-step colonization in Palestine. It finally led to open rebellion at the Sixth Zionist Congress in Basle in August, 1903. It erupted when Herzl submitted to the delegates for their consideration an offer from Joseph Chamberlain, British Colonial Secretary, to establish a large number of Jews on territory in the Uganda of East Africa. He argued in its favor that "the proposal means an autonomous Jewish settlement area in East Africa, with a Jewish administration, Jewish local

government and a Jewish chief officer at its head; all naturally under sovereign British supervision."

This proposal caused a furor. Delegates from Russia bitterly accused Herzl of betraying the Zionist cause, of trying to

Group photograph of Herzl and colleagues at opening of the Sixth Zionist Congress in Basle in 1903. (1) Israel Zangwill, noted English writer; (2) Theodor Herzl's mother; (3) Dr. Max Nordau, a famous intellectual journalist of the day, who lent his oratorical skill and prestige to the new Zionist movement and, next to Theodor Herzl himself, was the most influential and striking personality in the Zionist world; (4) Theodor Herzl; (5) Dr. Max Bodenheimer, the leader of the German Zionists; (6) Oskar Marmorek, a noted architect and a member of the first Zionist Executive; (7) David Wolfsohn, closest associate and friend of Herzl and his successor as President of the World Zionist Organization; (8) Professor Emanuel Mandelstamm, an early leader of the *Hovevei Zion* movement in Russia who was prominent in Jewish communal affairs in that country; (9) L. J. Greenberg, editor of the *Jewish Chronicle* of London; (10) Professor Otto Warburg, famous botanist and later Nobel Prize winner whom Herzl persuaded to join actively in the Zionist movement.

divert the Jews from establishing their homeland in their historic *Eretz Yisrael.* In vain he tried to defend his position: "Admittedly, this is not Zion, and never can be. It is only an auxiliary settlement scheme. . . . It is and remains only an emergency measure . . . and is intended to prevent the loss of dispersed parts of the nation."

The indignation of the Russian delegates could not be stilled. They withdrew in a body, joined by other opposition delegations. While Herzl obtained a nominal majority in a test vote, it proved only a Pyrrhic victory—the delegations representing the majority of *shekel*-paying members had bolted!

In fact, at a special conference held later in Kharkov under Menachem Mendel Ussishkin's leadership, the Russian Zionists repudiated the Uganda proposal and demanded greater emphasis on practical colonization in Palestine. Although Herzl finally submitted to the dissidents' demands and became reconciled with them, the excitement and the strain caused by the acrimonious dispute completely wore him out. He died on July 3, 1904, stricken by heart disease at the age of forty-four.

Another important consequence of the clash on the Uganda issue was the withdrawal of a number of prominent members from the Zionist Organization. Led by Israel Zangwill and Professor Mandelstamm, they formed the Jewish Territorial Organization (ITO), which until the issuance of the Balfour Declaration sought energetically, but in vain, to obtain a suitable Jewish territory in Asia or Africa.

Left. Menachem Ussishkin, veteran Zionist leader and long-time President of the Jewish National Fund. *Right.* Yoshua Hankin, early agricultural pioneer, who was instrumental in making the most important land purchases for the Fund. He was called "The Redeemer of the Emek" because of the large land purchases he negotiated in the Emek Jezreel after 1921. As early as 1897 at the First Zionist Congress, the plan for the Jewish National Fund had been proposed by its originator, Professor Hermann Schapira (1840-1898), a noted mathematician at the University of Heidelberg. Its object was to "redeem" by purchase large land tracts in Palestine and to develop them for the establishment of agricultural settlements. Its goal at first was modest, resolute and simple: "another Jew, another *dunam* (¼-acre), another cow." It was not until 1908, however, that it began actual operations with the first purchase of land for the Judean Plain settlement of Ben Shemen where the Herzl Forest was planted. By 1948, when the State was founded, the Jewish National Fund had already redeemed, in all parts of Palestine, a total of 926,000 *dunams* of land on which it had established 83,000 agricultural settlers in 233 settlements. It had also planted 5,000,000 trees in a denuded country desperately in need of reforestation.

Aaron David Gordon (1856-1922) went to Palestine as an agricultural settler in 1904 at the relatively advanced age of 48. He became the most ardent champion of manual labor and inspired several generations of pioneers to follow his example. His belief in collective living prompted him to take the lead in 1909 in the establishment of the first *kvutzah* or *kibbutz*, as it is variously called, at Deganiah (Place of Corn) in the Jordan Valley. The *kvutzah* Gordonia was named in his memory, and he is known as the Father of the Kibbutz.

"The Dignity of Labor"

While the Zionist movement continued to hold to the political program its founder, Theodor Herzl, had given it, it began to lay more emphasis on colonization in Palestine itself. This marked a partial return to the policies of the "Practicals" of the old *Hovevei Zion*.

The struggle of the early settlers with the soil in Palestine had proven in some instances well nigh disastrous. Not even the millions which Baron Rothschild poured into several of the settlements in order to keep them alive had accomplished much. Even the romantics and the idealists among the pioneers wilted before the difficulties they had to face—poverty,

Group of wine-press workers in 1914 standing before the Carmel Wine Company cellars in the colony Rishon-le-Zion which had been founded in 1882. The center figure is David Ben-Gurion, who went to Palestine from Poland in 1906. He had helped establish the Labor Zionist movement in Palestine and thus, as one of its principal leaders, achieved political power.

the niggardliness of nature, the ravages of malaria and, not least, their lack of training as farmers. The disheartened "Lovers of Zion" now began to call the land of their dreams a "land of corpses and graves." Even the dignity of manual labor, so traditional among Jews, had fallen into disrepute

Left. Ber Borochov (1881-1919) was one of the founders of the *Poale Zion* movement. He served as its theoretical leader and drew up its political program. At the Eighth Zionist Congress he succeeded in uniting all the *Poale Zion* organizations into a World Union. The *Histradrut*, the Palestine Federation of Labor and its political arm, the *Mapai* Party, are today part of the *Poale Zion* movement. *Right.* Dr. Nachman Syrkin (1868-1924). Beginning in 1909, with Ber Borochov, he became an intellectual leader of the Labor Zionist movement. He came to the United States in 1907 where he remained active in the *Paole Zion* organization.

in the settlements. Baron Rothschild's administrators had frowned upon the colonists' doing their own work. They shared the colonial bureaucrats' typical attitude, and the myth of the superiority of Europeans had to be preserved at all costs. The colonists were to be gentlemen-managers only—the Arab "natives" were to do the digging and the plowing.

This was the situation into which the next wave of immigrants came during the "Second *Aliyah*" of 1904-1914. They constituted a new type of settlers, young students and intellectuals from Russia and Poland, in the main members of the *Poale Zion* (Labor Zionist) movement. Some held strongly democratic, even socialist views. They found little in common with the older discouraged settlers and so pursued paths of their own. To work productively with their hands, to lead the simple wholesome life of tillers of the soil, and to earn their bread by the sweat of their brows were ideals they hoped in time to translate into a national pattern for the entire Jewish people.

The first editorial board of the Labor Journal *Achdut* (Unity) in 1912. Seated at left is Joseph Chaim Brenner, one of the most gifted of modern Hebrew writers, who preferred to earn his livelihood as a worker. During the Arab riots in 1921 against the Jews in Jaffa, he was murdered. The colony Givath Brenner (Brenner's Hill) in Judea was founded in his honor by the Jewish National Fund in 1928. Seated next to Brenner are David Ben-Gurion and Isaac Ben-Zvi. The latter had founded, with Ber Borochov, the *Poale Zion* Party in 1905 in Russia. A Hebrew scholar and writer, he served as President of the *Vaad Leumi* (National Council) of Palestine from 1931. Upon the death of Dr. Chaim Weizmann in 1952 he was chosen President of Israel.

An open-air meeting held in 1908 to decide on the founding of Tel-Aviv. This metropolis was then only a stretch of gray sand dunes outside the Arab city of Jaffa.

World War I

The world clash of armies shattered the peace of the Zionist movement. Armed eastern European Zionists faced armed central European Zionists from opposition trenches. More than ever, the tragedy of Jewish destiny was underscored. In Palestine the *Yishuv* (Jewish community) seemed doomed. When Turkey entered the war on the side of Germany, the

Djemal Pasha (with beard), the Turkish commander on the Near Eastern front, before the Mosque of Omar with General von Falkenhayn, German Commander of the *Asienkorps* in the Eastern theatre of war (1915).

Jews of Palestine were certain that they were trapped. The Governor of Syria and Palestine, the intelligent but half-demented Djemal Pasha, happened also to be Commander-in-Chief of the Fourth Imperial Army of Turkey. He arrested the foremost Zionist leaders and deported a number of them, including David Ben-Gurion and the present head of the State in Israel. Yitzhak Ben Zvi, who found a haven in the United States. Because they were not Turkish citizens, he ordered 12,000 Jews expelled from the country. Furthermore, he approved a decree of January 21, 1915, reading: "The Exalted Empire in its resentment of the provoking element which is planning to create in the Palestinian section of the Ottoman Empire a Jewish government under the name of 'Zionism' . . . orders the confiscation of all Zionist stamps, flags and cheques of the Anglo-Palestine Company, which are circulated among these elements, and furthermore, orders all the Zionist societies and organizations to disband."

Jews hanging on scaffolds erected by the Turks before the Jaffa city hall in the spring of 1917. The military in the foreground are the Turkish executioners in Djemal Pasha's army.

Captain Joseph Trumpeldor (1880-1920). With Vladimir Jabotinsky he had organized the Zion Mule Corps for the British Army in 1915. Its 650 Jewish members fought at the Dardanelles during the Gallipoli campaign. Later, after the Corps was disbanded in 1916, he went to London to help Jabotinsky form the Jewish Legion. He met a heroic death defending the frontier colony of Tel-Hai in upper Galilee against maurauding Arabs on March 1, 1920. His grave at Tel-Hai has become a national shrine for pilgrims in Israel.

When the Egyptian Expeditionary Force (E.E.F.), under General Sir Archibald Murray, invaded Palestine from Egypt early in the spring of 1916, Djemal Pasha started an unrelenting "spy hunt" among the Jews. He had many imprisoned and tortured. He even shot and hanged a number upon the merest suspicion of sympathy for the English.

Vladimir (Zeev) Jabotinsky (1880-1940) in the English Army uniform of the Jewish Legion in 1918. A famous Zionist orator and journalist, soon after the Balfour Declaration in favor of a Jewish national home in Palestine had been issued, he persuaded the Zionist leaders and the British War Office in London to allow him to organize the Jewish Legion. About three thousand volunteers, a large number from the United States and Canada, were recruited by Jabotinsky, aided by two other members of the Legion—Isaac Ben-Zvi and David Ben-Gurion. These volunteers were formed into three battalions of the Royal Fusiliers (38th, 39th and 40th) and collectively called the Jewish Legion, or "The Judeans." Units of the Legion took part in the final phase of the war which culminated in the attack on Es-Salt in September, 1918, under General Allenby.

The 39th Battalion Royal Fusiliers of the Jewish Legion marching into the Herzl Forest at Ben-Shemen in Judea, on *Chamishah Asar Bishvat*, the Jewish Arbor Day, 1919, where each soldier planted a memorial tree.

The principal Zionist negotiators in London, 1917: Dr. Chaim Weizmann, at the time a professor of chemistry at the University of Manchester; Dr. Nahum Sokolow; Yehiel Tchlenov (center), leader of the Russian Zionists.

Throughout the war, negotiations had gone on in London for a Jewish homeland in Palestine between the foremost Zionist leaders—Ussishkin, Tchlenov, Sokolow and Weizmann—and members of the British government. When, finally, in February, 1917, the Foreign Office expressed its readiness to fulfill the Zionist objectives provided its Allies gave their consent, Dr. Nahum Sokolow, "the diplomat" of the Zionist movement, was sent to obtain concurrence from the Pope and from the French and the Italian governments. In this he succeeded. Although the United States was not yet officially at war with the Central Powers, through the mediation of U. S. Supreme Court Justice Louis D. Brandeis, President Woodrow Wilson expressed his support of the projected Jewish Homeland.

On November 2, 1917, Arthur James Balfour, British Foreign Secretary, wrote to Lord Rothschild the momentous letter that has become known as the Balfour Declaration.

Lord Arthur James Balfour.

Foreign Office,
November 2nd, 1917

Dear Lord Rothschild,

I have much pleasure in conveying to you, on behalf of His Majesty's Government, the following declaration of sympathy with Jewish Zionist aspirations which has been submitted to, and approved by, the Cabinet

"His Majesty's Government view with favour the establishment in Palestine of a national home for the Jewish people, and will use their best endeavours to facilitate the achievement of this object, it being clearly understood that nothing shall be done which may prejudice the civil and religious rights of existing non-Jewish communities in Palestine, or the rights and political status enjoyed by Jews in any other country".

I should be grateful if you would bring this declaration to the knowledge of the Zionist Federation.

The Balfour Declaration.

"National Home"

The turbulent history of the Zionist efforts to establish a Jewish National Home in Palestine cannot be understood without a knowledge of the circumstances surrounding the Balfour Declaration. As soon as the Declaration was issued, rumblings of discontent over the planned establishment of the Jewish National Home in Palestine started reverberating throughout the Arab world. Arab nationalists appeared before the Peace Conference at San Remo and spoke in opposition to granting the Palestine Mandate to Britain. It was their indignant claim that Palestine had been promised to them as an Arab state and not to the Jews.

To forestall the possibility of later misunderstanding, Dr. Chaim Weizmann, the head of the Zionist Commission, had been completely circumspect. He had conferred, almost as soon as he had arrived in Palestine a year before in April, 1918, with Emir Feisal, son and heir of King Hussein of Hedjaz. Together they had drawn up and signed, on January 3, 1919, a treaty of friendship. In this pact the Emir had declared his sympathetic interest in the establishment of the Jewish National Home. He also expressed his approval of the large-scale immigration of Jews that was being planned and of their settlement on the land, but with the single proviso that the interests of the Arab population would not be affected adversely thereby.

Yet, to the surprise of the Zionist delegation at the Peace Conference, the Arab objectors to the Mandate suddenly revealed for the first time the existence of a secret correspondence entered into early in 1915 between Sir Henry MacMahon, British High Commissioner in Egypt, and the Grand Sherif Hussein of Mecca, afterwards King of Hedjaz. In it the Sherif —in consequence of a prior understanding negotiated with the famous British Intelligence agent, Col. "T. E. Lawrence of Arabia"—committed himself to start a diversionary revolt against the Turks whose entry into the war on the side of Germany was regarded as imminent. In repayment for this aid, the British government, on its part, promised to support at the proper time the Arab claims for an independent state to be established in a specified territory. But MacMahon's political promises were couched in ambiguous phraseology. There was no mention of Palestine in them. Yet the Arabs insisted that Palestine was categorically meant and included in the bargain with the Sherif.

It was not long before the Zionist leaders discovered that they, too, had been adroitly misled in their expectations. The Balfour Declaration also had been phrased in verbal ambiguities which made possible various legalistic interpretations of both its general intentions and its specific promises. The behind-the-scenes diplomatic origins of this curious document first came to light years later. In 1937 a Palestine Royal Commission, which had been appointed to study the causes for the intense Arab-Jewish hostility that had erupted the year before in bloody rioting and pogroms by armed Arab bands and street mobs, reported to the British government: "In the evidence he gave before us, Mr. Lloyd-George, who was Prime Minister at that time, stated that . . . the launching of the Balfour Declaration at that time was 'due to propagandist reasons.'" These "propagandist reasons," explained Lloyd-George, were decided upon by the British Cabinet because of the threat of an Allied defeat. England stood in need of all possible help. "In particular, Jewish sympathy [*viz.*, shown by the British government for the Jews] would confirm the sup-

port of the American Jewry. . . ." In return, continued the former Prime Minister, Zionist leaders promised "to do their best to rally Jewish sentiment and support throughout the world to the Allied cause."

With undiplomatic frankness the Royal Commission expressed its opinion that the term *National Home* was deliberately made ambiguous: "We have been permitted to examine the records which bear upon the question and it is clear to us that the words 'the establishment in Palestine of a National Home' were the outcome of a compromise between those Ministers who contemplated the ultimate establishment of a Jewish State and those who did not." Winston Churchill made no bones about it when he presented his interpretation of the term: "When it is asked what is meant by the development of a Jewish National Home in Palestine, it may be answered . . . the further development of the existing Jewish Community. . . ." To show that on this subject there was no difference of opinion between Tory and Labourite, Ramsay MacDonald, then Prime Minister, issued in 1930 a White Paper (the Jews bitterly called it "Black Paper") in which he gave his unqualified support to Churchill's interpretation.

Chalutzim

The post-war period was full of promise for the projected Jewish Homeland in Palestine. Impatiently the Zionist movement waited for the legalization by the Allied Supreme Council of their project so that at long last it could begin the large-scale settlement operations the Balfour Declaration had sanctioned. Even before the San Remo Peace Conference had assigned the mandate for Palestine to Great Britain on April 25, 1920, the Zionist bodies were already represented in an official advisory capacity to the British Administration in Jerusalem. A Zionist Commission, headed by Dr. Chaim Weizmann, was authorized in March, 1918, to confer with the British in all matters concerning "the establishment of the Jewish National Home." In 1921 this Commission was transformed into the Zionist Executive representing all political factions.

Before the outbreak of the world conflict the Jewish population of Palestine had been unofficially estimated at nearly 100,000. By the time it had ended, little more than 50,000 were left. A number had succumbed to the normal civilian ravages of war, to famine and disease. But many thousands had left the country either because they were ordered expelled by Djemal Pasha or because life under his despotic rule had become insupportable. The number of pioneer settlers and workers had also dwindled. When the *Histadrut*, the Labor Federation of Palestine, was being created in 1920, the combined membership of the four separate groups that took part in its amalgamation was only 4,333.

With the end of the war a new immigration wave from Europe was started on its course. During 1918-25 there were 60,000 settlers; 84,000 arrived during 1925-35. Towns began to boom: Tel-Aviv and Haifa grew into small cities. New businesses were opened; small factories began to hum, and the thud of hammers in construction work on new dwellings and schoolhouses resounded from Dan in the north to Beersheba in the southern Negev wilderness.

Still, the most important work went on among the *chalutzim* in the agricultural settlements. The romantic dream of the "Lovers of Zion" with its back-to-the-land call continued to retain its hold on the young. But to those who believed in

307

Immigrants arriving at the port of Haifa in 1925.

rooting Jewish life in the soil it appeared as neither romantic nor as a dream. One hundred new settlements were successfully founded in the tiny land in the eighteen years after the issuing of the Balfour Declaration. If the settlers had not been helped, they would probably have failed. But the various Zionist organizations and agencies throughout the world, maintained by Jewish mass-support, sustained them in their difficulties. This was especially true of the *Keren Kayemeth* (Jewish National Fund), which purchased and prepared the land for the settlements; of the *Keren Hayesod* (Palestine Foundation Fund), which financed them until they could become self-supporting, and of *Hadassah*, founded by Henrietta Szold in the United States, which provided them with medical care and public health services.

The great majority of the *chalutzim* were young. Many

Chalutzim, many of them cultured and university-trained, laying stones for a road along Lake Tiberias early in the 1920's. This was a cooperative public works project conducted by the *Histadrut,* by arrangement with the Mandatory Government and the Zionist organizations.

A visiting nurse of *Hadassah* calling on a patient in the early 1920's. *Hadassah* was founded in 1912 in New York by Henrietta Szold and began operations in Palestine the following year. It established a chain of nursing centers in every district. Visiting nurses extended maternity and infant care to Jews, Christians, Mohammedans and unbelievers alike. *Hadassah* also carried on an intensive campaign against trachoma in the schools, in the Arab villages and among adults in the towns.

were imbued with labor and socialist ideals, belonged to *Poale Zion, Zeire-Zion, Hapoel Hatzair* and *Hechalutz.* Many also were conservatives, middle-class General Zionists and Orthodox *Mizrachi* adherents. In fact, in 1924 there were two farm settlements founded by the *Hasidic rebbes* of Kosnitz and Yablona. Their disciples with their families had followed them from Poland into the Holy Land and made the daily cultivation of the soil a part of their "service for the Lord."

Rabbi Abraham Isaac Kook (1864-1935). A leader of the Orthodox *Mizrachi* Zionists, he was a defender of the dignity of labor and on occasion upheld the secularist *chalutzim* against the die-hard pietists in Palestine. Under the British Mandatory Government he served officially as the *Ashkenazic* Chief Rabbi of Palestine. He was universally revered.

But it must not be assumed that all came as idealists to Palestine. For instance, beginning with 1924 there was a striking increase in the number of brokers, traders and shopkeepers whom the cold pogrom had frozen out of Poland. Some of these turned to productive labor and callings and helped build up the legitimate trade and industry of the country. Others, however, went in search of "an easy *piastre*." Together with fortune-hunters from the United States and other countries they engaged in feverish land speculations. They created a synthetic boom in real estate, especially in Tel-Aviv, with inflationary results that were deplored by the rest of the *Yishuv.*

Tillers of the Soil

Chalutziot, or pioneering on the land, has been considered the keystone to the arch which supports the State of Israel. The development of a farming population has been deemed the most basic requirement for placing Jewish national life there on a wholesome and balanced basis. The return of the Jews to the soil constituted more than a policy of certain Zionist leaders of two generations. It was also the fervent wish of thousands of plain Jews the world over, who year after year would drop their modest coins into the blue collection boxes (*pushkas*) of the Jewish National Fund for the purpose of hastening "the land redemption" of Palestine by purchase. The *Hechalutz* movement in eastern and central European countries arose in response to this ideal evaluation of the role of the agricultural worker in the land of Israel.

Thus, almost from the very start, groups of energetic young men and women, many with good education and trade skills, banded together with the intention of living cooperatively on the land. Most of the time their farming settlements took on the additional character of military outposts on a lonely frontier. The "conquest of labor," the driving motivation of all agricultural settlers, was inevitably combined with the practical conquest of the land for the future Jewish Commonwealth. They entered into those territories which by ordinary standards were considered unprofitable, forbidding and even dangerous. They were undaunted by malaria, drought, crop failure, hunger and the quite frequent attacks by marauding

Arab bands. Those who suffered in the process of the struggle with the ungenerous soil had the comforting reassurance that they were pioneers building for a brighter future.

Most of the hundreds of agricultural settlements in Israel today are organized on either cooperative or socialist-labor principles. The patterns they follow were set by pioneers of previous *aliyahs*. The most common forms are: the *kibbutz* (formerly known as *kvutzah*), the collective settlement; the *moshav ovdim*, the workers' cooperative or small-holders' settlement; and the *moshav-shitufi*, a type of settlement which combines features of both the *kibbutz* and the *moshav ovdim*.

Yemenite settler working a modern combine in Maoz Zurim.

The *kibbutz* is socialistic in character. All its land is collectively owned and worked and its profits are shared equally. Its members, women as well as men, pool their labor. The education and care of the *kibbutz* children are undertaken collectively, since mothers are taken up with field and other work. It operates on four fundamental principles: 1. The land of the settlement, purchased by the Jewish National Fund, is

Lubavitcher *Hasidim* from Russia, who settled in the abandoned Arab village of Safariya. Former townspeople and tradesmen, in Israel they were taught to operate agricultural machinery.

to be considered national property. 2. Self-labor: Unlike private colonists who hire outside labor, usually Arab, the members of the *kibbutz* consider themselves morally obligated to live by their own toil. 3. Mutual aid: The welfare of the individual is to be considered as the welfare of the entire community. 4. Collective production marketing and consumption to insure greater economies and efficiency.

The *moshav-ovdim*, the workers' cooperative or small-holders' settlement, resembles the *kibbutz* in a number of ways. However, it is less socialistic and more individualistic than the latter. Each settler owns his own piece of land. On it he builds his house and cultivates the rest of it in any man-

An orange grove in a settlement on land furnished by the Jewish National Fund. The cultivation of citrus fruits in the central coastal plain of Israel is unique in the entire Middle East. It is the country's oldest and most valuable crop, because of its industrial by-products and also because there is a ready export market for it. Before World War II, 15 million cases of oranges, grapefruit, lemons and tangerines were exported each year. But during the War with the Arabs the groves suffered great damage and destruction. In 1951 less than 5,000,000 cases were sent out of the country. Besides citrus fruits Israel also produces grapes, olives, plums, apricots, bananas, dates, figs and almonds.

ner he chooses. Yet many of the collective features of the *kibbutz* are present here, too. For instance, all its members make cooperative use of expensive farm machinery: tractors, combines, incubators and cold storage. Alike with the *kibbutz*, it also benefits from the cooperative institutions established by *Histadrut*, the General Labor Federation, for marketing produce, for purchasing supplies, for obtaining credit and for extending comprehensive medical services.

The settlement of Nahalal in the Valley of Jezreel. The site on which it stands was originally swampland and was reclaimed only through exceptional toil and hardship. It is chiefly a citrus-growing center.

The *moshav-shitufi*, although it works its land collectively like the *kibbutz*, offers even more freedom to the individual settler than the *moshav ovdim*. It, too, utilizes the cooperative institutions created by *Histadrut*. Also, like the *moshav ovdim*, it lays primary stress on a more complete home life than does the collectivistic *kibbutz*.

By the end of 1951, the *kibbutz* was represented by 214 settlements with a total population of 73,000. The *moshav ovdim* claimed 180 settlements with a population of 63,000, and the *moshav-shitufi*, 27 settlements with 3,000. In addition, there were 39 agricultural colonies worked by middle-class families with hired labor according to the standard practices of all privately owned farms. About 80% of all agricultural settlements in Israel have been established on land purchased and prepared by the Jewish National Fund, and held by it in perpetual trust for the nation.

Planting potatoes in the settlement of Kfar Menahem.

Water

For many years, many people had discounted the possibility that a large Jewish community in Palestine could maintain itself on land that was three-quarters barren waste of sand and stone, with most of its hills deforested and its soil unbelievably eroded. But those who knew the land and were buttressed by the opinions of agricultural scientists had faith

Giant water pipeline being laid in the Negev wilderness. After three years of intensive scouting and scientific study of the soil, water resources, climate and flora in the Negev, the Jewish National Fund in 1946 established there 14 new settlements on the same day.

that the desert could once more be made to flower. What they thought it required was great patience, hard labor, much money and the unfaltering application of scientific methods in order to restore the fertility of the depleted soil.

As in Bible times, one of the major problems was that of water. Wherever there was an adequate supply of it, by means of proper irrigation and a soil conservation program along modern lines, the wilderness could be reclaimed. This basic agricultural truth was demonstrated time and again by the

Professor L. Picard, famous geologist of the Hebrew University, inspecting the drilling operations for water in Beth Guvrin in the Negev desert.

spectacular accomplishments of many of the Jewish settlements. These were transformed into little garden spots in the midst of the surrounding wilderness.

It was the general assumption for a long time that Palestine did not have enough water resources for irrigation. This view was exploded in recent years by teams of hydrologists and geologists. With the aid of modern machinery they found water even in regions such as the Negev where it was never before believed to be. Scientists today have completed a blueprint for building eight separate systems of irrigation canals. They are to constitute an *underground* water reservoir system. By means of conduits and central engineering controls it will be able to provide sufficient water to every part of the country. The claim is being made that it is a matter of a short period of time only when the entire Negev desert, which constitutes about half of Israel, will be turned into a fruitful area supporting at least a million of farming population.

Conflict with the Arabs

The controversy that raged over the Balfour Declaration through the years generated ill-will toward the Jews among the Arabs of Palestine. Their nationalist leaders, and especially Haj Amin al-Husseini, the *Mufti*, or Moslem religious head in

Chalutzim of a new frontier settlement in the wilderness showing hospitality to Bedouin tribesmen.

Arab villagers entertaining Jewish settlers who have just consummated the purchase of a tract of land from them. Many of these settlers learned to speak Arabic and took an enlightened interest in Arabic traditions and ways of life. This attitude often resulted in mutual respect and trust.

Jerusalem, constantly incited them with charges that the Jews meant to take their homes and holy places away from them and to drive them out of Palestine. To the embarrassment of the Zionist leaders, there existed no responsible organized

Bedouins waiting for treatment at the malaria station run by medical scientists of the Hebrew University in Jerusalem.

Zionist leaders meeting in 1929 in Jerusalem with friendly sheiks from Trans-Jordan. Seated are Dr. Chaim Weizmann and Dr. Chaim Arlosoroff, labor leader of Palestine, who was one of the staunchest proponents of Arab-Jewish friendship. Ironically enough, he was struck down by an Arab assassin only a short time after this meeting. Moshe Sharett, later Israeli Foreign Minister, is seen at the extreme right, standing. *Reproduced with the kind permission of La-Am Israel Publishing Co. Ltd.*

body among the Palestine Arabs with whom to conciliate or negotiate. The only Arabs who were making themselves vocal were unscrupulous demagogues, nationalist terrorists and spokesmen for the feudal *effendis.* From 1920 on, there was an incessant chain-reaction of incidents of violence, of arson,

The *Mufti* Haj Amin al-Husseini.

snipings, bombings, ambushes, assassinations and even well-organized pogroms in all of which the guiding hand of the *Mufti* was evident. The British Mandatory Government, which was resentful of the Jews' persistence in seeing their own interpretation of the Balfour Declaration carried out, showed itself hostile to the *Yishuv* from the very start. It did very

little to prevent the outbreaks or to give protection to those attacked. In consequence, Palestine Jewry had to look to its own self-defense.

Feudal System

The chief source of Arab opposition to the creation of a Jewish homeland in Palestine came from the *effendis,* the privileged land-owning class. Since time immemorial they had been the feudal rulers of the oppressed Arab peasantry, the *felaheen.* The latter were treated as serfs. They lived in wretched mud hovels in the villages that were owned by the *effendis,* ravaged by hunger and disease and kept in total ignorance. These *effendis* feared that civilized standards of life

Left. An *effendi* standing beside his American-made car with chauffeur. *Right.* A *felah* clearing field of stones before plowing.

and work and the humane relationships within the democratic group existence of the Jewish settlements might prove a dangerous example for the *felaheen.* Furthermore, as a result of the labor performed by the Arab villagers in their free time in Jewish communities, their earning capacities had risen spectacularly. In order to defend their vested interests of cheap labor and a submissive peasantry, the *effendis* banded together, and allied with the ever-growing number of nationalists among the better-educated and well-to-do Arabs in the towns and cities, they waged a relentless and often savage warfare which was aimed at driving the Jews out of Palestine. It was of this element that the *Mufti* became the embattled leader.

In 1930, after the entire country had been convulsed by rioting and after one hundred thirty-three Jews had been killed by Arab mobs, the British government conducted several investigations. It finally issued the Passfield "White Paper" and then placed drastic curbs on Jewish immigration.

The Haganah

Ever since Captain Joseph Trumpeldor and his comrades-in-arms fell defending Tel-Hai in Upper Galilee against Arab marauders in 1920, the Jews of the *Yishuv* decided to look to their own defense. They had never placed any reliance on the British Mandatory Government to give them adequate protection against Arab attacks. In fact, the League of Nations in 1930 had sharply reprimanded the government for failure to protect the Jewish population during the riots of 1929. This time, in the middle 1930's, the *Yishuv* greatly strengthened the *Haganah* in both numbers and arms. By 1936 this defense force counted 25,000.

311

A *Haganah* cavalry patrol helping to defend the widely separated Jewish settlements against armed Arab bands during the disturbances of 1936-39.

"Tower and Stockade"

As part of its general defense against the anticipated Arab attacks, the *Yishuv* rushed the construction of the now legendary "tower and stockade" settlements in strategic areas and along the frontiers. These outposts were manned by the most determined of the *chalutzim*. They were literally erected overnight. Everything was planned in advance along the most efficient modern lines. Half-built sections of watchtowers and wooden skeletons for stockades, lumber, hardware and other necessary supplies and tools were loaded into a convoy of trucks. Volunteers would be mobilized from the nearest Jewish settlements for construction work. Before dawn the convoy

While the volunteers were building the "tower and stockade" settlements the men of the *Haganah* stood guard against surprise Arab attacks.

A "tower and stockade" settlement going up.

would proceed to the selected site and the labor would begin as members of *Haganah* stood guard. The work went on feverishly, urgently, for attacks by Arabs sometimes interrupted their labor. Therefore, everything important had to be reasonably completed before nightfall. When darkness fell, the projector fixed on top of the watchtower would be turned on, lighting up the entire area. Then the men and women of the convoy moved off into the darkness, leaving behind a small but determined band of permanent settlers.

A "tower and stockade" settlement.

The Conspiracy

With the rise of Hitler to power in Germany, all subsequent events in Palestine seemed to lead inexorably to a crisis. There were two major factors working along parallel lines toward an explosion. The 1930's saw a new kind of immigrant *aliyah* to Palestine. Of the 265,000 Jews who arrived during that period, 60,000 were refugees from Germany: a great many industrialists, chemists, engineers, research scientists, doctors, technicians, musicians and teachers. They established some twenty agricultural settlements of their own while many of them joined already existing Jewish farm communities. The impact of this able and cultured group on the total life of the *Yishuv* was dramatic. The economy made striking gains. All fields of culture hummed as they had never done before.

The Arab nationalists and the *effendis* could not help but take stock of this. The thing they dreaded most—a Jewish National Home—not only was taking clearer shape but nothing they could do seemed able to prevent it. At this point they began receiving weighty support from a new quarter. The Grand *Mufti*, it was widely charged, had reached an understanding with the Nazi and Italian Fascist Governments, whereby the Arab Nationalists agreed to make trouble for the British in Palestine. They were also instructed, it was alleged, to accelerate their hostile campaign against the Jews. For these purposes, reports had it, they were well supplied with German and Italian money and with arms smuggled into the country.

The leaders of the Jewish community were convinced of this plotting among the reactionary Arab circles for a civil war. They took steps to frustrate it.

Organized Terrorism

Despite the energetic steps of the *Yishuv*, widespread Arab violence flared up in well-organized fashion throughout the country in 1936. There was an interminable series of am-

Arab riot in Jaffa, 1936, during which a number of Jews were killed.

bushes and snipings at cars and buses on the highways. There were street riots and attacks on Jewish settlements. Killings took place on the streets in broad daylight. This terrorism was openly carried out under the direction of the *Mufti* and the Arab Higher Committee. Although there were large British detachments garrisoned in Palestine, the systematic violence continued unabated until 1939 when World War II started.

The Betrayal

Unable, or unwilling, to check the continuing violence, the British government appointed the six-member Peel Commission to re-examine the acerbated problem of Arab-Jewish relations. After many hearings the Commission declared in its report of July, 1937, that the Mandate was unworkable. In its place it recommended the partition of the country between Jews and Arabs: the Jews to get the coastal plain, the Emek and Galilee. All holy places were to be under British control. As if to emphasize their rejection of the plan for partition, even in principle, the Arab nationalists intensified their terroristic campaign against the Jews. The British government, angered by this display of open defiance, ordered the *Mufti* arrested and the Arab Higher Committee outlawed. The *Mufti* escaped to Lebanon but he continued to direct the disturbances in Palestine from there. In 1938 the Mandatory Government felt itself forced to place the country under military administration. Finally, in a desperate quandary in which it was placed between the two contending forces, the British government decided to gamble on a compromise solution which it implemented in its White Paper of May, 1939. By allowing 15,000 Jewish immigrants annually for only a period of five years and by empowering the High Commissioner to curb drastically the purchase of land by Jews, it brought forth the charge from the latter that the British government had reneged on its solemn promises made in the Balfour Declaration.

The consequences of the White Paper proved catastrophic to Jews. Thousands of refugees fleeing across the Mediterranean were prevented by the British from landing in Palestine. Many perished: 250 lost their lives in an explosion on the *Patria* in the harbor at Haifa; all except one of the 769 passengers on the *Struma*, a badly leaking old ship, were drowned in the Black Sea after neither the British in Palestine nor the Turks would let them land.

The *Irgun*

In opposition to official Zionist policy, which he steadily attacked as being too cooperative with the British and too conciliatory with the Arabs, Vladimir Jabotinsky founded his separatist "New Zionist Organization" in Vienna in 1935. He also started forming that same year the para-military *Irgun Zvai Leumi* (National Military Organization). His program was simplicity itself: to force the English to go home, to immobilize the Arabs, to bring in one million Jewish settlers in one year, and to establish without delay a Jewish State on *both sides* of the Jordan. After the White Paper of 1939 his proposal for a Jewish countermeasure was—"illegal immigration." Because of the political aims of the New Zionists (later the *Herut* party) and because of the terrorist direct-action methods of the *Irgun*, they were widely accused by other Zionists of being fascistic. This charge they indignantly denied.

Vladimir Jabotinsky inspects (in New York) a unit of his youthful followers in the B'rith Trumpeldor Organization. He died only a few months later on August 3, 1940, at Camp Betar near Hunter, New York.

The "Illegals"

The White Paper of 1939, despite the Jewish Agency's appeal for "self-restraint" and the avoidance of violence, completely disenchanted all those who had entertained any lingering hopes that the British government could be persuaded by legal and peaceful means to fulfill the provisions of the Mandate. The Jewish community was inflamed as never before. In a joint declaration by the *Vaad Leumi* (National Council) and the Jewish Agency on May 18, 1939, the British were warned: ". . . this treacherous policy will not be tolerated . . . nor [will we] recognize . . . any callous restriction of Jewish immigration. . . . The homeless will find their way here, and every Jew in this land will readily welcome them."

For the first time there was widespread sympathy among the Jews of Palestine for the direct-action methods of the *Irgun* and of its minor offshoot, the Stern Group. The latter, a secret terrorist band, estimated at no more than several hundred members, operated under the leadership of the young Hebrew poet, Abraham Stern. It now declared war to the death against the British authorities, arguing that by preventing German refugee immigrants from entering the country Britain was in effect serving as an "accomplice of Hitler's crimes . . . and should be fought with undiminished vigor." And so the Sternists, but especially the more numerous Irgunites, initiated a campaign of systematic terror against the British with assassinations, bombings and kidnappings. At first they were anxious to win mass sympathy and support for their operations. They pointed out, cogently enough, that the White Paper of 1939, with its complete surrender to the Arab nationalists' demands, had come about only as a result of the latter's campaign of terror. However, the brutality with which the Jewish terrorist groups carried out their own operations eventually shocked and alienated most of the public support for them in the *Yishuv*.

"Illegals" crowded into a rubber raft off the coast of Italy, pulling up under cover of darkness to the ship they named *Al Tafchidunu* ("They cannot frighten us"). When they arrived at Haifa in December, 1947, the British authorities would not allow them to land, but sent them to the detention camp in Cyprus. Shipload after shipload of Jews escaping Nazi Europe came hopefully to Palestine in unbelievably overcrowded and unseaworthy boats. Due to the clandestine nature of their voyages, their departures from Mediterranean ports had to be kept secret and were carried on under the most disadvantageous conditions.

It was against this background of violence and public disorder that the illegal immigration of Jews to Palestine began in the spring of 1939. Despite all the difficulties and the dangers they were obliged to run, 113,000 desperate and often defiant "illegals" entered Palestine by 1947. In retaliation the British Colonial Office halted the immigration quota of 15,000 it permitted annually. It also sharply rebuked the Jewish Agency for its "lawless" conduct. To this the Agency retorted: "It is not the Jewish refugees returning to their home-

A fleet of ships loaded with thousands of "illegals" detained in Haifa harbor, August, 1946. The British naval patrols kept a sharp watch on all ships bringing "illegals." Those that were intercepted were brought into the harbor of Haifa under "arrest" and their human contraband was sent to the detention camp in Cyprus. No matter what stern curbs the British adopted, this immigration, with an historically unprecedented resolution, contined to flow on.

land who are violating the law but those who are endeavoring to deprive them of the supreme right of every human being." The British government's reply to this display of independence was to clap collective fines on those Jewish communities it suspected of aiding the illegal immigration. There also took place a man-hunt for the "illegals," with mass screening and arrests to facilitate the inquisition. Simultaneously, the British coastal patrols were strengthened by land and by sea.

The fight over immigration now became the focal point in the struggle for a Jewish National Home, and it waxed more determined and also more merciless with time. In 1945 the English-trained *Palmach*, the commando arm of the *Haganah*, in a rare instance of collaboration with the *Irgun* and the Sternists, struck forcefully in guerrilla raids at British installations that had been erected to curb the entry of the illegal immigrants.

British detention camp on the island of Cyprus.

Members of *Haganah* bringing in illegal immigrants from a ship discreetly anchored off the coast of Palestine. The *Yishuv* became passionately devoted to the task of smuggling the new arrivals into the country. A remarkable "underground railroad" was established by *Haganah* for this purpose. It worked with great efficiency and resourcefulness.

Exodus 1947 pulling into Haifa harbor. Nothing so dramatized the plight of the immigrants as the incident of the *Exodus 1947*. The winter and spring of 1947 had seen 11,000 "illegals" enter Palestine. Under British and United Nations pressure a sharp curb was placed in European ports on ships departing for Palestine. Yet several broke through this blockade. Among these was the *Exodus 1947*. Carrying the incredible number of 4,550 refugees, this small boat was "arrested" by a British warship on July 18 of that year and was escorted into Haifa harbor. The capture was made in the customary manner the British employed at that time. They rammed her, plowing a hole into her side. Finally, when the ship was moored at the dock and the British tried to board her the passengers put up a stubborn resistance. Three Jews were killed and about a hundred were injured. The hazards the immigrants, as well as the ships' crew, had to endure on the journey to Palestine were an epic in themselves. Leaking tubs for the greater part, some of the boats broke up or foundered in severe storms. The extreme overcrowding on board, the hunger, thirst and illness caused much suffering and even death to some. But the severest ordeal was the frustration which so many of them were to meet at journey's end. Tantalizingly, they were able to see the Promised Land yet were prevented by the British from entering it.

English soldiers carrying off a wounded Jew after the battle on board the *Exodus*. The whole world was shocked when Ernest Bevin, then Foreign Minister in the Labour Government, in order "to make an example of this ship" ordered all its passengers returned to the D.P. camps in Germany from which they had come.

The Terror

The outbreak of World War II, in 1939, brought an uneasy truce in the three-cornered struggle for Palestine among the English, the Jews and the Arabs. At the 21st Zionist Congress in Geneva in August, 1939, Dr. Chaim Weizmann explained this political concession on the part of the Jews: " . . . above our regret and bitterness are higher interests. What the democracies are fighting for is the minimum . . . necessary for Jewish life." The *Irgun*, too, was willing to lay aside its terroristic activities for the duration. Tens of thousands of Jews, many of them victims of the Nazis, eagerly offered to take up arms against them. Of about 130,000 of both sexes who registered with the Jewish Agency as wanting to serve with the British armed forces, only 30,000 were accepted and trained as combat troops, principally for service in the Mediterranean theatre of operations.

Scene at the 21st Zionist Congress in Geneva, August, 1939, when Hitler's declaration of war was announced. Middle row, left to right: Moshe Shertok (Sharett), David Ben-Gurion and Dr. Chaim Weizmann. *Reproduced with the kind permission of La-Am Israel Publishing Co. Ltd.*

However, as a climax was approaching in the world conflict in 1944, a renewed Arab outbreak of arson and terror instigated by the Nazis rent the country. It raged unabated until 1946, when it rose to flood-tide. The *Irgun* and the Freedom Fighters (Sternists) promptly matched Arab violence with Jewish violence. Under its militant new leader, Menahem Beigin, a former Warsaw lawyer and Zionist Revisionist leader who had come to Palestine with the Polish army of General Anders, the *Irgun* waged an accelerated war of retaliation. Yet the principal fire of the Jewish terrorist organizations was leveled at the British Mandatory Government: at its civilian authorities, its police and military units. While the Freedom Fighters "specialized" in the assassination of English officials, the *Irgun* engaged in systematic bombings

Dov Gruner, *Irgunist* hero, who was sentenced by a British military court to die by hanging early in 1947. When the British commander, General Barker, refused the condemned man permission to appeal for royal clemency, the *Irgun* retaliated by kidnapping and holding as hostages two prominent Englishmen. The following day, General Barker gave the *Irgunite* permission to appeal to the Privy Council. The hostages were then promptly released. But Dov Gruner was led to the gallows three months later with a ringing cry of defiance at the British. His hanging deeply affected Jews throughout the world as well as in Palestine.

of government offices and attacks on the mobile police stations in Jerusalem, Tel-Aviv and Haifa. To replenish its depleted finances, the *Irgun*, allegedly by means of threats, kidnappings and beatings, was able to collect sizable "contributions" from Jewish businessmen. The Freedom Fighters, equally uninhibited, robbed Jewish banks in broad daylight in Tel-Aviv and other places. These acts attributed to the *Irgun* and the Freedom Fighters did not add to their popularity in the *Yishuv*.

Rescuers digging for the dead and injured in the debris of what was once the Atlantic Hotel in Jerusalem, following the explosion that took place there on February 22, 1948.

And so, as the months passed, one act of violence followed another in a steadily mounting chain-reaction of ferocity for which the Arab terrorists, the British authorities and the Jewish "direct actionists" were equally responsible. A climax was reached when members of the *Irgun* blasted the British Government Offices at the King David Hotel in Jerusalem on July 22, 1946. The explosion killed eighty and wounded seventy more British civil service employees. This outrage led to a marked rise in anti-Semitic feeling in England itself.

Goaded into exasperation by the *Irgun* terror he could not control, Lieutenant-General Sir Evelyn Barker issued an order to the 80,000 English troops stationed in Palestine, forbidding them to buy in Jewish shops. This boycott, the military order commented, would punish "the Jews in a way where it would hurt them most, by striking at their pockets and showing our contempt for them." This created an international furor.

The leaders of the *Yishuv* were dismayed. The Jewish Agency and other Zionist bodies publicly repudiated and deplored the activities of the *Irgun* and the Freedom Fighters. Dr. Chaim Weizmann called on the Jewish community to cut out the "cancer in the body politic of Palestine Jewry" or "it will devour the Movement and the *Yishuv* and will destroy all that we have built up." From that time on, the Jewish Agency, with the aid of the *Haganah,* cooperated with the English police in tracking down both the members and the hideouts of the *Irgun* and the Freedom Fighters. This type of collaboration with "the enemy" stirred up considerable bitterness in the *Yishuv* and also among Jews in the United States where indignation with British anti-Zionist policy had earned widespread sympathy for the *Irgun* and its direct-action methods.

The crisis in Palestine led to a near paralysis of the country.

Crowd in Tel-Aviv on November 29, 1947, celebrating the United Nations decision on a partition plan.

Law and order had almost broken down. Desperately the British struggled to disarm the combatants, but without success. The United States government brought strong pressure to bear on the British to find a rapid solution to the Palestine problem. Finally the British government announced formally to the United Nations that the Mandatory system was unworkable. The General Assembly then agreed on a partition plan for separate Jewish and Arab States in Palestine, with Jerusalem as an international city. The Jews accepted the partition plan, for with all its territorial limitations and inequities, it nevertheless legally assured a Jewish State in Palestine with the unequivocal backing of the world.

The Arab leaders acted in a quite contrary manner: they angrily rejected the United Nations partition plan. As if in direct answer, they unleashed a storm of violence throughout Palestine.

Arab mob burning Jewish shops and goods in Jerusalem after the United Nations declaration.

Medinath Israel

On May 14, 1948, after most of the British Army had departed from Palestine, the British High Commissioner, Lieut.-General Sir Allan Cunningham, boarded a British naval vessel at Haifa. With his going, the Mandatory Government came to an end after twenty-six years of turbulent rule.

Proclamation of Independence on May 14, 1948, establishing the State of Israel.

On that day the National Council, representing all elements of the Jews of the *Yishuv,* gathered at the Tel-Aviv Museum. It listened to David Ben-Gurion read the Proclamation of Independence establishing the Jewish State which thenceforth

The Provisional Council of the State of Israel.

was to be known as *Medinath Israel.* Almost immediately the United States government accorded the new Jewish State *de facto* recognition. Three days later the Soviet Union went one diplomatic step further and granted Israel *de jure* acceptance. Other countries followed suit quickly. The Council elected a Provisional Council of State with Dr. Chaim Weizmann as President and David Ben-Gurion as Prime Minister.

The Eve of Invasion

The concerted attacks by Arab bands, which followed the adoption of the Partition Plan by the United Nations on November 29, 1947, showed that they had been well prepared in advance. During the subsequent six weeks there were two thousand casualties.

The United Nations had sent its Palestine Commission to take over the administration of the country when the Mandatory Government would terminate its rule on May 14, 1948. Its main task then would be to supervise the orderly establishment of separate Arab and Jewish states according to the terms of the Partition Plan. Four separate times within two and a half months the Commission formally complained to the United Nations that the British authorities refused to cooperate with it, and that this policy of political sabotage was bound to lead to war.

Young *Haganah* members holding back Jewish youths from clashing with Arabs in Jerusalem. Ever since 1936, the slogan of the *Haganah* against all acts of Arab terror had been *havlagah*, "self-restraint."

Until this time the *Haganah* had practiced its well-known creed of *havlagah*, self-restraint. But when it became apparent, as the disturbances continued, that the Arabs were set upon a full-scale war, the *Haganah* rushed into feverish preparations to meet whatever blows from the enemy were impending. On March 9, 1948, it issued a mobilization call for all able-bodied men from seventeen to forty-five.

In preparation for the struggle, *Haganah* not only called for volunteers but began to draw upon its secret caches of arms and ammunition. A member of *Haganah* opening an arms cache.

The shape of unfolding events became clearer in only a matter of weeks. Arab bands at an early date had seized most of Old Jerusalem. From their vantage points there they laid siege to the New City in which 90,000 Jews were living. The intention of the Arab strategists was to isolate and starve into submission Jewish New Jerusalem by cutting the main highway to Tel-Aviv. Those Jews still trapped in the Jewish quarter of the Old City continued to hold out, stubbornly defended by small units of the *Haganah* and the *Irgun*. The

road to Tel-Aviv had been mined for ambush by the Arabs and was being heavily patrolled by them. But *Haganah* was determined to bring food and supplies to the besieged Jews of Jerusalem. It could do so, however, only by armed convoys of trucks. Its drivers and escorts accordingly suffered heavy casualties during December, 1947, and January, 1948. The road to Jerusalem seemed effectively blocked.

Jewish police of Tel-Aviv, aided by *Haganah* members, capturing an Arab sniper.

Young *Haganah* fighters led away by British soldiers after being found in possession of arms during the flare-up of violence in the border streets between Arab Jaffa and Jewish Tel-Aviv.

An English policeman supervising a Jew searching an Arab and an Arab searching a Jew for concealed arms before a Jerusalem post office.

317

A Jewish armored truck ambushed along the Jerusalem-Tel-Aviv highway by an Arab band whose leader is pumping bullets into the prostrate Jewish driver lying beside the truck. The roads of Palestine became too dangerous for travel during 1947-48. Organized bands of Arab irregulars ambushed Jewish vehicles, even armored trucks and cars, along the main highways. The British advised the Jews to stay at home. But in the line of duty to bring supplies to the far-flung settlements, hundreds of Jewish drivers daily risked their lives—and lost them, too.

Mechanics of *Histadrut* putting armor-plate on truck in preparation for conflict.

Armed convoy of *Haganah*, with supplies for the besieged Jews of Jerusalem, preparing to leave Tel-Aviv.

Mount Castel

Toward the end of March, the *Haganah* launched a major operation to capture the Arab strong point on Mount Castel, which commanded the Tel-Aviv-Jerusalem road. On April 2nd, after repeated attacks, they finally dislodged the Arabs and reopened the road.

At about the same time, an army of irregular Iraqi and Syrian volunteers, under the command of the notorious Nazi-trained Fawzi al-Kaukji, seized a number of Jewish settlements in northern Galilee. But two *Haganah* battalions, under

Members of *Haganah* standing guard on top of Mount Castel.

the command of Brigadier Epstein, rushed to the scene and routed Kaukji's army in open battle on April 9, 1948, at the Jewish settlement of Mishmar ha-Emek, which is situated near the site of the Biblical Armageddon.

Students standing guard at the Hebrew University on Mount Scopus overlooking territory in the hands of Jordan's Arab Legion.

Kaukji's "calling card" painted on the walls of Jewish settlements he attacked.

Reproduced with the kind permission of La-Am Israel Publishing Co. Ltd.

Arab Refugees

The Arab population of Palestine, by and large, was neither prepared nor inclined for the struggle. Its poverty and misery under the *effendis* and the sheiks did not predispose it to fight "patriotically" for their interests. Its tragedy was indeed boundless, caught in the vise between the two contending forces. Given the choice between war with the Jews and developing Palestine peacefully with them in neighborliness most of them probably would have chosen the latter course. But being fed with atrocity stories about the Jews, which were sedulously spread among them by the Arab leaders, they were literally afraid of their lives. Upon the defeat of the Arabs at Mount Castel and the rout of the famous Kaukji, a mass-hysteria spread among them. This was finally climaxed by a disastrous act of the *Irgun* and the Freedom Fighters. Unauthorized, they launched a surprise attack on April 9, 1948,

318

on the Arab village of Deir Yessin and killed 250 Arabs—men, women and children—in what was subsequently described as a massacre. The Jewish Agency expressed "its horror and disgust at the barbarous manner in which this action was carried out." But in the days following, the Arab radios broadcast the news in all its horrible details, even enlarging on it.

Arab refugees in flight, resting along the highway.

The consequences were unexpected, as far as the Arab leaders were concerned. Instead of lashing the Arab population into enthusiasm for a war of vengeance, it had quite the opposite effect. In tens of thousands the Arabs began pouring out of the villages in panic flight. They glutted all the highways—a mass of human misery driven on by unreasoning fear and confusion. From that time on, the war for Palestine was no longer fought by the Arabs of that country but by the invading armies of neighboring Arab governments.

Israeli and Druze officers at a party given in the home of a Druze sheik. Not all Arabs were unsympathetic to Israel during the invasion. This was especially true of the Druze tribesmen who lived in the hills of Northern Galilee and on Mount Carmel. Several Druze units volunteered to fight for the Jewish State. They were incorporated into the Defense Army of Israel.

War with the Arab States

The creation of the Jewish State on May 14, 1948, was the rocket which served as a signal to the armies of the seven Arab states—Iraq, Syria, Lebanon, Trans-Jordan, Saudi Arabia, Yemen and Egypt—to cross the borders of Israel as invading forces.

At the time, *Haganah*, which had been renamed the Defense Army of the State of Israel, had a striking strength of about 20,000, including a considerable number of women. It had, also, about the same number of militia assigned to the defense of Jewish settlements and villages. Against it was arrayed a total of 35,000 combat and irregular troops belonging to the seven Arab states. The invading forces overesti-

Lieutenant-Colonel Moshe Dayan, Military Commander of Jerusalem, and Colonel Yigal Yadin. *Haganah* became the youngest national army in the world with the youngest group of commanders as well. Colonel Yigal Yadin became Chief of Operations of the General Staff of the Defense Army at 32. Brigadier Mordecai Makleff was appointed Chief of Staff at 29. Brigadier Chaim Ladkov became commander of the Air Force at 35. Youngest of all was Commander Mordechai Limon, who was designated Head of the Israeli Navy at 27.

mated their chances for easy victory and underestimated their foe's military capabilities and potential. Although at first the Arab soldiers were better equipped and numerically superior, their hearts were not in the struggle. Palestine was not their country. The opposite was true of the defenders. They were fighting for their homes and their homeland, supported by a patriotic Jewish community fused together for the emergency by a common goal. Almost all of them had fought during the

Israeli soldiers in street fighting.

World War either in the British or in other Allied Armies, including that of the United States. Thousands of the younger men and women had previously received excellent military training in the *Haganah* in preparation for this very national crisis. Then, too, the Israeli Defense Army enjoyed the advantage of a high degree of military and administrative coordination and possessed the technical skills required for modern warfare.

Although at first hard pressed for arms and ammunitions, now that the British were gone and the naval blockade had been lifted, the Israeli Defense Army was free to import badly needed arms and ammunition from abroad. The biggest supply came from Czechoslovakia by air-lift: 75-millimeter field guns, small tanks, Bren automatic rifles and machineguns. Within several months the Israeli Army became a regular and well-equipped field force with effective striking power.

On every front, except that held in Central Palestine by the British-trained and -led Arab Legion of Jordan, the invaders gave an astonishing display of disorganization and ineptitude. They showed, also, a marked unwillingness to fight. The Arab Legion, however, made a determined effort to capture Jerusalem. It invested the walled Old City on May 18, 1948, and ringing the Jewish-inhabited New City, started to besiege it. In the meantime, planning to isolate New Jerusalem, a Trans-

Above. Hasidic recruits practicing with automatic arms. *Right.* A pious soldier in the field. The whole *Yishuv* organized itself into what was virtually a defense army. It was considered a patriotic war for the homeland. There was widespread consciousness among the people that the struggle was only repeating in 1948 what the Maccabees had done in the days of the Second Temple. The war effort, therefore, was total. It called for the active participation of every man, woman and child in city, town, village and settlement. In emulation of the Zealots (*Hasidim*), who rose up in arms under the Maccabees against the invading forces of Antiochus Epiphanes, the ultra-Orthodox youth of Israel, too, volunteered for the army.

Above. An elderly guard at the entrance of an agricultural settlement. *Right.* Boys and girls filling sand bags for defense. The agricultural settlements, from the northernmost hills of Galilee to the southernmost point in the Negev wilderness, were fully mobilized for self-defense from grandfathers down to school children.

Above. An underground chicken coop. *Right.* An underground shelter in a settlement. As a result of the attacks by armed Arab units, many Jewish settlements had to carry on much of their daily living underground. Ingenuity provided for underground hospitals and even chicken coops.

Jordan contingent seized Latrun, a strategic point at the western end of the Bab-el-Wad defile which lay along the Jerusalem-Tel-Aviv highway. It captured, also, the Lydda airport and the town of Ramleh. Thus Jerusalem was completely cut off from Tel-Aviv and no aid could reach the Jewish defenders. Realizing the hopelessness of their position, the latter surrendered after ten days of bitter fighting.

In the end, however, the Israeli General Staff succeeded in outmaneuvering the Arab Legion. It hurriedly built a new road which by-passed Latrun and other Arab positions. This was named, with a glow of national pride by Israelis, "The Road of Courage." On June 11th the first convoy bearing food and medical supplies from Tel-Aviv safely reached New

A soldier of the Arab Legion of Trans-Jordan. The Legion had been created and trained by the British under Brigadier Glubb "Pasha." Of all Arab invading armies it was the only competent and cohesive force, and showed skill in action and maneuver.

Mrs. E. Margalith, Acting Principal of the Nurses' Training School of *Hadassah*, conferring with Mother Superior Jeanne d'Arc of the Convent of St. Joseph de l'Apparition and Reverend Father Lavergne. During the war the Nurses' Training School was hospitably given quarters at the Convent. The work of *Hadassah* in caring for the sick and wounded during the war was considered of prime importance. Due to the fact that the *Hadassah* Hospital, together with the Hebrew University on Mount Scopus, had been cut off by the Arab Legion of Jordan, it was forced to operate in another part of Jerusalem.

Count Bernadotte (left), a short time before his murder. He is conferring with General Lundstorm, his Chief Observer. An unfortunate incident of the war was the assassination in Jerusalem on September 17, 1949, by an unknown Jewish terrorist, of Count Folke Bernadotte, United Nations Mediator for Palestine.

Jerusalem to relieve the 90,000 Jews besieged there. In order to make more secure for the future the "Jerusalem Corridor" connecting with Tel-Aviv and the coastal plain, the government of Israel hurriedly put up eight new tower-and-stockade settlements there to serve as fortified outposts.

On the very day (June 11) that the Israeli Army broke the siege of New Jerusalem, the Supreme Council of the United Nations, through its mediator, Count Folke Bernadotte, ordered a four weeks' truce. But when the truce came to an end the struggle was immediately resumed. However, the fighting was more sporadic than it had been before and was constantly diminishing in force.

Defeat of the Invaders

On November 18, 1948, the government of Israel accepted the Armistice Resolution voted by the United Nations. But the Egyptian Army, from its positions in Gaza and other coastal towns, persisted in harassing the isolated Jewish settlements in the southern Negev. It staged several damaging air raids on Tel-Aviv. Thereupon, the Israeli Army turned its attention to the Egyptians. After ten days of fighting, the *Palmach*, under Colonel Sadeh, captured Beersheba, the stra-

Colonel Yitzchak Sadeh, commander of the *Palmach*, the famous Israeli commando force.

tegic center of the Negev. On January 7, 1949, the Security Council of the United Nations issued a Cease-Fire Order to Israel and to the Arab states, and the war was practically at an end. Long before, during the preceding summer, King Abdullah of Jordan had considered pulling out of the useless and expensive war but the other Arab states and the Arab League were reluctant to end it. The hard realities had to be faced sooner or later and the Arab states finally entered, separately, into truce negotiations with Israel.

Truce

Negotiators for the Egyptian and Israeli Armies met with Acting U. N. Mediator Dr. Ralph Bunche on the Island of Rhodes. They agreed on truce terms on February 22nd. Sub-

Dr. Ralph Bunche (center) reading the agreed truce terms between Israel and Jordan to negotiators of both countries on April 3, 1949.

sequently, truce terms were signed separately by Israel with Lebanon on March 23rd, with Trans-Jordan on April 3rd, and with Syria on July 20th.

When the war ended, the State of Israel found itself with a considerably larger territory than the United Nations Palestine Partition Plan had carved out for it. This increase it

Map of Palestine showing the boundaries of the State of Israel as established by the truce with the Arab States. The areas with vertical shading represent the additional territory it gained in military operations. Jerusalem, however, remained divided—the Old City in Arab Trans-Jordan and the New City in Israel, but surrounded by the former on three sides.

Parade in Tel-Aviv to honor the Israeli Defense Forces for their victory. Not only the Jews of the *Yishuv* but also those throughout the world were immensely stirred by the triumphant defense of Israel. It released a flood of enthusiastic support for the new State in all countries among Jews and Christians alike.

insisted on retaining on the grounds that it had won it at terrible cost in a war forced on it by aggressor nations.

The First Election

With the fighting ended, and even before any formal truce had been signed with the Arab states, the Provisional Government of Israel called for a General Election to take place on January 25, 1949. The voting was to be for 120 deputies to the unicameral legislative assembly, the *Knesset*. Seats were to be apportioned to the various political groups participating under the proportional representation system.

A bewildered voter, scanning the posters of some of the 21 separate political parties which took part in the historic first election of Israel.

The election campaign was subsequently described as "fabulous." There were twenty-one political party lists carrying the staggering total number of 1,288 candidates. The Arabs of Israel, who had remained, also took part in the elections. Moreover, for the first time in the history of Palestine, Arab women were allowed to vote. Out of a total of 506,500 eligible voters, 440,000 Jews, Arabs and Christians cast their secret ballots.

Jewish and Arab members of the *Knesset* (Parliament) in amicable discussion.

The largest number of votes (35%) was won by the *Mapai* (Israel Workers Party), representing the *Histadrut*, the General Federation of Labor. The *Mapai*, moderately Social-Democratic in character, and comparable to the British Labour Party, won 46 out of the 120 seats in the *Knesset*. The second largest number of seats, 19, was won by *Mapam* (United Workers' Party), a coalition of several Left-Wing Socialist Parties. The United Religious Front won 16 seats. This Party was a coalition of four organizations: *Mizrachi* (Middle Class Orthodox), *Hapoel Hamizrachi* (the Labor Division of *Mizrachi*), *Agudath Israel* (Association of Israel,

ultra-Orthodox), and *Poale Agudath Israel* (Labor Division of *Agudath Israel*).

Fourth in strength, 14 seats, went to *Herut* (Freedom Party). This group, under the leadership of Menachem Beigin, became the political arm of the *Irgun*. The General Zionists, the middle-class Center Party to which Dr. Chaim Weizmann belonged, won only 7 seats. The middle-of-the-road Progressives won 5 seats. The Communist Party of Israel won 4 seats, and the United List of *Sephardim* and Oriental Communities also won 4 seats. The Arab Democratic Party of Nazareth, allied with *Mapai*, won 2 seats. There were a number of other minor parties with one or two seats each in the Knesset.

As a result of the election, a new government, the first democratically elected body in the new state, was formed. It consisted of the following: Prime Minister and Minister of Defense, David Ben-Gurion (*Mapai*); Minister of Trade and Industry, Yaakov Geri (non-partisan); Minister of Communications, Dov Joseph (*Mapai*); Minister of Agriculture, Pinhas

The three Justices of the first Supreme Court of Israel (left to right): Professor Rabbi S. Assaf, Rector of the Hebrew University; Dr. M. Smoira, President of the Court; I. Olshan.

Lubianiker (*Mapai*); Minister of Social Welfare, Golda Myerson (*Mapai*); Minister for Religious Affairs, Rabbi Leib Maimon (*Religious*); Minister of Finance, Eliezer Kaplan (*Mapai*); Minister of Justice, Pinhas Rosen (*Progressive*); Minister of Education and Culture, David Remez (*Mapai*); Minister for Police, Behor Shitreet (*Sephardim*); Minister of Interior, Health, Immigration, Moshe Shapiro (*Religious*); and Minister for Foreign Affairs, Moshe Sharett (*Mapai*).

The four parties constituting the government coalition were *Mapai*, the Religious Front, the Progressives and the *Sephardim*.

On January 25, 1949, the *Knesset* elected Dr. Chaim Weizmann as the First President of Israel.

Recognition

On May 11, 1949, the United Nations admitted Israel as its fifty-ninth member. By the end of the year, 58 states had recognized the Israeli government—42 *de jure* and 16 *de facto*.

At the end of the war, out of the 859,000 Arabs who had formerly lived in Israeli territory only 133,000 were left. Of those who had taken flight, 470,000 were said to be in Arab Palestine, 100,000 in Lebanon, 75,000 in Jordan and 70,000 in Syria. This created a serious economic and social problem. To aid these refugees, the United Nations and Works Agency for Palestine Refugees was established on November 16, 1949.

Those Arabs who remained in the country did not isolate themselves from the Jewish community but took part in the first election of Israel.

Members of the first Israeli Delegation seated in the United Nations (left to right): Arthur Lourie, Israeli Consul-General in New York; Major Aubrey Eban, head of the Israeli Delegation to the U. N.; and Moshe Sharett, Foreign Minister of Israel.

Ingathering

Kibbutz Galuyot (the Ingathering of the Exiles), as it was called, became the primary concern of the new State of Israel immediately after its founding on May 14, 1948. The considerations behind this gigantic project were both military and economic. Principally it was in order to increase the defense potential of the country. The doors were, therefore, flung wide open for immigration. Under the stimulation and with the financial help of the World Zionist movement and several Jewish relief agencies, foremost of which was the Joint Distribution Committee, there took place a rapid immigration of tens of thousands of new settlers from all the five continents, but especially from central and eastern Europe.

The Jewish population of Israel at the time stood at 742-355. But in the eight months between May and December of 1948, there arrived 101,000 immigrants. In 1949 there were 239,000; in 1950 only 169,000; in 1951, it was 173,901. However, by 1952 the torrent had subsided to a mere trickle—only 23,370. This brought the Jewish population to 1,450,000 by the end of 1952, representing about 12.6% of all the Jews in the world. The Arabs in Israel then numbered 170,000, the increase of 37,000 since the end of the war being due to a return of refugees.

A young orphan as he disembarks at an Israeli port, early in 1949. One of the most heartrending as well as stirring aspects of immigration into Israel was that of *Youth Aliyah.* Founded in the middle 1930's, for the rescue of Jewish children and youths in Nazi Germany, under the auspices of the Jewish Agency, this action became the special responsibility of *Hadassah,* aided by the Mizrachi Women's Organization and Pioneer Women. Since it began, *Youth Aliyah* brought to Israel some 60,000 children and youths, most of them orphaned by Nazi genocide.

The explanation for the sharp decline of the "ingathering" is not hard to find. For one thing, immigration from Communist countries and from central Europe had practically ceased. However, perhaps the principal cause for the "drying up" was what might figuratively be described as "population indigestion." A tiny undeveloped country, the State of Israel has an area of only 8,048 square miles and a great part of it

consists of stony wilderness and desert. The great influx of population which had occurred in such a short period of time created a number of staggering social, economic and cultural problems. There were also unwholesome tensions existing among the various ethnic communities. Jews were coming

"Behold, if there be any sorrow like unto my sorrow." Every ship that arrived from Europe brought joy to some Jews already in Israel. But it also brought grief and frustration to many others. Thousands of families were happily reunited after years of bitter separation and wandering. Each time a boat docked in Haifa or Tel-Aviv, a great crowd would gather near it. Hopefully and anxiously they would scan the faces of those disembarking, in search of beloved ones.

from every country in the world. They were bringing with them, by and large, their own poverty, languages, customs, standards of living and levels of civilization. The cultural disparities, for example, between the doctors and musicians from Vienna and the sheep-herders who had been cave-dwellers in the Atlas Mountains of Tripolitania can well be imagined. In addition to the hundreds of thousands of European Jews, there had been transported to Israel during the last few years almost the entire Jewish community of Iraq—122,500. The

Coffin of Theodor Herzl lying in state beside the sea at Tel-Aviv. Most of those who arrived in Israel felt they were coming home. Among these was one who had also expressed his longing to "come home" to the Land of Israel, but that was fifty years before. In his last will and testament, Theodor Herzl, the founder of Political Zionism, and therefore the real founder of the State of Israel, had asked that his body be laid to rest next to that of his father in the Jewish cemetery in Vienna "to remain there until the Jewish people will carry my remains to Palestine." Just as Joseph's body was carried back to the Land of Canaan by the Israelites when they departed from Egypt more than thirty centuries before, so did the modern Israelites do with the body of their leader. The State of Israel brought Theodor Herzl's last remains to the Jewish Homeland. Amidst solemn public rites participated in by the entire nation they were laid in the earth of the land of his desiring.

Yemenites—45,000 strong—had been transported by air-lift "Operation Magic Carpet" into what was virtually a new world. There were also large concentrations of Iranian Jews, Moroccan and Tunisian Jews, Jews of Kurdistan, India and many other remote places. These groups, culturally backward, had little enough in common with one another, but infinitely less so with the predominant community of Jews of European origin.

It required time, patience and great effort to fuse such a conglomeration of ethnic groups into a single nation. The immigrants first had to be prepared and trained for settlement and economic absorption in town, village or *kibbutz*. Nor could they manage without at least a smattering of modern Hebrew, the national language of Israel. Most important of all, the great majority of them had to be taught how to work at modern trades. Those who wished to cultivate the land required some basic training in agriculture.

These manifold problems and tasks, unprecedented in the Jewish people's experience, were greatly aggravated by the wretched physical condition of so many arrivals, especially of those who had been in concentration camps for years. The primary task was to restore their health. In consequence, they taxed all the resources and ingenuity of the infant State of Israel and of the *Yishuv* itself. Whatever was accomplished could not have been realized without the large-scale financial aid which came pouring in from the organized Jewry of many countries, especially from the United States through the campaigns of the United Jewish Appeal and of the Israel Bond drive.

Immigrant Camps

To receive the new arrivals, the Jewish Agency, on whom this responsibility fell, opened reception camps for their temporary care. This was at a time when Israel was engaged in a life-and-death struggle with the invading armies of the seven Arab states. Therefore, it could give but glancing attention to the immigrants. The camps consisted in the main of the most wretched barracks and shacks with only primitive sanitation and offering few creature comforts to the tired and harassed newcomers.

The immigrants had to endure an enforced and destructive idleness. Week after week they waited, often in vain, to find a useful place for themselves in the community. The great overcrowding, the discomforts, the poor administration of the camps due to inexperience or incompetence caused a corroding restlessness and sometimes a feeling of not being wanted. On the other hand, the financial burden was very heavy. (At one time there were as many as 130,000 immigrants in the reception camps.) For these and other reasons, the Jewish Agency broke up the reception camps and placed all newcomers in *ma'abarot* (plural for *ma'abara*—transition camp).

These transition camps showed decided advantages over the old camps. They were established in the vicinity of cities or larger agricultural settlements in order to make the transition into the new life easier and quicker. Each family was given, whenever available, separate quarters: a hut or a tent. The family unit had to do its own housekeeping, thus providing its members with a sense of more normal living. In the meantime, with the assistance of the Jewish Agency, they were expected to prepare themselves for settlement in some job, business or profession. One great difficulty was that the country was going through a severe housing shortage. Even

A family dining together in "its corner" in the old-type reception camp.

Shoemakers plying their trade in the "business center" at the reception camp in Keryath Shmuel.

Immigrants arriving at a transition camp.

A hut in a *ma'abara*. The *ma'abarot* varied in size. Some held as many as 10,000 temporary tenants. These lived in a curious assortment of tents and huts made of all kinds of materials—fabric, wood, aluminum sheeting and cement blocks.

when the immigrants were able to secure employment, thousands could find no roof for their heads. Therefore, they were obliged to continue living in the *ma'abarot*.

These difficult conditions progressively caused demoralization, wretchedness and tension which sometimes erupted with unhappy results. However, with time, money and experience, after the war's end the Jewish Agency succeeded in a partial alleviation of the housing problem. It put up thousands of

Two Yemenite women crossing the "Red Sea" at the Beth Lid Camp during the heavy rainy season, January, 1950. The camp held 10,000 immigrants.

A malaria fighter in the Emek.

small huts. It also launched a series of public works projects such as road-building, swamp-draining and irrigation in order to keep the able-bodied usefully occupied for themselves and also for the nation. Morale lifted perceptibly.

The Economy

The Government of Israel, as soon as the State was established, found itself facing a dilemma it could not avoid. In order to survive, it had to expand its economy as rapidly as possible and initiate large-scale industrialization. On the other hand, such an expansion depended on an increase in its financial and human resources. But here arose the difficulty—the greater the volume of immigration the more ruinous would become the financial drain and the larger the imports that would be required.

Food was the crucial factor. The agriculture of the country, considering the sharp rise in the population, was not developed enough to make Israel as yet self-sufficient. It was estimated that at first fully 85% of all bread grains and fats, 100% of sugar and 63% of fish had to be imported. In addition, almost all the fuel, wool, cotton, rubber, ores, metals, alloys and industrial equipment had to be brought into the

A student of the Agricultural Institute of the Hebrew University checking egg production on a farm. After the truce in 1949 a count showed 33,000 cattle, 70,000 sheep and goats, 8,000 horses and mules and 2,000 asses in Israel.

country. Naturally, imports far exceeded exports. The result was a disastrous though not unexpected unbalancing of the economy, marked by an inflationary spiral intensified by the inflationary trends generally operating in the world. A black market in currency and goods appeared in Israel, adding to the crisis. The government had no choice but to enter on an "austerity" and self-denial program which caused much hardship and wide discontent.

To aggravate matters, although a military truce had been arranged with the Arab states in 1949, the "cold war" with them went on ceaselessly. The Arab boycott caused dents in the Israeli economy. However, it was the huge Jewish immigration which was the major cause of the economic crisis. For months the majority of newcomers were of little productive usefulness. On the contrary, it required large sums of money to feed, house and take care of them. This resulted in a harmful diversion of finances and skills badly needed for industrialization. The long-range investments in public works, such as forestation, the drainage of swamps and road-building, were mostly for the future.

A typical *Tnuva* center. The *Histadrut*, through its affiliate *Tnuva*, acts as the central cooperative marketing agency for all the labor settlements and for most of the others as well. *Tnuva* operates centers for egg grading, fruit packing and processing, modern dairies and storage plants. At the same time, the *Histadrut* operates *Hamashbir Hamerkazi*, a cooperative purchasing agency which also serves the settlements.

The government, alert to the dangers, did everything possible to attract foreign investors. It induced an inflow of $168,000,000 of new capital into Israel and the establishment of 608 industrial enterprises, a number by leading American firms, from April, 1950, to September, 1951. Most of these ventures were in heavy industry, chemicals, building materials and farm machinery. An additional source of revenue for various industrial enterprises was furnished by the United Israel Appeal (later a part of the United Jewish Appeal) in the United States. Still this did not suffice, and in May, 1951, the

Fishermen of the settlement Maoz Haim on Lake Tiberias.

Government of Israel floated its $500,000,000 Independence Bond Issue in the United States. This money was to make up part of the budget of one and a half billion dollars that the Government of Israel had set itself for the following three-year period to absorb new immigrants and to place the economy on more secure foundations. Nor must it be overlooked that, in addition, Israel had received from the United States

$70,000,000 as a grant-in-aid. Moreover, on February 25, 1951, Israel and the United States signed a Point Four Agreement for technical assistance.

The settlement negotiated between the West German Bonn Government and the Conference on Jewish Material Claims Against Germany resulted in an agreement for the payment of $822,000,000. This represented restitution for the Jewish property that had been taken away by the Nazis. The Bonn government promised to pay this indemnity in goods, over a twelve-year period, to the Israeli government for the cost of settlement of the refugees in Israel.

In connection with the restitution agreement, the proposal, when first broached, caused great controversy and even disorders in the *Yishuv*. The Arab states, too, tried to bring political and trade pressures upon Germany in order to prevent ratification by the Bonn Parliament.

Natural Resources

The great hope of Israel's economy lies in its still untapped natural resources. Despite the assertions of the skeptics, geologists of the Hebrew University are persuaded that there lies a vast mineral wealth hidden deep in the ground. They ultimately expect to find oil in the Negev. The Dead Sea alone, it is claimed, contains a fabulous amount of chemical deposits: potassium chloride (2 billion metric tons), magnesium bromide (980 million tons), sodium chloride (12 billion tons), magnesium chloride (22 billion tons), calcium chloride (6 billion tons). In the Huleh Lake swamp region, which was being drained early in 1953, there are said to be 20 million tons of peat. Other raw materials available are salt, sulphur, bituminous limestone, gypsum, dolomite, manganese, copper, basalt, marble and phosphates.

Balfour Forest, largest forestation project in Israel. Of the total land area of Israel nearly two-thirds is non-arable at the present time due to centuries of neglect and abuse. One of the primary means of preventing further erosion and for reclaiming the waste lands is forestation.

Copper mining in the Negev on the site of King Solomon's mines.

Working in the quarry of the famous Ain Harod settlement, founded in 1921.

Industry

Every month new products of the national industries appear on the Israeli market. A partial listing of products will give an idea of the range of undertakings in the country.

Heavy Industry: Iron foundries, the manufacture of metal piping.

Textiles: Spinning, weaving, finishing, dyeing.

Leather: Tanning, shoe manufacturing, harness and saddle making, handicrafts.

Plastics: Nylon ware, Bakelite.

Chemicals: Pharmaceutical products, paints, dyes, waxes, soaps and cosmetics.

Foods: Milling, canning, preserving, oil pressing, candy-making.

Building Materials: Hardware, cement, concrete blocks, plywood, composition sheeting, glass, ceramics, furniture, tools and sanitary equipment.

The Shemen Oil Factory, the largest producer of soaps and edible oils in the country, in which *Hamashbir Hamerkazi* (Central Wholesale Purchasing Cooperative), an affiliate of *Histadrut*, owns a half interest.

Two Jews and an Arab consult a bulletin board of Consolidated Refineries in Haifa. This Arab is one of 12,000 members who form the Israel Labor League, an Arab affiliate union of *Histadrut*.

The nearly completed Ruttenberg Power Station in Haifa Bay which utilizes the water of the Jordan and the Yarkon Rivers. Most of the electric power in Israel is supplied by the Palestine Electric Corporation which owes its existence to the pioneering vision of Pinchas Ruttenberg, the famous engineer-*chalutz*. The company operates two power houses, one at Haifa and another at Tel-Aviv, both using oil-burning steam turbines.

326

Among the many new industries is that of diamond-cutting and polishing. It is already employing some 2,000 workers in four factories.

A breakdown of the 438,000 workers in Israel in a study made January 1, 1951, shows: agriculture—70,000; building and public works—30,000; industry—90,000; communications —53,000; business and finance—84,000; free professions—36,-000; in government service—75,000.

The "Tournalayer." This is a house-builder on wheels. Israelis call it fondly "the machine that lays a house like an egg." It is brought to any site desired. There concrete is poured into a giant mold for a complete house.

A textile printing plant in Tel-Aviv.

The Cities

Except for Tel-Aviv—which is a new all-Jewish city displaying some of the metropolitan features of Paris, Vienna and New York—in most of the cities of Israel, the Orient and the Occident, the ancient and the contemporary often meet in fantastic incongruity. However, all Israeli cities show unmistakably the impact of a half hundred separate strains of civilization which the Jews from every part of the world brought there with them. Sometimes these cultural contrasts create a bewildering picture of disharmony. At other times, they also reveal the first signs of the national integration that already is in the process of materializing. The new cities of Israel are gradually acquiring an individuality of their own. In their new additions they sometimes represent the most modern trends in city-planning, in styles of architecture and in the civilized amenities of life.

Israeli engineers testing the boiler of a reconditioned locomotive.

The Damascus Gate in Jerusalem.

The Nesher Cement Works in Haifa in which *Histadrut* holds a half interest. This is among the key industries in the country. *Histadrut*, the General Federation of Labor in Israel, has established industries in which it employs some 13,000 of its own union members. In addition, through its central holding company, *Hevrat Haovdim*, it owns stock in various industrial enterprises in conjunction with private industrialists, the Government of Israel and the Jewish Agency. Israeli labor's capitalist enterprises involve the metal industry, building materials, glass, textiles, shoes, chemicals, cement, cosmetics, soap and foodstuffs.

The Kingsway, the commercial center of Haifa. More than 150,-000 Jews lived in the city in 1951. The construction of the fine harbor in Haifa in 1933 made that city the logical center for the concentration of many of the heavy industrial enterprises of the country. In 1935 the city became the terminus for the great pipeline carrying crude oil from Mosul, 354 miles away, a factor in the British Government's great reluctance to surrender the Mandate.

The Jewish quarter of Mea Shefarim in Old Jerusalem. For centuries pious Jews of Europe came to the Holy Land to die and to be buried alongside their forefathers in the vast Jewish grave-yard in the Valley of Jehoshaphat.

Tel-Aviv's beach, on the Mediterranean.

View of modern Jerusalem. Out of a total population of 160,000 inhabiting both Old and New Jerusalem, the latter part of the city, which is new and almost entirely Jewish, counted in 1951 more than 117,000. Built in the progressive spirit of Israel, it has been growing very rapidly. As the capital of the country, it is still the national center of Jewish life although the population and wealth of Tel-Aviv since its merger with Jaffa may be almost three times as great.

Announcing the time of the arrival of the Sabbath.

Diesengoff Square in Tel-Aviv, named after the city's late mayor. Tel-Aviv is the metropolis of Israel, its bustling center for commerce, light industry and culture. A handsome modern city, it counted in 1951 more than 210,000 in its all-Jewish population.

It derives additional importance from the next-door proximity of the Arab city of Jaffa which has a population of some 100,000. Since the mass-flight of Arabs during the war, many Jews have settled in that city, now a part of Tel-Aviv.

A *Kupat Cholim* medical center of *Histadrut*. Fully half of all inhabitants of Israel receive comprehensive medical services from *Kupat Cholim*.

Street scene in modern Israel.

quite a number of doctors, nurses and physical therapists among the refugees from Germany and Austria.

Israel has, including the hospitals of *Hadassah*, forty-nine general hospitals, ten hospitals for lung diseases, twenty-one institutions for the mentally ill, three hospitals for chronic diseases and one hospital for lepers. These figures do not include the network of Israeli Army hospitals nor the hospitals of *Malben*, the health system operated by the American Joint Distribution Committee for the rehabilitation of the handicapped, the aged and the sick among the new immigrants.

Henrietta Szold, at 82, addressing the graduating class of the Henrietta Szold School of Nursing in Jerusalem.

Health

One of the unusual features of Jewish life in Israel is the preoccupation of both the government and the organizations in the *Yishuv* with the health of the population. Prevention of disease, along the most progressive public health lines, is given equal importance with medical therapy. There were

Courtyard at the Hadassah University Hospital on Mount Scopus in Jerusalem. Ground was broken in 1953 for a large new medical center to be situated on the University's new campus at Ein Karem, 10 miles outside Jerusalem.

The American Zionist Medical Unit of Hadassah in Jerusalem in 1918. The first medical and health service in the *Yishuv* was established by *Hadassah*, the American Women's Zionist Organization. During World War I, it sent a contingent of American Jewish doctors and nurses to Palestine. Not only in its hospitals in Jerusalem and elsewhere but also in its clinics and visiting nurse service throughout the country, it gave free treatment to thousands of poor Jews, Arabs and Christians. It also fought a determined battle to control malaria and trachoma by means of sanitary engineering aided by much research.

CULTURE

The Arts

A *bet tarbut* (house of culture) seems to be almost as indispensable in each Israeli settlements as its water-tower or powerhouse. Among large sections of the Israeli population, especially among the *chalutzim* in the settlements and among the student youth, the cultivation of the arts and sciences is an essential element of life.

The attitude of the *Yishuv* as a whole toward the development of a new form of Jewish civilization in Israel, with its roots in the old heritage, was incorporated in the Four-Year Plan the *Knesset* (Parliament) drew up in 1949. The Ministry for Education was instructed to provide "the assurance of a high cultural standard for every man and woman in Israel." One of its many tasks was to be "the encouragement of literary, scientific and artistic activity. . . ."

This preoccupation with culture must be considered as merely a part of the dynamic upsurge of Jewish national life. Out of the complex of the many ethnic groups and their diverse strains of cultures present in Israel today, there are evolving specific new forms of Jewish civilization. Israel's cultural influence, too, is radiating outward into all Jewish communities throughout the world. It may be said to be acting as a catalyst binding them closer together.

Art

Artists of every country, school and manner have settled in Israel where they are sinking their creative roots in the new Jewish life evolving there. The works they are producing, except in the employment of local scene or theme, reveal as yet no characteristics of a national art. Generally, the art trends today are universal. Like French or American artists, the artists of Israel, too, follow in this direction. Styles vary from the academic to the surrealist.

Art exhibition in Israel.

There are art museums and galleries in Tel-Aviv, Jerusalem, Haifa and Safed. Traveling exhibits rotate among all the settlements and are shown in each local *bet tarbut* (house of culture). A number of art schools, the oldest of which is Bezalel

The synagogue in the old settlement of Hedera (Gedera). In a country still as young as Israel, a daring new style of architecture is bound to be accepted with less esthetic controversy then it would meet with elsewhere.

Art School in Jerusalem, are training a new generation of artists for Israel.

Best known among contemporary painters and sculptors in Israel are: Reuben Rubin, Mordecai Morkady, Nahum Guttman, Joseph Zaritsky, Chaim Glicksberg, Miron Sima, Moshe Castel, David Hendler, Marcel Janco, Mordecai Ardon-Bronstein, Shimshon Holzman and the lately deceased sculptor Zeev Ben-Zvi.

Music

The influx of a large number of musicians, quite a few distinguished concert artists, orchestral conductors, instrumentalists and teachers, has accelerated the development of musical audiences and tastes in Israel. Amateur symphony orchestras and chamber music ensembles have been formed everywhere, some even in the most remote farm settlements.

Composers of talent have been coming forward constantly during the last twenty-five years: Paul Ben-Haim, Odeon Partos, Eric Walter Sternberg, Joseph Kaminski, M. Mahler Kalkstein, Alexander Uriah Boskovich, Yitzchak Edel, Marc Lavry, Verdina Shlonsky, Frank Pelleg and Ben Zion Orgad.

But the supreme expression of Israel's musical life is the Israel Philharmonic Orchestra which was founded in 1936 by the late Bronislaw Hubermann, the eminent violinist. A number of the world's distinguished conductors and artists have performed with it.

Arturo Toscanini conducting the Israel Philharmonic Orchestra at its debut in 1936.

Musicale after work in one of the settlements. The high level of culture in Israel is nowhere better illustrated than in the farming settlements. Intelligent, educated and under the continuing spell of the Jewish tradition of learning, many of the young settlers have created around themselves a daily existence which is rich in cultural values.

The Opera House in Tel-Aviv. It presents operatic productions from both classical and modern repertories.

A children's theatre in the old *Kibbutz* of Degania. The elders sometimes outnumber the children at the performances.

The Theatre

Israelis are enthusiastic theatre-goers. Their sophisticated taste calls for literary plays of substance. There are three Hebrew-language theatres which respond to this demand. The most important of them is the *Habimah*, which although founded in Moscow after the revolution, transferred its activities to Tel-Aviv in 1927. It has a classical-literary repertory and a company of distinguished actors. The Labor Theatre's Dramatic Studio, *Ohel*, has devoted itself largely to the production of plays with Biblical themes. The most recent drama institution is the Chamber Theatre *Matate* (the Broom). Its forte is the light satirical play.

Dancing the *hora*, the most popular of all the national Israeli folk-dances. Its great vogue is due as much to its uninvolved dance movements and its community character as it is to its infectious liveliness.

Habimah Theatre, Tel-Aviv.

Ballet dancers with the Israel Philharmonic Orchestra, performing in the open-air theatre of the Hebrew University. In the distance stretch the Desert of Judea, the Dead Sea, and the Hills of Moab.

The famous actress Rovina in *Habimah's* production of *Oedipus Rex*.

Rachel Nadav, a Yemenite, one of the foremost Israeli dancers, in her composition, "Going to the Well."

The Dance

An extraordinary development in the cultural life of Israel today is the emergence of the dance in all its forms—ballet, esthetic and folk—as a popular art-expression and a means of group entertainment. In an atmosphere charged with a resurgent national consciousness, the folk-dance, the folk-song and the folk-story have claimed the affections of the Israelis.

All the arts in Palestine draw heavily from folk-art forms and idioms. Folk-dancing is a national passion and pastime. Everybody who is young dances, in groups—an unconscious yearning for group solidarity. The dances are all derivative: principally Hasidic, Yemenite, Russian and Arab. The most popular dance is the *hora* which is danced from Dan to Elath.

331

Once a year there is even a great folk-dance festival in the "Dance Village" of Dalia in the Hills of Ephraim where some 100,000 folk-dance enthusiasts converge in trains, buses, cars, wagons and on muleback.

Literature

The new Hebrew literature, its roots sunk in its national habitat, is still too young to be assessed. Already there are found hundreds of professional writers of every description who aim to interpret in their works the character and aspirations of the new Jewish life in Israel. Notwithstanding its poverty, the *Yishuv* has witnessed a Hebrew cultural renaissance and is experiencing an unappeased appetite for Hebrew books and periodicals. Despite the labor and paper shortage, the presses have been running off as many as 750 titles a year. Most popular are works of fiction and literary anthologies. Oddly enough, books of verse often sell very well. Published, also, are a considerable number of technical and reference works, textbooks, encyclopedias and translations of foreign works.

Among the most admired Hebrew writers living in Israel today are: Yaacov Kahn, Y. D. Berkowitch, Yehudah Burla, S. J. Agnon, Joseph Klausner, Moshe Smilansky, Avigdor Hameiri, Isaac Shenberg, Chaim Hazaz, Uri Zvi Greenberg, Yitzchak Lamdan, Sh. Shalom, Abraham Shlonsky, Yaacov Fichman, David Shimonovitch, Asher Barash, Eliezer Steinman, Nathan Alterman, Leah Goldberg and Rachel.

The Press

The diversity of tongues in Israel, despite the fact that in time everybody learns to speak Hebrew, has resulted in a profusion of newspapers and periodicals. There are sixteen morning and three afternoon daily newspapers, twelve in Hebrew and seven in other languages. In addition, there are sixty weeklies and bi-weeklies and ninety monthly and quarterly periodicals.

The leading newspapers are *Davar*, published by *Histadrut; Doar Hayom,* the organ of the agricultural settlements; and the independent English-language *Palestine Post.*

The Hebrew labor newspaper, *Davar,* rolling off its high-speed press.

Education

The educational needs and problems of the population of Israel are as complicated as the variegated segments that compose it. Considering the presence in large numbers of culturally undeveloped Jewish ethnic groups, especially those from Iraq, Yemen, Iran and North Africa, what is required perhaps is as much re-education as education. This has to start from the ground up, for thousands among the newcomers are illiterate.

In striking contrast to them are the Europeans. The patterns of culture which they brought with them into Israel are generally of a high order. Moreover, the Zionist movement, ever since the Lovers of Zion came as pioneers to Palestine in 1881, developed its own traditions of learning and culture. Various intellectual streams thus met and mingled and brought to fruition the diverse educational values and institutions of present-day Israel.

Hebrew University

The most important institution of higher education in Israel is the Hebrew University in Jerusalem. As long ago as 1882 the mathematician, Professor Hermann Schapira, the father of the Jewish National Fund, proposed such a university. A Zionist leader of a later generation, also a noted scientist, Dr. Chaim Weizmann, became the real creator of this university.

Lord Balfour delivering the principal address at the opening of the Hebrew University on Mount Scopus in Jerusalem on April 1, 1925. (Seated around the table, left to right): Chaim Nachman Bialik, foremost Hebrew poet; Achad Ha'Am, famed exponent of "Cultural Zionism"; *Sephardic* Chief-Rabbi Uzziel; *Ashkenazic* Chief-Rabbi Kook; Lord Plumer, the British High Commissioner; Sir Herbert Samuel, his predecessor as the first High Commissioner of Palestine; and Dr. Chaim Weizmann.

When the institution opened on April 1, 1925, its first Chancellor was Dr. Judah L. Magnes, the New York Reform rabbi, but it had only a small faculty and student body. In 1951, under the Chancellorship of Dr. Selig Brodestky, it had 1,862 students and a faculty of 290, many of them internationally prominent scholars and scientists. Besides its faculties of Humanities and Science, the university also had a school of Medicine, a Law School and an Agricultural College. Its library holds the largest collection of Hebraica and Judaica in the world.

Weizmann Institute

As a distinguished research chemist, Dr. Chaim Weizmann realized quite early that the meager natural resources of Palestine would have to be compensated for by intensive scientific

Three students (the boy on the right is a Druze) chatting between classes at the Hebrew University in Jerusalem. The university, where instruction is carried on in Hebrew, is open to students of all faiths and races and encourages fraternization.

A class of English army doctors at the university. The civilian in the right foreground was then the chancellor of the university, the late Dr. Judah L. Magnes. During World War II the Medical School of the Hebrew University gave special courses in tropical medicine, war-surgery and camp-sanitation to British army doctors stationed with units in the Middle East.

research linked with the practical requirements of industry. In 1933 Dr. Weizmann's long-cherished dream for a scientific research institute materialized when the Zieff Institute, later the Weizmann Institute, was opened at Rehoboth. With the aid of sixty scientists, the majority of them chemists, Dr. Weizmann launched an important study of the processes of fermentation. The institute has a Department of Isotope Research and also a Department of Applied Mathematics. Its researches in pure science have been quite spectacular. After the war with the Arabs it greatly expanded its program. It has become one of the most important research institutions of its kind in the world.

Using an electronic microscope at the Weizmann Institute in Rehoboth.

Technion

The principal technical institution in Israel is *Technion* (Hebrew Technical College) in Haifa. Founded in 1912 as a technical high school, it expanded and included a higher institution in 1924. The college today has four departments: Civil Engineering, Industrial (i.e., Mechanical and Electrical) Engineering, the Weizmann Institute of Chemical Engineering, and the School of Architecture.

The *Technion* in Haifa.

The S. S. *Har Zion* (Mount Zion) and its Jewish skipper. One of the first ships to fly the Jewish national flag, it was sunk by a Nazi submarine in the Battle of the Atlantic. A merchant marine with seafaring personnel is being developed in Israel. A nautical school was first established at the *Technion* in Haifa in 1938 by the Maritime Department of the Jewish Agency in conjunction with the Israel Maritime League. It teaches marine engineering and is preparing its students both for the merchant marine and for the small Israeli Navy.

Hebrew for "Foreigners"

Adult education finds much support in Israel. A unique adult education institution is Beth Berl. The various organizations in the *Yishuv* operate their own adult education programs, including courses in every trade and calling and in the field of general culture. But one of the most urgent adult studies for the new arrivals is a working knowledge of Hebrew. The Jewish Agency itself opened thirty-four language-boarding schools called *Ulpanim* in which intensive four-to six-month courses in Hebrew are given. The *Histadrut* adult education center in Tel-Aviv also gives courses in the Hebrew language.

Elementary Schools

Before the State was established, the schools of Israel were largely under the partisan supervision of three political groups: the *Histadrut,* the Orthodox religious organizations, and the General Zionist schools. This pattern has continued to this day but under government over-all supervision and control. In 1951 the elementary schools that had been established by *Histadrut* were attended by 43% of all school children in the country. The point of view of their education was secular but Jewish national in content.

The *Mizrachi*, with 18%, had a religious educational coloration. The General Zionist schools, with 28%, emphasized a liberal education in conjunction with Jewish culture. Another

7% was controlled by *Agudat Israel*, which had an ultra-Orthodox orientation. In addition, there were a number of independent schools of all kinds. When the Government of Israel passed its compulsory education law for all children of elementary school age, it also affected Arab children. In 1951 there were 27,000 Arab children attending elementary schools established by the government. The increase in school attendance in Israel was spectacular: in 1948 the enrollment was 96,000; in 1951 it soared to 310,000.

An *Ulpan* boarding school at Nahariya for teaching Hebrew to immigrants in concentrated study of 12-14 hours daily. The *Ulpanim* are run by the Jewish Agency.

Children of 14 nationalities, but of one people, at the Bessie Gotsfeld Children's Village and Farm School in Raanana. This village is supported by the *Mizrachi* Women's Organization of America, a religious-Zionist group. The children came from the following countries: last row, left to right, Greece, Germany, Romania, Czechoslovakia, Yemen and Syria. Middle row, left to right, Algiers, Morocco, Holland and Iraq. Front row, Hungary, Yugoslavia, Belgium and Italy.

Children planting seedlings on *Chamishah Asar Bishvat* (the Jewish "Arbor Day"). The planting of trees—a symbol of life and its eternal renewal—is an act of national necessity in the urgent forestation program of Israel.

"Tomorrow's a wonderful day!" Its children are Israel's most valuable natural resource.

Funeral of President Chaim Weizmann, November 11, 1952.

Inauguration of Yitzhak Ben-Zvi as second president of Israel on December 10, 1952.

CONTINUITY

From the primeval days of the Patriarch Abraham, "the first Hebrew," to the Jewish child born today in an Israeli settlement or in a Brooklyn tenement, winds the course of Jewish history, labyrinthine, baffling in its complexities. Yet through all of it is traceable a continuity which, through ceaseless tribulation and adversity, has remained unbroken for at least four millenniums. Whatever the biologic variations, geographic dispersions, cultural fusions and religious differences the Jews of the world reveal today, nonetheless, they present a cohesiveness—*as a people*. This is an historic phenomenon perhaps without parallel.

How is one to explain this miracle of survival in Jewish identity?

The life of a people is much like that of an individual: its span of duration is unpredictable and is determined by a variety of internal and external factors. Why it is that one people survives the chemism of change and the buffetings of experience and another succumbs to them poses a difficult question to the student of history. The dynamics that rule the life and death of peoples are still largely unknown. At best one may only speculate about them, but tentatively, cautiously, lest one fall into the error of dogmatism.

To be sure, the Egyptians under the Pharaohs were a more numerous people than the Jews. They constituted a world power of great magnitude and influence. They could claim a culture which, in more than one way, was superior to that of the Jews. Yet their identity as a people was washed away by the tides of change and their unique culture absorbed into the collective anonymity of the civilization of mankind.

For centuries the great empires of the Assyrians and the Babylonians held the destiny of the Jews in their hands. Their material civilization was much superior to that of the Jews, yet they, too, passed the zenith of their power and influence and fell into the dust-bin of history.

Incomparable in their intellectual, artistic and scientific development were the ancient Greeks. Yet Hellas and its Golden Age vanished, with only its broken relics left to be enshrined in the classic museum of memory, although its cultural heritage entered into the bloodstream of Western civilization.

Was there an ancient people so aggressive, efficient and capable as the Romans? Their emperors, generals, legislators, engineers and architects were certain they were building their empire and their unique civilization to endure for all time. But *sic transit gloria mundi*—they, too, disappeared into limbo and their cultural estate, finding no lineal heir, was passed down to posterity at large.

But take the Jews—a people who were always insignificant in numbers. When they had a country, it was small and poor, serving as a vassal to more powerful neighbors and as a prey for its own rulers. When they became homeless wanderers, they were always at the mercy of the cruel, the rapacious or the unthinking. It is doubtful whether at any time there existed a people who were more tormented, more intolerably exposed to the vicissitudes and vengeance of a world that spurned them. Yet the Jews survived! How did that happen? By what inner strength and through what good fortune?

Good fortune the Jews rarely had, nor were they often the recipient of the benevolence of mankind. But they found the inner strength to endure. Their will to live, their *élan vital* as a people, surged powerfully within them. It had a spiritual, a moral propulsion, which is why, although persecuted and massacred, they managed to outlive their enemies who sat in the sun.

There were undoubtedly many factors which for thousands of years contributed to their stubborn refusal to die as a people. Perhaps the most powerful preserver of the Jewish identity was the Jewish religion. In theory and practice, in study and devotion, it represented at its best a synthesis of every group drive, social ideal and cultural striving of the Jewish people. It had the character of an all-comprehensive loyalty and consecration. The Jews considered themselves "a nation of priests." Their religion embraced both fear and love of God. It elevated righteousness as the greatest good and love of man as being synonymous with the love of God. It also engendered a fervent attachment to the land of Zion, stimulated among Jews a consciousness and patriotic devotion to "peoplehood" rarely or perhaps never quite equaled among the ancients. To die *al-kiddush ha-shem*, to sanctify the Name of God as a martyr, a tradition adopted by the early Jewish Christians, became a national Jewish ideal. It was considered as valid when suffered in defense of the Jewish community and people as of the Jewish religion. How powerfully felt these religious-patriotic sentiments were may be read in the accounts of the revolts of the Maccabees and of Bar-Kochba and of the siege of Jerusalem by the Romans. It may also be found in the martyrologies of the Jews of the Middle Ages in Europe and, although in modern secular settings, its ancient overtones may be clearly heard in the chronicles of the Battle of the Warsaw Ghetto and of the war of the Jews of the new State of Israel against the Arab invaders.

Another important factor in the preservation of the Jewish people was their wide scattering throughout the world. Already in the days of Roman rule over the Jews we find a *Talmudic* sage observing with grim satisfaction that, providentially, the Jews had been dispersed in many far-flung countries, so that if destroyed in one place they managed to survive in others. Consequently, he concluded, the cruel Romans were powerless to annihilate the Jewish people. Life and history, as demonstrated by the failure of the monstrous genocide plan of Hitler and the Nazis, has borne out the truth of this assertion.

Paradoxical as it may sound at first, it was the enemies of the Jews who had a large share in the preservation of the Jewish identity. The more they tried to force them to abandon their religion, the more fiercely the Jews embraced it; the more ruthless their methods of coercion, the more stubbornly the Jews resisted them and the more convinced they were that the Jewish religion was the superior religion morally and ethically. The more relentless their enemies' hatred and persecution, the closer the Jews clung to one another, the more compelling their need for group solidarity. By keeping the Jews isolated in the medieval ghetto and in the *mellahs* of North Africa, the oppressors of the Jews, Christians and Mohammedans alike, helped to preserve their traditional group-life and at the same time effectively insulated them against assimilationist influences and the temptations of conversion and biologic fusion.

This pictorial history of the Jewish people is a record of their struggle for survival and of their triumphant continuity.

SELECTED ENGLISH BIBLIOGRAPHY

General Reference

Apocrypha and Pseudoepigrapha of the Old Testament, ed. R. H. Charles and others. Oxford, 1913.

Baron, Salo W., *Social and Religious History of the Jews*. Revised and new edition. 2 vols., New York, 1952.

Bevan, E. R., and Charles Singer (eds.), *Legacy of Israel*. Oxford, 1927.

Daily Prayer Book: With Commentary, Introductions and Notes. ed. Joseph H. Hertz. New York, 1948.

Encyclopedia of Jewish Knowledge, ed. Jacob De Haas. New York, 1938.

Finkelstein, Louis (ed.), *The Jewish People: Past and Present*. 4 vols., New York, 1946.

Frisch, Ephraim, *An Historical Survey of Jewish Philanthropy*. New York, 1924.

Graetz, Heinrich, *History of the Jews*. 5 vols., Philadelphia, 1891-92.

Grayzel, Solomon, *A History of the Jews*. Philadelphia, 1947.

Holy Scriptures, The. The Jewish Publication Society translation. Philadelphia, 1917.

Jacobs, Joseph, *Jewish Contributions to Civilization*. Philadelphia, 1919.

Jewish Encyclopedia. 12 vols., New York, 1901-06.

Josephus, *Jewish Antiquities*, v. 4-7, Loeb Classical Library. London, 1926-43.

Learsi, Rufus, *Israel: A History of the Jewish People*. Cleveland, 1949.

Margolis, M., and Marx, A., *A History of the Jews*. Philadelphia, 1927.

Osterly, W. O. E., and T. H. Robinson, *History of Israel*. 2 vols., Oxford, 1932.

Roth, Cecil, *The Jewish Contribution to Civilization*. Cincinnati, 1940.

Roth, Cecil, *A Short History of the Jewish People*. London, 1948.

Sachar, Abram L., *A History of the Jews*. Revised edition. New York, 1953.

Universal Jewish Encyclopedia. 10 vols., New York, 1939-43.

Waxman, Meyer, *A History of Jewish Literature from the Close of the Bible to Our Own Days*. 4 vols., New York, 1930-41.

Who Are the Jews?

Birnbaum, Salomo, "Jewish Languages" [In *Essays in Honor of the Very Rev. Dr. J. H. Hertz*. London, 1943].

Boas, Franz, "Are the Jews a Race?", in *World Tomorrow*, v. 6, no. 1 (1923).

Coon, Carleton S., *The Races of Europe*. New York, 1939.

Fishberg, Maurice, *The Jews: A Study of Race and Environment*. New York, 1911.

Huxley, J. S., and A. C. Hadden, *We Europeans*. London, 1935.

Klineberg, Otto, *Race Differences*. New York, 1935.

Radin, Paul, *The Racial Myth*. New York, 1934.

Tenenbaum, Joseph, *Races, Nations and Jews*. New York, 1934.

Zeitlin, Solomon, *The Jews: Race, Nation, or Religion?* Philadelphia, 1936.

Biblical and Post-Biblical Jewish Life

Ginzerg, Eli, *Studies in the Economics of the Bible; slavery, the Sabbatical year and the Jubilee Year*. Philadelphia, 1932.

Pedersen, Johannes, *Israel, Its Life and Culture*. London, 1926.

Radin, Max, *The Life of the People in Biblical Times*. Philadelphia, 1929.

Wallis, Louis, *Sociological Study of the Bible*. Chicago, 1927.

Archaeology and the Bible

Albright, W. F., *Archaeology of Palestine and the Bible*. New York, 1932.

Albright, W. F., *Archaeology and the Religion of Israel*. Baltimore, 1942.

Biblical Archaeologist (quarterly). Published by the American Schools of Oriental Research. New Haven, 1938.

Finegan, Jack, *Light from the Ancient Past, the archaeological background of the Hebrew-Christian religion*. Princeton, 1946.

Garstang, John, *The Foundations of Bible History: Joshua–Judges*. New York, 1931.

Gaster, Theodor H., *Thespis; ritual, myth and drama in the ancient Near East*. New York, 1950.

Meek, T. J., *Hebrew Origins*. New York, 1936.

Petrie, W. M. Flinders, *Egypt and Israel*. London, 1911.

Radin, Paul, *Monotheism Among Primitive Peoples*. London, 1924.

Wright, G. E., and F. V. Filson, *Atlas to the Bible*. The Westminster Press, 1945.

Historic Judaism

Abrahams, Israel, "Jewish Interpretation of the Old Testament" [In *The People and the Book*, Arthur S. Peake (ed.). Oxford, 1925].

Bamberger, B. J., *Proselytism in the Talmudic Period*. Cincinnati, 1939.

Finkelstein, Louis, *The Pharisees*. Philadelphia, 1940.

Ginzberg, Louis, *Religion of the Jews at the Time of Jesus*. [In *Hebrew Union College Annual*, v. 1 (Cincinnati, 1924)].

Herford, R. Travers, *The Pharisees*. New York, 1924.

Kohler, Kaufmann, *Jewish Theology Historically and Systematically Considered*. New York, 1918.

Maimonides, Moses, *Guide for the Perplexed*. New York, 1946.

Mendelssohn, Moses, *Jerusalem: a Treatise on Ecclesiastical Authority and Judaism*. 2 vols., London, 1838.

Moore, George Foote, *The Literature of the Old Testament*. New York, 1913.

Moore, George Foote, *Judaism in the First Centuries of the Christian Era*. 2 vols., Cambridge, Mass., 1927.

Schechter, Solomon, *Studies in Judaism*. Three Series. Philadelphia, 1908-24.

Weber, Max, *Ancient Judaism*. Glencoe, Ill., 1952.

Welch, A. C., *Post-Exilic Judaism*. Edinburgh, 1934.

Wolfson, Harry A., *Philo: Foundations of Religious Philosophy, Judaism, Christianity and Islam*. 2 vols., Cambridge, Mass., 1947.

Literature of the *Talmud*

Ausubel, Nathan, *A Treasury of Jewish Folklore*. New York, 1948.

Cohen, A., *Everyman's Talmud*. London, 1934.

Danby, Herbert, *The Mishnah*. Oxford, 1933.

Gaster, Moses, *Agada: the Exempla of the Rabbis*. London, 1924.

Ginzberg, Louis, *Legends of the Jews*. 7 vols., New York, 1913-38.

Ginzberg, Louis, *Students, Scholars and Saints*. Philadelphia, 1928.

Montefiore, Claude G., and H. Loewe, *A Rabbinic Anthology*. London, 1938.

Newman, Louis, and Samuel Spitz, *The Talmudic Anthology*. New York, 1945.

Pirke Aboth (The Sayings of the Jewish Fathers). W. O. E. Oesterley (translator). London, 1919.

Strack, Hermann, *Introduction to Talmud and Midrash*. Philadelphia, 1945.

Ancient Jewish Art and Music

Leveen, Jacob, *The Hebrew Bible in Art*. London, 1944.

Osterley, W. O. E., "Music of the Hebrews" [In *The Oxford History of Music*, v. 7]. Oxford, 1929.

Preliminary Report on the Synagogue at Dura-Europos. New Haven, 1936.

Reifenberg, A., *Ancient Hebrew Arts*. New York, 1950.

Reifenberg, A., *Ancient Hebrew Seals*. London, 1950.

Rosenau, Helen, *The Architectural Development of the Synagogue*. Published by Courtauld Institute of Art, University of London.

Rostovtzev, M. I., *Dura-Europos and Its Art*. Oxford, 1938.

Sachs, Curt, *The Rise of Music in the Ancient World, East and West*. New York, 1943.

Saminsky, Lazare, *Music of the Ghetto and the Bible*. New York, 1934.

Sukenik, E. L., *Ancient Synagogues in Palestine and Greece*. Linden, 1934.

Sukenik, E. L., *The Ancient Synagogue of Beth Alpha*. London, 1932.

Hellenistic [Graeco-Roman] Age

Bickerman, E., *The Maccabees*. New York, 1947.

Cohen, Boaz, "Civil Bondage in Jewish and Roman Law" [In *Louis Ginzberg Jubilee Volume*. New York, 1945].

Gordis, Robert, *Social Background of Wisdom Literature* [In *Hebrew Union College Annual*, v. 18]. Cincinnati, 1943-44.

Gressman, H., "Jewish Life in Ancient Rome," in *Jewish Studies in Memory of Israel Abrahams*. New York, 1927.

Josephus: *Wars of the Jews* [In, Josephus, Flavius: *Collected Works*. H. St. J. Thackeray (tr.). Loeb Classical Library, v. 1. London, 1926-43].

Josephus: *Wars of the Jews*. [In, Josephus, Flavius: *Collected Works*. H. St. J. Thackeray (tr.). Loeb Classical Library. vs. 2 and 3. London, 1926-43].

Lieberman, S., *Hellenism in Jewish Palestine*. New York, 1950.

Mazur, B. D., *Studies of Jewry in Greece*. Athens, 1935.

Mommsen, Theodor, *The Provinces of the Roman Empire, from Caesar to Diocletian*. London, 1909.

Rostovtzev, M. I., *The Social and Economic History of the Hellenistic world*. 3 vols., Oxford, 1941.

Jewish Influences on Christianity

Eisler, Robert, *The Messiah Jesus and John the Baptist*. New York, 1931.

Friedländer, Gerald, *Jewish Sources of the Sermon on the Mount*. London, 1911.

Jacobs, Joseph, *Jesus as Others Saw Him; a retrospect, A.D. 54*. New York, 1925.

Kautsky, Karl, *Foundations of Christianity*. New York, 1925.

Klausner, Joseph, *Jesus of Nazareth*. New York, 1926.

Kohler, Kaufmann, *Origins of the Synagogue and the Church*. New York, 1929.

Loewe, H. M. J. (ed.), *Judaism and Christianity*. 2 vols., London, 1937.

Montefiore, Claude J. G., *Rabbinic Literature and Gospel Teachings*. London, 1930.

Montefiore, Claude J. G. (ed.), *The Synoptic Gospels*. 2 vols., London, 1927.

Oesterley, W. O. E., *The Gospel Parables in the Light of Their Jewish Background*. New York, 1936.

Oesterley, W. O. E., *Jewish Background of the Christian Liturgy*. Oxford, 1925.

Oesterley, W. O. E., *Jews and Judaism during the Greek Period: the background of Christianity*. New York, 1941.

Pfleiderer, Otto, *Christian Origins*. New York, 1906.

Radin, Max, *The Trial of Jesus of Nazareth* (juridical). Chicago, 1931.

Zeitlin, Solomon, *Who Crucified Jesus?* New York, 1942.

Jewish Life in the Middle Ages

General Reference

Gaster, Moses, *Hebrew Illuminated Bibles of the 9th and 10th centuries*. London, 1901.

Gaster, Moses, *The Ketubah; a chapter from the history of the Jewish people*. Berlin, 1923.

Glatzer, Nahum (ed.), *In Time and Eternity: A Jewish Reader*. New York,

Husik, I., *History of Medieval Jewish Philosophy*. New York, 1916.

Kauffmann, David, "Art in the Synagogue" [In *Jewish Review*, v. IX].

Landsberger, Franz, *History of Jewish Art*. Cincinnati, 1946.

Lane-Poole, Stanley, *History of Egypt in the Middle Ages*. London, 1914.

Lowenthal, Marvin, *A World Passed By*. Philadelphia, 1933.

Marcus, Jacob R., *The Jew in the Medieval World: A Source-Book (315-1791)*. Cincinnati, 1938.

Millgram, A. E. (ed.), *Anthology of Medieval Hebrew Literature*. Philadelphia, 1935.

Rabinowitz, L., *Jewish Merchant Adventurers. A Study of the Radanites*. London, 1948.

Rosenau, W., *Jewish Biblical Commentators*. Baltimore, 1906.

Schwarz, Leo W., *Memoirs of My People*. New York, 1943.

Starr, Joshua, *The Jews in the Byzantine Empire, (641-1204 C.E.)*. Athens, 1939.

Wischnitzer-Bernstein, Rahel, "Documents of Jewish Art" [In *Jewish Quarterly Review*, 1935].

The Medieval Jewish Community

Abrahams, Israels, *Jewish Life in the Middle Ages*. Philadelphia, 1896.

Baron, Salo W., *The Jewish Community, its history and structure to the American Revolution*. Philadelphia, 1942.

Finkelstein, Louis, *Jewish Self-Government in the Middle Ages*. New York, 1924.

Frisch, Ephraim, *An Historical Survey of Jewish Philanthropy, from the earliest times to the 19th century*. New York, 1924.

Kohler, Kaufmann, *The Historical Development of Jewish Charity*. Chicago, 1903.

Philipson, David, *Old European Jewries*. Philadelphia, 1894.

Shohet, D. M., *The Jewish Court in the Middle Ages*. New York, 1931.

Church and Synagogue

Grayzel, Solomon, *The Church and the Jews in the 13th Century*. Philadelphia, 1933.

Parkes, J. W., *The Jews in the Medieval Community*. London, 1938.

Ritual Murder Libel and the Jew. The report by Cardinal Lorenzo Ganganelli (Pope Clement XIV). Cecil Roth (ed.). London, 1934.

Williams, A. L., *Adversus Judaeos, A Bird's-Eye View of Christian Apologiae until the Renaissance*. Cambridge, England, 1935.

Zunz, Leopold, *The Suffering of the Jews during the Middle Ages*. New York, 1907.

Judaism and Islam

Arnold, Thomas, and Alfred Guillaume, *The Legacy of Islam*. Oxford, 1931.

Fischel, W. J., *Jews in the Economic and Political Life of Medieval Islam*. London, 1937.

Italy

Amram, D. W., *The Makers of Hebrew Books in Italy*. Philadelphia, 1909.

Baron, Salo W., "Azariah de Rossi's Attitude to Life." [In *Jewish Studies in Memory of Israel Abrahams*]. New York, 1927.

Roth, Cecil, *The History of the Jews of Italy*. Philadelphia, 1946.

Vogelstein, Hermann, *Rome*. Philadelphia, 1940.

Babylonia and Spain

Essays on Maimonides, an octocentennial volume. Salo W. Baron (ed.). New York, 1941.

Husik, Isaac, "Studies in Gersonides" [In *Jewish Quarterly Review*. Philadelphia, 1917-18].

Katz, Solomon, *The Jews in the Visigothic and Frankish Kingdoms of Spain and Gaul*. Cambridge, Mass., 1937.

Malter, Henry, *Saadia Gaon, his life and works*. Philadelphia, 1921.

Neuman, Abraham A., *The Jews in Spain*. 2 vols., Philadelphia, 1942.

Saadia (Gaon) Studies. Published by the *Jewish Quarterly Review* in Commemoration of the One Thousandth anniversary of the death of Saadia Gaon. Edited by Abraham A. Neuman and Solomon Zeitlin. Philadelphia, 1943.

Yellin, D., and I. Abrahams, *Maimonides*. Philadelphia, 1946.

The Inquisition—Marranos

Adler, E., *Auto-da-fé and Jew*. Oxford, 1908.

Lea, Henry Charles, *A History of the Inquisition in Spain*. New York, 1906.

Roth, Cecil, *A History of the Marranos*. Philadelphia, 1932.

Roth, Cecil, *The Spanish Inquisition*. London, 1937.

Amsterdam Ghetto

Bloom, Herbert I., *The Economic Activities of the Jews of Amsterdam in the 17th and 18th Centuries*. Williamsport, 1937.

Wolfson, Harry A., *Philosophy of Spinoza*. 2 vols., Cambridge, Mass., 1934.

England

Friedman, Lee M., *Robert Grosseteste and the Jews*. Cambridge, Mass., 1934.

Goodman, Paul, *Bevis Marks in History*. London, 1934.

Jacobs, Joseph, *The Jews of Angevin England*. London, 1893.

Roth, Cecil, *History of the Jews in England*. Oxford, 1941.

Starrs and Jewish Charters Preserved in the British Museum. Israel Abrahams, Rev. Canon H. P. Stokes and Herbert Loewe, (editors). 3 vols., Cambridge, England, 1930-32.

Wolf, Lucien, *Menasseh ben Israel's Mission to Oliver Cromwell*. London, 1901.

Germany and Austria

Grunwald, M., *Vienna*. Philadelphia, 1936.

Kisch, Guido, "The Jewry Law of the *Sachsenspiegel*" [In *Occident and Orient,* studies in honor of *Haham* Dr. M. Gaster's 80th birthday. London, 1936].

Kisch, Guido, *The Jews in Medieval Germany*. A Study of their Legal and Social Status. Chicago, 1949.

Liber, Maurice, *Rashi*. Philadelphia, 1906.

Lowenthal, Marvin, *The Jews of Germany*. A Story of Sixteen Centuries. Philadelphia, 1936.

Ma'aseh Buch; book of Jewish tales and legends. 2 v. Philadelphia, 1924.

Memoirs of Glückel of Hameln. Marvin Loewenthal (translator). New York, 1932.

Prague

The Old Jewish Cemetery of Prague. Published by the Jewish Museum of Prague, 1947.

Volavkova, Hana, *The Synagogue Treasures of Bohemia and Moravia*. Prague, 1949.

Russia and Poland

Aronson, Chill, "Wooden Synagogues of Poland" [In *Menorah Journal*. New York, 1937].

Dubnow, Simon, *History of the Jews in Russia and Poland*. 3 vols., Philadelphia, 1916-20.

Loukomski, G. K., *Jewish Art in European Synagogues*. London, 1947.

Slousch, Nahum, "The Origin of the East European Jews" [In *Menorah Journal,* New York, Oct., 1923].

Wooden Synagogues in Poland. Illustrated catalogue, Tel-Aviv Museum. 1941.

Jews in Medieval Science

Friedenwald, Harry, *The Jews in Medicine*. 2 vols., Baltimore, 1944.

Gandz, Solomon, *Studies in Hebrew Mathematics and Astronomy* [in *Proceedings of the American Academy for Jewish Research,* v. IX (1939), pp. 5-55].

Sarton, George, *Introduction to the History of Science*. 2 vols., Baltimore, 1927-31.

Schleiden, M. J., *The Importance of the Jews for the Preservation and Revival of Learning During the Middle Ages*. London, 1911.

Schleiden, M. J., *The Sciences among the Jews before and during the Middle Ages*. Baltimore, 1883.

Singer, Charles, *A Short History of Science to the Nineteenth Century*. Oxford, 1941.

Lecky, William E. H., *History of the Rise and Influence of the Spirit of Rationalism in Europe*. 2 vols., New York, 1886.

Cabala and Hasidism

Buber, Martin, *Jewish Mysticism*. London, 1931.

Greenstone, Julius H., *The Messiah Idea in Jewish History*. Philadelphia, 1906.

Kastein, Joseph, *The Messiah of Ismir, Sabbatai Zevi*. New York, 1931.

Minkin, Jacob S., *The Romance of Hasidism*. New York, 1935.

Scholem, Gershom G., *Major Trends in Jewish Mysticism*. New York, 1946.

Silver, Abba Hillel, *A History of Messianic Speculation in Israel,* from the First through the Seventeenth Centuries. New York, 1927.

Wallis, W. D., *Messiahs, Their Role in Civilization* (comparative anthropology). Washington, D. C. 1943.

The Zohar. Tr. Harry Sperling and Maurice Simon. 4 vols., London, 1931-34.

Religious Rites, Ceremonies and Customs

Friedländer, Gerald, *Laws and Customs of Israel*. London, 1934.

Goldin, Hyman E., *The Jewish Woman and Her Home*. New York, 1941.

Goodman, Philip, *The Purim Anthology*. Philadelphia, 1949.

Greenberg, Betty D., and Althea O. Silverman, *The Jewish Home Beautiful*. New York, 1941.

Idelsohn, A. Z., *The Ceremonies of Judaism*. Cincinnati, 1929.

Idelsohn, A. Z., *Jewish Music*. New York, 1929.

Idelsohn, A. Z., *Jewish Liturgy*. New York, 1932.

Levinger, Elma E., *With the Jewish Child in Home and Synagogue,* New York, 1930.

Millgram, A. E., *Sabbath, the Day of Delight*. Philadelphia, 1944.

Schauss, Hayyim, *The Jewish Festivals*. Cincinnati, 1938.

Lost Tribes and Remote Communities

Adler, E. N., *Jews in Many Lands*. London, 1905.

Ananthakrishna Ayyar, L. K., *Jews of Cochin* [in *Cochin Tribes and Castes,* v. 2, pp. 408-11. Madras, 1909-12].

Ausubel, Nathan (ed.), "The Ten Lost Tribes," in *A Treasury of Jewish Folklore,* pp. 540-59. New York, 1948.

Fischel, Walter J., "Israel in Iran," in *The Jews,* v. III, pp. 817-58, ed. Louis Finkelstein. Philadelphia, 1949.

Gaster, Moses, *The Samaritans: Their History, Doctrines and Literature*. Oxford, 1925.

Godbey, A. H., *Lost Tribes a Myth*. Durham, N. C., 1930.

Kehimkar, H. S., *The History of the Bene-Israel of India*. Tel-Aviv, 1937.

Leslau, Wolf, *Falasha Anthology*. New Haven, 1951.

Mandelbaum, David G., *Jewish Way of Life in Cochin* [in *Jewish Social Studies,* v. 1, pp. 421-60].

Nemoy, Leon, *Karaite Anthology*. New Haven, 1952.

Rosenau, W., *Ezekiel 37:15-23; What Happened to the Ten Tribes?* [in: Hebrew Union College Jubilee Volume, pp. 79-88. Cincinnati, 1925].

Sassoon, David Solomon, *A Short History of the Jews of Baghdad*. Letchworth, England, 1949.

Slouschz, Nahum, *Travels in North Africa*. Philadelphia, 1927.

White, W. C., *Chinese Jews*. 3 vols., Toronto, 1942.

Modern Period

General Reference

Cohen, Israel, *Jewish Life in Modern Times*. London, 1929.

Janowsky, Oscar J., *Jewish and Minority Rights*. New York, 1937.

Jewish Emancipation: a selection of documents. Raphael Mahler (ed.). American Jewish Committee. New York, 1941.

Kulischer, E. M., *Jewish Migrations*. New York, 1943.

Newman, H. (ed.), *The Real Jew, Some Aspects of the Jewish Contribution to Civilization*. London, 1925.

Robison, Sophia M., and Joshua Starr (eds.), *Jewish Population Studies*. New York, 1943.

Ruppin, Arthur, *The Jewish Fate and Future*. London, 1940.

Ruppin, Arthur, *The Jews in the Modern World*. New York, 1934.

Wiener, Leo, *The History of Yiddish Literature*. New York, 1899.

The Nature of Anti-Semitism

Lazare, Bernard, *Anti-Semitism, Its History and Causes*. New York, 1903.

Parkes, James W., *The Jew and His Neighbor: A Study of the Causes of Anti-Semitism*. London, 1931.

Pinson, Koppel J., "Anti-Semitism after World War I," in *Encyclopedia Britannica,* 1952 edition, v. 2, pp. 78-78J.

Pinson, Koppel (ed.), *Essays on Anti-Semitism*. New York, 1942.

Sachar, A. L., *Sufferance Is the Badge*. New York, 1939.

Segel, B. W., *The Protocols of the Elders of Zion—the Greatest Lie in History*. New York, 1934.

Simmel, Ernst, *Anti-Semitism: A Social Disease*. New York, 1946.

Wolf, Lucien, *The Myth of the Jewish Menace in World Affairs; the Truth about the Forged Protocols of the Elders of Zion*. London, 1921.

France—Dreyfus Case

Dreyfus, Alfred, *Five Years of My Life*. New York, 1901.

Friedman, Lee M., *Zola and the Dreyfus Case*. Boston, 1937.

Posener, S., *Adolphe Crémieux*. Philadelphia, 1940.

Modern Germany

Corti, Egon C., *The Rise of the House of Rothschild*. New York, 1928.

Ewen, Frederic (ed.), *The Poetry and Prose of Heinrich Heine*. New York, 1948.

Heine, Heinrich, *Memoirs*. London, 1910.

Hensel, Sebastian, *The Mendelssohn Family*. New York, 1882.

Lowenthal, Marvin, *The Jews of Germany*. A Story of Sixteen Centuries. Philadelphia, 1936.

Maimon, Solomon, *An Autobiography*. Boston, 1888.

Marcus, Jacob R., *The Rise and Destiny of the German Jews*. Philadelphia, 1934.

Memoirs of Moses Mendelssohn, the Jewish Philosopher. M. Samuels (ed.). London, 1827.

Meyer, Bertha, *Salon Sketches: Biographical Studies of Berlin Salons of the Emancipation*. New York, 1938.

Myerson, Abraham, and Isaac Goldberg, *The German Jew*. New York, 1933.

Walter, Hermann, *Moses Mendelssohn, Critic and Philosopher*. New York, 1930.

Germany Under Hitler

Black Book, The. The Nazi Crime Against the Jewish People. Published by the Jewish Black Book Committee. New York, 1946.

Brady, Robert A., *The Spirit and Structure of German Fascism*. New York, 1937.

Children in Bondage: A Survey of Child Life in the Occupied Countries of Europe. London, 1942.

Heiden, Konrad, *A History of National Socialism*. New York, 1935.

Hitler, Adolf, *Hitler's Speeches*. New York, 1942.

Hitler, Adolf, *Mein Kampf* (unexpurgated English edition). New York, 1939.

Hitler, Adolf, *Hitler's Speeches*. New York, 1941.

Liptzin, Solomon, *Germany's Stepchildren*. Philadelphia, 1948.

Osborne, Sidney, *Germany and Her Jews*. London, 1939.

Rauschning, Hermann, *The Voice of Destruction*. New York, 1940.

Schuman, Frederick L., *The Nazi Dictatorship*. New York, 1939.

Schwarz, Leo W., *The Root and the Bough;* the epic of an enduring people. New York, 1949.

Syrkin, Marie, *Blessed Is the Match*. Philadelphia, 1947.

Tartakower, Arieh, and Kurt Grossman, *The Jewish Refugee*. New York, 1944.

Warhaftig, Zorach, *Uprooted, the Story of Displaced Persons*. New York, 1946.

Weinreich, Max, *Hitler's Professors*. New York, 1946.

England, Canada, South Africa

Brandes, Georg, *Lord Beaconsfield*. London, 1880.

Goodman, Paul, *Moses Montefiore*. Philadelphia, 1943.

Hyamson, A. M., *A History of the Jews in England*. London, 1929.

Macaulay, Thomas B., *Speech on the Civil Disabilities of the Jews*. London, 1875.

Maurois, André, *Disraeli;* a picture of the Victorian Age. New York, 1928.

Modder, Montagu F., *The Jew in the Literature of England*. Philadelphia, 1944.

Picciotto, James, *Sketches of Anglo-Jewish History*. London, 1875.

Hart, Arthur D., *The Jew in Canada*. Toronto, 1926.

Rosenberg, Louis, *Canada's Jews*. Montreal, 1939.

Sack, Benjamin G., *History of the Jews in Canada*. Montreal, 1945.

Hermann, Louis, *A History of the Jews in South Africa*. Johannesburg, 1935.

Russia and Poland Under the Tsars

Dubnow, Simon, *History of the Jews in Russia and Poland*. 3 vols., Philadelphia, 1916-20.

Errera, L., *The Russian Jews: Extermination or Emancipation?* London, 1894.

Frederic, Harold, *The New Exodus: A Study of Israel in Russia*. London, 1892.

Greenberg, Louis, *The Jews in Russia*. New Haven, 1944.

Heschel, Abraham, *The Earth Is the Lord's; the Inner World of the Jew in East Europe*. Wood engravings by Ilya Schor. New York, 1950.

Raisin, J. S., *The Haskalah Movement in Russia*. Philadelphia, 1913.

Rubinow, I. M., "Economic Condition of the Jews in Russia," in *Bulletin of the Bureau of Labor*, No. 72, pp. 487-583. Washington, D. C., 1907.

Samuel, Maurice, *The World of Sholom Aleichem*. New York, 1943.

Tenenbaum, Joseph, *In Search of a Lost People; the old and the new Poland*. New York, 1948.

Wolf, Lucien, *The Legal Sufferings of the Jews in Russia*. London, 1912.

Soviet Russia

Dennen, Leon, *Where the Ghetto Ends*. New York, 1932.

Fischer, Louis, *Machines and Men in Russia*. New York, 1934.

Kunitz, Joshua, *Russian Literature and the Jew*. New York, 1929.

Lamont, Corliss, *The Peoples of the Soviet Union*. New York, 1946.

Lamont, Corliss, *Soviet Russia and Religion*. New York, 1936.

The Massacres and Other Atrocities Committed against the Jews in Southern Russia. Israel Goldberg (ed.). American Jewish Congress. New York, 1920.

Mikhailov, Nicholas, *Soviet Russia: The Land and Its People*. New York, 1948.

Pares, Bernard, *Russia*. Revised edition. London, 1953.

Stewart, George, *The White Armies of Russia*. New York, 1933.

Webb, Sidney and Beatrice, *Soviet Communism*. 2 vols., London, 1935.

Yarmolinsky, Avrahm, *The Jews and Other National Minorities under the Soviets*. New York, 1928.

United States

American Jewish Yearbook Annuals. New York.

Antin, Mary, *The Promised Land*. Boston, 1912.

Baron, H. S., *Haym Salomon, Son of Liberty*. New York, 1941.

Bernheimer, Charles, *The Russian Jew in the United States*. Philadelphia, 1905.

Brown, Francis J., and Joseph S. Roucek, *Our Racial and National Minorities*. New York, 1937.

Davidson, Gabriel, *Our Jewish Farmers*. New York, 1943.

Forster, Arnold: *A Measure of Freedom*. New York, 1950.

Fortune Magazine, *Jews in America*. New York, 1936.

Freehof, Solomon B., *Reform Jewish Practice and Its Rabbinic Background*. Cincinnati, 1944.

Friedman, Lee M., *Jewish Pioneers and Patriots*. Philadelphia, 1942.

Goldberg, Isaac, *Major Noah*. Philadelphia, 1936.

Gordis, Robert, *Conservative Judaism*. New York, 1945.

Grinstein, Hyman B., *The Rise of the Jewish Community of New York*, Philadelphia, 1945.

Huhner, Leon, *The Life of Judah Touro*. Philadelphia, 1946.

Janowsky, Oscar I. (ed.), *The American Jew: A Composite Portrait*. New York, 1942.

Kaplan, Mordecai M., *Judaism as a Civilization?* New York, 1934.

Kaplan, Mordecai M., *The Meaning of God in Modern Jewish Religion*. New York, 1937.

Karpf, Hyman J., *Jewish Community Organization in the U. S.* New York, 1939.

Kaufman, Yehezkel, "Ocupational Structure of Jews," in *Contemporary Jewish Record*, New York, 1939.

Lebeson, Anita, *Jewish Pioneers in America*. New York, 1938.

Levinger, Lee J., *A History of the Jews in the United States*. Cincinnati, 1935.

Lipsky, Louis, *Thirty Years of American Zionism*. New York, 1927.

Masserman and Baker, *The Jew Comes to America*. New York, 1933.

Marcus, Jacob Rader, *Early American Jewry*. Philadelphia, 1951.

Pool, Dr. David De Sola, *Portraits Etched in Stone: Early Jewish Settlers [1682-1831]*. New York, 1952.

Publications of the American Jewish Historical Society, 1893-to date.

Reznikoff, Charles, *The Jews of Charleston*. Philadelphia, 1950.

Ribalow, Harold U., *The Jew in American Sports*. New York, 1948.

Riis, Jacob A., *The Battle with the Slum*. New York, 1902.

Riis, Jacob A., *How the Other Half Lives; Studies among the tenements of New York*. New York, 1890.

Steinberg, Milton, *A Partisan Guide to the Jewish Problem*. New York, 1945.

Wiernik, Peter, *History of the Jews in America*. New York, 1912.

Wirth, Louis, *The Ghetto*. Chicago, 1928.

Zionism and Israel

Ahad Ha-Am, *Essays, Letters and Memoirs*. Oxford, 1946.

Barer, Shlomo, *The Magic Carpet*. New York, 1952.

Bentwich, Norman, *Israel*. New York, 1952.

Brandeis, Louis D., *The Jewish Problem: How to Solve It*. New York, 1915.

Crum, Bartley C., *Behind the Silken Curtain*. New York, 1947.

De Gaury, Gerald, *The New State of Israel*. London, 1952.

Dunner, Joseph, *The Republic of Israel*. New York, 1950.

Goodman, Paul, and A. D. Lewis (eds.), *Zionism: problems and views*. London, 1916.

Gordon, A. D., "Work and Culture" [in *Rebirth*, ed. Ludwig Lewisohn]. New York, 1935.

Gottheil, Richard, *Zionism*. Philadelphia, 1914.

Halkin, Simon, *Modern Hebrew Literature*. New York, 1950.

Hess, Moses, *Rome and Jerusalem*. New York, 1943.

Herzl, Theodor, *Diaries*. New York, 1929.

Herzl, Theodor, *The Jewish State*. New York, 1941.

Hurewitz, J. C., *The Struggle for Palestine*. New York, 1950.

Jabotinsky, Vladimir, *The Story of the Jewish Legion*. New York, 1945.

Katznelson-Rubashow, Rachel, *The Plow Woman [Pioneer Woman]*. New York, 1932.

Klausner, Joseph, *A History of Modern Hebrew Literature (1785-1930)*. London, 1932.

Learsi, Rufus, *Fulfillment: the Epic Story of Zionism*. Cleveland, 1951.

Lehrman, Hal, *Israel*. New York, 1951.

Lowdermilk, Walter C., *Palestine: Land of Promise*. New York, 1944.

McDonald, James G.: *My Mission in Israel*. New York, 1951.

Muenzner, Gerhard, *Labor Enterprise in Palestine*. New York, 1947.

Pinsker, Leo, *Auto-Emancipation*. New York, 1944.

Sacher, Harry, *Israel*. New York, 1952.

St. John, Robert, *Tongue of the Prophets; the Life Story of Eliezer Ben Yehuda*. New York, 1952.

Stone, I. F., *This Is Israel*. New York, 1948.

Weizmann, Chaim, *Trial and Error*. New York, 1949.

INDEX

Ramleh seized by Arab Legion, 320
Raphael's *Apollo on Mount Parnassus*, 103
Raphaelson, Samson, 296
Raphall, Rabbi Morris Jacob, 279
Rapoport, Abraham Menachem, 104
Rashi Chapel in Worms, 119
Rashi of Troyes, 70, 107, 115, 217
Rathenau, Emil, 162; Walter, 162, 170
Rau, Phil, 291
Rauschning, Herman, 256
Raynal, David, 155
Re, Egyptian sun-god, 12
Reading, Lord, 184
Rebbe, the, 146
Rechabites, 43, 60
Recife (Pernambuco), 212
"Reconstruction," American Jewish, 290
Red Sea, 5, 24, 49
Ree, Anton, 196; Julius, 196
Reed, Florence, 296
Reform Judaism, 161, 173, 178, 277, 278, 290
Refugees, U. S. quota laws for German, 299; German, in Bolivia, 213; German, in Brazil, 212; German, in Chile, 213; German, in Uruguay, 215; Jewish, in Switzerland, 202
Regnier, Henri de, 236
Rehabilitation of displaced persons, 266
Rehoboam, King, 25, 34, 59
Rehoboth, 301
Reichstein, Tadeus, 202
Reichswehr, German, 254, 255
Reiner, Fritz, 295
Reinhardt, Max, 165, 166, 174, 253
Reisen, Abraham, 240, 288
Religious freedom in U.S.A., 274, 276
Remak, Robert, 167
Remez, David, 322
Renaissance, 94, 102, 103, 104
Repentance, Jewish doctrine of, 57, 58
Rephidim, 30, 31
Resh Lakish, 78
Resurrection, 80
Reuben, Jacob's son, 18; tribe of, 38
Reubeni, Prince David, 141, 142, 300
Reuchlin, Johann, 123, 141
Reuter's News Agency, 185
Revel, Dr. Bernard, 290
Revere, Giuseppe, 200
Revolt against Moses, 32; against Nazis, 265; against Rome, 81, 89; Jeroboam's second, 59; Maccabean, 79; of 66 C.E., 87
Revolution of 1848, 173, 174, 178
Rezin, King of Damascus, 62
Rhaze's *Liber Continens*, 147
Rhineland, 95
Rhodes, Cecil, 190
Ribbentrop, von, 268
Ricardo, David, 181, 182
Rice, Elmer, 296
Rickover, Rear-Adm. Hyman G., 292
Ries, Peter, 169
Riess, Elias E., 292
Riesser, Gabriel, 159, 163, 164
Riga, 259, 265
Rilke, Rainer Maria, 174
Rimalho, Joao, 211
Rimonim, 71
Rindfleisch Massacres, 96, 134
Rishon-le-Zion, 301, 304
Risorgimento, 198, 199, 200
Ritt, Joseph R., 292
Ritual murder slander, 95, 96, 97, 117, 126, 133, 134, 177, 183, 235, 236
Rivera family of Newport, R. I., 272; Jacob Rodriguez, 272
Robespierre, 152
Robinson, Edward G., 296
Rocamora, *Fra* Vincente de, 112
Rocca, Enrico, 200
"Rochester Israelite" (Sherenbeck), 181
Rodgers, Richard, 294, 295
Rodrigues, Olinde, 155
Rogachevsky, Gen. Samuel, 259
Roman Carnival, 102; Ghetto, demolition of, 199; Jews humiliated by Popes, 101, 102; legions, 80, 87, 89, 90; party, Jewish, 80, 88, 90
Romania, 204, 205, 257, 268, 283
Romains, Jules, 155
Romanin, Samuel, 201
Romans, 78, 80, 81, 82, 87, 88, 114
Romberg, Moritz Heinrich, 167; Sigmund, 294
Rome, 45, 55, 81, 83, 84, 87, 89, 91, 98, 99, 100, 101, 102
Rome, Harold, 294
Romulus, 20
Ronald, Sir Landon, 183
Rose, Maj-Gen. Maurice, 258
Rosen, Max, 295
Rosenau, Milton Joseph, 293
Rosenberg, Dr. Alfred, 255, 256, 259, 268; Isaac, 185
Rosenbloom, Maxie, 297
Rosenfeld, Morris, 288; Yoinah, 240
Rosenfeldt, Leopold, 196
Rosenholz, Arkady P., 247
Rosenthal, Moritz, 174
Rosenwald, Julius, 248, 280, 281
Rosh Hashanah, 15, 57, 58
Rosh Pinah, colony, 301; synagogue in Winnipeg, 189
Ross, Barney, 297
Rossi, Salamone, 103, 161
Roth, Henry, 293
Rothenberg, Morris, 289
Rothenstein, Sir William, 185
Rothschild, Baron Edmond de, 304, 305; Lionel de, 182; Lord, 306; Meir Anschel, 162; Nathan M., 180; Baron Salomon, 171, 173, 174
Rothschilds, English, 302; French, 155
Rovina, 331
Rubenson, Robert, 197
Rubin, Edgar, 196; Reuben, 330
Rubinstein, Anton, 241, 253; Artur, 244, 294, 296; Nicolai, 241
Rüdiger, Bishop of Speyer, 119
Rudolph of Hapsburg, Emperor, 97
Rudolph the monk, 119
Ruhr industrialists, 254, 255
Rukeyser, Muriel, 293
Rukhimovich, Moisei L., 247
Rumkowski, 261
Rundstedt, Field Marshal von, 261
Russell, Bertrand, 241; Henry, 183
Russia (*see also* U.S.S.R), expulsion of Jews, 132; mass emigration of Jews, 234, 235, 282, 283; in medieval, 129, 130, 131, 132; Provisional Government (Kerensky), 247; Tsarist, 183, 230, 231, 232, 233, 234, 235, 236, 237, 238, 239, 240, 241
Russification, of Jews in 19th century, 231, 233; of Soviet Jews, 253
Ruthard, Archbishop, 119
Ruttenberg, Pinchas, 326
Ruttenberg Power Stations, Israel, 326
Ryazanov, 247

Saadya Gaon, 94, 105
Sabatarias of Chile, 213
Sabbatai Zevi, 142, 143
Sabbath, the, 73, 74, 75, 83, 219; in Israel, 328
Sacerdoti, Chief Rabbi Angelo, 202
Sachar, Dr. Abram L., 291
Sacher-Masoch, 174
Sachs, Bernard, 293; Kurt, 176
Sachsenhausen, Nazi death camp, 260
Sachsenspiegel, Dresden, 95
Sacrifices in Temple on *Yom Kippur*, 58
Sadducees, 80, 82, 87
Sadeh, Col. Yitzchak, 321
Safed, 141
Sahara Desert Jews, 226, 227
St. Charles, French ship, 270
Saint-Jean, Regnault de, 152
St. Petersburg Conservatory of Music, 241
Saint-Saens, 155
Saladin the Great, 114, 150
Saloman, Geskel, 196, 197; Nota, 196; Siegfried, 196
Salomon, Haym, 272, 273
Salomons, David, 180, 182; Sir Julius, 191
Salomonsen, Carl L., 196
Salonières, Viennese Jewish, 172
Saloniki Jews, 209, 210
Salten, Felix, 174
Salvador, Francis, 273
Samacoff (Bulgaria) synagogue, 206
Samaria, 59, 61, 62, 63, 68
Samaritans, the, 63, 68, 228
Samarkand, 220
Sambatyon River, 217
Saminsky, Lazare, 294
Samoilowitsch, Rudolph, 252
Samson, Judge of Israel, 40, 41, 42
Samuel ben Solomon, 115
Samuel ibn Nagdela (Samuel ha-Nagid), 105
Samuel, Judge of Israel, 34, 42, 46; Harold, 185; Sir Herbert (Viscount Samuel), 183, 184, 332; Sir Marcus (Viscount Bearsted), 182; Maurice, 293
Sanhedrin, 80, 87, 89; Napoleon's, 153, 198
Sansecondo, Jacopo, 103
Santiago (Chile), 213
Sao Paulo synagogue, 212
Saphir, Moritz, 174
Sapir, Edward, 294
Sarah, the Matriarch, 13, 15
Sarajevo synagogue, 207, 208
Sarffati, Isaac, 207; Margheritta, 201
Sargon II, King, 63, 217
Sarnoff, Brig.-Gen. David, 297
Sassoon, Siegfried, 185
Satan, cabalist's war on, 140
Satz, Ludwig, 288
Saul, King, 46, 47, 48, 49
Savoir, Alfred, 155
Sayings of the Fathers, 74
Schanzer, Carlo, 201
Schapira, Prof. Hermann, 304, 332
Schapiro, J. Salwyn, 294
Schechter, Prof. Solomon, 290
Scheinman, Aaron L., 247
Schenck, Joseph M., 296; Nicholas, 296
Schenker, Heinrich, 176
Schick, Dr. Bela, 292
Schiff, Jacob H., 281
Schildkraut, Joseph, 296; Rudolf, 166, 174
Schirach, Baldur von, 268
Schlesinger, Arthur, Jr., 294; Frank, 292
Schloss, O. M., 293
Schlossberg, Joseph, 286
Schnabel, Arthur, 174
Schneour, Zalman, 302
Schneor-Zalman of Liadi, Rabbi, 145
Schnitzler, Arthur, 174
Schoenberg, Arnold, 165, 174
Scholarship, medieval Jewish, 148
Schomberg, Adm. Sir Alexander, 180, 187
Schreiner, Abraham, 176
Schubert, Franz, 173
Schück, Prof. Henrik Emil, 197
Schulberg, Budd, 293
Schurz, Carl, 292
Schvartzman, O., 253
Schwartz, Arthur, 294; Delmore, 293; Maurice, 288
Schwarz, David, 168, 169; Samuel, 110
Schwarzbard, Samuel, trial of, 246
Science, Jewish attitude toward, 147; Jews in medieval, 147, 148
Scientists, Jewish, in Tsarist Russia, 241
Scot, Michael, 116
Scott, Sir Walter, 281
Scotus, Duns, 106
Scribes (*see Soferim*)
"Season of Repentance," 57
Secularism among Russian Jews, 239
Seder, the, 27, 28, 29
Sefer ha-Hasidim, 141
Sefer Torah, 58, 70, 71, 72, 85, 238
Sefer Yetzira, 139
Seidenberg, A., 292
Seipel, Monsignor, 177
Seixas, Capt. Abraham, 275; Rev. Gershom Mendes, 274, 275, 277; Capt. Moses B., 275; Capt. Solomon, 275
Segal, Isaac, 138; Vivienne, 297
Segre, Rabbi Isaac Benzion, 198
Sekhmet, Egyptian goddess, 9
Seleucid Empire, 78
Self-government, in medieval Germany, 121, 124; in medieval Poland, 135
Seligman, Edwin R. A., 293; Georg, 196; J. & W., & Co., 280
Selvinsky, 253
Selwyn, Edgar, 295
Selznick, Louis J., 296
Semitic types, ethnic, 7
Senator, Hermann, 167
Senderowitz, Charles, 196
Seneca, the Stoic philosopher, 73
Senesch, Hannah, 264, 265
Senior, Abraham, 110
Sennacherib, King, 63, 64
Sephardim, 113, 118, 180, 186, 187, 195, 271
Septuagint version of Bible, 69, 77, 78
Sereni, Enzo, 265
Serlin, Oscar, 295
Servi Camerae (*see* "King's Chattels")
Servitus Judeorum, 120
Seti I, King, 25
Settlements, foreign Judean, 77, 85, 87, 91
Severus, Julius, 90
Seville Golden Tower, 108
Shaar Hashomayim Congregation, Montreal, 188
Shaaray Zion Synagogue, Montreal, 189
Shahn, Ben, 294
Shakespeare in Yiddish, 181
Shalachmones (*see Purim*)
Shalmaneser III, King, 61
Shalmeneser V, 63
Shalom, Sh., 332
Shamash, Babylonian sun-god, 13, 25
Shapiro, Harry, 294; Karl, 293; L., 240; Moshe, 322
Sharett (Shertok), Moshe, 311, 315, 322, 323
Shavuoth, 36, 56
Shaw, Irwin, 293, 296
Shearith Israel Congregation, Montreal, 187; New York, 270, 271, 275, 277
Sheba, Queen of, 52
Shechem (Nablus), 18, 59, 228
Shechinah, 54
Sheftall, Mordecai, 272
Shekel, the Zionist, 302
Shem Ha-meforesh, 145
Shemen Oil Co., Israel, 326
Shenberg, Isaac, 332
Sheshbazzar, 55, 68
Sheyn, Grigory, 252
Shiloh, sanctuary of, 38, 42, 49
Shimonovitch, David, 332
Shinwell, Emanuel, 183
Shipman, Samuel, 296
Shishak, King (Sheshonk), 25, 34, 53, 59
Shitreet, Behor, 322
Shklovsky, Victor, 253
Shlakhta, 134, 135
Shlom the mint-master, 125
Shlonsky, Abraham, 332; Verdina, 330
Shmuel, Ahron ben, 294
Shmuelbuch (Book of Samuel), 123
Shofar, the, 15, 57, 58, 86, 129
Sholom Aleichem, 240, 252, 253; Library in Biro-bidjan, 249; School in Buenos Aires, 214
Shomronim, 228
Shore, Dinah, 297
Shtadlan (*see* Court Jew)
Shubert, J. J., 295; Lee, 295; Sam S., 295
Shumlin, Herman, 295
Siberia, political prisoners, 233, 236
Sicily, medieval, 99
Sidney, Sylvia, 296
Siege of Jerusalem, 87, 88
Siesbye, Oskar, 196
Siloam, pool of, 64, 65
Silva, Antonio José da, 212; Francisco Maldonado da, 215
Silver, Rabbi Abba Hillel, 289
Silver Shirts, 257
Silvers, Phil, 297
Silvester, Johann, Cardinal of Prague, 97
Sima, Miron, 330
Simchat Torah (*Simchas Torah*), 72
Simeon bar Yochai, 139
Simon, Dr. James, 2; Joseph, 272
Simonsen, Chief Rabbi, Copenhagen, 195, 196
Simonson, Lee, 295
Simms family, Cape Colony, 190
Simson, Eduard von, 163
Sinai, Mount, 31, 32, 33, 36
Singer, Al, 297; Paul, 170
Sinzheim, Rabbi David, 153
Sirota, *chazzan* of Warsaw, 239
Sisera, 39
Sklar, George, 293
Skoropadsky, Gen., 245
Skulnik, Menasha, 288
Slansky, Rudolf, 251
Slaveocracy, Egyptian, 9
Slavery in U. S., Jewish position, 278, 279
Slaves in Egypt, Semitic, 22
Slavophile movement in Russia, 233, 234, 235, 236
Sloman family, Cape Colony, 190
Slonimski, Antoni, 244; Chaim Selig, 241
Slovakia, modern, 146
Smigly-Rydz, Marshal, 242
Smilansky, Moshe, 332
Smoira, M., 322
Smolenskin, Peretz, 302
Smushkevich, Gen. Jacob, 258
Smyrna (Ismir), 210
Sobibor, Nazi death camp, 265
Sobieski, Jan, King, 137
Sociedad Hebraica Argentina, 215
Society for the Promotion of Jewish Culture and Science, 160, 162
Sodom and Gomorrah, 14
Sofer, Rabbi Moses, 178
Soferim, 68, 69, 71
Sofia, Great Synagogue, 206
Sokolnikov, Grigory V., 247
Sokolow, Nahum, 302, 306
Solis-Cohen, Solomon, 292
Solomon, Abraham, 185; Rabbi Abraham ben, 195; ben Isaac (*see* Rashi), 115; ibn Gabirol, 106; King, 6, 7, 44, 50, 51, 52, 53, 57, 62; Rebecca, 185; Sir Richard, 190; Saul, 190; Justice Saul, 190; Simeon, 185; V. L., 191; Sir William Henry, 190
Solomons, Levi, 187; Solomon J., 185
Sonnenfels, *Freiherr* Joseph von, 171, 174
Sonnenthal, Adolph, 174
Sonnino, Sidney, 200
"Sons of Liberty," 272
Sons of Zion, 290
South Africa, 190, 256, 257
Soutine, Chaim, 155
Soviet (*see also* U.S.S.R), decree against anti-Semitism, 245; -Israeli relations, 251, 252; intermarriage among Jews, 253; legation in Israel, 252; restrictions against religious education, 250
Soviets evacuate Jews before Nazi advance, 258; opposed by Zionists and Orthodox, 250; war on Zionism, 251
Soyer, Moses, 294; Raphael, 294
Spain, 53, 93, 98, 105-112
Spalato Jewish cemetery, 208
Spaniolish (*see Ladino*)
Spanish Armada, defeat of, 111
Spektor, Mordecai, 240, 288
Spewack, Bella, 296; Samuel, 296
Speyer & Co., 162, 280
Spielleute, 122, 238
Spinoza, Baruch, 112, 113
Spire, André, 155
Stahl, Friedrich Julius, 163, 164
Star and moon worship, Babylonian, 8
Starhemberg, Prince, 177
Staszow, 243
Statue of Liberty, N. Y., 293
Stein, Gertrude, 293
Steinberg, Isaac N., 247
Steinman, Eliezer, 332
Steinschneider, Moritz, 162, 164
Stern, Abraham, 241, 313; G. B., 184, 185; Isaac, 295; Lina, 252; Otto, 292
Stern Group, 313, 314, 315, 316, 318
Sternberg, Eric Walter, 330
Sterne, Maurice, 294

ACKNOWLEDGMENTS

The author wishes to acknowledge his deep indebtedness to a host of individuals, public and private organizations, art and archaeological museums, private picture collections and U. S. Government departments and bureaus. Also to foreign diplomatic representatives and government services, educational and cultural institutions, university, public and private libraries, news picture agencies, photographic services and individual photographers.

I am grateful to my publishers for their unflagging faith in this difficult project. First and foremost, my appreciation is due to Nat Wartels, President of Crown Publishers, for his broad vision and understanding, and for the numerous contributions with which he has enriched this work. Also valuably associated with the making of the book from its very inception was the editor, Herbert Michelman. Virginia Soskin gave the manuscript her zealous editorial attention and corrections. Bertha Krantz was painstaking in hunting down errors in text and in picture placement. Adrian Shapiro and Budd Urquhart showed skill and resourcefulness in overcoming technical difficulties of make-up. Helen Straeubel gave valuable editorial assistance. I also wish to express thanks to Jerome Meyers, Barbara Lea, Ruth Popofsky, Irene Greenberg, Dorothy Botkin, Sue Frisbie and Jane Behrman for their help.

Sincere thanks are due to Rabbi Philip Goodman of the Jewish Book Council of America for the generous assistance he gave me in every way possible, including a critical reading of the text. Similarly, special acknowledgment is made for their careful reading of the manuscript to Dr. I. Keyfitz, Professor of Oriental Languages, Literature and History at Bible College, University of Missouri, to Dr. Sarah Feder, sociologist and President of *Pioneer Women*, and to Abraham Berger, historian and assistant chief of the New York Public Library's Jewish Division, for reading the Biblical section. Needless to say, the sole responsibility for views expressed in this book rests with the author.

Invaluable and generous help was given me by the following individuals: Menashe Vaxer, scholar and Jewish book dealer; Bernard Postal, historian, who made available to me his extensive personal picture file; Judge and Mrs. Louis Shapiro; Rabbi Arthur A. Chiel; Rabbi I. Edward Kiev; Dr. A. Mibashan, editor of *Eretz Israel* (Buenos Aires); and, not least, my wife, Marynn Older Ausubel, who participated in the shaping of this book in all of its many aspects, and who has left her own deep imprint upon it.

Libraries and Archives: Special and grateful acknowledgment is made to the Jewish Theological Seminary Library, Rabbi Gerson D. Cohen, Librarian, Edith Brodsky, Public Information Department, and especially to Anna Kleban, who made available to me the notable Picture Collection of the Jewish Theological Seminary Library. Also to the American Jewish Historical Society and Rabbi Isidore S. Meyer, Librarian-Editor, for making available pictures from the collections of Captain N. Taylor Phillips, U.S.A., A. S. W. Rosenbach, Blanche Moses, Lee M. Friedman and Amelia Mayhoff; to the Frick Art Reference Library; American Jewish Committee Library, Mr. Henry Alderman, Librarian, and especially to Therese Benston of the staff; to Temple Emanuel Library and Mary Kiev, Librarian; to the American Jewish Archives and Dr. Jacob R. Marcus, Director; to Zionist Archives and Library; to the Archives of the Yiddish Scientific Institute (YIVO) and Rebecca Tcherikower; to the Picture Collection of the Jewish Welfare Board and Dr. Samuel Freeman; to the Hillel Foundation Center of Brooklyn College and Rabbi Herman Pollack, Director; to the Library of Congress—Prints and Photographs

Division; to the *Bibliothèque Nationale*, Paris; to National Archives and Records Service, Washington, D. C.; to Public Archives of Canada; to Hebrew University and National Library, Jerusalem; to New York Public Library and its various divisions, especially the *Jewish Division*, Dr. Joshua Bloch, chief, and the members of his staff, Marie Coralnik, Dora Steinglass and Fanny Spivack; the *Slavonic Division*, Dr. Alfred Berlstein, chief of the Polish section, and Rissa Yachnin and Lola Kovarsky of the staff; the *Theatre Division* and Garrison P. Sherwood; the *Print Room* and Elizabeth E. Roth; the *Picture Reference Collection;* the *Music Division;* the *Art and Architecture Division;* the Photostat and Photography Service; and the Seward Park Branch of the New York Public Library; to Yeshiva University and Florence Goldman of the Public Relations Department; to Columbia University and M. Halsey Thomas, Curator of *Columbiana;* to the South African Jewish Sociological and Historical Society and S. A. Rochlin, Archivist; to the United States Naval Academy and Captain Wade DeWeese, U. S. Navy (Ret.); to Brandeis University, and Dr. Abram S. Sachar, President; to Hebrew University in Jerusalem; to the College of the City of New York, Public Relations Bureau; to the Jewish Library, Montreal, and M. Ravitch; to the Hebrew Union College—Jewish Institute of Religion and Rabbi I. Edward Kiev, Librarian; and to Rutgers University.

Museums, Art Galleries and Archaeological Institutes: Thanks are due to the British Museum and to Dr. Jacob Leveen, Deputy Keeper of Oriental Printed Books and Manuscripts; the Jewish Museum of the Jewish Theological Seminary and Dr. Stephen S. Kayser, Director, and Frank J. Darmstaedter, Photographer; the Oriental Institute of the University of Chicago; the Yale University Art Gallery; the *Kunstmuseum*, Basle; Department of Antiquities, Cairo; *Rijkmuseum Van Oudheden Te Leiden;* Metropolitan Museum of Art; Jewish Museum, London; Museum of Jewish Antiquities, Hebrew University; The *Louvre;* Wadsworth Atheneum, Hartford; Boston Museum of Fine Arts; Detroit Institute of Arts; Pennsylvania Academy of Fine Arts; Lewis S. Hine, Memorial Collection, and Walter Rosenblum; Collection of M. Cottin; Collection of M. Zagaisky; Collection of Alfred Rubens (London); Collection of Dr. Abraham Schwadron (Jerusalem); National Portrait Gallery (London); Redwood Library and Athenaeum Collection, Newport, Rhode Island; *Shearith Israel* Synagogue Collection; Museum of the City of New York Collection; the Historical Society of Pennsylvania; and the *Museo Egizio,* Turin.

Governmental and Diplomatic Agencies: French Press and Information Service and Jeanne Boisacq; Netherlands Information Service and Henriette Van Nierop; Yugoslav Books and Information Center and Dr. Lujo Goranin-Weissmann; the Australian Ambassador, P. C. Spender; Australian News and Information Bureau and R. M. Younger, Director; United Nations Photographic and Visual Information Section and George N. Allen, Photo Librarian; Danish Information Office and C. H. W. Hasselriis, Director; The American-Swedish News Exchange and Holger Lundbergh, Director; Belgian Government Information Center and Denise Dunn; UNRRA Photographs; Spanish State Tourist Office; Israel Office of Information and Abraham Harman, Director; British Information Services and Irene A. Egan; Legation of the Romanian People's Republic; Polish Information Bureau; United States Department of Defense; SHAEF; OWI; Bureau of Engineering, Chicago Department of Public Works; and the Federal Art Project,

W.P.A., Photographic Division, and Arnold Eagle, Photographer.

Organizations and Publications: United Palestine (Israel) Appeal and Harold E. Steinberg, Public Relations Director, and his assistant, Sylvia S. Percoff; American Friends of the Hebrew University in Jerusalem and Rita Z. Blume; American Committee for the Hebrew University, Weizmann Institute of Science and Technion, and High Salpeter, Executive Secretary; American Jewish Joint Distribution Committee and Irving R. Dickman, Publicity Director; United Jewish Appeal, and Dr. Joseph Schwartz, Executive Vice-President, and George Silverman, Public Relations Director; *Hadassah*, and Mina Brownstone, Director of Promotion, and Fay Spiro, her assistant; Jewish National Fund, and Dr. S. Margoshes, Director of Public Relations, and Jane Halkin; National Jewish Welfare Board and Bernard Postal, Director of Public Information; American Jewish Congress and Dr. Joseph Schwartz, Executive American ORT Federation and Paul Bernick, Executive Secretary; National Committee for Labor Israel, and Nachum Gutman and Anne Marantz, Public Relations Department; *Mizrachi* Women's Organization of America and Marc Siegel, Director of Public Relations; American Jewish Congress and Dr. Jacob Freid; Canadian Jewish Congress and David Rome and Louis Rosenberg; Jewish Agency for Palestine and Victor Bernstein, Director of Public Relations; *Poale Zion,* and Pinchas Cruso, and Simone Silberman; American Committee for OSE and Dr. Leon Wulman; Jewish Agricultural Aid Society; Amalgamated Clothing Workers of America, and Edmund Fisher and Richard Rohman; International Ladies' Garment Workers Union and Harry Rubenstein, Photographer; Hebrew Immigrant Aid Society and Martin A. Bursten, Director, Press and Public Relations; *Histadruth Ivrit* and Samuel J. Borowsky; The Union of American Hebrew Congregations and Rabbi Samuel M. Silver; *Israel Speaks* and Gertrude Halpern, Editor; *Eretz Israel* (Buenos Aires) and Dr. A. Mibashan, *Editor; La'Am Israel* Publishing Company, Ltd., Tel-Aviv; *The New York Times;* Bonnier Publishing House, Stockholm; Schocken Books, Inc., Radio Corporation of America, Victor Division, and Dale Ford; Hurok Attractions; Philharmonic Symphony Society of New York; Bishop W. C. White and the University of Toronto Press; RKO Radio Pictures, Inc., *Jewish Daily Forward;* Columbia Artists Management, Inc.; Viking Press; Harcourt, Brace and Company; Farrar, Straus and Young; World Publishing Company; and Random House.

Thanks are also due to Dr. Philip Friedman, Ilsa Hofmann, Dr. Selman A. Waksman, Dr. Arthur Wendt, Dr. Wolf Leslau, Ben Shahn, Ernest Bloch, Abbo Ostrowsky, Dr. I. Alcalay, Lessing Rosenwald, Dr. Bela Schick, Lillian Hellman, James D. Proctor, Ralph Pulitzer, Arthur M. Loew, the Hon. Herbert H. Lehman, Henry "Hank" Greenberg, Dorothy Schiff, Ira Gershwin, Miss Ben Yehuda, Benny Goodman, Eleanor B. Dworkin, Arthur Miller, Bruno Walter, Michael Ress, Sam Maness, David Sohn, Ethel Older, Dr. and Mrs. Herman Ausubel, Dr. and Mrs. Moses Ausubel, and Albert Kahn, Associated Architects and Engineers, Detroit. Thanks are also due the Weiman and Lester photo processing house, and Janina Lester, Michael D. Lester, Henry Weiman, Barnett Singer and Joyce Kent, for excellent reproductions.

The author has made every effort to communicate with all individuals, institutions and organizations that might have legitimate rights or interests in the illustrations appearing in this book. If he has failed to make proper acknowledgments to anyone or has overlooked any rights, it has been entirely inadvertent, and he asks to be forgiven.